# Lecture Notes in Computer Science 15884

The series Lecture Notes in Computer Science (LNCS), including its subseries Lecture Notes in Artificial Intelligence (LNAI) and Lecture Notes in Bioinformatics (LNBI), has established itself as a medium for the publication of new developments in computer science and information technology research, teaching, and education.

LNCS enjoys close cooperation with the computer science R & D community, the series counts many renowned academics among its volume editors and paper authors, and collaborates with prestigious societies. Its mission is to serve this international community by providing an invaluable service, mainly focused on the publication of conference and workshop proceedings and postproceedings. LNCS commenced publication in 1973.

Michał Baczyński · Bernard De Baets ·
Michal Holčapek · Vladik Kreinovich ·
Jesús Medina
Editors

# Advances in Fuzzy Logic and Technology

14th Conference of the European Society for Fuzzy Logic and Technology, EUSFLAT 2025, Riga, Latvia, July 21–25, 2025
Proceedings, Part II

Springer

*Editors*
Michał Baczyński
University of Silesia in Katowice
Katowice, Poland

Bernard De Baets
Ghent University
Ghent, Belgium

Michal Holčapek
University of Ostrava
Ostrava, Czech Republic

Vladik Kreinovich
The University of Texas at El Paso
El Paso, TX, USA

Jesús Medina
University of Cádiz
Cádiz, Spain

ISSN 0302-9743 ISSN 1611-3349 (electronic)
Lecture Notes in Computer Science
ISBN 978-3-031-97227-0 ISBN 978-3-031-97228-7 (eBook)
https://doi.org/10.1007/978-3-031-97228-7



This Springer imprint is published by the registered company Springer Nature Switzerland AG
The registered company address is: Gewerbestrasse 11, 6330 Cham, Switzerland

# Preface

It is with great pleasure that we present the proceedings of the 14th Conference of the European Society for Fuzzy Logic and Technology (EUSFLAT 2025), held in Riga, Latvia, from July 21 to 25, 2025. This biennial conference continued the tradition of bringing together researchers, practitioners, and students from around the world who work in the broad area of fuzzy logic and related fields, including soft computing, computational intelligence, uncertainty modeling, and approximate reasoning. The event served as a platform for the exchange of ideas, dissemination of new results, and the strengthening of collaborations across academic, scientific, and industrial domains.

Nearly 26 years ago, the inaugural EUSFLAT-ESTYLF Joint Conference was convened in Palma de Mallorca from September 22 to 25, 1999. That event marked the first official conference of the European Society for Fuzzy Logic and Technology (EUSFLAT), following its establishment earlier that same year. Since then, the Society has organized successful conferences in Leicester (2001), Zittau (2003), Barcelona (2005), Ostrava (2007), Lisbon (2009), Aix-les-Bains (2011), Milan (2013), Gijón (2015), Warsaw (2017), Prague (2019), Bratislava (2021), and again Palma de Mallorca (2023). The fourteenth edition was hosted in Riga, organized by the University of Latvia, in cooperation with EUSFLAT.

The papers included in these proceedings underwent a rigorous peer-review process. Each submission was reviewed by at least two qualified experts, using a single-blind review protocol and adhering to strict conflict-of-interest policies. In addition, all submissions were carefully evaluated by the program chairs. As a result of this review process, 53 submissions were accepted and are presented across the two volumes of the proceedings. Topics covered include, but are not limited to, fuzzy sets and systems, knowledge representation, fuzzy control, decision-making, machine learning, data analysis, and applications in engineering, economics, and the social sciences.

The EUSFLAT conference series has served as a central forum for the community since its inception, promoting interdisciplinary collaboration and addressing new challenges in science and technology through fuzzy logic and soft computing. The 2025 edition stood out not only for the quality of its scientific contributions but also for its location – Riga, a city known for its rich cultural heritage, architectural beauty, and its growing role as a hub for science and innovation in the Baltic region. The Local Organizing Committee worked tirelessly to ensure a warm, efficient, and memorable experience for all participants.

In addition to regular paper sessions, EUSFLAT 2025 featured invited talks by distinguished researchers, special sessions on emerging topics, tutorials, and panel discussions. These components were designed to offer attendees a well-rounded and intellectually stimulating experience that combined depth with breadth. The program included keynote lectures by:

- Bernard De Baets (Ghent University, Belgium),
- Irina Perfilieva (University of Ostrava, Czech Republic),

- Humberto Bustince (Public University of Navarre, Spain),
- Óscar Cordón (University of Granada, Spain),
- Katarzyna Kaczmarek-Majer (Systems Research Institute, Polish Academy of Sciences, Warsaw, Poland),
- Ulrich Bodenhofer (University of Applied Sciences Upper Austria, Hagenberg, Austria),
- Andris Ambainis (University of Latvia, Latvia).

We are deeply grateful to all authors for submitting their research and sharing their insights with the community. We sincerely thank the reviewers and Program Committee members for their time, expertise, and thoughtful feedback, and we acknowledge the special session organizers for their initiative and commitment. Our appreciation also goes to the invited speakers for their inspiring presentations and to the session chairs for their essential role in ensuring the smooth flow of the technical program. Special thanks go to the Local Organizing Committee members for their dedication in preparing and hosting the conference. Their professionalism, attention to detail, and hospitality were instrumental in creating a successful and enjoyable event.

Last but not least, we would like to dedicate these proceedings to the late Alexander Šostak, who was an exemplary member of our society and a great researcher, and who was very happy and delighted that this fourteenth edition was going to be held in his city. Unfortunately, he is no longer with us, but his magnificent research group, and Olga Grigorenko in particular, have made great efforts for the organization of a splendid conference that would have made Alexander very proud. We hope that these proceedings will not only serve as a record of the work presented at EUSFLAT 2025, but will also stimulate future research, foster continued dialogue, and encourage new developments in the field of fuzzy logic and soft computing.

May 2025

Michał Baczynski
Bernard De Baets
Michal Holčapek
Vladik Kreinovich
Jesús Medina

# Organization

## General Chairs

| | |
|---|---|
| Martin Štěpnička | University of Ostrava, Czech Republic |
| Susana Montes | University of Oviedo, Spain |
| Svetlana Asmuss | University of Latvia, Latvia |

## Organizing Chairs

| | |
|---|---|
| Olga Grigorenko | University of Latvia, Latvia |
| Slawomir Zadrozny | Polish Academy of Sciences, Poland |

## Publication Chairs

| | |
|---|---|
| Jesús Medina | University of Cádiz, Spain |
| Michal Baczynski | University of Silesia in Katowice, Poland |

## EUSFLAT Programme Chairs

| | |
|---|---|
| Bernard De Baets | Ghent University, Netherlands |
| Vladik Kreinovich | University of Texas at El Paso, USA |
| Michal Holčapek | University of Ostrava, Czech Republic |

## Publicity Chairs

| | |
|---|---|
| Vladik Kreinovich | University of Texas at El Paso, USA |
| Katarzyna Kaczmarek-Majer | Polish Academy of Sciences, Poland |

## Advisory Board

| | |
|---|---|
| Radko Mesiar | Slovak University of Technology in Bratislava, Slovakia |
| Janusz Kacprzyk | Polish Academy of Sciences, Poland |

| | |
|---|---|
| Vilém Novák | University of Ostrava, Czech Republic |
| Marek Reformat | University of Alberta, Canada |
| Gabriella Pasi | University of Milano-Bicocca, Italy |
| Przemyslaw Grzegorzewski | Warsaw University of Technology, Poland |
| Susana Vieira | Universidade de Lisboa, Portugal |
| María Ángeles Gil | University of Oviedo, Spain |
| Peter Sussner | University of Campinas, Brazil |

## Organizing Committee

| | |
|---|---|
| Elīna Buliņa | University of Latvia, Latvia |
| Reinis Isaks | University of Latvia, Latvia |
| Māris Krastiņš | University of Latvia, Latvia |
| Ingrīda Uļjane | University of Latvia, Latvia |
| Mārtiņš Zemlītis | University of Latvia, Latvia |

## SS1: Interval Uncertainty. Organizers

| | |
|---|---|
| Martine Ceberio | University of Texas at El Paso, USA |
| Christoph Lauter | University of Texas at El Paso, USA |
| Vladik Kreinovich | University of Texas at El Paso, USA |

## SS2: Representing and Managing Uncertainty: Different Scenarios, Different Tools. Organizers

| | |
|---|---|
| Davide Ciucci | University of Milano-Bicocca, Italy |
| Chris Cornelis | Ghent University, Belgium |
| Jesús Medina | University of Cádiz, Spain |
| Dominik Slezak | University of Warsaw, Poland |

## SS3: Mathematical Fuzzy Logic. Organizers

| | |
|---|---|
| Matteo Bianchi | Università degli Studi di Milano, Italy |
| Tommaso Flaminio | IIIA-CSIC, Barcelona, Spain |
| Amanda Vidal | IIIA-CSIC, Barcelona, Spain |

## SS4: Soft Methods in Statistical Inference and Data Analysis. Organizers

| | |
|---|---|
| Przemyslaw Grzegorzewski | Warsaw University of Technology, Poland |
| Katarzyna Kaczmarek-Majer | Polish Academy of Sciences, Poland |
| Antonio Calcagni | University of Padova, Italy |

## SS5: Fuzzy Implication Functions. Organizers

| | |
|---|---|
| Michal Baczyński | University of Silesia in Katowice, Poland |
| Balasubramaniam Jayaram | Indian Institute of Technology Hyderabad, India |
| Raquel Fernández-Peralta | Universitat de les Illes Balears, Spain |

## SS6: Information Fusion Techniques Based on Aggregation Functions, Preaggregation Functions and their Generalizations. Organizers

| | |
|---|---|
| Humberto Bustince | Universidad Publica de Navarra, Spain |
| Graçaliz Pereira Dimuro | Universidade Federal do Rio Grande, Brazil |
| Javier Fernández | Universidad Publica de Navarra, Spain |
| Tiago da Cruz Asmus | Universidade Federal do Rio Grande, Brazil |
| Giancarlo Lucca | Universidade Católica de Pelotas, Brazil |
| Benjamin Bedregal | Universidade Federal do Rio Grande do Norte, Brazil |

## SS7: Fuzzy Metric Spaces and their Generalizations: Theory and Applications. Organizers

| | |
|---|---|
| Juan José Miñana | Universitat Politècnica de València, Spain |
| Jesús Rodríguez López | Universitat Politècnica de València, Spain |
| Almanzor Sapena | Universitat Politècnica de València, Spain |

## SS8: New Contexts in Aggregation Theory. Organizers

| | |
|---|---|
| Bernard De Baets | Ghent University, Belgium |
| Raúl Pérez-Fernández | University of Oviedo, Spain |

## SS9: Modeling Complex Dynamics: Adapting Analytical Tools for Diverse Scenarios. Organizers

| | |
|---|---|
| Martina Daňková | University of Ostrava, Czech Republic |
| Babak Shiri | Neijiang Normal University, China |
| Zahra Alijani | University of Ostrava, Czech Republic |
| Petra Števuliáková | University of Ostrava, Czech Republic |

## SS10: Soft Computing, Uncertainty and Imprecision in Image Processing. Organizers

| | |
|---|---|
| Irina Perfilieva | University of Ostrava, Czech Republic |
| Javier Montero | Universidad Complutense de Madrid, Spain |
| Humberto Bustince | Universidad Publica de Navarra, Spain |
| Isabelle Bloch | Sorbonne Université, France |
| Olivier Strauss | Université de Montpellier, France |
| Carlos Lopez Molina | Public University of Navarra, Spain |

## SS11: Fuzzy Relations and Applications. Organizers

| | |
|---|---|
| Halis Aygün | Kocaeli University, Turkey |
| Elif Güner | Kocaeli University, Turkey |
| Ingrīda Uļjane | University of Latvia, Latvia |
| Oscar Valero | University of the Balearic Islands, Spain |

## SS12: The Role and Value of Information in Decision Making

| | |
|---|---|
| Dmitry Gromov | University of Latvia, Latvia |

## SS13: Generalized Quantifiers, Logical Syllogisms and Applications. Organizers

| | |
|---|---|
| Vilém Novák | University of Ostrava, Czech Republic |
| Petra Murinová | University of Ostrava, Czech Republic |
| Karel Fiala | University of Ostrava, Czech Republic |

## SS4: Advancements and Applications of Fuzzy Theory and Fuzzy Control. Organizers

| | |
|---|---|
| Chin-Wang Tao | National Ilan University, Taiwan |
| Chen-Chia Chuang | National Ilan University, Taiwan |

## Program Committee

| | |
|---|---|
| Akbarzadeh-T., M.-R. | Ferdowsi University of Mashhad, Iran |
| Acampora, Giovanni | Università degli Studi di Napoli Federico II, Italy |
| Aliev, Rafik Aziz | Azerbaijan State Oil and Industry University, Azerbaijan |
| Allahviranloo, Tofigh | Istinye University, Turkey |
| Alijani, Zahra | University of Ostrava, Czech Republic |
| Alonso, Jose Maria | Universidad de Santiago de Compostela, Spain |
| Angelov, Plamen | Lancaster University, UK |
| Asmus, Tiago da Cruz | Universidade Federal do Rio Grande, Brazil |
| Asmuss, Svetlana | University of Latvia, Latvia |
| Atanassov, Krassimir | Bulgarian Academy of Sciences, Bulgaria |
| Balas, Valentina | Academy of Romanian Scientists, Romania |
| Baczyński, Michal | University of Silesia in Katowice, Poland |
| Bargiela Andrzej | University of Nottingham, UK |
| Bedregal, Bejamin | Universidade Federal do Rio Grande do Norte, Brazil |
| Beliakov, Gleb | Deakin University, Australia |
| Běhounek, Libor | University of Ostrava, Czech Republic |
| Bělolávek, Radim | Palacký University Olomouc, Czech Republic |
| Bianchi, Matteo | Università degli Studi di Milano, Italy |
| Bloch, Isabelle | Sorbonne Université, CNRS, France |
| Bobillo, Fernando | Universidad de Zaragoza, Spain |
| Bordogna, Gloria | Consiglio Nazionale delle Ricerche, Italy |
| Boffa, Stefania | University of Milano-Bicocca, Italy |
| Bouchon-Meunier, Bernadette | Sorbonne Université, France |
| Bronselaer, Antoon | Ghent University, Belgium |
| Bustince, Humberto | Universidad Pública de Navarra, Spain |
| Calvo, Tomasa | Universidad de Alcalá, Spain |
| Calganì, Antonio | University of Padova, Italy |
| Carlsson, Christer | Institute for Advanced Management Systems Research, Finland |
| Carvalho, Joao Paulo | Universidade de Lisboa, Portugal |
| Castellano, Giovanna | Università degli studi di Bari Aldo Moro, Italy |

| | |
|---|---|
| Castillo, Oscar | Tijuana Institute of Technology, Mexico |
| Ceberio, Martine | University of Texas at El Paso, USA |
| Chen, Guoqiang | Tsinghua University, China |
| Ciucci, Davide | University of Milano-Bicocca, Italy |
| Cordero, Pablo | Universidad de Málaga, Spain |
| Cordón, Oscar | Universidad de Granada, Spain |
| Cornelis, Chris | Ghent University, Belgium |
| Dankova, Martina | University of Ostrava, Czech Republic |
| De Baets, Bernard | Ghent University, Belgium |
| De Tré, Guy | Ghent University, Belgium |
| De Cock, Martine | University of Washington, Tacoma, USA |
| Diaz, Irene | Universidad de Oviedo, Spain |
| Dick, Scott | University of Alberta, Canada |
| Dimuro, Graçaliz | Universidade Federal do Rio Grande, Brazil |
| Dubois, Didier | Centre National de la Recherche Scientifique, France |
| Durante, Fabrizio | Università del Salento, Italy |
| Escano, Juan Manuel | Universidad de Sevilla, Spain |
| Ekel, Petr | Pontifícia Universidade Católica de Minas Gerais, Brazil |
| Fernandez, Javier | Universidad Pública de Navarra, Spain |
| Fiala, Karel | University of Ostrava, Czechia |
| Figueroa-García, Juan C. | Universidad Distrital Francisco José de Caldas, Colombia |
| Flaminio, Tommaso | IIIA - CSIC, Spain |
| Gaeta, Matteo | Università degli Studi di Salerno, Italy |
| Gagolewski, Marek | Deakin University, Poland |
| Garibaldi, Jonathan M. | University of Nottingham, UK |
| Gerla, Brunella | Università degli Studi dell'Insubria, Italy |
| Godo, Lluis | Artificial Intelligence Research Institute, IIIA - CSIC, Spain |
| Gomide, Fernando | Universidade Estadual de Campinas, Brazil |
| Greco, Salvatore | University of Catania, Italy |
| Grigorenko, Olga | University of Latvia, Latvia |
| Gromov, Dmitry | University of Latvia, Latvia |
| Grzegorzewski, Przemyslaw | Warsaw University of Technology, Poland |
| Güner, Elif | Kocaeli University, Turkey |
| Halaš, Radomír | Palacký University Olomouc, Czech Republic |
| Halčinová, Lenka | University of Pavol Jozef Šafárik, Slovakia |
| Halis, Aygün | Kocaeli University, Turkey |
| Hall, Larry | University of South Florida, USA |
| Herrera, Francisco | Universidad de Granada, Spain |

| | |
|---|---|
| Herrera-Viedma, Enrique | Universidad de Granada, Spain |
| Hirota, Kaoru | Beijing Institute of Technology, Japan |
| Holčapek, Michal | University of Ostrava, Czech Republic |
| Holeňa, Martin | Czech Academy of Sciences, Czech Republic |
| Huellermeier, Eyke | Ludwig Maximilian University of Munich, Germany |
| Hutník, Ondrej | Pavol Jozef Šafárik University, Slovakia |
| Inuiguchi, Masahiro | Osaka University, Japan |
| Ishibuchi, Hisao | Southern University of Science and Technology, China |
| Jayaram, Balasubramaniam | Indian Institute of Technology Hyderabad, India |
| Jin, Lesheng | Nanjing Normal University, China |
| Kaczmarek-Majer, Katarzyna | Polish Academy of Sciences, Poland |
| Kacprzyk, Janusz | Polish Academy of Sciences, Poland |
| Kahraman, Cengiz | Istanbul Technical University, Turkey |
| Kalina, Martin | Slovak University of Technology, Slovakia |
| Kaymak, Uzay | Eindhoven University of Technology, Netherlands |
| Keller, Jim | University of Missouri, USA |
| Kerre, Etienne | Ghent University, Belgium |
| Khastan, Alireza | Institute for Advanced Studies in Basic Sciences, Iran |
| Kim, Sungshin | Pusan National University, South Korea |
| Klawonn, Frank | Ostfalia University of Applied Sciences, Germany |
| Klement, Erich Peter | Johannes Kepler University Linz, Austria |
| Koczy, Laszlo T. | Budapest University of Technology and Economics, Hungary |
| Kolesárová, Anna | Slovak University of Technology, Slovakia |
| Kreinovich, Vladik | University of Texas at El Paso, USA |
| Krídlo, Ondrej | Pavol Jozef Šafárik University, Slovakia |
| Kruse, Rudolf | Otto von Guericke University Magdeburg, Germany |
| Lauter, Christophe | University of Alaska Anchorage, USA |
| Lesot, Marie-Jeanne | Sorbonne Université, France |
| Li, Jun | University of China, China |
| Liu, Xinwang | Southeast University, China |
| Loia, Vincenzo | University of Salerno, Italy |
| López-Molina, Carlos | Universidad Pública de Navarra, Spain |
| Lu, Jie | Australian Artificial Intelligence Institute, Australia |
| Lucca, Giancarlo | Catholic University of Pelotas, Brazil |
| Luo, M. | China Jiliang University, China |
| Madrid, Nicolas | University of Cádiz, Spain |

| | |
|---|---|
| Magdalena Layos, Luis | Universidad Politécnica de Madrid, Spain |
| Marcelloni, Francesco | University of Pisa, Italy |
| Marsala, Christophe | Sorbonne University, France |
| Martínez, Luis | Universidad de Jaén, Spain |
| Masulli, Francesco | University of Genoa, Italy |
| Massanet, Sebastia | Universitat de les Illes Balears, Spain |
| Medina, Jesús | Universidad de Cádiz, Spain |
| Mendel, Jerry | University of Southern California, USA |
| Merigo, Jose | University of Chile, Chile |
| Mesiar, Radko | Slovak University of Technology, Slovakia |
| Michalíková, Alzbeta | Matej Bel University, Slovakia |
| Miñana, Juan José | Universitat Politècnica de València, Spain |
| Možkoš, Jiří | University of Ostrava, Czech Republic |
| Montero, Javier | Universidad Complutense de Madrid, Spain |
| Montes, Susana | Universidad de Oviedo, Spain |
| Moreno-García, Juan | University of Castilla-La Mancha, Spain |
| Murinová, Petra | University of Ostrava, Czech Republic |
| Navara, Mirko | Czech Technical University, Czech Republic |
| Nguyen, Hung T. | University of Connecticut, USA |
| Niskanen, Vesa | University of Helsinki, Finland |
| Noguera, Carles | University of Siena, Italy |
| Novák, Vilém | University of Ostrava, Czech Republic |
| Nurmi, Hannu | University of Turku, Finland |
| Oh, Sung-Kwun | Suwon University, South Korea |
| Ojeda-Aciego, Manuel | Universidad de Málaga, Spain |
| Olivas, José Angel | Universidad de Castilla-La Mancha, Spain |
| Pal, Nikhil K. | Indian Statistical Institute, Kolkata, India |
| Pal, Sankar R. | Indian Statistical Institute, Kolkata, India |
| Pasi, Gabriella | University of Milano-Bicocca, Italy |
| Pedrycz, Witold | University of Alberta, Canada |
| Pókala, Barbara | University of Silesia in Katowice, Poland |
| Pérez-Fernández, Raúl | Universidad de Oviedo, Spain |
| Perfilieva, Irina | University of Ostrava, Czech Republic |
| Petrosino, Alfredo | University of Naples Parthenope, Italy |
| Platoš, Jan | Technical University of Ostrava, Czechia |
| Pocs, Jozef | Pavol Jozef Šafárik University, Slovakia |
| Portmann, Edy | University of Fribourg, Switzerland |
| Prade, Henri | Centre national de la recherche scientifique, France |
| Ralescu, Dan | University of Cincinnati, USA |
| Ralescu, Anca | University of Cincinnati, USA |
| Reformat, Marek | University of Alberta, Canada |

| | |
|---|---|
| Riera-Clapés, Juan Vicente | Universitat de les Illes Balears, Spain |
| Rodriguez, Rosa María | University of La Laguna, Spain |
| López, Jesús Rodríguez | University Pablo de Olavide, Spain |
| Romero, Francisco P. | Universidad de Castilla-La Mancha, Spain |
| Rovetta, Stefano | University of Genova, Italy |
| Ruiz-Aguilera, Daniel | Universitat de les Illes Balears, Spain |
| Sadeghian, Alireza | Toronto Metropolitan University, Canada |
| Sanchez, Daniel | Universidade Estadual de Campinas, Brazil |
| Sapena, Almanzor | Polytechnic University of Valencia, Spain |
| Seising, Rudolf | Deutsches Museum, Germany |
| Serrano-Guerrero, Jesús | Universidad de Castilla-La Mancha, Spain |
| Skowron, Andrzej | University of Warsaw, Poland |
| Slezak, Dominik | University of Warsaw, Poland |
| Słowiński, Roman | Poznań University of Technology, Poland |
| Snášel, Václav | Technical University of Ostrava, Czechia |
| Šostak, Alexander | University of Latvia, Latvia |
| Sotirov, Sotir | Paisii Hilendarski University of Plovdiv, Bulgaria |
| Sozzo, Sandro | University of Udine, Italy |
| Šešelja, Branimir | University of Novi Sad, Serbia |
| Štěpnička, Martin | University of Ostrava, Czech Republic |
| Števuliáková, Petra | University of Ostrava, Czech Republic |
| Straccia, Umberto | Istituto di Scienza e di Tecnologie dell'Informazione, Italy |
| Strauss, Olivier | University of Montpellier, France |
| Stupňanová, Andrea | Slovak University of Technology, Slovakia |
| Su, Shun-Feng | National Taiwan University of Science and Technology, Taiwan |
| Sussner, Peter | Universidade Estadual de Campinas, Brazil |
| Szmidt, Eulalia | Polish Academy of Sciences Poland |
| Takáč, Zdenko | Slovak University of Technology, Slovakia |
| Torra, Vicenç | Umeå University, Sweden |
| Tsai, Ching-Chih | National Chung Hsing University, Taiwan |
| Uļjane, Ingrīda | University of Latvia, Latvia |
| Valero, Oscar | University of the Balearic Islands, Spain |
| Verdegay, José Luis | Universidad de Granada, Spain |
| Vetterlein, Thomas | Johannes Kepler University Linz, Austria |
| Verma, Amanda | UNITY College of Teacher Education, India |
| Vidal, Amanda | Artificial Intelligence Research Institute, Spain |
| Watada, Junzo | Waseda University, Japan |
| Wilbik, Anna | Maastricht University, Netherlands |
| Yager, Ronald R. | Iona University, USA |
| Ying, Hao | Wayne State University, USA |

| | |
|---|---|
| Yoon, Jin Hee | Sejong University, South Korea |
| Zadrozny, Sławomir | Systems Research Institute, Poland |
| Zemankova, Andrea | Slovak Academy of Sciences, Slovakia |
| Zhang, Guangquan | University of Technology Sydney, Australia |

## Additional Reviewers

Sérgio Marcelino
Paolo Baldi
Kavit Nanavati

## Sponsoring Institutions

EUSFLAT (European Society for Fuzzy Logic and Technology)
Investment and Tourism Agency of Riga, Latvia
University of Latvia, Faculty of Exact Sciences and Technology, Department of Mathematics, Latvia
MDPI AG, Basel, Switzerland
Latvian Council of Science, project "A fuzzy logic based approach to the value of information estimation in optimal control problems under uncertainty with applications to ecological management", project No. lzp-2024/1-0188.

# Contents – Part II

**Modeling Complex Dynamics: Adapting Analytical Tools for Diverse Scenarios**

Adaptive Fuzzy Level Set Algorithm for Bitcoin Realized Volatility Modeling and Forecasting ........ 3
*Leandro Maciel, Guilherme Freitas, Vinicius Nazato, and Fernando Gomide*

Unconstrained Parametrization of Proper Symplectic Decomposition for Learning Hamiltonian Dynamics ........ 15
*Jānis Bajārs, Dāvis Kalvāns, and Dmitry Gromov*

**New Contexts in Aggregation Theory**

Prioritized Preference Aggregation for Non-uniform Groups of Agents ........ 29
*Janusz Kacprzyk and Sławomir Zadrożny*

An Axiomatic Study of the Properties Satisfied by Methods for Ranking the Elements of a Poset ........ 41
*Ignacio Montes, Raúl Pérez-Fernández, and Bernard De Baets*

Goodness-of-Fit Tests to Location-Scale Families Based on OWA Functions ... 53
*Marina Iturrate-Bobes, Ignacio Montes, and Raúl Pérez-Fernández*

Multidimensional Aggregation and Measurement of Social Poverty ........ 66
*Marta Cardin*

Ontology Aggregation with Maximum Consensus Based on a Fuzzy Multi-criteria Group Decision-Making Method ........ 76
*Lydia Castronovo, Giuseppe Filippone, Mario Galici, Gianmarco La Rosa, and Marco Elio Tabacchi*

**Representing and Managing Uncertainty**

How to Deal with High-Impact Low-Probability Events: Theoretical Explanation of the Empirically Successful Fuzzy-Like Technique ........ 91
*Juan Ulloa, Aaron Velasco, Olga Kosheleva, and Vladik Kreinovich*

Some Results on Fuzzy Basis of Fuzzy Lie Algebras ........................ 98
*Giuseppe Filippone, Mario Galici, Gianmarco La Rosa, and Marco Elio Tabacchi*

Visual Comparison of Inclusion Measures ........................ 110
*Patryk Żywica, Anna Stachowiak, and Joanna Siwek*

Implication Construction Methods on Bounded Lattices ........................ 122
*Ümıt Ertuğrul, Funda Karaçal, and Kübra Karacaır*

Idea Management and Game Theory with Uncertain Payoffs ........................ 134
*Inese Bula, Elīna Miķelsone, Līga Peiseniece, Astrīda Rijkure, Aivars Spilbergs, and Inga Uvarova*

On Direct Systems of Implications with Graded Attributes ........................ 146
*Manuel Ojeda-Hernández and Domingo López-Rodríguez*

Robust Decisions: Bridging the Quantitative-Qualitative Gap ........................ 158
*Sébastien Destercke and Agnès Rico*

**Soft Methods in Statistical Inference and Data Analysis**

A Soft Clustering Method Derived from the Probabilistic Interpretation of Fuzzy C-Means ........................ 173
*Davide Cazzorla and Corrado Mencar*

Alpha-Maxmin Classification with an Ensemble of Structural Restricted Boltzmann Machines ........................ 185
*Davide Petturiti and Maria Rifqi*

FLIRT–An Algorithm to Enhance a Regression Model with Federated Learning and GAN-Based Resampling ........................ 198
*Przemysław Grzegorzewski and Maciej Romaniuk*

Modeling Treatment Effect with Fuzzy Data ........................ 211
*Przemyslaw Grzegorzewski*

Resampling Approaches for Multivariate Random Interval Numbers ........................ 223
*Maciej Romaniuk*

## Type 2 Fuzzy Sets

A Decision-Making Framework Based on Intersection and Similarity Measures for Type-2 Fuzzy Sets ........ 237
*Pedro Huidobro, Francisco Javier Talavera, Susana Cubillo, Carmen Torres-Blanc, Pablo Hernández-Varela, and Jorge Elorza*

About T-Norms and T-Conorms on New Preorders in Type-2 Fuzzy Sets ...... 249
*Pablo Hernández-Varela, Francisco Javier Talavera, Carmen Torres-Blanc, Susana Cubillo, Pedro Huidobro, and Jorge Elorza*

## Advancements and Applications of Fuzzy Theory

Enhanced Anti-Money Laundering Transaction Monitoring via Fuzzy Equivalence in Rule-Based Systems ........ 263
*Igor Rodin and Jelizaveta Jelinska*

An Enhanced Multi Criteria Decision Making Model for Delivery Locker Placement Using TOPSIS and Einstein Operators in a Pythagorean Fuzzy Framework ........ 275
*Gvantsa Tsulaia*

How to Share a Success, How to Share a Crisis, and How All This is Related to Fuzzy ........ 288
*Olga Kosheleva and Vladik Kreinovich*

Prostate Cancer Diagnosis: A Geometric Approach Based on the Beer Index ... 299
*M. A. Serra-Moll, A. Mir-Fuentes, A. Burguera Burguera, and O. Valero*

**Author Index** ........ 311

# Contents – Part I

**Fuzzy Relations and Applications**


Functors from Fuzzy Structures Categories into Categories of Fuzzy Topological Spaces with Continuous Fuzzy Relations ........ 3
*Jiří Močkoř*

On the Existence of Non-trivial Monometrics on Betweenness Relations: Some Sufficient Conditions ........ 15
*Kavit Nanavati, Megha Gupta, and Balasubramaniam Jayaram*

A Few Notes to the Fuzzy Best-Worst Method ........ 26
*Jana Špirková and Igor Kollár*

Chatbots with Character - An Implementation of Fuzzy Conversational Character Computing ........ 39
*Sophie Hundertmark, Ramón Christen, and Edy Portmann*

Generating Modular Relaxed Pseudo-metrics by Aggregation ........ 54
*M. D. M. Bibiloni-Femenias, G. Jaume-Martin, and O. Valero*

Incomplete Preference Relation Analysis for Multi-granular Group Decision-Making Systems ........ 66
*José Ramón Trillo, Juan Carlos González-Quesada, Francisco Mata, Ignacio Javier Pérez, and Francisco Javier Cabrerizo*

On Metric Aggregation Functions and Fuzzy Decision-Making ........ 78
*M. A. Serra-Moll, O. Martorell-Cunill, C. Mulet-Forteza, and O. Valero*

On Modular Fuzzy Equivalences, Aggregation and Modular Pseudo-metrics ........ 91
*G. Jaume-Martin, M. D. M. Bibiloni-Femenias, and O. Valero*

On the Impossibility of Universally Transforming Similarity Metrics into Partial Metrics ........ 104
*A. Mir-Fuentes and O. Valero*

**Fuzzy Transforms**

A Natural Extension of F-Transform to Triangular and Triangulated Domains Necessitates the Use of Triangular Membership Functions .......... 117
*Hana Zámečníková, Irina Perfilieva, Olga Kosheleva, and Vladik Kreinovich*

Locally Modified Multivariate $F^m$-Transform: Theoretical Background and Possible Applications .......... 127
*Martins Kokainis and Svetlana Asmuss*

**Generalized Quantifiers, Logical Syllogisms and Applications**

Using Intermediate Quantifiers to Reduce the Number of Linguistic Rules for Diagnosing Mood Disorders from Incomplete Data .......... 141
*Lucas Dantas de Oliveira and Peter Sussner*

Verification of Validity of Generalized Logical Syllogisms Applying the Contraposition .......... 153
*Karel Fiala and Petra Murinová*

Verification of Validity of Logical Syllogisms Generated by Cube of Opposition Using Extended Peterson's Rules .......... 166
*Petra Murinová and Vilém Novák*

**Fuzzy Entropy**

A Study of the Fuzzy Differential Entropy .......... 181
*Zuzana Ontkovičová and Vicenç Torra*

Towards Probabilistic Entropies for Interval Valued Fuzzy Sets .......... 193
*Christophe Marsala and Bernadette Bouchon-Meunier*

**Fuzzy Metric Spaces and Their Generalizations**

Fuzzy Equivalence Based Metrizable Space .......... 207
*Reinis Isaks and Olga Grigorenko*

On Fuzzy Metrics Constructed from Metrics and their Topology .......... 219
*Juan-José Miñana and Simona Talia*

Some Metric-Like Structures and $\oplus$-Based Semi (Pseudo) Metric-Like .......... 229
*Şuara Onbaşıoğlu Altuhovs and Banu Pazar Varol*

## Information Fusion Techniques

Idempotence and Internality of Aggregations of Random Variables . . . . . . . . . . . 245
*Juan Baz, Irene Díaz, and Susana Montes*

Input Importance in Aggregation Theory by Means of Dependence Stochastic Orders . . . . . . . . . . . 258
*Juan Baz and Franco Pellerey*

Insights into the $q$ Exponent in Power Measure with Choquet-Based Generalizations for Classification Problems . . . . . . . . . . . 270
*Giancarlo Lucca, Tiago C. Asmus, Cedric Marco-Detchart, Helida S. Santos, Heloisa A. Camargo, Adenauer C. Yamin, Renata H. S. Reiser, Humberto Bustince, Alice Pintanel, and Graçaliz P. Dimuro*

Measuring Representativeness Through Coverage Degrees and Indexes . . . . . . . 282
*Inmaculada Gutiérrez, J. Tinguaro Rodríguez, Xabier González, Daniel Gómez, Javier Montero, and Humberto Bustince*

Understanding Data Properties in the Mallows Model: Impact of Voter Count Variability . . . . . . . . . . . 294
*Mario Villar, Noelia Rico, and Irene Díaz*

## Mathematical Fuzzy Logic

Foulis Quantales and Complete Orthomodular Lattices . . . . . . . . . . . 309
*Michal Botur, Jan Paseka, and Richard Smolka*

On Some Properties of Tabular Varieties of MTL-Algebras and Their Decidability . . . . . . . . . . . 322
*Stefano Aguzzoli and Matteo Bianchi*

On the Non-falsity and Threshold Preserving Variants of MTL Logics . . . . . . . . 335
*Francesc Esteva, Joan Gispert, and Lluís Godo*

Quantitative Lockean Thesis and its Logical Representation . . . . . . . . . . . 347
*Tommaso Flaminio and Lluis Subirana*

**Author Index** . . . . . . . . . . . 359

# Modeling Complex Dynamics: Adapting Analytical Tools for Diverse Scenarios

# Adaptive Fuzzy Level Set Algorithm for Bitcoin Realized Volatility Modeling and Forecasting

Leandro Maciel[1(✉)], Guilherme Freitas[2], Vinicius Nazato[1], and Fernando Gomide[3]

[1] School of Economics, Business, Accounting and Actuary, University of São Paulo, São Paulo, Brazil
{leandromaciel,vini_simoes}@usp.br
[2] Institute of Matemathics and Statistics, University of São Paulo, São Paulo, Brazil
gv.freitas2003@usp.br
[3] School of Electrical and Computer Engineering, University of Campinas, Campinas, Brazil
gomide@unicamp.br

**Abstract.** This paper addresses a novel approach to cryptocurrency risk management. An adaptive fuzzy model based on level sets is suggested to model and forecast the realized volatility of Bitcoin. The model, referred to as adaptive level set model (ALSM), is a rule-based fuzzy inference system that uses the concept of level sets to determine the model output in a data-driven and adaptive manner. One-step-ahead forecasts of realized volatility generated by the ALSM model are evaluated in terms of accuracy and compared to alternative machine learning models, an evolving fuzzy model, and the heterogeneous autoregressive (HAR) model. HAR serves as the baseline for realized volatility forecasting evaluation. The results indicate that the ALSM model achieves the highest accuracy among all competing approaches, highlighting its potential as a valuable tool to assist investors in forecasting risk in the Bitcoin market.

**Keywords:** Adaptive Fuzzy Modeling · Realized Volatility · Level Set · Bitcoin · Forecasting

## 1 Introduction

In January 2025, CoinMarketCap[1] reported that the cryptocurrency market has reached a total market capitalization of USD 3.5 trillion. Bitcoin (BTC) remains

[1] Source: https://coinmarketcap.com. Access on 28th January, 2025.

Supported by the Brazilian National Council for Scientific and Technological Development (CNPq) grant 302467/2019-0 and by the Ripple Impact Fund, a donor-advised Silicon Valley Community Foundation fund, for grant 2018-196450(5855), as part of the University Blockchain Research Initiative, UBRI.


M. Baczyński et al. (Eds.): EUSFLAT 2025, LNCS 15884, pp. 3–14, 2025.
https://doi.org/10.1007/978-3-031-97228-7_1

the dominant cryptocurrency in this market. These figures highlight the consolidation of cryptocurrencies in the global financial market as digital assets that have become integral parts of investment portfolios [10,16,19].

One of the main characteristics of the cryptocurrency market is its significant volatility compared to other markets such as stocks and commodities [1]. The volatility of a financial asset refers to the variability in its price returns. In finance, volatility is a crucial factor as it measures one of the key elements in decision making: the risk-return trade-off of assets. In addition, volatility is widely used in risk management, portfolio construction, and asset pricing [8,24,30].

In the cryptocurrency market, volatility is influenced by technological advances, market sentiment, and regulatory changes [31]. Among these factors, market sentiment plays a central role [20]. Volatility is an unobservable variable that must, therefore, be estimated using models. Approaches to volatility modeling include [11]:

1. Historical methods to estimate volatility via the standard deviation of past returns data using exponential smoothing methods such as the exponential weighted moving average (EWMA) model [17];
2. Financial econometrics approaches such as generalized autoregressive heteroskedasticity (GARCH) time series models, which assumes a generating process for volatility to capture stylized facts observed in financial return series such as high kurtosis and volatility clustering [22];
3. Stochastic volatility methods that asset price dynamics using stochastic differential equations [12];
4. Implied volatility approaches that extract return variance information from the prices of market-traded assets such as option contracts [7];
5. Realized volatility-based (RV) mechanisms to calculate return variability from the intraday prices using heterogeneous autoregressive (HAR) regression framework [6].

Recent studies in the literature suggest that realized volatility-based models give important information to estimate risk measures, especially due to their ability to capture intraday fluctuations [5,13]. In the case of highly volatile dynamics of cryptocurrencies intraday variability becomes even more critical and essential for risk analysis and asset pricing.

Many researchers have addressed cryptocurrency volatility modeling and forecasting. For instance, the relevance of volatility spillover effects among cryptocurrencies to forecast realized volatility of Bitcoin is investigated in [25]. Incorporation of external predictive information from other cryptocurrency markets to forecast realized volatility of Bitcoin is pursued in [29].

Various GARCH models and HAR Bitcoin volatility models are evaluated in [5]. The results indicate that exponential GARCH and asymmetric power GARCH outperform other GARCH models, while HAR models based on realized variance consistently surpass GARCH models that rely on daily data, especially for short-term volatility forecasts. [14] compares Bitcoin volatility forecasting with traditional econometric and machine learning models. Deep learning models outperform GARCH models across different forecasting horizons.

[4] analyzes the role of daily indices in forecasting Bitcoin volatility compared with monthly and weekly indices. Daily indices of economic policy uncertainty (EPU) and geopolitical risk (GPR) outperformed monthly indices in explanatory power and predictive accuracy. Combining indices with different frequencies significantly improved predictive performance.

This paper advances the current state of the art by introducing a new algorithmic approach to model and forecast the realized volatility of Bitcoin, namely, the adaptive level set fuzzy modeling (ALSM). Originally outlined in [21], the method consists of a rule-based fuzzy model whose outputs, differently from the linguistic and functional fuzzy rule-based models, are computed using output functions associated with each rule of the rule base. The ALSM model uses the concept of level sets – first introduced in [28] – and uses data to develop a function that maps activation levels of the rules into values in the output space [21]. The approach is adaptive, processing the data sequentially, which makes it particularly suitable to model time-varying dynamic systems, such as financial asset volatility market dynamics. In fact, [23] demonstrates the predictive power of the ALSM model to forecast future asset prices. This paper evaluates the ALSM model in forecasting the realized volatility of Bitcoin. It contributes to the literature on volatility modeling by offering an innovative approach and demonstrating the usefulness of fuzzy models in providing effective solutions in highly uncertain and complex environments, such as the cryptocurrency market. Using intraday Bitcoin data with a 5-minute frequency, the paper computes one-step-ahead forecasts of realized volatility. The results of the ALSM model are compared with HAR as the baseline model, and with alternative machine learning and evolving fuzzy forecasters.

The paper is organized as follows. Section 2 addresses the ALSM model. Section 4 presents the methodology, including data, alternative predictive models, and evaluation metrics of predictive quality. The results are addressed in Sect. 4.2. Section 5 concludes the paper summarizing its contributions and suggesting issues for future investigation.

## 2 Fuzzy Adaptive Level Set Modeling

This section briefly reviews the conceptual idea of fuzzy level-set-based modeling and an adaptive algorithm to develop fuzzy rule-based models from data.

### 2.1 Fuzzy Level Set Modeling

The level set method uses fuzzy rule-based models of the form

$$\mathcal{R}_i : \text{ if } \mathbf{x} \text{ is } \mathcal{A}_i \text{ then } y \; is \; \mathcal{B}_i, \tag{1}$$

where $i = 1, 2, \ldots, N$, and $\mathcal{A}_i$ and $\mathcal{B}_i$ are convex fuzzy sets with membership functions $\mathcal{A}_i(\mathbf{x}) : \mathcal{X} \to [0, 1]$ and $\mathcal{B}_i(y) : \mathcal{Y} \to [0, 1]$, respectively.

The development of fuzzy rule-based models needs the specification of the number of rules $N$, the membership functions for the antecedent variables $\mathcal{A}_i(\mathbf{x})$, and the membership functions $\mathcal{B}_i(y)$ of the consequent variables of each rule $\mathcal{R}_i$. Knowledge-based, grid, hierarchical, or clustering procedures can be used to granulate the input-output space and to determine the membership functions. Once the membership functions $\mathcal{A}_i$ and $\mathcal{B}_i$ are given, the fuzzy level set modeling method proceeds as follows [28].

Given input data $\mathbf{x} \in \mathcal{X}$:

1. Compute the activation level $\tau_i$ of each rule $\mathcal{R}_i$
$$\tau_i = \mathcal{A}_i(\mathbf{x}). \tag{2}$$
2. For each level $\tau_i$, find the corresponding level set $\mathcal{B}_{\tau_i}$
$$\mathcal{B}_{\tau_i} = \{y | \tau_i \leq \mathcal{B}_i(y)\} = [y_{il}, y_{iu}]. \tag{3}$$
where $y_{il}$ and $y_{iu}$ are the bounds of the interval for which $\mathcal{B}_i(y)$ is greater than or equal to $\tau_i$.
3. Compute the midpoint of the level set
$$m_i(\tau_i) = \frac{y_{il} + y_{iu}}{2}. \tag{4}$$
4. Compute the model output $\hat{y}$ as
$$\hat{y} = \frac{\sum\limits_{i=1}^{N} \tau_i m_i(\tau_i)}{\sum\limits_{i=1}^{N} \tau_i}. \tag{5}$$

Figure 1 summarizes the idea. The expression (5) is a particular case of a general mapping $\mathcal{F} : [0, 1] \to \mathcal{Y}$ in which $\mathcal{F}_i(\tau_i) = m_i(\tau_i)$, called the output function, is the midpoint of the interval $\mathcal{B}_{\tau_i} = [y_{il}, y_{iu}]$. In the example of Fig. 1, if $m_i$ is computed for all $x \in \mathcal{X}$, then the output function is the affine function $\mathcal{F}_i$ in $[0, 1] \times \mathcal{Y}$. Other choices are possible, especially in data-driven modeling frameworks. The reason to adopt the midpoint is discussed in [18].

In general, level set fuzzy models use output functions to produce outputs $\hat{y}$
$$\hat{y} = \frac{\sum_{i=1}^{N} \tau_i \mathcal{F}_i(\tau_i)}{\sum_{i=1}^{N} \tau_i} = \mathcal{F}(\tau). \tag{6}$$

Note that $\mathcal{F}$ maps membership degrees to elements of the output domain $\mathcal{Y}$, which is very different from what is done by linguistic and functional fuzzy models.

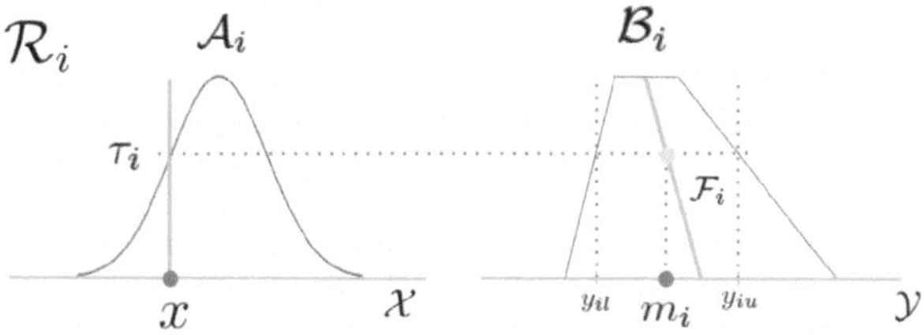


**Fig. 1.** Fuzzy level set modeling.

Data-driven level set fuzzy modeling [17] relies on a data set $\mathcal{D} = \{(\mathbf{x}^k; y^k)\}$, $\mathbf{x}^k \in R^p$, $y^k \in R$ such that $y^k = f(\mathbf{x}^k)$, for $k = 1, 2, \ldots, K$, to develop a fuzzy model $\mathcal{F}$ that approximates the function $f$ in $\mathcal{D}$. There is no need to specify $\mathcal{B}_i$ because the output functions $\mathcal{F}_i$ in (6) can be estimated from $\mathcal{D}$. This paper assumes affine output functions

$$\mathcal{F}_i(\tau_i) = v_i \tau_i + w_i. \tag{7}$$

The coefficients $v_i$ and $w_i$ can be estimated using any proper procedure, for example, the recursive correntropy-based least squares algorithm.

## 2.2 Recursive Correntropy Least Squares Algorithm

The algorithm adopted in this paper employs a correntropy-based recursive least squares algorithm [23, 26] to compute the coefficients of the output functions of the rules. The details of the algorithm are as follows.

Let $\mathbf{x}^k$ be an input data and $\tau_i^k = \mathcal{A}_i(\mathbf{x}^k)$ the activation level of $i$-th rule in step $k$. Therefore, from (6) and (7), the output of the model $\hat{y}^k$ at step $k$ is expressed as

$$\hat{y}^k = \frac{\tau_1^k(v_1^k \tau_1^k + w_1^k)}{s^k} + \ldots + \frac{\tau_N^k(v_N^k \tau_N^k + w_N^k)}{s^k}, \tag{8}$$

with the normalization factor $s^k = \sum_{i=1}^N \tau_i^k$.

Let $\boldsymbol{\theta}^k = [v_1^k, w_1^k, \ldots, v_N^k, w_N^k]^T$ be the vector with coefficients of the output functions of all $N$ rules, and

$$\mathbf{a}^k = [(\tau_1^k)^2/s^k, \tau_1^k/s^k, \ldots, (\tau_N^k)^2/s^k, \tau_N^k/s^k], \tag{9}$$

denotes the vector of normalized activation levels of the $N$ rules. The recursive least squares algorithm based on correntropy proceeds as follows:

Initialize: $\boldsymbol{\theta}^0 = 0$, $\mathbf{P}^0 = \alpha\mathbf{I}$

For each step $k = 0, \ldots K$:

1. Read the data pair $(\mathbf{x}^k; y^k)$ .
2. Compute the estimation error $e^k = \mathbf{a}^k \boldsymbol{\theta}^k - y^k$.

3. Set:

$$\psi^k = \frac{1}{\sqrt{2\pi}\zeta^3}\exp\left(-\frac{|e^k|^2}{2\zeta^2}\right), \tag{10}$$

in which $\zeta$ is a user-selected value that determines the width of the kernel.
4. Compute the activation levels $\tau_i^k = A_i(\mathbf{x}^k)$, $i = 1, \ldots, N$, and form the activation vector $\mathbf{a}^k$, as in (9).
5. Compute the gain matrix:

$$\mathbf{P}^k = \frac{1}{\lambda}\left(\mathbf{P}^{k-1} - \frac{\psi^k \mathbf{P}^{k-1}(\mathbf{a}^k)^T \mathbf{a}^k \mathbf{P}^{k-1}}{\lambda + \psi^k \mathbf{a}^k \mathbf{P}^{\mathbf{k}-1}(\mathbf{a}^k)^T}\right), \tag{11}$$

where $\lambda \in [0, 1]$ is a forgetting factor.
6. Update the coefficients of the output functions:

$$\boldsymbol{\theta}^{k+1} = \boldsymbol{\theta}^k + \psi^k \mathbf{P}^k (\mathbf{a}^k)^T (y^k - \mathbf{a}^k \boldsymbol{\theta}^k). \tag{12}$$

7. Compute the model output $\hat{y}^{k+1}$ using the expression

$$\hat{y}^{k+1} = \mathbf{a}^k \boldsymbol{\theta}^{k+1}. \tag{13}$$

The procedure requires initial estimates for the coefficients $\boldsymbol{\theta}^0$, and the initial gain matrix $\mathbf{P}^0$. Usually $\boldsymbol{\theta}^0 = \mathbf{0}$, and $\mathbf{P}^0 = \alpha\mathbf{I}$, where $\alpha$ is a sufficiently large constant, e.g., $10^3$. The parameter $\lambda$ is the forgetting factor that weighs the data instances in the sequence. A smaller $\lambda$ places more emphasis on recent data, allowing the algorithm to track time-varying behaviors more [15]. Membership functions and their parameters can be chosen using fuzzy clustering or domain knowledge.

# 3 Volatility Modeling and Forecasting Models

## 3.1 Volatility Modeling

This study analyzes the modeling and forecasting of Bitcoin's (BTC) realized volatility. The realized volatility on day $t$, $RV_t$, is defined as [2]:

$$RV_t = \sqrt{\sum_{j=1}^{n} r_{t,j}^2}, \tag{14}$$

where $r_{t,j} = \ln(p_{t,j}) - \ln(p_{t,j-1})$, $j = 1, \ldots, n$, are the intraday BTC log-returns, $p_{t,j}$ is the price of BTC on day $t$ at time $j$, and $n$ represents the number of intraday returns on day $t$.

Intraday data at a 5-minute frequency are used. Each day's data is discretized for the trading hours, which start at 5:00 AM and end at 12:00 PM. Thus, there are a total of 288 prices in a single day, implying that $n = 288$.

### 3.2 Heterogeneous Autoregressive Regression

The baseline forecast approach considered is the HAR model of [9]. The HAR method is an additive cascade model of volatility components defined over different time periods. This model effectively captures key empirical features of financial returns – long memory, fat tails, and self-similarity – in a parsimonious manner. Interestingly, the literature has highlighted the strong forecasting performance of HAR [6,9,27].

The HAR model is defined by [9]:

$$RV_{t+1} = \beta_0 + \beta_1 RV_t + \beta_2 RV_t^{(w)} + \beta_3 RV_t^{(m)} + \epsilon_t, \tag{15}$$

where $\beta_0$, $\beta_1$, $\beta_2$, and $\beta_3$ are parameters estimated using ordinary least squares; $RV_t^{(w)}$ and $RV_t^{(m)}$ represent the weekly and monthly realized volatilities, respectively; and $\epsilon_t$ is a white noise error term.

$RV_t^{(w)}$ and $RV_t^{(m)}$ are calculated as, respectively:

$$RV_t^{(w)} = \frac{1}{5}\left(RV_t + RV_{t-1} + RV_{t-2} + RV_{t-3} + RV_{t-4}\right), \tag{16}$$

$$RV_t^{(m)} = \frac{1}{22}\left(RV_t + RV_{t-1} + RV_{t-2} + RV_{t-3} + \ldots + RV_{t-21}\right). \tag{17}$$

By considering daily, weekly and monthly realized volatility, this approach accounts for realized volatility over time horizons longer than one day. The aim is to recognize the heterogeneity among traders. It identifies three primary volatility components: short-term traders with daily or higher trading frequency, medium-term investors who typically rebalance their positions weekly, and long-term agents with a characteristic time horizon of one month or more [9].

### 3.3 Machine Learning and Evolving Fuzzy Models

In addition to the HAR model, used as a baseline, and the ALSM model, which is the approach suggested in this paper, the following methods are also considered: Multilayer Perceptron (MLP) neural network, Support Vector Regression (SVR), and the evolving Takagi-Sugeno model (eTS+) [3]. SVR and MLP are traditional machine learning techniques, eTS+ is an adaptive fuzzy rule-based model that processes data sequentially, and continuously updates its structure and functionality as new data are input.

Similar to the HAR approach, one-step-ahead forecasts from SVR, MLP, eTS+, and ALSM are generated as:

$$RV_{t+1} = f\left(RV_t, RV_t^{(w)}, RV_t^{(m)}\right), \tag{18}$$

where $f(\cdot)$ represents the respective mapping function for each model (SVR, MLP, eTS+, and ALSM)[2].

[2] Regarding the notation used in Sect. 2: $y = RV_{t+1}$ and $\mathbf{x} = (RV_t, RV_t^{(w)}, RV_t^{(m)})$.

The form of (18) follows the same structure as the HAR approach. Alternatively, for SVR, MLP, eTS+, and ALSM, we also assess the following form:

$$RV_{t+1} = f\left(RV_t, RV_{t-1}, \dots, RV_{t-p}\right), \tag{19}$$

where $p$ is the number of lagged realized volatilities values considered.

## 4 Computational Results

This section presents the data used in the study, the accuracy evaluation metrics of the predictive models, and the main results.

### 4.1 Data and Error Measures

The data used in this paper consist of intraday Bitcoin price quotes at a 5-minute frequency. They were extracted from the Binance API (Application Programming Interface)[3], one of the leading cryptocurrency trading platforms worldwide. The dataset spans from 1/1/2018 to 11/30/2024, totaling 725,877 intraday quotes. This period was selected based on data availability at the time of extraction.

The one-step-ahead forecasts produced by the models are compared using the root mean squared error (RMSE) and mean absolute error (MAE) measures

$$\text{RMSE} = \sqrt{\frac{1}{T}\sum_{t=1}^{T}\left(RV_t - \hat{RV}_t\right)^2}, \qquad \text{MAE} = \frac{1}{T}\sum_{t=1}^{T}\left|RV_t - \hat{RV}_t\right|,$$

where $RV_t$ is the actual realized volatility at time $t$ and $\hat{RV}_t$ is the corresponding predicted value produced by the forecasters; $T$ denotes the sample size.

### 4.2 Forecasting Performance Evaluation

The data were split into in-sample and out-of-sample sets. The in-sample period spans from January 1, 2018, to September 26, 2020, comprising a total of 1,000 observations, was used to train the models. The out-of-sample period, from September 27, 2020, to November 30, 2024, consisting of 1,526 observations, was used to evaluate the forecasting performance of the models. The data split rate follows the recommendation of [9] for developing HAR models, i.e., using 1,000 observations for training. One-step-ahead forecasts were obtained sequentially by re-estimating the model parameters each day while maintaining a fixed rolling window of 1,000 observations. It is important to highlight that this approach was only applied to the HAR, SVR, and MLP models. In contrast, the

[3] Source: https://binance-docs.github.io/apidocs/spot/en/#general-api-information. Access on December 4th, 2024.

eTS+ and ALSM models are inherently adaptive, meaning that they update their parameters whenever a new datum is input.

The models are developed considering two approaches. The first approach uses the same input variables as the HAR model, as in (18), while the second considers lags of the realized volatility itself as input, as in (19).

The SVR model uses the same input variables as the HAR (SVR3), with a regularization parameter value of 50, a penalty of 0.001 in the loss function, and a radial basis function (RBF) kernel. This same parametrization was used for the SVR model considering two-lag inputs, referred to as SVR2.

Similarly, the MLP uses the same inputs as the HAR model, MLP3, and also considers two-lag realized volatilities as input, denoted by MLP2. In both cases, the neural networks employ a single hidden layer with 10 neurons and ReLU activation function, and a linear output layer. The training was conducted using the backpropagation algorithm.

The eTS+ with the same three inputs as HAR, denoted eTS+3, uses a hyperparameter value of 0.05 which is the threshold needed to evaluate the quality of the clustering structure. In the two-lags ($p = 2$) input, denoted eTS+2 it uses $p = 2$ and a hyperparameter value of 0.07.

The ALSM with the same three inputs as HAR, denoted ALSM3, uses two rules with Gaussian membership functions, with a forgetting factor value of 0.99. The ALSM with two-lags input, denoted ALSM2, also uses two rules with Gaussian membership functions and a forgetting factor of 0.99.

Table 1 summarizes the forecasting performance of the methods in terms of error measures. The bold values indicate the best-performing model, the one with the lowest error measure. Among the models that follow the same structure as the HAR model – i.e., those that use past daily, weekly, and monthly realized volatility as inputs (SVR3, MLP3, eTS+3, and ALSM3) – the adaptive level set fuzzy model exhibited the lowest RMSE error metric (see Table 1). Based on the same metric, only the eTS+3 and ALSM3 models outperform the baseline HAR model. In terms of MAE, SVR3 achieves the best performance, and all proposed approaches surpass the HAR model.

**Table 1.** Forecasting performance evaluation

| Method | HAR | SVR2 | SVR3 | MLP2 | MLP3 | eTS+2 | eTS+3 | ALSM2 | ALSM3 |
|---|---|---|---|---|---|---|---|---|---|
| RMSE | 0.0372 | 0.0433 | 0.0431 | 0.0447 | 0.0389 | 0.0362 | 0.0361 | **0.0346** | 0.0353 |
| MAE | 0.0123 | 0.0115 | **0.0113** | 0.0149 | 0.0121 | 0.0119 | 0.0117 | 0.0115 | 0.0115 |

When considering models that use lagged daily realized volatility as inputs, the ALSM model remains the most accurate approach, yielding the lowest RMSE value (see Table 1). Notably, ALSM2 is the most precise among the alternative strategies in terms of RMSE. Again, based on this metric, the fuzzy models (eTS+2 and ALSM2) outperform the HAR model. Regarding MAE, SVR2 and ALSM2 exhibit the lowest error values.

Overall, the adaptive fuzzy approach appears as an effective method to forecast the realized volatility of Bitcoin. Figure 2 shows the daily forecasts generated by the two-lag ALSM model, highlighting its potential for risk management.

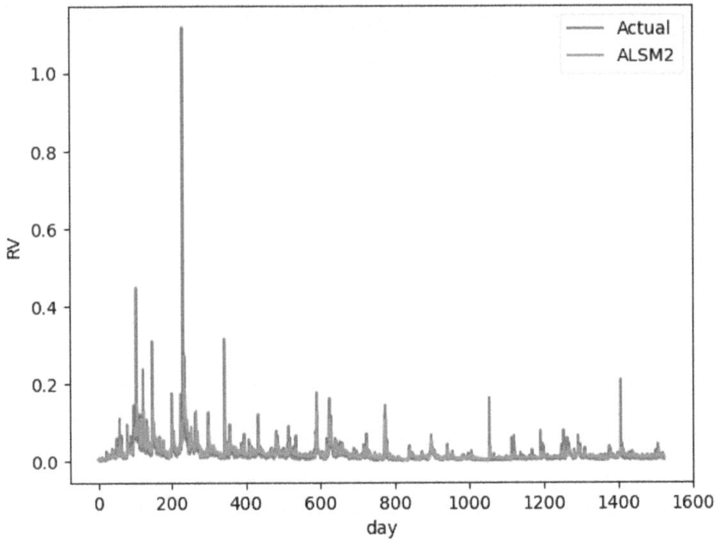


**Fig. 2.** ALSM daily forecasts for the two-lag inputs model (ASLM2).

## 5 Conclusion

The volatility of financial asset returns is a crucial risk measure in finance. Developing accurate models for volatility modeling and forecasting has been a persistent challenge for researchers, particularly for highly volatile, riskier assets such as cryptocurrencies. This paper has addressed a novel approach to forecast Bitcoin volatility using an adaptive fuzzy model based on the concept of level sets. The model is a fuzzy rule-based inference system whose outputs are computed using output functions that map the activation levels of the inputs into values in the output space.

Computational experiments focused on short-term, one-step-ahead, forecasting of the realized volatility of Bitcoin using intraday data. The performance of the adaptive level set model was compared with machine learning techniques and an evolving fuzzy model. The baseline model adopted was the heterogeneous autoregressive regression model – a widely used model in the realized volatility literature. The results suggest that the level set-based algorithmic approach achieves the highest performance. Future work should explore the use of the level set-based algorithm in other markets and asset classes and the evaluation of the results in economic terms. The use of market sentiment variables in adaptive fuzzy modeling is also an issue to be investigated.

**Acknowledgement.** The authors gratefully acknowledge the valuable comments provided by the anonymous reviewers.

## References

1. Ahmed, M.S., El-Masry, A.A., Al-Maghyereh, A.I., Kumar, S.: Cryptocurrency volatility: a review, synthesis, and research agenda. Res. Int. Bus. Financ. **71**, 102472 (2024)
2. Andersen, T.G., Bollerslev, T., Diebold, F.X., Labys, P.: The distribution of realized exchange rate volatility. J. Am. Stat. Assoc. **96**(453), 42–55 (2001)
3. Angelov, P.: Evolving Takagi-Sugeno fuzzy systems from data streams (eTS+). In: Angelov, P., Filev, D., Kasabov, N. (eds.) Evolving intelligent systems: Methodology and applications, pp. 21–50. Wiley & IEEE Press, Hoboken, NJ, USA (2010)
4. Aras, S., Özdemir, M.O., Çılgın, C.: Can joint modelling of external variables sampled at different frequencies enhance long-term bitcoin volatility forecasts? Financ. Res. Lett. **73**, 106679 (2025)
5. Øverland Bergsli, L., Lind, A.F., Molnár, P., Polasik, M.: Forecasting volatility of bitcoin. Res. Int. Bus. Financ. **59**, 101540 (2022)
6. Branco, R.R., Rubesam, A., Zevallos, M.: Forecasting realized volatility: does anything beat linear models? J. Empir. Financ. **78**, 101524 (2024)
7. Chen, T., Deng, J., Nie, J.: Implied volatility slopes and jumps in bitcoin options market. Oper. Res. Lett. **55**, 107135 (2024)
8. Chun, D., Cho, H., Ryu, D.: Volatility forecasting and volatility-timing strategies: a machine learning approach. Res. Int. Bus. Financ. **75**, 102723 (2025)
9. Corsi, F.: A simple approximate long-memory model of realized volatility. J. Financ. Economet. **7**(2), 174–196 (2009)
10. Cui, T., Ding, S., Jin, H., Zhang, Y.: Portfolio constructions in cryptocurrency market: a CVaR-based deep reinforcement learning approach. Econ. Model. **119**, 106078 (2023)
11. Degiannakis, S., Floros, C.: Methods of Volatility Estimation and Forecasting, pp. 58–109. Palgrave Macmillan UK, London (2015)
12. Harasheh, M., Bouteska, A.: Volatility estimation through stochastic processes: evidence from cryptocurrencies. North Am. J. Econ. Finan. **75**, 102320 (2025)
13. Hu, N., Yin, X., Yao, Y.: A novel HAR-type realized volatility forecasting model using graph neural network. Int. Rev. Financ. Anal. **98**, 103881 (2025)
14. Huang, Z.C., Sangiorgi, I., Urquhart, A.: Forecasting bitcoin volatility using machine learning techniques. J. Int. Finan. Markets. Inst. Money **97**, 102064 (2024)
15. Jung, L.: System Identification: Theory for the User. Pearson, Upper Saddle River (1999)
16. Ko, H., Son, B., Lee, J.: Portfolio insurance strategy in the cryptocurrency market. Res. Int. Bus. Financ. **67**, 102135 (2024)
17. Lahmiri, S.: Modeling and predicting historical volatility in exchange rate markets. Phys. A **471**, 387–395 (2017)

18. Leite, D., Gomide, F., Yager, R.: Data driven fuzzy modeling using level sets. In: Proceedings of the IEEE International Conference on Fuzzy Systems, Padova, Italy (2022)
19. Li, D., Shi, Y., Xu, L., Xu, Y., Zhao, Y.: Dynamic asymmetric dependence and portfolio management in cryptocurrency markets. Financ. Res. Lett. **48**, 102829 (2022)
20. Lin, X., Meng, Y., Zhu, H.: How connected is the crypto market risk to investor sentiment? Financ. Res. Lett. **56**, 104177 (2023)
21. Maciel, L., Ballini, R., Gomide, F.: Adaptive level set fuzzy modeling. In: NAFIPS International Conference on Fuzzy Systems, Soft Computing, and Explainable AI, South Padre Island, TX, USA (2024). in press
22. Maciel, L.: Cryptocurrencies value-at-risk and expected shortfall: do regime-switching volatility models improve forecasting? Int. J. Finan. Econ. **26**(3), 4840–4855 (2021)
23. Maciel, L., Ballini, R., Gomide, F.: Adaptive fuzzy modeling and forecasting of financial time series. In: 2024 IEEE Symposium on Computational Intelligence for Financial Engineering and Economics (CIFEr), pp. 1–7 (2024)
24. Oh, D.H., Park, Y.H.: Garch option pricing with volatility derivatives. J. Bank. Finan. **146**, 106718 (2023)
25. Qiu, Y., Wang, Y., Xie, T.: Forecasting bitcoin realized volatility by measuring the spillover effect among cryptocurrencies. Econ. Lett. **208**, 110092 (2021)
26. Rong, H., Yang, Z., Wong, P.: Robust and noise insensitive recursive maximum correntropy-based evolving fuzzy system. IEEE Trans. Fuzzy Syst. **28**(9), 2277–2284 (2020)
27. Xiao, J., Wen, F., Zhao, Y., Wang, X.: The role of us implied volatility index in forecasting Chinese stock market volatility: evidence from HAR models. Int. Rev. Econ. Finan. **74**, 311–333 (2021)
28. Yager, R.: An alternative procedure for the calculation of fuzzy logic controller values. J. Jpn. Soc. Fuzzy Theory Syst. **3**(4), 736–746 (1991)
29. Yi, Y., He, M., Zhang, Y.: Out-of-sample prediction of bitcoin realized volatility: do other cryptocurrencies help? North Am. J. Econ. Finan. **62**, 101731 (2022)
30. Zhang, Y., He, M., Wang, Y., Wen, D.: Model specification for volatility forecasting benchmark. Int. Rev. Financ. Anal. **97**, 103850 (2025)
31. Zhang, Z., Zhao, R.: Good volatility, bad volatility, and the cross section of cryptocurrency returns. Int. Rev. Financ. Anal. **89**, 102712 (2023)

# Unconstrained Parametrization of Proper Symplectic Decomposition for Learning Hamiltonian Dynamics

Jānis Bajārs(✉), Dāvis Kalvāns, and Dmitry Gromov

Faculty of Science and Technology, University of Latvia,
Jelgavas Street 3, Riga 1004, Latvia
{janis.bajars,davis.kalvans,dmitry.gromov}@lu.lv

**Abstract.** Symplecticity-preserving neural networks such as SympNets have been proposed to learn the flow of symplectic Hamiltonian dynamics and to obtain qualitatively better long-term predictions. Computationally, learning high-dimensional problems still poses a great challenge. Structure-preserving dimensionality reduction methods have been developed to improve computational efficiency, such as proper symplectic decomposition (PSD), to preserve the inherent geometric properties of the system when learning Hamiltonian dynamics. Several near-optimal PSD solutions, such as a cotangent lift solution, have also been constructed. In this work, we propose a symplecticity-preserving unconstrained parametrization of the symplectic lift matrices, such that the dimensionality reduction can be learned simultaneously with learning Hamiltonian dynamics in the dimension-reduced phase space. With this approach, we obtain more accurate numerical results, especially long-term predictions, compared to learning dimension-reduced dynamics with the previously introduced constant PSD cotangent lift solution.

**Keywords:** Hamiltonian systems · Structure-preserving neural networks · Learning dynamics · Proper symplectic decomposition · Dimensionality reduction

## 1 Introduction

The development of efficient numerical algorithms is an active area of research. With their significant increase in popularity, machine learning algorithms have also gained considerable recognition for being able to model complex dynamical systems from data, being viewed as having universal approximation properties. Along with the vast development and recognition in the past few decades of geometric or structure-preserving numerical integration methods [10], there has also been increased interest in the development of physics-informed and structure-preserving data-driven algorithms [3,8,11,14,19,20,23]. This interest stems from the fact that such data-driven methods have improved qualitative predictions, especially long-term predictions, in approximating the solutions of


M. Baczyński et al. (Eds.): EUSFLAT 2025, LNCS 15884, pp. 15–26, 2025.
https://doi.org/10.1007/978-3-031-97228-7_2

complex dynamical systems such as the Hamiltonian systems introduced in Sect. 2.

As the flow of a Hamiltonian system is *symplectic*, the authors of [14] proposed symplecticity-preserving neural network architectures called SympNets, described in Sect. 3. SympNets are universal approximators and can approximate symplectic flows and maps with high accuracy. Apart from Hamiltonian dynamics, structure-preserving algorithms have also been developed for learning Poisson, phase-volume-preserving, and time-reversible dynamics [3,11,21,23].

Learning the flow of a high-dimensional dynamical system can be a very challenging task that demands high computational power. If the dynamics can be modeled well in a low-dimensional subspace of the phase space, as in the case of the nonlinear localized *discrete breathers* (DBs) of the Hamiltonian lattice dynamics [4–6], then an optimal dimensionality reduction method will significantly decrease the training and prediction computational times by requiring smaller neural networks with fewer parameters. Objectively, dimensionality reduction methods should also preserve the inherent geometric structure of the system [4,5,18].

The proposed dimensionality reduction technique, *proper symplectic decomposition* (PSD), for learning Hamiltonian dynamics is considered in Sect. 4. PSD was originally proposed in [18] to obtain reduced-order Hamiltonian systems and was recently considered in conjunction with SympNets to learn Hamiltonian dynamics [4,5] and in the data-driven model reduction method with the Hamiltonian operator inference approach [20]. The authors of [18] also proposed exactly symplectic but suboptimal PSD solutions such as the *cotangent-lift* PSD solution, which may not necessarily be the best PSD solution when learning symplectic dynamics. In Sect. 5, we provide theoretical results for an unconstrained parametrization of *symplectic lift* matrices, allowing it to be learned simultaneously with learning Hamiltonian dynamics in dimension-reduced phase space.

Numerical results considering the unconstrained parametrization of symplectic lift matrices and learning discrete breather solutions are illustrated in Sect. 6. The numerical results show that learning a structure-preserving linear dimensionality reduction transformation alongside the flow of Hamiltonian dynamics yields significantly better long-term predictions compared to learning dynamics with the cotangent-lift solution. The conclusions of this work are summarized in Sect. 7.

## 2 Hamiltonian Systems

In this research, we are concerned with learning from given dynamics data the flow of a canonical Hamiltonian system described in the general form [1,7]

$$\frac{\mathrm{d}x}{\mathrm{d}t} = J_{2d}\nabla_x H(x), \quad x(0) = x_0, \tag{1}$$

where the time-dependent solution $x = (q, p)^T : [0, +\infty) \to \Omega \subset \mathbb{R}^{2d}$ consists of the conjugate variables $q \in \mathbb{R}^d$ and $p \in \mathbb{R}^d$, which are the position and momentum variables, respectively, and $x_0 = (q(0), p(0))^T$ is the initial condition. The matrix $J_{2d} \in \mathbb{R}^{2d\times 2d}$ is an invertible even-dimensional skew-symmetric matrix

$$J_{2d} = \begin{bmatrix} 0_d & I_d \\ -I_d & 0_d \end{bmatrix}, \tag{2}$$

where $I_d \in \mathbb{R}^{d\times d}$ and $0_d \in \mathbb{R}^{d\times d}$ are the $d$-dimensional identity and zero matrices. It follows that $J_{2d}^{-1} = J_{2d}^T = -J_{2d}$.

The Hamiltonian $H$ is the quantity conserved along the solutions of the system (1), i.e., $\frac{\mathrm{d}H}{\mathrm{d}t} = 0$. In addition to the Hamiltonian conservation, the flow $\phi_t$ of the Hamiltonian system (1), such that $x(t) = \phi_t(x_0)$, $x(t+s) = \phi_{t+s}(x_0) = \phi_t(\phi_s(x_0))$, for all $s, t \in [0, +\infty)$, and $x(0) = \phi_0(x_0) = x_0$, is *symplectic*, i.e., the equation

$$\frac{\partial \phi_t(x_0)}{\partial x_0}^T J_{2d} \frac{\partial \phi_t(x_0)}{\partial x_0} = J_{2d} \tag{3}$$

holds for all $t$ and $x_0 \in \Omega$ for which the flow $\phi_t$ is defined. From (3), we can also derive that the flow of the Hamiltonian system (1) is phase-volume-preserving.

## 3 Learning Hamiltonian Dynamics

To learn the flow $\phi_t$ of the Hamiltonian dynamics (1), or its discrete counterpart, we first consider the given dynamics data of the Hamiltonian system in the form of snapshot matrices. The first matrix is

$$X = \left[x_0\ \phi_h(x_0)\ \phi_{2h}(x_0)\ \phi_{3h}(x_0)\ \ldots\ \phi_{(K-1)h}(x_0)\right] \in \mathbb{R}^{2d\times K}, \tag{4}$$

where $h$ is the data sampling time interval, $K$ is the number of snapshots or observations, and the $j$th column of the matrix $X$ is $X^j = \phi_{(j-1)h}(x_0)$, for all $j = 1, \ldots, K$, which is the solution of the Hamiltonian system (1) at the time $t = (j-1)h$.

In addition to the snapshot data matrix (4), we also define the snapshot matrix in the following form:

$$Y = \left[\phi_h(x_0)\ \phi_{2h}(x_0)\ \phi_{3h}(x_0)\ \ldots\ \phi_{(K-1)h}(x_0)\ \phi_{Kh}(x_0)\right] \in \mathbb{R}^{2d\times K}, \tag{5}$$

such that the $j$th column of the matrix $Y$ is $Y^j = \phi_{jh}(x_0)$, where $j = 1, \ldots, K$. Note that the discrete map between the data snapshot matrices, $\Phi_h : X \to Y$, such that $\Phi_h(X^j) = Y^j$, for all $j = 1, \ldots, K$, is a symplectic map since $\phi_h$ is.

Thus, it is justified and desired to model the flow of the Hamiltonian system given by the snapshot matrices (4) and (5) using neural networks preserving symplecticity. Therefore, we consider the so-called G – SympNets of the recently proposed symplecticity-preserving neural network architectures SympNets [14]. The construction of SympNets is based on the fact that the composition of symplectic maps (neural network modules) is also a symplectic map. In addition, SympNets have also been shown to be universal approximators, as proven by the authors of [14] and numerically demonstrated in other works, e.g., [3–5].

The neural networks G – SympNets are defined in the following form as the composition of $L$ symplectic maps $\mathcal{M}_\tau$:

$$\xi_\tau = \underbrace{\mathcal{M}_\tau \circ \mathcal{M}_\tau \circ \cdots \circ \mathcal{M}_\tau \circ \mathcal{M}_\tau}_{L\,\text{times}}, \tag{6}$$

where $L$ specifies the depth (number of layers) of the neural network, and the map $\mathcal{M}_\tau$ of a free parameter $\tau$, which, in our study, we set proportional to the data sampling time interval value $h$, i.e., $\tau = h/L$, is a composition of the so-called symplectic *Up* and *Low* gradient modules: $\mathcal{M}_\tau = \mathcal{M}_\tau^{Low} \circ \mathcal{M}_\tau^{Up}$. Both the *Up* and *Low* modules are invertible maps, which map a given system's state $(q, p)^T \in \mathbb{R}^{2d}$ to a new state $(Q, P)^T \in \mathbb{R}^{2d}$. The gradient modules in the explicit form are

$$Q = q + \tau W_p^T \mathrm{diag}(w_p)\sigma(W_p p + b_p), \quad P = p; \tag{7}$$

$$Q = q, \quad P = p - \tau W_q^T \mathrm{diag}(w_q)\sigma(W_q q + b_q), \tag{8}$$

which satisfy the symplecticity condition (3) for all $\tau \in \mathbb{R}$, $\sigma$ (continuously differentiable), $W_{q,p} \in \mathbb{R}^{m\times d}$, $w_{q,p} \in \mathbb{R}^m$, and $b_{q,p} \in \mathbb{R}^m$, where $m$ specifies the width of the neural network (6). In modules (7) and (8), $\sigma$ is a continuously differentiable activation function, and it is set to be the sigmoid function, as in [3–5,14].

In learning Hamiltonian dynamics with the neural networks G – SympNets (6), the *mean squared error* (MSE) loss function, also referred to as the *prediction loss function*, is minimized:

$$\mathcal{L}_{\text{pred}} = \frac{1}{K}\sum_{j=1}^{K} \|\tilde{Y}^j - \xi_\tau(\tilde{X}^j)\|_2^2, \quad \tilde{Y}^j = S^+ Y^j, \quad \tilde{X}^j = S^+ X^j, \tag{9}$$

where $\|\cdot\|_2^2$ is the Euclidean norm squared and $S^+ \in \mathbb{R}^{2r\times 2d}$ is a *symplectic projection* matrix from the $2d$-dimensional phase space to the reduced-order model dimension $2r$, where $r \leq d$. The projection matrix $S^+$ is defined through the *symplectic lift* matrix $S \in \mathbb{R}^{2d\times 2r}$ from the subspace of lower dimension $2r$ to the original state space with dimension $2d$, i.e., $X = S\tilde{X}$ and $Y = S\tilde{Y}$, which we discuss in more detail in Sect. 4. When learning without dimensionality reduction, the matrices $S$ and $S^+$ are just identity matrices $I_{2d}$.

## 4 Dimensionality Reduction with Proper Symplectic Decomposition

In this section, we describe *proper symplectic decomposition* (PSD) [18] for learning Hamiltonian dynamics with dimensionality reduction, i.e., to obtain the symplectic lift and projection matrices $S \in \mathbb{R}^{2d\times 2r}$ and $S^+ \in \mathbb{R}^{2r\times 2d}$, respectively, already stated in the prediction loss function (9).

Since the flow of a Hamiltonian system is symplectic, we also consider symplectic dimensionality reduction techniques in conjunction with learning dynamics, as suggested by the authors of [4,5]. The *symplectic lift*, which preserves the symplectic structure, is performed with a linear transformation matrix $S$ that satisfies the symplecticity constraint equation:

$$S^T J_{2d} S = J_{2r}, \tag{10}$$

where $J_{2r} = \begin{bmatrix} 0_r & I_r \\ -I_r & 0_r \end{bmatrix} \in \mathbb{R}^{2r\times 2r}$. The set of all symplectic lift matrices $S \in \mathbb{R}^{2d\times 2r}$ is a *real symplectic Stiefel manifold* [18], denoted by $Sp(2r, 2d)$. If $r = d$, then $Sp(2d) = Sp(2r, 2d)$, $S$ is a *symplectic* matrix, and we have a symplectic group, which is also a Lie group [16].

From (10), it follows that $\operatorname{rank}(S) = 2r$. Furthermore, (10) restricts the columns of $S$. By denoting with $s_i'$, $i = 1, \ldots, r$, the first $r$ columns, and with $s_i''$ the last $r$ columns of $S$, i.e., $S = \left[s_1' \ldots s_r' \; s_1'' \ldots s_r''\right]$, we have the following conditions:

$$(s_i')^T J_{2d}\, s_j' = 0, \quad i, j \in \{1, \ldots, r\}, \tag{11a}$$
$$(s_i'')^T J_{2d}\, s_j'' = 0, \quad i, j \in \{1, \ldots, r\}, \tag{11b}$$
$$(s_i')^T J_{2d}\, s_j'' = \delta_{ij}, \quad i, j \in \{1, \ldots, r\}. \tag{11c}$$

Note that $(s_i')^T J_{2d}\, s_i' = (s_i'')^T J_{2d}\, s_i'' = 0$ holds trivially for all $i = 1, \ldots, r$ due to the skew-symmetry of $J_{2d}$. Thus, conditions (11a) and (11b) yield $r(r-1)$ constraints. In addition, condition (11c) yields an additional $r^2$ constraints. Hence, the dimension of the real symplectic Stiefel manifold $Sp(2r, 2d)$ is $4dr - r(2r-1)$. Particularly, for $r = d$ we have that $\dim Sp(2d) = 2d^2 + d$.

Then, the *symplectic projection* matrix $S^+$ is defined through the lift matrix $S$ satisfying (10) as

$$S^+ = J_{2r}^T\, S^T J_{2d}. \tag{12}$$

Direct calculation shows that $S^+ S = \left(J_{2r}^T\, S^T J_{2d}\right) S = J_{2r}^T \left(S^T J_{2d}\, S\right) = J_{2r}^T J_{2r} = I_{2r}$, whereas for $r < d$, $SS^+ \neq I_{2d}$, which leads to errors from the dimensionality reduction when projecting training data into lower-dimensional phase space.

With PSD [18], we aim to find the symplectic lift and projection matrices $S$ and $S^+$ that minimize the *projection loss function*:

$$\mathcal{L}_{\text{proj}} = \frac{1}{K} \sum_{j=1}^{K} \|X^j - SS^+X^j\|_2^2, \tag{13}$$

subject to the symplecticity constraint (10).

To our and the authors of [18]'s best knowledge, there is no closed-form solution to this constrained optimization problem. Therefore, in [18], several suboptimal solutions were proposed, i.e., exact solutions with respect to the specific subsets of $Sp(2r, 2d)$. In particular, the *cotangent lift* solution (COT) yields significantly better results compared to non-structure-preserving dimensionality reduction techniques such as *proper orthogonal decomposition* (POD); see [4,5,18].

While the cotangent lift solution provides constant and easily computable symplectic lift and projection matrices, it may only be suboptimal in the set $Sp(2r, 2d)$. On the other hand, solving the general constrained optimization problem (13) with constraint (10) can be a computationally intensive task for problems with large dimensions $2d$.

In the context of learning Hamiltonian dynamics, in the search for the most optimal dimensionality reduction symplectic lift matrix $S \in Sp(2r, 2d)$, one may introduce an additional two loss functions, along with the prediction loss function (9), to train a symplectic neural network (6) in the dimension-reduced phase space and to learn the most optimal symplectic lift matrix $S$ while minimizing the projection error (13), along with the *symplecticity loss function* given by the Frobenius norm squared:

$$\mathcal{L}_{\text{symp}} = \|S^T J_{2d} S - J_{2r}\|_F^2. \tag{14}$$

In general, optimizing the current multi-task problem with the loss functions (9), (13), and (14) will, at best, yield only near-symplectic lift and projection matrices $S$ and $S^+$, respectively. To overcome this problem, in the following section, we propose an unconstrained parametrization of the symplectic lift matrices $S \in Sp(2r, 2d)$ such that $\mathcal{L}_{\text{symp}} = 0$, exactly.

# 5 Unconstrained Parametrization of Symplectic Lift Matrices

In this section, we describe and prove the main theoretical results of this paper and present symplecticity-preserving unconstrained parametrization of the symplectic lift matrices $S \in Sp(2r, 2d)$, such that the symplecticity loss function (14) is exactly zero by construction. The motivation for the proposed parametrization stems from the fact that any symplectic matrix can be factored into no more than 5 unit triangular symplectic matrices; see Theorem 5 of [12]. It is worth mentioning that other parametrizations of symplectic matrices exist; see, e.g., [9], but these are less suitable for the application within the machine learning framework.

It is easy to verify that the unit triangular matrices, $\begin{bmatrix} I_d & R \\ 0_d & I_d \end{bmatrix}$ and $\begin{bmatrix} I_d & 0_d \\ R & I_d \end{bmatrix}$, where $R \in \mathbb{R}^{d\times d}$, are symplectic matrices if and only if $R = R^T$. The authors of [13] have demonstrated that any symplectic matrix can be factored into no more than 9 such unit triangular symplectic matrices, which allows their unconstrained parametrization, whereas the authors of [12] extended their result by proving that it suffices to take only 5.

The following important proposition shows that multiplying a symplectic lift matrix by symplectic matrices yields a symplectic lift matrix.

**Proposition 1.** *If $S \in Sp(2r, 2d)$, $A \in Sp(2d)$, and $B \in Sp(2r)$, then the matrix $\tilde{S} = ASB \in Sp(2r, 2d)$.*

*Proof.* Direct calculation shows that $\tilde{S}^T J_{2d}\, \tilde{S} = (ASB)^T J_{2d}\, (ASB) = B^T (S^T (A^T J_{2d}\, A)\, S)\, B = B^T (S^T J_{2d}\, S)\, B = B^T J_{2r}\, B = J_{2r}$, i.e., matrix $\tilde{S}$ satisfies equation (10), which proves the statement of the proposition.

The next proposition states that multiplying a symplectic lift matrix from the right-hand side by a symplectic matrix does not contribute to the projection error (13).

**Proposition 2.** *If $\tilde{S} = SB$, where $S \in Sp(2r, 2d)$ and $B \in Sp(2r)$, then $\tilde{S} \in Sp(2r, 2d)$ and $\tilde{S}\tilde{S}^+ = SS^+$, or, in other words, the right-hand-side multiplication by a symplectic matrix does not change the value of the projection loss function* (13).

*Proof.* From Proposition 1, it follows that $\tilde{S} \in Sp(2r, 2d)$. Using the definition of the symplectic projection matrix $S^+$ (12), the fact that $B^T$ is also a symplectic matrix, and the skew-symmetry property of the matrix $J_{2r}$, we find that $\tilde{S}\tilde{S}^+ = \tilde{S}\, J_{2r}^T\, \tilde{S}^T J_{2d} = (SB)\, J_{2r}^T\, (SB)^T J_{2d} = S\, (B\, J_{2r}^T\, B^T)\, S^T J_{2d} = -S\, (B\, J_{2r}\, B^T)\, S^T J_{2d} = -S\, J_{2r}\, S^T J_{2d} = S\, (J_{2r}^T\, S^T J_{2d}) = SS^+$, which completes the proof.

For our main result, we define a constant symplectic lift matrix $\Pi \in Sp(2r, 2d)$ in the form

$$\Pi = \begin{bmatrix} I_{d\times r} & 0_{d\times r} \\ 0_{d\times r} & I_{d\times r} \end{bmatrix}, \tag{15}$$

where $I_{d\times r}$ is a block matrix of the form $I_{d\times r} = \begin{bmatrix} I_r & 0_{r\times(d-r)} \end{bmatrix}^T$. Essentially, the matrix $\Pi$ lifts a vector from a lower-dimensional vector space with dimension $2r$ to the vector space with dimension $2d$ by adding a required number of $2(d-r)$ zero components to the vector. For a $2d \times 2d$ matrix, the symplectic lift matrix (15) defines a projection onto its $1, \ldots, r$ and $d+1, \ldots, d+r$ columns. Thus, we can define the canonical projection $\pi : Sp(2d) \to Sp(2r, 2d)$ by $S = A\Pi$ for $A \in Sp(2d)$, where $S \in Sp(2r, 2d)$ follows from Proposition 1. The projection $\pi$ is surjective as any symplectic lift matrix can be transformed to $\Pi$ by applying at most $4r$ symplectic corrections, called symplectic transvections [2] (see also [17] for a detailed discussion).

Now we demonstrate and prove the main result of the paper.

**Theorem 1.** *Any symplectic lift matrix $S \in Sp(2r, 2d)$ can be factored and, thus, unconstrainedly parametrized, in the following form:*

$$S = \begin{bmatrix} I_d & \mathrm{diag}(a) \\ 0_d & I_d \end{bmatrix} \begin{bmatrix} I_d & 0_d \\ A_4 & I_d \end{bmatrix} \begin{bmatrix} I_d & A_3 \\ 0_d & I_d \end{bmatrix} \begin{bmatrix} I_d & 0_d \\ A_2 & I_d \end{bmatrix} \begin{bmatrix} I_d & A_1 \\ 0_d & I_d \end{bmatrix} \Pi, \tag{16}$$

*where $a \in \mathbb{R}^d$, all $A_{1,2,3,4} \in \mathbb{R}^{d\times d}$ are symmetric matrices, each parametrized by $d(d+1)/2$ parameters, and $\Pi$ is the constant projection matrix* (15).

*Proof.* The proof follows from the fact that any symplectic lift matrix $S \in Sp(2r, 2d)$ can be expressed as the product of a symplectic matrix $A \in S(2d)$ and the projection matrix $\Pi$ (15), where the symplectic matrix $A$ by Theorem 5 of [12] can be factored into no more than 5 unit triangular symplectic matrices, which completes the proof of the theorem.

In the following section, we use the result of Theorem 1 to learn Hamiltonian dynamics in a dimension-reduced phase space while simultaneously learning the parametrized symplectic lift matrix $S$ in the form (16), further abbreviated as a ParamS solution.

## 6 Numerical Results

In this section, we provide numerical verification of the proposed unconstrained parametrization of the symplectic lift matrices in Sect. 5 by learning a discrete breather solution of a one-dimensional crystal lattice model with 64 particles (i.e., $2d = 128$) considered in [4–6]. Discrete breathers are nonlinear spatially localized lattice excitations. See Fig. 1, which illustrates the numerically exact time-period discrete breather solution of the symplecticity-preserving Verlet numerical method applied to the Hamiltonian lattice equations. For more details on obtaining such solutions, see [5]. Discrete breather solutions provide a good means for learning dimension-reduced Hamiltonian systems using symplecticity-preserving dimensionality reduction methods in conjunction with SympNets. Thus, with (6), we are approximating the Verlet method's symplectic flow map in a dimension-reduced phase space. In what follows, the problem's parameters are as follows: the data sampling time step $h = 0.01$, and the number of snapshots $K = 80$, i.e., the data reconstruction time interval is $[0, 0.8]$, whereas all predictions are performed by choosing the initial condition at $t = 0.8$. The reduced model's dimension is $2r = 14$, and the neural network's (6) architecture consists of $L = 4$ layers and a width $m = 64$.

All numerical calculations are performed in Python with the open-source machine learning framework PyTorch on a 12th-generation Intel Core i7-12700KF computer with 64 GB of RAM. All models are trained with the batch Adam optimization method [15] considering the standard parameter values while employing exponential scheduling for the learning rate $\eta$, where the decay rate parameter $\gamma = e^{\log(\eta_2/\eta_1)/N_e}$ is calculated by specifying the initial and final learning rate values $\eta_1$ and $\eta_2$, respectively, for the fixed number of epochs $N_e$. We set $N_e = 10^6$ so that the prediction loss function (9) reaches values below $10^{-9}$, allowing us to obtain even greater precision in long-term predictions. In addition, for maximal accuracy, we use double-precision floating-point arithmetic.

The results with the PSD cotangent-lift solution are recalculated from [5] by setting $\eta_1 = 10^{-2}$ and $\eta_2 = 10^{-3}$, whereas for learning with the ParamS symplectic lift matrix (16), for the multi-task problem, we employ the loss balancing method [22] with the default parameter values for the total loss function: $\mathcal{L} = \lambda_1 \mathcal{L}_{\text{pred}} + \lambda_2 \mathcal{L}_{\text{proj}}$, where the weights $\lambda_{1,2}$ get updated after each $10^3$ epochs.

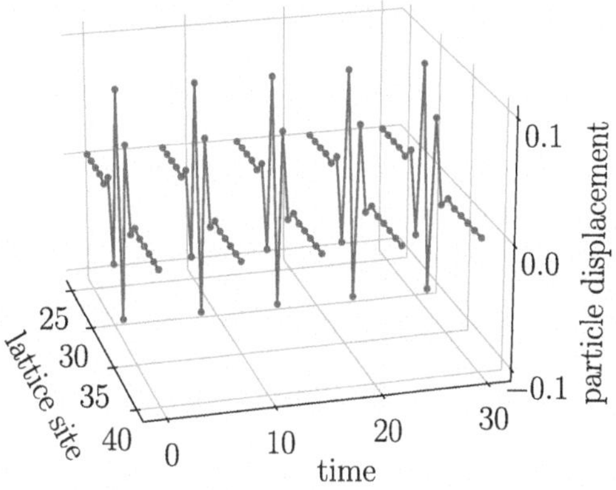


**Fig. 1.** Nonlinear localized discrete breather solution in the lattice of 64 particles. Particle displacement values are illustrated after each 10-wave period $T = 0.75$.

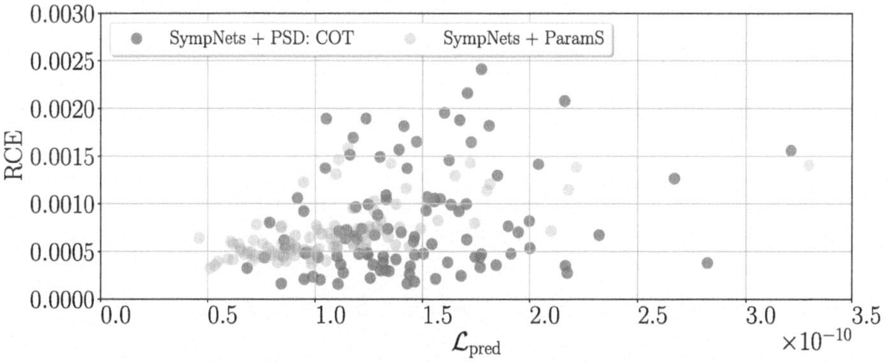


**Fig. 2.** Prediction loss values (9) versus the reconstruction errors for all 100 trained neural networks of both dimensionality reduction approaches; see text.

To ensure that the prediction loss values (9) agree well with the prediction loss values after $N_e = 10^6$ epochs using the PSD cotangent-lift solution (see Fig. 2), we found a need to reduce the learning rate by setting $\eta_1 = 10^{-3}$ and $\eta_2 = 10^{-4}$. For training SympNets, we initialize all weight values $W_q$, $W_p$, $w_q$, and $w_p$ from the normal distribution with mean zero and variance 0.01, while the initial bias values are set to zero; all parameters in the symplectic lift matrix (16) are chosen from the normal distribution with mean zero and variance 0.0001.

For the numerical comparison of both approaches for dimensionality reduction, we train 100 neural networks by considering different random weight initializations. In general, neural networks' predictions are highly dependent on the provided data, the weight initialization, the model parameter values (e.g., $L$ and $m$), the number of epochs $N_e$, the optimization method, and learning rate scheduling. Thus, not all trained models will yield the same results, and not all of them can produce qualitatively good long-term predictions. Training each

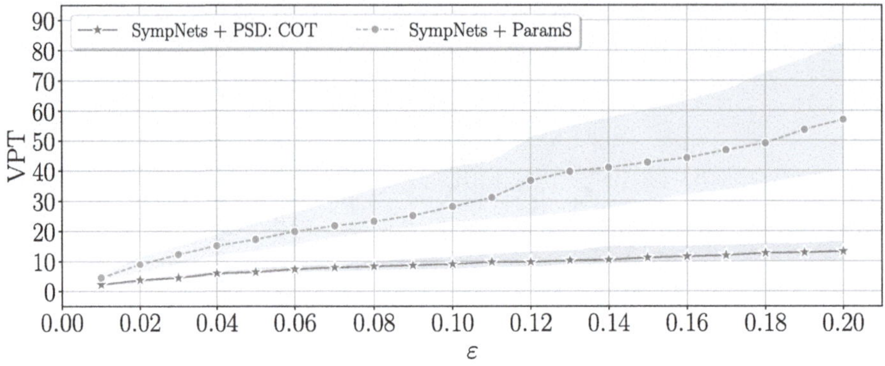


**Fig. 3.** The median of the valid prediction time and its 95% confidence interval as a function of the threshold value $\epsilon$ for both symplectic dimensionality reduction approaches; see text.

neural network model 100 times allows us to statistically quantify their overall performance.

The prediction performance of neural networks is investigated through the evaluation of the *valid prediction time* (VPT) defined based on the relative errors $RE(t_m)$ at time instances $t_m = hm$, where $m \in \mathbb{N}_0$, between the exact and predicted solution trajectories as a function of a threshold value $\epsilon > 0$, defined as time $T_\epsilon = \arg\max_{t_n} \{t_n = nh \mid RE(t_m) \leq \epsilon, \forall m \leq n,\ n, m \in \mathbb{N}_0\}$, whereas the *reconstruction error* (RCE) over the time interval $[0, 0.8]$ is computed as the averaged relative error: $\frac{1}{K}\sum_{k=1}^{K} RE(t_k)$. In Fig. 2, we plot the prediction loss (9) at the final epoch versus the reconstruction error for all trained neural networks and both dimensionality reduction methods. With the chosen training parameter values, we obtain comparable loss and reconstruction errors for both methods. From the illustrations, we have omitted the projection loss (13) values, which on average are approximately equal to $10^{-8}$.

To evaluate the performance of the long-term predictions of all trained neural networks of both symplecticity-preserving dimensionality reductions, in Fig. 3, we plot the median of the VPT and its 95% confidence interval as a function of the threshold value $\epsilon$. The numerical results indicate that, statistically, symplectic dimensionality reduction with the trained symplectic lift matrix (16) in conjunction with learning SympNets in dimension-reduced phase space will produce better long-term predictions. This holds even though the learned symplectic lift matrices are not necessarily the most optimal solutions to the proper symplectic decomposition constrained optimization problem.

## 7 Conclusions

In this work, we have proposed an unconstrained parametrization for the symplectic lift matrices. The optimal linear dimensionality reduction can be learned simultaneously with learning the flow of a Hamiltonian system using symplectic neural networks. In comparison to considering a suboptimal PSD solution for dimensionality reduction, the increased training time is balanced by the fact that the symplectic projection of training data is exactly symplectic, i.e., it has a symplectic loss function equal to zero, and by significant improvements in long-term predictions, as demonstrated by learning discrete breather dynamics in dimension-reduced phase space. With this work, we have provided analytical justification for the unconstrained parametrization and computational evidence concerning when the structure-preserving learning of high-dimensional problems can be further enhanced. This work stimulates further understanding and motivates the necessity for the development of structure-preserving data-driven dimensionality reduction methods, even beyond linear methods and Hamiltonian dynamics.

**Acknowledgements.** This research is funded by the Latvian Council of Science, project "Development of structure- and data-driven methods for analysis and control of complex dynamical systems", project No. lzp-2024/1-0207.

## References

1. Arnol'd, V.: Mathematical Methods of Classical Mechanics. Springer-Verlag New York (1989). https://doi.org/10.1007/978-1-4757-2063-1
2. Artin, E.: Geometric Algebra. Interscience Publishers, New York (1957)
3. Bajārs, J.: Locally-symplectic neural networks for learning volume-preserving dynamics. J. Comput. Phys. **476**, 111911 (2023). https://doi.org/10.1016/j.jcp.2023.111911
4. Bajārs, J.: Dimensionality reduction with proper symplectic decomposition for learning Hamiltonian dynamics. In: Sergeyev, Y.D., Kvasovitri, D.E., Astorino, A. (eds.) Numerical Computations: Theory and Algorithms, pp. 3–18. Springer Nature Switzerland, Cham (2025). https://doi.org/10.1007/978-3-031-81244-6_1
5. Bajārs, J., Kalvāns, D.: Structure-preserving dimensionality reduction for learning Hamiltonian dynamics. J. Comput. Phys. **528**, 113832 (2025). https://doi.org/10.1016/j.jcp.2025.113832
6. Bajārs, J., Kozirevs, F.: Data-driven intrinsic localized mode detection and classification in one-dimensional crystal lattice model. Phys. Lett. A **436**, 128071 (2022). https://doi.org/10.1016/j.physleta.2022.128071
7. Castaños, F., Gromov, D., Hayward, V., Michalska, H.: Implicit and explicit representations of continuous-time port-hamiltonian systems. Syst. Control Lett. **62**(4), 324–330 (2013). https://doi.org/10.1016/j.sysconle.2013.01.007
8. Celledoni, E., et al.: Structure-preserving deep learning. Eur. J. Appl. Math. **32**(5), 888–936 (2021). https://doi.org/10.1017/S0956792521000139
9. Dopico, F.M., Johnson, C.R.: Parametrization of the matrix symplectic group and applications. SIAM J. Matrix Anal. Appl. **31**(2), 650–673 (2009). https://doi.org/10.1137/060678221
10. Hairer, E., Lubich, C., Wanner, G.: Geometrical Numerical Integration: Structure-Preserving Algorithms for Ordinary Differential Equations, Springer Series in Computational Mathematics, vol. 31. Springer Berlin, Heidelberg (2006). https://doi.org/10.1007/3-540-30666-8

11. Jin, P., Zhang, Z., Kevrekidis, I., Karniadakis, G.E.: Learning Poisson systems and trajectories of autonomous systems via Poisson neural networks. IEEE Trans. Neural Netw. Learn. Syst., 1–13 (2022). https://doi.org/10.1109/TNNLS.2022.3148734
12. Jin, P., Lin, Z., Xiao, B.: Optimal unit triangular factorization of symplectic matrices. Linear Algebra Appl. **650**, 236–247 (2022). https://doi.org/10.1016/j.laa.2022.06.009
13. Jin, P., Tang, Y., Zhu, A.: Unit triangular factorization of the matrix symplectic group. SIAM J. Matrix Anal. Appl. **41**(4), 1630–1650 (2020). https://doi.org/10.1137/19M1308839
14. Jin, P., Zhang, Z., Zhu, A., Tang, Y., Karniadakis, G.E.: SympNets: intrinsic structure-preserving symplectic networks for identifying Hamiltonian systems. Neural Netw. **132**, 166–179 (2020). https://doi.org/10.1016/j.neunet.2020.08.017
15. Kingma, D.P., Ba, J.: Adam: A method for stochastic optimization. In: Bengio, Y., LeCun, Y. (eds.) 3rd International Conf. Learning Representations, ICLR 2015, San Diego, USA, 2015, Conference Track Proceedings (2015). http://arxiv.org/abs/1412.6980
16. Lee, J.M.: Introduction to Smooth Manifolds. Springer, second edn. (2012). https://doi.org/10.1007/978-1-4419-9982-5
17. Mackey, D.S., Mackey, N., Tisseur, F.: $\mathbb{G}$-reflectors: analogues of Householder transformations in scalar product spaces. Linear Algebra Appl. **385**, 187–213 (2004). https://doi.org/10.1016/j.laa.2003.07.009
18. Peng, L., Mohseni, K.: Symplectic model reduction of Hamiltonian systems. SIAM J. Sci. Comput. **38**(1), A1–A27 (2016). https://doi.org/10.1137/140978922
19. Raissi, M., Perdikaris, P., Karniadakis, G.: Physics-informed neural networks: a deep learning framework for solving forward and inverse problems involving nonlinear partial differential equations. J. Comput. Phys. **378**, 686–707 (2019). https://doi.org/10.1016/j.jcp.2018.10.045
20. Sharma, H., Wang, Z., Kramer, B.: Hamiltonian operator inference: physics-preserving learning of reduced-order models for canonical Hamiltonian systems. Physica D **431**, 133122 (2022). https://doi.org/10.1016/j.physd.2021.133122
21. Valperga, R., Webster, K., Turaev, D., Klein, V., Lamb, J.: Learning reversible symplectic dynamics. In: Firoozi, R., Mehr, N., Yel, E., Antonova, R., Bohg, J., Schwager, M., Kochenderfer, M. (eds.) Proc. 4th Annual Learning for Dynamics and Control Conference. Proceedings of Machine Learning Research, vol. 168, pp. 906–916. PMLR (2022). https://proceedings.mlr.press/v168/valperga22a.html
22. Wang, S., Sankaran, S., Wang, H., Perdikaris, P.: An expert's guide to training physics-informed neural networks (2023). https://arxiv.org/abs/2308.08468
23. Zhu, A., Zhu, B., Zhang, J., Tang, Y., Liu, J.: VPNets: volume-preserving neural networks for learning source-free dynamics. J. Comput. Appl. Math. **416**, 114523 (2022). https://doi.org/10.1016/j.cam.2022.114523

# New Contexts in Aggregation Theory

# Prioritized Preference Aggregation for Non-uniform Groups of Agents

Janusz Kacprzyk(✉) and Sławomir Zadrożny

Systems Research Institute, Polish Academy of Sciences,
Newelska 6, 01-447 Warsaw, Poland
{kacprzyk,zadrozny}@ibspan.waw.pl

**Abstract.** A novel approach to the important problem of aggregation of individual fuzzy preferences of a group of agents in a group decision process is presented. It is different than the traditional, widely employed aggregation based on the averaging, the weighed conjunction/disjunction, etc. of the respective preference degrees between pairs of options which stand for the uniformity of the group of agents in the sense that all testimonies of the agents are to be accounted for, even if the agents (and maybe also options) are assigned various importance degrees. The novel approach proposed here assumes that the group is not uniform in the above sense which implies that the testimonies of the most important agents are crucial and decisive, so that they should be followed, possibly ignoring testimonies of lower level agents, as it often happens in business or the military. Yager's approach to the so-called prioritized aggregation is employed. The results are very promising and can yield new vistas and perspectives for (fuzzy) preference based group decision making in complex groups of agents, notably authoritarian hierarchies.

**Keywords:** group decision making · fuzzy preference · fuzzy preference aggregation · prioritized aggregation

## 1 Introduction

In this paper we are concerned with some aspects of *group decision making* which is meant for our purposes as follows (cf. Nurmi [14], Nurmi and Kacprzyk [15], Nurmi, Kacprzyk and Fedrizzi [16], Kacprzyk, Fedrizzi and Nurmi [10]: we have a set of at least 2 options (alternatives, variants, ...), and a set of at least 2 agents, human (animate) or inanimate, e.g. software, cobots/robots, etc., who play the role of decision makers. Each agent provides his/her/its testimony which is assumed to be an individual preference relation. For generality, we assume that we have here the individual fuzzy preference relations the entries of which yield a degree of preference between a pair of options, from 1 standing for full preference for the first option of the pair over the second option, through, as it usually assumed, 0.5 for indifference between options, to 0 standing for full preference


M. Baczyński et al. (Eds.): EUSFLAT 2025, LNCS 15884, pp. 29–40, 2025.
https://doi.org/10.1007/978-3-031-97228-7_3

for the second option of the pair over the first one, with all intermediate values standing for partial preferences. For the purposes of this paper we assume, which is usually assumed in most works in the field, that the sum of preferences of the former option over the latter one and of the latter option over the former one is equal to 1.

Such individual fuzzy preferences can be directly employed for deriving *group decision solutions*, for instance, various cores or minimax sets (cf. Nurmi [14], Kacprzyk [9], Kacprzyk, Fedrizzi and Nurmi [10], Kacprzyk and Zadrożny [13]), etc.

However, there is also another direction in this field, that is, the individual fuzzy preference relations are not directly employed for deriving the solutions but are first aggregated to the social fuzzy preference relation which is meant in the same way as the individual fuzzy preference relations but concerns the preferences of the group as a whole. Then, the social fuzzy preference relation is used to derive group decision solutions exemplified by the consensus winners [14]. We are concerned with this type of decision making here.

It is easy to see that in our context, i.e. for the derivation of the group decision solutions on the basis of the social preference relation, the first, initial step, is to aggregate the individual fuzzy preference relations to obtain the social fuzzy preference relation. This is a general and very important problem in our context but also, more generally, in many multi-person decision making related contexts.

Among many traditionally employed aggregation methods, one can mention the following ones:

- *Arithmetic mean (averaging) aggregation* which boils down to the calculation, for each pair of options, of the average value of the preferences over this specific pair of options by all agents involved; this averaging type aggregation assumes the same importance of each agent and can readily be extended to include the importance degree, for instance, from 0, standing for not important at all to 1 standing for fully important, through all intermediate values between 0 and 1 standing for partially important; the OWA operator is defined by a vector of parameters, and via a proper choice of this parameters one obtains a number of other aggregation operators; weights, usually from $[0, 1]$ can be added;
- *Minimum and maximum aggregation* which boils down to the taking as the result the least or highest, respectively, value, of preference between each pair of options, for each agents; the minimum represent the fully pessimistic attitude while the maximum represents the fully optimistic attitude; also here weights, from $[0, 1]$ can be added;
- *Other aggregations* among which the following ones are often employed:
  - *Geometric mean aggregation* which is more resistant to extreme values than the arithmetic mean aggregation,
  - *Aggregation via the Ordered Weighted Averaging (OWA) operators* (cf. Yager [22], Yager and Kacprzyk [20], Yager, Kacprzyk and Beliakov [21], Kacprzyk, Yager and Merigó [12]) which makes it possible to assign weights (from 0 to 1) standing for the degrees of importance, meant as explained above, for each agent;

- *Choquet integral based aggregation* which makes it possible to handle complex interactions and dependencies between the arguments;
- *Sugeno integral based aggregation* which makes it possible to handle qualitative and ordinal preferences, etc.

The above mentioned aggregation operators, here to be applied to the aggregation of individual fuzzy preference relations, explicitly or implicitly assume that the agents whose preferences are to be aggregated are considered from some point of view to be the same, even if they are assigned various weights (importance) to them. Namely, even with different weights, the testimonies of the particular agents operate in the same manner meant as, for instance, a low testimony – i.e. a low preference degree between a pair of options – of an agent whose importance is high is anyway taken into account similarly as the testimony of any other agent, with a lower importance.

However, in many examples of real human groups the situation is different, that is, the testimony of a more important agent, especially if it is clear-cut, should be fully reflected in the social preferences. This situation is characteristic for many hierarchies, notably in the military or business fields, when the top level agents are real decision makers and their testimonies do count, and lower level agents have much less to say.

To formalize such a situation, we apply here – for developing a different type of aggregation of the individual fuzzy preference relations – an interesting approach proposed by Yager [18,19] called the *prioritized aggregation* which yields a new type of aggregation that can be adequate for many decision making processes, notably those considered here, i.e. for groups of agents hierarchically organized, i.e. forming a non-uniform group of agents, but additionally with a prioritization in the sense that a testimony of a more important agent should prevail over preferences of less important agents which is characteristic for many military, business, political, etc. settings.

We will first present the point of departure, that is the traditional averaging type preference aggregation, then present the application for this purpose of Yager's [18,19] prioritized aggregation scheme.

## 2 From the Individual to Social Fuzzy Preference Relations: The Problem of Aggregation

The point of departure in our context is based on the introduction of an *individual* and *social fuzzy preference relation.*

Let us have a set of $n \geq 2$ options, $S = \{s_1, \ldots, s_n\}$, and a set of $m \geq 2$ agents, $E = \{e_1, \ldots, e_m\}$; both are assumed finite. Then, an agent's $e_k \in E$ *individual fuzzy preference relation* in $S \times S$ assigns a value from $[0, 1]$ to the *preference degree* of one option over another.

Usually, some conditions are also to be satisfied, as, e.g., reflexivity, connectivity, (max-min) transitivity, etc. but we will not consider them here as we are primarily interested in a new aggregation scheme for the derivation of the *social fuzzy preference relations.*

An *individual fuzzy preference relation* of agent $e_k$, $R_k$, is given by its membership function $\mu_{R_k} : S \times S \longrightarrow [0,1]$ meant as

$$\mu_{R_k}(s_i, s_j) = \begin{cases} 1 & \text{if } s_i \text{ is definitely preferred to } s_j \\ c \in (0.5, 1) & \text{if } s_i \text{ is slightly preferred to } s_j \\ 0.5 & \text{in the case of indifference} \\ d \in (0, 0.5) & \text{if } s_j \text{ is slightly preferred to } s_i \\ 0 & \text{if } s_j \text{ is definitely preferred to } s_i \end{cases} \quad (1)$$

If the cardinality of $S$ (card($S$)) is small enough (as assumed here), an individual fuzzy preference relation of agent $e_k$, $R_k$, may conveniently be represented by an $n \times n$ matrix $R_k = [r^k_{ij}]$, such that $r^k_{ij} = \mu_{R_k}(s_i, s_j)$; $i, j = 1, \ldots, n$; $k = 1, \ldots, m$. $R_k$ is usually just assumed (also here) to be reciprocal, that is, $r^k_{ij} + r^k_{ji} = 1$, with $r^k_{ii} = 0$, for all $i, j, k$.

The *solution* to the group decision making problem may take different forms: a ranking of all options, the choice of a subset of the set of options (possibly a singleton) etc. - anyway, such a solution have to reflect the preferences of the group. The individual fuzzy preference relations, similarly as their non-fuzzy counterparts in traditional (non-fuzzy) group decision making, are a point of departure for most procedures for the derivation of solutions following 2 basic lines of reasoning (cf. Kacprzyk [9]):

- a *direct approach*

$$\{R_1, \ldots, R_m\} \longrightarrow \text{solution} \quad (2)$$

  that is, a group decision making solution is derived directly (without any intermediate steps) just from the set of individual fuzzy preference relations, and
- an *indirect approach*

$$\{R_1, \ldots, R_m\} \longrightarrow R \longrightarrow \text{solution} \quad (3)$$

  that is, from the set of individual fuzzy preference relations we form first a social fuzzy preference relation, $R$, which is then used to find a group decision making solution. The latter scheme is to be followed here, more specifically, its first step, the derivation of the social fuzzy preference relation.

There are many possible solution concepts for both schemes, cf. Nurmi [14], Kacprzyk, Fedrizzi and Nurmi [10]), Kacprzyk, Nurmi and Zadrożny [11], etc.:

- for the direct approach:
  - the *cores* which are sets of *non-dominated options*, i.e. those not defeated in *pairwise comparisons* by a required majority of agents,
  - the *minimax sets*, i.e. sets of options which in pairwise comparisons with any other option are defeated by the least number of agents,
- for the indirect approach:
  - the *consensus winner* which is basically a set of options that are preferred, by the whole group of agents, i.e. reflected by the social fuzzy preference relation, over a majority of the options.

For our purposes the main problem is first the derivation of the social fuzzy preference relation from the individual fuzzy preference relations, that is:

$$\{R_1, \ldots, R_m\} \longrightarrow R \tag{4}$$

In this paper we will not deal with theoretical aspects related to (4) referring an interested reader to, e.g., Billot [1]. First, we just assume as the point of departure for our next discussion the most straightforward, and most widely used approach to the derivation of the social fuzzy preference relation $R = [r_{ij}]$ given by:

$$r_{ij} = \begin{cases} \frac{1}{m} \sum_{k=1}^{m} a_{ij}^k & \text{if } i \neq j \\ 0 & \text{otherwise} \end{cases} \tag{5}$$

where

$$a_{ij}^k = \begin{cases} 1 \text{ if } r_{ij}^k > 0.5 \\ 0 \text{ otherwise} \end{cases} \tag{6}$$

Notice that $R$ obtained via (5) and (6) need not be reciprocal, i.e. $r_{ij} \neq 1 - r_{ji}$ does not have to hold, in general, but it can be shown that $r_{ij} \leq 1 - r_{ji}$, for each $i, j = 1, \ldots, n$. For other definitions and analyses of $R$, see, e.g., the classic works by Blin and Whinston [3], Billot [1], etc.

*Example 1.* Suppose that we have four agents, $k = 1, 2, 3, 4$, whose individual fuzzy preference relations are:

$R_1 =$

| | $j=$ 1 | 2 | 3 | 4 |
|---|---|---|---|---|
| $i=1$ | 0.0 | 0.3 | 0.7 | 0.1 |
| 2 | 0.7 | 0.0 | 0.6 | 0.6 |
| 3 | 0.3 | 0.4 | 0.0 | 0.2 |
| 4 | 0.9 | 0.4 | 0.8 | 0.0 |

$R_2 =$

| | $j=$ 1 | 2 | 3 | 4 |
|---|---|---|---|---|
| $i=1$ | 0.0 | 0.4 | 0.6 | 0.2 |
| 2 | 0.6 | 0.0 | 0.7 | 0.4 |
| 3 | 0.4 | 0.3 | 0.0 | 0.1 |
| 4 | 0.8 | 0.6 | 0.9 | 0.0 |

$R_3 =$

| | $j=$ 1 | 2 | 3 | 4 |
|---|---|---|---|---|
| $i=1$ | 0.0 | 0.5 | 0.7 | 0.1 |
| 2 | 0.5 | 0.0 | 0.8 | 0.4 |
| 3 | 0.3 | 0.2 | 0.0 | 0.2 |
| 4 | 0.9 | 0.6 | 0.8 | 0.0 |

$R_4 =$

| | $j=$ 1 | 2 | 3 | 4 |
|---|---|---|---|---|
| $i=1$ | 0.0 | 0.4 | 0.7 | 0.8 |
| 2 | 0.6 | 0.0 | 0.4 | 0.3 |
| 3 | 0.3 | 0.6 | 0.0 | 0.1 |
| 4 | 0.2 | 0.7 | 0.9 | 0.0 |

Then, using (5) and (6) we obtain the following social fuzzy preference relation

$R =$

| | $j=$ 1 | 2 | 3 | 4 |
|---|---|---|---|---|
| $i=1$ | 0.00 | 0.00 | 1.00 | 0.25 |
| 2 | 0.75 | 0.00 | 0.75 | 0.25 |
| 3 | 0.00 | 0.25 | 0.00 | 0.00 |
| 4 | 0.75 | 0.75 | 1.00 | 0.00 |

## 3 Idea of a Prioritized Aggregation

The idea of *prioritized aggregation* concerns the situation when we need to aggregate partial scores which are the satisfaction from some aspect of the case considered, these aspects are rank ordered from the most important to the least important, and the lack of satisfaction of a more important aspect cannot be (fully) compensated by the satisfaction of a less important aspects. This is a new approach to the aggregation of partial scores proposed in the seminal papers by Yager [18,19].

In our context of preference aggregation in a group of agents, we assume that there are agents of a different importance, organized in a hierarchy, at the top of the hierarchy there are the most important agents, e.g. top managers or top military commanders, and going down the hierarchy we have agents with a lower and lower importance, e.g. lower level business executives or lower level military commanders. Clearly, it is difficult, if not impossible, to override a testimony (preferences) of a higher level managers by testimonies of lower level managers. In the context of our work, such hierarchies are referred to as *prioritized sets of agents*. They can also be referred to as authoritarian hierarchies. For simplicity, we will call the aggregation in such a context a *prioritized aggregation*.

There are several known methods for incorporating importance weights within the aggregation process. It is, however, well known that there is no one, universal scheme to take into account the weights of aggregated arguments [5], i.e., the way the importance weights should be accounted for depends on the type of the aggregation implemented by a given operator. For example, in case of the conjunction/disjunction (minimium/maximum) type aggregation the following schemes are popular:

$$\mathrm{Wmin}_{w_1,\ldots,w_n}(a_1,\ldots,a_n) = \min_{i=1,\ldots,n} \max(1-w_i, a_i) \tag{7}$$

$$\mathrm{Wmax}_{w_1,\ldots,w_n}(a_1,\ldots,a_n) = \max_{i=1,\ldots,n} \min(w_i, a_i) \tag{8}$$

where $\max_{i=1,\ldots,n} w_i = 1$ [6].

The above formulas may be generalized using, for instance, the operators of $t$-norm/$t$-conorm and fuzzy implication($\mathtt{i}$)/co-implication($\mathtt{i}_c$) [7]. Then, one obtains:

$$\mathrm{Wmin}^{\wedge,i}_{w_1,\ldots,w_n}(a_1,\ldots,a_n) = \bigwedge_{i=1,\ldots,n} \mathtt{i}(w_i, a_i) \tag{9}$$

$$\mathrm{Wmax}^{\vee,\mathtt{i}_c}_{w_1,\ldots,w_n}(a_1,\ldots,a_n) = \bigvee_{i=1,\ldots,n} \mathtt{i}_c(1-w_i, a_i) \tag{10}$$

where $\bigwedge/\bigvee$ denote the $t$-norm/$t$-conorm operators applied to multiple arguments.

The (7)/(8), or (9)/(10), can be generalized by usuing the minimum/maximum $t$-norm/$t$-conorm operators and the implication/co-implication operators $\mathtt{i}(x,y) = \max(1-x, y)$ and $\mathtt{i}_c(x,y) = \min(1-x, y)$, respectively.

The above operators are *idempotent* [7] and under some additional assumptions as to properties of the implication/co-implication operators involved, and are also *monotonic*.

The formulas (7)–(8)) or, in a more general case, the formulas (9)–(10), implement the essence of the prioritized aggregation in the following sense. Let us first consider the minimum operator type aggregation. Then, the decisive factor is the smallest among the aggregated values as this value is taken as the result of the aggregation. Hence, in the prioritized aggregation scenario one should expect that if the most important among the aggregated values is small then this should be reflected in the result of the aggregation. This is exactly how the operator (7) works - in the extreme case when the smallest and, at the same time, the most important value is equal to 0, then the result of the aggregation is equal to 0, too. If less important value is small (even equal to 0) its value does not directly translates to the result of the whole aggregation. It is worth noticing that this does not apply to the large values being aggregated as, by the definition of the minimum operator, they do not influence the result of the aggregation in the same way as the low values. Thus, even if the most important value is equal to 1 still the result of the aggregation may be a small number.

Similar observations apply to the maximum operator type aggregation. In this case, the decisive factor is the largest among the aggregated values as it is taken as the result of the aggregation. Hence, in accordance with the prioritized aggregation semantics, if the most important among the aggregated values is large then this is reflected in the result of the aggregation carried out using (8). In the extreme case when the largest and, at the same time, the most important value is equal to 1, then the result of the aggregation is equal 1. If less important value is large (even equal to 1), then its value does not directly translates to the result of the whole aggregation. Again, this does not apply to the small values being aggregated as, by the definition of the maximum operator, they do not influence the result of the aggregation in the same way as the large values. Thus, even if the most important value is equal to 0, then still the result of the aggregation may be large.

The above mentioned novel methods for importance weights incorporation work well but for two different aggregation styles: either via minimum or maximum operator, respectively. However, in our case we need a method to:

- aggregate individual preferences into a social preference relation and, thus, the aggregation operator should be of the averaging type,
- the preferences are expressed on the so-called bipolar scale [8] and thus aiming at prioritized aggregation we need an aggregation scheme which observes strong opinions of the important agents at both ends of the scale, i.e., if an important agent expresses his or her preference for a pair of options either as a small number (e.g., 0) or a large number (e.g., 1), then it should be properly reflected in the resulting social (group) preference relation.

Hence, in our work we are concerned with maybe the most powerful scheme of the prioritized aggregation (cf. Yager [18,19]) which is well suited for the averaging type aggregation operators. We will use an agent related terminology since we are concerned with agents that constitute the group in which decision making is to take place but first the preference aggregation, is to proceed. The agents can clearly be humans or artificial, e.g. software agents or robots/cobots.

Let us remind the setting assumed in this work and slightly adjust it to the setting adopted in the original work by Yager [18,19]. Thus, first, we have:

- a set of $m$ agents, $E = \{e_1, \ldots, e_m\}$ and by $r_{ij}^k \in [0,1]$ we denote the degree of satisfaction of an aspect in question by agent $e_k$ (in the group decision making process context it is the preference degree for option $s_i$ over option $s_j$), $k = 1, 2, \ldots m$;
- the set of agents is rank ordered from the most important – meant as mentioned above that a testimony of a more important agent can override testimonies of a less important agent – to the least important one through intermediate cases, with $e_1$ denoting the most important and $e_m$ denoting the least important, such that:

$$e_k \text{ is more important than } e_l \text{ if and only if } k < l, \forall k, l \in \{1, 2, \ldots, m\} \quad (11)$$

Hence, in our context of preference aggregation, the set of aspects consists of the set of degree of preferences between the pairs of options.

Thus, for each pair of options $(s_i, s_j)$, we have a set of degrees of preferences of particular agents to aggregate:

$$P_{ij} = \{r_{ij}^k\} = \{r_{ij}^1, r_{ij}^2, \ldots, r_{ij}^m\} \quad (12)$$

and the aggregated preference degree, denoted as $r_{ij}$, is computed as the weighted average:

$$r_{ij} = \frac{\sum_{k=1}^m \mu_{ij}^k \cdot r_{ij}^k}{\sum_{k=1}^m \mu_{ij}^k} \quad (13)$$

where $\mu_{ij}^k$ is a weight of agent $e_k$ used for aggregating the elements of the set $P_{ij}$.

The main problem is now how to define the weights of agents, $\mu_{ij}^k$, to reflect the very idea of Yager's [18,19] prioritized aggregation. For each agent $e_k \in E$ and each set $P_{ij}$ separately, the importance weight is computed as follows. It depends on the position of agent $e_k$ in the order expressed by the user over the agents, and, both, on the weight computed for agent $e_{k-1}$ (with respect to the set $P_{ij}$), that is, who is of a greater priority (more important but in the prioritized rank ordering way) than agent $e_k$, as well as on the degree of preference $r_{ij}^{k-1} \in P_{ij}$ for option $s_i$ over option $s_j$ as seen by agent $e_{k-1}$.

That is, to aggregate the elements of the set $P_{ij}$, $i, j \in \{1, 2, \ldots, n\}$, for each agent $e_k$ we compute the importance weight $\mu_{ij}^k \in [0,1]$. The weights for the agents, which are rank ordered by the users with respect to their importance (which, for instance, results from the hierarchy present in the particular business, military, etc. company or organization), are computed as follows:

- for each set $P_{ij}$ the weight of the most important agent, $e_1$, is set to 1 (by definition), $\mu_{ij}^1 = 1$;

– the weights of the other, less important agents $e_2, e_3, \ldots, e_m$ are then calculated for $P_{ij}$ as:

$$\begin{aligned} \mu_{ij}^2 &= \mu_{ij}^1 \cdot r_{ij}^1 \\ \mu_{ij}^3 &= \mu_{ij}^2 \cdot r_{ij}^2 \\ &\ldots \\ \mu_{ij}^m &= \mu_{ij}^{m-1} \cdot r_{ij}^{m-1} \end{aligned} \tag{14}$$

for all $i, j = 1, 2, \ldots, n$.

The above basic scheme for importance weights calculation works well with respect to properly observing small preference degrees of the most important agents. Namely, if the most important agent $e_1$ expresses his preference for a pair of options $(s_i, s_j)$ as $r_{ij}^1 = 0$ then the weights of subsequent agents $e_i, i \geq 2$, are according to (14), automatically set to 0 and thus the aggregated preference degree for the pair of options $(s_i, s_j)$ becomes 0, too. However, if $e_1$ expresses his or her full preference for option $s_i$ over option $s_j$, i.e., $r_{ij}^1 = 1$ then the aggregated preference degree $r_{ij}$ still may be small.

Thus, we propose the following modification to the formula (14). The weight of agent $e_1$ is still always equal to 1, i.e., $\mu_{ij}^1 = 1, \forall i, j$, but the weights of the other, less important agents $e_i, i \in 2, \ldots, m$ are then:

$$\mu_{ij}^k = \mu_{ij}^{k-1} \cdot 2 \cdot |(|r_{ij}^{k-1} - 0.5| - 0.5)| \tag{15}$$

for all $j, k = 1, 2, \ldots, n$.

Now, according to (15), if the most important agent expresses clear-cut preferences for a pair of options $(s_i, s_j)$, i.e., either $r_{ij}^1 = 1$ or $r_{ij}^1 = 0$, then preferences of other agents are ignored and $r_{ij} = r_{ij}^1$. If, on the other hand, the most important agent $e^1$ does not have clear preferences with respect to such a pair of options, i.e., $r_{ij}^1 = 0.5$ then the weight of the second important agent becomes equal to 1.0 and he or her, or subsequent agents do have strong influence on the resulting aggregated preference degree $r_{ij}$. For the intermediary degrees of preferences expressed by the most important agent $e^1$ the remaining agents do exert some influence in determining the value of $r_{ij}$.

So far, we have tacitly assumed that the ordering of the agents (11) is a total linear order. However, in his original approach to the prioritized aggregation, Yager [18,19] assumes that the set of agents is weakly ordered, i.e., there may be ties between agents in their rank ordering. In particular, there may be a group of (equally) most important agents. This extension implies some changes to formulas which in turn requires a change to our modified formula (15).

Formally, in Yager [18] the agents are partitioned into $q$ distinct subsets $\{H_1, \ldots, H_q\}$ such that $H_u = \{e_{u1}, e_{u2}, \ldots, e_{um_u}\}$, $u \in \{1, \ldots, q\}$, $\sum_u m_u = m$, $\bigcup_{u=1}^q = E$. Now, the family of sets $H_u$ is rank ordered, i.e. they are linearly ordered in such a way that $H_1 > H_2 > \ldots H_q$ meaning that agents in the set $H_u$ are more important than all agents in sets $H_w$ for $w > u$, less important than all agents in sets $H_w$ for $w < u$, and within every set $H_u$ the agents are equally important. Now, the formula (13) takes the form:

$$r_{ij} = \frac{\sum_{u=1}^{q}(\sum_{w=1}^{m_u} \mu_{ij}^u \cdot r_{ij}^{uw})}{\sum_{u=1}^{q}\sum_{w=1}^{m_u} \mu_{ij}^u} \tag{16}$$

where $\mu_{ij}^u$ is a weight of an agent $e_{uw} \in H_u$ (all agents belonging to the same set $H_u$ have the same weight by definition) used for aggregating the elements of the set $P_{ij}$.

Next, the formula (14) is adjusted as follows:

- for each set $P_{ij}$ the weights of the most important agents, $e_{1w} \in H_1, w = 1,\ldots,m_1$, are set to 1 (by definition), $\mu_{ij}^1 = 1$;
- the weights of the other, less important agents $e_{uw} \in H_u, u = 2,\ldots,q$ are then calculated for $P_{ij}$ as:

$$\begin{aligned} \mu_{ij}^2 &= \mu_{ij}^1 \cdot \min_{w\in\{1,\ldots,m_1\}} r_{ij}^{1w} \\ \mu_{ij}^3 &= \mu_{ij}^2 \cdot \min_{w\in\{1,\ldots,m_2\}} r_{ij}^{2w} \\ &\ldots \\ \mu_{ij}^q &= \mu_{ij}^{q-1} \cdot \min_{w\in\{1,\ldots,m_{q-1}\}} r_{ij}^{q-1} \end{aligned} \tag{17}$$

for all $i, j = 1, 2, \ldots, n$.

Thus, now, according to the original Yager's [18,19] approach, the weight of agents belonging to a subset $H_u$ is a product of the weight of agents belonging to the subset $H_{u-1}$ and smallest degree of preference among degrees expressed by the agents to this subset. However, for our purposes we have to slightly revise this formula and thus we propose the following counterpart of formula (15):

$$\mu_{ij}^u = \mu_{ij}^{u-1} \cdot 2 \cdot |(|\frac{\sum_{w=1}^{m_{u-1}} r_{ij}^{(u-1)w}}{m_{u-1}} - 0.5| - 0.5)| \tag{18}$$

for all $j, k = 1, 2, \ldots, n$.

Hence, the formula (18) preserves the interpretation of the formula (15). For example, let subset of the most important agents $H_1$ contain 3 agents with degree of preferences for a pair of options $(s_1, s_2)$:

1. all equal to 1.0; then (18) yields weights $\mu_{12}^u$ for $u > 2$ equal to 0,
2. all equal to 0.0, what similarly to above mentioned case, produces weights equal to 0.

In our next papers practical applications of the presented novel method for the aggregation of individual fuzzy preference relations into a social fuzzy preference relation, which is then employed to derive group decision solution concepts (mainly various consensus winners) will be presented for some cases of strictly prioritized (authoritarian) hierarchies of agent exemplified by those in business, politics, military, etc.

There are many other prioritized operators known in the literature, notably various prioritization focused OWA (ordered weighted averaging) operators, cf. Yager [22], Yager and Kacprzyk [20], Yager, Kacprzyk and Beliakov [21], Kacprzyk, Yager and Merigó [12], Blanco-Mesa, Merig'o and Kacprzyk [2], etc. See also Dubois and Prade![?]. We will study their applicability in the context of the group decision making in our further works.

## 4 Concluding Remarks

We have presented a novel proposal to the important problem of aggregation of individual fuzzy preferences of a group of agents who are involved in a group decision process. The essence of the traditional, widely employed for years aggregation that has been based on the averaging (or some conjunctive/disjunctive types) of the respective preferences between pairs of options, which stands for the uniformity of the group of agents in the sense that all testimonies of the agents are to be taken into account, even if the agents (and maybe also options) are assigned various importance weights. In the new approach proposed here we have assumed that the group is not uniform in the above sense, that is, the agents operate in a strictly hierarchical (authoritarian) setting so that the testimonies of the most important agents are crucial and they, first of all, should be taken into account while constructing the social (group) preference. This situation is characteristic for many business, political and military systems. In our novel approach by Yager's [18, 19] so-called prioritized aggregation is employed. The idea is very promising and can yield new vistas and perspectives for (fuzzy) preference based group decision making in complex group of agents. An interesting extension for the future can be the use of other approaches to prioritized aggregation, e.g. by Wei and Tang [17] or Bouidghaghen at al. [4].

## References


1. Billot, A.: Aggregation of preferences: the fuzzy case. Theor. Decis. **30**, 51–93 (1991)
2. Blanco-Mesa, F., Merigó, J.M., Kacprzyk, J.: Bonferroni means with distance measures and the adequacy coefficient in entrepreneurial group theory. Knowl.-Based Syst. **111**, 217–227 (2016)
3. Blin, J.M., Whinston, A.B.: Fuzzy sets and social choice. J. Cybern. **3**(4), 28–36 (1973)
4. Bouidghaghen, O., Tamine-Lechani, L., Pasi, G., Cabanac, G., Boughanem, M., da Costa Pereira, C.: Prioritized aggregation of multiple context dimensions in mobile IR. In: Salem, M., Shaalan, K., Oroumchian, F., Shakery, A., Khelalfa, H. (eds.) AIRS 2011. LNCS, vol. 7097, pp. 169–180. Springer, Heidelberg (2011). https://doi.org/10.1007/978-3-642-25631-8_16
5. Kraft, D.H., Buell, D.A.: Fuzzy sets and generalized Boolean retrieval systems. Int. J. Man Mach. Stud. **19**(1), 45–56 (1983)
6. Dubois, D., Prade, H.: Weighted minimum and maximum operations in fuzzy set theory. Inf. Sci. **39**, 205–210 (1986)
7. Fodor, J., Roubens, M.: Fuzzy Preference Modelling and Multicriteria Decision Support. System Theory, Knowledge Engineering and Problem Solving, Kluwer Academic Publishers, Series D (1994)
8. Grabisch, M., Greco, S., Pirlot, M.: Bipolar and bivariate models in multicriteria decision analysis: Descriptive and constructive approaches. Int. J. Intell. Syst. **23**(9), 930–969 (2008)
9. Kacprzyk, J.: Group decision making with a fuzzy linguistic majority. Fuzzy Sets Syst. **18**(2), 105–118 (1986)

10. Kacprzyk, J., Fedrizzi, M., Nurmi, H.: Group decision making and consensus under fuzzy preferences and fuzzy majority. Fuzzy Sets Syst. **49**(1), 21–31 (1992)
11. Kacprzyk, J., Nurmi, H., Zadrozny, S.: Reason vs. rationality: from rankings to tournaments in individual choice. Trans. Comput. Collect. Intell. **27**, 28–39 (2017). https://doi.org/10.1007/978-3-319-70647-4_2
12. Kacprzyk, J., Yager, R.R., Merigo, J.M.: Towards human-centric aggregation via ordered weighted aggregation operators and linguistic data summaries: a new perspective on Zadeh's inspirations. IEEE Comput. Intell. Mag. **14**(1), 16–30 (2019)
13. Kacprzyk, J., Zadrożny, S.: Towards a general and unified characterization of individual and collective choice functions under fuzzy and nonfuzzy preferences and majority via the ordered weighted average operators. Int. J. Intell. Syst. **24**(1), 4–26 (2009)
14. Nurmi, H.: Approaches to collective decision making with fuzzy preference relations. Fuzzy Sets Syst. **6**(1), 249–259 (1981)
15. Nurmi, H., Kacprzyk, J.: On fuzzy tournaments and their solution concepts in group decision making. Eur. J. Oper. Res. **51**(2), 223–232 (1991)
16. Nurmi, H., Kacprzyk, J., Fedrizzi, M.: Probabilistic, fuzzy and rough concepts in social choice. Eur. J. Oper. Res. **95**, 264–277 (1996). https://api.semanticscholar.org/CorpusID:120373934
17. Wei, C., Tang, X.: Generalized prioritized aggregation operators. Int. J. Intell. Syst. **27**(6), 578–589 (2012)
18. Yager, R.R.: Prioritized aggregation operators. Int. J. Approximate Reasoning **48**(1), 263–274 (2008)
19. Yager, R.R.: Prioritized OWA aggregation. Fuzzy Optim. Decis. Making **8**, 245–262 (2009)
20. Yager, R.R., Kacprzyk, J.: The ordered weighted averaging operators: theory and applications (1997)
21. Yager, R.R., Kacprzyk, J., Beliakov, G. (eds.): Recent Developments in the Ordered Weighted Averaging Operators: Theory and Practice. Springer Science & Business Media (2011)
22. Yager, R.: On ordered weighted averaging aggregation operators in multicriteria decision making. IEEE Trans. Syst. Man Cybern. **18**(1), 183–190 (1988). https://doi.org/10.1109/21.87068

# An Axiomatic Study of the Properties Satisfied by Methods for Ranking the Elements of a Poset

Ignacio Montes[1], Raúl Pérez-Fernández[1(✉)], and Bernard De Baets[2]

[1] Departamento de Estadística e I.O. y D.M., Universidad de Oviedo, Oviedo, Spain
{imontes,perezfernandez}@uniovi.es
[2] KERMIT, Department of Data Analysis and Mathematical Modelling, Ghent University, Ghent, Belgium
bernard.debaets@ugent.be

**Abstract.** In discrete mathematics, an interesting problem that has called the attention of many scholars is that of ranking the elements of a given partially ordered set. In this contribution, we propose reasonable properties that a method for ranking the elements of a poset may satisfy and we study the relationships between these properties. Interestingly, it is shown how a plethora of additional properties may be borrowed from the field of social choice theory and, in particular, from the problem of the aggregation of rankings. Finally, we present three prominent methods for ranking the elements of a poset (namely, the averaged rank method, the mutual rank probabilities and the maximal method) and analyse which among the proposed properties each of these three methods satisfies.

**Keywords:** Poset · Averaged rank method · Mutual rank probabilities · Maximal method · Aggregation of rankings

## 1 Introduction

The problem of ranking the elements of a given partially ordered set (poset, for short), which consists of selecting the weak ordering that is the most compatible with a given poset, has recurrently called the attention of the scientific community [10]. Mainly of interest to the field of discrete mathematics, this problem has also been shown to be useful in fields of application such as chemistry [3,4] and, quite interestingly, some natural connections between this problem and the fields of voting theory [15] and stochastic orderings [14] have been recently explored.

Among the many methods that have been proposed for ranking the elements of a poset, three of the most common ones are: averaged rank method [22], mutual rank probabilities [7,8] and the maximal method [10]. The first two methods are related to the computation of the linear extensions of the poset, i.e., the chains that are compatible with the poset. In particular, the averaged rank method orders the elements according to the average position of each element in all the linear extensions, whereas the mutual rank probabilities method


M. Baczyński et al. (Eds.): EUSFLAT 2025, LNCS 15884, pp. 41–52, 2025.
https://doi.org/10.1007/978-3-031-97228-7_4

computes, for each pair of elements, the proportion of linear extensions in which each element appears at a better position than the other one. The former method follows a philosophy similar to the approach of Borda to voting theory [2] and the stochastic ordering of expected utility in statistics [16], whereas the latter method follows a philosophy similar to the approach of Condorcet to voting theory [5] and the stochastic ordering of statistical preference in statistics [9]. From a different perspective, the maximal method proceeds by firstly ranking the maximal elements of the poset and iteratively removing all maximal elements until all elements of the original poset are ranked. This approach aligns with the method of plurality in the context of voting theory [21] and the stochastic ordering of multivariate winning probabilities [13]. Thus, one may conclude that many ideas may be borrowed from the field of social choice theory and, in particular, from the problem of the aggregation of rankings.

In this contribution, we propose different properties that a method for ranking the elements of a poset may ideally fulfill. Some of these properties are basic, such as monotonicity or reversal symmetry, some of them are related to the structure of the poset, and some of them stem from the field of voting theory. After showing some connections between these properties, we analyse which properties are satisfied by each of the three methods for ranking the elements of a poset listed above.

The remainder of the manuscript is organised as follows. After introducing some basic definitions regarding posets in Sect. 2, in Sect. 3 we introduce the desirable properties that a method for ranking the elements of a poset may satisfy and we investigate the relationships between these properties. In Sect. 4, we formally present three common methods for ranking the elements of a poset: averaged rank method, mutual rank probabilities and the maximal method. The properties that each of these methods satisfy are also analysed within that section. We conclude the manuscript in Sect. 5 with some final comments.

## 2 Basics on Partially Ordered Sets

In this section we give an overview on partially ordered sets, or *posets* for short (see [6] for more details). A (finite) *poset* is a couple $(P, \leq)$ formed by a finite set $P$ and an order relation $\leq$ on $P$, i.e., a reflexive, antisymmetric and transitive relation on $P$. The strict part of $\leq$ is denoted by $<$. Two elements $x, y \in P$ are called *comparable* when either $x \leq y$ or $y \leq x$, otherwise they are called *incomparable*. Any subset $P' \subset P$ determines another poset $(P', \leq_{|P'})$, referred to as a *subposet*, where $\leq_{|P'}$ is the restriction of $\leq$ to the comparison of the elements in $P'$. The *dual* of a poset $(P, \leq)$ is another poset $(P, \geq)$ where $x \geq y$ if and only if $x \leq y$.

An element $x \in P$ is called *maximal* if there is no other element $y \in P$ such that $x \leq y$. Similarly, an element $x \in P$ is called *minimal* if there is no other element $y \in P$ such that $y \leq x$. Each element $x \in P$ determines two sets, the *principal ideal* and the *principal filter*, respectively denoted by $\downarrow x$ and $\uparrow x$ and defined by:

$$\downarrow x = \{y \in P \mid y \leq x\}, \qquad \uparrow x = \{y \in P \mid x \leq y\}.$$

An element $x \in P$ is said to be *covered by* another element $y \in P$, denoted by $x \lessdot y$, if $x < y$ and there exists no other element $z \in P \setminus \{x, y\}$ satisfying $x < z < y$. The covering relation $\lessdot$ characterises $\leq$ and can be used to give a graphical representation of the poset by means of the so-called *Hasse diagram.* In a Hasse diagram, the elements are presented in vertical tiers; a line between two elements means that the element situated in a lower tier is covered by the element situated in an upper tier.

*Example 1.* Consider the poset $(P, \leq)$ where $P = \{x_1, x_2, x_3, x_4, x_5, x_6\}$ and assume that the covering relation is given by:

$$\lessdot = \{(x_6, x_1), (x_4, x_2), (x_4, x_3), (x_5, x_1), (x_5, x_4)\}.$$

The corresponding Hasse diagram is shown in Fig. 1.

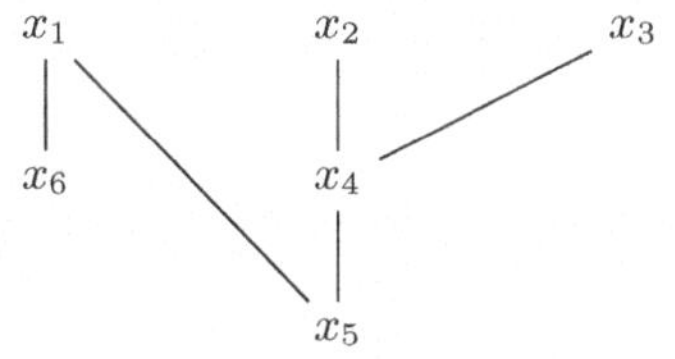


**Fig. 1.** Hasse diagram of the poset in Example 1.

The Hasse diagram shows the structure of the poset and allows us to see that $x_1$, $x_2$ and $x_3$ are maximal elements and $x_5$ and $x_6$ are minimal elements.

A poset $(P, \leq')$ is called an *extension* of $(P, \leq)$ if $x \leq y$ implies $x \leq' y$. A *chain* (or linear order) is a poset in which all the elements are comparable. A *linear extension* of a poset is an extension of the poset that is a chain. Here, we denote the set of all linear extensions of a poset $(P, \leq)$ by $E_{\leq}$. As an example, Table 1 presents all twenty six linear extensions of the poset presented in Example 1.

A *weak order* or *total preorder* is a couple $(P, \precsim)$ formed by a set $P$ and a complete, reflexive and transitive binary relation $\precsim$ on $P$. Any weak order relation $\precsim$ admits a partition into two binary relations:

**(i)** The strict part $\prec$, which is defined by $x \prec y$ if $x \precsim y$ and $y \not\precsim x$. Note that the relation $(\prec \cup =)$, denoted by $\preceq$ if no confusion can occur, is an order relation.

**(ii)** The symmetric part $\sim$, which is defined by $x \sim y$ if $x \precsim y$ and $y \precsim x$. Note that the relation $\sim$ is an equivalence relation, i.e., it is reflexive, transitive and symmetric.

**Table 1.** Linear extensions of the poset presented in Example 1.

| | |
|---|---|
| $e_1$: $x_5 < x_4 < x_3 < x_2 < x_6 < x_1$ | $e_2$: $x_5 < x_4 < x_2 < x_3 < x_6 < x_1$ |
| $e_3$: $x_5 < x_4 < x_3 < x_6 < x_2 < x_1$ | $e_4$: $x_5 < x_4 < x_2 < x_6 < x_3 < x_1$ |
| $e_5$: $x_5 < x_4 < x_6 < x_3 < x_2 < x_1$ | $e_6$: $x_5 < x_4 < x_6 < x_2 < x_3 < x_1$ |
| $e_7$: $x_5 < x_6 < x_4 < x_3 < x_2 < x_1$ | $e_8$: $x_5 < x_6 < x_4 < x_2 < x_3 < x_1$ |
| $e_9$: $x_6 < x_5 < x_4 < x_3 < x_2 < x_1$ | $e_{10}$: $x_6 < x_5 < x_4 < x_2 < x_3 < x_1$ |
| $e_{11}$: $x_5 < x_4 < x_3 < x_6 < x_1 < x_2$ | $e_{12}$: $x_5 < x_4 < x_2 < x_6 < x_1 < x_3$ |
| $e_{13}$: $x_5 < x_4 < x_6 < x_3 < x_1 < x_2$ | $e_{14}$: $x_5 < x_4 < x_6 < x_2 < x_1 < x_3$ |
| $e_{15}$: $x_5 < x_6 < x_4 < x_3 < x_1 < x_2$ | $e_{16}$: $x_5 < x_6 < x_4 < x_2 < x_1 < x_3$ |
| $e_{17}$: $x_6 < x_5 < x_4 < x_3 < x_1 < x_2$ | $e_{18}$: $x_6 < x_5 < x_4 < x_2 < x_1 < x_3$ |
| $e_{19}$: $x_5 < x_4 < x_6 < x_1 < x_3 < x_2$ | $e_{20}$: $x_5 < x_4 < x_6 < x_1 < x_2 < x_3$ |
| $e_{21}$: $x_5 < x_6 < x_4 < x_1 < x_3 < x_2$ | $e_{22}$: $x_5 < x_6 < x_4 < x_1 < x_2 < x_3$ |
| $e_{23}$: $x_6 < x_5 < x_4 < x_1 < x_3 < x_2$ | $e_{24}$: $x_6 < x_5 < x_4 < x_1 < x_2 < x_3$ |
| $e_{25}$: $x_6 < x_5 < x_1 < x_4 < x_3 < x_2$ | $e_{26}$: $x_6 < x_5 < x_1 < x_4 < x_2 < x_3$ |

As a generalisation of the notion of linear extension of a poset, a weak order $(P, \precsim)$ is called a *complete extension* of a poset $(P, \leq)$ if $x \leq y$ implies $x \precsim y$.

The *height* of an element $x \in P$, denoted by $h(x)$, is the number of elements below $x$, that is, $h(x) = |\downarrow x| - 1$, where $|\cdot|$ is used to denote the cardinality of a set. Analogously, the *dual height* of an element $x \in P$, denoted by $\overline{h}(x)$, is the number of elements above $x$, that is, $\overline{h}(x) = |\uparrow x| - 1$. A partition $\{P_1, \ldots, P_k\}$ of $P$, with $k$ being the maximum number of elements in a subposet of $P$ that is a chain, is called a *rank* [20] of $P$ if $y \lessdot x$ and $y \in P_i$ together imply $x \in P_{i+1}$. We denote by $\mathcal{P}(P)$ (or simply $\mathcal{P}$ if no confusion can occur) the set of all ranks of $P$. The maximum and minimum level of an element $x \in P$, denoted by $\overline{l}(x)$ and $\underline{l}(x)$, respectively, are defined as

$$\overline{l}(x) = \max\left\{i \mid \{P_1, \ldots, P_k\} \in \mathcal{P} \wedge x \in P_i\right\},$$
$$\underline{l}(x) = \min\left\{i \mid \{P_1, \ldots, P_k\} \in \mathcal{P} \wedge x \in P_i\right\}.$$

## 3 Methods for Ranking the Elements of a Poset

The problem of ranking the elements of a poset has attracted the attention of the scientific community for many years [4,10]. In this section we introduce some desirable properties that a method for ranking the elements of a poset may satisfy and we investigate the connection between these properties.

### 3.1 Desirable Properties

Consider $\precsim$ the weak order determined by a method for ranking the elements of a poset $(P, \leq)$. We start by mentioning two basic properties regarding symmetry and monotonicity.

**A1.Reversal symmetry:** If $y \precsim x$ in the weak order given for $(P, \leq)$, then $x \precsim' y$ in the weak order given for the dual poset $(P, \geq)$.

**A2.Monotonicity:** The weak order should be compatible with the relation $\leq$. Formally, if $y \leq x$, then $y \precsim x$.

Next, we mention some properties related to the structure of the poset. We start with two properties requiring the obtained weak order to be compatible with the (partial) order given by the principal filters and the principal ideals.

**A3.Ranking by principal filters:** The weak order is compatible with the inclusion between principal filters. Formally, if $\uparrow x \subseteq \uparrow y$, then $y \precsim x$.

**A4.Ranking by principal ideals:** The weak order is compatible with the inclusion between principal ideals. Formally, if $\downarrow y \subseteq \downarrow x$, then $y \precsim x$.

The following two properties require the obtained weak order to be compatible with the depth and the height.

**A5.Compatibility with the height:** The weak order is compatible with the height in the sense that the greater the height, the higher the ranking. Formally, if $h(y) \leq h(x)$, then $y \precsim x$.

**A6.Compatibility with the dual height:** The weak order is compatible with the dual height in the sense that the smaller the dual height, the higher the ranking. Formally, if $\overline{h}(x) \leq \overline{h}(y)$, then $y \precsim x$.

The last two properties regarding the structure of the poset require the obtained weak order to be compatible with the levels and dual levels.

**A7.Ranking by maximum levels:** The weak order is compatible with the maximum levels. Formally, if $\overline{l}(y) \leq \overline{l}(x)$, then $y \precsim x$.

**A8.Ranking by minimum levels:** The weak order is compatible with the minimum levels. Formally, if $\underline{l}(y) \leq \underline{l}(x)$, then $y \precsim x$.

The lastly proposed properties follow the philosophy of voting theory, and in particular of the problem of the aggregation of rankings, by considering the linear extensions $e = (P, \leq_e)$ of the poset $(P, \leq)$ as rankings to be aggregated into a weak order of interest. For instance, properties **A9** and **A10** are related to the majority winner [17,18] (not to be confused with the simple majority rule [11,12]), requiring that an element that appears at the first (resp. last) position in more than half of the linear extensions should be ranked at the first (resp. last) position.

**A9.Majority criterion:** If an element is at the first position in at least half of the linear extensions of $(P, \leq)$, it should be ranked at the first position. Formally, if there exists $x \in P$ such that $|\{e \in E_{\leq} \mid (y \leq_e x)(\forall y \in P)\}| > \frac{|E_{\leq}|}{2}$, then $y \precsim x$ for any $y \in P$.

**A10.Majority loser criterion:** If an element is at the last position in at least half of the linear extensions of $(P, \leq)$, then it should be ranked at the last position. Formally, if there exists $x \in P$ such that $|\{e \in E_{\leq} \mid (x \leq_e y)(\forall y \in P)\}| > \frac{|E_{\leq}|}{2}$, then $x \precsim y$ for any $y \in P$.

The next two properties also align with the philosophy of voting theory, but following the ideas of Condorcet [5] in which elements are compared pairwisely.

**A11. Condorcet criterion:** If an element $x$ beats any other element in at least half of the linear extensions, then it should be ranked at the first position. Formally, if there exists $x \in P$ such that $|\{e \in E_{\leq} \mid y \leq_e x\}| > \frac{|E_{\leq}|}{2}$ for any $y \in P$, then $y \precsim x$ for any $y \in P$.

**A12. Condorcet loser criterion:** If an element $x$ is beaten by any other element in at least half of the linear extensions, then it should be ranked at the last position. Formally, if there exists $x \in P$ such that $|\{e \in E_{\leq} \mid x \leq_e y\}| > \frac{|E_{\leq}|}{2}$ for any $y \in P$, then $y \precsim x$ for any $y \in P$.

Note that the Condorcet loser criterion is sometimes understood slightly differently in the context of social choice by requiring the Condorcet loser not to be ranked at the first position.

The final proposed property is a classical property in voting theory: independence of irrelevant alternatives [1]. Admittedly, there exist different variations of this property (see, e.g. [19]), we consider a version that fits the purpose of ranking the elements of a poset.

**A13. Independence of irrelevant alternatives:** The relative position of two elements within the weak order does not depend on other elements. Formally, consider $x, y \in P$ $(x \neq y)$ and $z \in P \setminus \{x, y\}$ such that either (i) $x < z$ and $y < z$, (ii) $z < x$ and $z < y$, or (iii) $x, z$ and $x, y$ are incomparable. If $y \precsim x$ in $(P, \leq)$, then $y \precsim x$ in the restriction to $P \setminus \{z\}$.

### 3.2 Relationships Between the Properties

In this subsection we establish some relationships between the properties introduced in the previous subsection. We start by showing that three of them, monotonicity and the ranking by principal filters and principal ideals, are equivalent.

**Proposition 1.** *The following statements are equivalent for a method for ranking the elements of a poset:*

**(i)** *It satisfies monotonicity (**A2**).*
**(ii)** *It satisfies the ranking by principal filters (**A3**).*
**(iii)** *It satisfies the ranking by principal ideals (**A4**).*

*Proof.* Assume that the ranking method satisfies monotonicity, and let $x$ and $y$ be two elements satisfying $\downarrow x \subseteq \downarrow y$. If both principal ideals coincide, then $x = y$. Otherwise, since $x \in \downarrow x$, $x$ also belongs to $\downarrow y$, and by definition $x \leq y$. By hypothesis we conclude that $x \precsim y$, and the method satisfies ranking by principal ideals. Conversely, assume that the method satisfies ranking by principal ideals and take $x, y \in P$ such that $x \leq y$. Since $\leq$ is transitive, $\downarrow x \subseteq \downarrow y$, and by hypothesis $x \precsim y$. The equivalence between monotonicity and ranking by principal filters follows analogously. □

Next, we also show that some of the properties imply monotonicity and, according to our previous proposition, also the ranking by principal filters and principal ideals.

**Proposition 2.** *If a method for ranking the elements of a poset satisfies any among compatibility with the height (***A5***), dual height (***A6***), ranking by maximum (***A7***) or minimum levels (***A8***), then it satisfies monotonicity (***A2***), ranking by principal filters (***A3***) and ranking by principal ideals (***A4***).*

*Proof.* Assume that the method for ranking the elements of a poset satisfies the compatibility with the height (**A5**), and consider $x, y \in P$ such that $y \leq x$. This implies that $\downarrow y \subseteq \downarrow x$, and consequently $h(y) \leq h(x)$, which using (**A5**) implies $y \precsim x$. Analogously, assume that the method for ranking the elements of a poset satisfies the compatibility with the dual height (**A6**), and consider $x, y \in P$ such that $y \leq x$. This implies that $\uparrow y \supseteq \uparrow x$, and consequently $\overline{h}(y) \geq \overline{h}(x)$, which using (**A6**) implies $y \precsim x$. Now, assume that the method for ranking the elements of a poset satisfies the ranking by maximum level (**A7**), and consider $x, y \in P$ such that $y \leq x$. This implies that if $x \in P_i$, then $y \in P_j$ with $j \leq i$, and using (**A7**), we get $y \precsim x$. Finally, assume that the method for ranking the elements of a poset satisfies the ranking by minimum level (**A8**), and consider $x, y \in P$ such that $y \leq x$. This implies that if $x \in P_i$, then $y \in P_j$ with $j \geq i$, and using (**A8**) we get $y \precsim x$. □

Finally, we show a connection between the Condorcet and majority (loser) criteria.

**Proposition 3.** *The following statements hold for a method for ranking the elements of a poset:*

**(i)** *If it satisfies the Condorcet criterion (***A11***), then it also satisfies the majority criterion (***A9***).*
**(ii)** *If it satisfies the Condorcet loser criterion (***A12***), then it also satisfies the majority loser criterion (***A10***).*

*Proof.* We prove that the Condorcet loser criterion implies the majority loser criterion; the proof of the other implication follows similarly. Assume that the method for ranking the elements of a poset satisfies the Condorcet loser criterion, and let $x \in P$ be an element such that $|\{e \in E_{\leq} \mid x \leq_e y\}| > \frac{|E_{\leq}|}{2}$. Thus, for any fixed $y^* \in P$, it holds that:

$$|\{e \in E_{\leq} \mid x \leq_e y^*\}| \geq |\{e \in E_{\leq} \mid (x \leq_e y)(\forall y \in P)\}| > \frac{|E_{\leq}|}{2},$$

and the Condorcet loser criterion implies that $x \precsim y^*$. This means that the method satisfies the majority loser criterion. □

# 4 Common Methods for Ranking the Elements of a Poset

In this section we present three among the most common methods that can be found in the literature for ranking the elements of a poset, namely the *Averaged rank method* [22], the *Mutual rank probabilities* [7] and the *Maximal method* [10]. We also investigate which properties among those presented in Sect. 3 are satisfied by each of these methods.

## 4.1 Averaged Rank Method

For each linear extension $e \in E_{\leq}$, we define the position $\mathrm{Pos}_e(x)$ of the element $x \in P$ in the linear extension $e = (P, \leq_e)$ as the number of elements in $P$ ranked at a better or equal position than $x$ in the chain determined by $\leq_e$:

$$\mathrm{Pos}_e(x) = \left|\{z \in P \mid x \leq_e z\}\right| .$$

For each element $x$, its average position $\mathrm{av}(x)$ is defined as:

$$\mathrm{av}(x) = \frac{1}{|E_{\leq}|} \sum_{e \in E_{\leq}} \mathrm{Pos}_e(x) .$$

The averaged rank method (see [3,22]) weakly orders the elements according to their average position. That is, it selects the complete extension $(P, \precsim_{\mathrm{av}})$ determined by $x \precsim_{\mathrm{av}} y$ if $\mathrm{av}(x) \geq \mathrm{av}(y)$. The complete extension is in general a weak order, and we consider the notation $x \prec_{\mathrm{av}} y$ when $\mathrm{av}(x) > \mathrm{av}(y)$ and $x \sim_{\mathrm{av}} y$ when $\mathrm{av}(x) = \mathrm{av}(y)$.

The next result shows the properties satisfied by this method. No other property holds (counterexamples are omitted due to space limitations).

**Proposition 4.** *The averaged rank method satisfies reversal symmetry (***A1***), monotonicity (***A2***) and ranking by principal filters (***A3***) and principal ideals (***A4***).*

*Proof. Reversal symmetry:* It is easy to see that $(P, \leq_e)$ is a linear extension of $(P, \leq)$ if and only if $(P, \geq_e)$ is a linear extension of its dual poset $(P, \geq)$. Hence, the position of $x$ in the chain determined by $\leq_e$ equals $(|P| + 1)$ minus the position of $x$ in the chain determined by $\geq_e$. Hence, $\mathrm{av}(y) \leq \mathrm{av}(x)$ in $(P, \leq)$ if and only if $\mathrm{av}(y) \geq \mathrm{av}(x)$ in the dual poset $(P, \geq)$.

*Monotonicity:* If $y \leq x$, then $y \leq_e x$ in any linear extension $e$ of the poset, hence $\mathrm{av}(x) \leq \mathrm{av}(y)$, implying $y \precsim_{\mathrm{av}} x$.

*Ranking by principal filters and principal ideals:* Since the averaged rank method satisfies monotonicity, Proposition 1 implies that it also satisfies ranking by principal filters and principal ideals. □

### 4.2 Mutual Rank Probabilities

Given a poset $(P, \leq)$, the mutual rank probability $p_{y<x}$ of $x \in P$ over a different element $y \in P$ is defined as the proportion of linear extensions of $(P, \leq)$ in which $y < x$, that is, $p_{y<x} = \frac{|\{e \in E_{\leq} | y \leq_e x\}|}{|E_{\leq}|}$. The method of mutual rank probabilities [8] selects as the complete extension $(P, \precsim_{\text{mr}})$ of $(P, \leq)$ the binary relation defined as $x \precsim_{\text{mr}} y$ if $p_{y<x} \leq \frac{1}{2}$. Note that the relation $\precsim_{\text{mr}}$ is not necessarily transitive and, therefore, its transitive closure needs to be considered if the aim is to obtain a complete extension of $(P, \leq)$. Again, we use the notation $x \prec_{\text{mr}} y$ and $x \sim_{\text{mr}} y$ for the strict and symmetric parts of $\precsim_{\text{mr}}$.

The next result shows the properties satisfied by this method. No other property holds (counterexamples are omitted due to space limitations).

**Proposition 5.** *The mutual rank probabilities method satisfies reversal symmetry (***A1***), monotonicity (***A2***), ranking by principal filters (***A3***) and principal ideals (***A4***), the majority (***A9***) and majority loser (***A10***) criteria, and the Condorcet (***A11***) and Condorcet loser (***A12***) criteria.*

*Proof. Reversal symmetry:* As argued before, $e = (P, \leq_e)$ is a linear extension of $(P, \leq)$ if and only if the dual $e = (P, \geq_e)$ is a linear extension of the dual poset $(P, \geq)$. Hence, $y \leq_e x$ if and only if $y \geq_e x$, meaning that $p_{y<x} \geq \frac{1}{2}$ in $(P, \leq)$ if and only if $p_{y>x} \geq \frac{1}{2}$ in the dual poset $(P, \geq)$.

*Monotonicity:* If $y \leq x$, then $y \leq_e x$ for any linear extension $e$, implying that $p_{y<x} \geq \frac{1}{2}$ and consequently $y \precsim_{\text{mr}} x$.

*Ranking by principal filters and principal ideals:* Since the mutual rank probabilities method satisfies monotonicity, Proposition 1 implies that it also satisfies ranking by principal filters and principal ideals.

*Condorcet criterion:* It is satisfied by definition.

*Majority:* Since the mutual rank probabilities method satisfies the Condorcet criterion, by Proposition 3 it also satisfies the majority criterion.

*Condorcet loser criterion:* It is satisfied by definition.

*Majority loser:* Since the mutual rank probabilities method satisfies the Condorcet loser criterion, by Proposition 3 it also satisfies the majority loser criterion. □

### 4.3 Maximal Method

Given a poset $(P, \leq)$, the maximal method [10] is an iterative method that proceeds as follows. Denote the set of maximal elements of $\leq$ in $P$ by $M_1$, the set of maximal elements of $\leq$ restricted to $P \setminus M_1$ by $M_2$ and, iterating while possible, the set of maximal elements in the restriction of $\leq$ to $P \setminus \cup_{j=1}^{i-1} M_j$ by $M_i$. The maximal method selects as the complete extension $(P, \precsim_{\max})$ of $(P, \leq)$ the weak order given by $x \precsim_{\max} y$ if $x \in M_i$ and $y \in M_j$ for $i \geq j$. In particular, it follows that $x \prec_{\max} y$ if $i > j$ and $x \sim_{\max} y$ if $i = j$.

The following result shows the properties satisfied by the maximal method. No other property holds (counterexamples are omitted due to space limitations).

**Proposition 6.** *The maximal method satisfies monotonicity (***A2***), ranking by principal filters (***A3***) and principal ideals (***A4***), the majority criterion (***A9***) and the Condorcet criterion (***A11***).*

*Proof. Monotonicity:* If $y \leq x$ and $x \in M_i$, then $y \in M_j$ for $j \geq i$, meaning that $y \precsim_{\text{mm}} x$.

*Ranking by principal filters and principal ideals:* Since the maximal method satisfies monotonicity, Proposition 1 implies that it also satisfies ranking by principal filters and principal ideals.

*Majority criterion:* If $x$ appears in at least half of the linear extensions at the first position, this means that it is a maximal element, hence the maximal method gives $y \precsim_{\text{mm}} x$ for any other $y$, where $y \prec_{\text{mm}} x$ whenever $y$ is also a maximal element and $y \sim_{\text{mm}} x$ otherwise.

*Condorcet criterion:* We first prove that, if there exists $x \in P$ such that $p_{y<x} \geq \frac{1}{2}$ for any other $y$, this means that $x$ is a maximal element of $P$. Assume that $x$ is not maximal, then there exists $y \in P$ such that $x < y$, which implies that $p_{y<x} = 0$, a contradiction. Hence, since $x$ is a maximal element, the maximal method gives $y \precsim_{\text{mm}} x$ for any other $y$, where $y \prec_{\text{mm}} x$ whenever $y$ is also a maximal element and $y \sim_{\text{mm}} x$ otherwise. □

## 5 Conclusions

In this work we have presented different properties that methods for ranking the elements of a poset may desirably satisfy. Additionally, we have compared three common methods for ranking the elements of a poset (namely, the averaged rank method, mutual rank probabilities and the maximal method) in terms of the properties they satisfy. Table 2 presents a summary of the properties satisfied by each method. It can be concluded that mutual rank probabilities and the maximal method fulfill a richer variety of properties than the averaged rank method. Notably, the maximal method does not fulfill the property of reversal symmetry (**A1**); however, a dual method could be proposed by iteratively ranking the minimal elements so that the maximal method agrees with the weak order given by this dual method for the dual poset. Interestingly, this dual method will satisfy the majority loser (**A10**) and Condorcet loser (**A12**) criteria instead of the majority (**A9**) and Condorcet (**A11**) criteria.

**Table 2.** Summary of the properties satisfied by the averaged rank method, mutual ranking probabilities and the maximal method.

| | **Averaged ranking** | **Mutual rank probabilities** | **Maximal method** |
|---|---|---|---|
| **A1.**Reversal symmetry | ✓ | ✓ | ✗ |
| **A2.**Monotonicity | ✓ | ✓ | ✓ |
| **A3.**Ranking by principal filters | ✓ | ✓ | ✓ |
| **A4.**Ranking by principal ideals | ✓ | ✓ | ✓ |
| **A5.**Compatibility with the height | ✗ | ✗ | ✗ |
| **A6.**Compatibility with the dual height | ✗ | ✗ | ✗ |
| **A7.**Ranking by maximum levels | ✗ | ✗ | ✗ |
| **A8.**Ranking by minimum levels | ✗ | ✗ | ✗ |
| **A9.**Majority criterion | ✗ | ✓ | ✓ |
| **A10.**Majority loser criterion | ✗ | ✓ | ✗ |
| **A11.**Condorcet criterion | ✗ | ✓ | ✓ |
| **A12.**Condorcet loser criterion | ✗ | ✓ | ✗ |
| **A13.**Independence of irrelevant alternatives | ✗ | ✗ | ✗ |

As an interesting matter for future studies, this contribution opens the door to introducing more properties that a method for ranking the elements of a poset may desirably satisfy by mimicking properties used within the context of the aggregation of rankings in the field of social choice theory. Future research questions also relate to the study of impossibility theorems showing whether some of the proposed properties are incompatible and to the search for new or existing methods that satisfy each of the proposed properties separately (thus guaranteeing that all properties are achievable).

**Acknowledgments.** This contribution is part of grant PID2022-140585NB-I00 funded by MICIU/AEI/10.13039/501100011033 and "FEDER/UE". Bernard De Baets received funding from the Flemish Government under the "Onderzoeksprogramma Artificiële Intelligentie (AI) Vlaanderen" programme.

**Disclosure of Interests.** The authors have no competing interests to declare that are relevant to the content of this article.

## References

1. Arrow, K.J.: Social Choice and Individual Values, 2nd edn. Yale University Press, New Haven (1963)
2. Borda, J. C. de: Mémoire sur les élections au scrutin. Histoire de l'Académie Royale des Sciences, Paris (1781)

3. Brüggemann, R., Simon, U., Mey, S.: Estimation of averaged ranks by extended local partial order models. MATCH. Commun. Math. Comput. Chem. **54**, 489–517 (2005)
4. Brüggemann, R., Voigt, K.: Basic principles of Hasse diagram technique in chemistry. Comb. Chem. High Throughput Screening **11**, 756–769 (2008)
5. Condorcet, M.: An essay on the application of probability theory to pluralty decision making: an election between three candidates. Reprinted in 1989. Sommerlad, F. and McLean, I. (eds.) (1785)
6. Davey, B.A., Priestley, H.A.: Introduction to Lattices and Order. Cambridge University Press, Cambridge (2002)
7. De Baets, B., De Meyer, H., De Loof, K.: On the cycle transitivity of the mutual rank probability relation of a Poset. Fuzzy Sets Syst. **161**, 2695–2708 (2010)
8. De Loof, K., De Baets, B., De Meyer, H., Brüggemann, R.: A hitchhiker's guide to Poset ranking. Comb. Chem. High Throughput Screening **11**, 734–744 (2008)
9. De Shuymer, B., De Meyer, H., De Baets, B., Jenei, S.: On the cycle-transitivity of the dice model. Theor. Decis. **54**, 261–285 (2003)
10. Fishburn, P.C., Gehrlein, W.V.: A comparative analysis of methods for constructing weak orders from partial orders. J. Math. Sociol. **4**, 93–102 (1975)
11. Inada, K.: The simple majority decision rule. Econometrica **37**, 490–506 (1969)
12. May, K.O.: A set of independent necessary and sufficient conditions for simple majority decision. Econometrica **20**, 680–684 (1952)
13. Montes, I., Montes, S., De Baets, B.: Multivariate winning probabilities. Fuzzy Sets Syst. **362**, 129–143 (2019)
14. Montes, I., Pérez-Fernández, R., de Baets, B.: A correspondence between methods for ranking elements of a poset and stochastic orderings. In: Lesot, M.J., et al. (eds.) Information Processing and Management of Uncertainty in Knowledge-Based Systems. IPMU 2024. Lecture Notes in Networks and Systems, vol. 1174, pp. 321–332 (2024)
15. Montes, I., Rademaker, M., Pérez-Fernández, R., De Baets, B.: A correspondence between voting procedures and stochastic orderings. Eur. J. Oper. Res. **285**, 977–987 (2020)
16. Morgenstern, O., Von Neumann, J.: Theory of Games and Economic Behavior. Princeton University Press, Princeton (1953)
17. Nurmi, H.: Comparing Voting Systems. Reidel, Dordrecht (1987)
18. Pérez-Fernández, R., de Baets, B.: The superdominance relation, the positional winner, and more missing links between Borda and Condorcet. J. Theor. Polit. **31**, 46–65 (2018)
19. Ray, P.: Independence of irrelevant alternatives. Econometrica **41**, 987–991 (1973)
20. Stanley, R.P.: Quotients of peck Posets. Order **1**, 29–34 (1984)
21. Staveley, E.S.: Greek and Roman Voting and Elections. Cornell University Press, New York (1972)
22. Winkler, P.: Average height in a partially ordered set. Discret. Math. **39**, 337–341 (1982)

# Goodness-of-Fit Tests to Location-Scale Families Based on OWA Functions

Marina Iturrate-Bobes(✉), Ignacio Montes, and Raúl Pérez-Fernández

Department of Statistics and O.R. and Mathematics Didactics, University of Oviedo, Oviedo, Spain
{iturratemarina,imontes,perezfernandez}@uniovi.es

**Abstract.** Skewness coefficients are measures for quantifying the degree of asymmetry of a random variable. Different authors have proposed several skewness coefficients, most of which are positioned within the axiomatic definition introduced by Oja. This contribution presents a general family of skewness coefficients based on OWA functions. After showing that this family fits within Oja's axiomatic definition of a skewness coefficient, we present a sample version of this coefficient, study its asymptotic distribution, and use it for defining a goodness-of-fit test to a location-scale family.

**Keywords:** Skewness coefficient · OWA function · Goodness-of-fit · Location-scale family

## 1 Introduction

A fundamental step in data analysis is to properly summarise the available data. For such purpose, one may resort to many different types of data summaries such as measures of location, dispersion, skewness and kurtosis. In this work, we focus on data summaries related to skewness, which measure the degree in which the data is asymmetric. This is of relevance to the field of Statistics since symmetry of a random variable is oftentimes considered to be a desirable property and, actually, it is a necessary condition for some non-parametric statistical tests such as Wilcoxon signed-rank test [15].

On this matter, various authors such as Pearson [12], Charlier and Edgeworth [4,6], Yule [17] and Bowley [1] have proposed different measures, referred to as skewness coefficients, for evaluating and comparing random variables in terms of the degree in which they fail to fulfil the property of symmetry. In this contribution, we propose a family of skewness coefficients based on the aggregation of population quantiles and demonstrate that, under some minimal requirements on the distribution of the random variable, all coefficients belonging to this family fit within the theoretical framework for skewness coefficients established by Oja [9]. A common consideration in this field is to assume that the random variables of interest are absolutely continuous. To be consistent with the literature, in this contribution we also make this assumption.


M. Baczyński et al. (Eds.): EUSFLAT 2025, LNCS 15884, pp. 53–65, 2025.
https://doi.org/10.1007/978-3-031-97228-7_5

Skewness coefficients have also attracted the interest of researchers in the context of statistical inference, so much so that studying its sample version has become a popular study subject for statisticians. For skewness coefficients within the proposed family, the sample version is constructed as the quotient between two OWA functions [16], which are a popular tool in aggregation theory [7]. Interestingly, the distribution of this sample version of the skewness coefficients based on OWA functions is proven to be asymptotically normal in this contribution. Finally, we propose to consider these statistics for constructing goodness-of-fit tests to location-scale families.

The rest of the contribution is organised as follows. After providing some preliminaries in Sect. 2, in Sect. 3 we present the proposed family of skewness coefficients. In Sect. 4, we explore a sample version of the skewness coefficient based on OWA functions, paying special attention to its asymptotic distribution and, in Sect. 5, we introduce goodness-of-fit tests to location-scale families and perform an experimental study to analyse its power. We conclude the paper with some final comments in Sect. 6.

## 2 Skewness Coefficients

A key property for describing random variables is that of symmetry. A random variable $X$ is said to be symmetric with respect to a point of symmetry $t \in \mathbb{R}$ if it holds that $P(X \geq t + x) = P(X \leq t - x)$ for any $x \in \mathbb{R}$. This means that $X - t$ and $t - X$ have the same distribution. Equivalently, the definition of symmetry can be stated in terms of the cumulative distribution function (cdf, for short) $F$, so that $X$ is symmetric with respect to a point of symmetry $t \in \mathbb{R}$ if it holds that $1 - F(t + x) + P(X = t + x) = F(t - x)$ for any $x \in \mathbb{R}$. In the particular case of absolutely continuous random variables, the definition of symmetry simplifies to $1 - F(t + x) = F(t - x)$ for any $x \in \mathbb{R}$. Additionally, considering the density function $f$, $X$ is symmetric with respect to $t \in \mathbb{R}$ if it holds that $f(t+x) = f(t-x)$ for any $x \in \mathbb{R}$. If a random variable $X$ is symmetric with respect to a point $t \in \mathbb{R}$, this point will necessarily coincide with the median (if it is unique) and the mean (if it exists). Related to symmetry we may find a stochastic order called the convex-transformation order [14]. An absolutely continuous random variable $X$ precedes another absolutely continuous random variable $Y$ in the convex-transformation order, denoted by $X \precsim Y$, if $G^{-1}(F(x))$ is convex for any $x$ in the support of $X$, where $F$ and $G$ are the cdfs of $X$ and $Y$, respectively, meaning that $X$ is less right-skewed than $Y$.

With the aim of quantifying the degree of asymmetry of a random variable, some measures known as skewness coefficients have been studied. These measures were formalised by Oja in 1981 [9, Def.5.4], who introduced the characterisation presented below. It must be remarked that this contribution exclusively focuses the study on absolutely continuous random variables, a common assumption in the literature.

**Definition 1.** *Let $\mathcal{L}(\Omega)$ be the set of absolutely continuous random variables defined from $(\Omega, \mathcal{A}, P)$ to $\mathbb{R}$. A skewness coefficient is a function $\gamma : \mathcal{L}(\Omega) \rightarrow \mathbb{R}$ that verifies the following properties:*

**O1.** $\gamma(X) = 0$ *if $X$ is symmetric.*
**O2.** $\gamma(cX + d) = \gamma(X)$ *for any $c, d \in \mathbb{R}$ with $c > 0$.*
**O3.** $\gamma(-X) = -\gamma(X)$.
**O4.** $\gamma(X) \leq \gamma(Y)$ *if $X \precsim Y$.*

It must be noted that the fact that a skewness coefficient is equal to 0 does not necessarily imply that the variable is symmetric since it is possible to find asymmetric variables for which the value of some skewness coefficients is 0. Also, even though it actually follows from axioms **O2** and **O3**, **O1** is typically still considered as an axiom to stress out this fact.

We can find the first skewness coefficient defined in the literature in 1895, when Pearson [12] introduced the coefficient $S_P(X) = \frac{\mu_X - Mo(X)}{\sigma_X}$, where $\mu_X$ and $Mo(X)$ are the population central measures mean and mode, respectively, and $\sigma_X$ is the population standard deviation. Some later coefficients are

$$\gamma_1(X) = \frac{E\left[(X-\mu_X)^3\right]}{\sigma_X^3} \qquad \gamma'_{Me(X)}(X) = 3 \cdot \frac{\mu_X - Me(X)}{\sigma_X}, \tag{1}$$

where $\gamma_1(X)$ was introduced by Charlier and Edgeworth [4,6] and $\gamma'_{Me(X)}(X)$ was given by Yule [17]. Additionally, Bowley [1] proposed a skewness coefficient based on the aggregation of the population quartiles $Q_1(X), Q_2(X)$ and $Q_3(X)$:

$$b(X) = \frac{Q_3(X) + Q_1(X) - 2Q_2(X)}{Q_3(X) - Q_1(X)}. \tag{2}$$

## 3 Skewness Coefficients Based on OWA Functions

There exist many different families of skewness coefficients, most of them being defined as the difference of two measures of central tendency divided by a dispersion measure. In this section, we will take as reference Bowley's skewness coefficient from Eq. (2) to define a new family of coefficients based on the aggregation of population quantiles.

**Definition 2.** *Let $\mathcal{L}(\Omega)$ be the set of absolutely continuous random variables defined from $(\Omega, \mathcal{A}, P)$ to $\mathbb{R}$. The following family of coefficients is defined:*

$$\gamma(X) := \frac{(\mathbf{v}^T\mathbf{C_p}(X) - \mathbf{w}^T\mathbf{C_p}(X)) - (\mathbf{w}^T\mathbf{C_p}(X) - \mathbf{v}^{r^T}\mathbf{C_p}(X))}{\mathbf{v}^T\mathbf{C_p}(X) - \mathbf{v}^{r^T}\mathbf{C_p}(X)}, \tag{3}$$

*where*

- $\mathbf{C_p}(X)$ *is a vector containing $m \in \mathbb{N}$ increasingly-ordered population quantiles of $X$, where $m$ is odd, verifying that if $C_p(X) \in \mathbf{C_p}(X)$ for a given $p \in ]0,1[$, then $C_{1-p}(X) \in \mathbf{C_p}(X)$.*

- $\mathbf{v}$ *is a weighting vector verifying that* $\mathbf{v}_i = 0$ *for any* $i \in \{1, \ldots, \lceil m/2 \rceil\}$ *and* $\mathbf{v}^r$ *is its inverted vector, that is, a vector where the elements are arranged in the opposite order.*
- $\mathbf{w}_{\lceil \frac{n}{2} \rceil} = 1$ *and* $\mathbf{w}_i = 0$ *for any* $i \neq \lceil m/2 \rceil$.

The conditions imposed to the quantiles assure that we are always including the median of the random variable: $\mathbf{C}_{\mathbf{p}_{\lceil \frac{m}{2} \rceil}}(X) = Me(X)$. This is consistent with several skewness coefficients in the literature that also include the median, such as those proposed by Yule (see $\gamma'_{Me(X)}$ in Eq. (1)), Bowley (see $b(X)$ in Eq. (2)) or Hinkley (see $\gamma_p$ in the forthcoming Eq. (4)).

For the sake of simplicity, the expression in Eq. (3) will be simplified to $\gamma(X) = \frac{\mathbf{a}^T \mathbf{C}_\mathbf{p}(X)}{\mathbf{b}^T \mathbf{C}_\mathbf{p}(X)}$, where $\mathbf{a} = \mathbf{v} - 2\mathbf{w} + \mathbf{v}^\mathbf{r}$ and $\mathbf{b} = \mathbf{v} - \mathbf{v}^\mathbf{r}$. Next, we demonstrate that the family of coefficients introduced in Definition 2 is well-defined.

**Proposition 1.** *The coefficient* $\gamma(X)$ *introduced in Definition 2 is well-defined for any absolutely continuous random variable* $X$.

*Sketch of Proof. The result follows from the fact that* $0 = \sum_{i=1}^{\ell} \mathbf{v}_i \leq \sum_{i=1}^{\ell} \mathbf{v}_i^r$ for any $\ell \in \{1, \ldots, \lfloor m/2 \rfloor\}$. *Additionally, since* $X$ *is an absolutely continuous random variable and the vector* $\mathbf{C}_\mathbf{p}(X)$ *is increasingly ordered, it holds that* $\mathbf{C}_{\mathbf{p}_i}(X) < \mathbf{C}_{\mathbf{p}_j}(X)$ *for any* $i, j \in \{1, \ldots, m\}$ with $i < j$. *In particular, it is concluded that the denominator is strictly positive.* ■

So far, we know that the coefficient $\gamma(X)$ introduced in Definition 2 is well-defined for any absolutely continuous random variable $X$, and no additional conditions were needed. However, with the aim of proving that this coefficient fulfils Oja's axioms listed in Definition 1 and that, therefore, it is a skewness coefficient, it is necessary to require some additional conditions concerning the distribution of the random variable. For this aim, it is convenient to introduce the following lemmas concerning linearity and symmetry properties of quantiles.

**Lemma 1.** *Let* $X$ *be a random variable and* $c, d \in \mathbb{R}$ *with* $c \neq 0$.

- *If* $c > 0$, *then it holds that* $C_p(cX + d) = c \cdot C_p(X) + d$ *for any* $p \in ]0, 1[$.
- *If* $c < 0$ *and* $X$ *is an absolutely continuous random variable whose cdf is strictly increasing on the preimage of the interval* $]0, 1[$, *then it holds that* $C_p(cX + d) = c \cdot C_{1-p}(X) + d$ *for any* $p \in ]0, 1[$.

**Lemma 2.** *Let* $X$ *be an absolutely continuous random variable that is symmetric with respect to* $t = 0$ *and whose cdf is strictly increasing on the preimage of the interval* $]0, 1[$. *It holds that* $C_p(X) = -C_{1-p}(X)$ *for any* $p \in ]0, 1[$.

The following result provides the requirements needed for the coefficient introduced in Definition 2 to satisfy Oja's axioms. For this aim, we denote by $\mathcal{L}'(\Omega)$ the set of absolutely continuous random variables whose cdf is strictly increasing on the preimage of the interval $]0, 1[$ and twice differentiable.

**Proposition 2.** *The coefficient defined by Eq.* (3) *restricted to* $\mathcal{L}'(\Omega)$ *fulfils Oja's axioms.*

*Sketch of Proof. The proof is divided into four parts:*

**O1.** *The result follows from Lemmas* 1 *and* 2 *and the properties of* $\mathbf{w}$ *(symmetric) and* $\mathbf{v}$ *as weighting vectors.*
**O2.** *The result follows from Lemma* 1.
**O3.** *The result follows from Lemma* 1.
**O4.** *Assume that* $X \precsim Y$. *Without loss of generality, we may assume that* $Me(X) = Me(Y) = 0$. $\gamma(X) \leq \gamma(Y)$ *is equivalent to:*

$$\sum_{1 \leq i < j \leq m} (\mathbf{a}_i \mathbf{b}_j - \mathbf{a}_j \mathbf{b}_i) \left( \mathbf{C}_{\mathbf{p}_i}(X)\mathbf{C}_{\mathbf{p}_j}(Y) - \mathbf{C}_{\mathbf{p}_j}(X)\mathbf{C}_{\mathbf{p}_i}(Y) \right) \leq 0 \, .$$

*This inequality holds because all the terms in the sum are zero or negative:*

- *If* $i, j < \lceil m/2 \rceil$ *or* $i, j > \lceil m/2 \rceil$, $\mathbf{a}_i \mathbf{b}_j - \mathbf{a}_j \mathbf{b}_i = 0$.
- *If* $i = \lceil m/2 \rceil$ *or* $j = \lceil m/2 \rceil$, *then* $\mathbf{C}_{\mathbf{p}_i}(X)\mathbf{C}_{\mathbf{p}_j}(Y) - \mathbf{C}_{\mathbf{p}_j}(X)\mathbf{C}_{\mathbf{p}_i}(Y) = 0$ *because either* $\mathbf{C}_{\mathbf{p}_i}(X) = \mathbf{C}_{\mathbf{p}_i}(Y) = 0$ *or* $\mathbf{C}_{\mathbf{p}_j}(X) = \mathbf{C}_{\mathbf{p}_j}(Y) = 0$.
- If $i < \lceil m/2 \rceil < j$, *then* $\mathbf{a}_i \mathbf{b}_j - \mathbf{a}_j \mathbf{b}_i = 2\mathbf{v}_j \mathbf{v}_i^{\tau} \geq 0$. *Moreover, both* $\mathbf{C}_{\mathbf{p}_i}(X)$ *and* $\mathbf{C}_{\mathbf{p}_i}(Y)$ *are negative and* $\mathbf{C}_{\mathbf{p}_j}(X)$ *and* $\mathbf{C}_{\mathbf{p}_j}(X)$ *are positive. Following the steps in* [8], *we deduce that* $\frac{\mathbf{C}_{\mathbf{p}_i}(Y)}{\mathbf{C}_{\mathbf{p}_i}(X)} \leq \frac{\mathbf{C}_{\mathbf{p}_j}(Y)}{\mathbf{C}_{\mathbf{p}_j}(X)}$, *but since* $\mathbf{C}_{\mathbf{p}_i}(X) < 0$, *we get* $\mathbf{C}_{\mathbf{p}_i}(X)\mathbf{C}_{\mathbf{p}_j}(Y) - \mathbf{C}_{\mathbf{p}_i}(Y)\mathbf{C}_{\mathbf{p}_j}(X) \leq 0$. ■

A particular case of this class of coefficients is the family introduced by Hinkley [10] in 1975 which was defined for a fixed $p \in ]0, 0.5[$ as

$$\gamma_p(X) = \frac{C_{1-p}(X) + C_p(X) - 2C_{0.5}(X)}{C_{1-p}(X) - C_p(X)}, \tag{4}$$

where the vector of quantiles is $\mathbf{C}_\mathbf{p}(X) = (C_p(X), C_{0.5}(X), C_{1-p}(X))^T$ and the weighting vector is $\mathbf{v} = (\mathbf{0}, \mathbf{0}, \mathbf{1})^\mathbf{T}$. Some popular skewness coefficients belong to the family of skewness coefficients introduced by Hinkley, e.g., Bowley's skewness coefficient [1] (considering $p = 0.25$) given in Eq. (2) and the octile skewness coefficient [2] (considering $p = 0.125$).

## 4 Sample Version

The main use of a skewness coefficient is to quantify the degree of asymmetry of a random variable. Nevertheless, we do not usually have information concerning the random variable but instead the available information is just a random sample of the random variable. Therefore, in order to quantify the asymmetry of a random sample in terms of the skewness coefficient $\gamma(X)$ introduced in Definition 2, it will be necessary to define its sample version.

**Definition 3.** *Let* $\mathbf{x} = (\mathbf{x}_1, \mathbf{x}_2, \ldots, \mathbf{x}_n)^T$ *be a random sample of size* $n \in \mathbb{N}$ *from an absolutely continuous random variable* $X \in \mathcal{L}(\Omega)$*. The sample version of the coefficient introduced in Eq. (2) is the function* $\hat{\gamma} : \mathbb{R}^n \to \mathbb{R}$ *given by:*

$$\hat{\gamma}(\mathbf{x}) := \frac{\mathbf{a}^T \widehat{\mathbf{C}_\mathbf{p}}(\mathbf{x})}{\mathbf{b}^T \widehat{\mathbf{C}_\mathbf{p}}(\mathbf{x})},$$

*where* $\widehat{\mathbf{C}_\mathbf{p}}(\mathbf{x}) = \left(\widehat{\mathbf{C}_{\mathbf{p}_1}}(\mathbf{x}), \ldots, \widehat{\mathbf{C}_{\mathbf{p}_m}}(\mathbf{x})\right)$ *is the sample estimate of* $\mathbf{C}_\mathbf{p}(X)$ *by means of the order statistic* $\widehat{\mathbf{C}_{\mathbf{p}_i}}(\mathbf{x}) = \mathbf{x}_{(\lceil n\mathbf{p}_i \rceil)}$ *for any* $i \in \{1, \ldots, m\}$*.*

Unfortunately, the sample version $\hat{\gamma}(\mathbf{x})$ may not be a well-defined expression even if the random sample comes from an absolutely continuous random variable whose cdf is strictly increasing on the preimage of the interval $]0,1[$ and twice differentiable. Therefore, some additional requirements concerning the sample size $n \in \mathbb{N}$ need to be adopted. On this matter, we present the following result that gives a sufficient condition on the sample size to guarantee that $\hat{\gamma}$ is well-defined.

**Proposition 3.** *The sample coefficient* $\hat{\gamma}(\mathbf{x})$ *is well-defined almost surely if the sample size* $n \in \mathbb{N}$ *verifies*

$$n \geq \left(\min_{i=1,\ldots,m-1} \mathbf{p}_{i+1} - \mathbf{p}_i\right)^{-1},$$

*where* $\min_{i=1,\ldots,m-1} \mathbf{p}_{i+1} - \mathbf{p}_i$ *is the smallest difference between the order of two consecutive quantiles of the vector* $\mathbf{C}_\mathbf{p}(X)$*.*

*Proof.* The sample coefficient is well-defined if $\widehat{\mathbf{C}_{\mathbf{p}_i}}(\mathbf{x}) < \widehat{\mathbf{C}_{\mathbf{p}_j}}(\mathbf{x})$ for any $i, j \in \{1, \ldots, m\}$ with $i < j$. This holds almost surely if $\lceil n\mathbf{p}_i \rceil < \lceil n\mathbf{p}_j \rceil$ for any $i \in \{1, \ldots, m-1\}$, condition that is satisfied when $n\mathbf{p}_{i+1} - n\mathbf{p}_i \geq 1$. The result follows from expressing the inequality in terms of $n$ and noting that the inequality holds for any $i \in \{1, \ldots, m-1\}$ whenever $n$ is greater than or equal to the maximum of the ratios between 1 and all the differences $\mathbf{p}_{i+1} - \mathbf{p}_i$. ■

Once the sample version of the coefficient is proven to be well-defined, it is convenient to study its distribution. The following theorem presents its asymptotic distribution.

**Theorem 1.** *Consider an absolutely continuous random variable* $X \in \mathcal{L}'(\Omega)$ *with density* $f$ *and the skewness coefficient* $\gamma(X) = \frac{\mathbf{a}^T \mathbf{C}_\mathbf{p}(X)}{\mathbf{b}^T \mathbf{C}_\mathbf{p}(X)}$*. It holds that:*

$$\sqrt{n}\left(\hat{\gamma}(\mathbf{x}) - \gamma(X)\right) \xrightarrow{\mathcal{D}} \mathcal{N}(0, \tau),$$

*where* $\xrightarrow{\mathcal{D}}$ *indicates convergence in distribution and*

$$\begin{aligned} \tau^2 = & \frac{4}{\left[(\mathbf{v}^T - \mathbf{v}^{r^T})\mathbf{C}_\mathbf{p}(X)\right]^4} \sum_{j=1}^{m} \sum_{i=1}^{m} \sigma^{ij} \left[\mathbf{v}_i(\mathbf{w}^T - \mathbf{v}^{r^T}) + \mathbf{v}^r_i(\mathbf{v}^T - \mathbf{w}^T)\right. \\ & \left. + \mathbf{w}_i(\mathbf{v}^{r^T} - \mathbf{v}^T)\right]\mathbf{C}_\mathbf{p}(X) \cdot \left[\mathbf{v}_j(\mathbf{w}^T - \mathbf{v}^{r^T}) + \mathbf{v}^r_j(\mathbf{v}^T - \mathbf{w}^T)\right. \\ & \left. + \mathbf{w}_j(\mathbf{v}^{r^T} - \mathbf{v}^T)\right]\mathbf{C}_\mathbf{p}(X), \end{aligned} \quad (5)$$

*for any* $i, j \in \{1, \ldots, m\}$ *with*

$$\sigma^{ij} = \frac{\min\{\mathbf{p}_i, \mathbf{p}_j\}(1 - \max\{\mathbf{p}_i, \mathbf{p}_j\})}{f(\mathbf{C}_{\mathbf{p}_i}(X))f(\mathbf{C}_{\mathbf{p}_j}(X))}.$$

*Sketch of Proof. The result follows from the multivariate delta method* [3, *Thm. 5.5.28.*] *and the asymptotic distribution of the empirical quantiles* [5], *where both results can be applied because* $X \in \mathcal{L}'(\Omega)$. *The values* $\sigma^{ij}$ *are given in* [13, *Sec. 2.3.3, Thm. B*]. ■

It must be remarked that the previous result does not only indicate the asymptotically normal distribution with known variance of the sample version $\hat{\gamma}(\mathbf{x})$ introduced in Definition 3, but also its asymptotic unbiasedness and consistency.

## 5 Goodness-of-Fit Tests to Location-Scale Families

Given a random sample $\mathbf{x}$ of size $n \in \mathbb{N}$ coming from an absolutely continuous random variable $X$ with unknown distribution, a goodness-of-fit test based on the skewness coefficients introduced in Definition 2 can be introduced when conditions of Theorem 1 are met and the sample size is large enough. In particular, this section will focus on goodness-of-fit tests to location-scale families. More precisely, the following hypotheses are considered:

$$\begin{cases} H_0 : \text{X belongs to the location-scale family } \mathcal{F}, \\ H_1 : \text{X does not belong to the location-scale family} \mathcal{F}. \end{cases}$$

Prominent examples of well-known goodness-of-fit tests to a location-scale family are normality tests like Anderson-Darling, Lilliefors and Shapiro-Wilk, whose main difference resides in the way in which the test statistic is defined. In the following subsection, a test statistic based on the coefficient introduced in Definition 2 will be used.

### 5.1 Formal Definition

According to axiom **O3** in Definition 1, skewness coefficients are location-scale invariant. Therefore, it becomes natural to construct a test statistic for a goodness-of-fit test to a location-scale family based on a skewness coefficient. In particular, the test statistic $\sqrt{n}\frac{\hat{\gamma}(\mathbf{x})-\gamma_{\mathcal{F}}}{\tau_{\mathcal{F}}}$ can be used, with $\gamma_{\mathcal{F}}$ the value of the skewness coefficient for the location-scale family under the null hypothesis and $\tau_{\mathcal{F}}$ defined as in Eq. (5) and being dependent on the location-scale family $\mathcal{F}$ under the null hypothesis.

**Proposition 4.** *The test statistic* $\sqrt{n}\frac{\hat{\gamma}(\mathbf{x})-\gamma_{\mathcal{F}}}{\tau_{\mathcal{F}}}$ *asymptotically follows a standard normal distribution when the null hypothesis is true and the conditions of Theorem 1 are met. Additionally, the asymptotic variance* $\tau^2_{\mathcal{F}}$ *coincides for any distribution belonging to the same location-scale family.*

*Sketch of Proof. The asymptotic distribution follows from Theorem* 1. *The fact that* $\tau^2_{\mathcal{F}}$ *coincides for any distribution belonging to the same location-scale family follows from the location-scale invariance of* $\gamma_{\mathcal{F}}$ *and the uniqueness of the convergence in distribution of* $\hat{\gamma}(\mathbf{x})$ *(Theorem* 1*).* ■

As a consequence of the previous result, the following rejection region can be considered at a significance level $\alpha \in ]0,1[$:

$$\mathrm{RR} = \left\{ \mathbf{x} \,\middle|\, |\hat{\gamma}(\mathbf{x}) - \gamma_{\mathcal{F}}| > \frac{\tau_{\mathcal{F}}}{\sqrt{n}} z_{1-\alpha/2} \right\}.$$

where $z_{1-\alpha/2}$ is the quantile of order $1 - \alpha/2$ of a standard normal distribution.

### 5.2 Experimental Analysis

For studying the behaviour of the presented goodness-of-fit tests, we provide an experimental analysis of its statistical power. We consider the problem of goodness-of-fit to three different location-scale families (normal, uniform and exponential, highlighted in gray in Tables 1, 2 and 3, respectively) for four samples sizes ($n \in \{10, 50, 100, 200\}$), and study the statistical power of goodness-of-fit tests based on five different skewness coefficients at several distributions (normal, uniform, Cauchy, logistic and exponential). More precisely, the considered skewness coefficients are of the form presented in Definition 2 with $\mathbf{w} = (0,0,1,0,0)^T$ and varying $\mathbf{v} = \lambda\,(0,0,0,1,0)^T + (1-\lambda)\,(0,0,0,0,1)^T$, where $\lambda \in \{0, 1/4, 1/2, 3/4, 1\}$. The statistical power of the tests is estimated by Monte Carlo simulation with $10^5$ replications, always working at a significance level $\alpha = 0.05$. Note that even though statistical powers are expected to be around 0.05 under the null hypothesis, lower values still indicate that the statistical tests are valid. For this reason, the interval $[0, 0.0511]$, which is the one-sided confidence interval at confidence level 0.95 for the parameter of the Bernoulli distribution for samples of size $10^5$ and mean 0.05, will be taken as a reference to indicate whether a test maintains the significance level or not. With the aim of facilitating the study, the values within this interval are highlighted in boldface and large values are highlighted in light and dark shades of red (if the powers are above 0.35 and 0.7, respectively) in Tables 1, 2 and 3. It is expected that the higher the sample size is, the closer the statistical power is to the significance level under the null hypothesis and the greater the statistical power is under the alternative hypothesis; since (i) the distribution of the test statistic is only known asymptotically and (ii) the variance of the test statistic decreases as the sample size increases.

**Case 1: Normal Distribution.** In this subsection, we explore goodness-of-fit tests to the normal distribution. It is expected that at the normal distribution the significance level $\alpha = 0.05$ is preserved. However, according to Oja's first axiom (Definition 1), the value of any skewness coefficient is 0 when a symmetric random variable is considered. Therefore, since the uniform, Cauchy and logistic distributions are symmetric as well as the normal distribution, any skewness coefficient takes the same value in all these families. Therefore, the obtained statistical powers are also expected to be low when considering samples from the uniform, Cauchy and logistic distributions.

Regarding the results presented in Table 1, we conclude that the tests behave in a similar manner (the significance level is preserved) at the normal and logistic distributions, however at the uniform distribution the powers are slightly higher than the considered significance level. On the other hand, the tests fail at preserving the significance level at the Cauchy distribution for most considered cases and exhibit the highest powers for all sample sizes at the exponential distribution, even reaching values close to 1 in some cases. It should be noted that higher powers are obtained for higher sample sizes, as expected. Additionally, it should be remarked that the test associated with the vector $\mathbf{v} = (0, 0, 0, 1, 0)^T$ exhibits the lowest power at all distributions.

**Table 1.** Statistical power of normal goodness-of-fit tests.

| Distribution | $n$ | $\mathbf{v} = (0,0,0,1,0)^T$ | $\mathbf{v} = (0,0,0,3/4,1/4)^T$ | $\mathbf{v} = (0,0,0,1/2,1/2)^T$ | $\mathbf{v} = (0,0,0,1/4,3/4)^T$ | $\mathbf{v} = (0,0,0,0,1)^T$ |
|---|---|---|---|---|---|---|
| Normal | 10 | **0.0000** | **0.0219** | **0.0357** | **0.0373** | **0.0344** |
| | 50 | **0.0457** | **0.0491** | 0.0514 | 0.0514 | **0.0504** |
| | 100 | **0.0502** | **0.0494** | **0.0490** | **0.0504** | **0.0486** |
| | 200 | **0.0489** | **0.0509** | **0.0490** | **0.0497** | **0.0498** |
| Uniform | 10 | **0.0000** | **0.0325** | **0.0506** | 0.0541 | **0.0486** |
| | 50 | **0.0492** | 0.0658 | 0.0702 | 0.0700 | 0.0662 |
| | 100 | 0.0541 | 0.0667 | 0.0694 | 0.0666 | 0.0665 |
| | 200 | 0.0535 | 0.0663 | 0.0713 | 0.0691 | 0.0648 |
| Cauchy | 10 | **0.0000** | **0.0406** | 0.0935 | 0.1205 | 0.1285 |
| | 50 | **0.0498** | 0.0736 | 0.1237 | 0.1566 | 0.1760 |
| | 100 | 0.0535 | 0.0775 | 0.1307 | 0.1685 | 0.1889 |
| | 200 | 0.0531 | 0.0760 | 0.1286 | 0.1681 | 0.1901 |
| Logistic | 10 | **0.0000** | **0.0205** | **0.0346** | **0.0385** | **0.0352** |
| | 50 | **0.0434** | **0.0470** | **0.0507** | 0.0531 | 0.0528 |
| | 100 | **0.0483** | **0.0463** | **0.0490** | **0.0506** | 0.0522 |
| | 200 | **0.0484** | **0.0472** | **0.0501** | **0.0510** | 0.0550 |
| Exponential | 10 | **0.0000** | 0.0997 | 0.1819 | 0.2070 | 0.2072 |
| | 50 | 0.1392 | 0.3457 | 0.5206 | 0.6196 | 0.6651 |
| | 100 | 0.2070 | 0.5604 | 0.7842 | 0.8743 | 0.9109 |
| | 200 | 0.3374 | 0.8045 | 0.9593 | 0.9871 | 0.9945 |

**Case 2: Uniform Distribution.** In this subsection, we explore goodness-of-fit tests to the uniform location-scale family. Again, since the uniform distribution is a symmetric distribution, the power of the different tests at the normal, uniform, Cauchy and logistic distributions are expected to be small, whereas the power at the exponential distribution is expected to be close to 1.

Regarding the results presented in Table 2, we can conclude that the tests exhibit statistical powers within the expected interval for any sample size and weighting vector $\mathbf{v}$ at the normal, uniform and logistic distributions. On the contrary, the powers obtained at the Cauchy distribution are higher and the significance level is preserved only when $\mathbf{v} = (0, 0, 0, 1, 0)^T$, for which the lowest powers are obtained. Finally, the results when testing uniformity (Table 2) at the exponential distribution are similar to the ones presented in Table 1 where normality was tested.

**Table 2.** Statistical power of uniform goodness-of-fit tests.

| Distribution | $n$ | $\mathbf{v} = (0,0,0,1,0)^T$ | $\mathbf{v} = (0,0,0,3/4,1/4)^T$ | $\mathbf{v} = (0,0,0,1/2,1/2)^T$ | $\mathbf{v} = (0,0,0,1/4,3/4)^T$ | $\mathbf{v} = (0,0,0,0,1)^T$ |
|---|---|---|---|---|---|---|
| Normal | 10 | **0.0000** | **0.0065** | **0.0165** | **0.0198** | **0.0200** |
| | 50 | **0.0398** | **0.0326** | **0.0338** | **0.0354** | **0.0352** |
| | 100 | **0.0459** | **0.0346** | **0.0324** | **0.0337** | **0.0349** |
| | 200 | **0.0441** | **0.0345** | **0.0347** | **0.0351** | **0.0364** |
| Uniform | 10 | **0.0000** | **0.0118** | **0.0259** | **0.0299** | **0.0296** |
| | 50 | **0.0433** | **0.0463** | **0.0507** | **0.0502** | **0.0486** |
| | 100 | **0.0498** | **0.0488** | **0.0487** | **0.0488** | **0.0479** |
| | 200 | **0.0482** | **0.0508** | **0.0499** | **0.0493** | **0.0498** |
| Cauchy | 10 | **0.0000** | **0.0169** | 0.0553 | 0.0809 | 0.0930 |
| | 50 | **0.0432** | 0.0538 | 0.0939 | 0.1268 | 0.1495 |
| | 100 | **0.0505** | 0.0565 | 0.1009 | 0.1357 | 0.1608 |
| | 200 | **0.0499** | 0.0575 | 0.0990 | 0.1371 | 0.1611 |
| Logistic | 10 | **0.0000** | **0.0071** | **0.0164** | **0.0199** | **0.0213** |
| | 50 | **0.0391** | **0.0316** | **0.0328** | **0.0349** | **0.0386** |
| | 100 | **0.0449** | **0.0328** | **0.0326** | **0.0333** | **0.0381** |
| | 200 | **0.0436** | **0.0341** | **0.0339** | **0.0365** | **0.0399** |
| Exponential | 10 | **0.0000** | **0.0403** | 0.1037 | 0.1380 | 0.1448 |
| | 50 | 0.1274 | 0.2956 | 0.4561 | 0.5589 | 0.6163 |
| | 100 | 0.1932 | 0.4995 | 0.7338 | 0.8413 | 0.8901 |
| | 200 | 0.3168 | 0.7659 | 0.9428 | 0.9826 | 0.9920 |

**Case 3: Exponential Distribution.** In this subsection, we consider goodness-of-fit tests to the exponential location-scale family. Unlike in the two previous cases, we now have a goodness-of-fit test to a location-scale family generated by an asymmetric distribution. Therefore, statistical powers within the confidence interval $[0, 0.0511]$ are expected at the exponential distribution and statistical powers close to 1 are expected at all other distributions.

Regarding the results presented in Table 3, we observe that the tests are able to preserve the significance level $\alpha = 0.05$ at the exponential distribution for any combination of sample size $n$ and weighting vector $\mathbf{v}$. On the contrary, the powers exhibited at the normal, uniform, Cauchy and logistic distributions are lower than expected. Even so, values higher than 0.7 are obtained for sizes $n = 100$ an $n = 200$ when the weighting vectors are $\mathbf{v} = (0, 0, 0, 1/4, 3/4)^T$ and $\mathbf{v} = (0, 0, 0, 0, 1)^T$, that is for weighting vectors that give more importance to the upper tails of the distribution. The lowest powers are obtained for smaller sample sizes and when $\mathbf{v} = (0, 0, 0, 1, 0)^T$.

### 5.3 Discussion

According to the obtained results, we conclude that the presented goodness-of-fit tests based on the family of skewness coefficients introduced in Definition 2 preserve the significance level under the null hypothesis in general. Even though the

**Table 3.** Statistical powers of exponential goodness-of-fit tests.

| Distribution | $n$ | $\mathbf{v} = (0,0,0,1,0)^T$ | $\mathbf{v} = (0,0,0,3/4,1/4)^T$ | $\mathbf{v} = (0,0,0,1/2,1/2)^T$ | $\mathbf{v} = (0,0,0,1/4,3/4)^T$ | $\mathbf{v} = (0,0,0,0,1)^T$ |
|---|---|---|---|---|---|---|
| Normal | 10 | **0.0032** | **0.0183** | **0.0444** | 0.0757 | 0.1037 |
| | 50 | 0.0685 | 0.2043 | 0.3730 | 0.5002 | 0.5868 |
| | 100 | 0.1310 | 0.4225 | 0.6866 | 0.8249 | 0.8860 |
| | 200 | 0.2569 | 0.7438 | 0.9464 | 0.9857 | 0.9948 |
| Uniform | 10 | **0.0036** | **0.0230** | 0.0526 | 0.0833 | 0.1118 |
| | 50 | 0.0694 | 0.2184 | 0.3760 | 0.4921 | 0.5718 |
| | 100 | 0.1378 | 0.4243 | 0.6708 | 0.8019 | 0.8652 |
| | 200 | 0.2578 | 0.7254 | 0.9285 | 0.9795 | 0.9916 |
| Cauchy | 10 | **0.0042** | 0.0514 | 0.1249 | 0.1793 | 0.2182 |
| | 50 | 0.0742 | 0.2449 | 0.4167 | 0.5142 | 0.5693 |
| | 100 | 0.1395 | 0.4447 | 0.6560 | 0.7494 | 0.7926 |
| | 200 | 0.2627 | 0.7274 | 0.8963 | 0.9432 | 0.9587 |
| Logistic | 10 | **0.0036** | **0.0176** | **0.0467** | 0.0812 | 0.1100 |
| | 50 | 0.0683 | 0.2045 | 0.3762 | 0.5037 | 0.5844 |
| | 100 | 0.1315 | 0.4236 | 0.6901 | 0.8245 | 0.8812 |
| | 200 | 0.2563 | 0.7463 | 0.9463 | 0.9865 | 0.9945 |
| Exponential | 10 | **0.0021** | **0.0048** | **0.0086** | **0.0127** | **0.0166** |
| | 50 | **0.0363** | **0.0399** | **0.0406** | **0.0424** | **0.0425** |
| | 100 | **0.0468** | **0.0445** | **0.0452** | **0.0439** | **0.0447** |
| | 200 | **0.0474** | **0.0471** | **0.0483** | **0.0476** | **0.0484** |

tests behave generally well, since the test statistic is solely based on a skewness coefficient, all these tests fail to distinguish location-scale families for which the value of the skewness coefficient is the same. For instance, these tests do not succeed in identifying whether the sample comes from one symmetric distribution or another. In such cases in which the skewness coefficient for the underlying distribution is the same (for instance, when considering symmetric distributions), we can monitor the value of the asymptotic variance $\tau^2$. In particular, the tests exhibit lower powers than those at the family under the null hypothesis if $\tau^2$ is smaller than the corresponding value for the distribution under the null hypothesis. This occurs, for instance, when we consider the power of uniformity tests at the normal and logistic distribution, for which the obtained powers are lower than those at the uniform distribution. Conversely, if $\tau^2$ is smaller than the corresponding value for the distribution under the null hypothesis, then the tests will not succeed in maintaining the significance level and, thus, will detect more often that we are not under the null hypothesis. This occurs, for instance, when we consider the power of normality tests at the uniform distribution.

## 6 Conclusions

In this contribution, we have taken as reference Hinkley's class of coefficients [10] to define a new family of skewness coefficients based on the aggregation of quantiles. This family successfully allows to quantify the asymmetry of an absolutely continuous random variable if its cdf is strictly increasing on the preimage of the interval $]0,1[$ and twice differentiable (see Propositions 1 and 2). In addition, we have also studied the asymptotic distribution of the sample version of the aforementioned family of skewness coefficients (see Theorem 1), which has been used for introducing goodness-of-fit tests to location-scale families. In this direction, we have carried out some experiments considering varying weighting vectors, sample sizes and underlying distributions to analyse the statistical power of normal, uniform and exponential goodness-of-fit tests. We conclude that the proposed tests behave well under the null hypothesis and successfully detect when we are under an alternative hypothesis for which the value of the skewness coefficient is different than that under the null hypothesis. Interestingly, as they are solely based on the use of a skewness coefficient, the presented tests fail to detect that we are under the alternative hypothesis when considering distributions with the same value of the skewness coefficient than the distribution under the null hypothesis. Future work will explore jointly exploiting skewness and some other shape measures such as kurtosis. In this direction, Jarque and Bera [11] already defined a test statistic for testing for normality based on the aggregation of Pearson's skewness coefficient [12] and a kurtosis coefficient.

**Acknowledgments.** This contribution is part of grant PID2022-140585NB-I00 funded by MICIU/AEI/10.13039/501100011033 and "FEDER/UE".

**Disclosure of Interests.** The authors have no competing interests to declare that are relevant to the content of this article.

## References

1. Bowley, A.L.: Elements of Statistics, 4th edn. Scribner, New York (1920)
2. Brys, G., Hubert, M., Struyf, A.: A comparison of some new measures of skewness. In: Developments in Robust Statistics, pp. 98–113. Springer, Heidelberg (2003)
3. Casella, G., Berger, R.L.: Statistical Inference, 2nd edn. Duxbury Advance Series, Boston (2008)
4. Charlier, C.: Über das Fehlergesetz. Arkiv för Matematik, Astronomi och Fysik **2**(20), 1–35 (1905)
5. Eberl, A., Klar, B.: Asymptotic distributions and performance of empirical skewness measures. Comput. Stat. Data Anal. **146**, 106939 (2020)
6. Edgeworth, F.Y.: The law of error. Trans. Cambridge Phil. Soc. **20**, 36–65 and 113–114 (1904)
7. Grabisch, M., Marichal, J.-L., Mesiar, R., Pap, E.: Aggregation Functions. Cambridge University Press, Cambridge (2009)
8. Groeneveld, R.A., Meeden, G.: Measuring skewness and kurtosis. J. R. Stat. Soc. Ser. D (Stat.) **33**(4), 391–399 (1984)
9. Hannu, O.: On location, scale, skewness and kurtosis of univariate distributions. Scand. J. Stat. **8**, 154–168 (1981)
10. Hinkley, D.V.: On power transformations to symmetry. Biometrika **62**, 101–11 (1975)
11. Jarque, C.M., Bera, A.K.: A test for normality of observations and regression residuals. Int. Stat. Rev. **55**(2), 163–172 (1980)
12. Pearson, K.: Contributions to mathematical theory of evolution II: skew variations in homogeneous material. Trans. R. Phil. Soc. Serie A **186**, 343–414 (1895)

13. Serfling, R.J.: Approximation Theorems of Mathematical Statistics. John Wiley & Sons, New York (2009)
14. Van Zwet, W.R.: Convex Transformations of Random Variables. Mathematisch Centrum, Amsterdam (1964)
15. Wilcoxon, F.: Individual comparisons by ranking methods. Biometr. Bull. **1**(6), 80–83 (1945)
16. Yager, R.R.: On ordered weighted averaging aggregation operators in multicriteria decision making. IEEE Trans. Syst. Man Cybern. **18**(1), 183–190 (1988)
17. Yule, G.U.: An Introduction to the Theory of Statistics, 2nd edn. Griffin, London (1912)

# Multidimensional Aggregation and Measurement of Social Poverty

Marta Cardin[(✉)]

Department of Economics, Ca' Foscari University of Venice,
Sestiere Cannaregio 873, Venezia, Italy
mcardin@unive.it

**Abstract.** Multidimensional poverty and deprivation measures are increasingly used in academic research and policy evaluations. Recognizing the multidimensional nature of well-being and poverty is essential for these assessments. This paper explores various categories of social poverty and deprivation measures, employing an axiomatic framework to analyze cases where the only information available for each attribute is whether an individual is deprived of it or not.

**Keywords:** multidimensional poverty · multidimensional inequality · supermodular functions · OWA · OWMax · SMSD indicator

## 1 Introduction

Poverty is often understood in terms of income, but true deprivation extends far beyond financial constraints. Multidimensional poverty considers various aspects of human well-being, including access to education, healthcare, nutrition, clean water, housing, and basic services. This broader approach recognizes that people can experience poverty in multiple ways simultaneously, even if they are not classified as "poor" based only on income. By bridging empirical data with theoretical frameworks, a recent approach seeks to offer a more holistic understanding of poverty beyond traditional income-based measures.

In this paper, our aim is to introduce a multidimensional approach to analyzing the level of poverty within a society. Every year, the United Nations publishes a comprehensive report on poverty covering at least 100 developing countries, while many individual nations release official estimates of their own poverty levels. At the same time, a large body of theoretical research has proposed various indices to assess poverty and deprivation within societies.

We consider an achievement matrix representing society, where each row corresponds to an individual's deprivation across various dimensions, and each column reflects the deprivation levels of different individuals within a specific dimension. We use the so-called row-first approach, in which the elements of each row are first aggregated to obtain an overall measure of the corresponding individual's poverty. Subsequently, a poverty measure is applied to assess the overall


M. Baczyński et al. (Eds.): EUSFLAT 2025, LNCS 15884, pp. 66–75, 2025.
https://doi.org/10.1007/978-3-031-97228-7_6

poverty level of society. We also discuss an approach to measuring inequality in multidimensional poverty that considers OWA functions. The characterization of OWA functions that are symmetric Choquet integrals has been studied in [3,4]. and [13]. These operators have sparked interest among researchers in the field of composite indicators (see, for example, [8] and [11]).

In the second part of the paper, we examine a particular example of a Sugeno integral, a well-known and powerful tool for decision-making and aggregation, particularly in contexts where data are ordinal rather than numerical. Unlike traditional integrals, which rely on arithmetic operations, the Sugeno integral is based on the lattice operators max and min. This distinctive structure makes it especially suitable for scenarios where values are ranked rather than measured on a precise numerical scale. As a result, the Sugeno integral is widely applied in fields such as fuzzy logic, decision analysis, and multi-criteria evaluation, where handling qualitative or imprecise data is crucial. We consider symmetric operators that can be represented as Sugeno integrals. We are interested in proposing a multivariate version of the symmetric Sugeno integral in our framework, which turns out to be a generalization of a social poverty index used in Europe.

The Severe Material and Social Deprivation (SMSD) rate is an indicator used by the European Union (EU) to measure poverty and social exclusion beyond income-based assessments. It identifies individuals or households who experience significant deprivation in essential material and social aspects of life. A person is considered severely materially and socially deprived if they lack at least 7 of 13 predefined items that represent basic living conditions. The SMSD rate captures multiple dimensions of poverty, highlighting individuals who struggle not only financially but also socially. It is part of the EU's social inclusion and poverty reduction strategy and helps shape policies aimed at improving living standards and reducing inequalities. This measure complements income-based poverty indicators such as At Risk of Poverty (AROP) and helps provide a more comprehensive view of economic hardship in European societies.

The structure of the paper is as follows. In Sect. 2, we describe the framework that we use. In Sect. 3, we introduce our row-first model, while in Sect. 4, we examine measures of deprivation that incorporate inequality between individuals as a negative aspect of poverty. Finally, in Sect. 5, we present a generalization of the SMSD rate considered in the framework of the European Union Statistics on Income and Living Conditions (EU-SILC).

## 2 Basic Notation

We consider a society with $n$ individuals and a set of $m$ dimensions, in terms of which individuals, as well as social well-being and deprivation (e.g., related to income, education, health, etc.) are evaluated.

Let $N = \{1, \ldots, n\}$ and $M = \{1, \ldots, m\}$ denote the set of individuals and the set of attributes, respectively, where $m$ and $n$ are positive integers, $n \geq 2$. Thus, we assume that our society is given and fixed.

Several measures proposed in the literature assume that each of the multiple attributes considered is cardinally measurable. However, in many instances, only ordinal data are available. We examine the case where each individual's attributes are measured on an ordinal and binary scale. Specifically, for each dimension, there are only two possible values: 1 if the individual is deprived with respect to that feature, and 0 if they are not. Let $\mathcal{X}^m = \{0,1\}^m$ be the set of row vectors of length $m$ with entries in $\{0,1\}$ and let $\mathcal{X} = \{0,1\}^{m \times n}$ be the set of all matrices with entries in $\{0,1\}$ of dimension $n \times m$. We consider each individual $i$ to be represented by a row vector $\mathbf{x}_i \in \mathcal{X}^m$, consisting of $m$ attributes that is the achievement vector of the individual $i$. The social deprivation matrix $n \times m$ $\mathbf{X} = (x_{ij}) \in \mathcal{X}$ summarises the deprivation experienced by each individual $i$ in across the $m$ attributes.

For every matrix $X \in \mathcal{X}$, we use the following notation:

- for each $i \in N$, the row vector $\mathbf{x}_{i\bullet} = (x_{i1}, \ldots, x_{im})$ denotes the achievement vector of individual $i$ across all dimensions.
- for each $j \in M$ the column vector $\mathbf{x}^{\bullet j} = (x_{1j}, \ldots, x_{nj})$ denotes the achievement vector of all individuals along dimension $j$.

We also define the matrix $\mathbf{0}$ such that $x_{i,j} = 0$ for every $i, j$ and the matrix $\mathbf{1}$ such that $x_{ij} = 1$ for every $i, j$. Similarly, we define the row vectors $\mathbf{0}_m$ and $\mathbf{1}_m$ which are elements of $\mathcal{X}^m = \{0,1\}^m$.

We consider a *preorder* on $\mathcal{X}$ (or in the set $\mathcal{X}^m$ ) that means a transitive and complete binary relation in the set $\mathcal{X}$ or in $\mathcal{X}^m$. For all $X, Y \in \mathcal{X}$, $X \succeq Y$ for a preorder $\succeq$ is interpreted as indicating that social deprivation under $X$ is greater or equivalent to social deprivation under Y with the obvious interpretation for $X \succ Y$ and $X \sim Y$.

In this paper, we focus on quantifying social poverty using a numerical function $F \colon \mathcal{X} \to [0,1]$, which aggregates data both across individual dimensions and across individuals. For $\mathbf{X}, \mathbf{Y}$, $F(\mathbf{X}) \geq F(\mathbf{Y})$ is interpreted as the degree of poverty or deprivation that society has under $\mathbf{X}$ is at least as high as the degree of deprivation under $\mathbf{Y}$.

## 3 A Class of Multidimensional Poverty Rankings

There are various ways to construct a multidimensional deprivation index, as illustrated, for example, in [5]. One common method is the column-first aggregation technique, often used when attribute data come from multiple sources. This approach first aggregates deprivation levels across all individuals for each attribute, which corresponds to a column in the social deprivation matrix, and then combines these attribute-specific totals into an index. In contrast, the row-first method first aggregates each individual's deprivation across attributes (a row in the social deprivation matrix) before compiling individual deprivation scores into a comprehensive index. Although the row-first method requires a rich dataset with detailed information on each individual and attribute, it effectively captures the simultaneous deprivations that an individual experiences. In this study, we focus on indices constructed using the row-first aggregation approach. Then, we consider the following standard axioms defined with respect to a set $\mathcal{X}$ and a preorder $\succeq$ on it.

Anonimity. If $\mathbf{X}, \mathbf{Y} \in \mathcal{X}$, $\sigma$ is a permutation of the set $N$ and $\mathbf{y}_{ij} = \mathbf{x}_{\sigma(i),j}$ then $\mathbf{X} \sim \mathbf{Y}$.

Monotonicity. If $\mathbf{X}, \mathbf{Y} \in \mathcal{X}$ are such that $x_{ij} = y_{i,j}$ for every $(i,j) \neq (h,k)$ and $x_{h,k} > y_{h,k}$ then $\mathbf{X} \succeq \mathbf{Y}$.

Our key axiom is related to the preferences defined over the set of rows and is similar to the one proposed in [10]. This axiom implies that social preferences are increasing with respect to individual preferences.

Row Preferences. For all $i \in N$ there is a preorder $\succeq_i$ in $\mathcal{X}^m$ such that for every $\mathbf{X}, \mathbf{Y} \in \mathcal{X}$ if $\mathbf{x}_{k\bullet} = \mathbf{y}_{k\bullet}$ for every $k \in N, k \neq i$ then $\mathbf{X} \succ \mathbf{Y}$ if and only if $\mathbf{x}_{i\bullet} \succ_i \mathbf{y}_{i\bullet}$ and $\mathbf{X} \sim \mathbf{Y}$ if and only if $\mathbf{x}_{i\bullet} \sim_i \mathbf{y}_{i\bullet}$.

Note that Row Preferences is a separability property in our framework. The implications of the above axioms are summarized in the following proposition.

**Proposition 1.** *An order relation $\succeq$ defined in $\mathcal{X} = \{0,1\}^{m\times n}$ satisfies Anonimity, Monotonicity and Row Preferences if and only if there exists an increasing function $f\colon \mathcal{X}^m \to [0,1]$ such that*

$$\mathbf{X} \succeq \mathbf{Y} \quad \textit{if and only if} \quad \sum_{i=1}^{n} f(\mathbf{x}_{i,\bullet}) \geq \sum_{i=1}^{n} f(\mathbf{y}_{i,\bullet}) \tag{1}$$

*Proof.* It is straightforward to prove that an preorder relation defined in $\mathcal{X}$ defined by Eq. 1 and by an increasing function $f\colon \mathcal{X}^m \to [0,1]$, satisfies Anonimity, Monotonicity and Row Preferences.

To prove the converse, note that the set $\mathcal{X}$ is finite; therefore, there exists an increasing function $F\colon \mathcal{X} \to [0,1]$, $F(\mathbf{0}) = 0$, $F(\mathbf{1}) = 1$, and such that $F(\mathbf{X}) > F(\mathbf{Y})$ if and only if $X \succ Y$ and $F(\mathbf{X}) = F(\mathbf{Y})$ if and only if $X \sim Y$.

Moreover, by Row Preferences we have that

$$F\left(\begin{bmatrix}\mathbf{x}_{1\bullet}\\ \mathbf{0}_m\\ \vdots\\ \mathbf{0}_m\\ \vdots\\ \mathbf{0}_m\end{bmatrix}\right) - F\left(\begin{bmatrix}\mathbf{0}_m\\ \mathbf{0}_m\\ \vdots\\ \mathbf{0}_m\\ \vdots\\ \mathbf{0}_m\end{bmatrix}\right) = F\left(\begin{bmatrix}\mathbf{x}_{1\bullet}\\ \mathbf{x}_{2\bullet}\\ \vdots\\ \mathbf{x}_{i\bullet}\\ \vdots\\ \mathbf{x}_{n\bullet}\end{bmatrix}\right) - F\left(\begin{bmatrix}\mathbf{0}_m\\ \mathbf{x}_{2\bullet}\\ \vdots\\ \mathbf{x}_{i\bullet}\\ \vdots\\ \mathbf{x}_{n\bullet}\end{bmatrix}\right)$$

and so forth. Then it can be proved that

$$F(\mathbf{X}) = F\begin{pmatrix}\mathbf{x}_{1\bullet}\\ \vdots\\ \mathbf{0}_m\\ \vdots\\ \mathbf{0}_m\end{pmatrix} + \ldots + F\begin{pmatrix}\mathbf{0}_m\\ \vdots\\ \mathbf{x}_{i\bullet}\\ \vdots\\ \mathbf{0}_m\end{pmatrix} + \ldots F\begin{pmatrix}\mathbf{0}_m\\ \vdots\\ \mathbf{0}_m\\ \vdots\\ \mathbf{x}_{n\bullet}\end{pmatrix}$$

$= f(\mathbf{x}_{1\bullet}) + \cdots + f(\mathbf{x}_{i\bullet}) + \cdots + f(\mathbf{x}_{n\bullet})$. Then for every $i, 1 \leq i \leq n$ we define the function $f_j \colon \mathcal{X}^m \to [0,1]$ such that

$$f_i(\mathbf{x}) = F\left(\begin{bmatrix} \mathbf{0}_m \\ \vdots \\ \mathbf{x} \\ \vdots \\ \mathbf{0}_m \end{bmatrix}\right).$$

Then it can be easily proved that for every $i \in N$, $f_i(\mathbf{0}_m) = 0$ and $f_i(\mathbf{1}_m) = \dfrac{1}{n}$ and also that for every $\mathbf{X}, \mathbf{Y} \in \mathcal{X}$ if $\mathbf{x}_{k,\bullet} = \mathbf{y}_{k,\bullet}$ for every $k \in N, k \neq i$ then $\mathbf{X} \succ \mathbf{Y}$ if and only if $f_i(\mathbf{x}i\bullet) \geq f_i(\mathbf{y}_{i\bullet})$ and $\mathbf{X} \sim \mathbf{Y}$ if and only if $f_i(\mathbf{x}i\bullet) = f_i(\mathbf{y}_{i\bullet})$. By the Monotonicity property, these functions are increasing. Moreover, due to the Anonymity property, it is easy to prove that the same function $f$ applies to every $i$, $i \in N$. ■

From the proof of Proposition 1, we obtain that a preorder relation $\succeq$ defined on the set $\mathcal{X}$ of social deprivation matrices, which satisfies Anonymity, Monotonicity, and Column Preferences, can be represented by an index of social deprivation expressed as the sum of individuals' deprivation.

This index is a function $F \colon \mathcal{X} \to [0,1]$, satisfying $F(\mathbf{0}) = 0$, $F(\mathbf{1}) = 1$, and is given by

$$F(\mathbf{X}) = \sum_{i=1}^{n} f(\mathbf{x}_{i\bullet})$$

where $f \colon \mathcal{X}^m \to [0,1]$, $f(\mathbf{0}_m) = 0$ and $f(\mathbf{1}_m) = \dfrac{1}{n}$.

## 4 Multimensional Inequality and Supermodular Functions

A natural question to consider is whether inequality can be meaningfully incorporated into a class of poverty measures. The underlying idea that we want to consider is that a more unequal society is a poorer society. To address this, we first propose a definition of greater or lesser inequality within a society of $n$ individuals, where each individual's deprivation is measured across $m$ attributes. Our approach follows a method similar to that in [1] and [2] (see also [6] for the definition of Clustered Deteriorations). We begin by defining a general multidimensional transfer in $\mathcal{X}$. This definition will later be used in formulating subsequent definitions and axioms that constrain the function representing a given preorder.

If $\mathbf{X}, \mathbf{Y} \in \mathcal{X} = \{0,1\}^{m \times n}$ we say that $\mathbf{X}$ is a *transfer* of $\mathbf{Y}$ if there exist $i_1, i_2 \in N$ and $j_1, j_2 \in M$, $i_1 \neq i_2, j_1 \neq j_2$ such that $x_{i_1,j_1} = 1 = x_{i_1,j_2}$ and $x_{i_2,j_1} = 0 = x_{i_2,j_2}$ while $y_{i_1,j_1} = 1 = y_{i_2,j_2}$ and $y_{i_1,j_2} = 0 = y_{i_2,j_1}$, and $x_{i,j} = y_{i,j}$ when $i \in M \setminus \{i_1, i_2\}$ and $j \in N \setminus \{j_1, j_2\}$ .

Then we say that $\mathbf{X}$ is *more unequal* than $\mathbf{Y}$, denoted $X \succeq_I Y$, if $\mathbf{X}$ is obtained from $\mathbf{Y}$ through a sequence of transfers and we are interested in relations $\succeq$ in $\mathcal{X}$ such that if $X \succeq_I Y$ then $X \succeq Y$.

We briefly recall the definition of a supermodular function. If $L$ is a lattice, a function $f\colon L \to \mathbb{R}$ is said to be *supermodular* if, for every $a, b \in L$,

$$f(a \vee b) + f(a \wedge b) \geq f(a) + f(b).$$

In the following proposition, we characterize poverty measures with an additive representation that respects the inequality order. Note that $\mathcal{X}^m$ is a lattice in the component-wise order.

**Proposition 2.** *Let $F\colon \mathcal{X} \to [0,1]$ is a function, $F(\mathbf{0}) = 0$, $F(\mathbf{1}) = 1$ and such that*

$$F(\mathbf{X}) = \sum_{i=1}^{n} f(\mathbf{x}_{i,\bullet})$$

*for some function $f\colon \mathcal{X}^m \to [0,1]$. Then*

$$X \succeq_I Y \quad \text{implies that} \quad F(\mathbf{X}) \geq F(\mathbf{Y}) \tag{2}$$

*if and only if the function $f$ is a supermodular function.*

*Proof.* Let $\mathbf{X}, \mathbf{Y} \in \mathcal{X}$ such that $\mathbf{X}$ is a transfer of $\mathbf{X}$ then $F(\mathbf{X}) - F(\mathbf{Y}) = f(x_{i_1 1}, \ldots, x_{i_1 j_1}, \ldots, x_{i_1, j_2}, \ldots, x_{i_1 m}) + f(x_{i_2 1}, \ldots, x_{i_2 j_1}, \ldots, x_{i_2, j_2}, \ldots, x_{i_2 m}) - f(x_{i_1 1}, \ldots, y_{i_1 j_1}, \ldots, y_{i_1, j_2}, \ldots, x_{i_1 m}) - f(x_{i_2 1}, \ldots, y_{i_2 j_1}, \ldots, y_{i_2, j_2}, \ldots, x_{i_1 m}) = f(x_{i_1 1}, \ldots, 1, \ldots, 1, \ldots, x_{i_1 m}) + f(x_{i_2 1}, \ldots, 0, \ldots, 0, \ldots, x_{i_2, m}) - f(x_{i_1 1}, \ldots, 1, \ldots, 0, \ldots, x_{i_1 m}) - f(x_{i_2 1}, \ldots, 0, \ldots, 1, \ldots, x_{i_1, m})$.

Hence if $f$ is supermodular $F(\mathbf{X}) - F(\mathbf{Y}) \geq 0$ and so we can say that if $X \succeq_I Y$ then $F(\mathbf{X}) \geq F(\mathbf{Y})$.

Now let $F\colon \mathcal{X} \to [0,1]$ a function, $F(\mathbf{0}) = 0$, $F(\mathbf{1}) = 1$, $F(\mathbf{X}) = \sum_{i=1}^{n} f(\mathbf{x}_{i,\bullet})$ where $f$ is a function $f\colon \mathcal{X}^m \to [0,1]$ and such that Eq. 1 is satisfied.

If $\mathbf{x}, \mathbf{y} \in \mathcal{X}^m$ we define the two elements of $\mathcal{X}$, $\mathbf{W}, \mathbf{Z}$,

$$\mathbf{W} = \begin{pmatrix} \mathbf{x} \vee \mathbf{y} \\ \mathbf{x} \wedge \mathbf{y} \\ \mathbf{0}_m \\ \vdots \\ \mathbf{0}_m \end{pmatrix} \qquad \mathbf{Z} = \begin{pmatrix} \mathbf{x} \\ \mathbf{y} \\ \mathbf{0}_m \\ \vdots \\ \mathbf{0}_m \end{pmatrix}.$$

It can be easily proved that $\mathbf{W} \succeq_I \mathbf{Z}$ and so $F(\mathbf{W}) \geq F(\mathbf{Z})$. Since $F(\mathbf{W}) = f(x \vee \mathbf{y}) + f(\mathbf{x} \wedge \mathbf{y})$ and $F(\mathbf{Z}) = f(\mathbf{x}) + f(\mathbf{y})$ we have proved that $f(\mathbf{x} \vee \mathbf{y},) + f(\mathbf{x} \wedge \mathbf{y}) \geq f(\mathbf{x}) + f(\mathbf{y})$ and then $f$ is supermodular. ■ ■

A special class of aggregation operators are the so-called OWA operators (ordered weighted averaging operators) introduced in [12] and related to the Choquet integral [7]. We recall that the OWA function associated with the weighting vector $\mathbf{w} = (w_1, \ldots, w_m) \in [0,1]^m$ satisfying $\sum_{i=1}^{m} w_i = 1$ is the function $f\colon \mathbb{R}^m \to \mathbb{R}$ defined as

$$f_{\mathbf{w}}(\mathbf{x}) = \sum_{i=1}^{m} w_i x_{(i)} \tag{3}$$

where (.) is the permutation of $M$ such that $x_{(1)} \geq \cdots \geq x_{(m)}$.

We can also consider an OWA function defined in $\mathcal{X} = \{0,1\}^m$ as in 3 and then we can prove the following Proposition that is well known in the case of real intervals.

**Proposition 3.** *A function $f\colon \mathcal{X}^m \to \mathbb{R}$ defined as*

$$f_{\mathbf{w}}(\mathbf{x}) = \sum_{i=1}^{m} w_i x_{(i)}$$

*where $x_{(1)} \geq \cdots \geq x_{(n)}$ is supermodular if and only if $w_1 \leq \cdots \leq w_n$.*

*Proof.* We note that if $f_{\mathbf{w}}$ is supermodular and we take $\mathbf{x} = (1, 0, \ldots, 0)$ and $\mathbf{y} = (0, 1, \ldots, 0)$ then, by the definition of supermodularity, we have $f_{\mathbf{w}}(\mathbf{x} \vee \mathbf{y}) + f_{\mathbf{w}}(\mathbf{x} \wedge \mathbf{y}) \geq f_{\mathbf{w}}(\mathbf{x}) + f_{\mathbf{w}}(\mathbf{y})$. Since this implies $w_1 + w_2 \geq w_1 + w_1$, it follows that $w_1 \leq w_2$. Similarly, if we consider the two vectors $\mathbf{x} = (1, 1, 0, \ldots, 0)$ and $\mathbf{y} = (1, 0, 1, \ldots, 0)$, we can prove that if $f_{\mathbf{w}}$ is supermodular $w_2 \leq w_3$. Therefore, we conclude that the condition

$$w_1 \leq \cdots \leq w_n$$

must hold whenever the OWA function $f_{\mathbf{w}}$ is supermodular.

To prove the converse note that a function $f\colon \mathcal{X}^m \to \mathbb{R}$ is supermodular if and only every two-dimensional section of the function is a supermodular function. Moreover, consider an OWA function of the form

$$f_{\mathbf{w}}(\mathbf{x}) = \sum_{i=1}^{m} w_i x_{(i)}$$

such that $w_1 \leq \cdots \leq w_n$. Taking two vectors $\mathbf{x}$ and $\mathbf{y}$ that differ only for two components, we can easily prove that

$$f_{\mathbf{w}}(\mathbf{x} \vee \mathbf{y}) + f_{\mathbf{w}}(\mathbf{x} \wedge \mathbf{y}) \geq f_{\mathbf{w}}(\mathbf{x}) + f_{\mathbf{w}}(\mathbf{y})$$

which completes the proof. ■ ■

By Proposition 3, we can conclude that OWA functions can be used to define measures of social deprivation that capture inequality aversion.

## 5 A New Proposal

The **Severe Material and Social Deprivation (SMSD) rate** is an European Union Statistics on Income and Living Conditions (EU-SILC) that measures an enforced lack of essential and desirable items needed for an adequate life. It identifies individuals or households who experience significant deprivation in essential material and social aspects of life. A person is classified as severely deprived if they experience an enforced lack of at least 7 out of 13 deprivation items, which are divided into:

- **Household-level items**: Ability to handle unexpected expenses, afford a vacation, pay bills on time, eat adequate meals, keep the house warm, own a car, and replace furniture.
- **Individual-level items**: Internet access, purchasing new clothes, having two pairs of shoes, spending money on yourself, participating in leisure activities, socializing at least once a month.

This indicator is defined as the proportion of the population that experienced a lack of at least 7 of the 13 deprivation items. The SMSD indicator contributes to the at-risk-of-poverty or social exclusion rate within the EU 2030 target on poverty and social exclusion.

In this paper, our aim is to propose a generalization of the aforementioned European index, taking into account the situation of a given nation or society more comprehensively by considering the percentage of individuals experiencing the lack of $k$ elements as $k$ varies.

Recall that a fuzzy measure, also known as a normalized capacity or monotone measure, is a set function $\mu : 2^{\{1,2,\ldots,m\}} \rightarrow [0,1]$ that satisfies the following properties: $\mu(\emptyset) = 0$, $\mu(\{1,\ldots,m\}) = 1$, and $\mu(U) \leq \mu(V)$ for all subsets $U \subseteq V$. Given such a measure, the discrete Sugeno integral of a vector $\mathbf{x} \in [0,1]^m$ is defined as:

$$S_\mu(\mathbf{x}) = \bigvee_{k=1}^{n} x_{(k)} \wedge \mu(\{(1),(2),\ldots,(k)\})$$

where $x_{(1)} \geq x_{(2)} \geq \cdots \geq x_{(m)}$.

In this paper, we consider only one class of the widely used capacities, which are symmetric capacities. These are characterized by the property that if two subsets $U$ and $V$ have the same cardinality, then $\mu(U) = \mu(V)$. A symmetric capacity can be fully described by a vector $h$ of $n$ weights, where $0 \leq h_1 \leq h_2 \leq \cdots \leq h_n = 1$ and $h_k = \mu(\{(1),(2),\ldots,(k)\})$. This leads to the following formulation of the Sugeno integral:

$$S_h(x) = \bigvee_{k=1}^{m} x_{(k)} \wedge h_k,$$

which is also known as the Ordered Weighted Maximum (OWMax) operator [9]. It can be demonstrated that aggregation functions of this kind possess various desirable properties (see [9]).

Moreover, it can be easily proved that if $\mathbf{x} \in \{0,1\}^m$, that is $\mathbf{x} \in \mathcal{X}^m$ then

$$S_h(\mathbf{x}) = \text{OWMax}(\mathbf{x}) = h_k = \mu(\{(1),(2),\ldots,(k)\}) \tag{4}$$

where $x_{(1)} = x_{(2)} = \cdots = x_{(k)} = 1$ and $x_{(k+1)} = x_{(k+1)} = \ldots x_{(m)} = 0$.

So, the quantity $h_k = \mu(\{(1),(2),\ldots,(k)\}$ can be seen, in our framework, as a measure of the poverty experienced by an individual suffering from $k$ deprivations.

If $\mathbf{x} \in \mathcal{X}^m$, we define $n(\mathbf{x}) = \#\{w : x_w = 1\}$. That is, if $n(\mathbf{x}) \geq k$ then $x_{(k)} = 1$. Then if $\mathbf{X} \in \mathcal{X}$ and $1 \geq k \geq n$ let

$$p_k(X) = \frac{\#\{i : n(x_{i\bullet}) \geq k\}}{n}. \tag{5}$$

Based on these definitions, we introduce a multivariate variant of the OWMax operator in (4):

$$F(X) = \bigvee_{k=1}^{m} p_k(X) \wedge h_k \tag{6}$$

Then if for every $k, 1 \leq k \leq m$, $0 \leq h_k \leq 1, h_0 = 0, h_1 = 1$ $F$ is a function $F\colon \mathcal{X} \to [0,1]$, satisfying $F(\mathbf{0}) = 0$, $F(\mathbf{1}) = 1$. Moreover, $F$ satisfies the monotonicity property. This operator considers, for each value of $k$ the percentage of people who suffer from $k$ deprivations and the importance of experiencing $k$ deprivations.

It is important to note that the SMSD index corresponds to the case where $m = 13$, with $h_k = 1$ if $k \geq 7$ and $h_k = 0$ if $k < 7$, whereas in our more general approach the values $p_k(X)$ for every k, $1 \leq k \leq m$ are taken into account.

## 6 Conclusion

The main purpose of this paper is to introduce some important functionals studied in the field of aggregation theory, aimed at representing the level of poverty or deprivation in a society. We study several classes of social evaluation functions that measure societal poverty or deprivation. This involves aggregation not only across the various dimensions of individual poverty but also across individuals themselves. We consider the aggregation of binary indicators and study representations that are additive with respect to individuals. Additionally, we propose an index that generalizes the Severe Material and Social Deprivation (SMSD) rate used in the EU.

In our future research, we aim to explore broader assumptions. For instance, in this initial investigation, we treat all attributes defining an individual's or society's poverty level as equally important, resulting in the use of symmetric operators. However, this assumption will need to be revised for a more generalized approach. It would also be worthwhile to consider a framework in which some attributes are represented cardinally, while others are treated ordinally.

## References


1. Aouani, Z., Chateauneuf, A.: Multidimensional inequality and inframodular order. J. Math. Econ. **90**, 74–79 (2020)
2. Basili, M., Casaca, P., Chateauneuf, A., Franzini, M.: Multidimensional Pigou-Dalton transfers and social evaluation functions. Theor. Decis. **83**, 573–590 (2017)
3. Calvo, T., De Baets, B.: Aggregation operators defined by k-order additive/maxitive fuzzy measures. Int. J. Uncertain. Fuzz. Knowl.-Based Syst. **6**(06), 533–550 (1998)
4. Calvo, T., Kolesárová, A., Komorníková, M., Mesiar, R.: Aggregation operators: properties, classes and construction methods. In: Aggregation Operators: New Trends and Applications, pp. 3–104 (2002)
5. Dhongde, S., Dong, X.: Analyzing racial and ethnic differences in the USA through the lens of multidimensional poverty. J. Econ. Race Policy **5**(4), 252–266 (2022)
6. Dhongde, S., Pattanaik, P.K., Xu, Y.: Well-being, deprivation, and the great recession in the U.S.: a study in a multidimensional framework. Rev. Income Wealth **65**, S281–S306 (2019)
7. Grabisch, M.: Fuzzy integral in multicriteria decision making. Fuzzy Sets Syst. **69**(3), 279–298 (1995)
8. Libório, M.P., Martinuci, O.D.S., Ekel, P.I., Hadad, R.M., Lyrio, R.D.M., Bernardes, P.: Measuring inequality through a non-compensatory approach. GeoJournal **87**(6), 4689–4706 (2022)
9. Marichal, J.L.: On Sugeno integral as an aggregation function. Fuzzy Sets Syst. **114**(3), 347–365 (2000)
10. Mongin, P., Pivato, M.: Ranking multidimensional alternatives and uncertain prospects. J. Econ. Theory **157**, 146–171 (2015)
11. Shu, Z., Carrasco, R.A., García-Miguel, J.P., Sánchez-Montañés, M.: Multiple scenarios of quality of life index using fuzzy linguistic quantifiers: the case of 85 countries in Numbeo. Mathematics **10**(12), 2091 (2022)
12. Yager, R.R.: On ordered weighted averaging aggregation operators in multicriteria decision making. IEEE Trans. Syst. Man Cybern. **18**(1), 183–190 (1988)
13. Yager, R.R., Kacprzyk, J., Beliakov, G.: Recent developments in the ordered weighted averaging operators: theory and practice (2011)

# Ontology Aggregation with Maximum Consensus Based on a Fuzzy Multi-criteria Group Decision-Making Method

Lydia Castronovo[1,2(✉)], Giuseppe Filippone[2], Mario Galici[2], Gianmarco La Rosa[2], and Marco Elio Tabacchi[2,3]

[1] Dipartimento di Scienze Matematiche e Informatiche, Scienze Fisiche e Scienze della Terra, Università degli Studi di Messina, Messina, Italy
lydia.castronovo@studenti.unime.it

[2] Dipartimento di Matematica e Informatica, Università degli Studi di Palermo, Palermo, Italy
{giuseppe.filippone01,mario.galici,gianmarco.larosa, marcoelio.tabacchi}@unipa.it

[3] Istituto Nazionale di Ricerche Demopolis, Palermo, Italy

**Abstract.** In this work, we extend the integration of fuzzy logic in Multi-Criteria Group Decision-Making (MCGDM) problems and its application to ontologies. We define an MCGDM framework where experts assign scores and weights to ontology classes, and each one of them is assigned a fuzzy weight, reflecting their relative importance in the decision process. Each expert selects their best choice among the alternatives and a final best compromise $A^*$ is derived using a minimal mean distance operator, ensuring that the aggregated result optimally reflects expert opinions while minimizing deviations from individual preferences.

**Keywords:** Multi-Criteria Group Decision-Making · Fuzzy Ontology · Fuzzy method · Fuzzy multi-expert decision-making

## 1 Introduction

Ontologies play a crucial role in artificial intelligence, the semantic web, and information systems by providing structured knowledge representations that facilitate interoperability and reasoning [1,23]. However, classical ontologies lack mechanisms to handle vagueness and imprecision, which are inherent in real-world scenarios [12,24]. To address this, fuzzy ontologies extend traditional frameworks by incorporating fuzzy logic, enabling degrees of membership for concepts and relationships [31,33]. Fuzzy Description Logics (FDLs) enhance classical DLs by introducing truth degrees, allowing assertions with varying confidence levels [14,20]. This adaptation necessitates new reasoning methods, such as fuzzy subsumption and consistency checking, to manage partial inconsistencies


M. Baczyński et al. (Eds.): EUSFLAT 2025, LNCS 15884, pp. 76–87, 2025.
https://doi.org/10.1007/978-3-031-97228-7_7

[3]. Another important concept in the study of ontologies is the process of unifying knowledge from multiple sources while ensuring semantic coherence. Due to the broad range of applications of ontologies (see [7,15]), many approaches to ontologies aggregation are proposed in the literature. For example, ontology merging [9,22] has applications in Judgment Aggregation (JA) [8,11,18,19]. However, works like [25–27], that focus on JA aspects, do not incorporate fuzzy ontologies, a key feature of our approach. For what concern fuzzy ontology aggregation, [2,16] provide relevant insights. In [2], Bobillo and Straccia introduce aggregation operators within Fuzzy OWL 2, while Huitzil et al. in [16] develop *Fudge*, a tool for aggregating fuzzy datatypes.

Nevertheless, when integrating existing fuzzy ontologies, discrepancies in assigned membership values may arise, requiring a method to derive an optimal consensus. To achieve this, we extend the integration of fuzzy logic in Multi-Criteria Group Decision-Making (MCGDM) [30] and its application to ontologies [29], treating ontology classes as criteria and configurations as alternatives. Specifically, a finite set of expert is considered, each one of them is assigned a fuzzy weight $\tilde{\pi}_k$, reflecting their relative importance in the decision process. Each expert selects their best choice among the alternatives of the MCGDM, and a final best compromise $A^*$ is derived using a minimal mean distance operator, ensuring that the collective consensus accurately represents expert opinions while minimising deviations from individual preferences.

The paper is organised as follows. In Sect. 2, we recall the definitions of ontology and fuzzy ontology, and some basic notions on fuzzy numbers, t-norms and t-conorms, aggregation operators and the algorithms for MCDM and MCGDM. In Sect. 3 we present our method for fuzzy ontology aggregation through an MCGDM approach. In particular we introduce the concept of membership matrix and we propose an "overall best compromise" obtained as a weighted mean of the optimal alternatives of the experts. Then, in Sect. 4, to ensure that the final "best compromise" actually incorporates all the experts' opinions by also minimizing the deviation from each expert best choice, we proposed a best compromise based on minimal mean distance operator. Finally, in Sect. 5, we conclude and we point out future work.

## 2 Preliminaries

This section provides an overview of essential concepts that form the foundation of this paper, including ontologies, fuzzy ontologies, trapezoidal fuzzy numbers and their operations, as well as background on Multi-Criteria Group Decision-Making (MCGDM) problems and aggregation operators.

An *ontology* is a formal and structured knowledge representation within a specific domain, defining concepts, relationships, and axioms. It facilitates data integration, semantic search, interoperability, and decision support while enabling reasoning through logical rules and constraints.

**Definition 1.** *An* ontology $\mathcal{O}$ *can be described as a tuple* $\mathcal{O} = (\mathcal{C}, \mathcal{I}, R)$ *where:*

- $\mathcal{C} = \{C_1, \ldots, C_m\}$ *is a set of* $m$ *concepts (or classes);*
- $\mathcal{I} = \{I_1, \ldots, I_N\}$ *is a set of* $N$ *individuals such that, for all* $s = 1, \ldots, N$, $I_s \in C_j$*, for some* $j = 1, \ldots, m$*;*
- $R = \{R_1, \ldots, R_c\}$ *is a set of* $c$ *relations between the concepts* $\mathcal{C}$ *or the individuals* $\mathcal{I}$ *such that* $R_t \colon (\mathcal{C} \cup \mathcal{I} \times \ldots \times \mathcal{C} \cup \mathcal{I}) \mapsto \{\perp, \top\}$*, where* $\perp$ *is* ***false****, and* $\top$ *is* ***true*** *in classic boolean logic.*

However, classical ontologies struggle with vagueness and imprecision. *Fuzzy ontologies* address this by incorporating fuzzy logic, allowing degrees of membership and defining rules via fuzzy axioms and providing a more flexible representation of uncertainty. Formally, a fuzzy ontology is defined as follows ([29], see also [7,21])

**Definition 2 (cf. [5]).** *A* fuzzy ontology *can be described as a tuple* $\tilde{\mathcal{O}} = (\mathcal{I}, \mathcal{C}, R, F, A)$*, where:*

- $\mathcal{I} = \{I_1, \ldots, I_N\}$ *is a set of* $N$ *individuals.*
- $\mathcal{C} = \{C_1, \ldots, C_m\}$ *is a set of* $m$ *concepts or classes. For all* $j = 1, \ldots, m$, $C_j \in \mathcal{C}$ *is a fuzzy set on the domain of individuals, i.e.,* $C_j \colon \mathcal{I} \mapsto [0, 1]$*. The set of entities of the fuzzy ontology will be denoted by* $\mathcal{X}$*, i.e.,* $\mathcal{X} = \mathcal{C} \cup \mathcal{I}$*.*
- $R = \{R_1, \ldots, R_c\}$ *is a set of* $c$ *fuzzy relations on the domain of entities* $\mathcal{X}$ *such that, for all* $t = 1, \ldots, c$, $R_t \colon \mathcal{X}^l \mapsto [0, 1]$*, with* $l > 1$*.*
- $F$ *is the set of fuzzy relations on the set of entities* $\mathcal{X}$ *and a specific domain contained in* $D = \{integer, string, \ldots\}$*. In detail, they are functions such that each element* $f \in F$ *is a relation* $f \colon \mathcal{X}^{(l-1)} \times P \mapsto [0, 1]$ *where* $P \in D$*, and* $l > 1$*.*
- $A$ *is the set of axioms expressed in a proper logical language, i.e., predicates that constrain the meaning of concepts, individuals, relationships, and functions.*

A fuzzy number generalises a real number by representing a range of possible values, each with a membership degree between 0 and 1, defined by a membership function. Formally, it is a fuzzy subset of $\mathbb{R}$ (see e.g. [4,13]). For foundational concepts, the reader is referred to [17]. In this paper, we focus on trapezoidal fuzzy numbers, characterised by trapezoidal-shaped membership functions.

**Definition 3.** *A* trapezoidal fuzzy number *(TpFN)* $\tilde{n} = (a, b, c, d)$*, with* $a, b, c, d \in \mathbb{R}$ *and* $a \leq b \leq c \leq d$*, is a fuzzy number whose membership function* $\mu$ *has the following form:*

$$\tilde{n}(x) = \mu(x) = \begin{cases} \frac{x-a}{b-a}, & x \in [a, b] \\ 1, & x \in [b, c] \\ \frac{d-x}{d-c}, & x \in [c, d] \\ 0 & otherwise. \end{cases}$$

It is possible to define addition and multiplication between TpFNs as $(a, b, c, d) * (\alpha, \beta, \gamma, \delta) := (a * \alpha, b * \beta, c * \gamma, d * \delta)$, with $* \in \{+, \cdot\}$.

In the following, we recall the definitions of t-norm and t-conorm.

**Definition 4.** *A* t-norm *is a binary operator* $\odot$ *such that,* $\forall x, y, z \in [0, 1]$,

*(a)* $x \odot y = y \odot x$;
*(b)* $x \odot (y \odot z) = (x \odot y) \odot z$;
*(c)* $y \leq z \implies x \odot y \leq x \odot z$;
*(d)* $x \odot 1 = 1 \odot x = x$ *(1 is the neutral element).*

*A* t-conorm *is a binary operator* $\oplus$ *with the same properties as a t-norm except that its neutral element is* 0.

T-norms and t-conorms generalise the AND and the OR operators from classic Boolean logic. The most famous and used examples are Zadeh (Z), Probabilistic (P), and Łukasiewicz (L):

(1) $x \odot_Z y := \min(x, y)$ and $x \oplus_Z y := \max(x, y)$ [33]);
(2) $x \odot_P y := x \cdot y$ and $x \oplus_P y := x + y - xy$ (deduced within probabilistic theory);
(3) $x \odot_L y := \max(0, x + y - 1)$ and $x \oplus_L y := \min(1, x + y)$ [10].

In the framework of fuzzy logic, t-norms and t-conorms are widely used to model operations among fuzzy sets and their definition is also extended to fuzzy numbers. Indeed, let $\tilde{x} = (a, b, c, d)$ and $\tilde{y} = (\alpha, \beta, \gamma, \delta)$ are two TpFNs. We can define the t-norm, t-conorm, and exponentiation respectively as $\tilde{x} * \tilde{y} := (a * \alpha, b * \beta, c * \gamma, d * \delta)$, with $* \in \{\odot, \oplus\}$, and $\tilde{x}^{\tilde{y}} := (a^\alpha, b^\beta, c^\gamma, d^\delta)$.

Here, the operations on the right-hand side are, respectively, t-norm, t-conorm, and exponentiation applied component-wise to its components.

*Multi-Criteria Decision-Making* (MCDM) is a prominent branch of *decision-making* that focuses on evaluating multiple options and identifying the one that best aligns with predefined goals, objectives, values, and priorities.

A MCDM problem involves a set of $n$ *alternatives* $\mathcal{A} = \{A_1, A_2, \dots, A_n\}$ and a set of $m$ *criteria* $\mathcal{C} = \{C_1, C_2, \dots, C_m\}$. In this context, *alternatives* represent the available choices of action. Decision *criteria*, also referred to as *goals* or *attributes*, define the dimensions from which these alternatives are evaluated. Each alternative $A_i$ is evaluated with respect to each criterion $C_j$ using a *score* $a_{ij}$ , which indicates how well $A_i$ satisfies $C_j$. The aim of MCDM is to identify the optimal alternative $A^*$ with the highest level of desirability. Additionally, most MCDM methods require assigning a weight $w_j$ to each criterion $C_j$ to reflect their relative importance in the decision-making process. Typically, the weights are normalised to sum up to one, that is $\sum_{j=1}^{m} w_j = 1$. These weights reflect either the perspective of an individual decision-maker or a consensus derived from a group of experts. There is extensive literature on methods for assigning weights (see, e.g. [32]). Finally, the MCDM approach includes the assignment of a *final rank* $x_i$ to each alternative $A_i$, where $i = 1, 2, \dots, n$. This rank reflects the overall desirability or relevance of the alternative within the context of the decision problem. These rankings are essential for prioritising alternatives and guiding the decision maker toward the most suitable choice. Additionally, the relationship between the alternatives and criteria is often organised into a decision matrix.

As an example, we show the so-called *Weighted Sum Method* (WSM), one of the most classical methods in MCDM. Formally, let $x_i = \sum_{j=1}^{m} a_{ij} w_j$ for each $i = 1, 2, \ldots, m$. The alternatives $A_i$ are ranked in descending order based on their final ranking values $x_i$, with the optimal alternative $A^*$ being the one that achieves the highest ranking value, i.e.,

$$A^* = \arg\max_{A_i} x_i. \tag{1}$$

When the decision problem involves a group of decision makers selecting the most suitable alternative from a finite set of alternatives under multiple criteria, we are in the context of MCGDM. In this context, there is a need to understand how to join, incorporate, or appropriately consider their opinions to reach a consensus among them.

*Aggregation operators* are essential tools designed to combine and summarise a finite set of values (whether crisp or fuzzy) into a single representative value. Their primary purpose is to simplify or synthesise data, enabling tasks such as making collective decisions, computing overall assessments, or reducing complexity. These operators are particularly significant in solving MCGDM problems.

In general, an aggregation operator is a function $\mathbf{A}$ used to combine multiple inputs from a subinterval of $(-\infty, +\infty)$ into a single output within the same interval, which must satisfy some conditions. For simplicity and convenience, the inputs are usually taken within the unit interval $I = [0, 1]$, that is, an aggregation operator is generally considered as a function $\mathbf{A}\colon \bigcup_{p\in\mathbb{N}} I^p \to I$. It is worth noting that, in our case, this operator fits perfectly, as we aggregate (matrices of) membership degrees. The three fundamental properties of aggregation operators are the following (see, e.g., [6,28]).

**Definition 5.** *An* aggregation operator *is a function* $\mathbf{A}\colon \bigcup_{p\in\mathbb{N}} I^p \to I$ *that satisfies the following properties:*

*(P1)* ***Boundary conditions:*** $\mathbf{A}(0, \ldots, 0) = 0$ *and* $\mathbf{A}(1, \ldots, 1) = 1$.
*(P2)* ***Singleton aggregation:*** *As a convention, for every* $x \in [0, 1]$, $\mathbf{A}(x) = x$.
*(P3)* ***Monotonicity:*** *for any* $p \in \mathbb{N}$, *by setting* $\mathbf{A}_{(p)} := \mathbf{A}_{|I^p}$,
$x_1 \le y_1, \ldots, x_p \le y_p \Rightarrow \mathbf{A}_{(p)}(x_1, \ldots, x_p) \le \mathbf{A}_{(p)}(y_1, \ldots, y_p)$.

A basic example of an aggregation operator is the arithmetic mean $\mathbf{M}$ given by $\mathbf{M}(x_1, \ldots, x_p) = \frac{1}{p} \sum_{i=1}^{p} x_i$. Moreover, to define aggregation operators, additional desirable properties, such as continuity, commutativity, idempotency, and boundedness, are usually considered.

It is often necessary to introduce a weighting system for an aggregation operator, particularly in the context of MCGDM. Let $v_1, \ldots, v_p \in \mathbb{N}$ be integer weights and let $v = (v_1, \ldots, v_p)$ be the corresponding (non-zero) weighting vector. Given an aggregation operator $\mathbf{A}\colon \bigcup_{p\in\mathbb{N}} I^p \to I$, the weights $v_i$ can be incorporated as follows:

$$\mathbf{A}_{(p)}(x_1,\ldots,x_p) = \mathbf{A}_{(p)}(\underbrace{x_1,\ldots,x_1}_{v_1 \text{ times}},\underbrace{x_2,\ldots,x_2}_{v_2 \text{ times}},\ldots,\underbrace{x_p,\ldots,x_p}_{v_p \text{ times}}).$$

For example, integrating a weighting system $v = (v_1,\ldots,v_p)$ into the arithmetic mean $\mathbf{M}$, yields the well known *weighted arithmetic mean* $\mathbf{M}_v$ (with rational weights), defined as

$$\mathbf{M}_v(x_1,\ldots,x_p) = \sum_{i=1}^{p} w_i x_p, \tag{2}$$

where the weighting vector $w$ has components $w_i = \frac{v_i}{\sum_{j=1}^{p} v_j}$. For notation and definitions about aggregation operators, we refer the reader to [6].

## 3 Fuzzy MCGDM-Based Aggregation in Ontologies

In this section, we first introduce the notation used throughout this work, and then we describe our algorithm for ontology aggregation via fuzzy MCGDM.

Consider a fuzzy ontology $\tilde{\mathcal{O}}$ with classes $C_j$, $j = 1,\ldots,m$, and let $\mathcal{I}$ denote the set of individuals, with $|\mathcal{I}| = N$. Given a membership function $\mu_i$ defined on the pair $(\mathcal{I},\mathcal{C})$, the *membership matrix* $A_i$ is defined as the matrix $A_i = (\alpha_{i,sj})$, where $\alpha_{i,sj} = \mu_{i,C_j}(I_s)$ is the value of the $i$-th membership function of the individual $I_s \in \mathcal{I}$ with respect to the class $C_j$. Let $\mathcal{E} = \{E_1, E_2,\ldots,E_p\}$ denote the set of experts. In this framework, the criteria $\mathcal{C} = \{C_1, C_2,\ldots,C_m\}$ of the MCGDM are the classes of the ontology $\tilde{\mathcal{O}}$, while the alternatives $\mathcal{A} = \{A_1, A_2,\ldots,A_n\}$ are the *membership matrices* associated with the ontology $\tilde{\mathcal{O}}$. We emphasize that the alternatives are given a priori on the ontology and they are not tied to the experts of the decision problem.

For each expert $E_k$, where $k = 1,\ldots,p$, a decision matrix is constructed based on the available alternatives and criteria, as shown in Table 1. For every $i = 1,\ldots,n$ and $j = 1,\ldots,m$, the entry of the $k$-th decision matrix is the scores $a_{ij}^k$ which represents the evaluation assigned by expert $E_k$ to the alternative $A_i$ with respect to the criterion $C_j$.

Additionally, each expert $E_k$ assigns a weight $w_j^k$ to the class (criterion) $C_j$, reflecting its relative importance in the context of the decision problem from the expert's perspective. These weights are assumed to be normalised for each expert and are organised into a *weight matrix*, denoted by $W = (w_j^k)$.

This method can be extended by incorporating trapezoidal fuzzy numbers for weights, $\tilde{w}_j^k$, and scores, $\tilde{a}_{ij}^k$, of expert $E_k$ with $k = 1,\ldots,p$. First, the weights are normalised as TpFNs whose vertices are within $[0,1]$. Specifically, for a given expert $E_k$, let $\tilde{w}_j^k = (\tilde{\alpha}_j^k, \tilde{\beta}_j^k, \tilde{\gamma}_j^k, \tilde{\delta}_j^k)$, and let $\hat{\alpha}_k = \sum_{i=1}^m \tilde{\alpha}_i^k$, $\hat{\beta}_k = \sum_{i=1}^m \tilde{\beta}_i^k$, $\hat{\gamma}_k = \sum_{i=1}^m \tilde{\gamma}_i^k$, and $\hat{\delta}_k = \sum_{i=1}^m \tilde{\delta}_i^k$, then the normalized weight for the class $C_j$ is given by $w_j^k = \left(\frac{\tilde{\alpha}_j^k}{\hat{\alpha}_k}, \frac{\tilde{\beta}_j^k}{\hat{\beta}_k}, \frac{\tilde{\gamma}_j^k}{\hat{\gamma}_k}, \frac{\tilde{\delta}_j^k}{\hat{\delta}_k}\right)$, for each $j = 1,\ldots,m$.

Hence, we construct $p$ decision matrices, one for each expert, similarly to what was done in Table 1 in the crisp case. Each expert computes the final rank values for alternatives using, for example, a Simple Additive Weighting (SAW) method, treating weights and scores as TpFNs. The final fuzzy rank value for alternative $A_i$ is given by $\tilde{x}_i^k = \sum_{j=1}^{m} \tilde{a}_{ij}^k \tilde{w}_j^k$ for each $k = 1, \ldots, p$ and $i = 1, \ldots, n$.

To obtain crisp ranks, we defuzzify $\tilde{x}_i^k$ using a defuzzification method, such as Mean of Maximum (MOM), resulting in $x_i^k$. The optimal alternative for each expert $E_k$ is identified as $A_k^* = \arg\max_{A_i} x_i^k$.

**Table 1.** Decision matrix for the expert $E_k$ with respect to the classes of a fuzzy ontology. For every $i = 1, \ldots, n$, $x_i$ represents the final rank of alternative $A_i$.

| | $E_k$ | Criteria | | | |
|---|---|---|---|---|---|
| | | $w_1^k$ | $w_2^k$ | $\cdots$ | $w_m^k$ |
| Rank | Alternatives | $C_1$ | $C_2$ | $\cdots$ | $C_m$ |
| $x_1$ | $A_1$ | $a_{11}^k$ | $a_{12}^k$ | $\cdots$ | $a_{1m}^k$ |
| $x_2$ | $A_2$ | $a_{21}^k$ | $a_{22}^k$ | $\cdots$ | $a_{2m}^k$ |
| $\vdots$ | $\vdots$ | $\vdots$ | $\vdots$ | $\ddots$ | $\vdots$ |
| $x_n$ | $A_n$ | $a_{n1}^k$ | $a_{n2}^k$ | $\cdots$ | $a_{nm}^k$ |

The *overall best* compromise $A^*$ is determined by aggregating the experts' optimal alternatives. Assuming equal importance for all experts and using the arithmetic mean we get $A^* = \frac{1}{p}\sum_{k=1}^{p} A_k^*$. Alternatively, if experts are assigned different importance levels $\pi_k$ (assumed to be normalised), the weighted aggregation becomes

$$A^* = \sum_{k=1}^{p} \pi_k A_k^*. \tag{3}$$

The best compromise $A^*$ in Eq. (3) can be proven to be a membership matrix itself. The above process can also be expressed using aggregation operators. The best compromise matrix is denoted as $A^* = (\alpha_{sj}^*)$, $s = 1, \ldots, N$ and $j = 1, \ldots, m$, with elements determined using Eq. (2):

$$\alpha_{sj}^* = \mathbf{M}_{\{\pi_1, \pi_2, \ldots, \pi_p\}}(\alpha_{sj}^{1*}, \alpha_{sj}^{2*}, \ldots, \alpha_{sj}^{p*}). \tag{4}$$

Each element of the matrix $A^*$ represents the weighted aggregation of the corresponding elements from the matrices $A_1^*, \ldots, A_p^*$.

The previous algorithm can be applied in various scenarios. For example, it can be used to convert a crisp ontology into a fuzzy ontology by determining membership degrees for individuals in newly added fuzzy classes. This process relies on expert input or user surveys to handle uncertainty and imprecision effectively. Another application could be using the algorithm to aggregate results from multiple decision-making problems. For example, it can combine different evaluations of alternatives, such as identifying optimal countries for commercialisation or comparing employment rates in neighbouring regions, to produce a unified fuzzy ontology reflecting all perspectives.

## 4 Minimal Mean Distance Compromise

In this section, we present our algorithm for ontology aggregation using fuzzy MCGDM, aiming to determine the best overall compromise through a minimal mean distance operator (see Fig. 1 for the flowchart of the algorithm). This approach ensures that the final result incorporates all expert opinions while minimising deviations from their individual preferences.

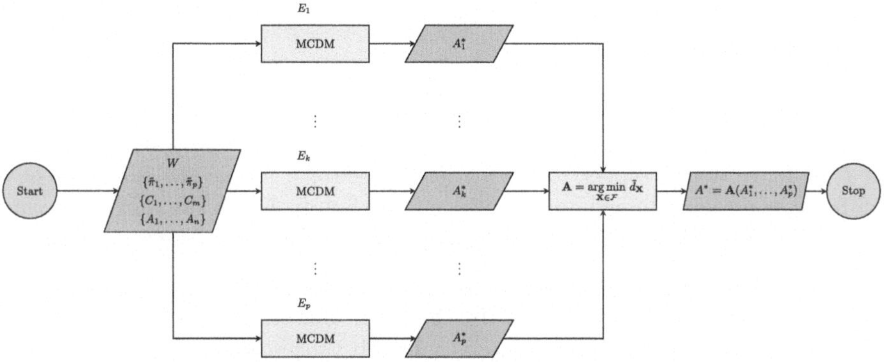


**Fig. 1.** Flowchart of the algorithm.

In the MCGDM setting of Sect. 3, suppose that each expert $E_k$ has selected their best choice $A_k^*$, and let us fix a t-norm $\odot$ and a t-conorm $\oplus$. Now, assume that the experts' importance levels are fuzzy trapezoidal numbers $\tilde{\pi}_k = (\alpha_k, \beta_k, \gamma_k, \delta_k)$, for $k = 1, \ldots, p$. A vector $\pi = (\tilde{\pi}_1, \ldots, \tilde{\pi}_p)$ is called a *weighting vector* (with respect to the t-conorm $\oplus$) if it satisfies $\bigoplus_{k=1}^{p} \tilde{\pi}_k = (1, 1, 1, 1) = 1$.

Since the weights are now fuzzy numbers, to determine the best overall compromise $A^*$, we aggregate the choices $A_k^*$, $k = 1, \ldots, m$, selected by the experts, using a suitable *fuzzy triangular aggregation operator* (see [28]) $\mathbf{A}$ to compute each entry $\alpha_{sj}^*$, that is

$$A^* = \mathbf{A}(A_1^*, \ldots, A_p^*). \tag{5}$$

One example is the *Fuzzy Triangular Weighted Averaging operator* (FTWA), given by:

$$\tilde{\mathbf{M}}_{(\tilde{\pi}_1, \ldots, \tilde{\pi}_p)}(y_1, \ldots, y_p) = \bigoplus_{k=1}^{p} (\tilde{\pi}_k \odot y_k). \tag{6}$$

This operator generalises the weighted arithmetic mean, and it follows the definition in [28], but in this case, we have fuzzy weights and crisp variables.

Since membership matrices are elements of $\mathbb{R}^{N \times m}$, where $N = |\mathcal{I}|$ and $m = |\mathcal{C}|$, we recall that the Euclidean distance between $A^*$ and each $A_k^*$ is

$$d_{\mathbf{A}}^k = d_{\mathbf{A}}(A^*, A_k^*) = \sqrt{\sum_{\substack{s=1,\ldots,N \\ j=1,\ldots,m}} \left(\alpha_{sj}^* - \alpha_{sj}^{k*}\right)^2}. \tag{7}$$

Additionally, we can consider the mean distance $\bar{d}_{\mathbf{A}} = \sum_{k=1}^{p} \frac{d_{\mathbf{A}}^k}{p}$, which depends on the aggregation operator $\mathbf{A}$ choosen in Eq. (5).

In this setting the goal is to select $A^*$ in a way that accurately reflects the collective opinions of all experts $E_k$, while minimising deviations from their individual choices. In other words, we seek to ensure that $A^*$ remains as close as possible to each $A_k^*$ in the Euclidean space $\mathbb{R}^{N\times m}$. This approach guarantees that the final compromise does not disproportionately favour any single expert's perspective but instead maintains a balanced representation of all viewpoints. To achieve this, we aim to find an aggregation operator $\mathbf{A}$ that minimises the mean distance, that is,

$$\mathbf{A} = \underset{\mathbf{X}\in \mathrm{FTW}_\pi(I^p)}{\arg\min}\ \bar{d}_{\mathbf{X}}, \tag{8}$$

where $\mathrm{FTW}_\pi(I^p)$ represents the set of all fuzzy triangular weighted operators on $I^p = [0,1]^p$ with respect to the weighting vector $\pi$. Since the existence of a minimum is not guaranteed, we consider a finite family $\mathcal{F} \subset \mathrm{FTW}_\pi(I^p)$, ensuring that an operator $\mathbf{A}$ minimizing $\bar{d}_{\mathbf{X}}$ exists. Then we have $\mathbf{A} = \underset{\mathbf{X}\in\mathcal{F}}{\arg\min}\ \bar{d}_{\mathbf{X}}$.

If multiple operators achieve the minimum, any of them can be chosen as they provide maximum consensus. In this case, one may introduce additional criteria to choose between two minimal mean distance operators.

**Definition 6.** *A* minimal mean distance compromise *is the aggregated matrix $A^* = \mathbf{A}(A_1^*, \ldots, A_p^*)$, where $\mathbf{A}$ is a minimal mean distance operator in an appropriately given family $\mathcal{F}$ of fuzzy triangular weighted operators.*

A natural choice for $\mathcal{F}$ includes fuzzy triangular versions of the weighted arithmetic and geometric means, respectively $\mathbf{M}$ and $\mathbf{G}$. Thus, the entries of the overall best compromise matrix $A^*$ in these two cases are computed as, respectively:

$$\alpha_{s,j}^* = \mathbf{M}_{(\tilde{\pi}_1,\ldots,\tilde{\pi}_p)}(\alpha_{s,j}^{1*}, \ldots, \alpha_{s,j}^{p*}) = \bigoplus_{k=1}^{p} \left(\tilde{\pi}_k \odot \alpha_{s,j}^{k*}\right),$$
$$\alpha_{s,j}^* = \mathbf{G}_{(\tilde{\pi}_1,\ldots,\tilde{\pi}_p)}(\alpha_{s,j}^{1*}, \ldots, \alpha_{s,j}^{p*}) = \bigodot_{k=1}^{p} \left(\alpha_{s,j}^{k*}\right)^{\tilde{\pi}_k}.$$

## 5 Conclusions

This work extends the integration of fuzzy logic in MCGDM [30] and its application to ontologies [29]. We introduced a fuzzy value-aggregation method for semantic preference unification, applying MCGDM to fuzzy ontologies. Given a fuzzy ontology $\tilde{\mathcal{O}}$ with classes $\mathcal{C} = \{C_1, \ldots, C_m\}$, a MCGDM problem was defined with a set of experts $\mathcal{E}$ and a set of alternatives $\mathcal{A}$. Here, alternatives are represented by membership matrices associated to different membership functions, and criteria correspond to ontology classes. Each expert $E_k$ assigned scores and weights to the ontology classes, expressed as qualitative values and converted into trapezoidal fuzzy numbers. Each expert $E_k$ is given a fuzzy weight $\tilde{\pi}_k$. A final best compromise $A^*$ was obtained by using a minimal mean distance operator, in order to reflect the collective opinions of all experts and to minimise deviations from their individual choices. This algorithm is well-suited for MCDM problems where the final choice can fall outside the set of predefined alternatives. For example, a company optimising office temperature may select any value within a reasonable range to balance comfort, energy efficiency, and health. However, this approach can also be applied when the final choice must be one of the given options, such as selecting a nuclear waste storage site, where an intermediate location may be geologically unstable or too close to a population centre. In such cases, the best choice is the predefined alternative closest to the minimal mean distance compromise.

**Acknowledgements.** Giuseppe Filippone, Mario Galici, Gianmarco La Rosa, and Marco Elio Tabacchi are supported by funding from the **Sustainability Decision Framework (SDF)** Research Project – CUP **B79J23000540005** – Grant Assignment Decree No. **5486** adopted on **2023-08-04**. Mario Galici and Gianmarco La Rosa are also supported by the **Gruppo Nazionale per le Strutture Algebriche, Geometriche e le loro Applicazioni (GNSAGA)** of the **Istituto Nazionale di Alta Matematica (INdAM)** "Francesco Severi". Lydia Castronovo is supported by the **Gruppo Nazionale per l'Analisi Matematica, la Probabilità e le loro Applicazioni (GNAMPA)** of the **Istituto Nazionale di Alta Matematica (INdAM)** "Francesco Severi". Lydia Castronovo and Marco Elio Tabacchi acknowledge financial support under the National Recovery and Resilience Plan (NRRP), Mission 4, Component 2, Investment 1.1, Call for tender No. 1409 published on 14.9.2022 by the Italian Ministry of University and Research (MUR), funded by the European Union – NextGenerationEU – Project Title **Quantum Models for Logic, Computation and Natural Processes (QM4NP)** – CUP **B53D23030160001** – Grant Assignment Decree No. **1371** adopted on **2023-09-01** by the Italian Ministry of University and Research (MUR).

## References


1. Antoniou, G., et al.: A Semantic Web Primer. The MIT Press, Cambridge (2012). isbn 0262018284
2. Bobillo, F., Straccia, U.: Aggregation operators for fuzzy ontologies. Appl. Soft Comput. **13**(9), 3816–3830 (2013). https://doi.org/10.1016/j.asoc.2013.05.008. issn: 1568–4946
3. Bobillo, F., Straccia, U.: Fuzzy description logics under Gödel semantics. Int. J. Approx. Reason. **50**(3), 494–514 (2009). https://doi.org/10.1016/j.ijar.2008.11.003
4. Buckley, J.J., Eslami, E.: An Introduction to Fuzzy Logic and Fuzzy Sets. In: Advances in Intelligent and Soft Computing, 1st edn, pp. X, 285. Physica Heidelberg (2002). https://doi.org/10.1007/978-3-7908-1799-7
5. Calegari, S., Ciucci, D.: Fuzzy ontology, fuzzy description logics and fuzzy-OWL. In: Masulli, F., Mitra, S., Pasi, G. (eds.) WILF 2007. LNCS (LNAI), vol. 4578, pp. 118–126. Springer, Heidelberg (2007). https://doi.org/10.1007/978-3-540-73400-0_15. isbn: 978-3-540-73400-0
6. Calvo, T., Mayor, G., Mesiar, R. (eds.): Aggregation Operators. New Trends and Applications. Studies in Fuzziness and Soft Computing, 1st edn, pp. XIV, 353. Physica Heidelberg (2002). https://doi.org/10.1007/978-3-7908-1787-4

7. Cross, V., Chen, S.: Fuzzy ontologies: state of the art revisited. In: Barreto, G.A., Coelho, R. (eds.) NAFIPS 2018. CCIS, vol. 831, pp. 230–242. Springer, Cham (2018). https://doi.org/10.1007/978-3-319-95312-0_20. isbn: 978-3-319-95312-0
8. Endriss, U.: Judgment aggregation. In: Brandt, F. et al. (eds.) Handbook of Computational Social Choice, pp. 399–426. Cambridge University Press, Cambridge (2016)
9. Flouris, G., et al.: Ontology change: classification and survey. Knowl. Eng. Rev. **23**(2), 117–152 (2008). https://doi.org/10.1017/S0269888908001367
10. Giles, R.: Łukasiewicz logic and fuzzy set theory. Int. J. Man-Mach. Stud. **8**(3), 313–327 (1976). https://doi.org/10.1016/S0020-7373(76)80003-X. https://www.sciencedirect.com/science/article/pii/S002073737680003X. issn: 0020-7373
11. Grossi, D., Pigozzi, G.: Judgment aggregation: a primer. In: Synthesis Lectures on Artificial Intelligence and Machine Learning, 1st edn, pp. XVII, 133. Springer, Cham (2014). https://doi.org/10.1007/978-3-031-01568-7
12. W3C OWL Working Group. OWL Web Ontology Language Overview (2004). https://www.w3.org/TR/owl-features/
13. Hájek, P.: Metamathematics of fuzzy logic. In: Trends in Logic, 1st edn, pp. VIII, 299. Springer, Dordrecht (1998). https://doi.org/10.1007/978-94-011-5300-3
14. Hájek, P.: Metamathematics of fuzzy logic, vol. 4. Springer, Heidelberg (1998). https://doi.org/10.1007/978-94-017-1866-7
15. Hepp, M.: Ontologies: state of the art, business potential, and grand challenges. In: Hepp, M., et al. (eds.) Ontology Management: Semantic Web, Semantic Web Services, and Business Applications, pp. 3–22. Springer US, Boston (2008). isbn: 978-0-387-69900-4. https://doi.org/10.1007/978-0-387-69900-4_1
16. Huitzil, I., et al.: Fudge: fuzzy ontology building with consensuated fuzzy datatypes. In: Fuzzy Sets and Systems 401 (2020). Fuzzy Measures, Integrals and Quantification in Artificial Intelligence Problems – An Homage to Prof. Miguel Delgado, pp. 91–112. issn: 0165-0114. https://doi.org/10.1016/j.fss.2020.04.001
17. van Laarhoven, P.J.M., Pedrycz, W.: A fuzzy extension of saaty's priority theory. Fuzzy Sets Syst. **11**(1), 229–241 (1983). issn: 0165-0114. https://doi.org/10.1016/S0165-0114(83)80082-7
18. List, C., Polak, B.: Introduction to judgment aggregation. J. Econ. Theory **145**(2), 441–466 (2010). issn: 0022-0531. https://doi.org/10.1016/j.jet.2010.02.001
19. List, C., Puppe, C.: Judgment aggregation: a survey. In: Anand, P., Pattanaik, P., Puppe, C. (eds.) Handbook of Rational and Social Choice. Oxford University Press, Cambridge (2009)
20. Lukasiewicz, T.: Fuzzy description logic programs under the answer set semantics for the semantic web. Fundamenta Informaticae **82**(3), 289–310 (2008). https://doi.org/10.3233/FI-2008-823
21. Manikandabalaji, M., Sivakumar, R.: Knowledge representation using fuzzy ontologies: a survey. IJCSNS **23**(12), 199 (2023). https://doi.org/10.22937/IJCSNS.2023.23.12.20
22. Noy, N., Musen, M.A.: PROMPT: algorithm and tool for automated ontology merging and alignment. In: AAAI/IAAI (2000)
23. Noy, N.F., McGuinness D.L.: Ontology development 101: a guide to creating your first ontology (2001). Accessed 10 Apr 2023. https://protege.stanford.edu/publications/ontology_development/ontology101-noy-mcguinness.html
24. Pan, J.Z.: OWL Working Group. OWL 2 Web Ontology Language Document Overview: W3C Recommendation 27 October 2009. English (2009)
25. Porello, D.: Judgement aggregation in non-classical logics. J. Appl. Non-Class. Logics **27**(1-2), 106–139 (2017). https://doi.org/10.1080/11663081.2017.1368846

26. Porello, D., Endriss, U.: Ontology merging as social choice. In: Leite, J., Torroni, P., Ågotnes, T., Boella, G., van der Torre, L. (eds.) CLIMA 2011. LNCS (LNAI), vol. 6814, pp. 157–170. Springer, Heidelberg (2011). https://doi.org/10.1007/978-3-642-22359-4_12. isbn: 978-3- 642-22359-4
27. Porello, D., et al.: Two approaches to ontology aggregation based on axiom weakening. In: Proceedings of the Twenty-Seventh International Joint Conference on Artificial Intelligence, IJCAI-18. International Joint Conferences on Artificial Intelligence Organization, July 2018, pp. 1942–1948 (2018). https://doi.org/10.24963/ijcai.2018/268
28. Simo, Y.F., Gwét, H.: Fuzzy triangular aggregation operators. Int. J. Math. Math. Sci. 2018(1), 9209524 (2018). https://doi.org/10.1155/2018/9209524
29. Straccia, U.: Foundations of Fuzzy Logic and Semantic Web Languages, 1st edn. Chapman and Hall/CRC (2013). https://doi.org/10.1201/b15460
30. Straccia, U.: Multi criteria decision making in fuzzy description logics: a first step. In: Velásquez, J.D., Ríos, S.A., Howlett, R.J., Jain, L.C. (eds.) KES 2009. LNCS (LNAI), vol. 5711, pp. 78–86. Springer, Heidelberg (2009). https://doi.org/10.1007/978-3-642-04595-0_10
31. Straccia, U.: Reasoning within fuzzy description logics. J. Artif. Intell. Res. **14**, 137–166 (2001). https://doi.org/10.1613/jair.825
32. Triantaphyllou, E.: Multi-Criteria Decision Making Methods: A Comparative Study, vol. 44 (2000). https://doi.org/10.1007/978-1-4757-3157-6. isbn: 978-1-4419-4838-0
33. Zadeh, L.A.: Fuzzy sets. Inf. Control **8**(3), 338–353 (1965). https://doi.org/10.1016/S0019-9958(65)90241-X. issn: 0019-9958

# Representing and Managing Uncertainty

# How to Deal with High-Impact Low-Probability Events: Theoretical Explanation of the Empirically Successful Fuzzy-Like Technique

Juan Ulloa[1], Aaron Velasco[2], Olga Kosheleva[3], and Vladik Kreinovich[1](✉)

[1] Department of Computer Science, University of Texas at El Paso, 500 W. University, El Paso, TX 79968, USA
{julloa,vladik}@utep.edu

[2] Department of Earth, Environmental, and Resource Sciences, University of Texas at El Paso, 500 W. University, El Paso, TX 79968, USA
aavelasco@utep.edu

[3] Department of Teacher Education, University of Texas at El Paso, 500 W. University, El Paso, TX 79968, USA
olgak@utep.edu

**Abstract.** When making decisions, it is important to take into account high-impact low-probability events. For such events, traditional probability-based approach – which considers the product of the probability $p$ that this event happens and the probability $P$ that a randomly selected building will be destroyed – often underestimates risks. Available data has lead to an empirical table that provides a more adequate risk estimate. Most of the entries in this table correspond to the fuzzy-like formula $\min(p, P)$. This paper explains this empirical result. Specifically, it explains both the effectiveness of the min formula – and also explains deviations from this formula.

**Keywords:** High-impact low-probability events · Fuzzy-like formulas · Hurwicz optimism-pessimism approach

## 1 Formulation of the Problem

**Need to Deal with High-Impact Low-Probability Events.** In many decision-making situations, we need to take into account high-impact low-probability events. For example:

- in civil engineering, we need to take into account the possibility of rare strong earthquakes that could destroy the designed buildings;
- in information security, we need to take into account the low-probability scenario in which the adversary can break through all our security barriers and thus, inflict a high-impact damage, etc.

How can we take such events into account?


M. Baczyński et al. (Eds.): EUSFLAT 2025, LNCS 15884, pp. 91–97, 2025.
https://doi.org/10.1007/978-3-031-97228-7_8

**Cannot We Use the Usual Risk-Based Approach?** At first glance, the solution is straightforward. According to decision theory (see, e.g., [2,3,7,10, 12,13,17]), in decision making, we should select the alternative for which the expected utility is the largest – i.e., in this case, that the expected loss is the smallest. The expected loss is equal to the product $p \cdot \ell$ of:

- the event's probability $p$ and
- the corresponding loss $\ell$.

So, this product should be the numerical measure that describes how we should take such events into account.

This measure can be described in purely probabilistic terms. For example, the earthquake's damage $\ell$ to a city can be described by multiplying:

- the probability $P$ that in this event, a randomly selected building will be damaged, and
- the average amount of damage $D$ to an affected building.

For $\ell = P \cdot D$, the expected loss $p \cdot \ell$ takes the form $p \cdot P \cdot D$, and is, thus, proportional to the product $p \cdot P$ of the two probabilities:

- the probability $p$ that such an event will occur, and
- the probability $P$ that this event will damage a randomly selected building.

**The Usual Risk-Based Approach Underestimates the Risk.** We want to estimate the probability that the event occurred *and* that it damaged the randomly selected building. The above product formula $p \cdot P$ is valid if these two events are independent. However, for high-impact low-probability events, there is often a correlation between these two events – which makes the product formula not valid.

Let us explain this on the example of earthquakes. In California or Japan, where reasonable-size earthquakes are frequent, everything is designed with this in mind, so such earthquakes do not cause any major damage. In contrast, in place like El Paso – where we live – earthquakes are very rare. As a result, many buildings are not designed with such earthquakes in mind. So, if a similar-strength earthquake happens in El Paso – and it will happen sometimes in the next few hundred years – it will cause a huge damage. Statistical estimates for $P$ mainly take into account most frequent events – i.e., mostly events from high-frequency zones like California. So, if we use these largely-California-based estimates to estimate El Paso risks, we will be strongly underestimating the risk.

**So What Can We Do: Empirically Successful Way to Take Such Events into Account.** Statistical analysis of numerous high-impact low-probability events was performed by researchers from the US National Institute of Standards and Technology (NIST). The results of their analysis are summarized in the NIST document [15]. Here is the main table from this document, see Table 1. In this table, VL means very low, L means low, M means moderate, H mean high, and VH means very high. For now, ignore the underlining – it is not from the original table, it was done by us, and it will be explained later:

**Table 1.** Empirical results

| p \ P | VL | L | M | H | VH |
|---|---|---|---|---|---|
| VL | L | L | L | L | L |
| L | VL | L | L | L | M |
| M | VL | L | M | M | H |
| H | VL | L | M | H | VH |
| VH | VL | L | M | H | VH |

With the exception of several entries from the first row and from the last column – entries that we underlined – all the entries fit the fuzzy-like formula $\min(p, P)$ (see, e.g., [1,6,11,14,16,20]) – as opposed to the above-mentioned probability-like product formula.

**But Why?** But why this empirical table has this particular form?

A naive answer is that in this case, naive fuzzy – with minimum – works better than naive probability – with the product. In other words, paraphrasing Orwell's "Animal Farm": fuzzy good, probability bad. But why is probability bad for low-frequency events – while it works perfectly well for the cases when the frequency is not low?

**What We Do in this Paper.** In this paper, we provide an explanation for the above empirical table.

- First, we explain, in detail, the non-underlined part of the table.
- Then, we provide qualitative arguments explaining why underlined entries in this table are different from minimum.

## 2 Our Explanation

**What Do We Know About the Desired Probability of Both Events Happening?** The expected loss is equal to the damage $D$ multiplied by the probability $t$ that both events occur:

- that the low-probability event happens, and
- that this event causes a randomly selected building to be destroyed.

All we know is the probabilities $p$ and $P$ of these two events. We know that there is a correlation between them, but we do not know the values of this correlation. In this case, all we know about the probability $t$ of both events happening is that this value must satisfy the following inequalities – first derived by Frechet (see, e.g., [18]):

$$\max(p + P - 1, 0) \le t \le \min(p, P). \tag{1}$$

We consider low-probability events, i.e., events for which $p \ll 1$. So, unless $P \approx 1$ – which is the case of the last column of or table – we have $p + P \le 1$ and thus, $\max(p + P - 1, 0) = 0$. In this case, the double inequality (1) takes the following form:

$$0 \le t \le \min(p, P). \tag{2}$$

**What Do We Know About the Expected Loss and the Expected Utility?** Because of the bounds (2) on the probability $t$, the expected loss $t \cdot D$ satisfies the following inequality:

$$0 \le t \cdot D \le \min(p, P) \cdot D. \tag{3}$$

So, for the expected utility $u$ – which is equal to minus the expected loss – we have the following inequality:

$$-\min(p, P) \le u \le 0. \tag{4}$$

In other words, all we know about the expected utility $u$ is that it is locates somewhere on an interval $[\underline{u}, \overline{u}]$, where

$$\underline{u} \stackrel{\text{def}}{=} -\min(p, P) \cdot D \text{ and } \overline{u} \stackrel{\text{def}}{=} 0. \tag{5}$$

**How Should be Make a Decision Under this Interval Uncertainty?** In situations when we only know the bounds on expected utility, decision theory recommends selecting an alternative with the largest possible value of the following combination

$$\alpha_H \cdot \overline{u} + (1 - \alpha_H) \cdot \underline{u}, \tag{6}$$

for some coefficient $\alpha_H \in [0, 1]$; see, e.g., [4,7,10]. This expression was first derived by the economist Leo Hurwicz – who later got Nobel prize for his research.

The coefficient $\alpha_H$ is known as the *optimism-pessimism parameter*. The name comes from the following:

- For $\alpha_H = 1$, the expression (6) turns into $\overline{u}$. This means that the decision maker only takes into account the best-case scenario and ignores all other possibilities. This is the case of extreme optimism.

- For $\alpha_H = 0$, the expression (6) turns into $\underline{u}$. This means that the decision maker only takes into account the worse-case scenario and ignores all other possibilities. This is the case of extreme pessimism.
- Intermediate values $\alpha_H$ mean that the decision maker takes different possible scenarios into account.

In particular, for the case when the interval is described by the formula (5), the Hurwicz's combination (6) takes the following form:

$$\alpha_H \cdot 0 + (1 - \alpha_H) \cdot (-\min(p, P) \cdot D) = -\min(p, P) \cdot (1 - \alpha_H) \cdot D.$$

So, the risk is proportional to the minimum $\min(p, P)$ – which is exactly what most entries in the above table say.

**Remaining Questions: Why Some Entries Differ from Min?** To complete our explanations, it is necessary to explain why in two cases: in the first row and in the last column – some entries differ from $\min(p, P)$. Let us explain these two cases one by one.

**Why Some Entries in the First Row are Different From Min?** Humans have a tendency to ignore low-probability events when making decisions. For example, in many papers, events with probability less than 5% were considered to be impossible – which led to so many irreproducible results that the American Statistical Association (ASA) had to issue a special statement about it [19]. In spite of this highly publicized statement, many practitioners continue to ignore low-probability events when making decisions.

Because of this phenomenon, there is a risk that a low-probability event will be ignored. To make sure that the event is *not* ignored, NIST researchers recommend to increase the probability $t$ for such cases, when $p$ is very low. This affects the first row of the above table – the row corresponding to events with very low (VL) probability.

**Why Some Entries in the Last Column are Different from Min?** As mentioned in [5,8,9], humans have a tendency to underestimate high probabilities when making decisions.

To counteract this subjective underestimation, NIST researchers proposed to increase recommended values $t$ for the case when the probability of damage is very high (VH) – which corresponds to the last column.

**Acknowledgments.** This work was supported in part by the National Science Foundation grants 1623190 (A Model of Change for Preparing a New Generation for Professional Practice in Computer Science), HRD-1834620 and HRD-2034030 (CAHSI Includes), EAR-2225395 (Center for Collective Impact in Earthquake Science C-CIES), and by the AT&T Fellowship in Information Technology.

It was also supported by a grant from the Hungarian National Research, Development and Innovation Office (NRDI), and by the Institute for Risk and Reliability, Leibniz Universitaet Hannover, Germany.

The authors are greatly thankful to Oscar Perez for his help and encouragement, and to the anonymous referees for valuable suggestions.

## References

1. Belohlavek, R., Dauben, J.W., Klir, G.J.: Fuzzy Logic and Mathematics: A Historical Perspective. Oxford University Press, New York (2017)
2. Fishburn, P.C.: Utility Theory for Decision Making. John Wiley & Sons Inc., New York (1969)
3. Fishburn, P.C.: Nonlinear Preference and Utility Theory. The John Hopkins Press, Baltimore (1988)
4. Hurwicz, L.: Optimality Criteria for Decision Making Under Ignorance. Cowles Commission Discussion Paper, Statistics, No. 370 (1951)
5. Kahneman, D.: Thinking, Fast and Slow. Farrar, Straus, and Giroux, New York (2011)
6. Klir, G., Yuan, B.: Fuzzy Sets and Fuzzy Logic. Prentice Hall, Upper Saddle River (1995)
7. Kreinovich, V.: Decision making under interval uncertainty (and beyond). In: Guo, P., Pedrycz, W. (eds.) Human-Centric Decision-Making Models for Social Sciences. SCI, vol. 502, pp. 163–193. Springer, Heidelberg (2014). https://doi.org/10.1007/978-3-642-39307-5_8
8. Lorkowski, J., Kreinovich, V.: Fuzzy logic ideas can help in explaining Kahneman and Tversky's empirical decision weights. In: Zadeh, L.A., Abbasov, A.M., Yager, R.R., Shahbazova, S.N., Reformat, M.Z. (eds.) Recent Developments and New Direction in Soft-Computing Foundations and Applications. SFSC, vol. 342, pp. 89–98. Springer, Cham (2016). https://doi.org/10.1007/978-3-319-32229-2_7
9. Lorkowski, J., Kreinovich, V.: Bounded Rationality in Decision Making Under Uncertainty: Towards Optimal Granularity. SSDC, vol. 99. Springer, Cham (2018). https://doi.org/10.1007/978-3-319-62214-9
10. Luce, R.D., Raiffa, R.: Games and Decisions: Introduction and Critical Survey. Dover, New York (1989)
11. Mendel, J.M.: Explainable Uncertain Rule-Based Fuzzy Systems. Springer, Cham (2024). https://doi.org/10.1007/978-3-031-35378-9
12. Nguyen, H.T., Kosheleva, O., Kreinovich, V.: Decision making beyond Arrow's 'impossibility theorem', with the analysis of effects of collusion and mutual attraction. Int. J. Intell. Syst. **24**(1), 27–47 (2009)
13. Nguyen, H.T., Kreinovich, V., Wu, B., Xiang, G.: Computing Statistics under Interval and Fuzzy Uncertainty. Springer Verlag, Berlin, Heidelberg (2012). https://doi.org/10.1007/978-3-642-24905-1
14. Nguyen, H.T., Walker, C.L., Walker, E.A.: A First Course in Fuzzy Logic. Chapman and Hall/CRC, Boca Raton (2019)
15. National Institute of Standards and Technology. Information Security: Guide for Conducting Risak Assessments. NIST Special Publication 800-30, Revision 1 (2012)
16. Novák, V., Perfilieva, I., Močkoř, J.: Mathematical Principles of Fuzzy Logic. Kluwer, Boston (1999)

17. Raiffa, H.: Decision Analysis. McGraw-Hill, Columbus (1997)
18. Sheskin, D.J.: Handbook of Parametric and Nonparametric Statistical Procedures. Chapman and Hall/CRC, Boca Raton (2011)
19. Wasserstein, R.L., Lazar, N.A.: The ASA's statement on p-values: context, process, and purpose. Am. Stat. **70**(2), 129–133 (2016). https://doi.org/10.1080/00031305.2016.1154108
20. Zadeh, L.A.: Fuzzy sets. Inf. Control **8**, 338–353 (1965)

# Some Results on Fuzzy Basis of Fuzzy Lie Algebras

Giuseppe Filippone[1], Mario Galici[1], Gianmarco La Rosa[1](✉), and Marco Elio Tabacchi[1,2]

[1] Dipartimento di Matematica e Informatica, Università degli Studi di Palermo, Palermo, Italy
{giuseppe.filippone01,mario.galici,gianmarco.larosa, marcoelio.tabacchi}@unipa.it

[2] Istituto Nazionale di Ricerche Demopolis, Palermo, Italy

**Abstract.** This work explores the application of fuzzy set theory to the study of algebraic structures, with a particular focus on Lie algebras. Since fuzzy Lie algebra can be regarded as fuzzy vector space, the foundational properties of these structures are investigated, with emphasis placed on the role of fuzzy basis. A selection of key results is presented, establishing necessary and sufficient conditions for a basis to be fuzzy, and providing concrete examples to illustrate how these findings can be applied in practice to fuzzy Lie subalgebras.

**Keywords:** Fuzzy set theory · Lie algebra · fuzzy Lie algebra · fuzzy basis · level set

## 1 Introduction

Since the 1965 publication of Zadeh's pioneering work on fuzzy set theory [19], the concept has played a pivotal role in various fields of mathematics, including logic, topology, probability, and computer science. Notably, its influence on algebra has been seminal, as evidenced by A. Rosenfeld's foundational 1971 study [14], which marked a significant milestone in this area. In this seminal study, Rosenfeld advanced the concept of fuzziness to algebraic structures, commencing with groups. Consequently, while Zadeh is widely acknowledged as the progenitor of fuzzy set theory, Rosenfeld is recognised as the trailblazer of fuzzy algebra. For a more comprehensive historical perspective, readers are directed to consult the references provided in [6].

Rosenfeld's foundational approach to introducing fuzziness into algebraic structures is rooted in the fundamental axiom that defines any algebraic system: the closure property of an operation adhering to a specific set of axioms. More explicitly, an algebraic structure—such as a group, ring, or field—is fundamentally composed of a set and an operation. Consequently, the critical aspect of integrating fuzzy set theory into algebraic structures lies in understanding how the operation interacts with fuzzy logic principles. The pioneering work of


M. Baczyński et al. (Eds.): EUSFLAT 2025, LNCS 15884, pp. 98–109, 2025.
https://doi.org/10.1007/978-3-031-97228-7_9

Zadeh established a framework for redefining set membership by replacing the traditional binary classification with a continuous scale ranging from 0 to 1.

To illustrate, consider an algebraic structure $(X, *)$, where $X$ is a set equipped with a binary operation $* : X \times X \to X$. Before imposing additional axioms, it is essential to first confirm that $X$ indeed is an algebraic structure. This validation relies on verifying the fundamental closure property, which states that for any $x_1, x_2 \in X$, the result of their operation, $x_1 * x_2$, must also belong to $X$. In a fuzzy algebraic setting, the notion of a fuzzy set is introduced, formalised as a function $\mu : X \to [0, 1] \subset \mathbb{R}$, representing the degree of membership of elements in $X$. Under this framework, the objective is to establish the condition that for all pairs $x_1, x_2 \in X$, the membership function satisfies $\mu(x_1 * x_2) \geq \min\{\mu(x_1), \mu(x_2)\}$. This constraint ensures that the product of two elements retains membership in $X$ to at least the same degree as the lesser of the two individual memberships.

As outlined above, Lie algebras are also algebraic structures, albeit with a more intricate framework compared to single-operation systems. Their complexity necessitates a more nuanced application of these fuzzy algebraic principles, further expanding the scope of this mathematical framework.

The aim of this short study is to provide a way to work out when a basis of a vector space (and consequently of a Lie algebra) can be used as a fuzzy basis. In order to achieve this, the Transfer Principle and fuzzy Lie algebras will be utilised. To accomplish this goal, Sect. 2 lays out the fundamental definitions and results required to make the exposition self-contained. Subsequently, the following section presents a collection of results related to the fuzzy basis of a Lie fuzzy subalgebra. The last two sections, on the other hand, focus on the applications of these results: Sect. 4 provides illustrative examples, while Sect. 5 summarizes the conclusions drawn from this study and suggests possible future research directions in line with its scope.

## 2 Theoretical Background

Lie groups are not linear structures, but rather curved manifolds. The power of Lie's theorem lies in simplifying the study of these objects by shifting their investigation to simpler ones. The basic idea, informally stated, is to associate a linear structure, primarily a vector space, with such complex objects as Lie groups, ensuring that this new structure inherits the group's properties. Furthermore, the results obtained on these linear structures should provide insight into the original Lie group. The solution to these questions can be found in Lie algebras, which are vector spaces on which an operation, known as the Lie brackets, is defined. The Lie bracket must satisfy two properties. The notion of Lie algebra originates from the study of continuous symmetries and transformations, playing a crucial role in various branches of mathematics and physics. The definition of Lie algebra became necessary and useful in order to formalise the structure and properties of these symmetries, and this has led to extensive research throughout the 20th century by scholars such as E. Cartan, W. Killing, and E. Levi. Lie algebras, although originally developed in an abstract setting, have applications in various fields such as the theory of differential equations (e.g., [3,13]), physics (e.g., [15,17]), and robotics (e.g., [4]). Moreover, while their definition has historically been linked to a geometric structure such as a Lie group, they are also studied purely from an algebraic perspective, which is the approach we will take here (Fig. 1).

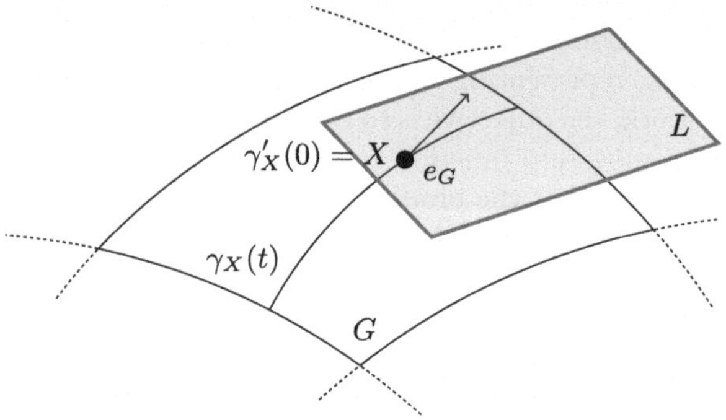


**Fig. 1.** The Lie algebra $L$ of the Lie group $G$.

**Definition 1.** *Let $\mathbb{F}$ be a field and let $L$ be a $\mathbb{F}$–vector space. The space $L$ is a Lie algebra over $\mathbb{F}$ if $L$ is equipped with a bilinear map, the Lie bracket, defined as follows:*

$$L \times L \to L$$
$$(x, y) \mapsto [x, y]$$

*satisfying the following properties:*

$$[x, x] = 0_L, \ \textit{for all } x \in L, \tag{1}$$
$$[x, [y, z]] + [y, [z, x]] + [z, [x, y]] = 0_L, \tag{2}$$

*for every $x, y, z \in L$.*

In this study, our focus will be on finite-dimensional Lie algebras, defined as those possessing a finite basis as vector spaces.

Following the definition of an algebraic structure, mathematicians define its substructures. These are defined as subsets that are themselves algebraic structures of the same type (for example, subgroups are subsets of a group that are also groups, etc.). Lie subalgebras are no exception to this rule; they are vector subspaces of a Lie algebra that are, in turn, Lie algebras. Samy El-Badawy Yehia first introduced the definition of a fuzzy Lie subalgebra of a Lie algebra in [18]. Nevertheless, we use the same notation of [1, Definitions 1.16 - 1.17].

**Definition 2 (cf. [1]).** *Let $L$ be a Lie algebra over a field $\mathbb{F}$. A fuzzy set $\mu \colon L \to [0, 1]$ is called a fuzzy Lie subalgebra of $L$ over a field $\mathbb{F}$ if*

1. $\mu(x + y) \geq \min\{\mu(x), \mu(y)\}$,
2. $\mu(ax) \geq \mu(x)$,
3. $\mu([x, y]) \geq \min\{\mu(x), \mu(y)\}$,

*for all* $x, y \in L$ *and* $a \in \mathbb{F}$.

Note that by 2), we obtain $\mu(-x) \geq \mu(x)$ and $\mu(0) \geq \mu(x)$ for all $x \in L$.

**Example 1.** *Let* $L$ *be the 2-dimensional non–abelian Lie algebra with basis* $\{e_1, e_2\}$ *and non–zero brackets* $[e_1, e_2] = e_1$. *By direct calculations, it is easy to see that the map*

$$\mu(x) = \begin{cases} 0.5, & \text{if } x = 0_L, \\ 0.1, & \text{otherwise}, \end{cases}$$

*defines a fuzzy Lie algebra structure over* $L$.

The initial condition outlines the fuzzy closure of the vector space addition operation, as previously described in the introduction. The subsequent condition asserts that scalar multiplication of a vector must also be closed, albeit in a fuzzy sense. Collectively, these two conditions delineate the definition of a fuzzy subspace of a vector space. Nevertheless, the final condition is of particular significance. Analogous to the first condition, it expresses the fuzzy closure of the Lie bracket. From now on we use the notation $\mu \leq L$ to say that $\mu$ is a fuzzy Lie subalgebra of $L$.

**Proposition 1.** *If* $\mu$ *is a fuzzy subspace of a vector space* $V$, *then*

1. $\mu(x) = \mu(-x)$,
2. $\mu(x - y) = \mu(0) \Rightarrow \mu(x) = \mu(y)$,
3. $\mu(x) < \mu(y) \Rightarrow \mu(x - y) = \mu(x) = \mu(y - x)$,

*for all* $x, y \in V$.

In conclusion of this section of the results, it is necessary to proceed by recalling the transfer principle for fuzzy sets. This was initially described in [9], and subsequently employed in [7] to prove and derive the following theorem, which is presented as it appears in [1]. We recall here that, for a fuzzy set $\mu \colon X \to [0, 1]$ and for any $t \in [0, 1]$, with $U(\mu, t)$ we will denote the *t-cut set* of $\mu$, that is

$$U(\mu, t) = \{x \in X \mid \mu(x) \geq t\}.$$

Finally, we observe that, although $\mu$ is a fuzzy set on $X$, the $t$-cut sets are crisp subsets of $X$.

**Theorem 1 (cf. [1])** *For a fuzzy subset* $\mu$ *of a vector space* $V$, *the following statements are equivalent.*

1. $\mu$ *is a fuzzy subspace of* $V$,
2. *each nonempty* $U(\mu, t)$ *is a subspace of* $V$.

## 3 Main Results

We will denote by $L$ a real Lie algebra and by $V$ a real vector space unless otherwise stated.

This section is dedicated to the presentation of the primary outcomes of this study. To commence, the following definition, which is presented in [12], is provided.

**Definition 3.** *Let $V$ be a fuzzy vector space. A set of vectors $\mathcal{B} = \{e_1, \ldots, e_n\}$ is fuzzy linearly independent if*

1. *$\{e_i\}_{i=1}^n$ are linearly indipendent,*
2. *$\mu(\sum_{i=1}^n a_i e_i) = \min_{i \in \{1,\ldots,n\}} \mu(a_i e_i)$,*

*for any $a_i \in \mathbb{R}$, with $i = 1, \ldots, n$.*

**Definition 4 (cf. [12]).** *A fuzzy basis for a fuzzy vector space $V$ is a fuzzy linearly independent basis for $V$.*

Therefore, in the context of a vector space, a crisp basis may be defined as a set of linearly independent vectors that span the space, whereas a fuzzy basis can be understood as a set of fuzzy linearly independent vectors that also span the space.

*Remark 1.* It is evident that a finite set of vectors forming a basis for a vector space $V$, that is, a maximal set of linearly independent vectors in $V$, is a set of fuzzy linearly independent vectors. Indeed, $a_i e_i \in V$ for every $i = 1, \ldots, n$, and $\sum_{i=1}^n a_i e_i \in V$. Hence $\mu(a_i e_i) = 1$ and $\mu(\sum_{i=1}^n a_i e_i) = 1$, thus obtaining that condition 2) in Definition 3 holds. In summary, we can say that being a crisp basis implies being a fuzzy basis.

We will denote by $\mu \leq L$ the fact that $\mu$ is a subspace (or a Lie subalgebra, as will be clear from the context) of $L$.

**Proposition 2.** *Let $\mu \leq L$. Then*

1. *$\mu(0_L) = \sup\{\mu(x) \mid x \in L\}$*
2. *$\mu(ax) = \mu(x)$, for any $a \in \mathbb{R}^*$ and for any $x \in L$.*
3. *For any $x, y \in L$ such that $\mu(x) \neq \mu(y)$, we have*

$$\mu(x + y) = \min\{\mu(x), \mu(y)\}.$$

*Proof.* 1. See the proof of Proposition 2.5 in [12].

2. By 2) in Definition 2, for every $a \in \mathbb{R}$ and $x \in L$, we have $\mu(ax) \geq \mu(x)$. If $a \neq 0$, then we can consider the vector $x' = \frac{1}{a}x$. Hence the inequalities above it is still true for $x'$, that is

$$\mu(ax') \geq \mu(x') \Rightarrow \mu(x) \geq \mu(\frac{1}{a}x).$$

By putting $b = \frac{1}{a}$, we proved that statement since $\mu(bx) \geq \mu(x)$ is always true, for every $b \in \mathbb{R}$ and $x \in L$.

3. See the proof of Proposition 2.4 in [12];

*Remark 2.* If $a_i = 0$, then $\mu(a_i e_i) = \mu(0_L) = \sup\{\mu(x) \mid x \in L\}$. Therefore, it is a reasonable assumption that all scalars $a_i$ are non-zero, given that the inequalities involved will concern the minimum of the memberships.

**Proposition 3.** *Let $\mu \leq L$, with $\mathcal{B} = \{e_1, \dots, e_n\}$ a fuzzy basis of the fuzzy vector space $\mu$. Suppose $e_1, \dots, e_k$, $k \leq n$, are the basis vector realising the minimum of $\mu$ in $\mathcal{B}$, that is $\mu(e_j) = \min_{i \in \{1,\dots,n\}} \mu(e_i)$, $j = 1, \dots, k$. Then the following inequality holds,*

$$\min_{i \in \{1,\dots,n\}} \mu(e_i) \geq \min \mu(x),$$

*for any $x \in L \setminus \mathrm{span}\{e_{k+1}, \dots, e_n\}$.*

*Proof.* Let $\mathcal{B} = \{e_1, \dots, e_n\}$ a basis of $L$. For every $x \in L \setminus \mathrm{span}\{e_{k+1}, \dots, e_n\}$, we put $x = \sum_{i=1}^{n} x_i e_i$, with $x_i \in \mathbb{R}$. Hence, there exists $j \in \{1, \dots, k\}$ such that $x_j \neq 0$. Thus,

$$\begin{aligned}\min_{i \in \{1,\dots,n\}} \mu(e_i) &= \min_{i \in \{1,\dots,n\}} \mu(x_i e_i) \\ &= \mu\left(\sum_{i=1}^{n} x_i e_i\right) \\ &= \mu(x) \geq \min \mu(x).\end{aligned}$$

The first equality follows from Proposition 2 and Remark 2, keeping in mind that $x_j \neq 0$ for some $j \in \{1, \dots, k\}$. The second equality follows from 2) in Definition 3.

The following result serves to reinforce the preceding one by considering the zero element of the vector space.

**Corollary 1.** *The following inequality holds*

$$\mu(0) \geq \min_{i \in \{1,\dots,n\}} \mu(e_i) \geq \min_{x \in L \setminus \{0_L\}} \mu(x).$$

To reach the purpose of this paper, we have to provide a definition of a fuzzy basis for Lie algebras to better establish the concept. To the best of our knowledge, such a definition does not appear in the existing literature, despite its seemingly natural formulation. In classical Lie theory, the basis of a Lie algebra is the basis of the vector space on which the Lie brackets are defined. The same approach will be adopted for fuzzy Lie algebra.

**Definition 5.** *Let $\mu \leq L$. A* fuzzy basis *for a fuzzy Lie algebra $L$ is a fuzzy linearly independent basis for the vector space on which the Lie algebra $L$ lies.*

For the sake of completeness, we provide here the definition of the dimension of a Lie algebra, which is essentially based on Definition 5.1 of [12].

**Definition 6.** *Let $\mu \leq L$. The dimension of the fuzzy Lie subalgebra $\mu$ is defined as*

$$\dim(\mu) = \sup_{\mathcal{B} \text{ a basis of } L} \left( \sum_{e \in \mathcal{B}} \mu(e) \right).$$

It is clear how, theoretically, the function dim associates a value in the interval $[0, +\infty)$ to a class of fuzzy Lie algebras. A fuzzy Lie algebra $\mu$ is finite–dimensional if and only if $\dim(\mu) < +\infty$.

**Theorem 2.** *Let $\mu \leq L$ and $\mathcal{B} = \{e_1, \ldots, e_n\}$ a basis of $L$ with $\mu(e_1) = a$ and $\mu(e_i) = b$, with $1 < i \leq n$ and $a \geq b$. The set $\mathcal{B}$ is a fuzzy basis of $\mu$ if and only if*

$$\mu(x) = \min_{i \in \{1,\ldots,n\}} \mu(e_i) = b, \tag{3}$$

*for every $x \in L \setminus \text{span}\{e_1\}$.*

*Proof.* Suppose $\mathcal{B}$ is a fuzzy basis of $\mu$ and let $x = \sum_{i=1}^{n} x_i e_i \in L \setminus \text{span}\{e_1\}$. Then

$$\mu(x) = \mu\left(\sum_{i=1}^{n} x_i e_i\right) = \min_{i \in \{1,\ldots,n\}} \mu(e_i) = b, \tag{4}$$

where the second equality comes from condition 2) of Definition 3. Hence, Eq. (3) holds.

Suppose that Eq. (3) holds. Since the elements $e_1, \ldots, e_n$ are linearly independent, we have to prove only 2) of Definition 3. Let $x = \sum_{i=1}^{n} x_i e_i$ be a generic element of $L$. If $x \in \text{span}\{e_1\}$, the argument is trivial. Let $x \in L \setminus \text{span}\{e_1\}$. Then,

$$\mu\left(\sum_{i=1}^{n} x_i e_i\right) = \mu(x) = b = \min_{i \in \{1,\ldots,n\}} \mu(x_i e_i). \tag{5}$$

Hence, $\mathcal{B}$ is a fuzzy basis of $\mu$.

*Remark 3.* In Theorem 2, of course, is valid for all basis such that all but one vectors give the minimum of $\mu$ in $\mathcal{B}$. For simplicity of notation, the other vector can be chosen to be the first one, i.e. the vector $e_1$.

Let us consider $t$–cut sets of a fuzzy subalgebra $\mu \leq L$, namely $U(\mu, t_1)$ and $U(\mu, t_2)$. These subsets of $L$ are subalgebras of $L$, by Thereom 1.6 in [1]. Actually, there are more; they are *ideals* of the Lie algebra $L$. In order to simplify the matter, the focus will not be directed towards fuzzy ideals, thus resulting in a weaker version of the original outcome.

**Theorem 3.** *A fuzzy set $\mu$ of a Lie algebra $L$ is its fuzzy Lie subalgebra if and only if each nonempty set $U(\mu, t)$ is a Lie subalgebra of $L$.*

Generally, two subspaces of a vector space (even before being subalgebras) always have at least one vector in their intersection, namely the zero vector. It is noteworthy to demonstrate that, without resorting to the techniques particular to linear algebra, we can substantiate this outcome for $t$–cut sets.

**Proposition 4.** *For every fuzzy Lie subalgebra $\mu$ of $L$ and each nonempty set $U(\mu,t)$, $0_L \in U(\mu,t)$.*

*Proof.* By 2) of Definition 2, with $a = 0$, we have already seen that $\mu(0_L) \geq \mu(x)$, for every $x \in L$. Then, we have

$$\mu(0_L) \geq \mu(x) \geq t,$$

for every $x \in U(\mu,t)$. Thus $0_L \in U(\mu,t)$.

**Corollary 2.** *If $t > \mu(0_L)$, then $U(\mu,t) = \emptyset$.*

We suppose now that $U(\mu,t_1) \cap U(\mu,t_2) = \{0_L\}$ and $t_1, t_2 \in [0,1]$, with $t_1 < t_2$. Then, we have a more precise description of the $t_1$–cut set $U(\mu,t_1)$, that is

$$U(\mu,t_1) = \{x \in L \mid t_2 \gneq \mu(x) \geq t_1\}. \tag{6}$$

Indeed, if $\mu(x) \geq t_2$, for every $x \in U(\mu,t_1) \setminus \{0_L\}$, we have $x \in U(\mu,t_2)$ with $x \neq 0_L$. Clearly, this is a contradiction. Then Eq. (6) holds, and we can summarise this result in the following.

**Proposition 5.** *Let $\mu \leq L$ and $t_1, t_2 \in [0,1]$, with $t_1 < t_2$. If $U(\mu,t_1) \cap U(\mu,t_2) = \{0_L\}$, then $U(\mu,t_1) = \{x \in L \mid t_2 \gneq \mu(x) \geq t_1\}$.*

The following definition of a partition of a closed interval $\mathbb{R}$ numbers will now be provided. While the definition of a partition can be given for a set in general (e. g. see [16]), in the context of the present discussion, such a definition would be too general and abstract.

**Definition 7.** *Let $[a,b] \subset \mathbb{R}$ a closed interval. A partition $\mathscr{P}$ of $[a,b]$ is a finite set of points $x_0 < x_1 < \cdots < x_{n-1} < x_n$, with $x_i \in [a,b]$ for every $i = 0,\ldots,n$, such that $x_0 = a$ and $x_n = b$. We will denote such a partition with $\mathscr{P}_n = \{x_0,\ldots,x_n\}$.*

*Remark 4.* If $n = 0$, we do not have a partition, this would imply that $x = a = b$ and the closed interval would collapse into a single point (without any assumption on $a$ and $b$). Alternatively, if we assume $a \neq b$, it can be shown that it is not logical to consider a partition consisting of a single element, as this would lead to the contradiction $x = a \neq b = x$.

Now, we are interested in the closed interval $[0,1]$. Thus, if we map each $x \in [a,b]$ to $\frac{x-a}{b-a}$, we obtain a partition of the interval $[0,1]$ induced by the partition on $[a,b]$. Moreover, by the injectivity of $f(x) = \frac{x-a}{b-a}$, the inequalities $x_0 < x_1 < \cdots < x_{n-1} < x_n$ are preserved. Therefore, since this can be done for any closed interval, we will assume, without loss of generality, that the partition is of the unit interval.

*Remark 5.* In general, if $t_1 < t_2$, then $U(\mu, t_2) \subset U(\mu, t_1)$ since $\mu(x) \geq t_2 \Rightarrow \mu(x) \geq t_1$.

By Proposition 5 and Remark 5, the following is proved.

**Theorem 4.** *Let $\mu \leq L$ and $t_1, t_2 \in [0, 1]$, with $t_1 < t_2$. Then, $U(\mu, t_1) \cap U(\mu, t_2) = \{0_L\}$ if and only if $U(\mu, t_2) = \{0_L\}$.*

By stressing the last result on a partition of the unit interval, one can prove the following.

**Theorem 5.** *Let $\mu \leq L$ and let $\mathscr{P}_n = \{t_0, \ldots, t_n\}$ be a partition of $[0, 1]$. If $U(\mu, t_i) \cap U(\mu, t_j) = \{0_L\}$, for every $0 \leq i < j \leq n$, then*

$$U(\mu, t_k) = \begin{cases} L, & \text{if } k = 0, \\ \{0_L\}, & \text{otherwise.} \end{cases}$$

*Proof.* We will prove this by induction on $n$. By Remark 4 the base of induction is $n = 1$, then we have the partition $\mathscr{P}^1 = \{0, 1\}$. Hence we have $U(\mu, 0) = \mu$ and, by hypothesis and Theorem 4, $U(\mu, 1) = \{0_L\}$. Let us assume that the result holds for $n - 1$ and prove it for $n$. The partition $\mathscr{P}^n = \{t_0 = 0, t_1, \ldots, t_{n-1}, t_n = 1\}$ induces the following descending chain of Lie subalgebras

$$U(\mu, 0) \supseteq U(\mu, t_1) \supseteq \cdots \supseteq U(\mu, t_{n-1}) \supseteq U(\mu, 1).$$

By inductive hypothesis we have

$$U(\mu, 0) \text{ and } U(\mu, t_k) = \{0_L\}, \text{ with } 1 \leq k \leq n - 1.$$

Since $U(\mu, t_i) \cap U(\mu, t_j) = \{0_L\}$, for every $0 \leq i < j \leq n$, then

$$U(\mu, 0) \cap U(\mu, t_n) = \{0_L\}.$$

Last intersection and Theorem 4 imply $U(\mu, 1) = \{0_L\}$.

## 4 Examples

One potential application of this approach is evident in verifying the basis of a fuzzy Lie algebra as a fuzzy basis, facilitated by the findings of the preceding section.

**Example 2.** *By Example 1 it easy to check that $\{e_1, e_2\}$ is a fuzzy basis of $\mu$. Indeed, $\mu(e_1) = \mu(e_2) = 0.1$ and, for every $x \in L \setminus \{0_L\}$, $\mu(x) = 0.1$, then Eq. (3) holds.*

**Example 3.** *This example is the Example 1.3 in [1]. Let* $L = \mathbb{R}^3$ *the 3-dimensional real vector space with Lie bracket* $[x, y] = x \times y$*, where* $x, y \in \mathbb{R}^3$*, that is the classical cross product. Then* $L = (\mathbb{R}^3, \times)$ *is a real Lie algebra. We define a fuzzy set* $\mu$ *on* $L$ *by*

$$\mu(x) = \begin{cases} 0.9 & \textit{if } x = (0,0,0), \\ 0.6 & \textit{if } x = (a,0,0), a \neq 0, \\ 0.2 & \textit{otherwise.} \end{cases}$$

*By direct calculations, it is easy to see that* $\mu$ *is a fuzzy Lie algebra. Moreover, with our results, we can easily check that* $\mathcal{B} = \{e_1, e_2, e_3\}$ *is a fuzzy basis of* $\mu$*. With the values above, we have* $\mu(e_1) = 0.6$*, and* $\mu(e_2) = \mu(e_3) = 0.2$*, then* $\min_{e_i \in \mathcal{B}} \mu(e_i) = 0.2 = \mu(x)$*, for every* $x \in \mathbb{R}^3 \setminus \{0_{\mathbb{R}^3}\}$*.*

## 5 Conclusions and Future Works

We have presented a series of results concerning fuzzy basis of fuzzy Lie algebra, or more generally, fuzzy vector spaces. We believe that these results contribute to a more profound understanding of the concept, and more importantly, facilitate the implementation of computational software. To the best of our knowledge, no official packages currently exist that handle computations and algorithms for fuzzy Lie algebra in the same way they do for their crisp counterparts. We have also provided illustrative examples demonstrating the application of the aforementioned results in determining the fuzzy nature of a given basis of a vector space.

Finally, we offer a concise discussion of potential future research directions that could build upon the present work.

- Introducing fuzzy Leibniz algebras: Leibniz algebras generalises Lie algebra by removing the requirement of the alternation property of the Lie bracket. The challenges associated with Lie algebra classification and integration as the tangent space of a smooth algebraic structure are also applicable to their fuzzy counterparts [2,8,11], and thus investigating them would be a natural extension of the current study.
- Exploring fuzzy derivations: While there is existing literature on the fuzzy version of Lie algebra homomorphisms, the same cannot be said for derivations. These play a fundamental role in Lie theory, and studying the derivations of a given Lie algebra is crucial—for instance, in the classification of solvable Lie algebra. Investigating fuzzy derivations would provide valuable insights into the structure of fuzzy Lie algebra.
- Furthermore, it would be worthwhile to extend the results obtained here to derivations of fuzzy Leibniz algebras [10], or even to the study of biderivations [5], which capture additional structural properties.
- Investigating induced subspace filtration: The investigation of induced subspaces filtrations is of significant interest in the field of algebraic topology.

In the context of Remark 4 and under certain assumptions, it is possible to define a filtration of subspaces, thereby establishing a structured hierarchy of fuzzy subspaces. These filtrations are of considerable importance in various algebraic settings, as they facilitate a more profound analysis of subspaces stability and facilitate the decomposition of the algebra into a hierarchical structure.

These findings underscore the potential for further theoretical developments and computational applications in the study of fuzzy Lie algebra.

**Acknowledgements.** All authors are supported by funding from the **Sustainability Decision Framework (SDF)** Research Project – CUP **B79J23000540005** – Grant Assignment Decree No. **5486** adopted on **2023-08-04**. The second and the third authors are also supported by the **Gruppo Nazionale per le Strutture Algebriche, Geometriche e le loro Applicazioni (GNSAGA)** of the **Istituto Nazionale di Alta Matematica (INdAM)** "Francesco Severi". Last author acknowledge financial support under the National Recovery and Resilience Plan (NRRP), Mission 4, Component 2, Investment 1.1, Call for tender No. 1409 published on 14.9.2022 by the Italian Ministry of University and Research (MUR), funded by the European Union – NextGenerationEU – Project Title **Quantum Models for Logic, Computation and Natural Processes (QM4NP)** – CUP **B53D23030160001** – Grant Assignment Decree No. **1371** adopted on **2023-09-01** by the Italian Ministry of University and Research (MUR).

## References

1. Akram, M.: Fuzzy lie algebras. In: Infosys Science Foundation Series, 1st edn, pp. XIX, 302. Springer, Singapore (2018). https://doi.org/10.1007/978-981-13-3221-0
2. Ayupov, S., Omirov, B., Rakhimov, I.: Leibniz algebras. In: Structure and Classification. CRC Press, Boca Raton (2020). https://doi.org/10.1201/9780429344336. isbn: 9780429344336
3. Cicogna, G., Gaeta, G.: Symmetry and Perturbation Theory in Nonlinear Dynamics. Lecture Notes in Physics Monographs, 1st edn, pp. XI, 212. Springer, Heidelberg (1999). https://doi.org/10.1007/3-540-48874-X
4. Coelho, P., Nunes, U.: Lie algebra application to mobile robot control: a tutorial. Robotica **21**(5), 483–493 (2003). https://doi.org/10.1017/S0263574703005149
5. Di Bartolo, A., La Rosa, G.: Biderivations of complete Lie algebras. J. Algebra Appl. **24**(1), 14 (2025). https://doi.org/10.1142/S0219498825500161. issn: 0219-4988
6. Filippone, G., et al.: Fuzziness and lie algebras. In: Marie-Jeanne, L., et al. (eds.) Information Processing and Management of Uncertainty in Knowledge-Based Systems, pp. 113–123. Springer, Cham (2025). isbn: 978-3-031-74000-8. https://doi.org/10.1007/978-3-031-74000-8_10
7. Katsaras, A.K., Liu, D.B.: Fuzzy vector spaces and fuzzy topological vector spaces. J. Math. Anal. Appl. **58**(1), 135–146 (1977). https://doi.org/10.1016/0022-247X(77)90233-5. issn: 0022-247X
8. Kinyon, M.K.: Leibniz algebras, Lie racks, and digroups. J. Lie Theory **17**(1), 99–114 (2007). issn: 0949-5932

9. Kondo, M., Dudek, W.A.: On the transfer principle in fuzzy theory. Mathware Soft Comput. **12**(1), 41–55 (2005)
10. La Rosa, G., Mancini, M.: Derivations of two-step nilpotent algebras. Commun. Algebra **51**(12), 4928–4948 (2023). https://doi.org/10.1080/00927872.2023.2222415. issn: 0092-7872
11. La Rosa, G., Mancini, M.: Two-step nilpotent Leibniz algebras. Linear Algebra Appl. **637**, 119–137 (2022). https://doi.org/10.1016/j.laa.2021.12.013. issn: 0024-3795
12. Lubczonok, P.: Fuzzy vector spaces. Fuzzy Sets Syst. **38**(3), 329–343 (1990). https://doi.org/10.1016/0165-0114(90)90206-L. issn: 0165-0114
13. Olver, P.J.: Applications of lie groups to differential equations. In: Graduate Texts in Mathematics, 1st edn, pp. XXVI, 500. Springer, New York (1986). https://doi.org/10.1007/978-1-4684-0274-2
14. Rosenfeld, A.: Fuzzy groups. J. Math. Anal. Appl. **35**(3), 512–517 (1971). https://doi.org/10.1016/0022-247X(71)90199-5. issn: 0022-247X
15. Sattinger, D.H., Weaver, O.L.: Lie Groups and algebras with applications to physics, geometry, and mechanics. In: Applied Mathematical Sciences, 1st edn, pp. X, 218. Springer, New York (1986). https://doi.org/10.1007/978-1-4757-1910-9
16. Stoll, R.R.: Set Theory and Logic. Courier Corporation (1979)
17. Woit, P.: Quantum Theory, Groups and Representations. An Introduction, 1st edn, pp. XXII, 668. Springer Cham (2017). https://doi.org/10.1007/978-3-319-64612-1
18. Yehia, S.E.: Fuzzy ideals and fuzzy subalgebras of Lie algebras. Fuzzy Sets Syst. **80**(2), 237–244 (1996). https://doi.org/10.1016/0165-0114(95)00109-3. issn: 0165-0114
19. Zadeh, L.A.: Fuzzy sets. Inf. Control **8**(3), 338–353 (1965). https://doi.org/10.1016/S0019-9958(65)90241-X. issn: 0019-9958

# Visual Comparison of Inclusion Measures

Patryk Żywica(✉), Anna Stachowiak, and Joanna Siwek

Faculty of Mathematics and Computer Science, Adam Mickiewicz University, Poznań, Poland
{bikol,aniap,jsiwek}@amu.edu.pl

**Abstract.** The concept of fuzzy set inclusion is essential in decision-making, classification, and natural language processing, yet comparing different inclusion measures remains a significant challenge. To address this, we propose a visualization method using contour plots to facilitate direct comparison of different inclusion measures. By analyzing rescaled fuzzy sets, we investigate how inclusion measures behave under various parameter settings. Several well-known measures, including those based on S- and R-implications, are examined. Understanding these computational and theoretical properties is critical for selecting efficient inclusion measures in practical applications, where optimizing model performance. This study contributes to the development of systematic approaches for evaluating inclusion measures.

**Keywords:** inclusion measures · inclusion measure visualization · inclusion measure comparison

## 1 Introduction

In all scientific disciplines, there has long been a need to compare certain objects. While some branches of science have sought to answer the question of the nature of similarity, others have required a precise, formal definition. Comparing two objects or events can be viewed as an attempt to determine the relationship between them. The most important and frequently used relationships among objects are similarity, difference, and inclusion. In the literature, the issue of object similarity has received the most attention [25].

In recent decades, fuzzy set theory has found applications in many areas of science and daily life. The need to compare fuzzy sets naturally arose at the very inception of the theory. Numerous methods have been developed, often based on those used for classical sets. The intensive development of fuzzy logic and its applications frequently requires the definition of new ways to compare objects [6]. This issue is particularly significant in computer-aided decision-making, classification, and natural language processing.

Although the issue of object comparison is crucial for many applications of this theory, fundamental concepts such as similarity and inclusion have not yet been unambiguously formalized, and multiple approaches to defining them


M. Baczyński et al. (Eds.): EUSFLAT 2025, LNCS 15884, pp. 110–121, 2025.
https://doi.org/10.1007/978-3-031-97228-7_10

currently coexist [5]. While some researchers in fuzzy logic strive to precisely define these concepts, others question this approach, arguing that imposing rigid frameworks limits practical applicability.

Unfortunately, comparing different inclusion measures is particularly challenging when they are not identical. However, the choice of an inclusion measure is crucial not only for the construction and quality of a model but also significantly affects its computational properties. For example, the way an inclusion measure is defined can have a substantial impact on computational complexity, particularly in calculations performed under uncertainty [26]. Therefore, conducting research on efficient methods for comparing inclusion measures is essential, as it can have practical implications, such as optimizing the runtime of models. This is especially relevant in real-world applications where computational efficiency is a critical factor in decision-making systems.

This paper explores fuzzy set inclusion measures, their mathematical foundations, and a novel visualization method. It begins with an introduction outlining the significance of inclusion measures, followed by formal mathematical definitions. A review of existing inclusion measures highlights their diversity and classification into set-theoretic and logic-based approaches. The proposed visualization method provides intuitive graphical insights into their behavior, which is demonstrated through example visualizations. The discussion section analyzes the results, comparing different inclusion measures and their computational implications.

## 2 Definitions

A fuzzy set $A$ in the universe $U$ is defined as a (classical) set of ordered pairs

$$A = \{(\mu_A(x), x) : x \in U\} , \tag{1}$$

where $\mu_A$ is the membership function of the fuzzy set $A$, and $\mu_A(x) \in [0,1]$ represents the degree of membership of the element $x$ in the fuzzy set $A$. For simplicity, for sets containing only one element $A = \{(a,x)\}$, we adopt the notation $A = a/x$. We denote by $FS(U)$ the family of all fuzzy sets in the universe $U$.

A function $t : [0,1] \times [0,1] \to [0,1]$ that satisfies the following conditions for all $a, b, c \in [0,1]$ [15]:

$$\begin{aligned}
&t(a,1) = a && \text{(neutral element)},\\
&a \le b \Rightarrow t(a,c) \le t(b,c) && \text{(monotonicity)},\\
&t(a,b) = t(b,a) && \text{(commutativity)},\\
&t(a,t(b,c)) = t(t(a,b),c) && \text{(associativity)}
\end{aligned}$$

is called a t-norm.

Similarly, a function $s : [0,1] \times [0,1] \to [0,1]$ that satisfies the following conditions for all $a, b, c \in [0,1]$ [15]:

$$\begin{aligned} &s(a,0) = a && \text{(neutral element)},\\ &a \le b \Rightarrow s(a,c) \le s(b,c) && \text{(monotonicity)},\\ &s(a,b) = s(b,a) && \text{(commutativity)},\\ &s(a,s(b,c)) = s(s(a,b),c) && \text{(associativity)} \end{aligned}$$

is called a t-conorm.

A function $\sigma : FS(U) \to [0,\infty)$ is called a scalar cardinality if it satisfies the following conditions for every $a, b \in [0,1]$, $A, B \in FS$, and $x, y \in U$ [24]:

1. $\sigma(1/x) = 1$, $\sigma(\{(1,x)\}) = 1$
2. $a \le b \implies \sigma(a/x) \le \sigma(b/y)$,
3. If $A \cap B = \emptyset$, then $\sigma(A \cup B) = \sigma(A) + \sigma(B)$.

There exists a simple characterization of all scalar cardinalities [24]. A function $\sigma$ is a scalar cardinality if and only if there exists a non-decreasing function $f : [0,1] \to [0,1]$ such that $f(0) = 0$ and $f(1) = 1$, for which

$$\sigma(A) = \sum_{x \in A} f(A(x)) \tag{2}$$

for any fuzzy set $A$. Such a function $f$ is called a prototype function (also referred to as a weight function). The most common weight function is the identity function id.

The relative cardinality of a fuzzy set represents the proportion of elements in one fuzzy set that also belong to another fuzzy set. This is why it is referred to as the relative cardinality of fuzzy set $A$ with respect to fuzzy set $B$, denoted as $\sigma(A|B)$, and defined as:

$$\sigma(A|B) = \frac{\sigma(A \cap B)}{\sigma(B)}. \tag{3}$$

A function $g : FS(U) \to [0,1]$ that satisfies the following conditions:

1. $g(\emptyset) = 0$,
2. $g(U) = 1$,
3. If $A \subseteq B$, then $g(A) \le g(B)$,

is called a fuzzy measure of a fuzzy set (also known as a scalar evaluator). It allows replacing a fuzzy set with a single scalar value. A fuzzy measure is called existential if $g(A) = 0$ if and only if $A = \emptyset$, and universal if $g(A) = 1$ if and only if $A = U$. An example of such fuzzy measure is:

$$g_{\sup}(A) = \sup_{u \in U} \mu_A(u), \tag{4}$$

while:

$$g_{\inf}(A) = \inf_{u \in U} \mu_A(u) \tag{5}$$

is a universal fuzzy measure.

The most commonly used implication operators are S-implications and R-implications [1,22]. The first family of implications arises by directly generalizing the implication known from classical logic:

$$a \Rightarrow b \equiv \overline{a} \vee b\,.$$

S-implication is obtained by replacing the disjunction operator with a t-conorm:

$$a \Rightarrow b = s(1 - a, b)\,.$$

The term "S-implication" originates from the use of a t-conorm $s$ in its definition. S-implications are often referred to as strong implications.

Many well-known fuzzy implications have been found to be S-implications. The Łukasiewicz implication is derived using the Łukasiewicz t-conorm:

$$a \Rightarrow_{\text{Łuk}} b = \min(1, 1 - a + b)\,.$$

The Kleene-Dienes implication is obtained by applying the maximum t-conorm:

$$a \Rightarrow_{\max} b = \max(1 - a, b)\,.$$

The family of R-implications arises from a generalization of the implication known in propositional logic:

$$a \Rightarrow b \equiv \sup\{x \in [0,1] : a \wedge x \leq b\}\,.$$

In the term "R-implication," the letter $R$ originates from residuated semi-groups, which emerge by replacing conjunction with a t-norm:

$$a \Rightarrow b = \sup\{x \in [0,1] : t(a,x) \leq b\}\,.$$

Many implications known from infinite-valued logic are R-implications. For example, applying the product t-norm yields the Goguen implication [10,11]:

$$a \Rightarrow_G b = \begin{cases} \min(1, \frac{b}{a})\,, & \text{if } a \neq 0 \\ 1, & \text{otherwise} \end{cases}$$

The Łukasiewicz implication can also be obtained as an R-implication using the Łukasiewicz t-norm.

The use of t-norms and t-conorms enables the definition of infinitely many implication operators. More than 40 different fuzzy implications have been proposed and analyzed in the literature [16,19]. Additionally, research has been conducted on selection criteria and the applicability of specific implications in various contexts [2–4,8,14,17,20,21,23].

## 3 Inclusion Measures

This section presents the most widely used inclusion measures, categorized into two main groups: set-theoretic and logic-based. This classification effectively reflects the two main approaches to defining inclusion measures [6]. The overview of inclusion measures developed over the years aims to highlight the diversity of this concept and the challenges associated with formally analyzing the relationships between different inclusion measures.

It is important to note that there is no universally accepted definition of an inclusion measure, similar to the case of similarity measures [5,26]. Consequently, the examples discussed here differ significantly in both construction methods and properties. Moreover, this section presents only a selection of existing inclusion measures and does not attempt to provide a comprehensive survey. Instead, the primary objective of this study is to propose a visualization method to compare different inclusion measures.

### 3.1 Set-Theoretic Approach

The simplest way to define the degree of inclusion of a classical set $X$ in a set $Y$, where $X \not\subseteq Y$, is as the ratio of the number of elements in $X$ to the number of elements present in either set

$$Sub(X,Y) = \frac{|X|}{|X \cup Y|}. \tag{6}$$

Under this definition, the degree of inclusion equals to 1 if and only if $X \subset Y$. This approach aligns with the definition of fuzzy set inclusion given by Zadeh:

$$A \subset B, \quad \text{if } \forall_{u \in U} \mu_A(u) \leq \mu_B(u). \tag{7}$$

However, the coefficient value is equal to 0 only when the sets $X$ and $Y$ are disjoint, which does not fully align with (7). However, this behavior is expected, as an inclusion measure should be able to take any intermediate values within the interval $[0, 1]$.

The use of t-norms other than the minimum and arbitrary fuzzy measures may lead to even greater deviations from Zadeh's definition of inclusion. The boundary values 0 and 1 may be attained for different fuzzy sets, similar to how they behave in classical set theory. For example, for many t norms, condition $A \cap B = \emptyset$ does not necessarily imply that supports of fuzzy sets $A$ and $B$ are disjoint.

Dubois and Prade proposed the following set of axioms that an inclusion measure should satisfy [7]:

1. $Sub(A, B) = 1$ if and only if $\overline{A} \cup B = U$,
2. if the sets $A$ and $B$ are disjoint, then $Sub(A, B) = 0$,
3. $Sub(A, B)$ depends on the value of $g(\overline{A} \cup B)$.

These assumptions led to the formulation of a general formula for the inclusion measure of fuzzy sets:

$$Sub_{g,s}(A,B) = \frac{g(\overline{A} \cup_s B) - g(\overline{A})}{1 - g(\overline{A})} \,. \tag{8}$$

The first two conditions contradict each other when $A = \emptyset$. On the one hand, $Sub(\emptyset, B) = 1$ because $\overline{\emptyset} = U$. On the other hand, since $\emptyset$ and $B$ are disjoint, the second condition implies $Sub(\emptyset, B) = 0$. To maintain consistency with classical set theory, we assume that $Sub(\emptyset, B) = 1$ and $Sub(A, \emptyset) = 0$, except in the case where $A = \emptyset$. Moreover, not all fuzzy measures of fuzzy sets and t-conorm-generated union operations substituted into (8) guarantee compliance with these axioms.

If the union operation of sets is generated by the Łukasiewicz t-conorm $s_{\text{Łuk}}$, and the fuzzy measure used is $g_{\text{id}}$, then from (8) we obtain the inclusion measure proposed by Kosko [18]:

$$\begin{aligned} Sub_{g_{\text{id}},s_{\text{Łuk}}}(A,B) &= \frac{g(\overline{A} \cup B) - g(\overline{A})}{1 - g(\overline{A})} = \frac{\sum_{u \in U} \min\left(\mu_A(u), \mu_B(u)\right)}{\sum_{u \in U} f(\mu_A(u))} \\ &= \frac{\sigma_f(A \cap_{t_{\min}} B)}{\sigma_f(A)} = Sub_{g_{\text{id}},\cap_{\min}}(A,B) \,. \end{aligned} \tag{9}$$

Kosko's inclusion measure can be generalized to other intersection operations generated by arbitrary t-norms, thereby yielding more restrictive inclusion measures such as $Sub_{g_{\text{id}},\cap_{\text{prod}}}(A,B)$ and $Sub_{g_{\text{id}},\cap_{\text{Łuk}}}(A,B)$. The fuzzy measures $g_{\text{inf}}$ and $g_{\text{sup}}$ can also be used in the construction of inclusion measures. For instance, $Sub_{g_{\text{sup}},s_{\text{Łuk}}}(A,B)$ satisfies all the proposed axioms, as does $Sub_{g_{\text{inf}},s_{F,\lambda}}(A,B)$.

The inclusion relation is reflexive. Unfortunately, this property is not satisfied by most inclusion measures defined using (8). This results from the fact that most popular families of t-norms are Archimedean, meaning that $t(a,a) < a$, which in turn implies $Sub(A,A) < 1$. An example of a reflexive inclusion measure is $Sub_{g_{\text{id}},s_{\text{Łuk}}}$.

Another property of inclusion measures is transitivity. If $A_1 \subseteq A_2 \subseteq A_3$, one might expect that $Sub(A_1, A_3) \geq Sub(A_2, A_3)$. In the case of $Sub_{g_{\text{inf}},s_{F,\lambda}}(A,B)$, this is indeed satisfied. However, for $Sub_{g_{\text{id}},s}(A,B)$, it is not.

### 3.2 Logic-Based Approach

Logic-based inclusion measures [12,13] utilize the interpretation of a fuzzy set's membership function as the degree of truth of the conclusion represented by that set. The fundamental method involves using an implication operator, which allows for the construction of both inclusion and similarity measures. In this approach, the degree of inclusion $A \subset B$ is assumed to be equal to the degree to which $A$ implies $B$. To compare two fuzzy sets, we define the inclusion coefficient for two membership degrees, denoted as $\equiv_{\subset}$. In the simplest case, the inclusion coefficient can be directly taken as the implication operator:

$$a \equiv_{\subset} b = a \Rightarrow b \,. \tag{10}$$

This approach corresponds to evaluating the degree to which $A$ entails $B$. The inclusion coefficient can be extended to the stronger form:

$$a \equiv_{\subset} b = \frac{1}{2} \cdot \left(a \Rightarrow b + \bar{b} \Rightarrow \bar{a}\right) . \tag{11}$$

The inclusion coefficient allows for the comparison of individual membership degrees. Thus, when comparing two fuzzy sets $A$ and $B$, we obtain a vector of the form:

$$v_{A,B} = \left[\mu_A(u_1) \equiv_{\subset} \mu_B(u_1), \cdots, \mu_A(u_n) \equiv_{\subset} \mu_B(u_n)\right] . \tag{12}$$

To compute an inclusion measure, this vector must be aggregated into a single real number within the interval $[0, 1]$. In a sense, this vector can be treated as a fuzzy set itself. Therefore, any fuzzy measure can be used for its aggregation.

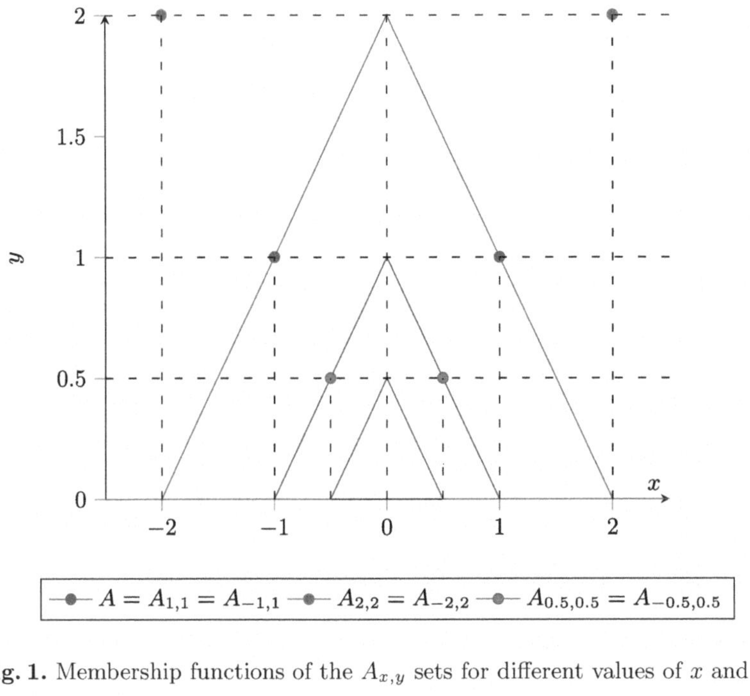


**Fig. 1.** Membership functions of the $A_{x,y}$ sets for different values of $x$ and $y$

# 4 Proposed Visualization Method

Inclusion measures defined using entirely different methods can sometimes be equivalent. Comparing different inclusion measures is particularly challenging when they are not identical. This section describes a method for visualizing inclusion measures using relatively simple contour plots. Graphical representations of selected inclusion measures are given in the next Section.

For any fuzzy set $A$ in the universe $U \subset \mathbb{R}$ and $x \neq 0$, $y \in \mathbb{R}$, we define the transformed fuzzy set $A_{x,y}$

$$\mu_{A_{x,y}}(u) = 1 \wedge y \cdot \mu_A\left(\frac{1}{x} \cdot u\right) . \tag{13}$$

Thus, the fuzzy set $A_{x,y}$ is a vertically and horizontally scaled version of the original set $A$. Naturally, the following equality holds: $A_{1,1} = A$. Figure 1 illustrates the sets $A_{x,y}$ for different values of $x$ and $y$.

To visualize inclusion measures, contour plots of the following two-argument function $f_A : \mathbb{R} \times [0, \frac{1}{\alpha}] \to [0, 1]$ will be used

$$f_A(x, y) = Sub(A_{|x|,y}, A) , \tag{14}$$

where $\alpha = \max_{u \in U} \mu_A(u)$.

The value of the function $f_A(x, y)$ represents the degree of inclusion of the fuzzy set rescaled in $A$. If the classical binary inclusion definition proposed by Zadeh is used as the inclusion measure, then the function $f_A$ takes the following form, regardless of the choice of the fuzzy set $A$:

$$f_A(x, y) = \begin{cases} 1 , & \text{if } |x|, y \leq 1 \\ 0 , & \text{otherwise} \end{cases} . \tag{15}$$

Any fuzzy set $A$ can be chosen for visualization. However, it should be both sufficiently representative and simple enough to avoid excessive complexity in the plots. For this reason, this study adopts a triangular fuzzy set $A$, whose membership function is given by:

$$\mu_A(x) = \begin{cases} \max(0, \frac{1+x}{2}) , & \text{if } x \leq 0 \\ \max(0, \frac{1-x}{2}) , & \text{if } x > 0 \end{cases} . \tag{16}$$

This choice ensures an intuitive, symmetric shape that is easy to interpret in the visualizations.

## 5 Example Visualizations

This section presents contour plots of the function $f_A$ for various inclusion measures defined in Sect. 3 for $x \in [-5, 5]$ and $y \in [0, 2]$. The visualizations consider t-norms and t-conorms from the Frank family with different parameter values [9]

$$t_\lambda^F(x, y) = \log_\lambda \left(1 + \frac{(\lambda^x - 1)(\lambda^y - 1)}{\lambda - 1}\right) . \tag{17}$$

The three fundamental t-norms and t-conorms – minimum, product, and Łukasiewicz – also belong to this family, corresponding to $p = 0$, $p = 1$, and $p = \infty$, respectively. These visualizations provide insights into the behavior of different inclusion measures and how they vary with respect to scaling transformations applied to fuzzy sets. Figure 2a presents classical inclusion measure proposed by Kosko (9). Figure 2b presents the general inclusion measure proposed by Dubois and Prade (8) generated by identity fuzzy measure and various Frank t-conorms. Figure 3 presents inclusion measures defined using simple inclusion coefficient (10) applied to S- (a) and R- (b) implications. The last Fig. 4 shows the inclusion measure constructed with extended inclusion coefficient (11).

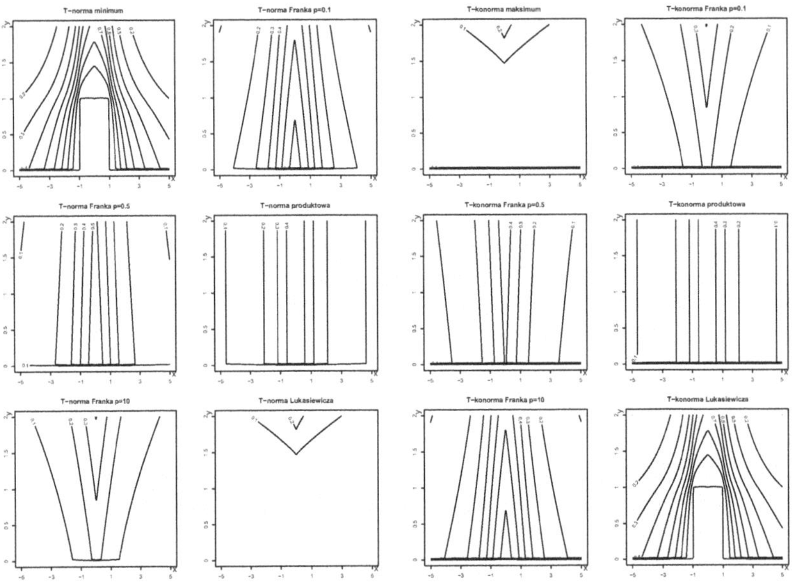


(a) (b)

**Fig. 2.** The contour plots of the inclusion measures $Sub_{g_{\mathrm{id}},\cap_t}$ and $Sub_{g_{\mathrm{id}},s}$, obtained using intersection operations generated by different t-norms and union operations generated by different t-conorms.

## 6 Discussion

One of the most noticeable differences in the inclusion measures analyzed is the impact of their construction method on their characteristics. Inclusion measures based on set theory behave fundamentally differently from those constructed using implication operators. A particularly interesting observation concerns the relationship between Kosko's inclusion measure and the one proposed by Dubois and Prade. These two inclusion measures appear to be inversely related with respect to the parameter $p$. The generated contour plots strongly suggest a significant dependence between them and may even indicate that a formal equivalence could be established.

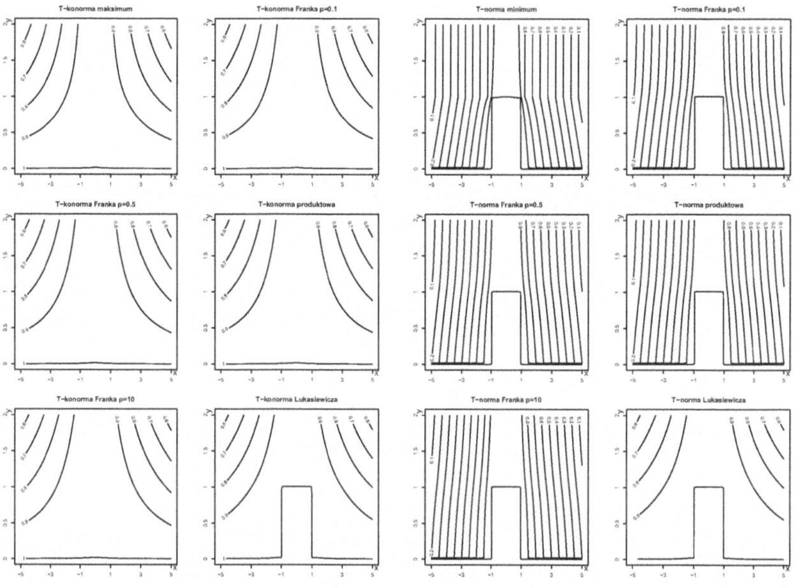


(a) (b)

**Fig. 3.** The contour plots of inclusion measures constructed with a simple inclusion coefficient, for S-implications and R-implications generated by different Frank t-norms and t-conorms.

For set-theoretic inclusion measures, the choice of t-norm or t-conorm has a profound effect on their characteristics. The variability induced by different t-(co)norms is considerably greater than what is observed in logic-based inclusion measures. This suggests that set-theoretic inclusion measures are more sensitive to the selected aggregation functions, whereas logic-based inclusion measures maintain a more stable structure across different configurations.

Among all inclusion measures analyzed, the one that is most intuitively in alignment with the natural concept of set inclusion is Kosko's inclusion measure with the minimum t-norm (top-left plot in Fig. 2a). Interestingly, a similar characteristic is observed across all inclusion measures analyzed based on implication operators. This consistency suggests that implication-based inclusion measures inherently capture an intuitive notion of inclusion, which remains stable across different logical formulations.

Another significant observation is that, despite the formal distinction between the simple and extended inclusion coefficients, the similarity measures derived from them exhibit only minimal differences across all six analyzed t-norms (Fig. 3b and 4). This suggests that, at least in some cases, using a more complex inclusion measure may not significantly impact the results of set comparisons or the performance of models relying on such inclusion measures. This finding could

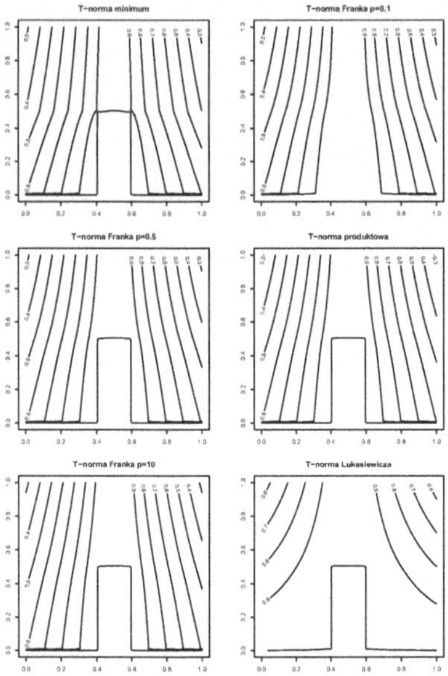


**Fig. 4.** The contour plots of inclusion measures constructed with the extended inclusion coefficient and R-implications generated by different Frank t-norms. The fuzzy measure $g_{\mathrm{id}}$ was used for aggregation.

be particularly relevant in practical applications where computational efficiency is a priority.

However, as illustrated in Fig. 3, the choice of different implication operators – despite using the same inclusion measure construction method – leads to entirely different characteristics. While for the Łukasiewicz t-(co)norm, the results remain consistent, as the parameter $p$ in the Frank family of t-(co)norms decreases, the differences become increasingly significant. For S-implications, the degree of inclusion decreases gradually and smoothly concerning both vertical and horizontal scaling. However, for R-implications, vertical scaling has almost no effect on the inclusion degree, regardless of the value of $p$. This highlights that the behavior of inclusion measures is not only a function of the aggregation method used but is also strongly influenced by the specific type of logical operator applied.

**Disclosure of Interests.** The authors have no competing interests to declare that are relevant to the content of this article.

## References

1. Baczyński, M., Jayaram, B.: Fuzzy Implications. Springer, Heidelberg (2008)
2. Baldwin, J.F., Pilsworth, B.: Axiomatic approach to implication for approximate reasoning with fuzzy logic. Fuzzy Sets Syst. **3**(2), 193–219 (1980)

3. Bandler, W., Kohout, L.J.: The use of checklist paradigm in inference systems. Fuzzy Logic Knowl. Eng. 95–111 (1986)
4. Bouchon, B.: Inferences with imprecisions and uncertainties in expert systems. Fuzzy Expert Systems. Addison-Wesley, New York (1987)
5. Couso, I., Garrido, L., Sánchez, L.: Similarity and dissimilarity measures between fuzzy sets: a formal relational study. Inf. Sci. **229**, 122–141 (2013)
6. Cross, V.V., Sudkamp, T.A.: Similarity and Compatibility in Fuzzy Set Theory: Assessment and Applications, vol. 93. Springer (2002)
7. Dubois, D., Prade, H.: A unifying view of comparison indices in a fuzzy set-theoretic framework. Fuzzy Sets and Possibility Theory: Recent Developments. Pergamon, New York (1982)
8. Dutta, A.: Reasoning with imprecise knowledge in expert systems. Inf. Sci. **37**(1), 3–24 (1985)
9. Frank, M.J.: On the simultaneous associativity of f (x, y) and x+ y- f (x, y). Aequationes Math. **19**, 194–226 (1979)
10. Gaines, B.R.: Foundations of fuzzy reasoning. Int. J. Man Mach. Stud. **8**(6), 623–668 (1976)
11. Goguen, J.A.: The logic of inexact concepts. Synthese **19**(3), 325–373 (1969)
12. Hirota, K., Pedrycz, W.: Handling fuzziness and randomness in process of matching fuzzy data. In: Proceedings of the Third IFSA Congress, pp. 97–100 (1989)
13. Hirota, K., Pedrycz, W.: Matching fuzzy quantities. IEEE Trans. Syst. Man Cybern. **21**(6), 1580–1586 (1991)
14. Kiszka, J., Kochanska, M., Sliwinska, D.: The influence of some parameters on the accuracy of a fuzzy model. Ind. Appl. Fuzzy Control 187–230 (1985)
15. Klement, E.P., Mesiar, R., Pap, E.: Triangular Norms, vol. 8. Springer (2013)
16. Klir, G., Yuan, B.: Fuzzy Sets and Fuzzy Logic, vol. 4. Prentice Hall, New Jersey (1995)
17. Kohout, L.J., Bandler, W.: How the checklist paradigm elucidates the semantics of fuzzy inference. In: IEEE International Conference on Fuzzy Systems, pp. 571–578. IEEE (1992)
18. Kosko, B.: Fuzziness vs. probability. Int. J. Gen. Syst. **17**(2-3), 211–240 (1990)
19. Lee, C.C.: Fuzzy logic in control systems: fuzzy logic controller. ii. IEEE Trans. Syst. Man Cybern. **20**(2), 419–435 (1990)
20. Magrez, P., Smets, P.: Fuzzy modus ponens: a new model suitable for applications in knowledge-based systems. Int. J. Intell. Syst. **4**(2), 181–200 (1989)
21. Mizumoto, M., Zimmermann, H.J.: Comparison of fuzzy reasoning methods. Fuzzy Sets Syst. **8**(3), 253–283 (1982)
22. Trillas, E., Valverde, L.: On mode and implication in approximate reasoning. Approx. Reason. Expert Syst. 157–166 (1985)
23. Whalen, T., Schott, B.: Alternative logics for approximate reasoning in expert systems: a comparative study. Int. J. Man Mach. Stud. **22**(3), 327–346 (1985)
24. Wygralak, M.: Cardinalities of Fuzzy Sets, vol. 118. Springer (2003)
25. Zeng, W., Li, H.: Inclusion measures, similarity measures, and the fuzziness of fuzzy sets and their relations. Int. J. Intell. Syst. **21**(6), 639–653 (2006). https://doi.org/10.1002/int.20152
26. Żywica, P., Baczyński, M.: An effective similarity measurement under epistemic uncertainty. Fuzzy Sets Syst. **431**, 160–177 (2022)

# Implication Construction Methods on Bounded Lattices

Ümıt Ertuğrul(✉), Funda Karaçal, and Kübra Karacaır

Department of Mathematics, Karadeniz Technical University, Trabzon, Turkey
uertugrul@ktu.edu.tr

**Abstract.** We present some construction methods to obtain fuzzy implications on a bounded lattice $L$ via two implications defined on sub-intervals of the bounded lattice $L$. Then, we take a step further this idea to produce fuzzy implications via given three implications. Moreover, many illustrative examples are included.

**Keywords:** Fuzzy implication · Construction method · Sub-interval · Bounded lattice

## 1 Introduction

In recent years fuzzy implication functions have been widely studied in terms of both theory and their applications. In the literature, it can be found many different construction methods to produce fuzzy implications [1–3,6,7]. One of the important aspect of obtaining a fuzzy implication is ordinal sums of fuzzy implications.

In Su et al. have offered a new class of fuzzy implications by means of the ordinal sum of a family of given implications on the unit interval $[0, 1]$ [10]. In [9], based on the construction of ordinal sum of overlap functions, two construction methods to produce a new fuzzy implication on the unit interval $[0, 1]$ from the given ones have been proposed for fuzzy implications. Two different classes of ordinal sum implications, called the minor ordinal sum and the major ordinal sum implications, on the unit interval $[0, 1]$ have been introduced and have been discussed the some properties satisfied by the new ordinal sums in [5].

In this study, we focus on ordinal sums of given two and three implications on bounded lattices. We believe it gives to insight into defining an ordinal sum construction for a finite number of implications.

The rest of this paper is organized as follows: In Sect. 2, we remind some main definitions, which are useful for our paper. In the Sect. 3, we give construction methods to obtain implications by means of implications defined on some sub-intervals of bounded lattices and add some examples from these construction methods. Finally, we finish with concluding remarks.


M. Baczyński et al. (Eds.): EUSFLAT 2025, LNCS 15884, pp. 122–133, 2025.
https://doi.org/10.1007/978-3-031-97228-7_11

## 2 Preliminaries

In this section, we list some basic notions and results which will be use in the paper.

**Definition 1.** *[4] Let $(L, \leq, 0, 1)$ be a bounded lattice and $a, b \in L$ with $a \leq b$. The subinterval $[a, b]$ is defined as*

$$[a, b] = \{x \in L \mid a \leq x \leq b\}.$$

Similarly, $(a, b] = \{x \in L \mid a < x \leq b\}$, $[a, b) = \{x \in L \mid a \leq x < b\}$ and $(a, b) = \{x \in L \mid a < x < b\}$ can be defined.

**Definition 2.** *[4] Let $(L, \leq, 0, 1)$ be a bounded lattice and $a, b \in L$. We use the notation $a \parallel b$ denote that $a$ and $b$ are incomparable. If $a$ and $b$ are comparable, we use the notation $a \nparallel b$.*

*In the following, $I_a$ denotes the set of all incomparable elements with $a$; i.e., $I_a = \{x \in L \mid x \parallel a\}$. $I_a^b$ denotes the set of elements that are incomparable with $a$ but comparable with $b$; i.e., $I_a^b = \{x \in L \mid x \parallel a \text{ and } x \nparallel b\}$. Similarly, $I_b^a$ denotes the set of elements that are incomparable with $b$ but comparable with $a$; i.e., $I_b^a = \{x \in L \mid x \parallel b \text{ and } x \nparallel a\}$. $I_{a,b}$ denotes the set of elements that are incomparable with both $a$ and $b$; i.e., $I_{a,b} = \{x \in L \mid x \parallel a \text{ and } x \parallel b\}$.*

**Definition 3.** *([8]) Let $(L, \leq, 0, 1)$ be a bounded lattice. A triangular (co)norm $T$ (briefly t-(co)norm) is a binary operation on $L$ which is commutative, associative, monotone and has neutral element 1 (0).*

Throughout the paper, we will denote by the notaion $\mathcal{T}$ ($\mathcal{S}$) the set of all triangular norms (triangular conorm) on a bounded lattice $L$.

*Example 1.* ([8]) Let $S_D(x, y) = \begin{cases} x, if\ y = 0 \\ y, if\ x = 0 \\ 1, \text{otherwise} \end{cases}$ and $T_\wedge(x, y) = x \wedge y$.

Then, $S_D \in \mathcal{S}$ and $T_\wedge \in \mathcal{T}$

**Definition 4.** *[9] A function $I : L^2 \to L$ on a bounded lattice $(L, \leq, 0, 1)$ is called an implication if it satisfies the following conditions:*

*(I1) $I$ is a decreasing operation on the first variable, that is, for every $x, z \in L$ with $x \leq z$, $I(z, y) \leq I(x, y)$ for all $y \in L$.*

*(I2) $I$ is an increasing operation on the second variable, that is, for every $y, z \in L$ with $y \leq z$, $I(x, y) \leq I(x, z)$ for all $x \in L$.*

*(I3) $I(0, 0) = 1$.*

*(I4) $I(1, 1) = 1$.*

*(I5) $I(1, 0) = 0$.*

Throughout the paper, we will denote by $\mathcal{F}$ the set of all implications on a bounded lattice $L$. Also, we will denote by $F_{[a,b]}$ the set of all implications on sublattice $[a, b]$ for $a, b \in L$ with $a \leq b$.

**Theorem 1.** *([2]) Let $(L, \leq, 0, 1)$ be a bounded lattice, $S : L^2 \to L$ be a t-conorm, $T : L^2 \to L$ be a t-norm, $I, J : L^2 \to L$ be implications and $a \in L$. The function $TS_a : L^2 \to L$ defined by, for all $x, y \in L$,*

$$TS_a(x, y) = T(S(a, I(x, y)), J(x, y)) \tag{1}$$

*is an implication.*

**Theorem 2.** *([7]) Let $(L, \leq, 0, 1)$ be a bounded lattice, $S : L^2 \to L$ be a t-conorm, $T : L^2 \to L$ be a t-norm, $I, J : L^2 \to L$ be implications, $N : L \to L$ be a negation and $a \in L$. The function $K^{I,J}_{a,T,S,N} : L^2 \to L$ defined by, for all $x, y \in L$,*

$$K^{I,J}_{a,T,S,N} = S(T(a, I(x, y)), T(N(a), J(x, y))) \tag{2}$$

*is an implication if and only if $S(a, N(a)) = 1$.*

**Theorem 3.** *([3]) Let $(L, \leq, 0, 1)$ be a bounded lattice, $a, b \in L$, $T \in \mathcal{T}$, $S \in \mathcal{S}$, $N \in \mathcal{N}$ and $J^a \in \mathcal{F}^{[0, a]}$. Then the function $I_{ab} : L^2 \to L$ defined by*

$$I_{ab}(x, y) = S(S(T(N(x), b), T(y, b)), J^a(T(x, a), T(y, a))), \tag{3}$$

*is an implication if and only if $S(a, b) = 1$.*

## 3 Ordinal Sum of Two (Three) Implications on a Bounded Lattice

**Theorem 4.** *Let $(L, \leq, 0, 1)$ be a bounded lattice, $a \in L$, $R_1 \in \mathcal{F}_{[0,a]}$, $R_2 \in \mathcal{F}_{[a,1]}$ and define the binary operation $\mathcal{R}^1_{R_1 R_2} : L^2 \to L$ given, for all $x, y \in L$, as*

$$\mathcal{R}^1_{R_1 R_2}(x, y) = \begin{cases} R_1(x, y) & \text{if } (x, y) \in (0, a] \times [0, a], \\ 1 & \text{if } (x, y) \in (\{0\} \times L) \cup ((0, a] \cup I_a) \times (a, 1], \\ a & \text{if } (x, y) \in (L \backslash \{0\}) \times I_a, \\ 0 & \text{if } (x, y) \in ((a, 1] \cup I_a) \times [0, a], \\ R_2(x, y) & \text{if } (x, y) \in (a, 1] \times (a, 1]. \end{cases} \tag{4}$$

*Then, $\mathcal{R}^1_{R_1 R_2} \in \mathcal{F}$.*

*Proof.* **(I1)** Let $x, y, z \in L$ with $x \leq y$, we need to prove that $\mathcal{R}^1_{R_1 R_2}(y, z) \leq \mathcal{R}^1_{R_1 R_2}(x, z)$. Whenever $(x, y) \in (0, a]^2 \cup (a, 1]^2 \cup (I_a)^2$, (I1) is clear. Also, it is obvious when $x = 0$. From the fact that $\mathcal{R}^1_{R_1 R_2}(y, z) = 0$ when $y \in L \backslash [0, a]$, $z \in [0, a]$, and $\mathcal{R}^1_{R_1 R_2}(x, z) = 1$ when $x \in L \backslash (a, 1]$, $z \in (a, 1]$, and $\mathcal{R}^1_{R_1 R_2}(y, z) = a = \mathcal{R}^1_{R_1 R_2}(x, z)$ when $z \in I_a$, $x, y \in L \backslash \{0\}$, (I1) is directly obtained.

**(I2)** Let $x, y, z \in L$ with $x \leq y$, we need to prove that $\mathcal{R}^1_{R_1 R_2}(z, x) \leq \mathcal{R}^1_{R_1 R_2}(z, y)$. Whenever $(x, y) \in [0, a]^2 \cup (a, 1]^2 \cup (I_a)^2$, (I2) is clear. Also, it is obvious when $z = 0$. Then, the proof can be split into all remain possible cases as in the following.

1. Let $x \in [0, a]$.
1.1. $y \in (a, 1]$,
1.1.1. If $z \in (0, a]$, then $\mathcal{R}^1_{R_1R_2}(z, x) = R_1(z, x) \leq 1 = \mathcal{R}^1_{R_1R_2}(z, y)$.
1.1.2. If $z \in (a, 1]$, then $\mathcal{R}^1_{R_1R_2}(z, x) = 0 \leq R_2(z, y) = \mathcal{R}^1_{R_1R_2}(z, y)$.
1.1.3. If $z \in I_a$, then $\mathcal{R}^1_{R_1R_2}(z, x) = 0 \leq 1 = \mathcal{R}^1_{R_1R_2}(z, y)$.
1.2. $y \in I_a$,
1.2.1. If $z \in (0, a]$, then $\mathcal{R}^1_{R_1R_2}(z, x) = R_1(z, x) \leq a = \mathcal{R}^1_{R_1R_2}(z, y)$.
1.2.2. If $z \in (a, 1] \cup I_a$, then $\mathcal{R}^1_{R_1R_2}(z, x) = 0 \leq a = \mathcal{R}^1_{R_1R_2}(z, y)$.
2. Let $x \in I_a$ and $y \in (a, 1]$.
2.1. If $z \in (0, a] \cup I_a$, then
$\mathcal{R}^1_{R_1R_2}(z, x) = a \leq 1 = \mathcal{R}^1_{R_1R_2}(z, y)$.
2.2. If $z \in (a, 1]$, then $\mathcal{R}^1_{R_1R_2}(z, x) = a \leq R_2(z, y) = \mathcal{R}^1_{R_1R_2}(z, y)$.
I3, I4 and I5 are obtained directly from the definition of $\mathcal{R}^1_{R_1R_2}$.
Thus, $\mathcal{R}^1_{R_1R_2} \in \mathcal{F}$

*Example 2.* Consider the bounded lattice $(L_1, \leq, 0, 1)$ characterized by the Hasse diagram in Fig. 1, the functions $R_1$ and $R_2$ on $[0, x_4]$ and $[x_4, 1]$ shown in Table 1 and Table 2, respectively. We can easily verify that $R_1$ and $R_2$ are implications on corresponding sub-intervals.

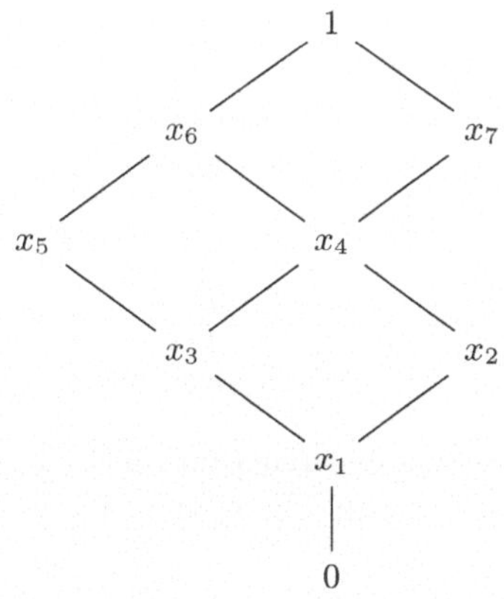


**Fig. 1.** Lattice diagram of $L_1$.

**Table 1.** The implication $R_1$ on $[0, x_4]$

| $R_1$ | 0 | $x_1$ | $x_2$ | $x_3$ | $x_4$ |
|---|---|---|---|---|---|
| 0 | $x_4$ | $x_4$ | $x_4$ | $x_4$ | $x_4$ |
| $x_1$ | $x_2$ | $x_2$ | $x_2$ | $x_4$ | $x_4$ |
| $x_2$ | $x_1$ | $x_1$ | $x_2$ | $x_3$ | $x_4$ |
| $x_3$ | $x_1$ | $x_1$ | $x_2$ | $x_3$ | $x_4$ |
| $x_4$ | 0 | $x_1$ | $x_2$ | $x_3$ | $x_4$ |

**Table 2.** The implication $R_2$ on $[x_4, 1]$

| $R_2$ | $x_4$ | $x_6$ | $x_7$ | 1 |
|---|---|---|---|---|
| $x_4$ | 1 | 1 | 1 | 1 |
| $x_6$ | $x_7$ | 1 | $x_7$ | 1 |
| $x_7$ | $x_6$ | $x_6$ | 1 | 1 |
| 1 | $x_4$ | $x_6$ | $x_7$ | 1 |

By the method presented in Theorem 4, where $a = x_4$, we can obtain an implication $\mathcal{R}^1_{R_1R_2}$ on $L_2$ shown in Table 3.

**Table 3.** The implication $\mathcal{R}^1_{R_1R_2}$ on $L_1$.

| $\mathcal{R}^1_{R_1R_2}$ | $0$ | $x_1$ | $x_2$ | $x_3$ | $x_4$ | $x_5$ | $x_6$ | $x_7$ | $1$ |
|---|---|---|---|---|---|---|---|---|---|
| $0$ | $1$ | $1$ | $1$ | $1$ | $1$ | $1$ | $1$ | $1$ | $1$ |
| $x_1$ | $x_2$ | $x_2$ | $x_2$ | $x_4$ | $x_4$ | $x_4$ | $1$ | $1$ | $1$ |
| $x_2$ | $x_1$ | $x_1$ | $x_2$ | $x_3$ | $x_4$ | $x_4$ | $1$ | $1$ | $1$ |
| $x_3$ | $x_1$ | $x_1$ | $x_2$ | $x_3$ | $x_4$ | $x_4$ | $1$ | $1$ | $1$ |
| $x_4$ | $0$ | $x_1$ | $x_2$ | $x_3$ | $x_4$ | $x_4$ | $1$ | $1$ | $1$ |
| $x_5$ | $0$ | $0$ | $0$ | $0$ | $0$ | $x_4$ | $1$ | $1$ | $1$ |
| $x_6$ | $0$ | $0$ | $0$ | $0$ | $0$ | $x_4$ | $1$ | $x_7$ | $1$ |
| $x_7$ | $0$ | $0$ | $0$ | $0$ | $0$ | $x_4$ | $x_6$ | $1$ | $1$ |
| $1$ | $0$ | $0$ | $0$ | $0$ | $0$ | $x_4$ | $x_6$ | $x_7$ | $1$ |

*Remark 1.* Let the bounded lattice $(L_1, \leq, 0, 1)$ characterized by the Hasse diagram in Fig. 1, $T = T_\wedge$, $S = S_D$ and the implication $J^{x4} = R_1$ on $[0, x_4]$ shown in Table 1. Consider the negation $N = N_1$ shown in formula (5). We have $I_{x_41}(x_4, x_4) = 1$ by applying the method presented in Theorem 3, where $a = x_4$, $b = 1$. Also, we know $\mathcal{R}^1_{R_1R_2}(x_4, x_4) = x_4$ from Table 3. Then, $\mathcal{R}^1_{R_1R_2}$ and $I_{ab}$ may not be the same in general.

$$N_1(x) = \begin{cases} 0, & if\ x = 1 \\ 1, & if\ x = 0 \\ x_4, & \text{otherwise.} \end{cases} \tag{5}$$

We also obtain another two construction methods as follows. They can be proven in similar fashion as done in Theorem 4. Thus, we omit their proofs.

**Theorem 5.** *Let $(L, \leq, 0, 1)$ be a bounded lattice, $a, b \in L$ with $a \leq b$, $R_1 \in \mathcal{F}_{[0,a]}$, $R_2 \in \mathcal{F}_{[a,1]}$ and define the binary operation $\mathcal{R}^2_{R_1R_2} : L^2 \to L$ given, for all $x, y \in L$, as*

$$\mathcal{R}^2_{R_1R_2}(x, y) = \begin{cases} R_1(x, y) & if\ (x, y) \in (0, a] \times [0, a], \\ 1 & if\ (x, y) \in (\{0\} \times L) \cup (0, a] \times ((a, 1] \cup I_a) \cup I_a \times (a, 1], \\ a & if\ (x, y) \in (I_a \cup (a, 1]) \times I_a, \\ 0 & if\ (x, y) \in ((a, 1] \cup I_a) \times [0, a], \\ R_2(x, y) & if\ (x, y) \in (a, 1] \times (a, 1]. \end{cases} \tag{6}$$

*Then, $\mathcal{R}^2_{R_1R_2} \in \mathcal{F}$.*

**Theorem 6.** *Let $(L, \leq, 0, 1)$ be a bounded lattice, $a, b \in L$ with $a \leq b$, $R_1 \in \mathcal{F}_{[0,a]}$, $R_2 \in \mathcal{F}_{[a,1]}$ and define the binary operation $\mathcal{R}^3_{R_1R_2} : L^2 \to L$ given, for all $x, y \in L$, as*

$$\mathcal{R}^3_{R_1R_2}(x,y)=\begin{cases} R_1(x,y) & \textit{if } (x,y)\in(0,a]\times[0,a],\\ 1 & \textit{if } (x,y)\in(\{0\}\times L)\cup(0,a]\times((a,1]\cup I_a)\cup I_a\times((a,1]\cup I_a),\\ a & \textit{if } (x,y)\in(I_a\cup(a,1])\times I_a,\\ 0 & \textit{if } (x,y)\in((a,1]\cup I_a)\times[0,a],\\ R_2(x,y) & \textit{if } (x,y)\in(a,1]\times(a,1]. \end{cases} \tag{7}$$

*Then,* $\mathcal{R}^3_{R_1R_2}\in\mathcal{F}$.

Considering the construction methods from two implications on sub-intervals to the whole lattice, we give the following methods for obtaining an implication on a lattice from three implications on sub-intervals of the lattice. In this way, we hope to gain insight into obtaining a new ordinal sum construction method for implications from a finite number of implications on the sub-intervals.

**Theorem 7.** *Let* $(L,\leq,0,1)$ *be a bounded lattice,* $a,b\in L$ *with* $a\leq b$, $R_1\in\mathcal{F}_{[0,a]}$, $R_2\in\mathcal{F}_{[a,b]}$, $R_3\in\mathcal{F}_{[b,1]}$ *and define the binary operation* $\mathcal{R}^1_{R_1R_2R_3}:L^2\to L$ *given, for all* $x,y\in L$, *as*

$$\mathcal{R}^1_{R_1R_2R_3}(x,y)=\begin{cases} R_1(x,y) & \textit{if } (x,y)\in(0,a]\times[0,a],\\ 0 & \textit{if}(x,y)\in(L\backslash[0,a])\times[0,a],\\ a & \textit{if } (x,y)\in((b,1]\cup I_{a,b}\cup I_b^a)\times(a,b]\cup(L\backslash\{0\})\times(I_a^b\cup I_{a,b}),\\ R_2(x,y) & \textit{if } (x,y)\in(a,b]\times(a,b],\\ R_3(x,y) & \textit{if } (x,y)\in(b,1]\times(b,1],\\ b & \textit{if } (x,y)\in((0,a]\cup I_a^b)\times(a,b]\cup(L\backslash\{0\})\times I_b^a,\\ 1 & \textit{if } (x,y)\in\{0\}\times(L\backslash(b,1])\cup(L\backslash(b,1])\times(b,1]. \end{cases} \tag{8}$$

*Then,* $\mathcal{R}^1_{R_1R_2R_3}\in\mathcal{F}$.

*Proof.* I3, I4 and I5 are obtained directly from the definition of $\mathcal{R}^1_{R_1R_2R_3}$.

**(I1)** Let $x,y,z\in L$ with $x\leq y$, we need to prove that $\mathcal{R}^1_{R_1R_2R_3}(y,z)\leq\mathcal{R}^1_{R_1R_2R_3}(x,z)$. Whenever $(x,y)\in(0,a]^2\cup(a,b]^2\cup(b,1]^2\cup(I_a^b)^2\cup(I_b^a)^2\cup(I_{a,b})^2$, (I1) is clear. Since $\mathcal{R}^1_{R_1R_2R_3}(y,z)=0$ when $y\in L\backslash[0,a]$, $z\in(0,a]$, and $\mathcal{R}^1_{R_1R_2R_3}(x,z)=1$ when $x\in(L\backslash(b,1])$, $z\in(b,1]$, (I1) is directly obtained. Also, it is obvious when $x=0$. Then, the proof can be split into all remain possible cases as in the following.

If $x,z\in\{0\}$, $z\in I_a^b\cup I_{a,b}$, $\mathcal{R}^1_{R_1R_2R_3}(y,z)=a=\mathcal{R}^1_{R_1R_2R_3}(x,z)$. Similarly $\mathcal{R}^1_{R_1R_2R_3}(y,z)=b=\mathcal{R}^1_{R_1R_2R_3}(x,z)$ when $z\in I_b^a$.

1. Let $x\in(0,a]$.

1.1. If $y\in(a,b]$ and $z\in(a,b]$, then $\mathcal{R}^1_{R_1R_2R_3}(y,z)=R_2(y,z)\leq b=\mathcal{R}^1_{R_1R_2R_3}(x,z)$.

1.2. $y\in(b,1]\cup I_b^a\cup I_{a,b}$ and $z\in(a,b]$, then $\mathcal{R}^1_{R_1R_2R_3}(y,z)=a\leq b=\mathcal{R}^1_{R_1R_2R_3}(x,z)$.

1.3. If $y\in I_a^b$ and $z\in(a,b]$, then $\mathcal{R}^1_{R_1R_2R_3}(y,z)=b=\mathcal{R}^1_{R_1R_2R_3}(x,z)$.

2. Let $x\in(a,b]$.

2.1. If $y\in(b,1]\cup I_b^a$ and $z\in(a,b]$, then $\mathcal{R}^1_{R_1R_2R_3}(y,z)=a\leq R_2(x,z)=\mathcal{R}^1_{R_1R_2R_3}(x,z)$.

3. Let $x\in I_a^b$.

3.1. If $y \in (a,b]$ and $z \in (a,b]$, then $\mathcal{R}^1_{R_1R_2R_3}(y,z) = R_2(y,z) \leq b = \mathcal{R}^1_{R_1R_2R_3}(x,z)$.

3.2. If $y \in (b,1] \cup I^a_b \cup I_{a,b}$, and $z \in (a,b]$, then $\mathcal{R}^1_{R_1R_2R_3}(y,z) = a \leq b = \mathcal{R}^1_{R_1R_2R_3}(x,z)$.

4. Let $x \in I^a_b$.

4.1. If $y \in (b,1]$ and $z \in (a,b]$, then $\mathcal{R}^1_{R_1R_2R_3}(y,z) = a = \mathcal{R}^1_{R_1R_2R_3}(x,z)$.

5. Let $x \in I_{a,b}$.

5.1. If $y \in (b,1] \cup I^a_b$ and $z \in (a,b]$, then $\mathcal{R}^1_{R_1R_2R_3}(y,z) = a = \mathcal{R}^1_{R_1R_2R_3}(x,z)$.

**(I2)** Let $x, y, z \in L$ with $x \leq y$, we need to prove that $\mathcal{R}^1_{R_1R_2R_3}(z,x) \leq \mathcal{R}^1_{R_1R_2R_3}(z,y)$. Whenever $(x,y) \in [0,a]^2 \cup (a,b]^2 \cup (b,1]^2 \cup (I^b_a)^2 \cup (I^a_b)^2 \cup (I_{a,b})^2$, (I2) is clear. Also, it is obvious for $z = 0$. Then, the proof can be split into all remain possible cases as in the following.

1. Let $x \in [0,a]$. If $z \in (a,b] \cup (b,1] \cup I_a \cup I_b$, then $\mathcal{R}^1_{R_1R_2R_3}(z,x) = 0$, i.e., (I2) is obvious. Let us investigate the rest of possible cases.

1.1. If $y \in (a,b]$ and $z \in (0,a]$, then $\mathcal{R}^1_{R_1R_2R_3}(z,x) = R_1(z,x) \leq b = \mathcal{R}^1_{R_1R_2R_3}(z,y)$.

1.2. If $y \in (b,1]$ and $z \in (0,a]$, then $\mathcal{R}^1_{R_1R_2R_3}(z,x) = R_1(z,x) \leq 1 = \mathcal{R}^1_{R_1R_2R_3}(z,y)$.

1.3. If $y \in I^b_a \cup \in I_{a,b}$, and $z \in (0,a]$, then $\mathcal{R}^1_{R_1R_2R_3}(z,x) = R_1(z,x) \leq a = \mathcal{R}^1_{R_1R_2R_3}(z,y)$.

1.4. $y \in I^a_b$, $z \in (0,a]$, then $\mathcal{R}^1_{R_1R_2R_3}(z,x) = R_1(z,x) \leq b = \mathcal{R}^1_{R_1R_2R_3}(z,y)$.

2. Let $x \in (a,b]$.

2.1. Let $y \in (b,1]$. If $z \in (0,a] \cup (a,b] \cup I_a \cup I_b$, then $\mathcal{R}^1_{R_1R_2R_3}(z,y) = 1$, i.e., (I2) is obvious. Let us investigate the rest of possible cases.

2.1.1. If $z \in (b,1]$, then $\mathcal{R}^1_{R_1R_2R_3}(z,x) = a \leq R_3(z,y) = \mathcal{R}^1_{R_1R_2R_3}(z,y)$.

2.2. $y \in I^a_b$,

2.2.1. If $z \in (0,a] \cup I^b_a$, then $\mathcal{R}^1_{R_1R_2R_3}(z,x) = b = \mathcal{R}^1_{R_1R_2R_3}(z,y)$.

2.2.2. If $z \in (a,b]$, then $\mathcal{R}^1_{R_1R_2R_3}(z,x) = R_2(z,x) \leq b = \mathcal{R}^1_{R_1R_2R_3}(z,y)$.

2.2.3. If $z \in (b,1] \cup I^a_b \cup I_{a,b}$, then $\mathcal{R}^1_{R_1R_2R_3}(z,x) = a \leq b = \mathcal{R}^1_{R_1R_2R_3}(z,y)$.

3. Let $x \in I^b_a$

3.1. $y \in (a,b]$,

3.1.1. If $z \in (0,a] \cup I^b_a$, then $\mathcal{R}^1_{R_1R_2R_3}(z,x) = a \leq b = \mathcal{R}^1_{R_1R_2R_3}(z,y)$.

3.1.2. If $z \in (a,b]$, then $\mathcal{R}^1_{R_1R_2R_3}(z,x) = a \leq R_2(z,y) = \mathcal{R}^1_{R_1R_2R_3}(z,y)$.

3.1.3. If $z \in (b,1] \cup I^a_b \cup I_{a,b}$, then $\mathcal{R}^1_{R_1R_2R_3}(z,x) = a = \mathcal{R}^1_{R_1R_2R_3}(z,y)$.

3.2. $y \in (b,1]$,

3.2.1. If $z \in (0,a] \cup (a,b] \cup I^b_a \cup I^a_b \cup I_{a,b}$, then $\mathcal{R}^1_{R_1R_2R_3}(z,x) = a \leq 1 = \mathcal{R}^1_{R_1R_2R_3}(z,y)$.

3.2.3. If $z \in (b,1]$, then $\mathcal{R}^1_{R_1R_2R_3}(z,x) = a \leq R_3(z,y) = \mathcal{R}^1_{R_1R_2R_3}(z,y)$.

3.3. If $y \in I^a_b$ and $z \in L\backslash\{0\}$, then $\mathcal{R}^1_{R_1R_2R_3}(z,x) = a \leq b = \mathcal{R}^1_{R_1R_2R_3}(z,y)$.

3.4. If $y \in I_{a,b}$ and $z \in L\backslash\{0\}$, then
$\mathcal{R}^1_{R_1R_2R_3}(z,x) = a = \mathcal{R}^1_{R_1R_2R_3}(z,y)$.

4. Let $x \in I^a_b$ and $y \in (b,1]$.

4.1. If $z \in (0,a] \cup (a,b] \cup I^b_a \cup I^a_b \cup I_{a,b}$, then $\mathcal{R}^1_{R_1R_2R_3}(z,x) = b \leq 1 = \mathcal{R}^1_{R_1R_2R_3}(z,y)$.

4.2. If $z \in (b,1]$, then $\mathcal{R}^1_{R_1R_2R_3}(z,x) = b \leq R_3(z,y) = \mathcal{R}^1_{R_1R_2R_3}(z,y)$.

5. Let $x \in I_{a,b}$.

5.1. $y \in (b, 1]$,

5.1.1. If $z \in (0, a] \cup (a, b] \cup I_a^b \cup I_b^a \cup I_{a,b}$, then $\mathcal{R}^1_{R_1R_2R_3}(z, x) = a \leq 1 = \mathcal{R}^1_{R_1R_2R_3}(z, y)$.

5.1.2. If $z \in (b, 1]$, then $\mathcal{R}^1_{R_1R_2R_3}(z, x) = a \leq R_3(z, y) = \mathcal{R}^1_{R_1R_2R_3}(z, y)$.

5.2. If $y \in I_b^a$ and $z \in L \backslash \{0\}$, then $\mathcal{R}^1_{R_1R_2R_3}(z, x) = a \leq b = \mathcal{R}^1_{R_1R_2R_3}(z, y)$.

Thus, $\mathcal{R}^1_{R_1R_2R_3} \in \mathcal{F}$.

The structure of the implication $\mathcal{R}^1_{R_1R_2R_3}$ given in formula (8) in Theorem 7 can be summarized as in Fig. 2.

| | $0$ – $a$ | $a$ – $b$ | $b$ – $1$ | $I_a$ | $I_b^a$ |
|---|---|---|---|---|---|
| $I_b^a$ | $b$ | $b$ | $b$ | $b$ | $b$ |
| $I_a$ | $a$ | $a$ | $a$ | $a$ | $a$ |
| $b$ – $1$ | $1$ | $1$ | $R_3(x, y)$ | $1$ | $1$ |
| $a$ – $b$ | $b$ | $R_2(x, y)$ | $a$ | $b$ | $a$ |
| $0$ – $a$ | $R_1(x, y)$ | $0$ | $0$ | $0$ | $0$ |

**Fig. 2.** The implication $\mathcal{R}^1_{R_1R_2R_3}$ on $L$.

*Example 3.* Consider the bounded lattice $(L_2, \leq, 0, 1)$ characterized by the Hasse diagram in Fig. 3, the functions $R_1$, $R_2$ and $R_3$ on $[0, x_3]$, $[x_3, x_7]$ and $[x_7, 1]$ shown in Table 4, Table 5 and Table 6, respectively. We can easily verify that $R_1$, $R_2$ and $R_3$ are implications on corresponding sub-intervals.

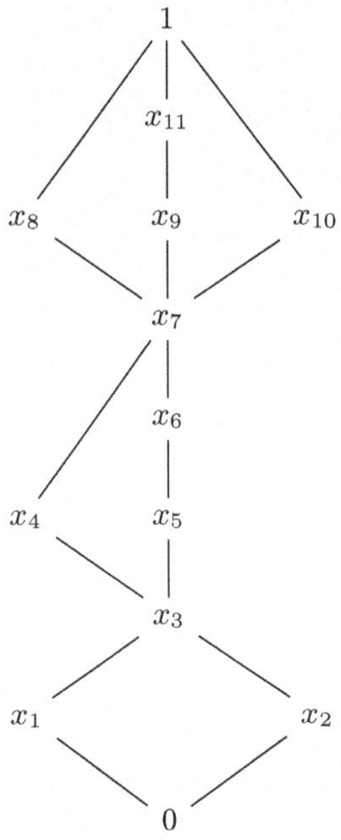


**Fig. 3.** Lattice diagram of $L_1$.

**Table 4.** The implication $R_1$ on $[0, x_3]$

| $R_1$ | 0 | $x_1$ | $x_2$ | $x_3$ |
|---|---|---|---|---|
| 0 | $x_3$ | $x_3$ | $x_3$ | $x_3$ |
| $x_1$ | 0 | $x_3$ | $x_2$ | $x_3$ |
| $x_2$ | 0 | $x_2$ | $x_3$ | $x_3$ |
| $x_3$ | 0 | 0 | 0 | $x_3$ |

**Table 5.** The implication $R_2$ on $[x_3, x_7]$

| $R_2$ | $x_3$ | $x_4$ | $x_5$ | $x_6$ | $x_7$ |
|---|---|---|---|---|---|
| $x_3$ | $x_7$ | $x_7$ | $x_7$ | $x_7$ | $x_7$ |
| $x_4$ | $x_3$ | $x_7$ | $x_5$ | $x_6$ | $x_7$ |
| $x_5$ | $x_3$ | $x_7$ | $x_7$ | $x_7$ | $x_7$ |
| $x_6$ | $x_3$ | $x_7$ | $x_5$ | $x_7$ | $x_7$ |
| $x_7$ | $x_3$ | $x_4$ | $x_5$ | $x_6$ | $x_7$ |

**Table 6.** The implication $R_3$ on $[x_7, 1]$.

| $R_3$ | $x_7$ | $x_8$ | $x_9$ | $x_{10}$ | $x_{11}$ | 1 |
|---|---|---|---|---|---|---|
| $x_7$ | 1 | 1 | 1 | 1 | 1 | 1 |
| $x_8$ | $x_{10}$ | 1 | 1 | $x_{10}$ | 1 | 1 |
| $x_9$ | $x_{11}$ | 1 | 1 | 1 | 1 | 1 |
| $x_{10}$ | $x_8$ | $x_8$ | 1 | 1 | 1 | 1 |
| $x_{11}$ | $x_9$ | 1 | $x_9$ | 1 | 1 | 1 |
| 1 | $x_7$ | $x_7$ | $x_7$ | $x_7$ | $x_7$ | 1 |

By the method presented in Theorem 7, where $a = x_3, b = x_7$, we can obtain an implication $\mathcal{R}^1_{R_1 R_2 R_3}$ on $L_1$ shown in Table 7.

**Table 7.** The implication $\mathcal{R}^1_{R_1R_2R_3}$ on $L_2$.

| $\mathcal{R}^1_{R_1R_2R_3}$ | $0$ | $x_1$ | $x_2$ | $x_3$ | $x_4$ | $x_5$ | $x_6$ | $x_7$ | $x_8$ | $x_9$ | $x_{10}$ | $x_{11}$ | $1$ |
|---|---|---|---|---|---|---|---|---|---|---|---|---|---|
| $0$ | $1$ | $1$ | $1$ | $1$ | $1$ | $1$ | $1$ | $1$ | $1$ | $1$ | $1$ | $1$ | $1$ |
| $x_1$ | $0$ | $x_3$ | $x_2$ | $x_3$ | $x_7$ | $x_7$ | $x_7$ | $x_7$ | $1$ | $1$ | $1$ | $1$ | $1$ |
| $x_2$ | $0$ | $x_2$ | $x_3$ | $x_3$ | $x_7$ | $x_7$ | $x_7$ | $x_7$ | $1$ | $1$ | $1$ | $1$ | $1$ |
| $x_3$ | $0$ | $0$ | $0$ | $x_3$ | $x_7$ | $x_7$ | $x_7$ | $x_7$ | $1$ | $1$ | $1$ | $1$ | $1$ |
| $x_4$ | $0$ | $0$ | $0$ | $0$ | $x_7$ | $x_5$ | $x_6$ | $x_7$ | $1$ | $1$ | $1$ | $1$ | $1$ |
| $x_5$ | $0$ | $0$ | $0$ | $0$ | $x_7$ | $x_7$ | $x_7$ | $x_7$ | $1$ | $1$ | $1$ | $1$ | $1$ |
| $x_6$ | $0$ | $0$ | $0$ | $0$ | $x_7$ | $x_5$ | $x_7$ | $x_7$ | $1$ | $1$ | $1$ | $1$ | $1$ |
| $x_7$ | $0$ | $0$ | $0$ | $0$ | $x_4$ | $x_5$ | $x_6$ | $x_7$ | $1$ | $1$ | $1$ | $1$ | $1$ |
| $x_8$ | $0$ | $0$ | $0$ | $0$ | $x_3$ | $x_3$ | $x_3$ | $x_3$ | $1$ | $1$ | $x_{10}$ | $1$ | $1$ |
| $x_9$ | $0$ | $0$ | $0$ | $0$ | $x_3$ | $x_3$ | $x_3$ | $x_3$ | $1$ | $1$ | $1$ | $1$ | $1$ |
| $x_{10}$ | $0$ | $0$ | $0$ | $0$ | $x_3$ | $x_3$ | $x_3$ | $x_3$ | $x_8$ | $1$ | $1$ | $1$ | $1$ |
| $x_{11}$ | $0$ | $0$ | $0$ | $0$ | $x_3$ | $x_3$ | $x_3$ | $x_3$ | $1$ | $x_9$ | $1$ | $1$ | $1$ |
| $1$ | $0$ | $0$ | $0$ | $0$ | $x_3$ | $x_3$ | $x_3$ | $x_3$ | $x_7$ | $x_7$ | $x_7$ | $x_7$ | $1$ |

*Remark 2.* Let the bounded lattice $(L_2, \leq, 0, 1)$ characterized by the Hasse diagram in Fig. 3, $T = T_\wedge$, $S = S_D$ and the implication $J^{x_3} = R_1$ shown in Table 4. Consider the negation $N = N_2$ shown in formula (9). We have $I_{x_3x_7}(x_4, x_4) = 1$ by applying the method presented in Theorem 3, where $a = x_3$, $b = x_7$. Also, we know $\mathcal{R}^1_{R_1R_2R_3}(x_4, x_4) = x_7$ from Table 7. Then, $\mathcal{R}^1_{R_1R_2R_3}$ and $I_{ab}$ may not be the same in general.

$$N_2(x) = \begin{cases} 0, & if\ x = 1 \\ 1, & if\ x = 0 \\ x_3, & \text{otherwise.} \end{cases} \tag{9}$$

In the following theorems, we present some construction methods for the implications, which are different from the method in Theorem 7. We do not include their proofs since they can be proven similarly to Theorem 7.

**Theorem 8.** *Let $(L, \leq, 0, 1)$ be a bounded lattice, $a, b \in L$ with $a \leq b$, $R_1 \in \mathcal{F}_{[0,a]}$, $R_2 \in \mathcal{F}_{[a,b]}$, $R_3 \in \mathcal{F}_{[b,1]}$ and define the binary operation $\mathcal{R}^2_{R_1R_2R_3} : L^2 \to L$ given, for all $x, y \in L$, as*

$$\mathcal{R}^2_{R_1R_2R_3}(x, y) = \begin{cases} R_1(x, y) & if\ (x, y) \in (0, a] \times [0, a], \\ 0 & if (x, y) \in (L \backslash [0, a]) \times [0, a], \\ a & if\ (x, y) \in ((b, 1] \cup I_b^a) \times (a, b] \cup (L \backslash \{0\}) \times (I_a^b \cup I_{a,b}), \\ R_2(x, y) & if\ (x, y) \in (a, b] \times (a, b], \\ R_3(x, y) & if\ (x, y) \in (b, 1] \times (b, 1], \\ b & if\ (x, y) \in ((0, a] \cup I_a^b \cup I_{a,b}) \times (a, b] \cup (L \backslash \{0\}) \times I_b^a, \\ 1 & if\ (x, y) \in \{0\} \times (L \backslash (b, 1]) \cup (L \backslash (b, 1]) \times (b, 1]. \end{cases} \tag{10}$$

*Then, $\mathcal{R}^2_{R_1R_2R_3} \in \mathcal{F}$.*

**Theorem 9.** *Let* $(L, \leq, 0, 1)$ *be a bounded lattice,* $a, b \in L$ *with* $a \leq b$, $R_1 \in \mathcal{F}_{[0,a]}$, $R_2 \in \mathcal{F}_{[a,b]}$, $R_3 \in \mathcal{F}_{[b,1]}$ *and define the binary operation* $\mathcal{R}^3_{R_1R_2R_3} : L^2 \to L$ *given, for all* $x, y \in L$, *as*

$$\mathcal{R}^3_{R_1R_2R_3}(x,y) = \begin{cases} R_1(x,y) & \text{if } (x,y) \in (0,a] \times [0,a], \\ 0 & \text{if} (x,y) \in (L \backslash [0,a]) \times [0,a], \\ a & \text{if } (x,y) \in ((b,1] \cup I^a_b \cup I_{a,b}) \times (a,b] \cup (L \backslash \{0\}) \times I^b_a, \\ R_2(x,y) & \text{if } (x,y) \in (a,b] \times (a,b], \\ R_3(x,y) & \text{if } (x,y) \in (b,1] \times (b,1], \\ b & \text{if } (x,y) \in ((0,a] \cup I^b_a) \times (a,b] \cup (L \backslash \{0\}) \times (I^a_b \cup I_{a,b}), \\ 1 & \text{if } (x,y) \in \{0\} \times (L \backslash (b,1]) \cup (L \backslash (b,1]) \times (b,1]. \end{cases} \tag{11}$$

*Then,* $\mathcal{R}^3_{R_1R_2R_3} \in \mathcal{F}$.

**Theorem 10.** *Let* $(L, \leq, 0, 1)$ *be a bounded lattice,* $a, b \in L$ *with* $a \leq b$, $R_1 \in \mathcal{F}_{[0,a]}$, $R_2 \in \mathcal{F}_{[a,b]}$, $R_3 \in \mathcal{F}_{[b,1]}$ *and define the binary operation* $\mathcal{R}^4_{R_1R_2R_3} : L^2 \to L$ *given, for all* $x, y \in L$, *as*

$$\mathcal{R}^4_{R_1R_2R_3}(x,y) = \begin{cases} R_1(x,y) & \text{if } (x,y) \in (0,a] \times [0,a], \\ 0 & \text{if} (x,y) \in (L \backslash [0,a]) \times [0,a], \\ a & \text{if } (x,y) \in ((b,1] \cup I^a_b) \times (a,b] \cup (L \backslash \{0\}) \times I^b_a, \\ R_2(x,y) & \text{if } (x,y) \in (a,b] \times (a,b], \\ R_3(x,y) & \text{if } (x,y) \in (b,1] \times (b,1], \\ b & \text{if } (x,y) \in ((0,a] \cup I^b_a \cup I_{a,b}) \times (a,b] \cup (L \backslash \{0\}) \times (I^a_b \cup I_{a,b}), \\ 1 & \text{if } (x,y) \in \{0\} \times (L \backslash (b,1]) \cup (L \backslash (b,1]) \times (b,1]. \end{cases} \tag{12}$$

*Then,* $\mathcal{R}^4_{R_1R_2R_3} \in \mathcal{F}$.

## 4 Conclusions

In this paper, several construction methods of fuzzy implications on bounded lattices are presented. We started investigating a construction method for fuzzy implications on a bounded lattice $L$ base on two implications on sub-intervals of the bounded lattice $L$. Then, by modifying the result, we obtained another two methods. Furthermore, we generated the construction methods applying on three implications on sub-intervals of the lattice. In our future work, we also hope that we will obtain ordinal sum construction method of fuzzy implications by finite number or countably infinite number of fuzzy implications on sub-intervals of the lattices.

## References


1. Neres, F., Bedregal, B., Santiago, R.: Bi-aggregated contrapositivisation: a new contrapositivisation technique for fuzzy implications. Fuzzy Sets Syst. **466**, 108427 (2023)
2. Karaçal, F., Kesicioğlu, M.N., Ertuğrul, Ü.: The implications obtained by two given implications on bounded lattices. Int. J. Gen. Syst. **50**(3), 281–299 (2021)
3. Karaçal, F., Karacair, K.: Some implication operators on bounded lattices. Int. J. Gen. Syst. **53**(7–8), 898–927 (2024)

4. Birkhoff, G.: Lattice Theory. American Mathematical Society Colloquium Publishers, Providence (1967)
5. Frazao, H., Santiago, L., Pinheiro, J., Milfont, T., Canuto, A.: Two classes of ordinal sum implications. Comput. Appl. Math. **43**, 220 (2024)
6. Baczyński, M., Jayaram, B.: Fuzzy Implications, Studies in Fuzziness and Soft Computing, vol. 231. Springer, Heidelberg (2008)
7. Kesicioğlu, M.N., Ertuğrul, Ü., Karaçal, F.: Generalized convex combination of implications on bounded lattices. Iran. J. Fuzzy Syst. **17**(6), 75–91 (2020)
8. Klement, E.P., Mesiar, R., Pap, E.: Triangular Norms. Kluwer Academic Publishers, Dordrecht (2000)
9. Baczyński, M., Drygaś, P., Krśol, A., Mesiar, R.: New types of ordinal sum of fuzzy implications. In: 2017 IEEE International Conference on Fuzzy Systems (FUZZ-IEEE), Naples, Italy (2017). https://doi.org/10.1109/FUZZ-IEEE.2017.8015700
10. Su, Y., Xie, A., Liu, H.: On ordinal sum implications. Inf. Sci. **293**(6), 251–262 (2015)

# Idea Management and Game Theory with Uncertain Payoffs

Inese Bula[1,2](✉), Elīna Miķelsone[3], Līga Peiseniece[3], Astrīda Rijkure[4], Aivars Spilbergs[3], and Inga Uvarova[3]

[1] Faculty of Science and Technology, University of Latvia, Jelgavas Street 3, Riga 1004, Latvia
inese.bula@lu.lv
[2] Institute of Mathematics and Computer Science, University of Latvia, Raina bulv. 29, Riga 1048, Latvia
[3] BA School of Business and Finance, K. Valdemara Street 161, Riga 1013, Latvia
{elina.mikelsone,liga.peiseniece,aivars.spilbergs,inga.uvarova}@ba.lv
[4] Faculty of Economics and Social Sciences, University of Latvia, Aspazijas bulv. 5, Riga 1050, Latvia
astrida.rijkure@lu.lv

**Abstract.** Idea management is a system that helps to generate, develop, and implement ideas. Organizations usually use idea management systems to supplement their innovation management processes. Idea management takes place at the forefront of innovation management. One of the stages of the idea management process is the acceptance and rejection of ideas. Idea generators (e.g., employees of Company X) and idea acceptors (e.g., managers of Company X) can be seen as two players with potentially different opinions. The payoffs of these players are uncertain, so the decision to accept or reject an idea can be made in various ways. In this article, we outline a possible solution using bimatrix games or extensive form games.

**Keywords:** Idea management · Normal-form game · Extensive-form game · Nash equilibrium · Uncertain payoff

## 1 Introduction

Game theory studies situations of competition and cooperation between several involved parties by using mathematical methods [13]. Game theory is a branch of applied mathematics that provides tools for analyzing situations in which parties, called players, make decisions that are interdependent. This interdependence causes each player to consider the other player's possible decisions, or strategies, in formulating strategy. A solution to a game describes the optimal decisions of the players, who may have similar, opposed, or mixed interests, and the outcomes that may result from these decisions. You can read about various aspects of game theory at [1,4,8,12,13].


M. Baczyński et al. (Eds.): EUSFLAT 2025, LNCS 15884, pp. 134–145, 2025.
https://doi.org/10.1007/978-3-031-97228-7_12

Game theory has a wide range of applications in economics, in social problems research, in political voting systems, in computer science (see [4]). Game theory was developed extensively in the 1950s. The notable works of John Nash [10] and [11] on the existence of equilibrium also belong to this time period. Many Nobel prizes in economics have been awarded for achievements in game theory. In 1994, Nash was awarded the Nobel Prize in Economics.

Review [14] suggests that game theory is a very useful tool for modelling project management scenarios. In this article, we will try to apply game theory concepts to the analysis of idea management.

Idea management focuses primarily on creating, developing, and implementing ideas. The aim is to create value from these ideas and turn them into reality [16]. The term idea management is sometimes confused with innovation management. Innovation management is the process through which an organization manages and implements innovation. Idea management, on the other hand, is a sub-process of innovation management. It is a system that helps to generate, develop, and implement ideas. Organizations usually use idea management systems to supplement their innovation management processes. Idea management takes place at the forefront of innovation management [16].

One of the stages of the idea management process is the acceptance and rejection of ideas (see Fig. 3 below). Idea generators and idea acceptors can be considered as two players. They may have common goals, but they may also have different opinions. The payoffs of these players are generally uncertain. In this article, we will develop a possible solution for decision making with bimatrix games or with extensive form games.

The paper is organized as follows. In Sect. 2, we first provide some concepts, definitions, and theorems from game theory that are used throughout the paper. In Sect. 3, we introduce the possibilities of analyzing idea management with game theory tools that include uncertain payoffs functions. Finally, we provide some conclusions, remarks, and ideas for future work.

## 2 Some Definitions and Results from Game Theory

Game theory can be viewed as a mathematical modelling of strategic interactions, making it one of the most powerful analytical tools in economics, especially microeconomics, and in the social sciences. Game theory can offer guidance to decision makers and help develop and implement effective strategies. In this chapter, we will describe the game theory concepts and results that we will use later in the article.

Let $N = \{1, 2, ..., n\}$ be the finite set of players. Each player $i \in N$ has a pure strategy (activities) set $S_i$. In general case, the sets $S_i$ may possess any structure (a finite set of elements, a subset of $\mathbf{R}^n$, etc.). As a result, player $i$ obtain the payoffs $u_i$.

**Definition 1 ([4,8]).** *A normal-form game is an object*

$$\Gamma = \{N, S_1, ..., S_n, u_1, ..., u_n\},$$

*where $S_i$ designates the sets of strategies of players $i \in N$ and $u_i$ indicates their payoff functions, $u_i : S = S_1 \times S_2 \times ... \times S_n \to \mathbf{R}$, $i \in N$.*

We define the strategies that maximize a player's payoff, while fixing the combination of all other players' strategies. $s_i \in S_i$ denotes one strategy of player $i$, while $s_{-i} \in S_{-i} = S_1 \times S_2 \times ... \times S_{i-1} \times S_{i+1} \times ... \times S_n$ represents one strategy combination from all other players without player $i$.

**Definition 2** ([1,4,8,13]). *A strategy combination $(s_1^*, s_2^*, ..., s_n^*) \in S$ is a Nash equilibrium if, for any player $i \in N$*

$$\forall s_i \in S_i \quad u_i(s_i^*, s_{-i}^*) \geq u_i(s_i, s_{-i}^*).$$

Nash equilibrium is one of the possible solutions in games. Nash equilibrium does not exist in all normal-form games.

*Example 1.* Let's look at a two-player normal-form two games, illustrated by a payoff bimatrices in Table 1a) and b).

**Table 1.** Payoff bimatrices of Example 1: a) two Nash equilibria, b) there is no Nash equilibrium.

a)

| | $s_{21}$ | $s_{22}$ |
|---|---|---|
| $s_{11}$ | $(3,4)$ | $(\mathbf{5},\mathbf{5})$ |
| $s_{12}$ | $(\mathbf{4},\mathbf{4})$ | $(3,3)$ |

b)

| | $s_{21}$ | $s_{22}$ |
|---|---|---|
| $s_{11}$ | $(4,4)$ | $(3,5)$ |
| $s_{12}$ | $(3,4)$ | $(5,3)$ |

In both cases, player 1 has two strategies $s_{11}$ and $s_{12}$, while player 2 has two strategies $s_{21}$ and $s_{22}$. The games differ in that for player 1, the payoffs of strategies $s_{11}$ and $s_{12}$ in Table 1b) are swapped compared to Table 1a). In the first case, there are two Nash equilibria $(s_{12}, s_{21})$ and $(s_{11}, s_{22})$, but in the case of Table 1b), no Nash equilibrium exists. ■

In normal-form games, it is assumed that each player chooses his own strategy regardless of the opponent's choice and tries to maximize his payoff. However, it should be noted that the payoff of any player depends on both his strategy and the opponent's strategy. But there are games in which players can move sequentially and observe or partially observe each other's activities. Such situations are better modeled by so-called extensive-form games.

**Definition 3** ([8]). *An extensive-form game with complete information is a pair $\Delta = \{N, G\}$, where $N = \{1, 2, ..., n\}$ indicates the set of players and $G = \{X, Z\}$ represents a directed graph without cycles (a finite tree) having the initial node $x_0$, the set of nodes (positions) $X$ and $Z(x)$ as the set of nodes directly following node $x$.*

Figure 1 demonstrates the tree of such a game with the initial state $x_0$ and two players. At the initial node $x_0$, player 1 makes his move $s_{11}$ or $s_{12}$. Then, at nodes $A$ and $B$, player 2 makes a move. After player 2's move, the game ends. One of the terminal nodes with the corresponding payoff vector has been reached - the first coordinate is the payoff for player 1, the second coordinate is the payoff for player 2.

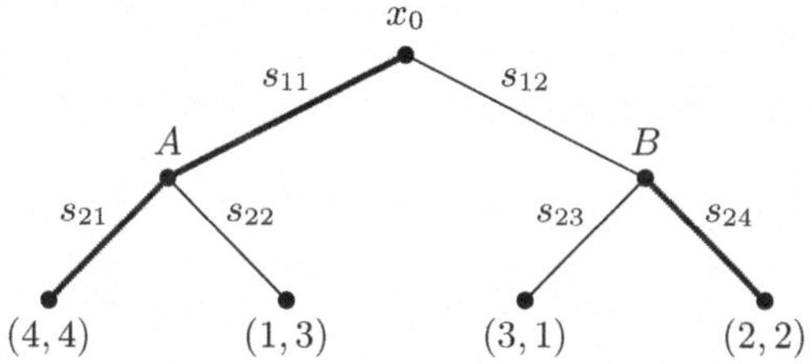


**Fig. 1.** The tree of an extensive-form game $\Delta$ with complete information.

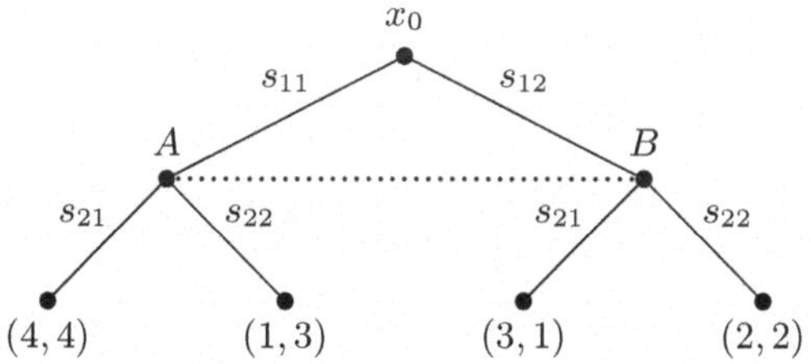


**Fig. 2.** The tree of an extensive-form game $\Delta$ with imperfect information.

The notion of information sets are used to model imperfect information. In the present example in Fig. 1 the game is with complete information - both players know each other's moves and possible order, and know the payoff vectors. Imperfect (incomplete) information can occur if a player does not observe another player's move or has forgotten his previous moves. Figure 2 player 2 does not know what move player 1 has made. For nodes A and B to be truly undecidable for player 2, the possible moves at both nodes must be the same. In that case, player 2 has two actions, namely $s_{21}$ and $s_{22}$. We call the two connected nodes an information set of player 2. If the game is with complete information, then all the players' information sets consist of a single node. In Fig. 1 player 2 has two information sets, but in Fig. 2 only one information set.

In a game in extensive-form, it is extremely important to distinguish between actions and strategies. An action is a possible move of a player at an information set. In the game in Fig. 1 player 1 has the actions $s_{11}$ and $s_{12}$ and player 2 has the actions $s_{21}$ and $s_{22}$, and $s_{23}$ and $s_{24}$. Player 1's strategies match his actions because player 1 only has to make a move in one node. Player 2 has to take actions at two nodes, so he comes up with a plan in advance of what he will do at each node if he gets there. He has 4 strategies $s_{21}s_{23}$, $s_{21}s_{24}$, $s_{22}s_{23}$ and $s_{22}s_{24}$.

**Definition 4** ([13]). *A strategy of player is a list of actions, exactly one at each information set of that player.*

In games of complete information extensive-form, the solution can be found by backward induction. First, all terminal nodes with payoff vectors are considered from the point of view of the player who had the last chance to make a move. In the case of Fig. 1, this is player 2. At each node available to him (here $A$ and $B$), player 2 evaluates the move that gives the greater payoff: at node $A$ it is $s_{21}$ and at node $B$ it is $s_{24}$ (see Fig. 1 bold lines). This means that player 1 has the opportunity to achieve only the payoff vectors $(4, 4)$ and $(2, 2)$. Since $4 > 2$, player 1 makes move $s_{11}$. We have obtained the solution of the game $(s_{11}, s_{21}s_{24})$.

But in a game like Fig. 2 the Nash equilibrium cannot be found by backward induction. In extensive-form games with incomplete information with 2 players, a reduction to a bimatrix game is required.

**Theorem 1** ([1]). *For any finite extensive-form game $\Delta$ of complete information, the solution by backward induction is a Nash equilibrium of $\Delta$.*

If it is necessary to find all Nash equilibria in an extensive-form game, then one can construct a payoff bimatrix. This is convenient for two or three players with a small number of actions, but in the general case one must analyze the game tree itself.

## 3 Game Theory Application to Idea Management

Idea management is generally a long and time-consuming process. However, in all cases, one of the stages of the idea management process is the acceptance and rejection of ideas (see generic model of the idea management process in Fig. 3). Idea generators and idea acceptors can be considered as two players with possibly different opinions.

Let us assume in the simplest case that player 1 - the idea generator - has created two ideas. The task of player 2 - the idea acceptor - is to evaluate the created ideas. We will assume here that player 2 always has only two strategies: accepted ideas and rejected ideas. The situation 'deferred ideas' (see Fig. 3) is considered as a case when an idea is accepted or rejected, but is not possible separately.

The evaluation of an idea by the generator and the acceptor may differ. Moreover, when proposing or rejecting an idea, it has not yet been implemented, and it is not known exactly how much benefit it will bring. Both players can make

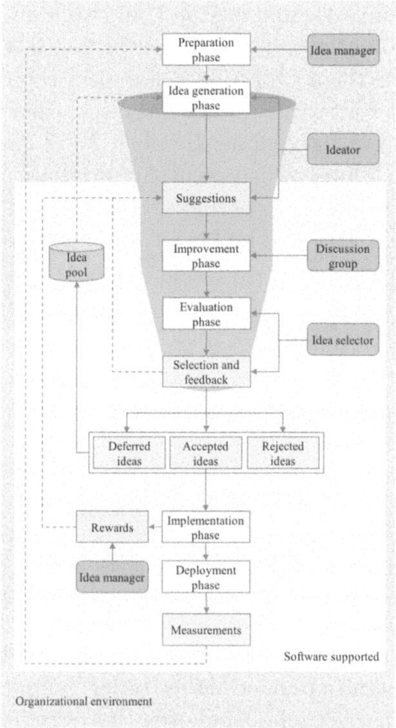


**Fig. 3.** Generic model of the idea management process (figure from [3]).

assessments from their positions in all four cases (idea 1, accept), (idea 1, reject), (idea 2, accept), (idea 2, reject). Usually the evaluation is a number, for example, profit. But it can also be a moral satisfaction expressed on some numerical scale, for example, between 0 and 100. It is quite logical that in both cases, if we apply it to idea management, the payoff will be imprecise and at best can be assessed from above and below. As a result, we can write the payoff as an interval, see Table 2.

**Table 2.** Bimatrix game with interval payoffs.

| | $s_{21}$ - accept | $s_{22}$ - reject |
|---|---|---|
| $s_{11}$ - idea 1 | $([\underline{a_1}, \overline{a_1}], [\underline{a_2}, \overline{a_2}])$ | $[\underline{b_1}, \overline{b_1}], [\underline{b_2}, \overline{b_2}]$ |
| $s_{12}$ - idea 2 | $[\underline{c_1}, \overline{c_1}], [\underline{c_2}, \overline{c_2}]$ | $[\underline{d_1}, \overline{d_1}], [\underline{d_2}, \overline{d_2}]$ |

In [6], authors developed a methodology for solving two-person zero-sum games where the payoffs were expressed with intervals (i.e., data having lower and upper bounds), see also [5]. Two-person non-zero sum game under interval and unknown payoffs is investigated in [15]. Unfortunately, we have not yet found a way to interpret the potential solution. However, successful interpretations with interval data using game theory have been found in the papers [2,17].

If each player's payoff intervals do not intersect, then the given game can be considered an ordinary bimatrix game. If it is a $2 \times 2$ game, then four different numbers assigned to each interval in ascending order are sufficient. On the other hand, if the intervals are intersect, perhaps writing down the payoffs in interval form wasn't the best idea. It would be better to immediately arrange all possible events in a certain order from least desirable to most desirable and attach certain different numbers from smallest to largest to this arrangement. As a result, obtain a payoff bimatrix as shown in Table 3.

**Table 3.** Payoff bimatrix, $a_1 > c_1$, $a_2 > b_2$.

| | $s_{21}$ - accept | $s_{22}$ - reject |
|---|---|---|
| $s_{11}$ - idea 1 | $(\mathbf{a_1}, \mathbf{a_2})$ | $(b_1, b_2)$ |
| $s_{12}$ - idea 2 | $(c_1, c_2)$ | $(d_1, d_2)$ |

It would be reasonable to assume that one of the ideas, say the first one, from player 1 (idea generator) has a higher order value than the other idea, so $a_1 > c_1$. If player 2 (idea acceptor) believes that accepting this 1st idea gives a greater payoff than rejecting it, then $a_2 > b_2$, and a single Nash equilibrium $(s_{11}, s_{21})$ is formed. However, this does not correspond to the idea management model, where one should accept both ideas, reject both, or accept one and reject the other. In principle, this means that in a bimatrix game two Nash equilibria would be desirable and both of them are achieved, for example, it could look like this (Table 4):

**Table 4.** Payoff bimatrix with two Nash equilibria.

| | $s_{21}$ - accept | $s_{22}$ - reject |
|---|---|---|
| $s_{11}$ - idea 1 | $(\mathbf{4}, \mathbf{4})$ | $(1, 3)$ |
| $s_{12}$ - idea 2 | $(3, 1)$ | $(\mathbf{2}, \mathbf{2})$ |

Classically, a bimatrix game means that both players choose one strategy from their strategy set and it is played simultaneously. In practice, it is a game with incomplete information - although both players know the payoff matrix, the choice of strategies is unknown. If we allow for the possibility that after generating ideas, both player 1 and player 2 independently create their own payoff matrix and then a joint bimatrix is created, then we can probably find the Nash equilibrium of the game as the best solution. Unfortunately, Nash equilibrium does not exist in all bimatrix games.

A better interpretation of the idea management model could be achieved with the extensive-form game with complete information, because then there exists at least one Nash equilibrium, which can be found by backward induction (Theorem 1). The extensive-form game tree includes time dynamics. Only when ideas are generated (and a payoff is attached to them from the generator's side) does the company's management begin evaluating them and make a decision to accept or reject them.

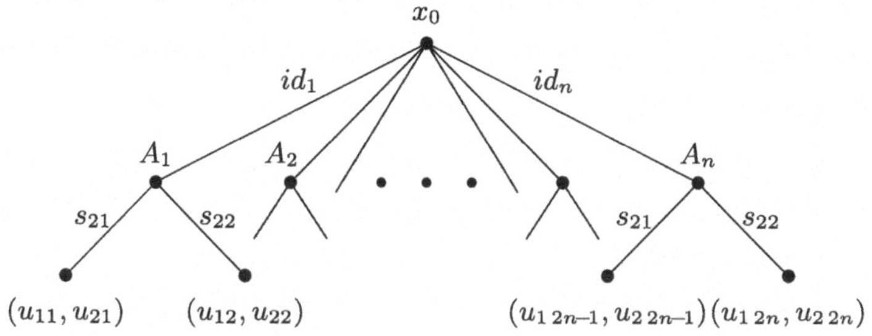


**Fig. 4.** The tree of an extensive-form game with $n$ ideas.

Figure 4 shows a game tree in which the idea generator offers $n$ ideas (strategies $id_i$, $i = 1, ..., n$) and each of the ideas in nodes $A_i$, $i = 1, ..., n$, is reviewed by the idea acceptor, making move $s_{21}$ - accept or move $s_{22}$ - reject.

The normal-form game, whose payoff bimatrix was given in Table 4, corresponds to the extensive-form game tree in Fig. 2. It is a game with imperfect information. If we assume that for player 2, nodes $A$ and $B$ each have their own information set, then we obtain a complete information game as in Fig. 1. By backward induction, we obtain only one Nash equilibrium $(s_{11}, s_{21}s_{24})$ with the payoff vector $(4, 4)$. Since there is no correct correspondence with Table 4, the second Nash equilibrium from the extensive-form is not obtained.

The idea acceptor's choice of move at node $A_i$ depends on his perceptions of the payoff of the $i$-th idea, accepting or rejecting this idea. Theoretically, it can be assumed that the payoff of rejection is 0, but the payoff of acceptance can be both a positive and a negative number. In the case of a positive number, the idea is accepted, and in the case of a negative number - rejected. A positive number interprets a good idea, the implementation of which, from the idea acceptor's point of view, will bring benefits to the company, while a negative number interprets an idea, the implementation of which, from the idea acceptor's point of view, will bring losses to the company. If the payoff of acceptance is 0, then an unequivocal decision on acceptance or rejection of the idea is not made with regard to the specific idea. To avoid such a situation, the acceptor of ideas must express an opinion about each idea: a positive number - it is accepted, a negative number - the idea is rejected. This number is recorded as the payoff of player 2 when performing the action 'accept'. But for the action 'reject', the payoff is the number 0. When performing backward induction, if the acceptance evaluation is a negative number, a rational player will choose payoff 0, which corresponds to rejecting the idea.

The idea generator may have a completely different opinion about the payoffs of ideas. Here too, it can be assumed that the payoff of rejecting an idea is 0. But since the idea is offered, the payoff of accepting it will always be positive. It is possible that the payoff is an unspecified quantity. To make a decision about which ideas will actually be implemented, it is enough for the idea generator to be able to arrange the proposed ideas in a strict order from their point of view with the least payoff to the idea with the greatest payoff.

Under the described conditions, if the idea acceptor has placed a positive payoff on at least one idea, a Nash equilibrium will be obtained in the extensive-form game that will result in one feasible idea.

*Example 2.* We illustrate the described situation with an example. We assume that the idea generator offers 4 ideas, in his opinion the values of the payoff function $u_1$ are as follows

$$u_1(id_1) = 1 < u_1(id_2) = 2 < u_1(id_3) = 3 < u_1(u_4) = 4.$$

The opinion of the idea acceptor, on the other hand, is as follows

$$u_2(id_1) = -1,\ u_2(id_2) = 2,\ u_2(id_3) = 3,\ u_1(u_4) = 1.$$

Figure 5 shows a game tree for this situation.

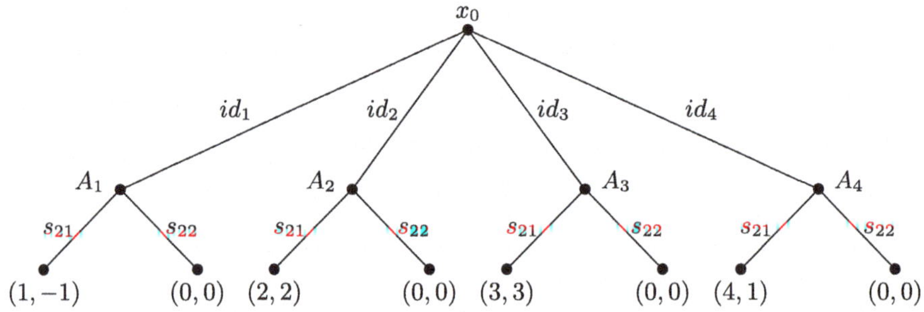


**Fig. 5.** The tree of an extensive-form game with 4 ideas.

Figure 6 shows how to find the Nash equilibrium by backward induction. First, the idea acceptor (player 2) rejects idea 1 (actions $s_{22}$ in node $A_1$), but accepts (actions $s_{21}$ in nodes $A_2$, $A_3$ and $A_4$) the other three. The idea generator (player 1) then compares the potential payoffs 0, 2, 3, 4 and chooses the move that gives him the greatest payoff, which is $id_4$. A Nash equilibrium $(id_4, s_{22}s_{21}s_{21}s_{21})$ with the payoff vector $(4, 1)$ is obtained.

The result obtained in this case is a Nash equilibrium that is the most desirable idea from the idea generator's side, but the least desirable idea accepted by the idea acceptor. ■

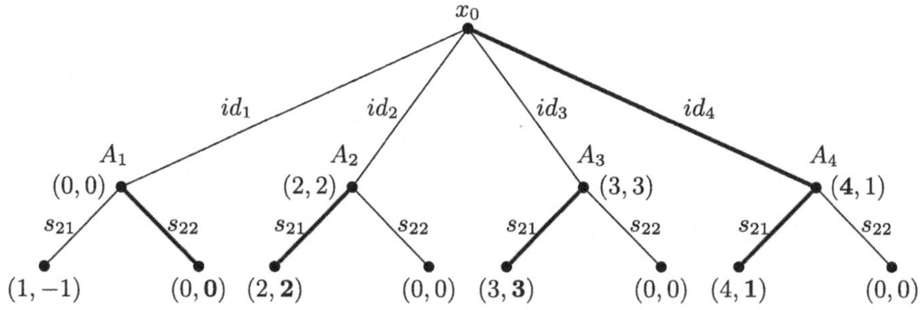


**Fig. 6.** Finding Nash equilibrium.

From Example 2 and the proposed description of the extensive-form game application in idea management, it follows that

1) provided that at least once the idea acceptor has chosen to accept the action, there exists a Nash equilibrium with the proposed idea;
2) if the idea acceptor has accepted $m$ of ideas, but can only implement $k$, where $k < m$, then of the $m$ accepted ideas, those $k$ ideas that have the largest payoff from the idea generator should be implemented.

The conclusion for the second case can be obtained inductively, by first removing the branch from the game tree whose idea is accepted for implementation. And this can continue until $k$ ideas are found for implementation.

This article contributes to the discussion of Lozano [7] that applied game theory tools—such as the Prisoner's Dilemma, Tragedy of the Commons, and Nash Equilibrium—to illustrate how cooperation leads to better long-term outcomes. While our research contributes with the demonstration of how strategic decision-making under uncertainty can influence long-term business and innovation strategies and the idea management. A key addition to earlier research is the role of uncertainty in decision-making. The uncertain payoff structures explored provide a more nuanced view of collaboration, highlighting that players may not always have full information about the potential benefits of cooperative sustainability efforts. It can be suggested that collaborative decision-making processes can be structured through iterative game-theoretic frameworks.

## 4 Conclusion

In game theory, it is usually assumed that a single solution is realized in a given game. This article presents the idea that the solution is obtained by constructing, for example, a payoff bimatrix and analysing all Nash equilibrium—ideally, two equilibrium in a $2 \times 2$ game. A bimatrix game is essentially a game with imperfect information, as it assumes that players make their moves simultaneously. However, this approach is not suitable for the idea management model.

In contrast, in extensive-form games, a decision must be made for each subgame, and the resulting Nash equilibrium will provide a more accurate description of the desired situation. In games of complete information extensive-form, at least one Nash equilibrium will always be found. Even if the game has more levels than the cases considered in this article, at least one Nash equilibrium will be obtained, which can potentially give a feasible idea.

From a mathematical standpoint our research highlights how game theory can be applied to decision-making under uncertainty. The study utilises bimatrix games and extensive-form games to model interactions between idea generators and idea acceptors. The research highlights the limitations of normal-form games, which assume simultaneous decisions with fixed payoffs, and suggests that extensive-form games provide a more accurate representation of idea management processes by incorporating sequential decision-making and uncertain payoffs. The application of extensive-form games aligns well with agile innovation processes, where iterative decision-making allows firms to adjust strategies dynamically. The study also illustrates the use of backward induction as a method to derive optimal strategies, ensuring rational decision-making despite the presence of uncertainty.

From an innovation management and business strategy perspective, the study provides valuable insights into the strategic acceptance and rejection of ideas within organisations. It frames idea evaluation as a competitive yet cooperative process, where different stakeholders (idea generators and evaluators-acceptors) have differing incentives and uncertain outcomes. By incorporating game theory, the paper offers a structured method for decision-makers to optimise the selection process of innovative ideas.

This research contributes to multidisciplinary knowledge by bridging game theory, innovation and idea management. It demonstrates that the mathematical rigor rigour of game theory can be effectively integrated into managerial decision-making in business environments when considerinf considering new ideas and innovation. Moreover, by focusing on uncertainty in payoffs, it extends traditional economics and decision-making models to accommodate subjective and evolving preferences, making it relevant for fields such as innovation and entrepreneurship studies.

One of the key digital tools supporting companies in their idea management efforts is web-based idea management systems. The study by [9] shows how companies can leverage the benefits of platforms, such as web-based idea management systems, to achieve superior quality and quantity of ideas generated from stakeholders involved in these platform ecosystems. In future research, we could investigate whether the final decisions in web-based idea management systems are in accordance with the Nash equilibrium of idea generators and idea acceptors.

A future research direction may involve the integration of two key perspectives—leveraging game theory (for example, Bayesian games) to enhance sustainability initiatives while extending its application to innovation and strategic decision-making under uncertainty. Such a comprehensive framework would facilitate a more robust modeling of the interplay between innovation management, collaboration, and sustainability. Further attention should be given to applying uncertain payoff structures to real-world sustainability initiatives, ensuring that both short-term and long-term sustainability benefits and impacts are adequately considered.

**Acknowledgments.** The research is financed by the Recovery and Resilience Facility project "Internal and External Consolidation of the University of Latvia" (No. 5.2.1.1.i. 0/2/24/I/CFLA/007), Grant No. LU-BA-PA-2024/1-0036 "Sustainable Idea management".

**Disclosure of Interests.** The authors have no competing interests to declare that are relevant to the content of this article.

## References

1. Fujiwara-Greve, T.: Non-Cooperative Game Theory. Monographs in Mathematical Economics, vol. 1. Springer Japan (2015)
2. Huang, Y., He, X., Dai, Y., Wang, Y.-M.: Hybrid game cross efficiency evaluation models based on interval data: a case of forest carbon sequestration. Expert Syst. Appl. **204**, 117521, 14 p (2022)
3. Gerlach, S., Brem, A.: Idea management revisited: a review of the literature and guide for implementation. Int. J. Innov. Stud. **1**, 144–161 (2017)
4. Laraki, R., Renault, J., Sorin, S.: Mathematical Foundations of Game Theory. Universitext, Springer Nature Switzerland AG (2019)
5. Li, D.F., Nan, J.X., Zhang, M.J.: Interval programming models for matrix games with interval payoffs. Optim. Methods Softw. **27**(1), 1–16 (2012)
6. Liu, S.T., Kao, C.: Matrix games with interval data. Comput. Ind. Eng. **56**(4), 1697–1700 (2009)
7. Lozano, R.: Collaboration as a pathway for sustainability. Sustain. Dev. **15**(6), 370–381 (2007)
8. Mazalov, V.: Mathematical Game Theory and Applications. Wiley (2014)
9. Mikelsone, E., Segers, J.P., Spilbergs, A.: Governance of web-based idea management system rewards: from the perspective of open innovation. J. Open Innov. Technol. Market Complexity **8**(2), 1–28 (2022)
10. Nash, J.: Equilibrium points in n-person games. Proc. Natl. Acad. Sci. **36**(1), 48–49 (1950)
11. Nash, J.: Non-cooperative games. Ann. Math. **54**, 286–295 (1951)
12. Osborne, M.J.: An Introduction to Game Theory. Oxford University Press (2003)
13. Peters, H.: Game Theory. A Multi-Leveled Approach. Springer Texts in Business and Economics, 2nd edn. Springer, Heidelberg (2015)
14. Piraveenan, M.: Applications of game theory in project management: a structured review and analysis. Mathematics (MDPI) **7**(9), 858, 31 p (2019)
15. Sohraiee, S., Lotfi, F.H., Anisi, M.: Two person games with interval data. Appl. Math. Sci. **4**(28), 1355–1365 (2010)
16. What is Idea Management and How to Do It? Blog in ORCHIDEA. https://info.orchidea.dev/innovation-blog/what-is-idea-management-and-how-to-do-it#process. Accessed 17 Feb 2025
17. Zhang, Q., Shu, L., Jiang, B.: Moran process in evolutionary game dynamics with interval payoffs and its application. Appl. Math. Comput. **446**, 127875, 16 p (2023)

# On Direct Systems of Implications with Graded Attributes

Manuel Ojeda-Hernández[1(✉)] and Domingo López-Rodríguez[2]

[1] Department of Computing Science, Umeå University, Umeå, Sweden
manueloh@cs.umu.se

[2] Depto. de Matemática Aplicada, Universidad de Málaga, Andalucía Tech, 29071 Málaga, Spain
dominlopez@uma.es

**Abstract.** In this paper the problem of defining direct systems of implications in the fuzzy setting is studied. The directness of systems allows a quick computation of the closure operator in cases such as Fuzzy Formal Concept Analysis. Characterizing these properties in algebraic terms is deeply linked to Simplification Logic. After the theoretical results, some thoughts on algorithms to provide direct systems are also considered.

**Keywords:** Fuzzy Formal Concept Analysis · Bases of implications · Simplification Logic

## 1 Introduction

Functional dependences, Horn clauses and implications play the role of if-then rules in different fields of mathematics, namely Relational Databases, Logic Programming and Formal Concept Analysis.

Formal Concept Analysis was introduced by Wille [20] in the eighties as a mathematical tool to store, manage and represent knowledge stored in relational data tables. Nevertheless, it is natural that some attributes can be neither true or false but allow some graduality. For instance, in a medical database, a patient can have a low, medium, high or very high fever. Thus, fuzzy Formal Concept Analysis (FFCA) was introduced, first by Burusco and Fuentes-González [8] where the set of truth values was a lattice, and then by Pollandt [17] and Bělohlávek [2,3], whose works focus on the use of a complete residuated lattice as the set of truth-values.

Computing the closure of an element via an implicational system is an iterative procedure that runs until a fixed point is reached [12]. Due to this iteration, two lines of research arise naturally: one being the study of which properties ensure that bases have as few implications as possible, these studies involve research on pseudointents and quasi-closed elements [13,15,19]; the other studies implicational systems that need only one iteration to compute the closure, the so-called direct systems [6,18]. This paper follows the latter.


M. Baczyński et al. (Eds.): EUSFLAT 2025, LNCS 15884, pp. 146–157, 2025.
https://doi.org/10.1007/978-3-031-97228-7_13

Despite the increase of computational complexity in the fuzzy setting and the amount of work done on the first line of research [4,5,15,16,19], there are few contributions on direct systems in the fuzzy setting. In this line we highlight the work of [10], which opened the field. Intuitively, even if direct systems are larger than the stem or Duquenne-Guigues basis, the implicational system computation is done all at once and from that point on closure computation is almost immediate. In cases where several closures have to be computed, direct systems arise as a suitable option.

In this paper, we present the definition of direct system of implications in the fuzzy setting. This property is characterized in algebraic terms and an algorithm to compute a direct system of implications from a complete system of implications is provided.

## 2 Preliminaries

In this section we will recall the notions needed to follow the results of the paper, which encompass FFCA, Fuzzy Attribute Simplification Logic and direct implicational systems.

### 2.1 Fuzzy Formal Concept Analysis

A fuzzy formal context is a tuple $\mathbb{K} = (G, M, I)$ where G and M are non-empty sets of objects and attributes, respectively and $I\colon G \times M \to L$ is a fuzzy relation between objects and attributes.

In this setting, $I(g, m)$ represents the degree to which object $g$ satisfies attribute $m$. For fuzzy sets of objects and attributes $X \in L^G, Y \in L^M$ we define the concept-forming operators $^{\uparrow}\colon L^G \to L^M$, $^{\downarrow}\colon L^M \to L^G$ by

$$X^{\uparrow}(m) = \bigwedge_{g\in G} X(g) \to I(g, m),$$

$$Y^{\downarrow}(g) = \bigwedge_{m\in M} Y(m) \to I(g, m).$$

These mappings form a fuzzy Galois connection and, as a consequence, both compositions $^{\uparrow\downarrow}$ and $^{\downarrow\uparrow}$ are closure operators. A pair $(A, B) \in L^G \times L^M$ is said to be a formal concept if $A^{\uparrow} = B$ and $B^{\downarrow} = A$. The set of all formal concepts is in fact a complete lattice, the so-called concept lattice. In FFCA there are two main knowledge structures, one is the already mentioned concept lattice and the other is the set of valid attribute implications.

An attribute implication is an expression of the form $A \to B$, read "$A$ implies $B$", where $A, B \in L^M$. An implication $A \to B$ is said to be valid if $B \subseteq A^{\downarrow\uparrow}$.

### 2.2 Fuzzy Attribute Simplification Logic

A fuzzy set $X \in L^M$ is said to be a model of an implication $A \to B$ if

$$\|A \to B\|_X = S(A, X) \to S(B, X) = 1.$$

The set of all models is denoted by $Mod(A \to B)$. A set of implications $T$ is called a theory. The models of $T$, denoted by $Mod(T)$ is a system of fuzzy sets defined by

$$Mod(T) = \{X \in L^M : \|A \to B\|_X = 1 \text{ for all } A \to B \in T\}$$

The validity of an implication $A \to B$ with respect to a theory $T$ is defined by

$$\|A \to B\|_T = \bigwedge_{X \in Mod(T)} \|A \to B\|_X.$$

Simplification Logic [11,14] arose as a means to obtain smaller, more readable attribute implications in FCA, with no loss of knowledge. This approach is deeply linked to the optimality of systems, as studied in the crisp case by Rodriguez et al. [18]. As a matter of fact, Bertet et al. gave a characterization result on direct-optimal systems, Theorem 2 in [7], that bears impressive similarities with the derivation rules of Simplification Logic.

Simplification Logic was extended to the fuzzy case in [1], where the set of truth-values was a complete residuated lattice $\mathbb{L} = (L, \vee, \wedge, 0, 1, \otimes, \to)$. The axioms and derivation rules of Fuzzy Attribute Simplification Logic (FASL) are introduced below, for all $A, B, C, D \in L^M, c \in L$,

`[Ax]` infer $AB \to A$, (Axiom)
`[Mul]` from $A \to B$ infer $c \otimes A \to c \otimes B$, (Multiplication)
`[Sim]` from $A \to B, C \to D$ infer $AC \setminus B \to D$, (Simplification)

where $\setminus : L \to L$ is an operation that satisfies for all $a, b, c \in L$

$$a \setminus b \leq c \text{ if and only if } a \leq b \vee c.$$

Note that, if $L$ is linear and $a \leq b$, then $a \setminus b = 0$. In this paper, the juxtaposition of two sets $X$ and $Y$ is used to simplify the notation for the union of those sets, i.e., $XY$ stands for $X \cup Y$.

The operation $\setminus$ is extended to fuzzy sets in a pointwise manner, that is, for any $A, B \in L^M, m \in M$

$$(A \setminus B)(m) = A(m) \setminus B(m).$$

The provability of FASL is denoted by $\vdash$, i.e., $T \vdash A \to B$ means that $A \to B$ is provable from $T$ using `[Ax]`, `[Mul]`, and `[Sim]`.

**Theorem 1** ([1]). *Let $L$ and $M$ be finite, let $T$ be a set of formulas. For the axiomatic system of FASL we have $T \vdash A \to B$ if and only if $\|A \to B\|_T = 1$.*

In FASL the following logical equivalences hold.

**Theorem 2** ([1]). *For any $A, B, C, D \in L^M$, the following equivalences hold true:*

`[DeEq]` $\{A \to B\} \equiv \{A \to B \setminus A\}$;
`[UnEq]` $\{A \to B, A \to C\} \equiv \{A \to BC\}$;
`[SiEq]` *If $A \subseteq C$ then* $\{A \to B, C \to D\} \equiv \{A \to B, A(C \setminus B) \to D \setminus B\}$.

### 2.3 Crisp Direct Bases

Given a system of implications $\Sigma = \{A \to B \mid A, B \subseteq M\}$, consider the operator $\pi_\Sigma \colon 2^M \to 2^M$ defined as,

$$\pi_\Sigma(X) = X \cup \bigcup\{B \mid A \subseteq X, A \to B \in \Sigma\}.$$

This operator is inflationary and isotone, which makes it a preclosure operator in the terms of Čech [9]. It is not a closure operator in general, since it is not necessarily idempotent. However, a closure operator can be obtained by iterating $\pi_\Sigma$. Thus, we obtain $\varphi_\Sigma \colon 2^M \to 2^M$ defined by

$$\varphi_\Sigma(X) = \pi_\Sigma(X) \cup \pi_\Sigma^2(X) \cup \pi_\Sigma^3(X) \cup \cdots .$$

**Definition 1.** *A system of implications $\Sigma$ is said to be direct if $\varphi_\Sigma(X) = \pi_\Sigma(X)$, for all $X \in L^M$, that is, if*

$$\varphi_\Sigma(X) = X \cup \bigcup\{B \mid A \subseteq X, A \to B \in \Sigma\}.$$

Direct systems of implications are of interest since they allow a fast computation of the closure operator. Whereas general systems of implications need several runs through all the implications to get the closure, direct system need only one. Therefore, there is a trade off between the cost of computing the direct system of implications, which is in general higher than others, and the cost of computing closures, which is much faster with direct systems of implications.

The following result characterizes the directness of an implicational system in terms of a single property.

**Lemma 1** ([18]). *An implicational system $\Sigma$ is direct if and only if it satisfies the following condition: for all $A \to B, C \to D \in \Sigma$, $b \in B \smallsetminus A$ and $d \in D \smallsetminus (A \cup C)$, if $b \in C$ then there exists $G \to H \in \Sigma$ such that $G \subseteq A \cup C$ and $d \in H$.*

## 3 Direct Systems of Implications in the Fuzzy Setting

In this section, the problem of defining and characterizing the directness of a system of implications in the fuzzy setting is studied. Notice that this line of research is different from the one in [10]. In the cited work, the authors consider implications of the form $A \xrightarrow{\vartheta} B$ where $A, B \subseteq M$, that is, both $A$ and $B$ are crisp sets and the truth value $\vartheta$ is the degree of validity of the implication, also called confidence in the setting of association rules. In this paper, an implication is, as defined in Sect. 2.1, an expression $A \to B$, where $A, B \in L^M$.

The nomenclature theory $T$ is commonly used in papers that deal with logic. Nevertheless, papers concerning systems of implications in general use $\Sigma$. From this point on, we will follow the notation of [18], and denote our systems of implications by $\Sigma$.

Throughout the rest of the paper, the complete residuated lattice $L$ will be a discretization of the unit interval, hence $L$ will be a finite numerical chain.

Given a theory $\Sigma$, define the operator $\pi_\Sigma\colon L^M \to L^M$ defined as,

$$\pi_\Sigma(X)(m) = X(m) \vee \bigvee\{S(A, X) \otimes B(m) \mid A \to B \in \Sigma\}.$$

Again, the closure operator is obtained by iteration. Thus, we obtain $\varphi_\Sigma\colon L^M \to L^M$ defined by

$$\varphi_\Sigma(X) = \pi_\Sigma(X) \cup \pi^2_\Sigma(X) \cup \pi^3_\Sigma(X) \cup \cdots .$$

**Definition 2.** *A system of implications $\Sigma$ is said to be direct if $\varphi_\Sigma(X) = \pi_\Sigma(X)$, for all $X \in L^M$, that is, if for all $m \in M$,*

$$\varphi_\Sigma(X)(m) = X(m) \vee \bigvee\{S(A, X) \otimes B(m) \mid A \to B \in \Sigma\}.$$

**Lemma 2.** *Let $L$ be a finite chain, $X \in L^M$, $\Sigma$ an implicational system and $m \in M$ such that $\pi_\Sigma(X)(m) > X(m)$. Then there exists an implication $G \to H \in \Sigma$ such that $\pi_\Sigma(X)(m) = S(G, X) \otimes H(m)$.*

*Proof.* By definition of implicational closure,

$$\pi_\Sigma(X)(m) = X(m) \vee \bigvee\{S(A, X) \otimes B(m) \mid A \to B \in \Sigma\}.$$

Since $L$ is linear and finite, the supremum is reached and is indeed a maximum. Thus, since $\pi_\Sigma(X)(m) > X(m)$, there exists an implication $G \to H \in \Sigma$ such that $S(A, X) \otimes B(m)$.

Notice that the use of a finite chains as the set of truth-values allows us to find one implication that fulfil the condition, rather that a collection of implications whose supremum reach the desired value. This will be of paramount importance throughout the rest of the section.

**Definition 3.** *Let us consider the following metric $p\colon \Sigma \times L^M \times L^M \to \mathbb{R}$ defined as*

$$p(A \to B, Y, X) = \sum_{\substack{x \in M \\ X(x) < S(A,Y) \otimes A(x)}} S(A, Y) \otimes A(x).$$

*Remark 1.* Observe that the sum is well-defined since $L$ is a discretization of the unit interval, therefore the truth values considered are real numbers. Also notice that $p(A \to B, Y, X) = 0$ if and only if $S(A, Y) \otimes A \subseteq X$.

In the crisp case, the directness of a system of implications is characterized by the so-called exchange condition, which is seen in Lemma 1. This condition is related to Simplification Logic, the use of [Sim] can be hinted by the nature of the formula. The following is an extension of the exchange condition to the fuzzy setting.

**Definition 4.** *An implicational system $\Sigma$ is said to satisfy the fuzzy exchange condition if for all pair implications $A \to B, C \to D \in \Sigma$, for all $m, n \in M$ and all $c, d \in L$, if $c \otimes B(m) > c \otimes A(m)$, $d \otimes D(n) > c \otimes A(n) \vee d \otimes C(n)$ and $d \otimes C(m) < c \otimes B(m)$ then there exists an implication $G \to H \in \Sigma$ such that*

$$S(G, c \otimes A \cup (d \otimes C \setminus c \otimes B)) \otimes H(n) \geq d \otimes D(n).$$

**Lemma 3.** *Let $\Sigma$ be an implicational system, $X, Y \in L^M$, $Y \subseteq \pi_\Sigma(X)$ and $C \to D \in \Sigma$ such that $S(C, Y) \otimes D(m) > \pi_\Sigma(X)(m)$ for some $m \in M$. If $\Sigma$ satisfies the fuzzy exchange condition and $p(C \to D, Y, X) > 0$ there exist an implication $G \to H \in \Sigma$ and a fuzzy set $Z \in L^M$ such that $p(G \to H, Z, X) < p(C \to D, Y, X)$. Moreover, the following inequality holds $S(G, Z) \otimes H(m) \geq S(C, Y) \otimes D(m)$.*

*Proof.* Let $\Sigma$ satisfy the fuzzy exchange condition, $C \to D \in \Sigma$, $X, Y \in L^M$ such that $Y \subseteq \pi_\Sigma(X)$, $S(C, Y) \otimes D(m) > Y(m)$ and $p(C \to D, Y, X) > 0$. Then, there exists an attribute $n \in M$ such that, $S(C, Y) \otimes C(n) > X(n)$.

Since $Y \subseteq \pi_\Sigma(X)$, by Lemma 2 there exists an implication $A \to B \in \Sigma$ such that $S(A, X) \otimes B(n) \geq S(C, Y) \otimes C(n)$. Hence, we have two implications $A \to B, C \to D \in \Sigma$ such that

$$\begin{aligned}
&S(A, X) \otimes A \to S(A, X) \otimes B,\\
&S(C, Y) \otimes C \to S(C, Y) \otimes D,\\
&S(A, X) \otimes B(n) \geq S(C, Y) \otimes C(n) > X(n) \geq S(A, X) \otimes A(n),\\
&S(C, Y) \otimes D(m) > \pi_\Sigma(X)(m) \geq Y(m) \geq S(C, Y) \otimes C(m).\\
&S(C, Y) \otimes D(m) > \pi_\Sigma(X)(m) \geq X(m) \geq S(A, X) \otimes A(m).
\end{aligned}$$

Thus, applying the fuzzy exchange condition there exists $G \to H \in \Sigma$ such that

$$S(G, S(A, X) \otimes A \cup S(C, Y) \otimes C \setminus S(A, X) \otimes B) \otimes H(m) \geq S(C, Y) \otimes D(m).$$

Hence, we have found an implication $G \to H$ and a set

$$Z = S(A, X) \otimes A \cup (S(C, Y) \otimes C \setminus S(A, X) \otimes B).$$

Assume $o \in M$ satisfies $X(o) < S(G, Z) \otimes G(o)$, then

$$\begin{aligned}
S(G, Z) \otimes G(o) &\leq Z(o)\\
&= S(A, X) \otimes A(o) \vee S(C, \pi_\Sigma(X)) \otimes C(o) \setminus S(A, X) \otimes B(o)\\
&\leq X(o) \vee S(C, Y) \otimes C(o) \setminus S(A, X) \otimes B(o)\\
&\leq S(C, Y) \otimes C(o) \setminus S(A, X) \otimes B(o)\\
&\leq S(C, Y) \otimes C(o).
\end{aligned}$$

In particular for $n \in M$, either $S(G, Z) \otimes G(n) \leq X(n)$ and $S(G, Z) \otimes G(n)$ is not summed or $X(n) < S(G, Z) \otimes G(n)$ is satisfied and we have

$$\begin{aligned}
S(G, Z) \otimes G(n) &\leq Z(n)\\
&\leq S(C, Y) \otimes C(n) \setminus S(A, X) \otimes B(n)\\
&< S(C, Y) \otimes C(n).
\end{aligned}$$

Therefore,

$$p(G \to H, Z, X) = \sum_{\substack{x \in M \\ X(x) < S(G,Z) \otimes G(x)}} S(G, Z) \otimes G(x)$$
$$< \sum_{\substack{x \in M \\ X(x) < S(A,Y) \otimes A(x)}} S(A, X) \otimes A(x) = p(A \to B, Y, X).$$

**Theorem 3.** *An implicational system $\Sigma$ is direct if and only if it satisfies the fuzzy exchange condition.*

*Proof.* For the direct implication, let $\Sigma = \{A_i \to B_i \mid i \in I\}$ be a direct implicational system (i.e. $\varphi_\Sigma = \pi_\Sigma$), $A \to B, C \to D \in \Sigma$ and $c, d \in L$. Then, by `[Mul]`, $c \otimes A \to c \otimes B$ and $d \otimes C \to d \otimes D$ are valid implications. In addition, applying `[Sim]`, we get $(c \otimes A \cup (d \otimes C \smallsetminus c \otimes B)) \to d \otimes D$ is a valid implication, that is,

$$d \otimes D \subseteq \varphi_\Sigma((c \otimes A \cup d \otimes C \smallsetminus c \otimes B)) = \pi_\Sigma((c \otimes A \cup (d \otimes C \smallsetminus c \otimes B))).$$

Assume there are $m, n \in M$ such that $c \otimes B(m) > c \otimes A(m)$, $d \otimes D(n) > c \otimes A(n) \vee d \otimes C(n)$ and $d \otimes C(m) < c \otimes B(m)$. Then,

$$d \otimes D(n) > c \otimes A(n) \vee d \otimes C(n) \geq (c \otimes A \cup (d \otimes C \smallsetminus c \otimes B))(n),$$

and since $\Sigma$ is direct by Lemma 2 there exists an implication $G \to H \in \Sigma$ such that

$$S(G, c \otimes A \cup (d \otimes C \smallsetminus c \otimes B)) \otimes H(n) \geq d \otimes D(n).$$

For the converse implication, let $\Sigma$ be an implicational system satisfying the fuzzy exchange condition. One must show that $\varphi_\Sigma(X) = \pi_\Sigma(X)$, or equivalently that $\pi_\Sigma(X) = \pi^2_\Sigma(X)$, or still equivalently (since $\pi_\Sigma$ is inflationary) that $\pi^2_\Sigma(X) \subseteq \pi_\Sigma(X)$. Assume that there exists $X$ with $\pi_\Sigma(X) \subsetneq \pi^2_\Sigma(X)$, i.e., there exists $m \in M$ such that

$$\pi_\Sigma(X)(m) < \pi^2_\Sigma(X)(m).$$

Then, by Lemma 2, there exists $A \to B \in \Sigma$ with $\pi_\Sigma(X)(m) < S(A, \pi_\Sigma(X)) \otimes B(m)$. Let us consider the metric in Definition 3 applied particularly on $A \to B$, $\pi_\Sigma(X)$ and $X$.

Recall that $p(A \to B, \pi_\Sigma(X), X) = 0$ if and only if $S(A, \pi_\Sigma(X)) \otimes A \subseteq X$, which gives $S(A, \pi_\Sigma(X)) \otimes B \subseteq \pi_\Sigma(X)$, a contradiction. Thus, one has $p(A \to B, \pi_\Sigma(X), X) > 0$ and we are in the conditions to apply Lemma 3 to get an implication $A_1 \to B_1 \in \Sigma$ and a set $Z_1 \in L^M$ such that $p(A_1, Z_1) < p(A, \pi_\Sigma(X))$ and

$$S(A_1, Z_1) \otimes B_1(m) \geq S(A, \pi_\Sigma(X)) \otimes B(m) > \pi_\Sigma(X)(m).$$

At this point, Lemma 3 can be applied iteratively until $p(A_k, Z_k) = 0$, convergence is ensured since both $L$ and $M$ are finite. In addition,

$$S(A_k, Z_k) \otimes B_k(m) \geq \cdots \geq S(A, \pi_\Sigma(X)) \otimes B(m) > \pi_\Sigma(X)(m).$$

Notice that this is a contradiction since $p(A_k, Z_k) = 0$ implies $S(A_k, Z_k) \otimes A_k \subseteq X$, therefore $S(A_k, Z_k) \otimes B_k(m) \leq \pi_\Sigma(X)(m)$. Hence, $\pi_\Sigma(X) = \pi^2_\Sigma(X)$ and $\Sigma$ is direct.

## 4 An Algorithm for the Construction of Direct Systems

In this section, we propose an algorithm that takes an implicational system as input and returns a direct system equivalent to the input. Throughout this section, we will suppose that the input system, $\Sigma$, is *reduced*, that is, in the right-hand side of the implications, no attribute appears with a degree equal to or lower than its degree in the corresponding left-hand side. Any implication $A \to B$ can be transformed (maintaining the logical equivalence) into reduced form via substitution by $A \to B \setminus A$ (using `[DeEq]`).

In the case of a reduced system of implications, the fuzzy exchange condition which characterizes the directness of the system can be rewritten in simpler terms:

**Lemma 4.** *A reduced implicational system $\Sigma$ satisfies the fuzzy exchange condition if for all pair of implications $A \to B, C \to D \in \Sigma$, for all $m, n \in M$ and all $c, d \in L$, if $d \otimes D(n) > c \otimes A(n)$ and $c \otimes B(m) > d \otimes C(m)$ then there exists an implication $G \to H \in \Sigma$ such that*

$$S(G, c \otimes A \cup (d \otimes C \setminus c \otimes B)) \otimes H(n) \geq d \otimes D(n).$$

The next result establishes which implications are needed for a system to become direct:

**Proposition 1.** *Let $\mathbb{K}$ be an $L$-fuzzy formal context and $A \to B, C \to D$ two valid implications. Then, the implication $G \to H$ given by*

$$\begin{aligned} G &= c \otimes A \cup (d \otimes C \setminus c \otimes B) \\ H &= (d \otimes D) \cap P = d \otimes D \setminus c \otimes A \end{aligned} \tag{1}$$

*is also valid in $\mathbb{K}$ and satisfies*

$$S(G, c \otimes A \cup (d \otimes C \setminus c \otimes B)) \otimes H(n) \geq d \otimes D(n)$$

*for all $n \in M$ where $d \otimes D(n) > c \otimes A(n)$.*

*Proof.* First, let us see that it is indeed a valid implication. Following the same reasoning as in Theorem 3, we obtain that $G = c \otimes A \cup (d \otimes C \setminus c \otimes B) \to d \otimes D$ is a valid implication. It suffices to use `[DeEq]` to arrive at $G \to d \otimes D \setminus c \otimes A$ being also valid.

Furthermore, if $n \in M$ is such that $d \otimes D(n) > c \otimes A(n)$, then:

$$\begin{aligned} S(G, c \otimes A \cup (d \otimes C \setminus c \otimes B)) \otimes H(n) &= 1 \otimes H(n) = H(n) = \\ &= (d \otimes D \setminus c \otimes A)(n) = d \otimes D(n) \end{aligned}$$

**Definition 5.** *Given two implications* $A \to B, C \to D$, *their* derived implication *for given* $\alpha, \beta \in L$, *is the implication* $G \to H$ *defined as in Eq. (1).*

The previous result leads us to propose an iterative algorithm for the construction of a direct system of implications from a general one. The pseudocode for this method is presented in the `DirectSystem` function in Algorithm 1.

**Algorithm 1:** `DirectSystem`$(\Sigma, L)$

$\Sigma :=$ `ReducedSystem`$(\Sigma)$<br>
**repeat**<br>
    $\mathcal{D} := \varnothing$<br>
    **foreach** $A \to B, C \to D \in \Sigma$ **do**<br>
        $\mathcal{D} := \mathcal{D} \cup$ `AddDerived`$(A \to B, C \to D, L)$<br>
    change, $\Sigma :=$ `Combine`$(\Sigma, \mathcal{D})$<br>
**until** change $=$ **false**<br>
**return** $\Sigma_d = \Sigma$

Broadly speaking, this algorithm begins by reducing the system of implications (transforming each $A \to B \in \Sigma$ into $A \to B \smallsetminus A$) and performs iterations consisting of two phases: in the first phase, all pairs $A \to B, C \to D \in \Sigma$ are explored, and all possible derived implications are accumulated in the set $\mathcal{D}$ (using the function `AddDerived`); in the second phase, $\Sigma$ and $\mathcal{D}$ are combined, checking whether further iterations are required due to the addition or modification of any implication. Once a fixed point is reached, no further iteration is necessary, and the algorithm returns the direct system $\Sigma_d$, which matches the last stored value of $\Sigma$.

We start with an auxiliary function, `AddDerived` (Algorithm 2), which adds the necessary implications $G \to H$ defined according to Eq. (1) for a pair of implications $A \to B, C \to D$, and all values $c, d \in L$.

**Algorithm 2:** `AddDerived`$(A \to B, C \to D, L)$

$\Sigma := \varnothing$<br>
**foreach** $c, d \in L$ **do**<br>
    **if** $d \otimes C \smallsetminus c \otimes B \neq \varnothing$ **and** $d \otimes D \smallsetminus c \otimes A \neq \varnothing$ **then**<br>
        $G := c \otimes A \cup (d \otimes C \smallsetminus c \otimes B)$<br>
        $H := d \otimes D \smallsetminus c \otimes A$<br>
        $\Sigma := \Sigma \cup \{G \to H\}$<br>
**return** $\Sigma$

It can be observed that a large number of derived implications are generated, on the order of $|L|^2$ for each pair of implications analyzed. However, it is not necessary to accumulate all of them, as there may already be an implication in the set $\Sigma$ with the same premise, in which case it would suffice to update the existing implication. This idea is implemented in the `Combine` method in Algorithm 3.

**Algorithm 3:** `Combine`$(\Sigma, \mathcal{D})$

change := **false**
**foreach** $A \to B \in \mathcal{D}$ **do**
  **if exists** $A \to B' \in \Sigma$ **then**
    **if** $B \nsubseteq B'$ **then**
      `// Old implication has been modified`
      change := **true**
      $\Sigma := \Sigma \setminus \{A \to B'\} \cup \{A \to B \cup B'\}$
  **else**
    `// New implication has been added`
    change := **true**
    $\Sigma := \Sigma \cup \{A \to B\}$
**return** change, $\Sigma$

Note that `Combine` returns two values. In addition to the combined system of implications, it also returns a boolean value indicating whether a significant change has occurred during the combination: the addition of a previously unconsidered implication or the update of an existing implication by modifying (increasing) its right-hand side. In both cases, a new iteration is required, which is why the value returned for the variable `change` is set to true. The importance of this method, beyond collecting all the accumulated implications, lies in its ability to help detect when the algorithm should terminate, as a direct system has been obtained.

**Lemma 5.** *Let $\Sigma$ be a system of implications and $\mathcal{D}$ the set of all implications derived from pairs of implications in $\Sigma$, and let* `change` *and $\Sigma_c$ be the values returned by executing* `Combine`$(\Sigma, \mathcal{D})$*. If the value of* `change` *is false, then $\Sigma_c$ is a direct system.*

*Proof.* Let $A \to B, C \to D \in \Sigma$ and appropriate values $c, d \in L$ and $n \in M$, and consider $G \to H \in \mathcal{D}$ such that

$$S(G, c \otimes A \cup (d \otimes C \setminus c \otimes B)) \otimes H(n) \geq d \otimes D(n),$$

which exists by the construction of $\mathcal{D}$. If `change` is false, then necessarily one of the following two situations occurs: either $G \to H \in \Sigma$ or there exists $G \to H' \in \Sigma$ with $H \subseteq H'$. In this case, this implication also satisfies:

$$S(G, c \otimes A \cup (d \otimes C \setminus c \otimes B)) \otimes H'(n) \geq d \otimes D(n),$$

due to the monotonicity of $\otimes$ and $H \subseteq H'$.

Therefore, for each pair of implications $A \to B, C \to D$ and appropriate values $c, d \in L$ and $n \in M$, there exists an implication $X \to Y \in \Sigma$ (with $X = G$ and $Y \in \{H, H'\}$ as described above) satisfying

$$S(X, c \otimes A \cup (d \otimes C \setminus c \otimes B)) \otimes Y(n) \geq d \otimes D(n),$$

that is, $\Sigma$ satisfies the fuzzy exchange condition. Therefore, $\Sigma_c = \Sigma$ is a direct system.

All these observations lead us to the main result of this section:

**Theorem 4.** *Given a L-fuzzy formal context, and a valid implication system $\Sigma$, the method* `DirectSystem` *in Algorithm 1 terminates and outputs $\Sigma_d$, a direct system, equivalent to $\Sigma$.*

*Proof.* From the fact that $M$ and $L$ are finite, it is easy to deduce that the method terminates, as, in the worst case, it would explore and produce all possible implications. The only condition to stop iterating is that the variable change takes a *false* value. By Lemma 5, this means that the output, $\Sigma_d = \Sigma$ at the last iteration, is a direct system. The equivalence between the original $\Sigma$ and $\Sigma_d$ is provided by the fact that all derived implications are logical consequences of $\Sigma$, and that the `Combine` method either keeps a derived implication unchanged or uses the `[UnEq]` rule to compose it with another implication, thus resulting in a valid implication.

Due to space limitations, we refer the reader to https://malaga-fca-group.github.io/fuzzy-direct-systems-example/ for the detailed trace of an application of this algorithm. Furthermore, the code for the algorithms, needed to replicate the results, is included in the same website.

## 5 Conclusions and Future Work

In this paper, the condition of directness of implicational systems in the fuzzy setting has been presented. In addition, this condition has been characterized in terms of one condition, which has allowed the development of an algorithm to turn an implicational system into a direct system. A proper study of computational complexity and performance of the algorithms is left for future work due to the space restrictions. The notion of direct-optimal system is also bound to be studied in a subsequent manuscript in order to obtain the most readable and interpretable system of implications without losing knowledge in the process.

**Acknowledgments.** The authors would like to thank Dr. Kira Adaricheva who inspired us to study this topic. This research is partially supported by the Kempe foundation, the State Agency of Research (AEI), the Spanish Ministry of Science, Innovation, and Universities (MCIU) and the European Social Fund (FEDER) through the research projects with reference JCSMK24-0053 (Kempe), PID2021-127870OB-I00 and (MCIU/AEI/FEDER, UE) and the VALID research project (PID2022-140630NB-I00 funded by MCIN/ AEI/ 10.13039/ 501100011033).

**Disclosure of Interests.** The authors declare no conflict of interest.

## References


1. Bělohlávek, R., Cordero, P., Enciso, M., Mora, A., Vychodil, V.: Automated prover for attribute dependencies in data with grades. Int. J. Approximate Reasoning **70**, 51–67 (2016)
2. Belohlavek, R.: Fuzzy concepts and conceptual structures: induced similarities. In: Joint Conference on Information Sciences 1998 Proceedings, vol. 1, pp. 179–182 (1998)
3. Bělohlávek, R.: Fuzzy Relational Systems. Springer, Cham (2002)
4. Bělohlávek, R., Vychodil, V.: Fuzzy attribute implications: computing non-redundant bases using maximal independent sets. In: Australasian Joint Conference on Artificial Intelligence, pp. 1126–1129. Springer, Cham (2005)
5. Bělohlávek, R., Vychodil, V.: Attribute implications in a fuzzy setting. In: Formal Concept Analysis: 4th International Conference, ICFCA 2006, Dresden, Germany, 13–17 February 2006. Proceedings, pp. 45–60. Springer, Cham (2006)
6. Bertet, K., Monjardet, B.: The multiple facets of the canonical direct unit implicational basis. Theor. Comput. Sci. **411**(22–24), 2155–2166 (2010). https://doi.org/10.1016/J.TCS.2009.12.021
7. Bertet, K., Nebut, M.: Efficient algorithms on the family associated to an implicational system. Discret. Math. Theor. Comput. Sci. **6** (2004)
8. Burusco, A., Fuentes-González, R.: The study of the $L$-fuzzy concept lattice. Mathware Soft Comput. **3**, 209–218 (1994)
9. Čech, E.: Topological spaces [revised edition] (1966)
10. Cordero, P., Enciso, M., Mora, A.: Directness in fuzzy formal concept analysis. In: International Conference on Information Processing and Management of Uncertainty in Knowledge-Based Systems, pp. 585–595. Springer, Cham (2018)
11. Cordero, P., Enciso, M., Mora, A., Vychodil, V.: Parameterized simplification logic I: reasoning with implications and classes of closure operators. Int. J. Gen. Syst. **49**(7), 724–746 (2020). https://doi.org/10.1080/03081079.2020.1831484
12. Ganter, B., Obiedkov, S.: Conceptual Exploration. Springer, Cham (2016)
13. Guigues, J., Duquenne, V.: Familles minimales d'implications informatives résultant d'une tables de données binaires. Mathématiques et Sciences Humaines **95**, 5–18 (1986)
14. Mora, A., Enciso, M., Cordero, P., Fortes, I.: Closure via functional dependence simplification. Int. J. Comput. Math. **89**, 510–526 (2012)
15. Ojeda-Hernández, M., Cabrera, I.P., Cordero, P.: Quasi-closed elements in fuzzy posets. J. Comput. Appl. Math. **404**, 113390 (2022). https://doi.org/10.1016/j.cam.2021.113390
16. Ojeda-Hernández, M., Cabrera, I.P., Cordero, P., Muñoz-Velasco, E.: On pseudointents in fuzzy formal concept analysis. In: International Conference on Conceptual Structures, pp. 36–40. Springer, Cham (2023)
17. Pollandt, S.: Fuzzy Begriffe: Formale Begriffsanalyse von unscharfen Daten. Springer, Heidelberg (1997)
18. Rodríguez-Lorenzo, E., Bertet, K., Cordero, P., Enciso, M., Mora, A.: Direct-optimal basis computation by means of the fusion of simplification rules. Discret. Appl. Math. **249**, 106–119 (2018). https://doi.org/10.1016/j.dam.2017.12.031
19. Vychodil, V., Bělohlávek, R.: Fuzzy attribute logic: attribute implications, their validity, entailment, and non-redundant basis. In: Proceedings of the Eleventh International Fuzzy Systems Association World Congress, vol. I (2005)
20. Wille, R.: Restructuring lattice theory: an approach based on hierarchies of concepts. In: Ordered Sets, pp. 445–470. Springer, Cham (1982)

# Robust Decisions: Bridging the Quantitative-Qualitative Gap

Sébastien Destercke[1(✉)] and Agnès Rico[2]

[1] Université de technologie de Compiègne, CNRS, Alliance Sorbonne Université, Heudiasyc, Compiègne, France
sebastien.destercke@hds.utc.fr
[2] ERIC, Université Lyon 1, Lyon, France
Agnes.Rico@univ-lyon1.fr

**Abstract.** When it comes to model uncertainty and make robust decision in the form of partial, set-valued recommendations, one can find a large literature on the topic for quantitative models but much less for qualitative models. This paper intends to partially solve this issue by taking notions from the quantitative world and transfer them to the qualitative one. In particular, we consider the transfer of decision rules based on lower probabilities and Choquet integral to decision rules based on fuzzy measures and Sugeno integral.

**Keywords:** Uncertainty · Decision making · Qualitative model · Sugeno integral · Fuzzy measures

## 1 Introduction

In uncertainty reasoning, decision making plays a quite important role, and has been considered from many different perspectives within many different theories. We can refer to [1] for an overview of decision making processes, including under uncertainty.

In the particular case where uncertainty is modelled by non-additive measures such as necessity measures and belief functions, or by more general models (e.g., lower previsions or choice functions [2]), there exists a quite extensive literature on how to make robust decisions, i.e., in the sense that the recommendation may come in the shape of a set of alternatives rather than as a single alternative when information turns out to be insufficient to identify a single optimal solution. One can refer to [3,8] for more focused reviews than in [1].

However, as far as we know, this literature does not have an equivalent in the qualitative world, where fuzzy measures and Sugeno integrals are the most commonly used tools. Our goal in this paper is to build upon the quantitative literature and to propose counterparts of the quantitative robust decision rules in the qualitative setting. More precisely, we assume that uncertainty is not represented quantitatively, but qualitatively by a pair of dual pessimistic and optimistic capacities (a.k.a. fuzzy measures) on an ordinal scale, and that the


M. Baczyński et al. (Eds.): EUSFLAT 2025, LNCS 15884, pp. 158–170, 2025.
https://doi.org/10.1007/978-3-031-97228-7_14

capacities and the alternative values are aggregated using the Sugeno integral. We will see that while some decision rules are straightforward to transpose, others require careful consideration, and do not necessarily map in a single concept.

Section 2 provides a reminder about both the quantitative and qualitative settings when it comes to represent uncertainty and compute aggregated values of alternatives within them. In this same section, we discuss the notion of core of a pair of qualitative, dual pessimistic and optimistic capacities, providing new definitions and properties. Section 3 is a reminder of the main elements of quantitative decision rules we want to transpose to the qualitative setting. Finally, Sect. 4 discusses extensions of the quantitative rules to the qualitative setting, as well as some of their properties.

## 2 Representing Information and Alternative Values in Quantitative and Qualitative Settings

In this part, we recall the main elements of the quantitative framework we will transpose to the qualitative world, as well as the main building blocks of this qualitative setting. Doing so also brings us to already discuss and characterise new notions within the qualitative setting, such as a new notion of core of capacities.

In general, we will consider a finite space $\Omega = \{\omega_1, \ldots, \omega_n\}$ of $n$ exclusive states, about which we are uncertain. We nevertheless assume that the actual value is within this space, meaning it is exhaustive.

### 2.1 Probability Sets

A common way to represent (convex) probability sets[1] is by specifying a lower probability $\underline{P} : 2^{\Omega} \to [0, 1]$ over the subsets $A \subseteq \Omega$, such that it is bounded, i.e., $\underline{P}(\emptyset) = 0, \underline{P}(\Omega) = 1$, and monotonic, i.e., $\underline{P}(A) \leq \underline{P}(B)$ if $A \subseteq B$. To the lower probability can be associated a dual upper probability $\overline{P}(A) = 1 - \underline{P}(A^c)$ where $A^c$ stands for the complement of $A$.

To a lower probability $\underline{P}$ can be associated a set of probabilities $\mathcal{M}(\underline{P})$, i.e., of additive measures $P$ that dominates $\underline{P}$ and are dominated by $\overline{P}$, that is

$$\mathcal{M}(\underline{P}) = \{P : \forall A \subseteq \Omega, \underline{P}(A) \leq P(A) \leq \overline{P}(A)\}. \tag{1}$$

We will call $\mathcal{M}(\underline{P})$ the core of $\underline{P}$. Note that since $\underline{P}$ and $\overline{P}$ are dual, we can use only one of them, as $P$ dominating $\underline{P}$ implies that it is dominated by $\overline{P}$, since the additive measures $P$ are also **auto-dual**, in the sense that $P(A) = 1 - P(A^c)$. Note that in this paper, we will only consider lower probabilities that are consistent, i.e., have a non-empty core and are the lower envelopes of the additive measures within it, i.e., $\underline{P}(A) = \inf_{P \in \mathcal{M}(\underline{P})} P(A)$ for any $A$.

---

[1] There are more general ways to define such sets, but we will restrict ourselves to lower probabilities here.

Now, if one considers a function or alternative $\boldsymbol{x} : \Omega \to \mathbb{R}$, where $x(\omega)$ is the reward one would get by choosing $\boldsymbol{x}$ if state $\omega$ is the true one, one can define from an additive measure $P$ an expectation operator $\mathbb{C}_P(\boldsymbol{x}) = \sum_{\omega \in \Omega} x(\omega)P(\{\omega\})$. Given a set $\mathcal{M}(\underline{P})$, one can then define lower and upper expectations of $x$ in the following way:

$$\underline{\mathbb{C}}(\boldsymbol{x}) = \min_{P \in \mathcal{M}(\underline{P})} \mathbb{C}_P(\boldsymbol{x}) \quad \text{and} \quad \overline{\mathbb{C}}(x) = \max_{P \in \mathcal{M}(\underline{P})} \mathbb{C}_P(\boldsymbol{x}). \tag{2}$$

In the case where a lower probability is also 2-monotone, that is $\underline{P}(A \cup B) + \underline{P}(A \cap B) \geq \underline{P}(A) + \underline{P}(B)$ for any pair $A, B$, the functions $\underline{\mathbb{C}}(\boldsymbol{x}), \overline{\mathbb{C}}(\boldsymbol{x})$ can be computed through the Choquet integral[2], that reads as follow: let $x_i := \boldsymbol{x}(\omega_i)$ and $\sigma$ be a permutation over $\{1, \ldots, n\}$ such that $x_{\sigma(1)} \leq x_{\sigma(2)} \leq \ldots \leq x_{\sigma(n)}$ and denote by $A_{\sigma(i)} = \{\sigma(i), \ldots, \sigma(n)\}$ the decreasing sequence of sets in terms of inclusion. Then the Choquet integral of $\boldsymbol{x}$ with respect to $\underline{P}$ is

$$\underline{\mathbb{C}}(\boldsymbol{x}) = \sum_{i=1}^{n} (x_{\sigma(i)} - x_{\sigma(i-1)}) \underline{P}(A_{\sigma(i)}) \tag{3}$$

with $x_{\sigma(0)} = 0$. The upper bound can be obtained by replacing $\underline{P}$ by $\overline{P}$.

### 2.2 Qualitative Capacities

In our previous case, alternatives and uncertainty could take values within a subset of $\mathbb{R}$, while in the standard qualitative setting they take values in an ordered scale $L = \{\lambda_0, \ldots, \lambda_t\}$. We assume that $L$ is equipped with an order-reversing map $\eta : L \to L$ such that $\eta$ is unique and $\eta(\lambda_i) = \lambda_{t-i}$. In order to have an obvious neutral element when needed, we will assume that $L$ has an odd number of elements, hence that $t$ is even and that $\lambda_{t/2}$ is the neutral element. An alternative is represented by a vector $\boldsymbol{x} : \Omega \to L$, $\boldsymbol{x} = (x_1, \ldots x_n) \in L^n$.

A capacity (or fuzzy measure) is a set function $\mu : 2^\Omega \to L$ such that: $\forall A, B \subseteq \Omega$, $A \subseteq B \implies \mu(A) \leq \mu(B)$, $\mu(\Omega) = \lambda_t$ and $\mu(\varnothing) = \lambda_0$, $\varnothing$ being the empty set of $\Omega$. The conjugate capacity of $\mu$ is denoted $\mu^c$. It is defined by $\forall A \subseteq \Omega$, $\mu^c(A) = \eta(\mu(A^c))$ where $A^c$ is the complement of $A$ in $\Omega$. Let $\mu$ and $\nu$ be two capacities of $\Omega$, we say that $\mu$ **dominates** $\nu$, denoted by $\mu \succcurlyeq \nu$, if $\forall A \subseteq \Omega$, $\mu(A) \geq \nu(A)$.

A capacity $\mu$ is said to be **optimistic** if it dominates its conjugate capacity: $\mu \succcurlyeq \mu^c$ and **pessimistic** if it is dominated by its conjugate capacity: $\mu \preccurlyeq \mu^c$. If $\mu$ is optimistic then $\mu^c$ is pessimistic and vice versa. A capacity $\mu$ is said to be **auto-dual** if $\mu = \mu^c$. In this case, one could consider that it is both optimistic and pessimistic. We will denote by $\mathcal{A}$ the set of auto-dual capacities.

**Sugeno Integral.** The Sugeno integral [7] is a qualitative aggregation method commonly used in multi-criteria decision making.

[2] This explains our choice of $\mathbb{C}$ to denote expectations.

Let us consider the vector $\boldsymbol{x} = (x_1, \cdots, x_n) \in L^n$, the Sugeno integral of $\boldsymbol{x} \in L^n$ with respect to a capacity $\mu$ on $2^\Omega$ is defined by

$$\mathbb{S}_\mu(\boldsymbol{x}) = \max_{A \subseteq \Omega} \min(\mu(A), \min_{i \in A} x_i). \tag{4}$$

Expression (4) has an apparent high complexity of $2^n$, as one would have to check an exponential number of events. Yet, it can be simplified in a much more tractable expression. Let us consider the permutation $\sigma$ such that $x_{\sigma(1)} \leq \ldots \leq x_{\sigma(n)}$ and the level sets - also called coalitions - $A_{\sigma(i)} = \{\sigma(i), \ldots, \sigma(n)\}$. Equation (4) can then be rewritten as

$$\mathbb{S}_\mu(\boldsymbol{x}) = \max_{i=1}^{n} \min(x_{\sigma(i)}, \mu(A_{\sigma(i)})), \tag{5}$$

which has now a linear complexity in $n$, meaning that the whole procedure is polynomial. Expression (5) can also be re-expressed as the median of $2n - 1$ values as

$$\mathbb{S}_\mu(\boldsymbol{x}) = median(x_1, \ldots, x_n, \mu(A_{\sigma(2)}), \ldots, \mu(A_{\sigma(n)})), \tag{6}$$

When considering a couple of pessimistic and optimistic measures $\mu, \mu^c$, $\mu \preccurlyeq \mu^c$, we will consider lower and upper Sugeno integrals with the following notations:

$$\underline{\mathbb{S}}_\mu(\boldsymbol{x}) = \mathbb{S}_\mu(\boldsymbol{x}) \text{ and } \overline{\mathbb{S}}_\mu(\boldsymbol{x}) = \mathbb{S}_{\mu^c}(\boldsymbol{x}) \tag{7}$$

that can be summarised as an "interval"[3] $[\underline{\mathbb{S}}_\mu(\boldsymbol{x}), \overline{\mathbb{S}}_\mu(\boldsymbol{x})]$.

**Core of a (Qualitative) Capacity.** In the quantitative context, the core of a pessimistic capacity $\mu$ can be expressed in two equivalent ways: either as the set of probabilities dominating the considered capacity, or as the core of auto-dual capacities $\nu$ such that $\mu \leq \nu \leq \mu^c$.

In the qualitative case, this coincidence of the two definitions does not hold anymore. First, the notion of additive capacity does not make a lot of sense on a purely ordinal scale, and it is customary to consider maxitive measures, a.k.a., possibility measures, as their counterpart. From such considerations one can then derive cores of $\mu$ or $\mu^c$ in terms of maxitive measures dominating them or being dominated by them [5,6].

While such approaches are quite interesting to approximate a given capacity $\mu$ or work with limited information about it, it will fail the property that dominating maxitive capacities of $\mu$ will be dominated by $\mu^c$. In other words, if a maxitive capacities $\Pi$ is such that $\mu \leq \Pi$, it will generally not imply that $\Pi \leq \mu^c$, which seems desirable if one wants to see $\mu \leq \mu^c$ as two bounding capacities of an uncertain situation.

This is why, rather than using the parallel between additive and maxitive capacities, we will prefer to extend the notion of core to the qualitative setting

[3] We make a small abuse of notation here, so to ease connection with the quantitative setting.

by considering the auto-dual nature of additive capacities in the quantitative case. Following this path, we define the auto-dual core $\mathcal{M}(\mu)$ of a pessimistic qualitative capacity $\mu$ as the set

$$\mathcal{M}(\mu) = \{\nu \in \mathcal{A} : \forall A \subseteq \Omega,\ \mu \leq \nu \leq \mu^c\}. \tag{8}$$

In our knowledge, such a definition has not been proposed before, so let us check that some natural properties of $\mathcal{M}(\mu)$ are satisfied, namely that it is not empty and that the bounds $\mu, \mu^c$ for each event can be reached by some elements of $\mathcal{M}(\mu)$.

**Proposition 1.** *$\mathcal{M}(\mu)$ is not empty, i.e., there is an auto-dual capacity $\nu$ with $\mu \leq \nu \leq \mu^c$.*

*Proof.* Let us consider the very simple capacity $\nu^*$ such that[4]

$$\nu^*(A) = \begin{cases} \mu(A) & \text{if } |A| \leq t/2 \\ \mu^c(A) & \text{if } |A| > t/2 \end{cases}$$

$\nu^*$ is inclusion monotonic by construction, as both $\mu$ and $\mu^c$ are, and as $\mu \leq \mu^c$ by assumption. It is also auto-dual, as for all events $A$ such that $|A| \leq t/2$, $A^c$ is such that $|A| > t/2$. Note also that $\mu \leq \nu^* \leq \mu^c$, which finishes the proof.

**Proposition 2.** *For any event $A$, there are auto-dual capacities $\underline{\nu}_A, \overline{\nu}_A \in \mathcal{M}(\mu)$ such that $\underline{\nu}_A(A) = \mu(A)$ and $\overline{\nu}_A(A) = \mu^c(A)$.*

*Proof.* We will only focus on the case $|A| \leq t/2$, the proof for the other case being similar. Note that in this case, the capacity built in the proof of Proposition 1 is such that $\underline{\nu}_A(A) = \mu(A)$.

To build $\overline{\nu}_A$, consider the simple capacity such that:

$$\overline{\nu}_A(B) = \begin{cases} \mu^c(B) & \text{if } A \subseteq B \\ \mu(B) & \text{if } B \subseteq A^c \\ \nu^*(B) & \text{else} \end{cases}$$

One can prove that this capacity is auto-dual, as all events $B$ with $A \subseteq B$ have their complement $B^c$ such that $B^c \subseteq A^c$, that this capacity is monotone and by definition we have $\overline{\nu}_A(A) = \mu^c(A)$.

This proves that whenever $\mu$ is pessimist in the qualitative setting, its core is non-empty, and its bounds are reached by some members of its core. This is already a departure from the quantitative case, where being pessimistic is necessary yet not sufficient to have a non-empty core of auto-dual capacities. Take for example the case where $\mathcal{X} = \{x_1, \ldots, x_4\}$ and where $\mu(A) = 1/3$ for all $A \subseteq \mathcal{X}$: $\mu$ is pessimistic, yet there is no probability giving more than $1/3$ to every element $x_i$. We can furthermore prove that, for any alternative $\boldsymbol{x} \in L^n$, the bounds (7) are reached by an element of the core $\mathcal{M}(\mu)$.

[4] Remind that for reading easiness we set $t$ to be even.

**Proposition 3.** *For any alternative $\boldsymbol{x}$, there are distinct auto-dual capacities $\underline{\nu_{\boldsymbol{x}}}, \overline{\nu_{\boldsymbol{x}}} \in \mathcal{M}(\mu)$ such that $\mathbb{S}_{\underline{\nu_x}}(\boldsymbol{x}) = \underline{\mathbb{S}}_\mu(\boldsymbol{x})$ and $\mathbb{S}_{\overline{\nu_x}}(\boldsymbol{x}) = \overline{\mathbb{S}}_\mu(\boldsymbol{x})$.*

*Proof.* We will make the proof for $\underline{\nu_{\boldsymbol{x}}}$ and $\mathbb{S}_{\underline{\nu_x}}(\boldsymbol{x})$, the proof in the other way being similar. For this, consider the median value $v_{med}$, and let us first prove that $v_{med}$ is between two values $\mu(A_{\sigma(i_0+1)}) \leq v_{med} \leq \mu(A_{\sigma(i_0)})$.

According to the definition, there exists $i_0$ such that $\mathbb{S}_\mu(\boldsymbol{x}) = \min(x_{\sigma(i_0)}, \mu(A_{\sigma(i_0)}))$.

- If $\mathbb{S}_\mu(\boldsymbol{x}) = \mu(A_{\sigma(i_0)})$ there exists $i$ such that $\mu(A_{\sigma(i)}) \leq \mu(A_{\sigma(i_0)})$ or $\mu(A_{\sigma(i_0)}) \leq \mu(A_{\sigma(i)})$ and the inequalities are satisfied. Now,
- If $\mathbb{S}_\mu(\boldsymbol{x}) = x_{\sigma(i_0)} \leq \mu(A_{\sigma(i_0)})$ then since Sugeno integral is a maximum we have $\min(x_{\sigma(i_0+1)}, \mu(A_{\sigma(i_0+1)})) \leq x_{\sigma(i_0)}$ which implies that $\mu(A_{\sigma(i_0+1)}) \leq x_{\sigma(i_0)}$ because $x_{\sigma(i_0)} \leq x_{\sigma(i_0+1)}$ and the inequalities are satisfied.

We have two cases:

- $|A_{\sigma(i_0)}| \leq t/2$, then we can take $\nu^*$ of Proposition 1, as it will not change the values before the median, and only increase the values of $\mu(A)$ after the median since $(\mu \leq \mu^c)$.
- $|A_{\sigma(i_0)}| > t/2$. We consider in this case the capacity $\overline{\nu}_{(A_{\sigma(i_0+1)})^c} = \overline{\nu}_{\{\omega_1, \cdots, \omega_{\sigma(i_0)}\}}$. We have $|\{\omega_1, \cdots, \omega_{\sigma(i_0)}\}| \leq t/2$ and

$$\overline{\nu}_{\{\omega_1,\cdots,\omega_{\sigma(i_0)}\}}(A) = \begin{cases} \mu^c(A) & \text{if } \{\omega_1, \cdots, \omega_{\sigma(i_0)}\} \subseteq A \\ \mu(A) & \text{if } A \subseteq \{\omega_1, \cdots, \omega_{\sigma(i_0)}\}^c \\ \nu^*(A) & \text{else} \end{cases}$$

  Again, we have not changed the values before the median, and only increased the values of $\mu(A)$ after the median.

**Corollary 1.** $\underline{\mathbb{S}}(\boldsymbol{x}) = \min_{\nu \in \mathcal{M}(\mu)} \mathbb{S}_\nu(\boldsymbol{x})$ *and* $\overline{\mathbb{S}}(\boldsymbol{x}) = \max_{\nu \in \mathcal{M}(\mu)} \mathbb{S}_\nu(\boldsymbol{x})$

*Proof.* We have $\underline{\mathbb{S}}(\boldsymbol{x}) = \mathbb{S}_{\underline{\nu_x}}(\boldsymbol{x}) \geq \min_{\nu \in \mathcal{M}(\mu)} \mathbb{S}_{\underline{\nu}}(\boldsymbol{x})$. by definition of the min. $\underline{\mathbb{S}}(\boldsymbol{x}) \leq \mathbb{S}_\nu(\boldsymbol{x})$ for all $\nu \in \mathcal{M}(\mu)$ so $\underline{\mathbb{S}}(\boldsymbol{x}) \leq \min_{\nu \in \mathcal{M}(\mu)} \mathbb{S}_{\underline{\nu}}(\boldsymbol{x})$. Given this double inequality, we have $\underline{\mathbb{S}}(\boldsymbol{x}) = \min_{\nu \in \mathcal{M}(\mu)} \mathbb{S}_\nu$. Similar proof for $\underline{\mathbb{S}}(\boldsymbol{x})$.

These results show that the space of dual capacities can describe any core, in the sense that any pair of pessimistic and optimistic

## 3 Quantitative Robust Decision Rules

Let us now recall the main robust decision rules that exist within the quantitative setting, so that we can explore their extensions to the qualitative one.

### 3.1 Definitions

Given a set $\mathcal{X} = \{\boldsymbol{x}^1, \ldots, \boldsymbol{x}^q\}$ of alternatives, a decision rule is a function $Dec : 2^{\mathcal{X}} \to 2^{\mathcal{X}}$ such that, given a subset $X$ of alternatives, will return a subset such that $Dec(X) \subseteq X$. In other words, a decision rule is a choice function. Assuming that our uncertainty is described by some 2-monotone lower probability $\underline{P}$, let us now define the most common robust decision rules derived from it [4,8]. The first three rules are based on pairwise comparison, and the last one on the selection of possible top elements of linear orders.

**Lattice-Based Rule.** Considering the partial order $\succ_L^{\underline{P}}$ such that

$$\boldsymbol{x}^i \succeq_L^{\underline{P}} \boldsymbol{x}^j \text{ iff } \underline{\mathbb{C}}(\boldsymbol{x}^i) \geq \underline{\mathbb{C}}(\boldsymbol{x}^j) \text{ and } \overline{\mathbb{C}}(\boldsymbol{x}^i) \geq \overline{\mathbb{C}}(\boldsymbol{x}^j), \tag{9}$$

the lattice-based decision rule is then

$$Dec_L^{\underline{P}}(X) = \{\boldsymbol{x} \in X : \nexists \boldsymbol{x}' \in X \text{ such that } \boldsymbol{x}' \succ_L^{\underline{P}} \boldsymbol{x}\}.$$

**Interval Dominance Rule.** Considering the partial order $\succ_I^{\underline{P}}$ such that

$$\boldsymbol{x}^i \succeq_I^{\underline{P}} \boldsymbol{x}^j \text{ iff } \underline{\mathbb{C}}(\boldsymbol{x}^i) \geq \overline{\mathbb{C}}(\boldsymbol{x}^j), \tag{10}$$

the interval dominance decision rule is then

$$Dec_I^{\underline{P}}(X) = \{\boldsymbol{x} \in X : \nexists \boldsymbol{x}' \in X \text{ such that } \boldsymbol{x}' \succ_I^{\underline{P}} \boldsymbol{x}\}.$$

**Difference Rule.** Considering the partial order $\succ_L$ such that

$$\boldsymbol{x}^i \succeq_D^{\underline{P}} \boldsymbol{x}^j \text{ iff } \underline{\mathbb{C}}(\boldsymbol{x}^i - \boldsymbol{x}^j) \geq 0, \tag{11}$$

which in the quantitative scale is equivalent to state that $\boldsymbol{x}^i \succeq_D \boldsymbol{x}^j$ for all $P \in \mathcal{M}(\underline{P})$. The difference dominance decision rule is then

$$Dec_D^{\underline{P}}(X) = \{\boldsymbol{x} \in X : \nexists \boldsymbol{x}' \in X \text{ such that } \boldsymbol{x}' \succ_D^{\underline{P}} \boldsymbol{x}\}.$$

**E-Admissibility Rule.** Given a precise probability, consider the precise rule $Dec_P(X) = \arg\max_{\boldsymbol{x} \in X} \mathbb{C}(\boldsymbol{x})$, which are the top elements of the order induced by $\mathbb{C}(\boldsymbol{x})$. The E-admissibility rule is then

$$Dec_E^{\underline{P}} = \cup_{P \in \mathcal{M}(\underline{P})} Dec_P(X)$$

### 3.2 Properties

In the rest of the paper, we will study two particular properties, that are monotonicity with respect to information gain (or monotonicity for short), and Pareto refinement. Let us enunciate both of these properties:

**Definition 1 (Monotonocity).** *Let us consider two lower probabilities $\underline{P}, \underline{P}'$ such that $\underline{P} \leq \underline{P}'$. Then a decision rule $Dec^{\underline{P}}$ is monotonic if*

$$Dec^{\underline{P}'}(X) \subseteq Dec^{\underline{P}}(X)$$

In other words, a decision rule is monotonic if gaining more information (as modelled by $\underline{P} \leq \underline{P}'$) can only lead us to reduce our set of recommended alternatives. This is in line with the idea of a robust or skeptical rule, that will only remove those alternatives that are certainly sub-optimal. The second property is Pareto refinement

**Definition 2 (Pareto refinment).** *Within $X$, consider the set $X_P$ of alternative Paretop dominated by another one in $X \setminus X_P$. Then a decision rule $Dec^{\underline{P}}$ refines Pareto if for any $\underline{P}$ we have*

$$Dec^{\underline{P}'}(X) \subseteq X \setminus X_P$$

In other words, a decision rule refines Pareto if we are guaranteed that it will not include any Pareto dominated option. This somehow ensures that our rule is not too conservative, i.e., will not recommend alternatives that are certainly sub-optimal.

We will also compare rules in terms of their decisiveness, saying that a decision rule $Dec$ is more decisive than a decision $Dec'$ if $Dec(X) \subseteq Dec'(X)$.

For the quantitative case, we have the following relations

$$\left.\begin{array}{l} Dec_E^{\underline{P}}(X) \\ Dec_L^{\underline{P}}(X) \end{array}\right\} \subseteq Dec_D^{\underline{P}}(X) \subseteq Dec_I^{\underline{P}}(X) \tag{12}$$

going from the most to the least decisive rules. Table 1 also summarises the properties satisfied by the different rules. One can see that $Dec_E^{\underline{P}}$ and $Dec_D^{\underline{P}}$ are the most satisfactory from this perspective, but they are also usually the most computationally demanding, which sometimes a sufficient reason to use, e.g., approximations.

**Table 1.** Decision rules and properties

| | $Dec_L^{\underline{P}}$ | $Dec_E^{\underline{P}}$ | $Dec_D^{\underline{P}}$ | $Dec_I^{\underline{P}}$ |
|---|---|---|---|---|
| Monotonicity | ✗ | ✓ | ✓ | ✓ |
| Pareto Refinment | ✓ | ✓ | ✓ | ✗ |

## 4 Qualitative Decision Rules

Let us now study the counterparts of the different quantitative decision rules within the qualitative setting. We will start with the rules that use the imprecise bounds over single alternatives, as they are easier to extend, before discussing the more complex rules that are the difference and E-admissibile rules.

We will now consider a set $\mathcal{X} = \{\boldsymbol{x}^1, \ldots, \boldsymbol{x}^q\}$ of alternatives defined over $L^n$, rather than over $\mathbb{R}$, together with a knowledge modeled by the pair $\mu \leq \mu^c$ of pessimistic and optimistic capacities.

### 4.1 Interval Bound Rules

Let us consider the interval bounds $[\underline{\mathbb{S}}(\boldsymbol{x}^i), \overline{\mathbb{S}}(\boldsymbol{x}^i)]$ given by Eq. (7). Then it is straightforward to extend the lattice and interval dominance rules.

**Definition 3 (Lattice-based rule).** *Considering the partial order* $\succ_L^\mu$ *such that*

$$\boldsymbol{x}^i \succeq_L^\mu \boldsymbol{x}^j \text{ iff } \underline{\mathbb{S}}(x^i) \geq \underline{\mathbb{S}}(x^j) \text{ and } \overline{\mathbb{S}}(x^i) \geq \overline{\mathbb{S}}(x^j),$$

*the lattice-based decision rule is then*

$$Dec_L^\mu(X) = \{\boldsymbol{x} \in X : \nexists \boldsymbol{x}' \in X \text{ such that } x' \succ_L^\mu x\}.$$

We can show that the Lattice bound criterion can be associated to a $\forall, \exists$ constraint on the auto-dual capacities of the core.

**Proposition 4.** $\boldsymbol{x}^i \succeq_L^\mu \boldsymbol{x}^j$ *if and only if*
$\forall \nu \in \mathcal{M}(\mu)\, \exists \nu' \in \mathcal{M}(\mu)$ *such that* $\mathbb{S}_\nu(\boldsymbol{x}^i) \geq \mathbb{S}_{\nu'}(\boldsymbol{x}^j)$ *and*
$\forall \nu \in \mathcal{M}(\mu)\, \exists \nu' \in \mathcal{M}(\mu)$ *such that* $\mathbb{S}_{\nu'}(\boldsymbol{x}^i) \geq \mathbb{S}_\nu(\boldsymbol{x}^j)$.

*Proof.* If $\boldsymbol{x}^i \succeq_L^\mu \boldsymbol{x}^j$ then
$\forall \nu \in \mathcal{M}(\mu)$ we have $\overline{\mathbb{S}}(\boldsymbol{x}^i) \geq \mathbb{S}_\nu(\boldsymbol{x}^i) \geq \underline{\mathbb{S}}(\boldsymbol{x}^i) \geq \underline{\mathbb{S}}(\boldsymbol{x}^j) = \mathbb{S}_{\underline{\nu}_x}(\boldsymbol{x}^j)$ where $\underline{\nu}_x \in \mathcal{M}(\mu)$.
$\forall \nu \in \mathcal{M}(\mu)$ we have $\underline{\mathbb{S}}(\boldsymbol{x}^j) \leq \mathbb{S}_\nu(\boldsymbol{x}^j) \leq \overline{\mathbb{S}}(\boldsymbol{x}^j) \leq \overline{\mathbb{S}}(\boldsymbol{x}^i) = \mathbb{S}_{\overline{\nu}_{x^i}}(\boldsymbol{x}^i)$ where $\underline{\nu}_{x^i} \in \mathcal{M}(\mu)$.
Reciprocally,
If $\forall \nu \in \mathcal{M}(\mu)\, \exists \nu' \in \mathcal{M}(\mu)$ such that $\mathbb{S}_\nu(\boldsymbol{x}^i) \geq \mathbb{S}_{\nu'}(\boldsymbol{x}^j)$ we have $\exists \nu' \in \mathcal{M}(\mu)$ such that $\underline{\mathbb{S}}(\boldsymbol{x}^i) = \mathbb{S}_{\underline{\nu}_{x^i}}(\boldsymbol{x}^i) \geq \mathbb{S}_{\nu'}(\boldsymbol{x}^j) \geq \underline{\mathbb{S}}(\boldsymbol{x}^j)$.
If $\forall \nu \in \mathcal{M}(\mu)\, \exists \nu' \in \mathcal{M}(\mu)$ such that $\mathbb{S}_{\nu'}(\boldsymbol{x}^i) \geq \mathbb{S}_\nu(\boldsymbol{x}^j)$ then
$\overline{\mathbb{S}}(\boldsymbol{x}^j) = \mathbb{S}_{\overline{\nu}_{x^j}}(\boldsymbol{x}^j) \leq \mathbb{S}_{\nu'}(\boldsymbol{x}^i) \leq \overline{\mathbb{S}}(\boldsymbol{x}^i)$.

**Definition 4 (Interval dominance).** *Considering the partial order* $\succ_I^\mu$ *such that*

$$\boldsymbol{x}^i \succeq_I^\mu \boldsymbol{x}^j \text{ iff } \underline{\mathbb{S}}(\boldsymbol{x}^i) \geq \overline{\mathbb{S}}(\boldsymbol{x}^j),$$

*the interval dominance decision rule is then*

$$Dec_I^\mu(X) = \{\boldsymbol{x} \in X : \nexists \boldsymbol{x}' \in X \text{ such that } \boldsymbol{x}' \succ_I^\mu \boldsymbol{x}\}.$$

We can show that this criterion is linked to a $\forall, \forall$ constraint on auto-dual capacities within the core.

**Proposition 5.** $\boldsymbol{x}^i \succeq_I^\mu \boldsymbol{x}^j$ *if and only if* $\forall \nu, \nu' \in \mathcal{M}(\mu)$ *we have* $\mathbb{S}_\nu(\boldsymbol{x}^i) \geq \mathbb{S}_{\nu'}(\boldsymbol{x}^j)$.

*Proof.* If $\boldsymbol{x}^i \succeq_I^\mu \boldsymbol{x}^j$ then $\forall \nu, \nu' \in \mathcal{M}(\mu)$ we have $\mathbb{S}_\nu(\boldsymbol{x}^i) \geq \underline{\mathbb{S}}(\boldsymbol{x}^i) \geq \overline{\mathbb{S}}(\boldsymbol{x}^j) \geq \mathbb{S}_{\nu'}(\boldsymbol{x}^j)$.

If $\forall \nu, \nu' \in \mathcal{M}(\mu)$ we have $\mathbb{S}_\nu(\boldsymbol{x}^i) \geq \mathbb{S}_{\nu'}(\boldsymbol{x}^j)$ we have $\mathbb{S}_{\underline{\nu}_{\boldsymbol{x}^i}}(\boldsymbol{x}^i) \geq \mathbb{S}_{\overline{\nu}_{\boldsymbol{x}^j}}(\boldsymbol{x}^j)$ i.e. $\underline{\mathbb{S}}(\boldsymbol{x}^i) \geq \overline{\mathbb{S}}(\boldsymbol{x}^j)$.

We can easily show that those rules suffer from the same defaults as their quantitative counterparts, i.e., the lattice rule is not monotonic with respect to information gain, and interval dominance may not refine the Pareto dominance.

*Example 1 (Non-monotonicity of lattice rule).* Let $\Omega = \{1, 2, 3\}$ and let $L = \{a, b, c, d, e\}$. Let us consider the capacity $\mu(\{1\}) = b$, $\mu(\{2\}) = a$, $\mu(\{3\}) = a$, $\mu(\{1, 2\}) = c$, $\mu(\{1, 3\}) = b$, $\mu(\{2, 3\}) = b$. It can be checked that $\mu < \mu^c$. Let us now consider the alternatives $\boldsymbol{x} = (a, d, e)$ and $\boldsymbol{y} = (e, d, a)$. Then we have

$$[\mathbb{S}_\mu(\boldsymbol{x}), \mathbb{S}_{\mu^c}(\boldsymbol{x})] = [b, d], \quad [\mathbb{S}_\mu(\boldsymbol{y}), \mathbb{S}_{\mu^c}(\boldsymbol{y})] = [c, d],$$

meaning that $\boldsymbol{y} \succ_L^\mu \boldsymbol{x}$. Now let us consider the capacity $\mu'$ such that $\mu'(\{1, 2\})) = \mu'(\{3\}) = c$ and $\mu' = \mu$ for the other events. Then we have $\mu \leq \mu' \leq \mu'^c \leq \mu^c$, showing that indeed $\mu'$ constitute a gain of information. However, we do have

$$[\mathbb{S}_{\mu'}(\boldsymbol{x}), \mathbb{S}_{\mu'^c}(\boldsymbol{x})] = [b, d], \quad [\mathbb{S}_{\mu'}(\boldsymbol{y}), \mathbb{S}_{\mu'^c}(\boldsymbol{y})] = [c, c],$$

meaning that $\boldsymbol{y} \succ\prec_L^{\mu'} \boldsymbol{x}$, i.e., $\boldsymbol{y}$ and $\boldsymbol{x}$ are incomparable, indicating that lattice rule is non-monotonic, as $Dec_L^\mu(\{\boldsymbol{y}, \boldsymbol{x}\}) = \{\boldsymbol{y}\}$ and $Dec_L^{\mu'}(\{\boldsymbol{y}, \boldsymbol{x}\}) = \{\boldsymbol{y}, \boldsymbol{x}\}$

*Example 2 (Non-Pareto refinment of interval dominance).* Let $\Omega = \{1, 2, 3\}$, $L \subseteq [0, 1]$ and $\mu$ be the capacity defined by $\mu(\{1\}) = \mu(\{2\}) = \mu(\{3\}) = 0$, $\mu(\{1, 2\}) = \mu(\{1, 3\}) = \mu(\{2, 3\}) = 0.4$ and 1 on $\Omega$. The conjugate capacity is $\mu^c(\{1\}) = \mu^c(\{2\}) = \mu^c(\{3\}) = 0.6$ and $\mu^c$ equals to 1 otherwise. We have $\mu \leq \mu^c$. Let us consider $\boldsymbol{x} = (1, 1, 0)$ and $\boldsymbol{y} = (1, 0, 0)$, we have $\boldsymbol{x} \geq \boldsymbol{y}$ but $\mathbb{S}_\mu(\boldsymbol{x}) = 0.4 < \mathbb{S}_{\mu^c}(\boldsymbol{y}) = 0.6.$, hence $\boldsymbol{x}$ and $\boldsymbol{y}$ are incomparable w.r.t. $\succeq_I^\mu$.

It is also rather direct to see that $\boldsymbol{x}^i \succeq_I^\mu \boldsymbol{x}^j \Rightarrow \boldsymbol{x}^i \succeq_L^\mu \boldsymbol{x}^j$, as in the precise case, hence that $Dec_L^\mu(X) \subseteq Dec_I^\mu(X)$.

As those decision rules suffer from the same defects as their precise counterparts, it remains desirable to extend the other decision rules to the qualitative setting. As such decision rules are more difficult to extend and to treat, and as we are bound to space constraints, we will focus on proposing such extensions and on providing the most immediate insights about them, leaving the complete study of their relations with other for another paper or an extension of this one.

### 4.2 Difference Rule

An issue of the difference rule as given by Eq. 11 is that it uses the difference $x^i - x^j$, which in the quantitative case is equivalent to say that the pairwise dominance between $x^i$ and $x^j$ is true for every auto-dual capacity dominating $\underline{P}$. This equivalence is no longer true in the qualitative case, and each of these view can give rise to two different notions: a first one that considers a qualitative notion of the difference between alternatives, and a second one that checks whether $x^i$ dominates $x^j$ for every capacity in $\mathcal{M}(\mu)$.

**Qualitative Difference,** Let us first propose how to perform the operation $x^i - x^j$ in a qualitative setting. Note that while it does not make sense to speak of the intensity of the difference, it is easy to speak of the sign of the difference, i.e., $x^i_k - x^j_k$ is positive if $x^i_k \geq x^j_k$ in $L$, and negative otherwise. It then makes sense to speak of the sign $sign(x^i_k - x^j_k)$ of the difference.

Provided that we have an odd number of elements in $L$, we first consider that $\lambda_{t/2}$ plays the role of "neutral" element, that is any $\lambda_j$ with $j > t/2$ is deemed positive as a reward, and negative when $j < t/2$. We then propose to define the difference $x^i - x^j$ as follows:

$$x^i_k - x^j_k = \begin{cases} \lambda_t & \text{if } sign(x^i_k - x^j_k) > 0 \\ \lambda_0 & \text{if } sign(x^i_k - x^j_k) < 0 \\ \lambda_{t/2} & \text{if } x^i_k = x^j_k \end{cases} \tag{13}$$

Given these definitions, we are now able to define our decision rule

**Definition 5 (Qualitative difference).** *Considering the partial order $\succ^{\mu}_{QD}$ such that*

$$\boldsymbol{x}^i \succeq^{\mu}_{QD} \boldsymbol{x}^j \text{ iff } \underline{\mathbb{S}}(x^i - x^j) \geq \lambda_{t/2},$$

*the qualitative difference decision rule is then*

$$Dec^{\mu}_{QD}(X) = \{\boldsymbol{x} \in X : \nexists \boldsymbol{x}' \in X \text{ such that } x' \succ^{\mu}_{QD} x\}.$$

*Remark 1.* Note that due to Eq. (6), the qualitative difference decision rule and its associated partial order are insensitive to the encoding of the difference in Eq. (13), as long as a negative difference is below $\lambda_{t/2}$, and a positive one above. Indeed, the sign of the median is independent of such an encoding.

**Core Dominance.** Core dominance is much more straightforward to define, as it relies upon a point-wise dominance for every auto-dual capacity within the core.

**Definition 6 (Core dominance).** *Considering the partial order $\succ^{\mu}_{CD}$ such that*

$$\boldsymbol{x}^i \succeq^{\mu}_{CD} \boldsymbol{x}^j \text{ iff } \mathbb{S}_{\nu}(x^i) \geq \mathbb{S}_{\nu}(x^j) \ \forall \nu \in \mathcal{M}(\mu),$$

*the core dominance decision rule is then*

$$Dec^{\mu}_{QD}(X) = \{\boldsymbol{x} \in X : \nexists \boldsymbol{x}' \in X \text{ such that } x' \succ^{\mu}_{CD} x\}.$$

While we leave a complete study as future work, we can already mention a rather straightforward relation between $\succeq_I^\mu$ and $\succeq_{CD}^\mu$.

**Proposition 6.** *Given a capacity $\mu$ and a set $\mathcal{X}$, we have the following implication: $\boldsymbol{x}^i \succeq_I^\mu \boldsymbol{x}^j \Rightarrow \boldsymbol{x}^i \succeq_{CD}^\mu \boldsymbol{x}^j$*

*Proof.* Clearly, for any $\nu \in \mathcal{M}(\mu)$, we will have $\underline{\mathbb{S}}_\mu(x) \leq \mathbb{S}_\nu(x) \leq \overline{\mathbb{S}}_\mu(x)$, hence if $\overline{\mathbb{S}}_\mu(x^j) \leq \underline{\mathbb{S}}_\mu(x^i)$, we will have $\mathbb{S}_\nu(x^j) \leq \overline{\mathbb{S}}_\mu(x^j) \leq \underline{\mathbb{S}}_\mu(x^i) \leq \mathbb{S}_\nu(x^i)$ for all $\nu \in \mathcal{M}(\mu)$.

### 4.3 E-Admissibility

As with the core dominance and the interval bound rules, extending E-admissibility to the qualitative case is rather straightforward, and give rise to the following definition.

**Definition 7 (Qualitative E-admissibility).** *Given an auto-dual capacity $\nu \in \mathcal{A}$, consider the rule $Dec_\nu(X) = \arg\max_{\boldsymbol{x} \in X} \mathcal{S}_\nu(\boldsymbol{x})$, which are the top elements of the order induced by $\mathcal{S}_\nu(\boldsymbol{x})$. The qualitative E-admissibility rule of $\mu$ is then*

$$Dec_E^\mu = \cup_{\nu \in \mathcal{M}(\mu)} Dec_\nu(X)$$

We also have a direct relation between our interval-valued decision rules and E-admmissibility.

**Proposition 7.** *Given a capacity $\mu$ and a set $\mathcal{X}$, we have the inclusion $Dec_E^\mu \subseteq Dec_{CD}^\mu$*

*Proof.* To prove this, let us show that if $\boldsymbol{x} \in Dec_E^\mu$, it must be in $Dec_{CD}^\mu$. First observe that if $\boldsymbol{x} \in Dec_E^\mu$, there is a capacity $\nu \in\in \mathcal{M}(\mu)$ such that $\mathcal{S}_\nu(x) \geq \mathcal{S}_\nu(y)$ for all $y \in \mathcal{X}$. From the definition of core dominance, it results that there is no $y$ such that $y \succ_C D^\mu x$, otherwise we would not have such a capacity $\nu$. Hence, $x$ must also be in $Dec_{CD}^\mu$.

## 5 Conclusion

In this paper, we have introduced qualitative adaptations of commonly used decision rules in the quantitative setting, and have studied some of their properties. The next step will be to study in detail the difference and E-admissibility rules, both regarding their properties, inter-relations and algorithmic resolution.

## References


1. Bouyssou, D., Dubois, D., Prade, H., Pirlot, M.: Decision Making Process: Concepts and Methods. John Wiley & Sons, Hoboken (2013)
2. de Cooman, G.: Coherent and archimedean choice in general banach spaces. Int. J. Approx. Reason. **140**, 255–281 (2022)
3. Denoeux, T.: Decision-making with belief functions: a review. Int. J. Approx. Reason. **109**, 87–110 (2019)
4. Destercke, S.: A decision rule for imprecise probabilities based on pair-wise comparison of expectation bounds. In: Combining Soft Computing and Statistical Methods in Data Analysis, pp. 189–197. Springer, Heidelberg (2010)
5. Dubois, D., Faux, F., Prade, H., Rico, A.: Qualitative capacities: basic notions and potential applications. Int. J. Approx. Reason. **148**, 253–290 (2022)
6. Grabisch, M.: Set Functions, Games and Capacities in Decision-Making (2016)
7. Sugeno, M.: Theory of Fuzzy Integrals and its Applications. PhD thesis, Tokyo Institute of Technology (1974)
8. Troffaes, M.: Decision making under uncertainty using imprecise probabilities. Int. J. Approx. Reason. **45**(1), 17–29 (2007)

# Soft Methods in Statistical Inference and Data Analysis

# A Soft Clustering Method Derived from the Probabilistic Interpretation of Fuzzy C-Means

Davide Cazzorla(✉) and Corrado Mencar

University of Bari Aldo Moro, Bari, Italy
d.cazzorla@phd.uniba.it, corrado.mencar@uniba.it

**Abstract.** The Bayesian interpretation of Fuzzy C-Means (FCM) opens the door to novel extensions of this technique for soft data clustering. In this paper, we propose a new method based on the minimization of negative log-likelihood of data samples, using basin-hopping and Powell method for minimization. Differently from FCM, we observed a more robust arrangement of prototypes, which could enable the assessment of the suitability of the chosen number of clusters. Moreover, the method enables the data-driven derivation of the fuzzification coefficient, which is directly related to the variance of the component densities. Experiments on synthetic data aim at comparing the proposed method with FCM, by showing benefits and limitations of the two techniques.

**Keywords:** Fuzzy C-Means · Soft Clustering · Maximum likelihood estimation · Fuzzification coefficient

## 1 Introduction

Soft clustering is an approach to clustering whereby the labels assigned to data points are permitted to assume values between zero and one, rather than being confined to binary values [3]. These values can be utilized to signify a degree of uncertainty in the assignment of the point to the cluster.

A widely used soft clustering method is Fuzzy C-Means (FCM) [1]. Since its formulation, FCM has been used in endless applications and extended in numerous variants thanks to its efficiency, robustness and simple definition [4,8].

FCM is usually analyzed within Fuzzy Set Theory, where clusters are fuzzy sets and membership degrees are intended as "degrees of sharing" [2], which may pose some interpretation difficulties when using FCM within Explainable AI. To address this problem, we recently analyzed FCM under the umbrella of probability theory, obtaining a theoretically sound interpretation of membership degrees [5]. The work opened the door to possible extensions of FCM that are coherent with this probabilistic interpretation.

In particular, the interpretation of membership degrees as posterior probabilities of clusters given data, enables their direct comparison with classical model-based clustering, like Gaussian Mixture Models (GMM). GMM parameters are


M. Baczyński et al. (Eds.): EUSFLAT 2025, LNCS 15884, pp. 173–184, 2025.
https://doi.org/10.1007/978-3-031-97228-7_15

typically estimated by maximum likelihood estimation using the expectation-maximization algorithm (EM); therefore, a consequent research question is whether it is possible to use likelihood for estimating the parameters of a mixture model that is defined with the same structure of FCM.

One key aspect of FCM is the fuzzification coefficient, usually denoted with $m$ and often set to a constant value (typically 2) [7]. Despite extensive research, there is still no widely accepted criterion for selecting the optimal fuzzification coefficient value. In fact, a constant value for the fuzzification coefficient may not be suitable for all datasets [9]. We hypothesize that the difficulties in setting a proper value of the fuzzification parameter lay in the lack of a clear interpretation of its value in the context of clustering. According to our probabilistic interpretation, the fuzzification coefficient is related to the expected variance of data points within a cluster [5]. Therefore, our second research question is whether the fuzzification coefficient can be estimated from data in agreement with its statistical interpretation.

To address these research questions, in this work, we describe a soft clustering method based on the probabilistic framework we proposed for FCM. We compare standard FCM with this new method, by showing similarities and differences in a simplified experimental scenario. Furthermore, we show that this method allows a data-driven estimation of the fuzzification coefficient with a sound probabilistic interpretation. These results may shed light on new approaches for a full data-driven and interpretable clustering method that is inspired by FCM.

In the next section, the preliminary notation and definitions are reported. In Sect. 3, the proposed soft-clustering method is presented, while in Sect. 4 some preliminary experiments on synthetic data are reported. Current limitations and indications for future development are outlined in Sect. 5.

## 2 Preliminaries

We provide a concise overview of the original FCM definition [1], in addition to discussing our earlier proposed probabilistic interpretation [5].

### 2.1 Fuzzy C-Means

Let $\mathbf{X}$ be a collection of $N$ items $x_j \in \mathbb{R}^n$ to be clustered in $c$ groups. Fuzzy C-Means (FCM) finds the prototypes $v_i$ and membership values $u_{ij}$ such that the following objective function is minimized:

$$J(\mathbf{U},\mathbf{V}) = \sum_{j}^{N}\sum_{i}^{c} u_{ji}^{m}||x_j - v_i||_2^2 \tag{1}$$

constrained to:

$$u_{ji} \in [0,1], \quad 1 \le j \le N, 1 \le i \le c,$$
$$\sum_{i}^{c} u_{ji} = 1, \quad 1 \le j \le N,$$
$$0 < \sum_{j}^{N} u_{ji} < N, \quad 1 \le i \le c$$

The fuzzification coefficient $m$ is fixed to a value in $(1, \infty)$. To minimize the objective function, an iterative procedure is adopted, which alternately calculates the membership values and the prototypes according to the following two equations:

$$u_{ji} = \frac{1}{\sum_{k}^{c} \left( \frac{||x_j - v_i||}{||x_j - v_k||} \right)^{\frac{2}{m-1}}} \tag{2}$$

$$v_i = \frac{\sum_j u_{ji}^m x_j}{\sum_j u_{ji}^m} \tag{3}$$

The procedure stops when the change of the prototypes or membership values is less than a value or when a certain number of iterations is reached.

### 2.2 Bayesian Interpretation of the Fuzzy C-Means

To derive a probabilistic interpretation of FCM, some assumptions are stated. First, it is assumed the data distribution follows a mixture model:

$$f(x|\theta) = \sum_{i}^{c} \Pr(C = i) f(x|C = i, \theta) \tag{4}$$

with $C$ the unknown class of the point and $\Pr(C = i)$ the mixing proportions.

Second, it is assumed that the component densities $f(x|C = i, \theta)$ are defined as follows:

$$f(x|C = i, \theta) = \frac{1}{K} ||x - v_i||^{-\beta} \quad \forall i \in [1, \cdots, c] \tag{5}$$

where $\theta = (v_1, \ldots, v_c, \beta)$ is the vector of parameters, consisting of the cluster prototypes $v_i$ and the parameter $\beta > 0$.

To be a proper density, it is furthermore assumed that the distance is bounded, i.e., $a \le ||x - v_i|| \le l$. With this last assumption, it is possible to derive the value of $K$ (see Appendix A). The implicit assumption in this density is that the prototypes must be at a certain distance from the data points, and that the points are concentrated around the prototype (Fig. 1).

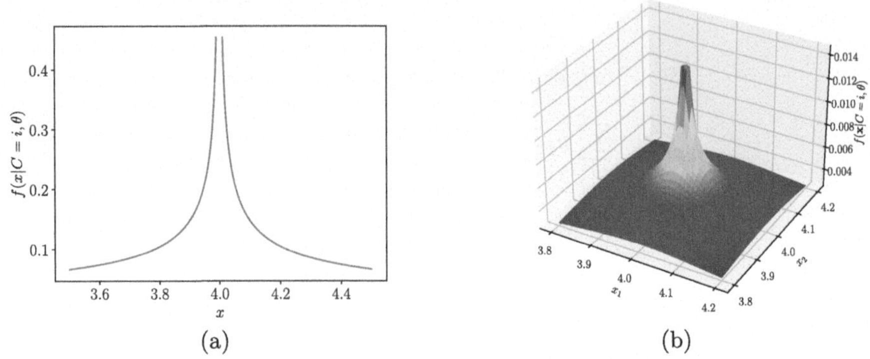


**Fig. 1.** Example of one-dimensional distribution (a) and two-dimensional distribution (b) of the component densities $f(\cdot|C = i, \theta)$.

Assuming that $\Pr(C = i) = 1/c\ \forall i \in [1, \cdots, c]$, the posterior probability of the model defined above is:

$$f(C = i|x_j, \theta) = \frac{f(x_j|C = i, \theta) f(C = i)}{\sum_k^c f(C = k, x_j|\theta)} \tag{6}$$

$$= \frac{||x_j - v_i||^{-\beta}}{\sum_k^c ||x_j - v_k||^{-\beta}} \tag{7}$$

$$= \frac{1}{\sum_k^c \left(\frac{||x_j - v_i||}{||x_j - v_k||}\right)^{\beta}} \tag{8}$$

It is possible to see that the posterior probability is the same as the membership function of the FCM by setting $\beta = \frac{2}{m-1}$. Thus, the results of the FCM can be seen in the context of probability theory.

# 3 Proposed Method

Given a set of samples $\mathbf{X} = \{x_1, x_2, \cdots, x_n\}$, the goal is to estimate the unknown parameters of the statistical model defined in (4). We estimate these parameters by minimizing the negative log-likelihood:

$$\theta^* = \arg\min_\theta \{-\log \mathcal{L}(\theta|\mathbf{X})\} = \arg\min_\theta \{-\log f(\mathbf{X}|\theta)\} \tag{9}$$

$$= \arg\min_\theta \left\{ -\log \prod_j f(x_j|\theta) \right\} \tag{10}$$

$$= \arg\min_{\beta>0, \mathbf{v}\in\mathbb{S}^c} \left\{ -\sum_j^N \log \sum_i^c \frac{1}{c}\frac{1}{K} ||x_j - v_i||^{-\beta} \right\} \tag{11}$$

where $\mathbb{S} = \mathbb{R}^n \setminus \{v \in \mathbb{R}^n | \, \|v - x_j\| \leq a, x_j \in \mathbf{X}\}$. (This constraint is required to avoid data samples as accumulation points.)

The structure of (11), as well as the non-trivial dependency of $K$ on $\beta$ (see Appendix A) does not allow a analytical solution to the optimization problem. Moreover, the log-likelihood function is not continuous, and its derivative approaches infinity when some prototypes get close to some data points. The landscape of the log-likelihood function can be locally considered "funnel-like" around the data samples, making its optimization challenging. For this reason, we choose to use the *basin-hopping* algorithm, which has been proven to be useful in cases where the function has complex funnel-type landscape [6].[1]

The basin-hopping algorithm is a global optimization algorithm that performs three steps in an iterative way. First, it perturbs the estimate of the parameters, then it performs a local minimization, and lastly it accepts or rejects the new candidate based on a test. In the SciPy implementation, the Metropolis test is used. For the local minimization algorithm, we choose the Powell's method, which is a conjugate direction method that does not require function derivatives. To force the algorithm to operate within $\mathbb{S}$, in practice, an infinite amount of negative log-likelihood is assigned to candidates that are within $a$ from any data points.

Notably, the log-likelihood in (11) is parameterized by $\beta$; therefore, its minimization leads to an optimal value of $\beta$ together with the optimal prototypes $v_i$. Since $\beta = {}^{2}\!/_{m-1}$, the optimization of the log-likelihood leads to finding an optimal value of the fuzzification coefficient $m$.

Interestingly, the fuzzification coefficient is related to the variance of the component density function. In fact, restricting the analysis to the one-dimensional case for the sake of clarity, we first notice that:

$$E_{X|i,\theta}[X] = \int_S x \cdot f(x|C = i, \theta) dx = v_i \tag{12}$$

where $S = [v_i - l, v_i - a] \cup [v_i + a, v_i + l]$. (This is easily established by noticing the symmetry of $f$ around $v_i$; see also Fig. 1.) Then, we derive:

$$V(X) = E_{X|i,\theta}\left[(X - E_{X|i,\theta}[X])^2\right] = \int_S (x - v_i)^2 \frac{1}{K} |x - v_i|^{-\beta} dx \tag{13}$$

$$= \frac{2}{K} \int_{v_i+a}^{v_i+l} (x - v_i)^{2-\beta} dx = \frac{2}{K} \frac{l^{3-\beta} - a^{3-\beta}}{3 - \beta} \tag{14}$$

for $\beta \neq 3$, and

$$V(X) = \int_S (x - v_i)^2 \frac{1}{K} |x - v_i|^{-3} dx = \frac{2}{K} \int_{v_i+a}^{v_i+l} (x - v_i)^{-1} dx \tag{15}$$

$$= \frac{2}{K} \Big( \log(l) - \log(a) \Big) \tag{16}$$

[1] A procedure for basin-hopping optimization is available in the SciPy library.

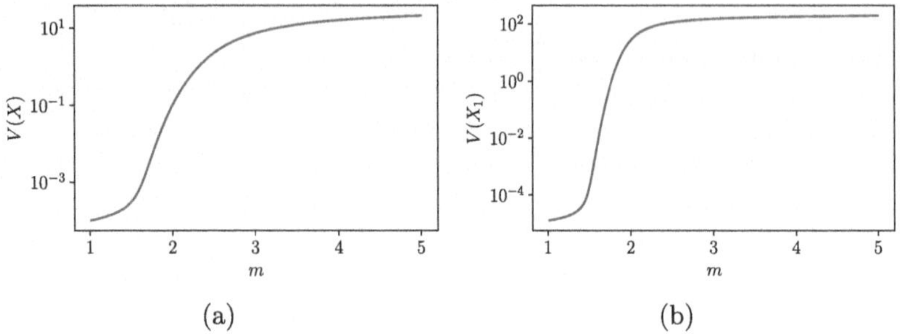


**Fig. 2.** Variance of the distribution of the component density (5) by varying $m$ in (a) the one-dimensional case, and (b) the two-dimensional one case. The variance was calculated assuming $a = 0.005$ and $l = 30$.

for $\beta = 3$.

As a consequence, optimizing the log-likelihood for $\beta$ (and $m$ accordingly) implies the search for the best value of common variance among all clusters. The relation between $m$ and variance is depicted in Fig. 2.

# 4 Experimental Results

We carried out initial tests to evaluate the proposed method against FCM. For this purpose, we utilized synthetic datasets in both one-dimensional and two-dimensional formats to visually emphasize the distinctions.

## 4.1 One-Dimensional Data

We employed a one-dimensional dataset to evaluate our proposed soft clustering approach against FCM, focusing on the resulting positions of the prototypes. Additionally, the data's low dimensionality allows for a visual inspection of the objective functions, facilitating comparison.

The experimental dataset, depicted with blue dots in Fig. 3, served as the basis for running the methods under the assumption of either two or three clusters. Apparently, data are grouped in three regions of high density, making the choice of three clusters the optimal.

In both scenarios, the methods were initialized using identical values for the parameters $m$ and $v_i$, for all $i \in [1, \cdots, c]$. Our method, however, also requires specifying the parameters $a$ and $l$, which we set as $a = 0.0005$ and $l = 20$. The choice of $l = 20$ was made because the clusters are situated within the range of $[-10, 10]$. The value of $a$ was chosen such that it is less than every pairwise distance (divided by two) between the data points.

In Fig. 3, the methods exhibit convergence to distinct prototypes, notably when dealing with two clusters only, while they almost coincide with three clusters. In particular, for FCM, one prototype aligns almost centrally between

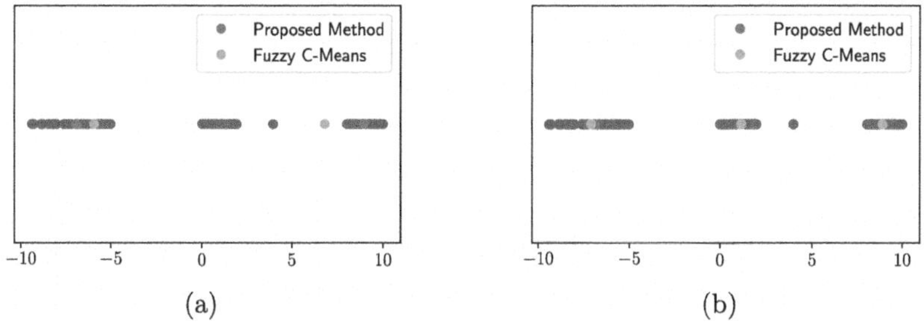


**Fig. 3.** Clustering results on a one-dimensional dataset with (a) two prototypes and (b) three prototypes. Data was generated from a mixture of 4 Uniform distributions defined on different intervals, $[-10, 10]$, $[-10, -5]$, $[0, 2]$ and $[8, 10]$.

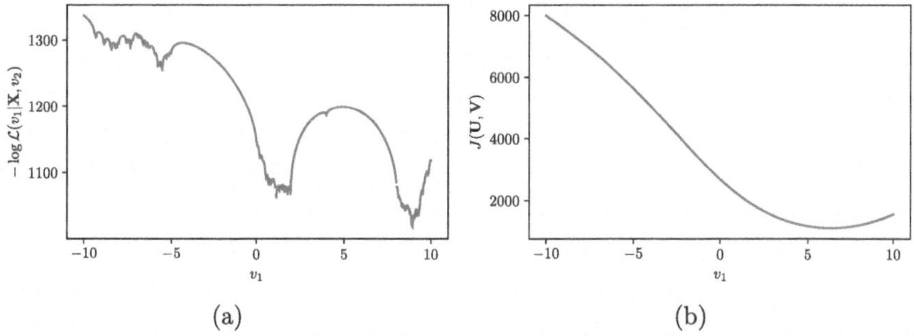


**Fig. 4.** (a) Negative Log-Likelihood (11) and (b) objective function of FCM (1), both evaluated by varying $v_1$ in $[-10, 10]$, while fixing $v_2 = -6.878$ and $m = 2$.

two regions of data. Conversely, our approach treats the central data cluster as noise. This divergence is evident in their respective objective function evaluations (Fig. 4). The negative likelihood reveals two minima: one within the central cluster and another in the right cluster, whereas the FCM objective function features a single minimum centered between the two clusters. On the other hand, the graphs indicate challenges in optimizing the negative likelihood due to its discontinuity and multiple local minima, whereas the smoother Fuzzy C-Means functional is more straightforward to optimize.

The variation in outcomes when utilizing merely two clusters highlights how our proposed technique significantly reduces the weight assigned to data points distant from the prototypes. This peculiar weighting is apparent in the assumed data distribution model of our method (Fig. 1). This feature can be beneficial in situations where the initial number of clusters does not accurately reflect the data distribution.

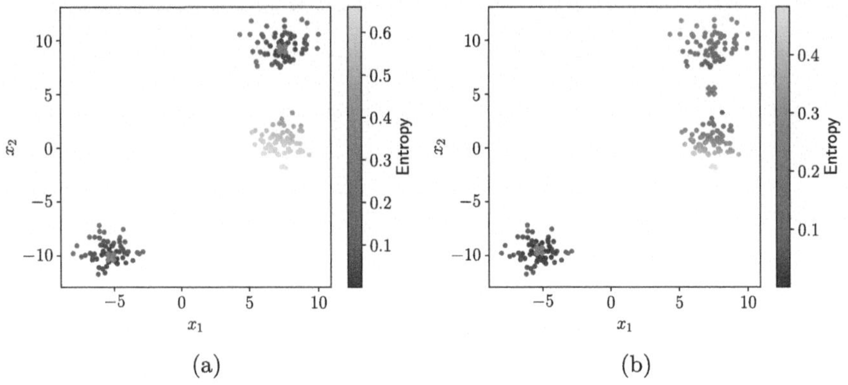


**Fig. 5.** Prototypes found by the proposed method (a) and FCM (b). Every data point is colored based on its entropy. The entropy of FCM was calculated using the probabilistic interpretation of the membership degrees.

### 4.2 Two-Dimensional Data

In this experiment, we evaluated the methods' outcomes when the number of clusters imposed on the data differs from what is naturally outlined by the data's density. Additionally, we empirically demonstrated that the estimated fuzziness parameter $m$ is influenced by the clusters' variance.

Analogous to the previous setting with one-dimensional data, we utilized a dataset composed of three clusters (Fig. 5, represented by colored circles) and analyzed the methods under the assumption that only two clusters exist. The methods were initialized using identical prototype values and $m = 2$. In our technique, given that the data spans $[-15, 15]$, we chose $l = 30$ to ensure the distribution encompasses the entire data space. The parameter $a = 0.001$ was set such that each pair of data points has distance greater than $2a$.

Referring to the outcomes depicted in Fig. 5, it is evident once more that the methods transition to distinct prototypes. Our proposed method treats one of the data clusters as noise, whereas FCM includes that cluster as a portion of a larger one. In this situation, our approach's results might be more favorable because the cluster's uncertainty, which lacks a prototype at its center, is properly elevated. This characteristic can be measured using entropy by analyzing the probability distribution of a specific data point across all clusters. We readily notice that the entropy of these data points exceeds that of others.

Ultimately, we assessed the methods on two additional 2D datasets where the clusters exhibit varying variances (Fig. 6). In the initial dataset, the clusters were drawn from two Gaussian distributions with a variance of 6.25, while in the second dataset, the clusters originated from Gaussian distributions with a 0.01 variance. Both methods were started with identical initial parameter values, resulting in comparable outcomes in each instance.

Examining the value $m$ derived from our method (Table 1), it becomes evident that a dataset with greater variance yields a larger estimated value for $m$.

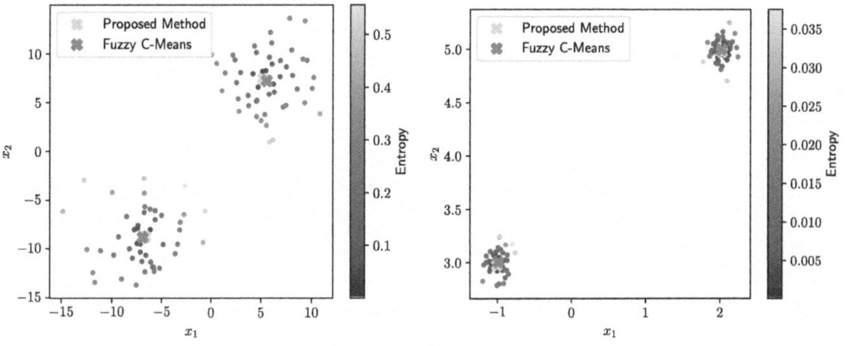


(a) (b)

**Fig. 6.** Prototypes derived by the two methods on synthetic datasets with different variance. Entropy was calculated using the results of our proposed method.

(Notice that the estimated variance differs from that used for generating data because the component density functions are not Gaussian.) This empirical evidence supports the idea that our approach successfully relates the estimated value of $m$ to the variance within the clusters. Determining the accurate value of $m$ is crucial for assessing metrics of uncertainty, including the entropy of individual data points.

**Table 1.** Estimated value of $m$ by the proposed method.

| Dataset | Est. $m$ | Variance |
|---|---|---|
| High Variance | 2.225 | 72.8 |
| Low Variance | 1.896 | 9.1 |

## 5 Conclusion

The suggested soft clustering method draws inspiration from FCM but is fundamentally based on a probabilistic framework, allowing the application of conventional probabilistic techniques, like minimizing negative log-likelihood, for clustering formation. This method offers fresh perspectives but also presents certain challenges.

Expressing the clustering optimization problem as minimizing the negative log-likelihood results in outcomes that differ from those of FCM. In this approach, cluster centers tend to gravitate more towards areas with high data density—unlike FCM—hence the averaging effect is reduced, particularly when the number of real clusters exceeds the set number of clusters.

This feature enhances the robustness of clustering, allowing for a potential examination of cluster validity by analyzing the entropy in data point assignments to clusters. Additionally, the suggested soft-clustering approach allows for the measurement of the fuzzification coefficient, which is linked directly to the (assumed) shared variance among clusters. This paves the way for future developments where each cluster can be characterized by its specific variance, and parameter uncertainty can be assessed through a comprehensive Bayesian framework.

The proposed method presents certain limitations that warrant additional research. In particular, the method requires specifying the value of two new hyperparameters. A study on how the results are affected by different hyperparameter values may help decide an appropriate value for them. Furthermore, the "funnel-like" nature of the log-likelihood function necessitates caution when applying a minimization technique. While basin-hopping optimization shows potential, it is essential to conduct comprehensive tests on larger datasets (in terms of both size and complexity) to evaluate the practicality and performance of this method in real-world applications.

## A The Value of *K*

We assume that the distance of any data point $x$ to the prototype $v$ is restricted in the interval $[a, l]$. We denote by $\mathbb{S}$ the subset of admissible data points. The goal is therefore to calculate the value of $K$ such that:

$$\int_{\mathbb{S}} \frac{1}{K} ||x - v||^{-\beta} dx = 1$$

### A.1 One-Dimensional Case

In the one-dimensional case, $\mathbb{S} = [v - l, v - a] \cup [v + a, v + l]$. Two cases are distinguished:

Case I: $\beta \neq 1$

$$\begin{aligned} K &= \int_{\mathbb{S}} |x - v|^{-\beta} dx = \int_{v+a}^{v+l} (x - v)^{-\beta} dx + \int_{v-l}^{v-a} (-x + v)^{-\beta} dx \\ &= \left.\frac{(x - v)^{1-\beta}}{1 - \beta}\right|_{v+a}^{v+l} - \left.\frac{(-x + v)^{1-\beta}}{1 - \beta}\right|_{v-l}^{v-a} \\ &= \frac{l^{1-\beta} - a^{1-\beta}}{1 - \beta} - \frac{a^{1-\beta} - l^{1-\beta}}{1 - \beta} = 2 \times \frac{l^{1-\beta} - a^{1-\beta}}{1 - \beta} \end{aligned}$$

Case II: $\beta = 1$

$$\begin{aligned} K &= \int_{\mathbb{S}} |x - v|^{-1} dx = \int_{v+a}^{v+l} \frac{1}{(x - v)} + \int_{v-l}^{v-a} \frac{1}{(-x + v)} \\ &= \log(x - v)\Big|_{v+a}^{v+l} - \log(-x + v)\Big|_{v-l}^{v-a} = 2\Big(\log(l) - \log(a)\Big) \end{aligned}$$

## A.2 Two-Dimensional Case

In the two-dimensional case, the region $\mathbb{S}$ corresponds to the difference between the two circles with radius $l$ and $a$ respectively, both centered at $v$. Given a data point $x = (x_1, x_2)$ and a prototype $v = (v_1, v_2)$, we use polar coordinates to simplify integration:

$$\begin{aligned}(x_1 - v_1)^2 + (x_2 - v_2)^2 &= r^2\\ x_1 - v_1 &= r\cos\varphi\\ x_2 - v_2 &= r\sin\varphi,\end{aligned}$$

Again, we distinguish two cases:
Case I: $\beta \neq 2$

$$K = \int_0^{2\pi}\int_a^l r^{-\beta} r\, dr\, d\varphi = \int_0^{2\pi} \frac{r^{2-\beta}}{2-\beta}\bigg|_a^l d\varphi = 2\pi\frac{l^{2-\beta} - a^{2-\beta}}{2-\beta}$$

Case II: $\beta = 2$

$$K = \int_0^{2\pi}\int_a^l \frac{1}{r} dr\, d\varphi = \int_0^{2\pi} \log r\bigg|_a^l d\varphi = 2\pi\left(\log l - \log a\right)$$

## A.3 $n$-Dimensional Case

In the general case, the region $\mathbb{S}$ is the $n$-dimensional ring between the two $n$-dimensional spheres with radius $l$ and $a$ respectively, both centered at $v$.

Using the polar coordinates, we obtain:

$$\begin{aligned}(x_1 - v_1)^2 + &(x_2 - v_2)^2 + \cdots + (x_n - v_n)^2 = r^2\\ x_1 - v_1 &= r\cos\varphi_1\\ &\vdots\\ x_n - v_n &= r\sin\varphi_1\sin\varphi_2\cdots\sin\varphi_{n-1},\end{aligned}$$

the integral becomes:

$$\begin{aligned}K &= \int_{\mathbb{S}} \|x - v\|^{-\beta} dx\\ &= \int_0^{2\pi}\int_0^{\pi}\cdots\int_0^{\pi}\int_a^l r^{-\beta} r^{n-1}\sin^{n-2}(\varphi_1)\sin^{n-3}(\varphi_2)\cdots\sin(\varphi_{n-2})dr d\varphi_i\cdots d\varphi_{n-1}\\ &= \int_a^l r^{n-\beta-1}dr\int_0^{2\pi}\int_0^{\pi}\cdots\int_0^{\pi}\sin^{n-2}(\varphi_1)\sin^{n-3}(\varphi_2)\cdots\sin(\varphi_{n-2})d\varphi_i\cdots d\varphi_{n-1}.\end{aligned}$$

As the second integral is the $n$-dimensional volume of the unit ball times $n$, the integral becomes:

Case I: $\beta \neq n$

$$K = \left.\frac{r^{n-\beta}}{n-\beta}\right|_a^l \frac{2\pi^{n/2}}{\Gamma(\frac{n}{2})} = \frac{2\pi^{n/2}}{\Gamma(\frac{n}{2})}\frac{l^{n-\beta} - a^{n-\beta}}{n-\beta}$$

Case II: $\beta = n$

$$K = \log(r)|_a^l \frac{2\pi^{n/2}}{\Gamma(\frac{n}{2})} = \frac{2\pi^{n/2}}{\Gamma(\frac{n}{2})}(\log l - \log a)$$

## References


1. Bezdek, J.C., Ehrlich, R., Full, W.: FCM: the fuzzy c-means clustering algorithm. Comput. Geosci. **10**(2–3), 191–203 (1984). https://doi.org/10.1016/0098-3004(84)90020-7
2. Ferraro, M.B., Giordani, P.: Possibilistic and fuzzy clustering methods for robust analysis of non-precise data. Int. J. Approximate Reasoning **88**, 23–38 (2017). https://doi.org/10.1016/j.ijar.2017.05.002
3. Ferraro, M.B., Giordani, P.: Soft clustering. WIREs Comput. Stat. **12**(1), e1480 (2020). https://doi.org/10.1002/wics.1480
4. Lu, J., Ma, G., Zhang, G.: Fuzzy machine learning: a comprehensive framework and systematic review. IEEE Trans. Fuzzy Syst. **32**(7), 3861–3878 (2024). https://doi.org/10.1109/TFUZZ.2024.3387429
5. Mencar, C., Castiello, C.: A Bayesian interpretation of fuzzy c-means. In: Massanet, S., Montes, S., Ruiz-Aguilera, D., González-Hidalgo, M. (eds.) Fuzzy Logic and Technology, and Aggregation Operators, vol. 14069, pp. 443–454. Springer, Cham (2023). https://doi.org/10.1007/978-3-031-39965-7_37
6. Olson, B., Hashmi, I., Molloy, K., Shehu, A.: Basin hopping as a general and versatile optimization framework for the characterization of biological macromolecules. Adv. Artif. Intell. **2012**, 1–19 (2012). https://doi.org/10.1155/2012/674832
7. Pal, N., Bezdek, J.: On cluster validity for the fuzzy c-means model. IEEE Trans. Fuzzy Syst. **3**(3), 370–379 (1995). https://doi.org/10.1109/91.413225
8. Ruspini, E.H., Bezdek, J.C., Keller, J.M.: Fuzzy clustering: a historical perspective. IEEE Comput. Intell. Mag. **14**(1), 45–55 (2019). https://doi.org/10.1109/MCI.2018.2881643
9. Zhou, K., Yang, S.: Fuzzifier selection in fuzzy c-means from cluster size distribution perspective. Informatica **30**(3), 613–628 (2019). https://doi.org/10.15388/Informatica.2019.221

# Alpha-Maxmin Classification with an Ensemble of Structural Restricted Boltzmann Machines

Davide Petturiti[1(✉)] and Maria Rifqi[2]

[1] Department of Economics, University of Perugia, Perugia, Italy
davide.petturiti@unipg.it
[2] LEMMA, Paris-Panthéon-Assas University, Paris, France
maria.rifqi@assas-universite.fr

**Abstract.** This article addresses a classification problem relying on an ensemble of Structural Restricted Boltzmann Machines (SRBMs). Each SRBM in the ensemble is trained by imposing structural constraints on the related weight matrix, so as to enforce sparsity, and results in a probabilistic classifier. Hence, given a new instance, the ensemble gives rise to a credal classifier where the classification is carried out relying on the alpha-maxmin criterion, depending on a pessimism index $\alpha \in [0, 1]$, and a $\beta$-quantile filtering of outliers. The paper presents an experimental analysis on artificial data sets to highlight the role of the parameters $\alpha$ and $\beta$ in the classification performances.

**Keywords:** Structural Restricted Boltzmann Machine · Ensemble · Classification · Alpha-Maxmin

## 1 Introduction

*Restricted Boltzmann Machines (RBMs)* are generative stochastic neural networks that can be used to learn a probability distribution from a given training set. Although they were initially introduced in the 1980's under the name of *harmoniums* [19], their major development and diffusion was reached in the 2000's after the systematic work of Hinton (see, e.g., [8,10]) who was awarded the 2024 Nobel prize in physics for his achievements on the topic.

An RBM is described by a bipartite graph, with all visible variables in one layer and all hidden variables in the other: visible variables are totally connected to hidden variables, while connections are not allowed in the same layer. Thus, such models can be also analyzed in the theory of probabilistic graphical models.

Nowadays, RBMs are a well-established framework, mostly used for generative purposes both as stand-alone models or as parts of more complex generative models. The initial restriction to binary variables has been removed; thus, they are currently able to work with binary, multinomial and Gaussian variables. Besides their generative purpose, RBMs have also been adapted to face classification tasks [13]: in detail, given a new instance $\mathbf{x}^*$, an RBM will return a


M. Baczyński et al. (Eds.): EUSFLAT 2025, LNCS 15884, pp. 185–197, 2025.
https://doi.org/10.1007/978-3-031-97228-7_16

*probabilistic classifier*, i.e., a conditional probability distribution $p(y|\mathbf{x}^*)$ on the possible values of the class $y$.

Besides being considered individually, ensembles of classical RBMs appeared in recent times both for classification [21] and for feature-based explanations [2], while implicit mixtures of RBMs were introduced in [16].

The training of an RBM is usually a delicate task [6] since we need to properly choose the number of hidden variables, next we need to learn a large amount of parameters, typically by a stochastic gradient descent algorithm, which is normally faced via the *Contrastive Divergence (CD)* technique [9]. Since RBMs are particular energy-based models, they can suffer from the *mode collapse* phenomenon [4]. Such phenomenon, together with a reduction of time complexity of the learning task, can be faced by imposing sparsity [3]. In this line, in [1] the authors introduced *Structural Restricted Boltzmann Machines (SRBMs)*, where some of the connections between hidden and visible nodes are removed due to domain knowledge.

In this paper, we start from the concept of SRBM and we adopt an exploratory approach by building an ensemble of SRBMs having different numbers of hidden variables and randomly generated structural constraints of sparsity. Given a new instance $\mathbf{x}^*$, the quoted ensemble will result in a set of conditional probability distributions $\tilde{p}(y|\mathbf{x}^*)$'s that give rise to a *credal classifier*. Notice that here, the $\tilde{p}(y|\mathbf{x}^*)$'s are generated by the corresponding joint Boltzmann probability distributions obtained by structural constrained energy functions.

Usually, credal classification is carried out with some forms of majority vote enforced through the *maximality* and *E-admissibility* rules (see, e.g., [17,18]). In this paper, we adopt a decision rule which is based on the envelopes of the credal set spanned by the $\tilde{p}(y|\mathbf{x}^*)$'s. In turn, in order to allow graded positions between systematic pessimism and optimism, we consider a *pessimism index* $\alpha \in [0, 1]$, and build the *(conditional) $\alpha$-JP mixture capacity* (where "JP" refers to Jaffray-Philippe) [12], which is a fuzzy measure generated by the lower and upper envelopes. Finally, we translate the classification problem as a maximization of the generated $\alpha$-JP mixture capacity. This particular choice agrees with the so-called *$\alpha$-maxmin* decision criterion due to Hurwicz [11] which is very well-known in decision making under uncertainty (see, e.g., [5]). The term $\alpha$-maxmin refers to the fact that the $\alpha$-JP capacity used in classification is an $\alpha$-mixture of set-wise minima and maxima of probability distributions in a credal set.

Following [17,18], we face the problem of possible disagreement in the ensemble, by adopting a *$\beta$-quantile filtering* of "outlier" distributions in the credal classifier, with respect to the distance from a reference representative distribution. The resulting ensemble classifier thus depends on the hyper-parameters $\alpha$ and $\beta$ and will be called *$(\alpha,\beta)$-SRBMs* classifier.

Due to space limitations, we limit our study to binary visible and hidden variables only, and carry out an experimental analysis on artificial data. Our experiments show that both hyper-parameters $\alpha$ and $\beta$ play a crucial role in the classification accuracy. Moreover, upon a preliminary exploratory grid search of optimal hyper-parameters, the classification performance we get can compete with standard ensemble classifiers on the analyzed artificial data.

The paper is structured as follows. Section 2 introduces Structural Restricted Boltzmann Machines and discusses their training. Section 3 presents the $(\alpha, \beta)$-SRBMs classifier, while Sect. 4.1 proposes an experimental analysis on artificial data. Finally, Sect. 5 draws some conclusions and future perspectives.

## 2 Structural Restricted Boltzmann Machines for Classification

Following [13], we assume that our training set is $\mathcal{D}_{train} = \{(\mathbf{x}_i, y_i)\}_{i=1}^N$, where $\mathbf{x}_i \in \{0,1\}^d$ and $y_i \in \{1, \dots, c\}$, with $c \geq 2$, in which $d$ is the number of binary features and $c$ is the number of classes. In what follows, given $y \in \{1, \dots, c\}$ we denote by $\mathbf{1}_y$ the corresponding one-hot encoding vector, where $\mathbf{1}_y$ is a $c$-dimensional binary vector such that $\mathbf{1}_y(j) = 1$ if $j = y$ and 0 otherwise.

A *Restricted Boltzmann Machine (RBM)* on the given data set will be hence composed of a vector of *visible* binary variables $\mathbf{v} = (\mathbf{1}_y, \mathbf{x}) \in \{0,1\}^{n_v}$ with $n_v = c + d$, and a vector of *hidden* binary variables $\mathbf{h} \in \{0,1\}^{n_h}$, where $n_v$ and $n_h$ are the numbers of visible and hidden variables, respectively.

The training of a generative RBM on the quoted training data set reduces to the minimization of the following negative log-likelihood:

$$\mathcal{L}_{gen}(\mathcal{D}_{train}) = -\sum_{i=1}^{N} \ln p(y_i, \mathbf{x}_i), \tag{1}$$

where the probability distribution $p(y, \mathbf{x})$ on $\{1, \dots, c\} \times \{0,1\}^d$ is obtained by marginalizing the *joint Boltzmann probability distribution* on $\{1, \dots, c\} \times \{0,1\}^d \times \{0,1\}^{n_h}$ such that:

$$p(y, \mathbf{x}, \mathbf{h}) = \frac{\exp(-E(y, \mathbf{x}, \mathbf{h}))}{Z(y, \mathbf{x}, \mathbf{h})}, \tag{2}$$

in which the normalization constant $Z(y, \mathbf{x}, \mathbf{h}) = \sum_{y,\mathbf{x},\mathbf{h}} \exp(-E(y, \mathbf{x}, \mathbf{h}))$ is the so-called *partition function*. In turn, the computation of $p(y, \mathbf{x}, \mathbf{h})$ is based on the *energy function*:

$$E(y, \mathbf{x}, \mathbf{h}) = -\mathbf{h}^T \mathbf{W} \mathbf{x} - \mathbf{b}^T \mathbf{x} - \mathbf{c}^T \mathbf{h} - \mathbf{d}^T \mathbf{1}_y - \mathbf{h}^T \mathbf{U} \mathbf{1}_y, \tag{3}$$

that depends on the parameter vector $\Theta = (\mathbf{W}, \mathbf{b}, \mathbf{c}, \mathbf{d}, \mathbf{U})$ in which $\mathbf{W} = (w_{jk}) \in \mathbb{R}^{n_h \times d}, \mathbf{b} = (b_i) \in \mathbb{R}^d, \mathbf{c} = (c_j) \in \mathbb{R}^{n_h}, \mathbf{d} = (d_y) \in \mathbb{R}^c, \mathbf{U} = (u_{jy}) \in \mathbb{R}^{n_h \times c}$.

The vectors $\mathbf{b}$ and $\mathbf{d}$ contain the biases of visible variables in $\mathbf{v}$ (referring to the decomposition in the sub-vectors $\mathbf{x}$ and $\mathbf{1}_y$, respectively), while $\mathbf{c}$ contains those of the hidden variables in $\mathbf{h}$. Matrixes $\mathbf{W}$ and $\mathbf{U}$ contain the weights of the connections between visible variables in $\mathbf{v}$ (referring to the decomposition in the sub-vectors $\mathbf{x}$ and $\mathbf{1}_y$, respectively) and hidden variables in $\mathbf{h}$. Notice that the energy function in (3) has a negative sign that is removed in (2).

The bipartite graph representing an RBM is a probabilistic graphical model [14] encoding a set of conditional independence statements through the graph separation criterion: visible variables are mutually independent given hidden variables and viceversa, under the joint Boltzmann probability distribution (2).

As is well-known (see, e.g., [13]), computing the joint distribution $p(y, \mathbf{x})$ is not tractable, essentially due to the computation of the partition function, but we can compute the conditional distribution $p(y|\mathbf{x})$ as:

$$p(y|\mathbf{x}) = \frac{\exp(d_y)\prod_j(1+\exp(c_j+u_{jy}+\sum_k w_{jk}x_k))}{\sum_y \exp(d_y)\prod_j(1+\exp(c_j+u_{jy}+\sum_k w_{jk}x_k))}. \tag{4}$$

Since the parameter space is pretty large, in the spirit of [1], we impose some sparsity on the matrices $\mathbf{W}$ and $\mathbf{U}$. For fixed binary matrices $\mathbf{E} = (e_{jk}) \in \{0,1\}^{n_h \times d}, \mathbf{F} = (f_{jy}) \in \{0,1\}^{n_h \times c}$, we consider the structural constrained energy function:

$$\tilde{E}(y, \mathbf{x}, \mathbf{h}) = -\mathbf{h}^T(\mathbf{W} \odot \mathbf{E})\mathbf{x} - \mathbf{b}^T\mathbf{x} - \mathbf{c}^T\mathbf{h} - \mathbf{d}^T\mathbf{1}_y - \mathbf{h}^T(\mathbf{U} \odot \mathbf{F})\mathbf{1}_y, \tag{5}$$

where $\odot$ denotes the component-wise matrix product. Following [1], we call the resulting RBM a *Structural Restricted Boltzmann Machine (SRBM)*.

We stress that the binary matrices $\mathbf{E}, \mathbf{F}$ are used as masks to force to zero some links between the visible and hidden variables in the vectors $\mathbf{v} = (\mathbf{1}_y, \mathbf{x})$ and $\mathbf{h}$, and this translates in imposing some further conditional independencies between variables in $\mathbf{v}$ and $\mathbf{h}$. In particular, this allows us to discard the parameters $w_{jk}$'s and $u_{jy}$'s corresponding to zeros, which refer to missing links between visible and hidden variables. Moreover, if $\mathbf{E}, \mathbf{F}$ reduce to the matrices only made up of 1's, then we recover Eq. (3). In [1], SRBMs are shown to have a faster training and better accuracy results, though requiring domain knowledge to tailor matrixes $\mathbf{E}, \mathbf{F}$ to available data.

Under the structural constraint given by $\mathbf{E}, \mathbf{F}$, the parameter vector becomes $\tilde{\Theta} = ((\mathbf{W} \odot \mathbf{E}), \mathbf{b}, \mathbf{c}, \mathbf{d}, (\mathbf{U} \odot \mathbf{F}))$ and, since $\mathbf{E}, \mathbf{F}$ are fixed, only non-null entries of $(\mathbf{W} \odot \mathbf{E})$ and $(\mathbf{U} \odot \mathbf{F})$ play a role. We also denote by $\tilde{p}(y, \mathbf{x}, \mathbf{h})$ the joint Boltzmann probability distribution computed as in (2) by replacing $E(y, \mathbf{x}, \mathbf{h})$ with $\tilde{E}(y, \mathbf{x}, \mathbf{h})$.

Working with $\mathbf{E}, \mathbf{F}$, the conditional probability distribution (4) becomes:

$$\tilde{p}(y|\mathbf{x}) = \frac{\exp(d_y)\prod_j(1+\exp(c_j+u_{jy}f_{jy}+\sum_k w_{jk}e_{jk}x_k))}{\sum_y \exp(d_y)\prod_j(1+\exp(c_j+u_{jy}f_{jy}+\sum_k w_{jk}e_{jk}x_k))}. \tag{6}$$

Following [9], we optimize the joint probability distribution $\tilde{p}(y, \mathbf{x})$ using *Contrastive Divergence (CD)* with a single step of Gibbs sampling by initializing the sampler with the current observation $(y_i, \mathbf{x}_i)$, since this is more appropriate for small training sets. The training consists then to cycle over the training observations $(y_i, \mathbf{x}_i)$'s by applying Algorithm 1, which is a straightforward adaptation of classical CD (see [8] and also [13]), in which $\sigma(x) = (1 + \exp(x))^{-1}$ is the *logistic function*.

*Remark 1.* In case of large training sets, a different approach proposed in [13] is to optimize directly $\tilde{p}(y|\mathbf{x})$.

As suggested in [1], the matrices $\mathbf{E}, \mathbf{F}$ should be used to enforce some domain knowledge in the training of an SRBM. In this paper, we will adopt an exploratory approach by randomly generating several matrices $\mathbf{E}^m, \mathbf{F}^m$, for $m = 1, \ldots, M$, with a controlled percentage of structural zeros, in order to train an ensemble of SRBMs.

**Algorithm 1.** Training of an SRBM over $(y, \mathbf{x})$ using Contrastive Divergence with a single step of Gibbs sampling initialized at a fixed observation.

▷ *input:* Given mask matrices $\mathbf{E}, \mathbf{F}$
▷ *input:* Training pair $(y_i, \mathbf{x}_i)$ and learning rate $\lambda$
▷ *output:* Updated parameter vector $\tilde{\Theta}$

*# Positive phase*
$(y^0, \mathbf{x}^0) := (y_i, \mathbf{x}_i)$
$\widehat{\mathbf{h}}^0 := \sigma(\mathbf{c} + (\mathbf{W} \odot \mathbf{E})\mathbf{x}^0 + (\mathbf{U} \odot \mathbf{F})\mathbf{1}_{y^0})$
*# Negative phase*
Sample $\mathbf{h}^0$ from $\tilde{p}(\mathbf{h}|y^0, \mathbf{x}^0)$
Sample $(y^1, \mathbf{x}^1)$ from $\tilde{p}(y^1, \mathbf{x}^1|\mathbf{h}^0)$
$\widehat{\mathbf{h}}^1 := \sigma(\mathbf{c} + (\mathbf{W} \odot \mathbf{E})\mathbf{x}^1 + (\mathbf{U} \odot \mathbf{F})\mathbf{1}_{y^1})$
*# Update*
**for each** component $\theta$ of $\tilde{\Theta}$ **do**
  $\theta := \theta - \lambda\left(\frac{\partial}{\partial\theta}\tilde{E}(y^0, \mathbf{x}^0, \widehat{\mathbf{h}}^0) - \frac{\partial}{\partial\theta}\tilde{E}(y^1, \mathbf{x}^1, \widehat{\mathbf{h}}^1)\right)$
**end for**
**return** Updated $\tilde{\Theta}$

## 3 Alpha-Maxmin Credal Classifier for SRBMs

Let us consider an ensemble composed of $M$ SRBMs, where the $m$-th SRBM is characterized by a pair $\mathbf{E}^m, \mathbf{F}^m$ of fixed binary matrices. After training, the $m$-th SRBM gives rise to a conditional probability distribution $\tilde{p}^m(y|\mathbf{x})$ on $\{1, \ldots, c\} \times \{0, 1\}^d$, for $m = 1, \ldots, M$, through Eq. (6). To avoid cumbersome notation, we identify each probability distribution on $\{1, \ldots, c\}$ with the corresponding $c$-dimensional vector in the $(c-1)$-dimensional standard simplex $\Delta_c$ and we write the vector $\mathbf{p}^m_{\mathbf{x}}$ in place of $\tilde{p}^m(\cdot|\mathbf{x})$.

Hence, for all $\mathbf{x} \in \{0, 1\}^d$, the SRBMs in the ensemble give rise to a *(conditional) credal set* [15]

$$\mathcal{P}(\mathbf{x}) = \{\mathbf{p}^m_{\mathbf{x}} : m = 1, \ldots, M\}. \tag{7}$$

In turn, following the terminology of [18], Eq. (7) defines a *credal classifier*, i.e., a mapping $\mathbf{x} \mapsto \mathcal{P}(\mathbf{x})$ that associates to every $\mathbf{x} \in \{0, 1\}^d$ a set of probability distributions on classes $\mathcal{P}(\mathbf{x}) \subseteq \Delta_c$.

The use of $\mathcal{P}(\mathbf{x})$ in classification can present some issues due to contrasting probability distributions belonging to this set. For this, in [17] the authors propose to discard a certain percentage of "outliers", according to a preference order induced by a suitable probabilistic divergence. Typical examples of the quoted divergence are:

**$L_p$ distance ($p \geq 1$):** $D_{L_p}(\mathbf{p}, \mathbf{q}) = \left(\sum_{k=1}^{c} |p_k - q_k|^p\right)^{\frac{1}{p}}$;

**Kullback-Leibler divergence:** $D_{KL}(\mathbf{p}, \mathbf{q}) = \sum_{k=1}^{c} p_k \ln\left(\frac{p_k}{q_k}\right)$.

For a fixed divergence $D$, the proposal of [17] is to compute a reference probability distribution by solving the optimization problem:

$$\mathbf{p}_{\mathbf{x}}^* = \arg\min_{\mathbf{p} \in \Delta_c} \sum_{m=1}^{M} D(\mathbf{p}, \mathbf{p}_{\mathbf{x}}^m), \tag{8}$$

that reduces to $\mathbf{p}_{\mathbf{x}}^* = \frac{1}{M}\sum_{m=1}^{M} \mathbf{p}_{\mathbf{x}}^m$, when the squared $L_2$ distance is adopted (as we do in this paper). They finally propose to rank increasingly the elements of $\mathcal{P}(\mathbf{x})$ according to their squared $L_2$ distance from $\mathbf{p}_{\mathbf{x}}^*$ and to restrict to the elements with distance less than or equal to the $\beta$-quantile of the distances, for a fixed $\beta \in [0, 1]$. The corresponding subset of $\mathcal{P}(\mathbf{x})$ will be denoted as

$$\mathcal{P}_\beta(\mathbf{x}) = \{\mathbf{p}_{\mathbf{x}}^{i_m} : m = 1, \ldots, M_\beta\}, \tag{9}$$

and will be referred to as *filtered credal classifier*, where filtering is intended with respect to distance "outliers".

Given a fixed instance $\mathbf{x}^* \in \{0, 1\}^d$, the filtered credal classifier $\mathcal{P}_\beta(\mathbf{x}^*)$ gives rise to the (conditional) lower and upper probabilities [20] defined, for all $A \subseteq \{1, \ldots, c\}$, as

$$\underline{P}_{\mathbf{x}^*}^\beta(A) = \min_{m=1,\ldots,M_\beta} \sum_{k \in A} p_{\mathbf{x}^*}{}_k^{i_m}, \tag{10}$$

$$\overline{P}_{\mathbf{x}^*}^\beta(A) = \max_{m=1,\ldots,M_\beta} \sum_{k \in A} p_{\mathbf{x}^*}{}_k^{i_m}. \tag{11}$$

The set functions $\underline{P}_{\mathbf{x}^*}^\beta$ and $\overline{P}_{\mathbf{x}^*}^\beta$ encode systematically pessimistic and optimistic attitudes towards uncertainty, respectively, and are *fuzzy measures*, since are grounded, normalized and monotonic with respect to set inclusion (see, e.g., [7]). Nevertheless, a more flexible approach is to consider a *pessimism index* $\alpha \in [0, 1]$ and introduce the *$\alpha$-JP mixture capacity* [12] defined as:

$$\nu_{\mathbf{x}^*}^{(\alpha,\beta)} = \alpha \underline{P}_{\mathbf{x}^*}^\beta + (1 - \alpha)\overline{P}_{\mathbf{x}^*}^\beta. \tag{12}$$

The fuzzy measure $\nu_{\mathbf{x}^*}^{(\alpha,\beta)}$ allows us to answer to any query concerning the uncertainty of the class of $\mathbf{x}^*$, by adopting the *alpha-maxmin criterion* due to

[11]. In turn, this consists in averaging extreme positions given by the filtered credal classifier $\mathcal{P}_\beta(\mathbf{x}^*)$ through $\alpha$. As a result, we derive an *alpha-maxmin credal classifier* by solving the optimization problem:

$$y^* \in \arg \max_{y \in \{1,\dots,c\}} \nu_{\mathbf{x}^*}^{(\alpha,\beta)}(\{y\}). \tag{13}$$

The training and test code for the proposed *alpha-maxmin ensemble SRBM classifier with $\beta$-quantile filtering ($(\alpha, \beta)$-SRBMs)* is available on `GitHub`[1].

## 4 Experimental Analysis

In this section we report the results of tests on artificial data sets with the purpose of highlighting the effect of parameters $\alpha$ and $\beta$ on classification tasks, together with a comparison with other two popular ensemble classifiers.

In all the experiments below, we consider an ensemble of SRBMs where the number of visible variables is $n_v = c + d$, with $c$ and $d$ determined by the input data set, and the number of hidden variables $n_h$ ranges in $\{n_v, \lfloor \frac{4}{3} n_v \rfloor, \lfloor \frac{5}{3} n_v \rfloor\}$. In this way, the parameter $n_h$ increases of multiples of $33.\overline{3}\%$ with respect to $n_v$.

### 4.1 The Effect of Structural Constraints, and $\alpha$ and $\beta$ on Accuracy

We consider an artificial data set $\mathcal{D} = \{(\mathbf{x}_i, y_i)\}_{i=1}^{500}$ of 500 observations, where the entries of each vector $\mathbf{x}_i \in \{0,1\}^d$ are generated as independent Bernoulli random variables with parameter $p = 0.25$. Next, the corresponding $y_i$ is obtained by applying the non-linear function

$$\varphi(\mathbf{x}) = \max_{k=1,\dots,d} k \cdot x_k, \tag{14}$$

and finally the values of $\varphi(\mathbf{x}_i)$'s are scaled and truncated to belong to the set $\{1, \dots, c\}$. We fix $d = 20$ and take $c = 5$, in a way to have a large feature space of $2^{20} = 1048576$ binary vectors and a large number of classes. The generated data set is unbalanced with 1.4% of class 1, 3.4% of class 2, 14.0% of class 3, 55.8% of class 4, and 25.4% of class 5.

In this multi-class problem, due to class unbalancing, we compute the precision, recall and F1 scores using the `micro` averaging scheme in `sklearn.metrics`. Under such averaging scheme, the three scores are computed globally by counting the total true positives, false negatives and false positives, so they coincide with accuracy. For this reason, we will limit to report accuracy curves.

To appreciate the effect of structural constraints, we first consider an ensemble of three standard RBMs, obtained by taking $\mathbf{E}, \mathbf{F}$ equal to the constant matrices entirely formed by 1's, whose number of hidden variables $n_h$ ranges in $\{n_v, \lfloor \frac{4}{3} n_v \rfloor, \lfloor \frac{5}{3} n_v \rfloor\}$.

We then compare it with an ensemble of nine SRBMs obtained by considering, for each value of $n_h$, three different SRBMs with structural matrices $\mathbf{E}, \mathbf{F}$ whose

[1] Public `GitHub` repository: https://github.com/itsdavide/EUSFLAT2025.

entries are generated as independent Bernoulli random variables with parameter $p$ in $\{0.99, 0.9, 0.85\}$. Both ensembles have been trained for 1000 epochs with a learning rate $\lambda = 0.15$ in a stratified 5-fold cross-validation.

Figure 1 shows the mean and standard deviation of accuracy as a function of the pessimism index $\alpha$. The mean accuracy of the ensemble of SRBMs dominates that of the ensemble of RBMs for $0 \leq \alpha \leq 0.6$, while the standard deviation intervals in the case of SRBMs are much wider, due to the larger ensemble.

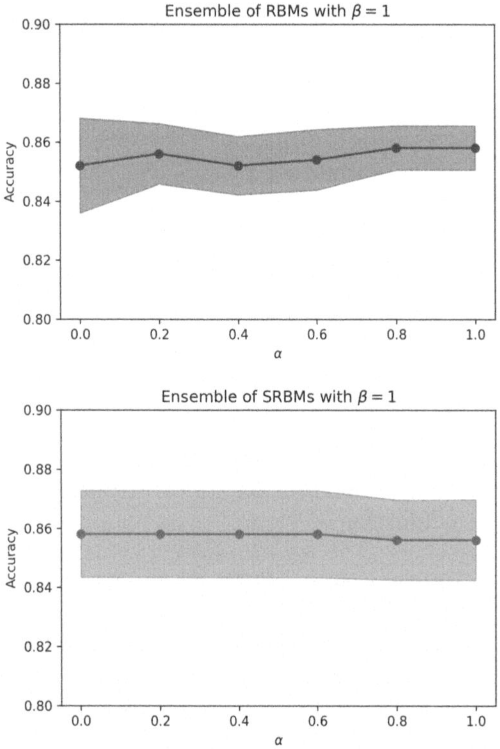


**Fig. 1.** Mean and standard deviation of accuracy as a function of $\alpha$ in a stratified 5-fold cross-validation, for an ensemble of three RBMs (top) and an ensemble of nine SRBMs (bottom), both with $\beta = 1$.

Next, we consider the effect of the outlier filtering by taking $\beta \in \{\frac{7}{9}, \frac{8}{9}\}$, i.e., by removing one or two outliers given by the previous ensemble of nine SRBMs. Figure 2 shows the mean and standard deviation of accuracy as a function of the pessimism index $\alpha$. By the graphs we can see that the best accuracy result in case of $\beta = \frac{8}{9}$ is obtained for $\alpha = 0.4$, while in case of $\beta = \frac{7}{9}$ this happens for $\alpha = 0.6$. We also notice that the accuracy performance in these last two cases dominates those obtained with the previous two ensembles, where $\beta = 1$.

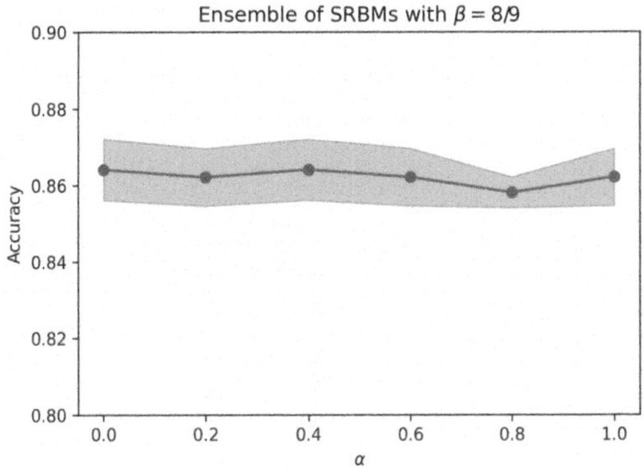


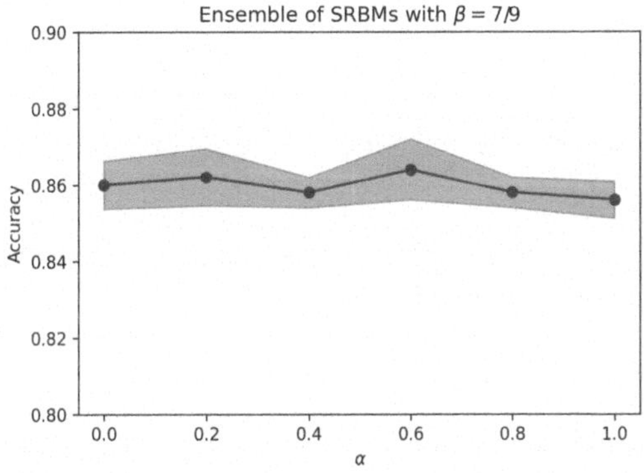


**Fig. 2.** Mean and standard deviation of accuracy as a function of $\alpha$ in a stratified 5-fold cross-validation, for an ensemble of nine SRBMs, respectively, with $\beta = \frac{8}{9}$ (top) and $\beta = \frac{7}{9}$ (bottom).

All graphs reported in Figs. 1 and 2 show that the pessimism index $\alpha$ has a direct impact on the obtained accuracy, and such parameter actually interacts with the structural constraints given by matrices $\mathbf{E}, \mathbf{F}$, as well as with the parameter of outlier filtering $\beta$.

### 4.2 Comparison with Other Ensemble Classifiers

We consider an artificial data set $\mathcal{D} = \{(\mathbf{x}_i, y_i)\}_{i=1}^{1000}$ of 1000 observations, where the entries of each vector $\mathbf{x}_i \in \{0,1\}^d$ are generated as independent Bernoulli random variables with parameter $p = 0.75$. Next, the corresponding $y_i$ is obtained by applying the non-linear function

$$\varphi(\mathbf{x}) = \sqrt{\sum_{k=1}^{d} k^2 \cdot x_k}, \tag{15}$$

and finally the values of $\varphi(\mathbf{x}_i)$'s are scaled and truncated to belong to the set $\{1, \ldots, c\}$. We generate several data sets relying on the described procedure, for

$c \in \{2, 3, 4\}$ and $d \in \{11, \ldots, 16\}$, so we change the representativeness of the generated data set. Figure 3 shows the class distribution for $d = 11$, highlighting that the three data sets are highly unbalanced.

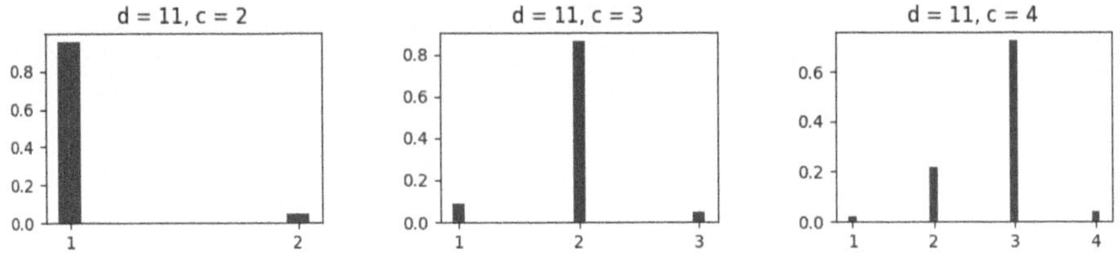


**Fig. 3.** Class distribution for $d = 11$ and $c \in \{2, 3, 4\}$.

We take as benchmarks the following ensemble classifiers implemented in the Python library `sklearn`[2]:

- Random Forest (RF) with hyper-parameters `max_depth` $= 5$, `n_estimators` $= 10$, `max_features` $= 1$, `random_state` $= 42$;
- AdaBoost (AB) with hyper-parameters `n_estimators` $= 10$, `random_state` $= 42$.

Our analysis is limited to RF and AB due to space limitations: other possible choices of ensemble classifiers are, e.g., Extra Trees, Gradient Boosting and Stacking.

We refer to an ensemble of SRBMs where, for each value of $n_h$ we consider three different SRBMs with structural matrices $\mathbf{E}, \mathbf{F}$ whose entries are generated as independent Bernoulli random variables with parameter $p$ in $\{0.99, 0.9, 0.85\}$. Hence, the final ensemble is composed of 9 heterogeneous SRBMs, which are trained for 10000 epochs with a learning rate of $\lambda = 0.1$.

We perform a stratified 5-fold cross-validation, in which, we restrict to $\mathcal{P}_\beta(\mathbf{x}^*)$ with $\beta = \frac{7}{9}$ and the alpha-maxmin decision rule is applied with $\alpha = 0.5$. Table 1 reports the mean and standard deviations in the stratified 5-fold cross-validation.

We point out that the choice of the number of epochs, $\lambda$, $\alpha$, and $\beta$ hyper-parameters has been executed after a preliminary grid search analysis.

As we can see from Table 1, $(\alpha, \beta)$-SRBMs always outperforms the other two ensemble classifiers for $c = 2$ and $c = 3$. In the case $c = 4$, $(\alpha, \beta)$-SRBMs always outperforms RF while its comparison with AB is won in four of the six data sets by $(\alpha, \beta)$-SRBMs and in the other two by AB.

[2] For RF we chose the hyper-parameter setting for classifier comparison reported in https://scikit-learn.org/stable/auto_examples/classification/plot_classifier_comparison.html, and we fixed the same size of the ensemble for AB, which is comparable to that of $(\alpha, \beta)$-SRBMs.

**Table 1.** Mean and standard deviation of accuracy in a stratified 5-fold cross-validation of data sets generated through function (14), for $c \in \{2, 3, 4\}$ and $d \in \{11, \ldots, 16\}$, with $\alpha = 0.5$ and $\beta = \frac{7}{9}$.

| | Classifier | $c = 2$ | $c = 3$ | $c = 4$ |
|---|---|---|---|---|
| $d = 11$ | RF | $95.2 \pm 0.2\%$ | $86.8 \pm 0.5\%$ | $77.7 \pm 2.3\%$ |
| | AB | $99.5 \pm 0.6\%$ | $87.5 \pm 1.9\%$ | $75.1 \pm 2.4\%$ |
| | $(\alpha, \beta)$-SRBMs | $\mathbf{100.0 \pm 0.0\%}$ | $\mathbf{91.2 \pm 1.9\%}$ | $\mathbf{78.6 \pm 1.8\%}$ |
| $d = 12$ | RF | $97.6 \pm 0.2\%$ | $92.3 \pm 0.2\%$ | $79.0 \pm 1.2\%$ |
| | AB | $97.4 \pm 1.2\%$ | $92.3 \pm 1.5\%$ | $\mathbf{82.9 \pm 1.7\%}$ |
| | $(\alpha, \beta)$-SRBMs | $\mathbf{100.0 \pm 0.0\%}$ | $\mathbf{93.4 \pm 0.2\%}$ | $79.8 \pm 1.6\%$ |
| $d = 13$ | RF | $97.6 \pm 0.2\%$ | $89.8 \pm 0.2\%$ | $78.8 \pm 0.9\%$ |
| | AB | $96.8 \pm 0.6\%$ | $91.0 \pm 1.4\%$ | $78.2 \pm 4.0\%$ |
| | $(\alpha, \beta)$-SRBMs | $\mathbf{100.0 \pm 0.0\%}$ | $\mathbf{92.1 \pm 0.6\%}$ | $\mathbf{80.9 \pm 1.5\%}$ |
| $d = 14$ | RF | $98.0 \pm 0.0\%$ | $90.0 \pm 0.3\%$ | $74.6 \pm 1.2\%$ |
| | AB | $98.0 \pm 0.0\%$ | $86.7 \pm 2.3\%$ | $72.3 \pm 2.4\%$ |
| | $(\alpha, \beta)$-SRBMs | $\mathbf{100.0 \pm 0.0\%}$ | $\mathbf{92.1 \pm 0.5\%}$ | $\mathbf{76.8 \pm 2.2\%}$ |
| $d = 15$ | RF | $98.9 \pm 0.2\%$ | $90.0 \pm 0.0\%$ | $75.2 \pm 1.0\%$ |
| | AB | $98.9 \pm 0.2\%$ | $88.8 \pm 2.2\%$ | $\mathbf{78.9 \pm 3.3\%}$ |
| | $(\alpha, \beta)$-SRBMs | $\mathbf{99.7 \pm 0.6\%}$ | $\mathbf{93.0 \pm 0.8\%}$ | $78.8 \pm 0.5\%$ |
| $d = 16$ | RF | $99.1 \pm 0.2\%$ | $87.2 \pm 0.2\%$ | $72.2 \pm 3.1\%$ |
| | AB | $99.1 \pm 0.2\%$ | $87.6 \pm 2.8\%$ | $72.0 \pm 3.5\%$ |
| | $(\alpha, \beta)$-SRBMs | $\mathbf{99.6 \pm 0.5\%}$ | $\mathbf{88.6 \pm 0.7\%}$ | $\mathbf{75.7 \pm 2.7\%}$ |

## 5 Conclusion

This paper discusses classification through an ensemble of SRBMs, the latter introduced in [1]. The ensemble approach allows us to address several important aspects in the training of a standard RBM as we can add to the ensemble SRBMs having different numbers of hidden variables and different structural constraints. We propose an ensemble classifier, namely $(\alpha, \beta)$-SRBMs, that relies on the $\alpha$-maxmin criterion [11] and the $\beta$-quantile filtering of outliers due to [17,18]. Due to space limitations, we tested our proposal on artificial data only, by considering two non-linear functional forms given by (14) and (15) for data generation. Our analysis on artificial data highlights the impact of parameters $\alpha$ and $\beta$ on accuracy, together with competitive performances with standard ensemble classifiers. As aim of future research, we plan a systematic experimental analysis on real data sets, together with a comparison with other credal classifier techniques presented in [18], as well as an execution time analysis. Other possible extensions concern the treatment of non-binary variables and the incorporation of bagging techniques.

**Acknowledgments.** The first author acknowledges the support of the MUR PRIN 2022 project 2022AP3B3B "Models for dynamic reasoning under partial knowledge to make interpretable decisions" (Finanziato dall'Unione europea - Next Generation EU, Missione 4 Componente 2, CUP J53D23004340006).

## References

1. Bidaurrazaga, A., Pérez, A., Santana, R.: Structural Restricted Boltzmann Machine for image denoising and classification. arXiv:2306.09628 (2023)
2. Borisov, V., Meier, J., van den Heuvel, J., Jalali, H., Kasneci, G.: A robust unsupervised ensemble of feature-based explanations using restricted Boltzmann machines. In: 1st Workshop on eXplainable AI Approaches for Debugging and Diagnosis (XAI4Debugging@NeurIPS2021), pp. 1–13 (2021)
3. Bresler, G., Buhai, R.D.: Learning restricted Boltzmann machines with sparse latent variables. In: Proceedings of 34th Conference on Neural Information Processing Systems (NeurIPS 2020), Vancouver, Canada, pp. 1–11 (2020)
4. Béreux, N., Decelle, A., Furtlehner, C., Rosseti, L., Seoane, B.: Fast, accurate training and sampling of Restricted Boltzmann Machines. arXiv:2405.15376v1 (2024)
5. Denux, T.: Decision-making with belief functions: a review. Int. J. Approximate Reasoning **109**, 87–110 (2019)
6. Fischer, A., Igel, C.: Training restricted Boltzmann machines: an introduction. Pattern Recogn. **47**(1), 25–39 (2014)
7. Grabisch, M.: Set Functions, Games and Capacities in Decision Making. Springer, Cham (2016)
8. Hinton, G.: Training products of experts by minimizing contrastive divergence. Neural Comput. **14**(8), 1771–1800 (2002)
9. Hinton, G.: A Practical Guide to Training Restricted Boltzmann Machines, pp. 599–619. Springer, Heidelberg (2012)
10. Hinton, G., Salakhutdinov, R.: Reducing the dimensionality of data with neural networks. Science **313**(5786), 504–507 (2006)
11. Hurwicz, L.: The Generalized Bayes Minimax Principle: A Criterion for Decision Making Under Uncertainty. Cowles Commission Discussion Paper **355** (1951)
12. Jaffray, J.Y., Philippe, F.: On the existence of subjective upper and lower probabilities. Math. Oper. Res. **22**(1), 165–185 (1997)
13. Larochelle, H., Bengio, Y.: Classification using discriminative restricted Boltzmann machines. In: McCallum, A., Roweis, S. (eds.) Proceedings of the 25th International Conference on Machine Learning (ICML), pp. 536–543 (2008)
14. Lauritzen, S.: Graphical Models. Clarendon Press, Oxford (1996)
15. Levi, I.: The Enterprise of Knowledge. MIT Press, Cambridge (1980)
16. Nair, V., Hinton, G.: Implicit mixtures of Restricted Boltzmann Machines. In: Proceedings of the 22nd International Conference on Neural Information Processing Systems, NIPS 2008, pp. 1145–1152 (2008)
17. Nguyen, V.L., Zhang, H., Destercke, S.: Learning sets of probabilities through ensemble methods. In: Bouraoui, Z., Vesic, S. (eds.) Symbolic and Quantitative Approaches to Reasoning with Uncertainty, pp. 270–283. Springer, Cham (2024)
18. Nguyen, V.L., Zhang, H., Destercke, S.: Credal ensembling in multi-class classification. Mach. Learn. **114**(1), 19 (2025)

19. Smolensky, P.: Information processing in dynamical systems: foundations of harmony theory. In: Parallel Distributed Processing: Explorations in the Microstructure of Cognition, vol. 1: Foundations, pp. 194–281. MIT Press (1986)
20. Walley, P.: Statistical Reasoning with Imprecise Probabilities. Chapman and Hall, London (1991)
21. Zhang, C.X., Zhang, J.S., Ji, N.N., Guo, G.: Learning ensemble classifiers via restricted Boltzmann machines. Pattern Recogn. Lett. **36**, 161–170 (2014)

# FLIRT–An Algorithm to Enhance a Regression Model with Federated Learning and GAN-Based Resampling

Przemysław Grzegorzewski[1,2] and Maciej Romaniuk[1,2(✉)]

[1] Faculty of Mathematics and Information Science,
Warsaw University of Technology, Koszykowa 75, 00-662 Warsaw, Poland
przemyslaw.grzegorzewski@pw.edu.pl
[2] Systems Research Institute Polish Academy of Sciences,
Newelska 6, 01-447 Warszawa, Poland
mroman@ibspan.waw.pl
[3] WIT Academy, Newelska 6, 01-447 Warszawa, Poland

**Abstract.** Federated learning is a notable method to combine efficient data analysis with privacy protection of data, mainly when legal regulations, privacy concerns, or competitive threats restrict data sharing between entities (clients). Instead, clients collaborate to solve the main problem through targeted updates coordinated by some central server. This paper proposes a novel approach combining federated learning, imputation phase, and resampling step to solve the regression problem. The MissForest method is employed during the imputation phase, while the resampling step utilizes an ML algorithm (GAN). The proposed approach is evaluated numerically on various synthetic and practice-oriented datasets. Subsequently, the associated errors related to the statistical properties of the regression models are measured and compared. The results demonstrate that the final model obtained through the proposed method outperforms client-based models in terms of these error metrics.

**Keywords:** Incomplete data · Model merging · Simulations · Machine learning · Imputation · GAN

## 1 Introduction

Nowadays, many institutions (organizations, enterprises, governments, etc.) continuously gather and analyze data to improve decision-making processes. However, constructing high-quality statistical models that can yield accurate conclusions and predictions usually requires a sufficiently large dataset to perform the necessary training and validation processes for those models. Unfortunately, some institutions do not have enough data to build models of sufficient quality on their own, and obtaining additional data from other entities may be impossible due to legal regulations, privacy requirements, competitive threats, etc. In such a situation, Federated Learning (FL) [8,19] may be a valuable tool to solve


M. Baczyński et al. (Eds.): EUSFLAT 2025, LNCS 15884, pp. 198–210, 2025.
https://doi.org/10.1007/978-3-031-97228-7_17

the task of interest to us. In FL, data is used by different institutions (also called "clients") to jointly build a model without exchanging local data. For this reason, FL can be seen as a privacy-preserving solution.

Similar approaches (e.g., federated systems, federated databases) have been studied widely in the literature [16], also in the fuzzy setting [13,19]. In [8], the FL is described as "a machine learning setting where multiple entities (clients) collaborate in solving a machine learning problem, under the coordination of a central server or service provider. Each client's raw data is stored locally and not exchanged or transferred; instead, focused updates intended for immediate aggregation are used to achieve the learning objective". This is where the main advantage of FL comes into play: the raw data is stored by the clients, but the overall model is improved by using data available to all parties, while only the client-based models are shared.

FL has been adapted to many problems, including supervised learning for regression models [10,18]. This paper proposes a new approach combining FL with an imputation phase and a resampling step based on a machine learning (ML) algorithm to obtain larger datasets and achieve a better quality model. The adopted sequence of steps of the proposed algorithm is the source of its name: **FLIRT** (**F**ederated **L**earning with **I**mputation and **R**esampling Algori**T**hms). It is worth noting that although we focus on the linear regression problem, FLIRT can be applied as a more general solution for other settings. As for the ML resampling method, we adopt the nonparametric Generative Adversarial Network (GAN) algorithm [1,5], which is widely used to increase the volume of available data [3].

The clients independently build models using their datasets in the proposed algorithm FLIRT. Then, these models and the overall characteristics of all datasets are transferred to the main server. Because the server has no initial data, it constructs its synthetic dataset (or reconstructs the initial sample somehow) with the random generation, imputation, and resampling steps using the obtained information. Next, these new data are utilized to create the overall regression model. Besides the main idea and the algorithm construction, FLIRT's properties were analyzed numerically for synthetic and more practically oriented datasets. It seems that the final model obtained by the server surpasses the clients' models in terms of the mean values of the absolute differences between the estimators of the models' coefficients. The same applies to the comparison of the number of significant variables between the server's model and the clients' counterparts.

This paper is organized as follows. In Sect. 2, the main algorithm for FLIRT with the necessary notation is introduced. The considered error measures between the estimated regression models and the benchmark (i.e., the overall model) are discussed in Sect. 3. Section 4 shows some numerical examples and analyses based on synthetic samples and various datasets from R packages. The paper is concluded with some final remarks and possible future research in Sect. 5.

## 2 Notation and Algorithm

Suppose there are $l$ clients denoted further by $A^1, \ldots, A^l$. Each client has its own dataset $D^1, \ldots, D^l$ containing $n_1, \ldots, n_l$ samples, respectively. Let $Y$ denote the dependent variable of interest, while $\mathbb{X} = (X_1, \ldots, X_s)$ stands for the set of all potential independent variables that the clients might consider.

In the first step of FLIRT (see Algorithm 1), each client $A^i$ uses his dataset $D^i$ to create his regression model $M^i$, say

$$Y = b_1^i X_1 + \ldots + b_s^i X_s + b_0^i + \varepsilon. \tag{1}$$

Usually, some independent variables (including the intercept) in $M^i$ may turn out to be irrelevant (statistically insignificant) based on the linear regression model (1). Thus, let $\mathbb{X}'^{,i}$ denote the subset of the statistically significant variables for the model developed by $A^i$. So as not to get lost in the considerations and at the same time to simplify the notation we keep the same numbering order of the variables for $\mathbb{X}'^{,i}$ as for $\mathbb{X}$, e.g., for $\mathbb{X}'^{,i} = (X_2'^{,i}, X_4'^{,i})$ only the second and fourth variable from $\mathbb{X}$ are statistically significant in model $M^i$.

Next, each client $A^i$ delivers to the central server the estimates $\hat{\mathbb{b}}^i = (\hat{b}_0^i, \ldots, \hat{b}_s^i)$ of the regression coefficients obtained in his model $M^i$, but limiting himself only to the statistically significant variables $\mathbb{X}'^{,i}$. He also delivers some descriptive statistics containing aggregated knowledge of the considered variables $\mathbb{X}'^{,i}$, like the respective means $\bar{X}_j^i$ and standard deviations $S_{X,j}^i$. This way, information related only to the statistically significant independent variables is transferred to the main server.

**Algorithm 1.** FLIRT – Federated Learning with Imputation and Resampling

**Require:** Datasets $D^1, \ldots, D^l$.
**Ensure:** Models $M^1, \ldots, M^l, \boldsymbol{M}, \boldsymbol{M}^*$.
*Clients:*
**for** $i = 1$ to $l$ **do**
  Evaluate the regression model $M^i$ and the set $\mathbb{X}'^{,i}$ based on $D^i$.
  Send the estimates of coefficients $\hat{\mathbb{b}}^i$ of the variables from $\mathbb{X}'^{,i}$ to the server.
  Send the means $\bar{X}_j^i$ and standard deviations $S_{X,j}^i$ of the variables from $\mathbb{X}'^{,i}$ to the server.
*Server:*
**for** $i = 1$ to $l$ **do**
  Generate the synthetic sample $\mathbb{Z}^i$ of the size $m$ based on $\hat{\mathbb{b}}^i, \bar{X}_j^i, S_{X,j}^i$ for $\mathbb{X}'^{,i}$.
Merge $\mathbb{Z}^1, \ldots, \mathbb{Z}^l$ into $\mathbb{Z}$.
Impute missing values in $\mathbb{Z}$.
Evaluate the regression model $\boldsymbol{M}$ based on $\mathbb{Z}$.
Resample the sample $\mathbb{Z}'$ of size $p$ using $\mathbb{Z}$.
Evaluate the regression model $\boldsymbol{M}^*$ based on $\mathbb{Z}^* = (\mathbb{Z}, \mathbb{Z}')$.

The following steps are executed by the server only. Firstly, the server creates its own dataset by generating random data based on each received model $M^i$.

For this purpose, the new synthetic values of variables $Y^{*,i}, X_1^{*,i}, \ldots, X_s^{*,i}$ are sampled.

Suppose $X_j^i$ for some $j$ is statistically significant in the model $M^i$, i.e., $X_j^i$ belongs to $\mathbb{X}'^{,i}$. Then the main server also has information about $\bar{X}_j^i$ and $S_{X,j}^i$. Then, $m$ values $X_{j,1}^{*,i}, \ldots, X_{j,m}^{*,i}$ are randomly generated form the uniform distribution on the interval

$$\left[\bar{X}_j^i - \frac{S_{X,j}^i}{2\sqrt{1/2}} S_{X,j}^i, \bar{X}_j^i + \frac{S_{X,j}^i}{2\sqrt{1/2}} S_{X,j}^i\right]. \tag{2}$$

It is easily seen that the expected value and standard deviation for such a uniform distribution are identical to their sample counterparts for $X_j^i$. The procedure mentioned above is repeated for all variables from $\mathbb{X}'^{,i}$. Additionally, $m$ realizations of the error $\varepsilon^i$ are generated, so we obtain a sample $\varepsilon_1^i, \ldots, \varepsilon_m^i$.

To simplify further notation, suppose all independent variables in $M^i$ are statistically significant. Then, following the procedure mentioned above, we obtain the vectors

$$\left(X_{1,k}^{*,i}, \ldots, X_{s,k}^{*,i}, \varepsilon_k^i\right), \quad k = 1, \ldots, m, \tag{3}$$

which consist of the randomly generated values for all independent variables and the corresponding errors. These vectors can be directly used to create $m$ values of the dependent variable $Y$ based on coefficients estimators obtained for $M^i$, i.e.,

$$Y_k^{*,i} = \hat{b}_1^i X_{1,k}^{*,i} + \ldots + \hat{b}_s^i X_{s,k}^{*,i} + \hat{b}_0^i + \varepsilon_k^i, \tag{4}$$

where $k = 1, \ldots, m$. The outputs (4) together with all the vectors (3) make a sample matrix

$$(\mathbb{Y}^{*,i}, \mathbb{X}^{*,i}, \varepsilon) = \begin{pmatrix} Y_1^{*,i} & X_{1,1}^{*,i} & \ldots & X_{s,1}^{*,i} & \varepsilon_1^i \\ Y_2^{*,i} & X_{1,2}^{*,i} & \ldots & X_{s,2}^{*,i} & \varepsilon_2^i \\ \ldots & & & & \\ Y_m^{*,i} & X_{1,m}^{*,i} & \ldots & X_{s,m}^{*,i} & \varepsilon_m^i \end{pmatrix} \tag{5}$$

with $m$ rows and $s+2$ columns related to the model $M^i$. Further on, we will utilize only $\mathbb{Z}^i = \left(\mathbb{Y}^{*,i}, \mathbb{X}^{*,i}\right)$, i.e., the matrix (5) without realizations of errors.

All generation steps described above are repeated for each model $M^i$, $i = 1, \ldots, l$. The new created matrices $\mathbb{Z}^1, \ldots, \mathbb{Z}^l$ are stacked column-wise to form a matrix $\mathbb{Z}$ of size $lm \times (s+1)$. Because certain independent variables may be statistically insignificant in some models $M^i$, some missing values (NAs) may appear in the output matrix $\mathbb{Z}$. In such a case, to take the next step, we must impute all these missing values to obtain the final dataset without any NAs. Therefore, some imputation techniques should be applied, like the MissForest algorithm [17].

Using $\mathbb{Z}$, we can resample additional values of both dependent and independent variables to obtain a new matrix $\mathbb{Z}'$ with $p$ rows and (as previously) $s+1$ columns. This resampling step aims to generate new samples "similar"' to those in $\mathbb{Z}$, but not originating directly from the models provided by the clients (here, e.g., GAN [1,5] can be applied).

In the last step, the main server combines two matrices column-wise into $\mathbb{Z}^* = (\mathbb{Z}, \mathbb{Z}')$ to estimate parameters of the global regression model $\boldsymbol{M}^*$ based on $\mathbb{Z}^*$. This way we obtain estimates $\hat{\mathbb{b}}^{\mathbf{M}^*} = (\hat{b}_0^{\mathbf{M}^*}, \ldots, \hat{b}_s^{\mathbf{M}^*})$ and the respective set of statistically significant independent variables $\mathbb{X}'^{,\mathbf{M}^*}$.

One can also verify whether the whole resampling step is necessary. Indeed, by the regression model $\boldsymbol{M}$ based only on $\mathbb{Z}$ we can evaluate the parameters of the model, i.e. $\hat{\mathbb{b}}^{\mathbf{M}} = (\hat{b}_0^{\mathbf{M}}, \ldots, \hat{b}_s^{\mathbf{M}})$ and a set of the statistically significant independent variables $\mathbb{X}'^{,\mathbf{M}}$, respectively.

## 3 Error Measures

To evaluate the quality of the introduced FLIRT algorithm, we assume that the whole dataset $D = \left(D^1, \ldots, D^l\right)$ consisting of all clients' subsets is known. Then we design a regression model $\mathcal{M}$ based on $D$, estimate its coefficients $\hat{\mathbb{b}}^{\mathcal{M}} = (\hat{b}_0^{\mathcal{M}}, \ldots, \hat{b}_s^{\mathcal{M}})$ and indicate which independent variables are statistically significant (i.e., we get $\mathbb{X}'^{,\mathcal{M}}$). Then, the obtained results serve as benchmarks to compare the "true" model $\mathcal{M}$ with models $M^1, \ldots, M^l$ delivered by the clients, and models $\boldsymbol{M}, \boldsymbol{M}^*$ created by the central server.

The respective errors are calculated as the mean values of the absolute differences between the coefficients estimators

$$\bar{b}^{m_1,m_2} = \frac{1}{s} \sum_{j=1}^{s} \left| \hat{b}_j^{m_1} - \hat{b}_j^{m_2} \right|, \tag{6}$$

and the weighted mean values

$$\bar{b}_w^{m_1,m_2} = \frac{1}{s} \sum_{j=1}^{s} \left| \frac{\hat{b}_j^{m_1} - \hat{b}_j^{m_2}}{\hat{b}_j^{m_2}} \right|, \tag{7}$$

where $m_1$ indicates the considered model and $m_2$–its benchmark counterpart. Similarly, one can check if the statistically significant variables are the same for $m_1$ and $m_2$ or not using the linear regression for the datasets related to $m_1$ and $m_2$, respectively.

In the following, we set $m_2 = \mathcal{M}$, so the overall regression linear model for the whole dataset $D$ will form the basis of our benchmark.

## 4 Numerical Studies

In this section, FLIRT is numerically examined with two kinds of datasets: the synthetic ones and those arising from the packages available in the R programming environment. To limit the size of the paper, only some results are provided (others are available upon reasonable request).

Three synthetic datasets *Set1, Set2, Set3* with $n = 400$ samples each were randomly generated. The sample size $m = 400$ can be considered as a moderate one. From our previous findings, $m$ should not be too small because the initial sample is then divided into parts, and the ML resampling algorithm (like GAN) shows problematic behavior when the training samples have too small sizes.

In the considered datasets values of independent variables $X_1, X_2$ and $X_3$, as well as the error $\varepsilon$ were independently drawn from some probability distributions described in Table 1, where $N(\mu, \sigma)$ stands for the normal distribution with the mean $\mu$ and standard deviation $\sigma$, $\text{Exp}(\lambda)$ is the exponential distribution with the parameter $\lambda$, $\Gamma(a, b)$ denotes the gamma distribution with the shape and scale parameters $a$ and $b$, respectively, $\mathcal{W}(a, b)$ is the Weibull distribution with the shape $a$ and scale $b$ parameters, and $\text{LN}(\mu, \sigma)$ denotes the lognormal distribution with the logarithm of location $\mu$ and the logarithm of scale $\sigma$. Then, the dependent variable $Y$ values were directly calculated based on the linear regression model (1) with the true values of the coefficients $b_1, b_2, b_3, b_0$ given in Table 1.

**Table 1.** Coefficients and random variables used to create synthetic datasets

| Dataset | $b_1; X_1$ | $b_2; X_2$ | $b_3; X_3$ | $b_0$ | Error |
|---|---|---|---|---|---|
| *Set1* | 1; $N(0, 4)$ | 2; Exp(2) | 3; $\Gamma(2, 4)$ | 5 | $N(0, 1)$ |
| *Set2* | 1; $\mathcal{W}(1.5, 1)$ | 2; LN(0.5, 1) | 0.5; $\Gamma(0.5, 1)$ | 10 | $N(0, 2)$ |
| *Set3* | 1; $\mathcal{W}(1.5, 1)$ | 10; Exp(2) | 0.1; $\Gamma(0.5, 1)$ | 10 | $N(0, 2)$ |

Next, each dataset was divided into four equal ($n_1 = n_2 = n_3 = n_4 = 100$) parts $D_1, \ldots, D_4$. They were treated as the respective datasets for the clients $A_1, \ldots, A_4$. Following the steps described in Sect. 2 the whole procedure was carried out, and all the models (i.e., $M_1, \ldots, M_4$–derived by the clients; $\boldsymbol{M}$ obtained after the generation step; $\boldsymbol{M}^*$ obtained after the resampling phase) were designed. To investigate the potential impact of datasets (the generated $\mathbb{Z}$ and resampled $\mathbb{Z}'$) size on the results, a sequence of increasing values $m = p = 50, 100, 200, 400, 800$ was also considered. The smallest value of $m = p$ in this sequence equals half the size of each part $D_1, \ldots, D_4$ and can be considered a small sample size. The biggest value of $m = p$ is eight times greater than the sizes of these parts and can be seen as the big sample size.

The `RGAN` package [12] in R was used during the resampling step. The parameter `noise_dim` responsible for the number of dimensions of the noise was equal to the total number of the independent variables in the considered model (e.g., three for the datasets *Set1*–*Set3*), and the number of training epochs `epochs` was set to 300. Other parameters had their default values.

Table 2 compares numbers of the significant variables (including the intercept) for all datasets, assuming the significance level $\alpha = 0.05$ for the respective t-tests in the regression analysis. A model is considered better if the number of its significant variables is closer to the counterpart for the overall model $\mathcal{M}$. We also compared the outputs using error measures described in Sect. 3. Then, in Figs. 1, 2, 3 and 4, the respective mean values $\bar{b}^{m_1,\mathcal{M}}$ of differences between estimated coefficients for the considered regression model $m_1$ and our benchmark $\mathcal{M}$ are plotted. They are functions of the increasing size $m = p$. In these figures, the following notation is used: *LMRes* means the error between the models $\boldsymbol{M}^*$ (with the generation and resampling steps) and $\mathcal{M}$ (the benchmark); *LMSubMerg* denotes the error between the models $\boldsymbol{M}$ (the generation phase only) and $\mathcal{M}$; *LMSub1* stands for the error between the models $M_1$ (the model obtained by the first client) and $\mathcal{M}$; *LMSub2* is the error between the models $M_2$ (the model from the second client) and $\mathcal{M}$, etc.

In the case of *Set1*, there were no differences between significant variables (including the intercept) for all the considered models (see Table 2). The errors $\bar{b}^{\cdot,\mathcal{M}}$ for $\boldsymbol{M}$ and $\boldsymbol{M}^*$ usually decreased for increasing $m$ and $p$ (see Fig. 1). However, the model with the only generation step clearly outperforms other models, including those of all clients. If the resampling step was included, the error was significantly higher apart from the case with the biggest sample $m = p = 800$. The same applies to the weighted mean error $\bar{b}_w^{\cdot,\mathcal{M}}$ (see Fig. 2).

**Table 2.** Numbers of significant variables

| Model | $m = p$ | *Set1* | *Set2* | *Set3* | *Carseats* | *Diamonds* |
|---|---|---|---|---|---|---|
| $\mathcal{M}$ | | 4 | 4 | 3 | 6 | 3 |
| $M_1$ | | 4 | 3 | 3 | 5 | 3 |
| $M_2$ | | 4 | 3 | 3 | 6 | 3 |
| $M_3$ | | 4 | 4 | 3 | 5 | 3 |
| $M_4$ | | 4 | 2 | 4 | 5 | 3 |
| $\boldsymbol{M}$ | 50 | 4 | 3 | 3 | 5 | 3 |
| $\boldsymbol{M}^*$ | 50 | 4 | 4 | 3 | 3 | 3 |
| $\boldsymbol{M}$ | 100 | 4 | 3 | 3 | 5 | 3 |
| $\boldsymbol{M}^*$ | 100 | 4 | 4 | 3 | 5 | 3 |
| $\boldsymbol{M}$ | 200 | 4 | 4 | 3 | 5 | 3 |
| $\boldsymbol{M}^*$ | 200 | 4 | 4 | 4 | 5 | 3 |
| $\boldsymbol{M}$ | 400 | 4 | 4 | 4 | 5 | 3 |
| $\boldsymbol{M}^*$ | 400 | 4 | 4 | 4 | 4 | 3 |
| $\boldsymbol{M}$ | 800 | 4 | 4 | 4 | 5 | 3 |
| $\boldsymbol{M}^*$ | 800 | 4 | 2 | 4 | 5 | 3 |

Case *Set2* is more complicated. The $\mathcal{M}$ model analysis indicates that all independent variables are statistically significant, contrary to models obtained by clients $M_2, M_4$. For $\boldsymbol{M}$ under increasing sample size $m$, all variables become significant (in line with $\mathcal{M}$), while for $\boldsymbol{M}^*$, the largest considered sample size $p = 800$ results in two statistically insignificant variables (with p-values greater

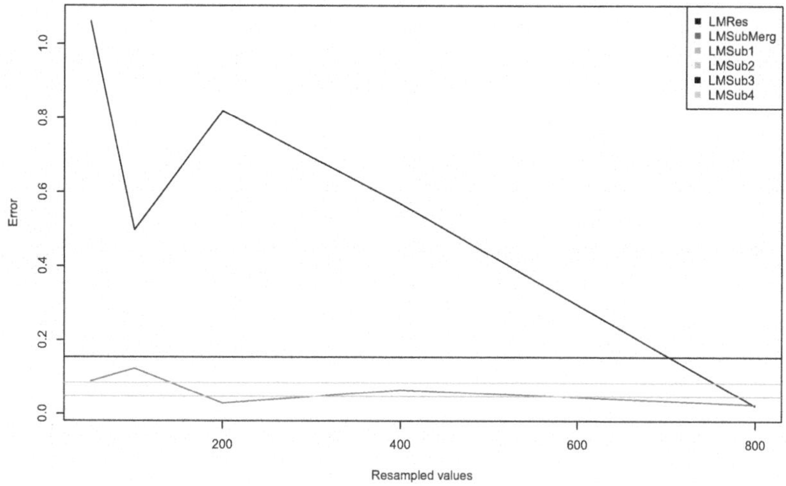


**Fig. 1.** Mean error of the coefficients as a function of $m = p$ for dataset *Set1*.

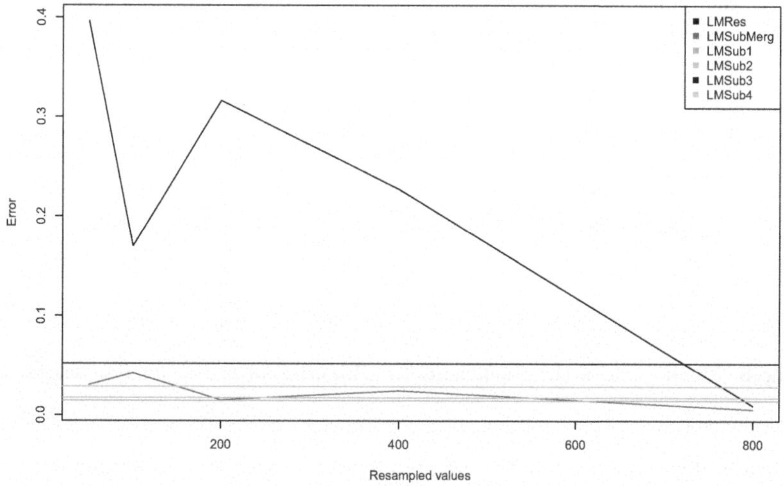


**Fig. 2.** Mean weighted error of the coefficients as a function of $m = p$ for dataset *Set1*.

than 0.1). On the other hand, errors treated as functions of the sample size behave similarly as for *Set1*. The generation step leads to better overall results, comparable with the clients' outputs (for lower $m$) and even surpassing them (for the biggest value of $m$). Considering the mean weighted error, the results were similar but a little worse for both $\boldsymbol{M}$ and $\boldsymbol{M}^*$.

In the case of *Set3*, the whole model $\mathcal{M}$ shows that $X_3$ is insignificant. The outputs were similar for $M_1$, $M_2$, and $M_3$, but for $M_4$, all independent variables were significant. Both for $\boldsymbol{M}$ and $\boldsymbol{M}^*$, all variables become statistically significant if sample sizes are large enough. It is worth paying attention to the behavior of errors (see Fig. 3). We obtain the U-shaped error function for $\boldsymbol{M}$, so the smallest differences are observed for moderate sample sizes ($m = 200 = 400$). The considered function decreases for $\boldsymbol{M}^*$, with the values close to the outputs for the clients if $p$ is large. The U-shaped weighted error function is also seen for $\boldsymbol{M}$, but for $\boldsymbol{M}^*$ is more unpredictable (see Fig. 4).

In our study, the datasets available in some R packages (i.e., *Carseats* from the package `ISLR` [7] and *Diamonds* included in the package `yarrr` [14]) were also considered. The same sequence $m = p$ was used for the generation and resampling steps to facilitate comparisons with the previously analyzed synthetic samples.

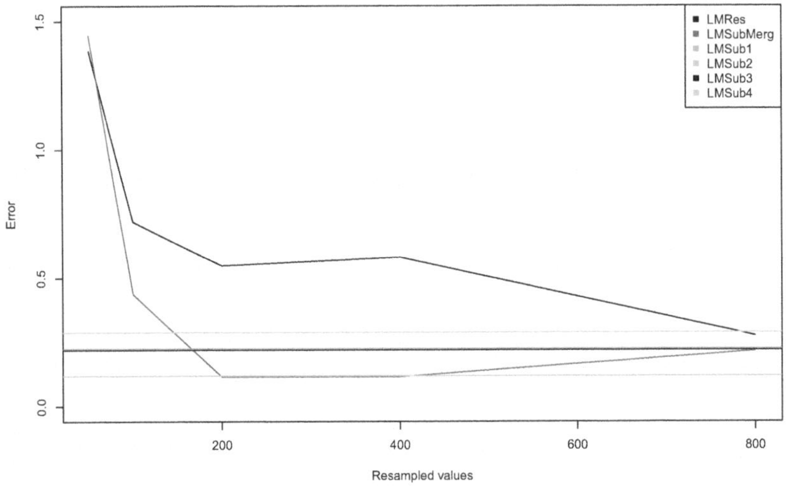


**Fig. 3.** Mean error of the coefficients as a function of $m = p$ for dataset *Set3*.

To simplify calculations, we considered only *Sales* as a dependent variable with *CompPrice, Income, Advertising, Price, Age, Intercept* as independent variables for *Carseats.* As before, the whole dataset was equally divided into four subsets (clients). Three models, $M_1$, $M_3$, and $M_4$, found the variable *Income* insignificant. Therefore, both $\boldsymbol{M}$ and $\boldsymbol{M}^*$ were closer to the benchmark except for the smallest sample size $m = p = 50$. The error functions for these two models behave in a somewhat predictable manner. The mean differences between coefficients are lower than their clients' counterparts for moderate or largest sample sizes. Once again, the model with the generation step only produces better results overall. The weighted error results were somewhat similar. However, $\bar{b}^{\boldsymbol{M},\mathcal{M}}$ was close to the clients' counterparts for the largest sample sizes.

For the *Diamonds* dataset, we examined a model with *value* as the dependent variable and two independent variables *weight* and *clarity.* All independent variables (including the intercept) were significant for all considered models. The

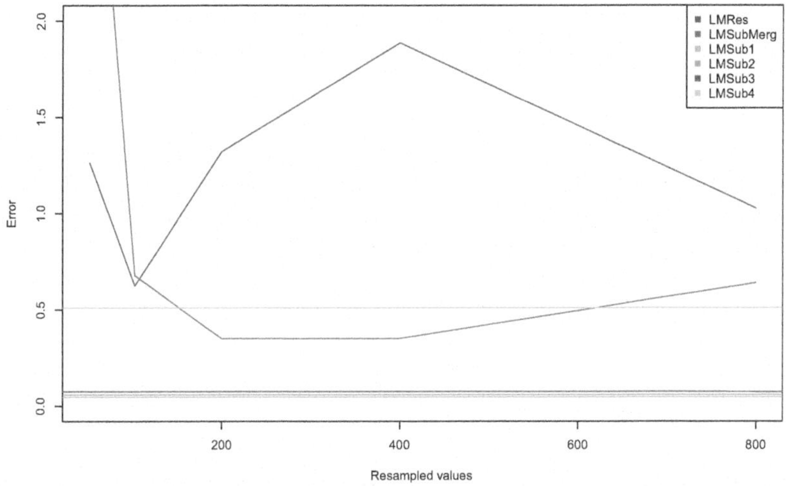


**Fig. 4.** Mean weighted error of the coefficients as a function of $m = p$ for dataset *Set3*.

errors for $\boldsymbol{M}$ also behaved desirably: they were smaller than their counterparts for the clients if the sample size was at least moderate. The same conclusions apply to the weighted errors.

We can roughly divide FLIRT into two parts based on execution time and numerical complexity. The first part, involving the construction of regression models and the generation step, is significantly faster than the second part–the resampling step–especially when a machine learning algorithm such as GAN is applied afterward. Examples of timing measurements, obtained using the R package `microbenchmark` [11] on *Set1* (laptop, Windows 11, Intel i7-8750H, 16 GB RAM, R 4.4.3), are provided in Table 3. The first part required about 6-21 milliseconds, showing no explicit dependency on the size $m$ of the generated synthetic sample $\mathbb{Z}^i$. In contrast, the second part took 100 up to almost 900 s, with execution time depending on the size $p$ of the resampled set $\mathbb{Z}'$. Thus, adopting a faster resampling method could offer substantial performance improvements.

**Table 3.** Examples of timing measurements for *Set1* (means)

| $m = p$ | Regression analysis and generation (ms) | Resampling step (s) |
|---|---|---|
| 50 | 21.1676 | 99.6422 |
| 100 | 5.9080 | 191.0296 |
| 200 | 21.3067 | 323.7671 |
| 400 | 8.9096 | 414.8706 |
| 800 | 6.4055 | 884.2524 |

## 5 Conclusions

An innovative approach to regression analysis based on federated learning (FL) supplemented with several additional steps is proposed. In particular, we added random generation of the server's dataset, imputation of the missing values existing there, and GAN was used as the enlarging technique. The proposed algorithm (FLIRT) was examined with different synthetic and more practically oriented datasets.

It seems that the final model produced by FLIRT surpasses the client-based models in terms of the mean differences between estimated parameters and the numbers of the significant variables (where the regression model with all data joined together was used as a benchmark). However, some caution is still advised. The best results were usually obtained for the server's moderately large dataset generation. Too small or too big samples may increase the error and worsen the overall behavior of the outputs. Interestingly, the resampling step provided with GAN does not improve the results noticeably. Sometimes, the generation and imputation steps offer the best solution (i.e., the model most similar to the benchmark).

Therefore, some other resampling approaches–both classical or proposed recently [2,4,6,15]–as well as various imputation algorithms [9] might be considered as possible directions in future research. Moreover, providing a ready-to-use R package implementing FLIRT is also our next step.

**Disclosure of Interests.** The author has no competing interests to declare relevant to this article's content.

## References


1. Creswell, A., White, T., Dumoulin, V., Arulkumaran, K., Sengupta, B., Bharath, A.A.: Generative adversarial networks: an overview. IEEE Signal Process. Mag. **35**(1), 53–65 (2018). https://doi.org/10.1109/MSP.2017.2765202
2. Davison, A.C., Hinkley, D.V.: Bootstrap Methods and their Application. Cambridge Series in Statistical and Probabilistic Mathematics. Cambridge University Press, Cambridge (1997). https://doi.org/10.1017/CBO9780511802843
3. Dzadz, N., Romaniuk, M.: Improving insurance catastrophic data with resampling and GAN methods. In: Atanassov, K.T., et al. (eds.) Uncertainty and Imprecision in Decision Making and Decision Support – New Advances, Challenges, and Perspectives. Springer, Heidelberg (2025)
4. Efron, B., Tibshirani, R.J.: An Introduction to the Bootstrap. No. 57 in Monographs on Statistics and Applied Probability. Chapman & Hall/CRC, Boca Raton (1993)
5. Goodfellow, I.: NIPS 2016 tutorial: generative adversarial networks (2017). https://arxiv.org/abs/1701.00160
6. Grzegorzewski, P., Hryniewicz, O., Romaniuk, M.: Flexible resampling for fuzzy data. Int. J. Appl. Math. Comput. Sci. **30**(2), 281–297 (2020). https://doi.org/10.34768/amcs-2020-0022
7. James, G., Witten, D., Hastie, T., Tibshirani, R.: An Introduction to Statistical Learning with Applications in R. Springer, New York (2021). https://doi.org/10.1007/978-1-0716-1418-1
8. Kairouz, P., et al.: Advances and open problems in federated learning. Found. Trends Mach. Learn. **14**(1–2), 1–210 (2021). https://doi.org/10.1561/2200000083
9. Little, R., Rubin, D.: Statistical Analysis with Missing Data. John Wiley & Sons, Inc., Hoboken (2022). https://doi.org/10.1002/9781119013563
10. McMahan, H.B., Moore, E., Ramage, D., Hampson, S., Arcas, B.A.: Communication-efficient learning of deep networks from decentralized data (2023). https://doi.org/10.48550/arXiv.1602.05629. https://arxiv.org/abs/1602.05629
11. Mersmann, O.: Microbenchmark: Accurate Timing Functions (2024). https://CRAN.R-project.org/package=microbenchmark, R package version 1.5.0
12. Neunhoeffer, M.: RGAN: Generative Adversarial Nets (GAN) in R (2022). https://CRAN.R-project.org/package=RGAN, R package version 0.1.1
13. Pekala, B., Szkola, J., Dyczkowski, K., Wilbik, A.: Federated similarity-based learning with incomplete data. In: 2023 IEEE International Conference on Fuzzy Systems (FUZZ), pp. 01–06 (2023). https://doi.org/10.1109/FUZZ52849.2023.10309757
14. Phillips, N.: yarrr: a companion to the e-Book "YaRrr!: The Pirate's Guide to R" (2017). https://CRAN.R-project.org/package=yarrr, R package version 0.1.5
15. Romaniuk, M., Hryniewicz, O.: Interval-based, nonparametric approach for resampling of fuzzy numbers. Soft. Comput. **23**(14), 5883–5903 (2018). https://doi.org/10.1007/s00500-018-3251-5
16. Sheth, A.P., Larson, J.A.: Federated database systems for managing distributed, heterogeneous, and autonomous databases. ACM Comput. Surv. **22**(3), 183–236 (1990). https://doi.org/10.1145/96602.96604
17. Stekhoven, D.J., Bühlmann, P.: MissForest-non-parametric missing value imputation for mixed-type data. Bioinformatics **28**(1), 112–118 (2011). https://doi.org/10.1093/bioinformatics/btr597

18. Wang, F., Zhu, H., Lu, R., Zheng, Y., Li, H.: A privacy-preserving and non-interactive federated learning scheme for regression training with gradient descent. Inf. Sci. **552**, 183–200 (2021). https://doi.org/10.1016/j.ins.2020.12.007
19. Wilbik, A., Grefen, P.: Towards a federated fuzzy learning system. In: 2021 IEEE International Conference on Fuzzy Systems (FUZZ-IEEE), pp. 1–6 (2021). https://doi.org/10.1109/FUZZ45933.2021.9494392

# Modeling Treatment Effect with Fuzzy Data

Przemyslaw Grzegorzewski[1,2](✉)

[1] Faculty of Mathematics and Information Science, Warsaw University of Technology, Koszykowa 75, 00-662 Warsaw, Poland
przemyslaw.grzegorzewski@pw.edu.pl

[2] Systems Research Institute Polish Academy of Sciences, Newelska 6, 01-447 Warsaw, Poland

**Abstract.** The treatment effect is a universal concept used in many fields. Regardless of the context, it is crucial to define the measure of the success of the intervention and the method of assessing the effect, which may require the use of various statistical methods. An additional challenge for analysts may be caused by imprecise data on the basis of which they are to assess the size of the treatment effect. It turns out that although the use of fuzzy sets to model imprecise data is something natural, further and deeper analysis of the treatment effect based on such data entails many difficulties. This contribution discusses how to deal with some these problems.

**Keywords:** Treatment effect · Fuzzy numbers · Fuzzy random variables · generalized Hukuhara difference · Estimation

## 1 Introduction

The term "treatment effect" refers to the change that occurs as a result of a specific action (procedure, intervention, or treatment). This concept is used both to determine whether the examined factor has any impact (i.e., the occurrence of a treatment effect) and to quantitatively assess the effectiveness of the implemented actions (i.e., the magnitude of the treatment effect).

The concept of treatment effect is encountered in many fields and areas. A typical example is clinical research aimed at evaluating the effectiveness of drugs. The term is also used in the context of assessing the success of surgical procedures or the effectiveness of physiotherapeutic interventions. In engineering and technology, the treatment effect refers to the impact of specific procedures on the performance of devices, systems, or materials - for example, improving engine efficiency through maintenance or tuning, the influence of heat treatment on material properties, or the effectiveness of diagnostic and repair procedures. In social sciences, the treatment effect is used to assess the outcomes of various interventions, such as evaluating the impact of changes in educational programs


M. Baczyński et al. (Eds.): EUSFLAT 2025, LNCS 15884, pp. 211–222, 2025.
https://doi.org/10.1007/978-3-031-97228-7_18

on student performance, the effectiveness of public campaigns promoting behavioral change, or the success of psychological therapies. Similarly, in economics and management, treatment effects are analyzed in relation to the introduction of specific strategies, policies, or reforms to determine their impact on economic growth, organizational efficiency, or market behavior.

Classical statistics has developed various tools for studying the effect of treatment based on precisely expressed real or binary data. In addition to such commonly used tools as the t-test or the Mann-Whitney-Wilcoxon test, there are also techniques designed for specific application areas. The situation is much worse when we deal with imprecise or, generally, uncertain data. And although it has been accepted for some time that such data are conveniently modeled using fuzzy sets, this does not solve the problem completely, because any modeling will only make sense if it is supplemented with effective analytical tools, mainly of statistical provenance.

In recent years, several tools have been developed to support statistical inference based on fuzzy data. We mean here some statistical tests referring to bootstrap or permutation techniques, which have proven to be very useful due to probabilistic difficulties encountered in the world of fuzzy random variables (see, e.g. [1–7,10]). However, in the context of the treatment effect, the statistical tools we know are basically used only to investigate whether this effect occurs at all, and not to assess the size of this effect.

One of the reasons for this state of affairs are arithmetic problems that appear in the space of fuzzy numbers. As is known, the set of fuzzy numbers equipped with Minkowski operations (addition and scalar multiplication) is not a linear space. The resulting problems with defining the subtraction operation translate directly into the problem of properly defining the treatment effect, which is perceived as the difference between the average value for the treatment sample and the control sample.

In this contribution, we address the problem of properly defining the treatment effect and estimating it based on fuzzy data (Sect. 3). For this purpose, we refer to various methods of determining the difference of fuzzy numbers and the consequences of adopting a given method (Sect. 4). From the point of view of our task, the best idea, in our opinion, is to use the generalized Hukuhara difference [12] (Sect. 5). Then we use the gH-difference to propose a desired definition of the fuzzy treatment effect (Sect. 6). Next, we suggest the estimator of the treatment effect based on fuzzy data and study its properties.

## 2 A Classical Statistical View of the Treatment Effect

In classical statistics the **treatment effect** represents a size of difference between groups, typically measured by the difference in means, medians, or proportions. Let $\mathbb{Y} = (Y_1, \ldots, Y_m)$ denote a sample from the so-called **treatment group**, and let $\mathbb{X} = (X_1, \ldots, X_n)$ represent a sample from the reference population, called the **control group**. Usually (but not always) we assume that observations in each sample are independent and identically distributed, as well as that these two samples are also independent.

Under the most common assumption that both samples are normally distributed, i.e., $X_1, \ldots, X_n$ i.i.d. $\mathrm{N}(\mu_X, \sigma)$ and $Y_1, \ldots, Y_m$ i.i.d. $\mathrm{N}(\mu_Y, \sigma)$, the treatment effect is defined by the difference of means, i.e.

$$\delta := \mu_Y - \mu_X. \tag{1}$$

Clearly, a natural point estimator of (1) is given by

$$\widehat{\delta} = \overline{Y} - \overline{X}. \tag{2}$$

Researchers are often interested not only in estimating the treatment effect but also in testing whether its value equals a predefined threshold, $\delta_0$. Formally, this involves testing the null hypothesis $H_0 : \delta = \delta_0$ of no effect, against the alternative $H_1 : \delta \neq \delta_0$ that some effect exists. A special case arises when $\delta_0 = 0$, where the primary goal is to determine whether the treatment effect is statistically significant. This framework can naturally be extended to incorporate one-sided alternatives, depending on the direction of interest. Under the assumptions stated above, the test statistic is defined as

$$T = \frac{\widehat{\delta} - \delta_0}{\sqrt{\frac{(n-1)s_X^2 + (m-1)s_Y^2}{n+m-2}}}. \tag{3}$$

It is well known that under the null hypothesis $H_0$, the test statistic (3) follows the t-distribution with $n+m-2$ degrees of freedom. Consequently, we reject $H_0$ if $|T| > t_{1-\alpha/2}^{[n+m-2]}$, where $t_\gamma^{[k]}$ denotes the $\gamma \cdot 100\%$ quantile of the t-distribution with $k$ degrees of freedom.

In practice, the assumption that both samples follow a normal distribution is rarely met. Additionally, the treatment under consideration may affect the second sample's distribution in ways beyond a simple shift in location. Moreover, in most cases, at least one of these distributions - if not both - is unknown. In such situations, nonparametric statistical methods provide a robust alternative. In particular, to test hypotheses about the treatment effect, we can employ, e.g. the well-known Mann-Whitney-Wilcoxon test. Notably, in the nonparametric framework, the treatment effect is typically assessed not as in (1), but using the difference in medians. However, even classical nonparametric tests become inadequate when the available data are not composed of precise real numbers or, at the very least, linearly ordered observations that can be ranked unambiguously. In cases where data are imprecise and modeled using fuzzy numbers or intervals - the latter being particularly valuable in engineering applications - the elements within the samples are only partially ordered. This limitation necessitates the use of alternative, non-classical methods in statistical inference. But actually, defining the treatment effect for imprecise data is also not a straightforward extension of the classical definition. Instead, it requires a fundamentally new approach, which will be explored further on.

## 3 Fuzzy Numbers

Given imprecise observations or measurements from experiments, we require a suitable tool to represent such data. A particularly effective approach for modeling imprecise values is the **fuzzy number**, which is characterized by a mapping $\widetilde{A}:\mathbb{R}\to[0,1]$, called a membership function, such that its $\alpha$-cuts defined by

$$\widetilde{A}_\alpha = \begin{cases} \{x\in\mathbb{R}:\widetilde{A}(x)\geqslant\alpha\} & \text{if } \alpha\in(0,1],\\ cl\{x\in\mathbb{R}:\widetilde{A}(x)>0\} & \text{if } \alpha=0, \end{cases} \tag{4}$$

are nonempty compact intervals for each $\alpha\in[0,1]$, where $cl$ is the closure operator. Thus, a fuzzy number can be represented either by its membership function $\widetilde{A}(x)$ or, equivalently, by the family of its $\alpha$-cuts, i.e. $\{\widetilde{A}_\alpha\}_{\alpha\in[0,1]}$. Two specific $\alpha$-cuts are of particular importance: $\widetilde{A}_1=\text{core}(\widetilde{A})$, called the **core**, which contains of all values fully compatible with the concept modeled by $\widetilde{A}$, and $\widetilde{A}_0=\text{supp}(\widetilde{A})$, called the **support**, which includes values that are partially compatible with $\widetilde{A}$ to some extent. The set of all fuzzy numbers is denoted by $\mathbb{F}(\mathbb{R})$.

Various types of fuzzy numbers have been extensively studied in the literature. Among them, the **LR fuzzy numbers** are one of the most widely used classes. A fuzzy number $\widetilde{A}$ is said to be an LR fuzzy number if its membership function can be expressed as follows

$$\widetilde{A}(x) = \begin{cases} 0 & \text{if } \ x<a_1,\\ L\left(\frac{x-a_1}{a_2-a_1}\right) & \text{if } \ a_1\leqslant x<a_2,\\ 1 & \text{if } \ a_2\leqslant x<a_3,\\ R\left(\frac{a_4-x}{a_4-a_3}\right) & \text{if } \ a_3\leqslant x<a_4,\\ 0 & \text{if } \ x\geq a_4, \end{cases} \tag{5}$$

where $L,R:[0,1]\to[0,1]$ are continuous and strictly increasing functions satisfying $L(0)=R(0)=0, L(1)=R(1)=1$, and $a_1,a_2,a_3,a_4\in\mathbb{R}$ such that $a_1\leqslant a_2\leqslant a_3\leqslant a_4$. Specifically, if $L$ and $R$ are the following linear functions

$$L(x)=\frac{x-a_1}{a_2-a_1},\quad R(x)=\frac{a_4-x}{a_4-a_3}, \tag{6}$$

the resulting fuzzy number is called a **trapezoidal fuzzy number**. It is fully characterized by its support and core, allowing it to be conveniently represented as $\widetilde{A}=\text{Tra}(a_1,a_2,a_3,a_4)$. Furthermore, if $a_2=a_3$, the fuzzy number reduces to a **triangular fuzzy number**.

Basic operations in $\mathbb{F}(\mathbb{R})$ are defined using $\alpha$-cut-wise operations on intervals. In particular, the sum of $\widetilde{A}\in\mathbb{F}(\mathbb{R})$ and $\widetilde{B}\in\mathbb{F}(\mathbb{R})$ with $\alpha$-cuts $\widetilde{A}_\alpha=[\widetilde{A}^L_\alpha,\widetilde{A}^U_\alpha]$ and $\widetilde{B}_\alpha=[\widetilde{B}^L_\alpha,\widetilde{B}^U_\alpha]$, respectively, is given by the Minkowski addition of $\alpha$-cuts, i.e. for all $\alpha\in[0,1]$ we have

$$(\widetilde{A}+\widetilde{B})_\alpha=\left[\widetilde{A}^L_\alpha+\widetilde{B}^L_\alpha,\widetilde{A}^U_\alpha+\widetilde{B}^U_\alpha\right],$$

while the product of $\widetilde{A} \in \mathbb{F}(\mathbb{R})$ by a scalar $\gamma \in \mathbb{R}$ is defined by the Minkowski scalar product for intervals, i.e. for all $\alpha \in [0,1]$ we obtain

$$(\gamma \cdot \widetilde{A})_\alpha = \left[\min\{\gamma \widetilde{A}^L_\alpha, \gamma \widetilde{A}^U_\alpha\}, \max\{\gamma \widetilde{A}^L_\alpha, \gamma \widetilde{A}^U_\alpha\}\right].$$

Although the formulas provided above are both conceptually and computationally straightforward, the Minkowski arithmetic presents several challenges for users. In particular, the algebraic structure $(\mathbb{F}(\mathbb{R}), +, \cdot)$ is not linear but rather semilinear because, in general, $\widetilde{A} - \widetilde{A} = \widetilde{A} + (-1 \cdot \widetilde{A}) \neq \mathbb{1}_{\{0\}}$, meaning that the opposite of $\widetilde{A}$ is not its additive inverse under the Minkowski addition. Moreover, the addition/subtraction property does not hold, as fuzzy numbers generally satisfy $(\widetilde{A} + \widetilde{B}) - \widetilde{B} \neq \widetilde{A}$. To address this issue, the Hukuhara difference [8] was introduced. It is defined as $\widetilde{C} \in \mathbb{F}(\mathbb{R})$ that satisfies

$$\widetilde{A} -_H \widetilde{B} = \widetilde{C} \quad \Longleftrightarrow \quad \widetilde{A} = \widetilde{B} + \widetilde{C}.$$

If the Hukuhara difference exists, it is unique. Clearly, $\widetilde{A} -_H \widetilde{A} = \mathbb{1}_{\{0\}}$. Moreover, $(\widetilde{A} + \widetilde{B}) -_H \widetilde{B} = \widetilde{A}$, $\forall \widetilde{A}, \widetilde{B} \in \mathbb{F}(\mathbb{R})$, i.e. the Hukuhara difference inverts the addition of fuzzy numbers. Unfortunately, the Hukuhara difference does not always exists.

Due to the aforementioned challenges with subtraction, differences are often replaced by distances in many applications. In$\mathbb{F}(\mathbb{R})$, numerous metrics can be defined, however, the most commonly used metric in statistical contexts is the distance given for any $A, B \in \mathbb{F}(\mathbb{R})$ as follows (see [13])

$$D^\lambda_\theta(\widetilde{A}, \widetilde{B}) = \left(\int_0^1 \left[(\operatorname{mid} \widetilde{A}_\alpha - \operatorname{mid} \widetilde{B}_\alpha)^2 + \theta \cdot (\operatorname{spr} \widetilde{A}_\alpha - \operatorname{spr} \widetilde{B}_\alpha)^2\right] d\lambda(\alpha)\right)^{1/2}, \quad (7)$$

where

$$\operatorname{mid} \widetilde{A}_\alpha = \frac{1}{2}\left(\widetilde{A}^L_\alpha + \widetilde{A}^U_\alpha\right) \quad \text{and} \quad \operatorname{spr} \widetilde{A}_\alpha = \frac{1}{2}\left(\widetilde{A}^U_\alpha - \widetilde{A}^L_\alpha\right) \quad (8)$$

denote the midpoint and the radius of the $\alpha$-cut $\widetilde{A}_\alpha$, respectively, and $\lambda$ is a normalized measure associated with a continuous distribution on $[0,1]$ which allows weighting the influence of $\alpha$-cuts. The parameter $\theta$ is a positive constant, that controls the relative impact of the distance between the spreads of the $\alpha$-cuts and the distance between their midpoints. Typically $\lambda$ is taken as the Lebesgue measure on $[0,1]$, but regardless of the choice of $(\lambda, \theta)$, the metric $D^\lambda_\theta$ is of $L^2$-type in $\mathbb{F}(\mathbb{R})$ and remains invariant to translations and rotations. Furthermore, $(\mathbb{F}(\mathbb{R}), D^\lambda_\theta)$ forms a separable metric space and for each fixed $\lambda$ all metrics $D^\lambda_\theta$ are topologically equivalent.

## 4 Fuzzy Random Variables

For statistical inference, a model is required that captures both aspects of uncertainty present in fuzzy data: fuzziness arising from data imprecision and randomness. To address this, Puri and Ralescu [11] introduced **fuzzy random variables**, also known as **random fuzzy numbers**.

Let $(\Omega, \mathcal{A}, P)$ be a probability space. A mapping $\widetilde{X} : \Omega \to \mathbb{F}(\mathbb{R})$ is a **random fuzzy number** if for all $\alpha \in [0,1]$ the $\alpha$-level function is a compact random interval. It can be shown that $\widetilde{X}$ is a random fuzzy number if and only if if and only if it is Borel measurable with respect to the $\sigma$-algebra generated by the topology induced by the metric $D_\theta^\lambda$.

The Aumann-type mean of a fuzzy random variable $\widetilde{X}$ is the fuzzy number $E(\widetilde{X}) \in \mathbb{F}(\mathbb{R})$ such that $\forall \alpha \in [0,1]$ the $\alpha$-cut $\big(E(\widetilde{X})\big)_\alpha$ is given by the Aumann integral of $\widetilde{X}_\alpha$, i.e.

$$\big(E(\widetilde{X})\big)_\alpha = \Big[\mathbb{E}(\mathrm{mid}\,\widetilde{X}_\alpha) - \mathbb{E}(\mathrm{spr}\,\widetilde{X}_\alpha), \mathbb{E}(\mathrm{mid}\,\widetilde{X}_\alpha) + \mathbb{E}(\mathrm{spr}\,\widetilde{X}_\alpha)\Big]. \tag{9}$$

A fuzzy random sample $\widetilde{\mathbb{X}} = (\widetilde{X}_1, \ldots, \widetilde{X}_n)$ is a finite sequence of random fuzzy numbers from the same distribution. Given $\widetilde{\mathbb{X}}$ we can determine the sample mean $\overline{\widetilde{X}} \in \mathbb{F}(\mathbb{R})$ defined by the following $\alpha$-cuts

$$\overline{\widetilde{X}}_\alpha = \left[\frac{1}{n}\sum_{i=1}^n \mathrm{mid}\,(\widetilde{X}_i)_\alpha - \frac{1}{n}\sum_{i=1}^n \mathrm{spr}\,(\widetilde{X}_i)_\alpha, \frac{1}{n}\sum_{i=1}^n \mathrm{mid}\,(\widetilde{X}_i)_\alpha + \frac{1}{n}\sum_{i=1}^n \mathrm{spr}\,(\widetilde{X}_i)_\alpha\right].$$

Transferring results from classical statistics to the fuzzy domain is challenging. The lack of well-established models for the distribution of fuzzy random variables complicates statistical reasoning significantly. Furthermore, there are currently no fully satisfactory Central Limit Theorems for fuzzy random variables that can be directly applied in decision-making. Standard nonparametric tests are also difficult to implement in the fuzzy framework, as they typically rely on ranks, whereas fuzzy numbers are not linearly ordered, and no universally accepted total ranking exists. Consequently, inference with fuzzy data requires innovative approaches, such as bootstrap methods (see, e.g., [1,2,10] or permutation tests [3–7]. Additionally, as mentioned earlier, the challenges associated with the subtraction of fuzzy numbers suggest that avoiding such operations whenever possible is strongly recommended. However, in some cases, this recommendation is impractical - precisely as in our current situation.

## 5 Some Consideration on the gH-Difference

Some of the tests mentioned above can be effectively used to determine whether a treatment effect exists by comparing the distance between the average behavior of observations in the test and control samples. However, these tests are not suitable for assessing the size of the treatment effect or for testing hypotheses about the size of the treatment effect. This limitation arises because the distance is always a non-negative quantity, and the direction (sign) of a treatment effect - often crucial for interpreting the studied phenomenon - cannot be directly inferred from it.

Furthermore, as previously noted, the set of fuzzy numbers lacks a linear order. The inequality of two fuzzy numbers may result not only from differences in their location but also from variations in their fuzziness and the shape of their membership functions. Therefore, defining the treatment effect in the contex6t of fuzzy data requires a careful approach that preserves the essence of the classical formulation (1) while also accounting for the unique characteristics of fuzzy data and the information they convey.

Since the definitions of the difference of fuzzy numbers used in Sect. 3 are unsatisfactory, it may be worthwhile to explore alternative approaches. An intriguing generalization was proposed by Stefanini [12], and we believe it merits further examination.

**Definition 1 (cf. [12]).** *Given $\widetilde{A}, \widetilde{B} \in \mathbb{F}(\mathbb{R})$, the* ***generalized Hukuhara difference*** *(gH-distance, in brief)of $\widetilde{A}$ and $\widetilde{B}$ is the fuzzy quantity $\widetilde{C} \in \mathbb{F}(\mathbb{R})$, it if exists, such that*

$$\widetilde{A} \ominus \widetilde{B} = \widetilde{C} \iff \left(\widetilde{A} = \widetilde{B} + \widetilde{C} \ \text{ or } \ \widetilde{B} = \widetilde{A} + (-1) \cdot \widetilde{C}\right). \tag{10}$$

It can be seen that if $\widetilde{A} \ominus \widetilde{B}$ and $\widetilde{A} -_H \widetilde{B}$ exist, then $\widetilde{A} \ominus \widetilde{B} = \widetilde{A} -_H \widetilde{B}$. If both conditions in (10) are satisfied simultaneously, then $\widetilde{C}$ is a crisp value. Moreover, $\widetilde{A} \ominus \widetilde{A} = \mathbb{1}_{\{0\}}$.

For calculations it is convenient to express the gH-difference in the $\alpha$-cut representation. Hence, assuming $\widetilde{C} = \widetilde{A} \ominus \widetilde{B}$, the $\alpha$-cuts of $\widetilde{C}$ are given by

$$\widetilde{C}_\alpha = \left[\min\left\{\widetilde{A}^L_\alpha - \widetilde{B}^L_\alpha, \widetilde{A}^U_\alpha - \widetilde{B}^U_\alpha\right\}, \max\left\{\widetilde{A}^L_\alpha - \widetilde{B}^L_\alpha, \widetilde{A}^U_\alpha - \widetilde{B}^U_\alpha\right\}\right]. \tag{11}$$

Let $\operatorname{len}(\widetilde{A}_\alpha) = \widetilde{A}^U_\alpha - \widetilde{A}^L_\alpha$ denote the $\alpha$-cut's length. This notation is used in the following theorem specifying conditions when the gH-difference exists.

**Theorem 1 (cf. [12]).** *Let $\widetilde{A}, \widetilde{B} \in \mathbb{F}(\mathbb{R})$ be two fuzzy numbers with $\alpha$-cuts $\widetilde{A}_\alpha$ and $\widetilde{B}_\alpha$, respectively. The gH-difference $\widetilde{A} \ominus \widetilde{B}$ exists if and only if one of the following two conditions (i) or (ii) is satisfied:*

$$(i) \begin{cases} \operatorname{len}(\widetilde{A}_\alpha) \geqslant \operatorname{len}(\widetilde{B}_\alpha) \ \forall \alpha \in [0,1], \\ \widetilde{A}^L_\alpha - \widetilde{B}^L_\alpha \text{ is increasing with respect to } \alpha, \\ \widetilde{A}^U_\alpha - \widetilde{B}^U_\alpha \text{ is decreasing with respect to } \alpha; \end{cases}$$

$$(ii) \begin{cases} \operatorname{len}(\widetilde{A}_\alpha) \leqslant \operatorname{len}(\widetilde{B}_\alpha) \ \forall \alpha \in [0,1], \\ \widetilde{A}^L_\alpha - \widetilde{B}^L_\alpha \text{ is decreasing with respect to } \alpha, \\ \widetilde{A}^U_\alpha - \widetilde{B}^U_\alpha \text{ is increasing with respect to } \alpha. \end{cases}$$

Note that conditions (ii) and (ii) of Theorem 1 are both valid if $\operatorname{len}(\widetilde{A}_\alpha) = \operatorname{len}(\widetilde{B}_\alpha)$ for all $\alpha \in [0,1]$ and in this case $\widetilde{A} \ominus \widetilde{B}$ is a crisp value.

Another useful conclusion from the Theorem 1 refers to trapezoidal fuzzy numbers. Namely, if $\widetilde{A} = \operatorname{Tra}(a_1, a_2, a_3, a_4)$ and $\widetilde{B} = \operatorname{Tra}(b_1, b_2, b_3, b_4)$ then $\widetilde{A} \ominus \widetilde{B}$ exists if and only if $a_1 - b_1 \leqslant a_2 - b_2 \leqslant a_3 - b_3 \leqslant a_4 - b_4$ or $a_1 - b_1 \geqslant a_2 - b_2 \geqslant a_3 - b_3 \geqslant a_4 - b_4$.

Last, but not least, we will derive formulas for expressing the gH-difference in the useful mid/spr representation.

**Lemma 1.** *Let $\widetilde{A}, \widetilde{B} \in \mathbb{F}(\mathbb{R})$ be two fuzzy numbers with $\alpha$-cuts $\widetilde{A}_\alpha$ and $\widetilde{B}_\alpha$, respectively. If the gH-difference $\widetilde{C} = \widetilde{A} \ominus \widetilde{B}$ exists, then the $\alpha$-cuts of $\widetilde{C}$ could be expressed as follows: $\widetilde{C}_\alpha = \left[\widetilde{C}^L_\alpha, \widetilde{C}^U_\alpha\right] = \left[\operatorname{mid} \widetilde{C}_\alpha - \operatorname{spr} \widetilde{C}_\alpha, \operatorname{mid} \widetilde{C}_\alpha + \operatorname{spr} \widetilde{C}_\alpha\right]$, where*

$$\operatorname{mid} \widetilde{C}_\alpha = \operatorname{mid} \widetilde{A}_\alpha - \operatorname{mid} \widetilde{B}_\alpha, \tag{12}$$

$$\operatorname{spr} \widetilde{C}_\alpha = \left|\operatorname{spr} \widetilde{A}_\alpha - \operatorname{spr} \widetilde{B}_\alpha\right|. \tag{13}$$

*Proof.* By (11)

$$\begin{aligned}
\widetilde{C}^L_\alpha &= \min\left\{\widetilde{A}^L_\alpha - \widetilde{B}^L_\alpha, \widetilde{A}^U_\alpha - \widetilde{B}^U_\alpha\right\} \\
&= \min\left\{\left[(\operatorname{mid} \widetilde{A}_\alpha - \operatorname{spr} \widetilde{A}_\alpha) - (\operatorname{mid} \widetilde{B}_\alpha - \operatorname{spr} \widetilde{B}_\alpha)\right],\right. \\
&\qquad \left.\left[(\operatorname{mid} \widetilde{A}_\alpha + \operatorname{spr} \widetilde{A}_\alpha) - (\operatorname{mid} \widetilde{B}_\alpha + \operatorname{spr} \widetilde{B}_\alpha)\right]\right\} \\
&= \min\left\{\left[(\operatorname{mid} \widetilde{A}_\alpha - \operatorname{mid} \widetilde{B}_\alpha) - (\operatorname{spr} \widetilde{A}_\alpha - \operatorname{spr} \widetilde{B}_\alpha)\right],\right. \\
&\qquad \left.\left[(\operatorname{mid} \widetilde{A}_\alpha - \operatorname{mid} \widetilde{B}_\alpha) + (\operatorname{spr} \widetilde{A}_\alpha - \operatorname{spr} \widetilde{B}_\alpha)\right]\right\} \\
&= \left(\operatorname{mid} \widetilde{A}_\alpha - \operatorname{mid} \widetilde{B}_\alpha\right) - \left|\operatorname{spr} \widetilde{A}_\alpha - \operatorname{spr} \widetilde{B}_\alpha\right|.
\end{aligned}$$

Similar transformations allow us to notice that

$$\begin{aligned}
\widetilde{C}^U_\alpha &= \max\left\{\widetilde{A}^L_\alpha - \widetilde{B}^L_\alpha, \widetilde{A}^U_\alpha - \widetilde{B}^U_\alpha\right\} \\
&= \left(\operatorname{mid} \widetilde{A}_\alpha - \operatorname{mid} \widetilde{B}_\alpha\right) + \left|\operatorname{spr} \widetilde{A}_\alpha - \operatorname{spr} \widetilde{B}_\alpha\right|.
\end{aligned}$$

Now, following expressions given in (8) we obtain

$$\begin{aligned}
\operatorname{mid} \widetilde{C}_\alpha &= \frac{1}{2}(\widetilde{C}^L_\alpha + \widetilde{C}^U_\alpha) = \operatorname{mid} \widetilde{A}_\alpha - \operatorname{mid} \widetilde{B}_\alpha, \\
\operatorname{spr} \widetilde{C}_\alpha &= \frac{1}{2}(\widetilde{C}^U_\alpha - \widetilde{C}^L_\alpha) = \left|\operatorname{spr} \widetilde{A}_\alpha - \operatorname{spr} \widetilde{B}_\alpha\right|,
\end{aligned}$$

which is the desired conclusion. □

## 6 Treatment Effect for Fuzzy Data

To define the treatment effect in the context of fuzzy data the most intuitive approach seems to be a generalization of statistical concepts rooted in practice, as discussed in Sect. 2.

**Definition 2.** *Let $\widetilde{X}_1, \ldots, \widetilde{X}_n$ and $\widetilde{Y}_1, \ldots, \widetilde{Y}_m$ denote two independent samples of random fuzzy numbers such that the Aumann expectations $E(\widetilde{X}), E(\widetilde{Y})$ for their corresponding distributions exist. In this case, the (fuzzy)* ***treatment effect*** *is defined as follows*

$$\Delta := E(\widetilde{Y}) \ominus E(\widetilde{X}). \tag{14}$$

Clearly, Definition 2 proposes a straightforward generalization of the classically perceived treatment effect given in (1). Therefore, a natural plug-in estimator of the treatment effect based on fuzzy data is given by

$$\widehat{\Delta} := \overline{\widetilde{Y}} \ominus \overline{\widetilde{X}}. \tag{15}$$

Obviously, just proposing a formula for an estimator is not enough if one does not say something about its properties. One of the basic and often desired properties of estimators considered in classical statistics is unbiasedness, which occurs when the expected value of the estimator is equal to the estimated parameter. If we wanted to transfer this definition to the fuzzy domain, we would have to demand that when estimating a fuzzy parameter $\theta$ using the estimator $\widehat{\theta} = \widehat{\theta}(\widetilde{\mathbb{X}})$, where $\widetilde{\mathbb{X}} = (\widetilde{X}_1, \ldots, \widetilde{X}_n)$ is a fuzzy random sample, the following equality holds

$$\left(E(\widehat{\theta})\right)_\alpha = \theta_\alpha, \quad \forall \alpha \in [0,1], \tag{16}$$

assuming, obviously, that all required expected values exist.

In practice, it's often challenging or unrealistic to expect a fuzzy estimator to match exactly the true fuzzy parameter due to sampling variability. In practice, it is often difficult or unrealistic to expect the fuzzy estimator to exactly match the true fuzzy parameter due to sampling variability. Therefore, in contrast to classical unbiasedness, in the presence of fuzzy data, we relax the equality to set inclusion, which leads to the following definition of so-called **weak unbiasedness** (or **set-valued unbiasedness**).

**Definition 3.** *Let $\widetilde{\mathbb{X}} = (\widetilde{X}_1, \ldots, \widetilde{X}_n)$ denote a fuzzy random sample from the distribution with a fuzzy parameter $\theta$. We say that the estimator $\widehat{\theta} = \widehat{\theta}(\widetilde{\mathbb{X}})$ is **weakly unbiased** if*

$$\theta_\alpha \subseteq \left(E(\widehat{\theta})\right)_\alpha, \quad \forall \alpha \in [0,1], \tag{17}$$

*provided all expectations exist.*

Hence weak unbiasedness means that the expected value of the fuzzy estimator is not necessarily equal to the fuzzy-valued parameter, but instead, as its superset, always contains (or covers) it. This is not only more practical than (16), further on called the *strong unbiasedness*, but it falls into the realm of so-called conservative estimators particularly useful in scenarios where underestimation can have significant negative consequences. It is worth noting that the same strategy is sometimes used in statistics based on interval data (see [9]).

**Theorem 2.** *If random intervals $\widetilde{X}$ and $\widetilde{Y}$ have a finite expectation and both the fuzzy treatment effect $\Delta$ and its fuzzy estimator $\widehat{\Delta}$ exist, then $\widehat{\Delta}$ is a weakly unbiased estimator of $\Delta$, i.e. $\left(E(\widehat{\Delta})\right)_\alpha \supseteq \Delta_\alpha$ for all $\alpha \in [0,1]$.*

*Proof.* By (9), for any $\alpha \in [0,1]$, we have

$$\left(E(\widehat{\Delta})\right)_\alpha = \left[\mathbb{E}(\operatorname{mid} \widehat{\Delta}_\alpha) - \mathbb{E}(\operatorname{spr} \widehat{\Delta}_\alpha), \mathbb{E}(\operatorname{mid} \widehat{\Delta}_\alpha) + \mathbb{E}(\operatorname{spr} \widehat{\Delta}_\alpha)\right], \tag{18}$$

where

$$\begin{aligned}\mathbb{E}(\operatorname{mid}\widehat{\Delta}_\alpha) - \mathbb{E}(\operatorname{spr}\widehat{\Delta}_\alpha) &= \mathbb{E}(\operatorname{mid}(\overline{\widetilde{Y}} \ominus \overline{\widetilde{X}})_\alpha) - \mathbb{E}(\operatorname{spr}(\overline{\widetilde{Y}} \ominus \overline{\widetilde{X}})_\alpha),\\ \mathbb{E}(\operatorname{mid}\widehat{\Delta}_\alpha) + \mathbb{E}(\operatorname{spr}\widehat{\Delta}_\alpha) &= \mathbb{E}(\operatorname{mid}(\overline{\widetilde{Y}} \ominus \overline{\widetilde{X}})_\alpha) + \mathbb{E}(\operatorname{spr}(\overline{\widetilde{Y}} \ominus \overline{\widetilde{X}})_\alpha).\end{aligned} \tag{19}$$

If observations $\widetilde{X}_1, \ldots, \widetilde{X}_n$ are identically distributed then $\mathbb{E}(\operatorname{mid}(\widetilde{X_i})_\alpha) = \mathbb{E}(\operatorname{mid}\widetilde{X}_\alpha)$ and $\mathbb{E}(\operatorname{spr}(\widetilde{X_i})_\alpha) = \mathbb{E}(\operatorname{spr}\widetilde{X}_\alpha)$, for all $i = 1, \ldots, n$, and $\forall \alpha \in [0,1]$. Similar conditions hold for $\widetilde{Y}_1, \ldots, \widetilde{Y}_m$. Therefore, following Lemma 1, we obtain

$$\begin{aligned}\mathbb{E}\Big(\operatorname{mid}(\overline{\widetilde{Y}} \ominus \overline{\widetilde{X}})_\alpha\Big) &= \mathbb{E}\Big(\operatorname{mid}\overline{\widetilde{Y}}_\alpha - \operatorname{mid}\overline{\widetilde{X}}_\alpha\Big) = \mathbb{E}\Big(\operatorname{mid}\overline{\widetilde{Y}}_\alpha\Big) - \mathbb{E}\Big(\operatorname{mid}\overline{\widetilde{X}}_\alpha\Big)\\ &= \mathbb{E}\Big(\frac{1}{m}\sum_{j=1}^{m}\operatorname{mid}(\widetilde{Y}_j)_\alpha\Big) - \mathbb{E}\Big(\frac{1}{n}\sum_{1=1}^{n}\operatorname{mid}(\widetilde{X}_i)_\alpha\Big)\\ &= \frac{1}{m}\sum_{j=1}^{m}\mathbb{E}\big(\operatorname{mid}(\widetilde{Y}_j)_\alpha\big) - \frac{1}{n}\sum_{1=1}^{n}\mathbb{E}\big(\operatorname{mid}(\widetilde{X}_i)_\alpha\big)\\ &= \mathbb{E}\big(\operatorname{mid}\widetilde{Y}_\alpha\big) - \mathbb{E}\big(\operatorname{mid}\widetilde{X}_\alpha\big).\end{aligned} \tag{20}$$

However, expectation and absolute value do not generally commute, i.e. for arbitrary random variables $Y$ and $X$ if their expectations exist, we have $\mathbb{E}|Y - X| \geqslant |\mathbb{E}(Y) - \mathbb{E}(X)|$. Hence, turning beck to Lemma 1, we have

$$\begin{aligned}\mathbb{E}\Big(\operatorname{spr}(\overline{\widetilde{Y}} \ominus \overline{\widetilde{X}})_\alpha\Big) &= \mathbb{E}\Big|\operatorname{spr}\overline{\widetilde{Y}}_\alpha - \operatorname{spr}\overline{\widetilde{X}}_\alpha\Big| \geqslant \Big|\mathbb{E}\Big(\operatorname{spr}\overline{\widetilde{Y}}_\alpha\Big) - \mathbb{E}\Big(\operatorname{spr}\overline{\widetilde{X}}_\alpha\Big)\Big|\\ &= \Big|\mathbb{E}\Big(\frac{1}{m}\sum_{j=1}^{m}\operatorname{spr}(\widetilde{Y}_j)_\alpha\Big) - \mathbb{E}\Big(\frac{1}{n}\sum_{1=1}^{n}\operatorname{spr}(\widetilde{X}_i)_\alpha\Big)\Big|\\ &= \Big|\frac{1}{m}\sum_{j=1}^{m}\mathbb{E}\big(\operatorname{spr}(\widetilde{Y}_j)_\alpha\big) - \frac{1}{n}\sum_{1=1}^{n}\mathbb{E}\big(\operatorname{spr}(\widetilde{X}_i)_\alpha\big)\Big|\\ &= \Big|\mathbb{E}\big(\operatorname{spr}\widetilde{Y}_\alpha\big) - \mathbb{E}\big(\operatorname{spr}\widetilde{X}_\alpha\big)\Big|.\end{aligned} \tag{21}$$

Thus combining (18)–(21) we obtain

$$\begin{aligned}\big(E(\widehat{\Delta})\big)_\alpha \supseteq \Big[&\mathbb{E}\big(\operatorname{mid}\widetilde{Y}_\alpha\big) - \mathbb{E}\big(\operatorname{mid}\widetilde{X}_\alpha\big) - \Big|\mathbb{E}\big(\operatorname{spr}\widetilde{Y}_\alpha\big) - \mathbb{E}\big(\operatorname{spr}\widetilde{X}_\alpha\big)\Big|,\\ &\mathbb{E}\big(\operatorname{mid}\widetilde{Y}_\alpha\big) - \mathbb{E}\big(\operatorname{mid}\widetilde{X}_\alpha\big) + \Big|\mathbb{E}\big(\operatorname{spr}\widetilde{Y}_\alpha\big) - \mathbb{E}\big(\operatorname{spr}\widetilde{X}_\alpha\big)\Big|\Big].\end{aligned} \tag{22}$$

On other hand, since $\Delta_\alpha = \big(E(\widetilde{Y}) \ominus E(\widetilde{X})\big)_\alpha$, by Lemma 1 we have

$$\begin{aligned}\operatorname{mid}\Delta_\alpha &= \operatorname{mid}\big(E(\widetilde{Y})\big)_\alpha - \operatorname{mid}\big(E(\widetilde{X})\big)_\alpha,\\ \operatorname{spr}\Delta_\alpha &= \big|\operatorname{spr}\big(E(\widetilde{Y})\big)_\alpha - \operatorname{spr}\big(E(\widetilde{X})\big)_\alpha\big|.\end{aligned} \tag{23}$$

Since $\left(E(\widetilde{Y})\right)_\alpha = \left[\mathbb{E}(\text{mid}\,\widetilde{Y}_\alpha) - \mathbb{E}(\text{spr}\,\widetilde{Y}_\alpha), \mathbb{E}(\text{mid}\,\widetilde{Y}_\alpha) + \mathbb{E}(\text{spr}\,\widetilde{Y}_\alpha)\right]$, hence keeping in mind (8) we find that

$$\begin{aligned}
\text{mid}\left(E(\widetilde{Y})\right)_\alpha &= \frac{1}{2}\Big(\big(\mathbb{E}(\text{mid}\,\widetilde{Y}_\alpha) - \mathbb{E}(\text{spr}\,\widetilde{Y}_\alpha)\big) + \big(\mathbb{E}(\text{mid}\,\widetilde{Y}_\alpha) + \mathbb{E}(\text{spr}\,\widetilde{Y}_\alpha)\big)\Big) \\
&= \mathbb{E}(\text{mid}\,\widetilde{Y}_\alpha), \\
\text{spr}\left(E(\widetilde{Y})\right)_\alpha &= \frac{1}{2}\Big(\big(\mathbb{E}(\text{mid}\,\widetilde{Y}_\alpha) + \mathbb{E}(\text{spr}\,\widetilde{Y}_\alpha)\big) - \big(\mathbb{E}(\text{mid}\,\widetilde{Y}_\alpha) - \mathbb{E}(\text{spr}\,\widetilde{Y}_\alpha)\big)\Big) \\
&= \mathbb{E}(\text{spr}\,\widetilde{Y}_\alpha).
\end{aligned}$$

Similarly, $\text{mid}\,\mathbb{E}(\widetilde{X}_\alpha) = \mathbb{E}(\text{mid}\,\widetilde{X}_\alpha)$ and $\text{spr}\,\mathbb{E}(\widetilde{X}_\alpha) = \mathbb{E}(\text{spr}\,\widetilde{X}_\alpha)$, so we can rewrite (23) as follows

$$\begin{aligned}
\text{mid}\,\Delta_\alpha &= \mathbb{E}(\text{mid}\,\widetilde{Y}_\alpha) - \mathbb{E}(\text{mid}\,\widetilde{X}_\alpha), \\
\text{spr}\,\Delta_\alpha &= \left|\mathbb{E}(\text{spr}\,\widetilde{Y}_\alpha) - \mathbb{E}(\text{spr}\,\widetilde{X}_\alpha)\right|.
\end{aligned} \tag{24}$$

Therefore, substituting (24) into (22) we obtain

$$\left(E(\widehat{\Delta})\right)_\alpha \supseteq \left[\text{mid}\,\Delta_\alpha - \text{spr}\,\Delta_\alpha, \text{mid}\,\Delta_\alpha + \text{spr}\,\Delta_\alpha\right] = \Delta_\alpha,$$

which is the desired conclusion. □

The reader has certainly noticed that the considerations presented so far referred to situations in which we assumed that a fuzzy treatment effect existed. However, no one can guarantee that this will always be the case (incidentally, it is worth noting that we do not have this problem in the case of interval data, since there the gH-difference always exists, see [12]). Fortunately, even if for a given pair of fuzzy numbers $\widetilde{A}$ and $\widetilde{B}$ there was no gH-difference (i.e. $\widetilde{A} \ominus \widetilde{B}$ not a fuzzy number), we can find an approximate solution. In fact, if the treatment effect $\Delta$ defined by (14) does not exist, then using the nested property of the $\alpha$-cuts we can approximate $\Delta$ by a fuzzy number $\Delta_{approx}$ defined as follows

$$\left(\Delta_{approx}\right)_\alpha := cl\left(\bigcup_{\beta \geqslant \alpha} \left(E(\widetilde{Y})\right)_\beta \ominus \left(E(\widetilde{X})\right)_\beta\right), \tag{25}$$

where $\alpha \in [0, 1]$ (see [12]). Similarly, if the treatment effect estimator $\widehat{\Delta}$ obtained from the formula (15) is not a proper fuzzy number, we may approximate it by a fuzzy number with the following $\alpha$-cuts

$$\left(\widehat{\Delta}_{approx}\right)_\alpha := cl\left(\bigcup_{\beta \geqslant \alpha} \left(\overline{\widetilde{Y}}\right)_\beta \ominus \left(\overline{\widetilde{X}}\right)_\beta\right). \tag{26}$$

## 7 Conclusions and Further Research

The treatment effect is a fundamental statistical concept widely used across various fields of research. In this paper, we have proposed a definition that extends this concept to accommodate imprecise data modeled by fuzzy numbers. This required addressing several challenges, but the resulting approach appears quite interesting. Its potential applications are also evident, which is crucial, as estimating the treatment effect alone is not sufficient. The next step in our research will focus on developing statistical tests to assess the size of the treatment effect.

## References


1. Blanco-Fernández, A., et al.: A distance-based statistical analysis of fuzzy number-valued data. Int. J. Approx. Reason. **55**(7), 1487–1501 (2014)
2. González-Rodríguez, G., Colubi, A., Gil, M.-A.: Bootstrap techniques and fuzzy random variables: synergy in hypothesis testing with fuzzy data. Fuzzy Sets Syst. **157**(19), 2608–2613 (2006)
3. Grzegorzewski, P.: Permutation k-sample goodness-of-fit test for fuzzy data. In: 2020 IEEE International Conference on Fuzzy Systems (FUZZ-IEEE), pp. 1–8 (2020). https://doi.org/10.1109/FUZZ48607.2020.9177765
4. Grzegorzewski, P.: Two-sample test for comparing ambiguity in fuzzy data. In: 2022 IEEE International Conference on Fuzzy Systems (FUZZ-IEEE), pp. 1–8 (2022). https://doi.org/10.1109/FUZZ-IEEE55066.2022.9882757
5. Grzegorzewski, P.: Paired sample test for fuzzy data. In: García-Escudero, L.A., et al.. (eds.) Building Bridges between Soft and Statistical Methodologies for Data Science, pp. 200–207. Springer, Heidelberg (2023). https://doi.org/10.1007/978-3-031-15509-3_27
6. Grzegorzewski, P., Gadomska, O.: Nearest neighbor tests for fuzzy data. In: 2021 IEEE International Conference on Fuzzy Systems (FUZZ-IEEE), pp. 1–6 (2021). https://doi.org/10.1109/FUZZ45933.2021.9494432
7. Grzegorzewski, P., Zacharczuk, M.: A new two-sample location test for fuzzy data. In: Massanet, S., Montes, S., Ruiz-Aguilera, D., González-Hidalgo, M. (eds.) Fuzzy Logic and Technology, and Aggregation Operators (EUSFLAT 2023, AGOP 2023). LNCS, vol. 14069, pp. 737–748. Springer, Heidelberg (2023). https://doi.org/10.1007/978-3-031-39965-7_61
8. Hukuhara, M.: Integration des applications measurables dont la valeur est un compact convexe. Funkcialaj Ekvacioj **10**, 205–223 (1967)
9. Li, B., Xiang, G., Kreinovich, V., Moscopoulos, P.: From Unbiased Numerical Estimates to Unbiased Interval Estimates. University of Texas at El Paso, Departmental Technical Reports (CS), 715 (2012)
10. Montenegro, M., Colubi, A., Casals, M., Gil, M.-A.: Asymptotic and bootstrap techniques for testing the expected value of a fuzzy random variable. Metrika **59**(1), 31–49 (2004)
11. Puri, M.-L., Ralescu, D.-A.: Fuzzy random variables. J. Math. Anal. Appl. **114**(2), 409–422 (1986)
12. Stefanini, L.: A generalization of Hukuhara difference and division for interval and fuzzy arithmetic. Fuzzy Sets Syst. **161**, 1564–1584 (2010)
13. Trutschnig, W., González-Rodríguez, G., Colubi, A., Gil, M.-A.: A new family of metrics for compact, convex (fuzzy) sets based on a generalized concept of mid and spread. Inf. Sci. **179**(23), 3964–3972 (2009)

# Resampling Approaches for Multivariate Random Interval Numbers

Maciej Romaniuk[1,2](✉)

[1] Systems Research Institute Polish Academy of Sciences, Newelska 6, 01-447 Warszawa, Poland
mroman@ibspan.waw.pl
[2] WIT Academy, Newelska 6, 01-447 Warszawa, Poland

**Abstract.** The classical bootstrap and similar methods are widely used to solve statistical problems. This paper considers four resampling methods specially tailored for the data consisting of many interval-valued variables. Two of these approaches are generalizations of the classical and smoothed bootstrap for such a particular case. The following two are non-parametric approaches that take into account possible dependencies within intervals for each variable and between the variables themselves. These algorithms are compared using numerical simulations, various error measures, and statistical tests to check their overall quality. It seems that particularly one of the considered resampling methods gives valuable bootstrapped samples.

**Keywords:** Interval-valued numbers · Bootstrap · Imprecise random values · Numerical simulations

## 1 Introduction

Starting from the classical bootstrap [5], many resampling methods were proposed for both real-valued (i.e., "crisp") data and imprecise (e.g., modeled by intervals or fuzzy numbers) values [9,10,14,16,19] together with the dedicated software packages, e.g., in R language [17,18]. They are widely used in statistical inference, e.g., statistical tests, estimation procedures, etc. [7,8].

In this paper, we proposed four resampling methods aimed at interval-valued random numbers (or *random intervals*, abbreviated further by RIs). Two of them are direct generalizations of the Efron's [5] and smoothed [20] bootstraps for the case of RIs. The next two approaches are non-parametric resampling methods explicitly tailored for RIs to generate bootstrap samples that are "similar but not completely the same" as the initial dataset. Such an "additional variability" (compared with the classical approach) helps solve many statistical problems [1]. Contrary to our previous paper [14], these new methods take into account the possible dependencies within the interval for each variable (e.g., caused by the existing relations between the ends of the interval or its mid-point) and between the variables themselves (e.g., related to the regression model generating these variables). Therefore, the proposed approaches are better suited for complex, multi-dimensional datasets consisting of RIs. Moreover, they are


M. Baczyński et al. (Eds.): EUSFLAT 2025, LNCS 15884, pp. 223–234, 2025.
https://doi.org/10.1007/978-3-031-97228-7_19

also non-parametric methods, so no additional assumptions about the data are necessary.

Extensive numerical analysis was performed for synthetic and real-life datasets with some dependencies among the variables to check the quality of these resampling methods. Various error measures and goodness-of-fit tests were proposed and applied during these simulations to highlight differences among the resampling algorithms. And it seems that one of them – *Unif1* – generates the best outputs if the criterion "similar but not completely the same" together with the applied error measures are taken into account.

This paper is organized as follows. In Sect. 2, some preliminaries concerning random intervals and resampling methods are discussed. In Sect. 3, new resampling algorithms for interval-valued numbers are introduced. Various error measures and statistical benchmarks are considered in Sect to compare their quality with the more classical approaches. 4. They are then used in numerical simulations for both the synthetic and real-life datasets in Sect. 5. Some concluding remarks are provided in Sect. 6.

## 2 Preliminaries

In this section, we recall some basic facts concerning the random intervals and resampling methods known in the literature.

**Definition 1.** *Let $X^L$ and $X^R$ be two random real-valued variables defined on the same sample space $\Omega$ such that $X^L(\omega) \leq X^R(\omega)$ for all $\omega \in \Omega$. Then $\boldsymbol{X} = \left[X^L, X^R\right]$ is called a random interval (RI for short) or random interval number. A random sample $\mathbb{X} = (\boldsymbol{X}_1, \ldots, \boldsymbol{X}_n)$ consists of $n$* iid *RIs.*

Such an RI can be characterized in two ways – using its left- and right end (i.e., $\boldsymbol{X} = \left[X^L, X^R\right]$ as in Definition 1) or with its spread (radius) $\operatorname{spr} \boldsymbol{X} = \left(X^R - X^L\right)/2$ and the mid-point (center of the interval) $\operatorname{mid} \boldsymbol{X} = \left(X^L + X^R\right)/2$.

Let $\mathbb{x} = (x_1, \ldots, x_n)$ be a realization of a real-valued random sample of size $n$ (so-called *the initial sample*). The Efron's bootstrap [5] is the most classical resampling method. In this case, the bootstrapped (secondary) sample $\mathbb{x}^* = (x_1^*, \ldots, x_m^*)$ is generated by drawing the values from $\mathbb{x}$ with repetitions and the constant probabilities $\frac{1}{n}$, where usually $m = n$. Then, the whole procedure can be repeated $B$ times, so we get the $i$-th bootstrapped sample $\mathbb{x}^{*,i} = \left(x_1^{*,i}, \ldots, x_m^{*,i}\right)$ for $i = 1, \ldots, B$.

Because of the known problems with the classical approach (e.g., repetitions of the same values, which may be undesirable in some settings), other resampling algorithms were proposed, e.g., the smoothed bootstrap [20]. In this method, instead of putting the samples drawn from $\mathbb{x}$ into $\mathbb{x}^*$ directly, some additional random noise is added to them. This noise is related to the specified kernel density (e.g., of the normal distribution).

## 3 Resampling Algorithms

Now, we present the four resampling algorithms for RIs. To simplify our notation, we focus on two variables $(\boldsymbol{X}, \boldsymbol{Y})$ only. However, our considerations can be generalized for more variables.

Then, let $(\mathbb{x}, \mathbb{y}) = ((\boldsymbol{x}_1, \boldsymbol{y}_1), \ldots, (\boldsymbol{x}_n, \boldsymbol{y}_n))$ be an initial sample consisting of $n$ pairs. Each of these pairs is the realization of RIs $(\boldsymbol{X}, \boldsymbol{Y})$ in the form $(\boldsymbol{x}_i, \boldsymbol{y}_i) = \left(\left(x_i^L, x_i^R\right), \left(y_i^L, y_i^R\right)\right)$, where $i = 1, \ldots, n$.

The first method (denoted by *Boot* further on, see Algorithm 1) is a direct generalization of the classical bootstrap [5] similar in some sense to the *pairwise bootstrap* [6]. Instead of the single value, the whole pair $(\boldsymbol{x}, \boldsymbol{y})$ is drawn from the initial sample with the constant probabilities $\frac{1}{n}$. Then, this pair is added to the output. This procedure is repeated $m$ times to get the bootstrapped sample $(\mathbb{x}^*, \mathbb{y}^*) = ((\boldsymbol{x}_1^*, \boldsymbol{y}_1^*), \ldots, (\boldsymbol{x}_m^*, \boldsymbol{y}_m^*))$, where $(\boldsymbol{x}_i^*, \boldsymbol{y}_i^*) = \left(\left(x_i^{*,L}, x_i^{*,R}\right), \left(y_i^{*,L}, y_i^{*,R}\right)\right)$. In the following, we focus on the case $m = n$ mimicking (in some way) the classical Efron's bootstrap to get the bootstrapped sample of the same size as its initial counterpart. However, values of $m$ other than $n$ can also be applied.

**Algorithm 1.** Method 1 – Classical bootstrap (*Boot*)

**Require:** The initial sample $(\mathbb{x}, \mathbb{y})$
**Ensure:** The bootstrapped sample $(\mathbb{x}^*, \mathbb{y}^*)$
1: **for** $i = 1, \ldots, m$ **do**
2: Randomly draw a pair $(\boldsymbol{x}, \boldsymbol{y})$ from $(\mathbb{x}, \mathbb{y})$ with the constant probabilities $1/n$
3: Add $(\boldsymbol{x}, \boldsymbol{y})$ to $(\mathbb{x}^*, \mathbb{y}^*)$

The second method (*Kern* for short, see Algorithm 2) is closely related to the *smoothed bootstrap* [20]. Firstly, the kernel density estimator is calculated using $(\mathbb{x}, \mathbb{y})$. Please note that the initial sample is a four-dimensional dataset. Then, the foursome $\left(x^{*,L}, x^{*,R}, y^{*,L}, y^{*,R}\right)$ is drawn from the obtained kernel and added to $(\mathbb{x}^*, \mathbb{y}^*)$. Of course, the outputs should be RIs, so the apparent conditions $x^{*,L} \leq x^{*,R}$ and $y^{*,L} \leq y^{*,R}$ have to be fulfilled. Once again, the whole procedure is repeated $m$ times to produce the bootstrapped sample.

The following two methods merge some general ideas from the pairwise and smoothed bootstraps and can be called *uniform perturbation resampling* approaches.

In the case of the first one (denoted by *Unif1* further on, see Algorithm 3), two new sets containing the spreads for both variables (i.e., $\operatorname{spr} \mathbb{x} = (\operatorname{spr} \boldsymbol{x}_1, \ldots, \operatorname{spr} \boldsymbol{x}_n)$ for $\boldsymbol{X}$, and $\operatorname{spr} \mathbb{y} = (\operatorname{spr} \boldsymbol{y}_1, \ldots, \operatorname{spr} \boldsymbol{y}_n)$ for $\boldsymbol{Y}$) are created. Next, the standard deviations $s(\operatorname{spr} \mathbb{x}), s(\operatorname{spr} \mathbb{y})$ for these two sets are calculated. Once again, a pair $(\boldsymbol{x}, \boldsymbol{y}) = \left(\left(x^L, x^R\right), \left(y^L, y^R\right)\right)$ is randomly drawn from the initial sample. Contrary to the *Boot* method, this pair is then modified. Four random variables (RV for short) are drawn from two different uniform distributions. The intervals of these probability distributions $(-ws(\operatorname{spr} \mathbb{x}), ws(\operatorname{spr} \mathbb{x}))$

---

**Algorithm 2.** Method 2 – Multivariate kernel resampling (*Kern*)

---

**Require:** The initial sample $(\mathrm{x}, \mathrm{y})$
**Ensure:** The bootstrapped sample $(\mathrm{x}^*, \mathrm{y}^*)$
1: Estimate the kernel $\mathcal{K}(\mathrm{x}, \mathrm{y})$
2: **for** $i = 1, \ldots, m$ **do**
3:    **repeat**
4:       Randomly draw a foursome $\left(x^{*,L}, x^{*,R}, y^{*,L}, y^{*,R}\right) \sim \mathcal{K}(\mathrm{x}, \mathrm{y})$
5:    **until** $x^{*,L} \leq x^{*,R}$ and $y^{*,L} \leq y^{*,R}$
6:    Add $(\boldsymbol{x}^*, \boldsymbol{y}^*) = \left(\left(x^{*,L}, x^{*,R}\right), \left(y^{*,L}, y^{*,R}\right)\right)$ to $(\mathrm{x}^*, \mathrm{y}^*)$

---

and $(-ws\,(\mathrm{spr}\,\mathrm{y}), ws\,(\mathrm{spr}\,\mathrm{y}))$ are given by the estimated standard deviations of the spreads for $\boldsymbol{X}$ and $\boldsymbol{Y}$, respectively, and user-defined parameter $w$. After drawing the first two *iid* RVs $Z^L, Z^R \sim U\left(-ws\,(\mathrm{spr}\,\mathrm{x}), ws\,(\mathrm{spr}\,\mathrm{x})\right)$, they are added to the left (i.e., $x^L$) and right end (i.e., $x^R$) of the previously selected interval $\boldsymbol{x}$. Hence, the new resampled value $\boldsymbol{x}^* = \left(x^{*,L}, x^{*,R}\right) = \left(x^L + Z^L, x^R + Z^R\right)$ is found. In the same manner, we generate $V^L, V^R \sim U\left(-ws\,(\mathrm{spr}\,\mathrm{y}), ws\,(\mathrm{spr}\,\mathrm{y})\right)$ and then obtain the second element of the output, i.e., $\boldsymbol{y}^* = \left(y^{*,L}, y^{*,R}\right) = \left(y^L + V^L, y^R + V^R\right)$.

Once again, the conditions $x^{*,L} \leq x^{*,R}$ and $y^{*,L} \leq y^{*,R}$ have to be fulfilled. Next, the obtained output $(\boldsymbol{x}^*, \boldsymbol{y}^*)$ is added to the bootstrapped sample.

---

**Algorithm 3.** Method 3 – Uniform perturbation resampling (*Unif1*)

---

**Require:** The initial sample $(\mathrm{x}, \mathrm{y})$
**Ensure:** The bootstrapped sample $(\mathrm{x}^*, \mathrm{y}^*)$
1: Calculate the spreads $\mathrm{spr}\,\mathrm{x} = (\mathrm{spr}\,\boldsymbol{x}_1, \ldots, \mathrm{spr}\,\boldsymbol{x}_n,), \mathrm{spr}\,\mathrm{y} = (\mathrm{spr}\,\boldsymbol{y}_1, \ldots, \mathrm{spr}\,\boldsymbol{y}_n)$
2: Calculate the standard deviations $s\,(\mathrm{spr}\,\mathrm{x}), s\,(\mathrm{spr}\,\mathrm{y})$
3: **for** $i = 1, \ldots, m$ **do**
4:    **repeat**
5:       Randomly draw a pair $(\boldsymbol{x}, \boldsymbol{y}) = \left(\left(x^L, x^R\right), \left(y^L, y^R\right)\right)$ from $(\mathrm{x}, \mathrm{y})$ with the constant probabilities $1/n$
6:       Generate $Z^L, Z^R \sim U\left(-ws\,(\mathrm{spr}\,\mathrm{x}), ws\,(\mathrm{spr}\,\mathrm{x})\right)$
7:       $x^{*,L} \leftarrow x^L + Z^L, x^{*,R} \leftarrow x^R + Z^R$
8:       Generate $V^L, V^R \sim U\left(-ws\,(\mathrm{spr}\,\mathrm{y}), ws\,(\mathrm{spr}\,\mathrm{y})\right)$
9:       $y^{*,L} \leftarrow y^L + V^L, y^{*,R} \leftarrow y^R + V^R$
10:   **until** $x^{*,L} \leq x^{*,R}$ and $y^{*,L} \leq y^{*,R}$
11:   Add $(\boldsymbol{x}^*, \boldsymbol{y}^*) = \left(\left(x^{*,L}, x^{*,R}\right), \left(y^{*,L}, y^{*,R}\right)\right)$ to $(\mathrm{x}^*, \mathrm{y}^*)$

---

There are two important differences between the *Unif1* approach and our last method (*Unif2* for short, see Algorithm 4). Firstly, the standard deviations are estimated for all four ends of $\boldsymbol{X}$ and $\boldsymbol{Y}$. Hence, we calculate the standard deviation $s\left(\mathrm{x}^L\right)$ based on $x_1^L, \ldots, x_n^L$, its counterpart $s\left(\mathrm{x}^R\right)$ for $x_1^R, \ldots, x_n^R$ and so on. Secondly, four different uniform distributions are used instead of only two. We independently generate $Z^L \sim U\left(-ws\left(\mathrm{x}^L\right), ws\left(\mathrm{x}^L\right)\right)$

and $Z^R \sim U\left(-ws\left(\mathbb{x}^R\right), ws\left(\mathbb{x}^R\right)\right)$. Next, the new bootstrapped interval value $\boldsymbol{x}^*$ is a summation result of the randomly drawn first element of the pair $(\boldsymbol{x}, \boldsymbol{y})$ and these generated values (i.e., $x^{*,L} = x^L + Z^L, x^{*,R} = x^R + Z^R$). In the same manner, $V^L \sim U\left(-ws\left(\mathbb{y}^L\right), ws\left(\mathbb{y}^L\right)\right), V^R \sim U\left(-ws\left(\mathbb{y}^R\right), ws\left(\mathbb{y}^R\right)\right)$ lead to the second interval value $\boldsymbol{y}^*$, where $y^{*,L} = y^L + V^L, y^{*,R} = y^R + V^R$. Once again, the conditions $x^{*,L} \leq x^{*,R}$ and $y^{*,L} \leq y^{*,R}$ have to be checked. Then, the new pair $(\boldsymbol{x}^*, \boldsymbol{y}^*)$ is added to the bootstrapped sample.

**Algorithm 4.** Method 4 – Uniform perturbation resampling (*Unif2*)

**Require:** The initial sample $(\mathbb{x}, \mathbb{y})$
**Ensure:** The bootstrapped sample $(\mathbb{x}^*, \mathbb{y}^*)$

```
Calculate the standard deviations s(x^L), s(x^R), s(y^L), s(y^R)
for i = 1, ..., m do
    repeat
        Randomly draw a pair (x, y) = ((x^L, x^R), (y^L, y^R)) from (x, y) with the
        constant probabilities 1/n
        Generate Z^L ~ U(-ws(x^L), ws(x^L)), Z^R ~ U(-ws(x^R), ws(x^R))
        x^{*,L} <- x^L + Z^L, x^{*,R} <- x^R + Z^R
        Generate V^L ~ U(-ws(y^L), ws(y^L)), V^R ~ U(-ws(y^R), ws(y^R))
        y^{*,L} <- y^L + V^L, y^{*,R} <- y^R + V^R
    until x^{*,L} <= x^{*,R} and y^{*,L} <= y^{*,R}
    Add (x^*, y^*) = ((x^{*,L}, x^{*,R}), (y^{*,L}, y^{*,R})) to (x^*, y^*)
```

Drawing the whole pair $(\boldsymbol{x}, \boldsymbol{y})$ in the *Unif1* and *Unif2* methods (as in the pairwise bootstrap) preserves the possible dependencies between variables. Perturbing the ends of the respective intervals with the additional random values from the uniform (hence non-informative) distributions (based on the variability characteristic of the dataset) leads to "different than in the initial sample but still similar" outputs. We still have the non-parametric setting, contrary to the multivariate kernel density (e.g., based on the Gaussian distribution, as in the *Kern* approach).

## 4 Error Measures

The quality of the considered resampling methods was checked using numerical simulations and various benchmarks. The first error measure $\text{MAE}^{\bar{X}}_{supp}$ is related to the mean absolute error (MAE) between the means for the respective ends of intervals of the initial $(\mathbb{x}, \mathbb{y})$ and bootstrapped $(\mathbb{x}^*, \mathbb{y}^*)$ samples, namely

$$\text{MAE}^{\bar{X}}_{supp} = \frac{1}{4}\left(\left|\bar{\mathbb{x}}^L - \bar{\mathbb{x}}^{*,L}\right| + \left|\bar{\mathbb{x}}^R - \bar{\mathbb{x}}^{*,R}\right| + \left|\bar{\mathbb{y}}^L - \bar{\mathbb{y}}^{*,L}\right| + \left|\bar{\mathbb{y}}^R - \bar{\mathbb{y}}^{*,R}\right|\right), \quad (1)$$

where $\bar{\mathbb{x}}^L = \frac{1}{n}\sum_{i=1}^n x_i^L, \bar{\mathbb{x}}^R = \frac{1}{n}\sum_{i=1}^n x_i^R, \ldots$, and we assume that both samples have the same size (i.e., $n = m$). To obtain the final value of $\text{MAE}^{\bar{X}}_{supp}$, the error (1) is then averaged for all the repetitions of the respective numerical experiment. Similar averaging is also applied for other error measures and p-values mentioned afterward.

In the same manner, MAE for the distance between the means of the mid-points can be calculated as

$$\mathrm{MAE}^{\bar{X}}_{mid} = \frac{1}{2}\left(\left|\overline{\mathrm{mid}\,\mathbb{x}} - \overline{\mathrm{mid}\,\mathbb{x}^*}\right| + \left|\overline{\mathrm{mid}\,\mathbb{y}} - \overline{\mathrm{mid}\,\mathbb{y}^*}\right|\right), \tag{2}$$

where $\overline{\mathrm{mid}\,\mathbb{x}} = \frac{1}{n}\sum_{i=1}^{n}\frac{1}{2}\left(x_i^L + x_i^R\right), \overline{\mathrm{mid}\,\mathbb{x}^*} = \frac{1}{n}\sum_{i=1}^{n}\frac{1}{2}\left(x_i^{*,L} + x_i^{*,R}\right)$ and so on. Instead of the means, the standard deviations can also be used. Then, we get $\mathrm{MAE}^S_{supp}$ in the case of the distance between the standard deviations for the ends of the intervals, and $\mathrm{MAE}^S_{mid}$ for the mid-points, respectively. These errors indicate the differences in the sample statistics between $(\mathbb{x}, \mathbb{y})$ and $(\mathbb{x}^*, \mathbb{y}^*)$ for "the most interesting points", like the end of the intervals and mid-points of RIs.

We are also interested in the similarities between the probability distributions. Therefore, the Kolmogorov-Smirnov (KS for short) two-sample goodness-of-fit tests are applied. Once again, we focus on the ends of the intervals and mid-points. In the first case, we get

$$p_{supp} = \frac{1}{4}\left(p\left(\mathbb{x}^L, \mathbb{x}^{*,L}\right) + p\left(\mathbb{x}^R, \mathbb{x}^{*,R}\right) + p\left(\mathbb{y}^L, \mathbb{y}^{*,L}\right) + p\left(\mathbb{y}^R, \mathbb{y}^{*,R}\right)\right), \tag{3}$$

where $p(w, v)$ denotes the p-value of the KS test between two samples $w$ and $v$. The output p-value in (3) is aggregated by averaging it for all ends of the intervals. Similarly, $p_{mid}$ is the averaged p-value for the KS tests based on the mid-points. Other aggregation approach for the KS test (i.e., the minimum for p-values calculated for the mid-points and spreads) was proposed in [12] in the case of the ontic RIs. Hence, such a p-value $p_{ont}$ is also calculated. We apply the averaging in (3) due to the simplicity of further calculations and some previous findings [13]. However, because of the dependency between the aggregated p-values, some more complex approaches [3,21] can also be used.

All of the p-values mentioned above should be as big as possible to show the accordance between the distributions of the initial and bootstrapped samples.

Because some kind of statistical dependency is assumed for $\boldsymbol{X}$ and $\boldsymbol{Y}$ in our numerical simulations, the resampling methods should also be compared in this regard. Therefore, we calculate the distances between the correlation coefficients for all ends of the intervals with

$$\begin{aligned}\mathrm{MAE}^r_{supp} = \frac{1}{8}\Big(&\left|\bar{r}\left(\mathbb{x}^L, \mathbb{x}^R\right) - \bar{r}\left(\mathbb{x}^{*,L}, \mathbb{x}^{*,R}\right)\right| + \left|\bar{r}\left(\mathbb{x}^L, \mathbb{y}^L\right) - \bar{r}\left(\mathbb{x}^{*,L}, \mathbb{y}^{*,L}\right)\right| + \\ &\left|\bar{r}\left(\mathbb{x}^L, \mathbb{y}^R\right) - \bar{r}\left(\mathbb{x}^{*,L}, \mathbb{y}^{*,R}\right)\right| + \left|\bar{r}\left(\mathbb{x}^R, \mathbb{y}^R\right) - \bar{r}\left(\mathbb{x}^{*,R}, \mathbb{y}^{*,R}\right)\right| + \\ &\left|\bar{r}\left(\mathbb{x}^R, \mathbb{y}^L\right) - \bar{r}\left(\mathbb{x}^{*,R}, \mathbb{y}^{*,L}\right)\right| + \left|\bar{r}\left(\mathbb{y}^L, \mathbb{y}^R\right) - \bar{r}\left(\mathbb{y}^{*,L}, \mathbb{y}^{*,R}\right)\right|\Big),\end{aligned} \tag{4}$$

where $\bar{r}\left(\mathbb{x}^L, \mathbb{x}^R\right) = \frac{1}{n}\sum_{i=1}^{n} r\left(x_i^L, x_i^R\right), \ldots,$ and $r(w, v)$ denotes the Pearson's correlation coefficient between two samples $w$ and $v$. A similar error for the mid-points $\mathrm{MAE}^r_{mid}$ is also obtained. We know the existing methods for calculating the correlations for RIs [15], but usually, they are numerically demanding or give only approximate results. Therefore, in some way mimicking the approach used in [12], the error $\mathrm{MAE}^r_{ont}$ based on the minimum for the errors of correlations for the spreads and mid-points is also found. All these "correlation" errors should be as low as possible for "the best" resampling approach.

## 5 Numerical Comparisons of the Algorithms

We started our numerical analysis using the synthetic samples consisting of two interval-valued variables $\boldsymbol{X}$ and $\boldsymbol{Y}$. To generate them, the approach known in the literature for fuzzy numbers [10,11,13,17] was adopted. Contrary to [14], this method does not require checking the additional conditions.

To construct the RI $\boldsymbol{X} = \left(x^L, x^R\right)$, we need three independent RVs, i.e.,

$$x^L = O - X^L, x^R = O + X^R, \tag{5}$$

where $O$ corresponds to the "origin" of $\boldsymbol{X}$ (so called *original* in the epistemic view for random fuzzy numbers [4]), and $X^L, X^R$ denote RVs that "blur" and "stretch" this value to give the whole interval. Because the second RI $\boldsymbol{Y} = \left(y^L, y^R\right)$ should be dependent (in some way and to some extent) on $\boldsymbol{X}$, then we apply the formula

$$y^L = O - Y^L + \delta + \varepsilon, y^R = O + Y^R + \delta + \varepsilon, \tag{6}$$

where $Y^L, Y^R$ are two new independent RVs, $\delta$ is the specified constant shift, and $\varepsilon$ is some random noise. In the following, two cases are considered – when $\varepsilon = 0$ is set ("stronger dependency" between $\boldsymbol{X}$ and $\boldsymbol{Y}$), and $\varepsilon \sim N(0, \sigma)$ ("weaker dependency"), where $N(\mu, \sigma)$ denotes the normal distribution with the mean $\mu$ and standard deviation $\sigma$.

The considered types of RIs are enumerated in Table 1, where $U(a, b)$ denotes the uniform distribution on the interval $[a, b]$, $\mathrm{Exp}(\lambda)$ – the exponential distribution with the rate intensity $\lambda$, $\Gamma(a, b)$ – the gamma distribution with the shape $a$ and scale $b$ parameters, $\mathcal{W}(a, b)$ – the Weibull distribution with the shape $a$ and scale $b$ parameters, and $\beta(a, b)$ – the beta distribution with the shape parameters $a, b$. These types are organized in pairs, where the first model is without the additional random error $\varepsilon$ and the second one (indicated with $P$ in its lower index) – with this error incorporated.

Small ($n = m = 10$) and relatively moderate ($n = m = 100$) sample sizes were generated for each modeled type. To diminish the random effects, in each experiment, 100 samples were generated, and then simulations were repeated $l = 1000$ times. The parameter $w$ in *Unif1* and *Unif2* was set to 0.1. The analysis was done with R language, and some functions from the package `kernelboot` [22] were used in the *Kern* algorithm.

To shorten the length of the paper, only some examples of tables are provided below. Other results are available upon reasonable request. In the tables, the best results (like the lowest errors or the biggest p-values) are written in bold text to facilitate reading.

**Table 1.** Types of the generated synthetic samples

| Type | $O$ | $X^L, X^R$ | $Y^L, Y^R$ | $\delta$ | $\varepsilon$ |
|---|---|---|---|---|---|
| $N/U$ | $N(0,1)$ | $U(0,0.6)$ | $U(0,0.6)$ | 4 | – |
| $N/U_P$ | $N(0,1)$ | $U(0,0.6)$ | $U(0,0.6)$ | 4 | $N(0,2)$ |
| $\Gamma/E$ | $\Gamma(2,2)$ | Exp(1/2) | Exp(1/3) | 3 | – |
| $\Gamma/E_P$ | $\Gamma(2,2)$ | Exp(1/2) | Exp(1/3) | 3 | $N(0,3)$ |
| $\mathcal{W}/\beta$ | $\mathcal{W}(1.5,1)$ | $\beta(5,1)$ | $\beta(2,2)$ | 3 | – |
| $\mathcal{W}/\beta_P$ | $\mathcal{W}(1.5,1)$ | $\beta(5,1)$ | $\beta(2,2)$ | 3 | $N(0,3)$ |

In general, *Boot* and *Unif1* give the lowest errors related to the MAE for the means and standard deviations (enumerated in the first four rows of Tables 2 and 3). The differences between these two methods are minimal, almost negligible in many cases. And *Unif2* is the third best, but with the slightly worse error values. Surprisingly, *Kern* gives the noticeable highest errors, far worse than other methods.

The estimated p-values (see the middle rows in Tables 2 and 3) favor the *Boot* method, and *Unif1* is slightly worse in this case. Once again, *Unif2* is the third best, with noticeably lower p-values than *Unif2*. And *Kern* gives the significantly smallest p-values. However, all of them are still far above the classical significance level of 0.05, so the null hypotheses in the KS tests can not be rejected.

For the errors related to the correlation coefficients, the results seem to be more ambiguous (compare the last rows in Tables 2 and 3). Depending on the situation and sample size, *Kern*, *Unif1* of *Boot* are the best methods. However, the differences between these algorithms are usually minimal. Only *Unif2* seems to be always "the worst".

**Table 2.** Error measures for the type $N/U$

| Method | $n=m=10$ | | | | $n=m=100$ | | | |
|---|---|---|---|---|---|---|---|---|
| | Boot | Kern | Unif1 | Unif2 | Boot | Kern | Unif1 | Unif2 |
| $\text{MAE}^{\bar{X}}_{supp}$ | 0.2426 | 0.3019 | **0.2411** | 0.2413 | **0.0801** | 0.0909 | 0.0803 | 0.0807 |
| $\text{MAE}^{\bar{X}}_{mid}$ | 0.2409 | 0.2997 | **0.2393** | **0.2393** | **0.0796** | 0.0902 | 0.0798 | 0.0800 |
| $\text{MAE}^{S}_{supp}$ | **0.1696** | 0.2491 | 0.1697 | 0.1701 | **0.0561** | 0.1314 | 0.0562 | 0.0562 |
| $\text{MAE}^{S}_{mid}$ | **0.1683** | 0.2473 | 0.1685 | 0.1688 | **0.0557** | 0.1304 | 0.0558 | 0.0558 |
| $p_{supp}$ | **0.8662** | 0.7277 | 0.8386 | 0.8284 | **0.8386** | 0.5981 | 0.7999 | 0.7733 |
| $p_{mid}$ | **0.8663** | 0.7259 | 0.8393 | 0.8320 | **0.8386** | 0.5942 | 0.8024 | 0.7837 |
| $p_{ont}$ | **0.7920** | 0.5989 | 0.7451 | 0.6994 | **0.7388** | 0.4583 | 0.6786 | 0.6062 |
| $\text{MAE}^{r}_{supp}$ | 0.0141 | **0.0138** | 0.0141 | 0.0157 | **0.0033** | 0.0034 | **0.0033** | 0.0042 |
| $\text{MAE}^{r}_{mid}$ | 0.0049 | **0.0047** | 0.0050 | 0.0055 | **0.0012** | **0.0012** | **0.0012** | 0.0015 |
| $\text{MAE}^{r}_{ont}$ | 0.1228 | 0.1234 | **0.1220** | 0.1262 | **0.0395** | 0.0397 | 0.0396 | 0.0402 |

**Table 3.** Error measures for the type $N/U_P$

| Method | $n = m = 10$ | | | | $n = m = 100$ | | | |
|---|---|---|---|---|---|---|---|---|
| | Boot | Kern | Unif1 | Unif2 | Boot | Kern | Unif1 | Unif2 |
| $\mathrm{MAE}^{\bar{X}}_{supp}$ | 0.3961 | 0.4935 | **0.3935** | 0.3958 | 0.1289 | 0.1458 | **0.1279** | 0.1290 |
| $\mathrm{MAE}^{\bar{X}}_{mid}$ | 0.3949 | 0.4920 | **0.3922** | 0.3942 | 0.1284 | 0.1453 | **0.1275** | 0.1285 |
| $\mathrm{MAE}^{S}_{supp}$ | 0.2685 | 0.4027 | **0.2668** | 0.2685 | 0.0907 | 0.2106 | **0.0906** | 0.0908 |
| $\mathrm{MAE}^{S}_{mid}$ | 0.2675 | 0.4015 | **0.2658** | 0.2674 | 0.0904 | 0.2099 | **0.0903** | 0.0905 |
| $p_{supp}$ | **0.8662** | 0.7304 | 0.8391 | 0.8267 | **0.8381** | 0.6023 | 0.8036 | 0.7732 |
| $p_{mid}$ | **0.8664** | 0.7297 | 0.8390 | 0.8315 | **0.8383** | 0.6013 | 0.8053 | 0.7841 |
| $p_{ont}$ | **0.7933** | 0.6024 | 0.7460 | 0.6720 | **0.7372** | 0.4633 | 0.6803 | 0.5260 |
| $\mathrm{MAE}^{r}_{supp}$ | 0.0977 | 0.0999 | **0.0968** | 0.0978 | 0.0333 | **0.0332** | **0.0332** | 0.0338 |
| $\mathrm{MAE}^{r}_{mid}$ | 0.0948 | 0.0969 | **0.0938** | 0.0941 | 0.0325 | 0.0324 | 0.0324 | 0.0326 |
| $\mathrm{MAE}^{r}_{ont}$ | 0.1577 | **0.1567** | 0.1572 | 0.1664 | 0.0516 | 0.0513 | **0.0512** | 0.0526 |

Hence, *Boot* produces the bootstrap samples that are the most "similar" to their initial counterparts. This result is evident in some way. However, *Boot* generates samples without their additional "perturbation" which may be undesirable, as mentioned previously. Therefore, *Unif1* seems to be the best method that produces "similar but not exactly the same" outputs. And there were no significant differences in the results between the models with "stronger dependency" (i.e., without the additional noise $\varepsilon$) and "weaker dependency" (with $\varepsilon$, respectively) as indicated by Tables 2 and 3.

We enrich our numerical analysis using real-life data with four variables based on the famous *Iris* dataset [2] available in R. These crisp numerical variables (i.e., *Sepal.Length, Sepal.Width, Petal.Length, Petal.Width*) were converted to intervals. It was done using the user-defined parameter $c = 0.2$, namely the formula $[(1-c)z_i, (1+c)z_i]$, where $z_i$ is the original crisp value.

In this more complex case, the general results are similar to the obtained previously (see Table 4). However, in many cases, there are exactly no differences between *Boot* and *Unif1* or even *Unif1* is favored (e.g., when MAEs for the means, standard deviations, and correlations are considered). Surprisingly, *Kern* gives significantly worse results (apart from MAEs for the correlations).

**Table 4.** Error measures for the dataset *Iris*

| Method | Boot | Kern | Unif1 | Unif2 |
|---|---|---|---|---|
| $\mathrm{MAE}^{\bar{X}}_{supp}$ | 0.0617 | 0.0721 | **0.0614** | 0.0619 |
| $\mathrm{MAE}^{\bar{X}}_{mid}$ | 0.0617 | 0.0721 | **0.0614** | 0.0619 |
| $\mathrm{MAE}^{S}_{supp}$ | **0.0301** | 0.1589 | **0.0301** | 0.0302 |
| $\mathrm{MAE}^{S}_{mid}$ | **0.0301** | 0.1589 | **0.0301** | 0.0302 |
| $p_{supp}$ | **0.8314** | 0.3101 | 0.8005 | 0.7636 |
| $p_{mid}$ | **0.8314** | 0.3077 | 0.8020 | 0.7773 |
| $p_{ont}$ | **0.8222** | 0.2119 | 0.4595 | 0.2730 |
| $\mathrm{MAE}^{r}_{supp}$ | **0.0247** | 0.0259 | **0.0247** | 0.0254 |
| $\mathrm{MAE}^{r}_{mid}$ | **0.0247** | 0.0259 | **0.0247** | 0.0248 |
| $\mathrm{MAE}^{r}_{ont}$ | **0.0269** | 0.0279 | 0.0272 | 0.0793 |

## 6 Conclusions

In this paper, we considered four resampling methods that were designed for the interval-valued data with many variables. Because of such a setting, the possible dependencies in the intervals for each variable and between the variables had to be incorporated into the resampling mechanism. Therefore, some answers to the problems mentioned in [14] as possible future research were given in this paper. Two completely original methods joined the ideas from the pairwise and smoothed bootstraps to give new non-parametric algorithms. After conducting the extensive numerical simulations, it seems that one of them (*Unif1*, namely) leads to the interesting results – the variability of the bootstrapped samples is more significant than for the classical bootstrap but with the general low values of the error measures.

Of course, some answers are still open. For example, other approaches (e.g., related to the regression analysis) to the problem of the existing possible dependencies in the interval-valued variables can be considered.

**Disclosure of Interests.** The author has no competing interests to declare that are relevant to the content of this article.

## References

1. Al Luhayb, A.S.M., Coolen-Maturi, T., Coolen, F.P.A.: Smoothed bootstrap methods for hypothesis testing. J. Stat. Theory Pract. **18**(1), 16 (2024). https://doi.org/10.1007/s42519-024-00370-x
2. Anderson, E.: The species problem in Iris. Ann. Mo. Bot. Gard. **23**(3), 457–509 (1936). https://doi.org/10.2307/2394164

3. Cinar, O., Viechtbauer, W.: The poolr package for combining independent and dependent p values. J. Stat. Softw. **101**(1), 1–42 (2022). https://doi.org/10.18637/jss.v101.i01
4. Couso, I., Dubois, D.: Statistical reasoning with set-valued information: ontic vs. epistemic views. Int. J. Approx. Reason. **55**, 1502–1518 (2014). https://doi.org/10.1016/j.ijar.2013.07.002
5. Efron, B., Tibshirani, R.J.: An Introduction to the Bootstrap. No. 57 in Monographs on Statistics and Applied Probability. Chapman & Hall/CRC, Boca Raton (1993). https://doi.org/10.1201/9780429246593
6. Freedman, D.A.: Bootstrapping regression models. Ann. Stat. **9**(6), 1218–1228 (1981). https://doi.org/10.1214/aos/1176345638
7. Gil, M.A., Montenegro, M., González-Rodríguez, G., Colubi, A., Casals, M.R.: Bootstrap approach to the multi-sample test of means with imprecise data. Comput. Stat. Data Anal. **51**(1), 148–162 (2006). https://doi.org/10.1016/j.csda.2006.04.018
8. González-Rodríguez, G., Montenegro, M., Colubi, A., Ángeles Gil, M.: Bootstrap techniques and fuzzy random variables: Synergy in hypothesis testing with fuzzy data. Fuzzy Sets Syst. **157**(19), 2608–2613 (2006). https://doi.org/10.1016/j.fss.2003.11.021
9. Grzegorzewski, P., Hryniewicz, O., Romaniuk, M.: Flexible bootstrap for fuzzy data based on the canonical representation. Int. J. Comput. Intell. Syst. **13**, 1650–1662 (2020). https://doi.org/10.2991/ijcis.d.201012.003
10. Grzegorzewski, P., Hryniewicz, O., Romaniuk, M.: Flexible resampling for fuzzy data. Int. J. Appl. Math. Comput. Sci. **30**(2), 281–297 (2020). https://doi.org/10.34768/amcs-2020-0022
11. Grzegorzewski, P., Romaniuk, M.: Bootstrap methods for epistemic data. Int. J. Appl. Math. Comput. Sci. **32**(2), 288–297 (2022). https://doi.org/10.34768/amcs-2022-0021
12. Grzegorzewski, P.: The Kolmogorov–Smirnov goodness-of-fit test for interval-valued data. In: Gil, E., Gil, E., Gil, J., Gil, M.Á. (eds.) The Mathematics of the Uncertain. SSDC, vol. 142, pp. 615–627. Springer, Cham (2018). https://doi.org/10.1007/978-3-319-73848-2_57
13. Grzegorzewski, P., Romaniuk, M.: Bootstrapped tests for epistemic fuzzy data. Int. J. Appl. Math. Comput. Sci. **34**(2), 277–289 (2024). https://doi.org/10.61822/amcs-2024-0020
14. Liubonko, Y., Romaniuk, M.: Discrete and smoothed resampling methods for interval numbers. In: Lesot, M.J., et al. (eds.) Information Processing and Management of Uncertainty in Knowledge-Based Systems, pp. 277–288. Springer, Cham (2025)
15. Opara, K.R., Hryniewicz, O.: Computation of general correlation coefficients for interval data. Int. J. Approx. Reason. **73**, 56–75 (2016). https://doi.org/10.1016/j.ijar.2016.02.007
16. Romaniuk, M., Hryniewicz, O.: Interval-based, nonparametric approach for resampling of fuzzy numbers. Soft. Comput. **23**, 5883–5903 (2019)
17. Romaniuk, M., Grzegorzewski, P.: Resampling fuzzy numbers with statistical applications: FuzzyResampling package. R J. **15**(1), 271–283 (2023). https://doi.org/10.32614/RJ-2023-036
18. Romaniuk, M., Grzegorzewski, P., Parchami, A.: FuzzySimRes: epistemic bootstrap – an efficient tool for statistical inference based on imprecise data. R J. **16**(2) (2024)

19. Romaniuk, M., Hryniewicz, O.: Discrete and smoothed resampling methods for interval-valued fuzzy numbers. IEEE Trans. Fuzzy Syst. **29**(3), 599–611 (2021). https://doi.org/10.1109/TFUZZ.2019.2957253
20. Silverman, B.W., Young, G.A.: The bootstrap: to smooth or not to smooth? Biometrika **74**(3), 469–479 (1987). https://doi.org/10.2307/2336686
21. Wilson, D.J.: Generalized mean p-values for combining dependent tests: comparison of generalized central limit theorem and robust risk analysis. Wellcome Open Res. **5**, 55 (2020)
22. Wolodzko, T.: kernelboot: Smoothed Bootstrap and Random Generation from Kernel Densities (2023). https://CRAN.R-project.org/package=kernelboot. R package version 0.1.10

# Type 2 Fuzzy Sets

# A Decision-Making Framework Based on Intersection and Similarity Measures for Type-2 Fuzzy Sets

Pedro Huidobro[1(✉)], Francisco Javier Talavera[2,3], Susana Cubillo[4], Carmen Torres-Blanc[4], Pablo Hernández-Varela[5], and Jorge Elorza[2,3]

[1] Departamento de Estadística e I.O. y Didáctica de la Matemática, Universidad de Oviedo, C. San Francisco, 3, 33003 Oviedo, Spain
huidobropedro@uniovi.es

[2] Departamento de Física y Matemática Aplicada, Facultad de Ciencias, Universidad de Navarra, C. Irunlarrea 1, 31008 Pamplona, Spain

[3] Institute of Data Science and Artificial Intelligence (DATAI), Universidad de Navarra, Edificio Ismael Sánchez Bella, Campus Universitario, 31009 Pamplona, Spain
ftalaveraan@alumni.unav.es, jelorza@unav.es

[4] Departamento de Matemática Aplicada, Universidad Politécnica de Madrid, 28660 Boadilla del Monte, Madrid, Spain
{scubillo,ctorres}@fi.upm.es

[5] Departamento de Ciencias Exactas, Facultad de Ingeniería, Arquitectura y Diseño, Universidad San Sebastián, Bellavista 7, 8420524 Santiago, Chile
pablo.hernandez@uss.cl

**Abstract.** This paper introduces a decision-making framework that employs Type-2 Fuzzy Sets (T2FS), focusing on normal and convex membership functions. Decisions are constructed using the intersection of T2FS representing constraints and objectives, and alternatives are ranked based on their similarity to the ideal decision using tailored similarity measures. A case study on hotel selection demonstrates the practical utility and robustness of the framework.

**Keywords:** Type-2 fuzzy sets · Decision-making · Similarity measures · Selecting best cities

## 1 Introduction

In 1965, Zadeh [22] introduced fuzzy sets, where the degree of membership of any element to a set is a value in the range $[0, 1]$. This concept has proven to be a powerful tool for modeling human knowledge and addressing imprecision. Later, Zadeh [23] proposed the first extensions of fuzzy sets, highlighting the importance of further developing this theory in order to address more complex issues, especially those related to decision-making processes.

One of the most significant extensions of fuzzy sets is type-2 fuzzy sets (T2FSs), introduced by Zadeh [21], where the membership function's value is itself a fuzzy set, enabling a more nuanced representation of uncertainty. This extension has attracted


M. Baczyński et al. (Eds.): EUSFLAT 2025, LNCS 15884, pp. 237–248, 2025.
https://doi.org/10.1007/978-3-031-97228-7_20

attention from researchers in the area of knowledge, see for instance [9], [10], or [15]. T2FSs have been applied in various fields, including decision-making, clustering, and data analysis.

A decision-making process typically involves three essential elements: a collection of alternatives, a set of constraints that define the feasible options among those alternatives, and a utility function that quantifies the gain or loss associated with each alternative. In many real-world scenarios, it is challenging to precisely define the objective function and constraints. As noted by Czogala and Zimmermann [6], fuzzy sets provide a valuable framework for managing this imprecision. Building on this foundation, T2FSs have been widely applied due to their ability to address both numerical and linguistic uncertainties [4].

Similarity measures (SMs) are indispensable tools in decision-making, clustering, and fuzzy analysis. These measures quantify the similarity between objects, with values ranging from 0 (no similarity) to 1 (complete identity). Over the years, numerous SMs for T2FSs have been proposed, including notable works by Wu and Mendel [17], Hao and Mendel [8], and Couso et al. [5]. However, integrating SMs into decision-making frameworks remains an open research area.

This paper introduces a novel decision-making framework based on T2FSs, where the ideal decision is constructed as the intersection of fuzzy alternatives, and each alternative is evaluated by its similarity to that ideal. While conceptually related to compromise programming [25], our method differs in key aspects: criteria and alternatives are modeled as T2FSs with normal and convex secondary membership functions; the ideal is computed via meet operations in the T2FS lattice, not pointwise minima; and alternatives are ranked using similarity measures tailored for T2FSs, such as extended restricted equivalence functions [7]. This yields a robust and interpretable approach to decision-making under uncertainty.

The remainder of the paper is structured as follows: Sect. 2 provides the necessary preliminaries on T2FS, Sect. 3 describes the proposed framework, Sect. 4 presents a case study, and Sect. 5 concludes with insights and future research directions.

## 2 Preliminaries

This section summarizes key concepts of fuzzy set theory, with a focus on T2FSs and the SMs relevant to our framework.

A type-1 fuzzy set (T1FS) $A$ on a universe $X$ is defined by a membership function $\mu_A : X \to [0,1]$, with $A = \{(x, \mu_A(x)) : x \in X\}$ [22]. The intersection and union of two fuzzy sets $A$ and $B$ are given by:

$$\mu_{A \cap B}(x) = \min(\mu_A(x), \mu_B(x)), \quad \mu_{A \cup B}(x) = \max(\mu_A(x), \mu_B(x)) \quad \forall x \in X.$$

Type-2 fuzzy sets, introduced by Zadeh, extend the classical fuzzy set theory by allowing the membership grades to be fuzzy sets themselves. This additional layer of uncertainty modeling makes them highly versatile for addressing complex problems involving imprecise or incomplete information.

**Definition 1** [21]. *A type-2 fuzzy set (T2FS) $\tilde{A}$ on a universe $X$ is defined by a membership function $\mu_{\tilde{A}}$ that maps each element $x \in X$ to a fuzzy set in $[0,1]$, denoted as $\mu_{\tilde{A}} : X \to [0,1]^{J_x}$, where $J_x \subseteq [0,1]$. The value $\mu_{\tilde{A}}(x)$ is referred to as the fuzzy grade and it is itself a fuzzy set in $[0,1]$.*

Without loss of generality, it is assumed that $J_x = [0,1]$ for all $x \in X$, since any value $y \notin J_x$ can simply be assigned $(\mu_{\tilde{A}}(x))(y) = 0$. The collection of all type-2 fuzzy sets defined on $X$ is represented as $T2FS(X) = \text{Map}(X, \mathbf{M} = [0,1]^{[0,1]})$. Similarly, the subset of type-2 fuzzy sets with membership values constrained to $M' \subseteq [0,1]^{[0,1]}$ is denoted by $T2FS_{M'}(X) = \text{Map}(X, M')$.

**Definition 2.** *A function $f \in \mathbf{M}$ is normal if,*

$$\sup\{f(x) : x \in [0,1]\} = 1$$

*and it is convex if for any $x \leq y \leq z$, the inequality:*

$$f(y) \geq f(x) \wedge f(z)$$

*holds, where the symbol $\wedge$ stands for the minimum.*

**L** will be the set of all normal and convex functions of **M**. Throughout this paper, the image of any element in a T2FS, is required to be in **L** (denoted $\tilde{A} \in T2FS_L(X)$). These restrictions ensure a complete lattice structure for T2FSs under the operations defined below.

**Definition 3** [16]. *The operations $\sqcup$ (extended maximum) and $\sqcap$ (extended minimum) are defined as follows:*

$$(f \sqcup g)(x) = \sup\{f(u) \wedge g(v) : u \vee v = x\},$$
$$(f \sqcap g)(x) = \sup\{f(u) \wedge g(v) : u \wedge v = x\},$$

These operations allow the construction of partial orders on the set of membership functions $\mathbf{M} = [0,1]^{[0,1]}$:

$$f \sqsubseteq g \iff f \sqcap g = f, \quad f \preceq g \iff f \sqcup g = g.$$

Additionally, when restricting to $L$, the two partial orders become equivalent:

$$f \sqsubseteq g \iff f \preceq g.$$

This follows from the fact that normal and convex functions satisfy $f \sqcap g = f \iff f \sqcup g = g$, ensuring a unified ordering in $L$.

In the context of fuzzy set theory, a fuzzy set $A$ is considered to be contained in another fuzzy set $B$ if and only if the membership function of $A$ is less than or equal to that of $B$ (see [22]). Extending this concept to type-2 fuzzy sets, containment can be defined by using an order relation.

**Definition 4** [16]. *Let $\tilde{A}$ and $\tilde{B}$ be two T2FSs, then:*

$$\tilde{A} \sqsubseteq \tilde{B} \text{ if and only if, for all } x \in X,\ \tilde{A}(x) \sqsubseteq \tilde{B}(x)$$

*Moreover, the functions $A \sqcap B \in T2FS(X)$ and $A \sqcup B \in T2FS(X)$ are respectively defined pointwise as $(A \sqcap B)(x) = A(x) \sqcap B(x)$ and $(A \sqcup B)(x) = A(x) \sqcup B(x)$ for all $x \in X$.*

## 2.1 Similarity Measures for Fuzzy Sets

This subsection provides an overview of similarity measures (SMs) for fuzzy sets, along with their foundational axiomatic principles. Due to their diverse range of applications, various axioms have been proposed in the literature to evaluate similarity, with the choice of specific axioms depending on the context of use. Some common properties associated with similarity measures in fuzzy set theory are the following [13, 14]:

- **Reflexivity:** $S(A,B) = 1$ if and only if $A = B$.
- **Symmetry:** $S(A,B) = S(B,A)$.
- **Transitivity:** If $A \subseteq B \subseteq C$, then $S(A,C) \leq S(B,C)$ and $S(A,C) \leq S(A,B)$.
- **Overlapping:** If $A \cap B \neq \emptyset$, then $S(A,B) > 0$; otherwise, $S(A,B) = 0$.

The values of similarity measures typically lie within the interval $[0,1]$, where values closer to 1 indicate a greater similarity.

It is important to note that not all these properties are mandatory for defining a similarity measure, as their applicability depends on the specific problem being addressed.

Another approach to defining similarity measures is through distance functions, where objects are considered more similar as their distance decreases [18].

Restricted equivalence functions offer an alternative perspective [3]. These functions, defined as mappings $REF : [0,1] \times [0,1] \to [0,1]$, satisfy the following conditions:

- $REF(x,y) = REF(y,x)$.
- $REF(x,y) = 1$ if and only if $x = y$.
- $REF(x,y) = 0$ when $x = 0$ and $y = 1$, or $x = 1$ and $y = 0$.
- $REF(x,y) = REF(c(x),c(y))$ for all $x,y \in [0,1]$, where $c$ is a strong negation.
- For all $x,y,z \in [0,1]$, if $x \leq y \leq z$, then $REF(x,z) \leq REF(x,y)$ and $REF(x,z) \leq REF(y,z)$.

Similarity measures for fuzzy sets can be derived by aggregating values obtained from restricted equivalence functions, with the aggregation function satisfying specific properties. These methods provide a flexible framework for measuring similarity in various contexts.

As an example, using the restricted equivalence function $REF(x,y) = 1 - |x-y|$ together with the arithmetic mean, the resulting similarity measure is obtained

$$S_{REF}^{T1}(A,B) = \frac{1}{n}\sum_{i=1}^{n}\left(1 - |A(x_i) - B(x_i)|\right)$$

## 2.2 Similarities for T2FSs

Several approaches have been developed to compute similarity between Type-2 Fuzzy Sets (T2FSs), often relying on different representations to manage their complexity. The most common ones include $\alpha$-planes, which slice the T2FS horizontally based on membership levels; z-slices, which divide the secondary membership domain vertically; and vertical slices, which fix primary domain values and analyze the corresponding secondary membership functions. These representations help transform T2FSs into structures more amenable to analysis, comparison, and computation.

Zhao et al. [24] introduced similarity measures based on $\alpha$-planes, allowing a detailed comparison of the fuzzy sets by analyzing their secondary membership functions at different $\alpha$ levels. These measures provide a fuzzy similarity set, which can then be defuzzified to obtain a numerical similarity value.

Hao and Mendel [8] proposed an alternative approach, where the similarity is first represented as a fuzzy set and subsequently reduced to a numerical value by computing its centroid. Similarly, McCulloch and Wagner [11, 12], and Yang and Lin [20], expanded these ideas using methods such as z-slices or vertical slice representations, offering additional tools for analyzing T2FSs.

While these methods are effective for capturing nuances in the comparison of type-2 fuzzy sets, their specific characteristics often make them more suited to particular applications.

We will focus on the method proposed by De Miguel et al. [7], which leverages extended restricted equivalence functions (EREFs) to compare the vertical slices of two T2FSs. This approach is notable for its use of cumulative functions, as described by Walker and Walker [16], to define the similarity. The method provides an interpretable and reliable measure of similarity, making it a compelling choice for the purposes of this work.

For a fixed $x$, the similarity measure is defined as:

$$S^{T2}_{EREF}\left(\tilde{A}(x,u),\tilde{B}(x,u)\right) = 1 - \frac{1}{2}\int_0^1 d\left(\tilde{A}(x)^L(u),\tilde{B}(x)^L(u)\right)du - \frac{1}{2}\int_0^1 d\left(\tilde{A}(x)^R(u),\tilde{B}(x)^R(u)\right)du$$

Here, $d$ denotes a distance metric, and $\tilde{A}(x)^L(u)$ and $\tilde{A}(x)^R(u)$ represent the left and right cumulative functions, respectively. The outcome is a fuzzy set of the form $T2SM(\tilde{A},\tilde{B}) = \{(x_i, S^{T2}_{EREF}(x_i)) : x_i \in X\}$, which is aggregated into a single numerical value.

## 3 Decision-Making Based on Type-2 Fuzzy Sets

This section introduces a decision-making methodology using T2FSs.

### 3.1 Decision-Making Framework

The literature includes various theories on the use of fuzzy sets in decision-making. Bellman and Zadeh [1] suggested that a decision could be seen as a combination of goals and constraints, treating these two concepts symmetrically and linking them with the "and" connective.

In classical fuzzy set theory, the membership degree of an element is typically assumed to be precisely known. However, real-world scenarios often involve uncertainty or incomplete information, where exact membership degrees are not available [2].

Following Bellman and Zadeh's approach for T1FSs [1], we will model constraints and goals as T2FSs over a set of alternatives, $X$. The decision $D$ is then represented as the intersection of all type-2 fuzzy goals and constraints, providing a more flexible framework for real-world scenarios.

Bellman and Zadeh [1] originally proposed that a decision is the result of the intersection between goals and constraints, ensuring that the selected alternative simultaneously satisfies all conditions. Similarly, Yager and Basson [19] extended this notion to fuzzy preference relations, reinforcing the idea that decision-making is guided by the aggregation of multiple criteria.

However, in our framework, we extend this classical perspective by considering type-2 fuzzy alternatives, where the universe consists of type-1 fuzzy criteria or constraints. This requires a refined interpretation of intersection: rather than simply ensuring simultaneous satisfaction of conditions, the intersection serves as a mechanism to construct an ideal alternative by consolidating the most consistent aspects of all available alternatives.

The intersection of alternatives represents the most *conservative* option, as it retains only the portion that is consistently valid across all alternatives. In other words, it ensures that the evaluated criteria are simultaneously satisfied by all alternatives. Since the membership degree in the intersection is always less than or equal to that of any individual alternative, this approach guarantees that the shared information is not overestimated by extreme values from certain alternatives, which could otherwise bias the decision-making process.

It is important to emphasize that the criteria in this study are modeled using the *opposite characteristic* to the one being assessed. For instance, if the objective is to determine the cleanest city, we do not directly model a "cleanliness" criterion; instead, we construct a "dirtiness" criterion, where the membership function indicates how dirty each alternative is. Consequently, selecting the alternative with the lowest membership in "dirtiness" indirectly identifies the cleanest city.

This inversion is crucial when computing the intersection of alternatives. Since intersection preserves the lowest membership values across all alternatives, it effectively identifies the alternative that minimizes undesired characteristics, such as dirtiness or distance to public transport. In this manner, the decision-making process ensures that the optimal choice is the one that best mitigates undesirable factors, aligning with the intended selection goal.

Our proposal is conceptually related to the classical idea of compromise solutions [25], where the objective is to select the alternative closest to an ideal point. However, our approach introduces significant differences: we use T2FSs with normal and convex secondary membership functions, ensuring a complete lattice structure; the ideal decision is computed via intersection in this lattice, not as pointwise minima; and instead of geometric distances, we use similarity measures specifically designed for T2FSs, such as those based on extended restricted equivalence functions.

**Definition 5.** *Let $X = \{x_1, \ldots, x_n\}$ be the set of criteria, and let $\tilde{A}_1, \ldots, \tilde{A}_p$ be the alternatives expressed as T2FSs over $X$. The decision-making framework is defined as follows:*

– ***Ideal Decision:*** *The intersection of all alternatives:*

$$\tilde{D} = \bigsqcap_{i=1}^{p} \tilde{A}_i.$$

- ***Optimal Decision:*** *The alternative* $\tilde{A}_i$ *that maximizes its similarity to the ideal decision:*

$$\tilde{D}^S = \{\arg\max_i S(\tilde{A}_i, \tilde{D})\}.$$

*Here,* $\arg\max_i S(\tilde{A}_i, \tilde{D})$ *denotes the alternative (or alternatives)* $\tilde{A}_i$ *for which the similarity measure* $S(\tilde{A}_i, \tilde{D})$ *attains its maximum value.*

This means that for each criterion $x$, the ideal alternative $\tilde{D}$ maintains the lowest compatible membership values across all alternatives.

Intuitively, this implies that $\tilde{D}$ is the most conservative representation of the decision, capturing only those characteristics that are consistently supported across all alternatives without generating contradictions.

The membership value $\tilde{D}(x)$ quantifies to what extent the criterion $x$ is satisfied. Once the ideal decision $\tilde{D}$ is obtained, the next step is to select the best alternative using the similarity measure.

A natural question that may arise is whether, instead of computing the intersection of alternatives, one could directly compare each alternative with the singleton $\tilde{0}$ (the set membership $\bar{0}(x) = \begin{cases} 1 \text{ if } x = 0 \\ 0 \text{ if } x \neq 0 \end{cases}$, across all criteria). At first glance, this approach might seem reasonable, as it would favor alternatives with the lowest membership in undesirable criteria. However, it has several drawbacks.

First, using the intersection as the ideal alternative allows us to maintain consistency with the original fuzzy representations of the criteria while comparing with the singleton $\tilde{0}$ ignores the inherent uncertainty structure present in the criteria and the way the alternatives interact. Since the intersection is formed by combining the given alternatives, it remains closer to the original data and better preserves the relationships between the criteria. This also leads to more meaningful similarity values, as alternatives are compared against a reference that is more representative of the decision space. In contrast, similarity values computed against the singleton $\tilde{0}$ would tend to be lower and potentially less informative, as this extreme reference might not reflect the actual variability among the alternatives.

Thus, employing the intersection as a reference not only ensures a structured and meaningful decision process but also allows for a more precise differentiation between alternatives, leveraging the original fuzzy information rather than discarding it.

A key challenge in type-2 fuzzy decision-making is that individual alternatives may exhibit high membership values in certain criteria without necessarily being the best overall choice. If an alternative were selected purely based on its membership values, it could lead to decisions that do not accurately reflect the overall decision space.

Intersection addresses this issue by:

- Ensuring that the ideal alternative $\tilde{D}$ retains only the information consistently supported by all alternatives, preventing biases from individual options.
- Providing a synthesized representation of the common structure among alternatives, rather than selecting an option based on isolated membership values.
- Allowing for an objective comparison using similarity measures, where the chosen alternative is the one that best fits the consolidated decision structure, rather than simply having the highest individual memberships.

*Example 1.* Suppose a company must decide where to establish a new plant among three possible locations. Each location is evaluated based on two criteria: real estate costs ($C_1$) and distance to suppliers ($C_2$). Due to uncertainty in the data, each location is modeled as a T2FS, where the criteria act as the T1FS. The membership functions for each criterion are given as trapezoidal T1FSs.

- $\tilde{A_1}(C) = \{\langle C_1, \text{tfm}(0.3, 0.4, 0.6, 0.7)\rangle, \langle C_2, \text{tfm}(0.4, 0.5, 0.7, 0.8)\rangle\}$.
- $\tilde{A_2}(C) = \{\langle C_1, \text{tfm}(0.5, 0.6, 0.7, 0.8)\rangle, \langle C_2, \text{tfm}(0.3, 0.4, 0.5, 0.6)\rangle\}$.
- $\tilde{A_3}(C) = \{\langle C_1, \text{tfm}(0.2, 0.3, 0.5, 0.6)\rangle, \langle C_2, \text{tfm}(0.4, 0.5, 0.6, 0.7)\rangle\}$.

Here, *tfm* stands for "trapezoidal fuzzy membership function", which is defined by four parameters: the left foot, left shoulder, right shoulder, and right foot of the trapezoid.

Next, we define the *ideal solution* as a T2FS that represents the best possible criteria values using the intersection:

$$\text{Ideal Solution} = \{\langle C_1, \text{tfm}(0.2, 0.3, 0.5, 0.6)\rangle, \langle C_2, \text{tfm}(0.3, 0.4, 0.5, 0.6)\rangle\}.$$

The final decision is based on the similarity between each location's aggregated intersection and the ideal solution. Here we used $S^{T2}_{EREF}$ with the arcotangent distance.

- $\tilde{A_1}$: Similarity value = 0.8750.
- $\tilde{A_2}$: Similarity value = 0.8845.
- $\tilde{A_3}$: Similarity value = 0.9500.

Thus, the optimal decision is $D^{\tilde{S^{T2}_{EREF}}} = \tilde{A_3}$.

This framework integrates T2FSs with decision-making principles, offering a robust method for handling uncertainty and complexity. Interestingly, some extensions of T1FSs–such as interval-valued fuzzy sets–can be viewed as particular cases of interval T2FSs. In such cases, our intersection and similarity operations remain valid with minor simplifications, showing that the framework is flexible and applicable to a broader class of fuzzy models.

## 4 Fuzzy Similarity Analysis for Airbnb Data in European Cities

This section shows an application of fuzzy similarity measures to analyze Airbnb data from various European cities[1]. The dataset includes features such as cleanliness, guest satisfaction, proximity to the city center, and distance to the nearest metro station. The objective is to assist in selecting the best city to visit based on these characteristics.

Each feature is modeled as a T2FS to capture variability and uncertainty. The four main features are:

- **Dirtiness**, derived as the complement of the cleanliness rating.
- **Dissatisfaction**, based on the satisfaction rating.
- **Distance to the city center**, normalized to a common scale.
- **Distance to the metro station**, normalized similarly.

[1] https://www.kaggle.com/datasets/cahyaalkahfi/airbnb-european-cities-join.

To construct the membership functions, we use trapezoidal representations based on the interquartile range. Instead of defining the core membership region using the minimum and maximum values, which can be highly sensitive to outliers, we adopt a more stable approach by using the first quartile (Q1, 25th percentile) and third quartile (Q3, 75th percentile). The resulting membership function is:

$$\mu(x) = \begin{cases} 0 & \text{if } x \leq a \text{ or } x \geq d, \\ \frac{x-a}{b-a} & \text{if } a < x \leq b, \\ 1 & \text{if } b < x < c, \\ \frac{d-x}{d-c} & \text{if } c \leq x < d. \end{cases}$$

where:
- $a$ = minimum observed value,
- $b$ = first quartile $Q_1$ (25th percentile),
- $c$ = third quartile $Q_3$ (75th percentile),
- $d$ = maximum observed value.

By using the interquartile range, we ensure that the membership function captures the central tendency of the data while reducing sensitivity to extreme values. This approach provides a more reliable representation of uncertainty, aligning with the fuzzy decision-making framework.

Figure 1 shows the updated T2FS membership functions for Amsterdam, illustrating the distribution of membership degrees for different features such as dirtiness, dissatisfaction, proximity to the city center, and proximity to the metro. Notably, the transition between membership levels is smooth due to the use of interquartile range for defining the fuzzy sets, leading to a more robust representation of uncertainty. The variability in the dirtiness metric continues to indicate significant fluctuations in Airbnb listing conditions across the city.

The decision set $\tilde{D}$ is constructed as the intersection of T2FSs representing each city's criteria. The similarity of each city to $\tilde{D}$ is then calculated using the EREF similarity measure with three different distance metrics:

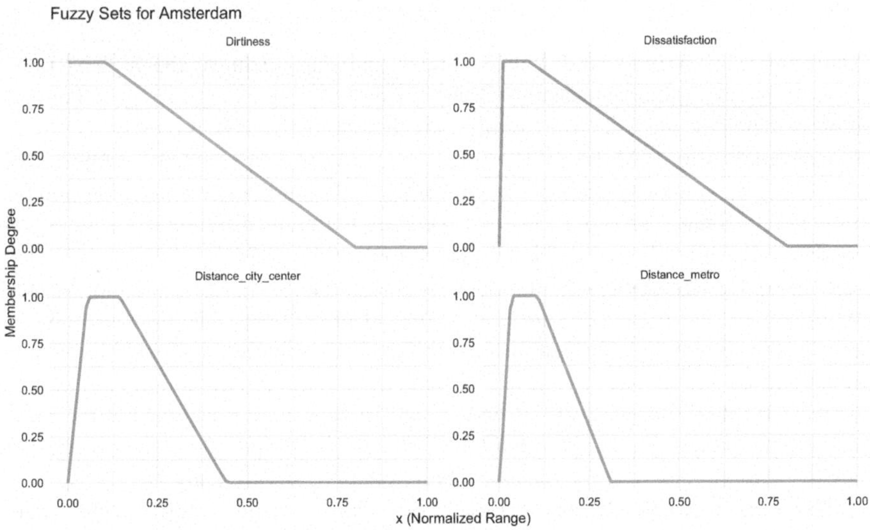


**Fig. 1.** Type-2 fuzzy membership functions for Amsterdam.

- **Arc Tangent Distance:** Computes similarity based on the difference in arc tangent transformed membership values, mitigating the effect of extreme values.
- **Euclidean Distance:** Measures similarity using the squared differences between membership values, highlighting larger discrepancies.
- **Absolute Distance:** Uses the absolute difference between membership values, providing a balanced sensitivity to variations.

Table 1 presents the rankings of cities according to these similarity measures.

**Table 1.** City rankings based on different similarity measures.

| City | $S^{T2}_{EREF}$ Arctan | $S^{T2}_{EREF}$ Euclid | $S^{T2}_{EREF}$ Abs |
|---|---|---|---|
| Amsterdam | 0.9722887 | 0.9745283 | 0.9476255 |
| Athens | **0.9896138** | **0.9948371** | **0.9807968** |
| Barcelona | 0.9785706 | 0.9859678 | 0.9595953 |
| Berlin | 0.9322810 | 0.9181165 | 0.8745033 |
| Budapest | 0.9480628 | 0.9508399 | 0.9065045 |
| Lisbon | 0.9724640 | 0.9786272 | 0.9489623 |
| London | 0.9457424 | 0.9401644 | 0.8971802 |
| Paris | 0.9859541 | 0.9925889 | 0.9725202 |
| Rome | 0.9744818 | 0.9779672 | 0.9511555 |
| Vienna | 0.9682433 | 0.9730278 | 0.9408334 |

The results in Table 1 can be interpreted as follows:

- **Dominance of Athens and Paris:** Athens and Paris achieve the highest rankings across all similarity measures. Their consistently high scores suggest that they closely match the ideal decision, reinforcing their attractiveness as preferred options.
- **Consistency Across Metrics:** The relative ranking of cities remains stable across the different similarity measures, indicating robustness in the decision-making framework. Small variations between methods highlight differences in their sensitivity to data distribution and local fluctuations.
- **Intermediate Performers:** Cities such as Barcelona, Rome, Lisbon, and Amsterdam demonstrate moderate similarity to the ideal decision. Their scores indicate reasonable alignment, although they exhibit greater variability compared to the top-ranked cities.
- **Lowest-Ranked Cities:** Berlin, London, and Budapest are positioned at the lower end of the ranking. These cities exhibit the lowest similarity scores, suggesting they are the least aligned with the ideal decision as defined in this study.
- **Differences Between Metrics:** While all three similarity measures provide consistent rankings, the Euclidean distance tends to be slightly more sensitive to outliers, whereas the arc tangent distance offers more stability. The absolute distance metric provides a balanced perspective, reinforcing the robustness of the results.

Athens and Paris emerge as the most similar cities to the ideal, while Berlin and London are the least aligned. The consistency in rankings across different measures confirms the validity of the proposed fuzzy decision-making framework, demonstrating its ability to evaluate and differentiate cities based on multiple criteria effectively.

## 5 Conclusions

This paper presented a decision-making framework based on type-2 fuzzy sets and similarity measures, offering a robust approach to handle uncertainty and imprecision in complex scenarios. By modeling decisions as the intersection of type-2 fuzzy sets and ranking alternatives through similarity scores, the methodology ensures a systematic and interpretable decision process.

This application to Airbnb data from European cities demonstrated the practical utility of the proposed framework. The results highlight the ability of type-2 fuzzy sets to capture nuanced variability and provide actionable insights in real-world decision-making.

Overall, this work bridges theoretical advancements in fuzzy set theory with practical applications, establishing type-2 fuzzy sets as a powerful tool for decision-making under uncertainty. The proposed framework is adaptable to diverse domains, enhancing decision quality and interpretability in scenarios where precision is limited.

**Acknowledgments.** This research was funded by the Spanish Ministerio de Ciencia e Innovación/AEI/EU FEDER Funds, grant numbers PID2021-122905NB-C22 and PID2022-139886NB-I00 and the Vicerrectoría de Investigación y Doctorados de la Universidad San Sebastián, Chile–USS–FIN–24–PASI–11. Francisco Javier Talavera acknowledges the grant from Asociación de Amigos de la Universidad de Navarra.

**Disclosure of Interests.** The authors have no competing interests to declare that are relevant to the content of this article.

## References

1. Bellman, R.E., Zadeh, L.A.: Decision-making in a fuzzy environment. Manage. Sci. **17**(4), B-141–B-164 (1970)
2. Bustince, H.: Interval-valued fuzzy sets in soft computing. Int. J. Comput. Intell. Syst. **3**(2), 215–222 (2010)
3. Bustince, H., Barrenechea, E., Pagola, M.: Restricted equivalence functions. Fuzzy Sets Syst. **157**(17), 2333–2346 (2006)
4. Bustince, H., et al.: A historical account of types of fuzzy sets and their relationships. IEEE Trans. Fuzzy Syst. **24**(1), 179–194 (2015)
5. Couso, I., Bustince, H., Sánchez, L.: A unified view of different axiomatic measures defined on $l$-fuzzy sets. IEEE Trans. Fuzzy Syst. **28**(8), 1878–1886 (2019)
6. Czogała, E., Zimmermann, H.J.: Decision making in uncertain environments. Eur. J. Oper. Res. **23**(2), 202–212 (1986)
7. De Miguel, L., et al.: Extension of restricted equivalence functions and similarity measures for type-2 fuzzy sets. IEEE Trans. Fuzzy Syst. **30**(9), 4005–4016 (2021)

8. Hao, M., Mendel, J.M.: Similarity measures for general type-2 fuzzy sets based on the $\alpha$-plane representation. Inf. Sci. **277**, 197–215 (2014)
9. Castillo, O., Amador-Angulo, L., Castro, J.R., Garcia-Valdez, M.: A comparative study of type-1 fuzzy logic systems, interval type-2 fuzzy logic systems and generalized type-2 fuzzy logic systems in control problems. Inf. Sci. **354**, 257–274 (2016)
10. Sanchez, M.A., Castillo, O., Castro, J.R.: Generalized type-2 fuzzy systems for controlling a mobile robot and a performance comparison with interval type-2 and type-1 fuzzy systems. Expert Syst. Appl. **42**(14), 5904–5914 (2015)
11. McCulloch, J., Wagner, C.: Measuring the similarity between zSlices general type-2 fuzzy sets with non-normal secondary membership functions. In: Proceedings of the IEEE International Conference on Fuzzy Systems (FUZZ-IEEE), pp. 461–468. IEEE, Vancouver (2016)
12. McCulloch, J., Wagner, C.: On the choice of similarity measures for type-2 fuzzy sets. Inf. Sci. **510**, 135–154 (2020)
13. Pappis, C.P., Karacapilidis, N.I.: A comparative assessment of measures of similarity of fuzzy values. Fuzzy Sets Syst. **56**(2), 171–174 (1993)
14. Rico, N., Huidobro, P., Bouchet, A., Díaz, I.: Similarity measures for interval-valued fuzzy sets based on average embeddings and its application to hierarchical clustering. Inf. Sci. **615**, 794–812 (2022)
15. Torres-Blanc, C., Martinez-Mateo, J., Cubillo, S., Magdalena, L., Talavera, F.J., Elorza, J.: Subsethood measures based on cardinality of type-2 fuzzy sets. Fuzzy Sets Syst. **499**, 109174 (2025)
16. Walker, C.L., Walker, E.A.: The algebra of fuzzy truth values. Fuzzy Sets Syst. **149**(2), 309–348 (2005)
17. Wu, D., Mendel, J.M.: Similarity measures for closed general type-2 fuzzy sets: overview, comparisons, and a geometric approach. IEEE Trans. Fuzzy Syst. **27**(3), 515–526 (2018)
18. Xu, Z.S., Chen, J.: An overview of distance and similarity measures of intuitionistic fuzzy sets. Internat. J. Uncertain. Fuzziness Knowl.-Based Syst. **16**(04), 529–555 (2008)
19. Yager, R., Basson, D.: Decision making with fuzzy sets. Decis. Sci. **6**(3), 590–600 (1975)
20. Yang, M.S., Lin, D.C.: On similarity and inclusion measures between type-2 fuzzy sets with an application to clustering. Comput. Math. Appl. **57**(6), 896–907 (2009)
21. Zadeh, L.A.: The concept of a linguistic variable and its application to approximate reasoning-I. Inf. Sci. **8**(3), 199–249 (1975)
22. Zadeh, L.A.: Fuzzy sets. Inf. Control **8**(3), 338–353 (1965)
23. Zadeh, L.A.: Outline of a new approach to the analysis of complex systems and decision processes. IEEE Trans. Syst. Man Cybern. **3**, 28–44 (1973)
24. Zhao, T., Xiao, J., Li, Y., Deng, X.: A new approach to similarity and inclusion measures between general type-2 fuzzy sets. Soft. Comput. **18**(4), 809–823 (2014)
25. Zeleny, M.: A concept of compromise solutions and the method of the displaced ideal. Comput. Oper. Res. **1**(5), 479–496 (1974)

# About T-Norms and T-Conorms on New Preorders in Type-2 Fuzzy Sets


Pablo Hernández-Varela[1(✉)], Francisco Javier Talavera[2,3], Carmen Torres-Blanc[4], Susana Cubillo[4], Pedro Huidobro[5], and Jorge Elorza[2,3]

[1] Departamento de Ciencias Exactas, Facultad de Ingeniería, Universidad San Sebastián, Bellavista 7, 8420524 Santiago, Chile
pablo.hernandez@uss.cl

[2] Departamento de Física y Matemática Aplicada, Facultad de Ciencias, Universidad de Navarra, C. Irunlarrea 1, 31008 Pamplona, Spain
ftalaveraan@alumni.unav.es, jelorza@unav.es

[3] Institute of Data Science and Artificial Intelligence (DATAI), Universidad de Navarra, Edificio Ismael Sánchez Bella, Campus Universitario, 31009 Pamplona, Spain

[4] Departamento de Matemática Aplicada a las TIC, Universidad Politécnica de Madrid, 28660 Boadilla del Monte, Madrid, Spain
{ctorres,scubillo}@fi.upm.es

[5] Departamento de Estadística e I.O. y Didáctica de la Matemática, Universidad de Oviedo, C. San Francisco, 3, 33003 Oviedo, Spain
huidobropedro@uniovi.es



**Abstract.** We propose two families of operators which could be used as triangular norms or conorms in the framework of type-2 fuzzy sets. We study their properties and present two new preorders for the set of functions from [0,1] to [0,1]. We show that the proposed operators satisfy the definition of t-norm and t-conorm, respectively, with the given preorders.



**Keywords:** Function from [0,1] to [0,1] · Convex function · Normal function · Type-2 fuzzy set · Preorder · Triangular norm · Triangular conorm


## 1 Introduction

Type-2 fuzzy sets (T2FSs) were first defined by L.A. Zadeh as a generalization of type-1 fuzzy sets (FSs) (see [21,22]). They are functions that map elements from the universe $X$ to $\mathbf{M}$, where $\mathbf{M}$ is the set of functions from [0,1] to [0,1]. Given the fact that FSs can be interpreted as particular cases of T2FSs, the accuracy for modeling certain situations is significantly higher when using T2FSs. This fact becomes more clear when we realize that the degree of membership of an element to a FS is given by a value in the interval $[0, 1]$ while the membership degrees for T2FSs are FSs in $[0, 1]$ (see for instance [13–16]).



M. Baczyński et al. (Eds.): EUSFLAT 2025, LNCS 15884, pp. 249–260, 2025.
https://doi.org/10.1007/978-3-031-97228-7_21

In this paper we consider T2FSs with membership degrees in some families of the set $\mathbf{M} = [0,1]^{[0,1]}$ of all functions from [0,1] to [0,1], but we will also focus our attention in $\mathbf{C}$ (set of convex functions of $\mathbf{M}$), $\mathbf{N}$ (set of normal functions of $\mathbf{M}$), and some subsets of $\mathbf{N}$. It should be noted that many properties satisfied by a function in the set $\mathbf{M}$, for example the commutativity of a binary operator, are directly satisfied in its subsets. Nevertheless, there are other properties that must be examined independently when we restrict ourselves to each subset, for example, the closure and boundary properties.

T-norms and t-conorms are widely known and used operators that can be defined over different extensions of FS. For example, Gehrke et al. in [6], defined t-norms and t-conorms on interval-valued fuzzy sets (IVFSs). Regarding T2FSs, Walker and Walker (see [16,17]) provided two new families of binary operations on $\mathbf{M}$ and determined that, under certain conditions, they are t-norms and t-conorms on $\mathbf{L}$ (set of normal and convex functions of $\mathbf{M}$). Moreover, some authors like Wu et al. (see [18,19]) and Hernández et al. (see [11,12]) have recently obtained different families of t-norms and t-conorms on $\mathbf{L}$, $\mathbf{C}$, $\mathbf{N}$ and some other subsets of $\mathbf{N}$.

The main goal of this paper is to define new operators on $\mathbf{M}$, which are extensions of some presented in [9]. We will impose the restriction of using the *product* t-norm and we check whether or not these operators satisfy the necessary axioms to be t-norms or t-conorms on $\mathbf{M}$ with respect to the two usual partial orders. In addition, we will define and determine two new preorders on $\mathbf{M}$, and then analyze if the mentioned extended families of operators turn out to be t-norms or t-conorms on $\mathbf{M}$, $\mathbf{C}$, $\mathbf{N}$ or some subsets of $\mathbf{N}$, with respect to these preorders.

The article is organized as follows. Section 2 establishes some definitions, notations and properties required for the rest of this work. More precisely, we review some definitions and properties of FSs, T2FSs and IT2FSs and provide some background on t-norms and t-conorms on such sets. Section 3 and Sect. 4 are the main parts of the contribution. In Sect. 3, the operations considered in [9], are extended by allowing the use of any t-norm in [0,1]. We will study the specific case of the *product* t-norm to check if these extensions satisfy the axioms of t-norm or t-conorm with respect to the two usual partial orders of $\mathbf{M}$. In Sect. 4 new relations on $\mathbf{M}$ are defined and it is proven that they are preorders in this set. In addition, it is studied if the operations analyzed in Sect. 3 turn out to be t-norms or t-conorms on all of $\mathbf{M}$ and some important subsets of $\mathbf{M}$ with respect to these new preorders. Section 5 summarizes the main results and states some conclusions.

## 2 Operations on Type-2 Fuzzy Sets

In this section, we present the definition of type-2 fuzzy set and we establish some important features and operations related to them. Throughout the paper, $X$ will be the set representing the universe of discourse. Additionally, $\leq$ will denote the usual order relation in the lattice of real numbers. $\vee$ and $\wedge$ will be the maximum and the minimum operators on the lattice $([0,1], \leq)$, respectively.

**Definition 1** *([15]). A type-2 fuzzy set (T2FS)* A *is characterized by a membership function:* $\mu_A : X \to \boldsymbol{M}$*, where* $\boldsymbol{M}$ *is the set of all functions from the interval* $[0,1]$ *to itself,* $\boldsymbol{M} = [0,1]^{[0,1]} = Map\,([0,1],[0,1])$*. That is,* $\mu_A(x)$ *is a fuzzy set on the interval* $[0,1]$ *and also the degree of membership of an element* $x \in X$ *to the set A. Therefore,* $\mu_A(x) = f_x$*, where* $f_x : [0,1] \to [0,1]$*.*

Next, let us present some subsets of $\mathbf{M}$ that we will consider in this work.

**Definition 2.** *A function* $f \in \boldsymbol{M}$ *is normal if* $\sup\{f(x) : x \in [0,1]\} = 1$ *and it is convex if for any* $x \le y \le z$*, the inequality:* $f(y) \ge f(x) \wedge f(z)$ *holds.*

The set of all normal functions of $\mathbf{M}$ will be denoted by $\mathbf{N}$, and the set of all convex functions of $\mathbf{M}$ will be denoted by $\mathbf{C}$. Other subsets of $\mathbf{M}$ studied in present work are: the set $\mathbf{L}$ of both convex and normal functions of $\mathbf{M}$, the set $\mathbf{K}$ of functions in $\mathbf{N}$ whose range is the set $\{0,1\}$ and the set $\mathbf{K}_c^F$ of functions in $\mathbf{K}$ whose support is a finite union of closed intervals.

The algebraic operations join, meet and complementation on $\mathbf{M}$, given in the next definition, were determined from Zadeh's Extension Principle [20,21].

**Definition 3** *([5,8,16]). The operations* $\sqcup$ *(extended maximum or join),* $\sqcap$ *(extended minimum or meet),* $\neg$ *(complementation) and the elements* $\bar{0}$ *and* $\bar{1}$ *are defined on* $\boldsymbol{M}$ *as follows:*

$$(f \sqcup g)(x) = \sup\{f(y) \wedge g(z) : y \vee z = x\}, \quad (f \sqcap g)(x) = \sup\{f(y) \wedge g(z) : y \wedge z = x\},$$

$$\neg f(x) = \sup\{f(y) : 1 - y = x\} = f(1-x),$$

$$\bar{0}(x) = \begin{cases} 1 & \text{if } x = 0, \\ 0 & \text{if } x \neq 0, \end{cases} \qquad \bar{1}(x) = \begin{cases} 1 & \text{if } x = 1, \\ 0 & \text{if } x \neq 1. \end{cases}$$

In the tuple $\mathbb{M} = (\mathbf{M}, \sqcup, \sqcap, \neg, \bar{0}, \bar{1})$, the absorption law is not satisfied in general and therefore it is not a lattice (see [8,16]). However, from the operations $\sqcup$ and $\sqcap$ we can define two partial orders on $\mathbf{M}$.

**Definition 4** *([15,16]). The relations* $\sqsubseteq$ *and* $\preceq$ *are defined on* $\boldsymbol{M}$ *as follows:*

$$f \sqsubseteq g \quad \text{if } f \sqcap g = f; \quad f \preceq g \quad \text{if } f \sqcup g = g.$$

In [15] was stablished that $\sqsubseteq$ and $\preceq$ are partial orders on $\mathbf{M}$.

The following definition and theorems were given in previous papers in order to simplify the operations on $\mathbf{M}$:

**Definition 5** *([5,8,16]). For each* $f \in \boldsymbol{M}$*, we define* $f^L, f^R \in \boldsymbol{M}$ *as follows:*

$$f^L(x) = \sup\{f(y) : y \le x\}, \quad f^R(x) = \sup\{f(y) : y \ge x\}.$$

The following characterizations for the partial orders were also shown in [16].

**Theorem 1** *([16]). Let* $f, g \in \boldsymbol{M}$*. Then:*

$$f \sqsubseteq g \Leftrightarrow (f^R \wedge g) \le f \le g^R, \quad f \preceq g \Leftrightarrow (g^L \wedge f) \le g \le f^L.$$

Note that the operation $\wedge$ and the order $\leq$ have the usual pointwise meaning in the set of functions, that is, $(f \wedge g)(x) = f(x) \wedge g(x)$ and $f \leq g$ if and only if $f(x) \leq g(x)$, for all $x \in [0,1]$.

**L** is a complete lattice and the partial orders $\sqsubseteq$ and $\preceq$ coincide. Furthermore, $\bar{0}$ and $\bar{1}$ are the minimum and the maximum, respectively (see [7,8,15,16] for more details). In this setting, our aim will be to find some operators acting as t-norms or t-conorms. They can be defined in any bounded poset as follows.

**Definition 6** [3,4]. *Let $(R, \leq_R, 0_R, 1_R)$ be a bounded poset. The binary operation $T: R^2 \rightarrow R$ is a t-norm on $R$ if:*

1. *$T(a,b) = T(b,a)$ for all $a, b \in R$ (commutativity),*
2. *$T(a, T(b,c)) = T(T(a,b),c)$ for all $a, b, c \in R$ (associativity),*
3. *$T(a, 1_R) = a$, for all $a \in R$ (neutral element),*
4. *Let $a, b, c \in R$ such that $b \leq_R c$, then $T(a,b) \leq_R T(a,c)$ (monotonicity).*

**Definition 7** [3,4]. *A binary operation $S: R^2 \rightarrow R$ is a t-conorm (triangular conorm) on the poset $(R, \leq_R, 0_R, 1_R)$ if the axioms 1, 2 and 4 of the t-norm and the axiom: 3'. $S(a, 0_R) = a$, for all $a \in R$, are satisfied.*

In [10,12] the two following families of binary operations on **M** were proposed. These operations are extensions of the ones given in [16,17].

**Definition 8** *([10,12]). Let $\star$ and $\triangle$ be continuous t-norms on $[0,1]$, and $\triangledown$ a continuous t-conorm on $[0,1]$. For each $f, g \in$ **M**, we define the binary operations $\blacktriangle$ and $\blacktriangledown$ as:*

$$(f \blacktriangle g)(x) = \sup\{f(y) \star g(z) : y \triangle z = x\}, \quad (f \blacktriangledown g)(x) = \sup\{f(y) \star g(z) : y \triangledown z = x\}.$$

In [12] it was shown that $\blacktriangle$ ($\blacktriangledown$) is a t-norm (t-conorm) on **L** given the order $\sqsubseteq$ (in this case $\sqsubseteq \equiv \preceq$).

## 3 Study of Two New Operations in C

In [9, Definition 13], the following novel operations $\perp$ and $\top$ were defined.

**Definition 9** *([9]). Let $f, g \in$ **M**, $\wedge$ the minimum t-norm in $[0,1]$, and $\blacktriangle$, $\blacktriangledown$ the operations given in Definition 8. The following operations are defined:*

$$f \perp g = \begin{cases} f & \text{if } g = \bar{1}, \\ g & \text{if } f = \bar{1}, \\ (f^L \wedge f^R) \blacktriangle (g^L \wedge g^R) & \text{otherwise,} \end{cases}$$

$$f \top g = \begin{cases} f & \text{if } g = \bar{0}, \\ g & \text{if } f = \bar{0}, \\ (f^L \wedge f^R) \blacktriangledown (g^L \wedge g^R) & \text{otherwise.} \end{cases}$$

In [9] it was proven that $\perp$ ($\top$) is t-norm (t-conorm) in some subsets of **M** such as **N**, **L**, **K** or $\boldsymbol{K}_c^{\boldsymbol{F}}$ with respect to the partial order $\sqsubseteq$ ($\preceq$). However, $\perp$ ($\top$) is not generally t-norm (t-conorm) in **C** with respect to $\sqsubseteq$ ($\preceq$). We propose then two new extensions of these operators in order to obtain t-norms and t-conorms in this subset.

**Definition 10.** *Let $f, g \in \boldsymbol{M}$, $\bar{\wedge}$ any t-norm in $[0,1]$, and $\blacktriangle$, $\blacktriangledown$ the operations given in Definition 8. We define the following operations:*

$$f \curlywedge g = \begin{cases} f & \text{if } g = \bar{1}, \\ g & \text{if } f = \bar{1}, \\ (f^L \bar{\wedge} f^R) \blacktriangle (g^L \bar{\wedge} g^R) & \text{otherwise}, \end{cases}$$

$$f \curlyvee g = \begin{cases} f & \text{if } g = \bar{0}, \\ g & \text{if } f = \bar{0}, \\ (f^L \bar{\wedge} f^R) \blacktriangledown (g^L \bar{\wedge} g^R) & \text{otherwise}. \end{cases}$$

Note that, in **C** and taking $\bar{\wedge} = \wedge$, we have $\perp = \curlywedge$ and $\top = \curlyvee$. Additionally, when we work restricted to **C**, it is known that $f = f^L \wedge f^R$, for all $f \in \mathbf{C}$ (see [16]). But, it is not generally true that $f = f^L \bar{\wedge} f^R$, for all $f \in \mathbf{C}$. Therefore, $\curlywedge$ and $\curlyvee$ are not necessarily equivalent to $\perp$ and $\top$ in this case.

In this section we will show that there are some situations where $\curlywedge$ and $\curlyvee$ are neither t-norms nor t-conorms in **C**. Nevertheless, in Sect. 4, we will study these operators for any t-norm $\bar{\wedge}$ by defining two new preorders that relax the conditions of the orders $\sqsubseteq$ and $\preceq$. In the first place we will show that the proposed operators are closed and well defined in **C**.

**Proposition 1.** *$\curlywedge$ and $\curlyvee$ are closed in $\boldsymbol{C}$.*

*Proof.* First, we will check that $f^L \bar{\wedge} f^R \in \mathbf{C}$, for all $f \in \mathbf{M}$, and for all t-norm $\bar{\wedge}$. Let $s = \sup\{f(x) \mid x \in [0,1]\}$. It is easy to check that, for any $x \in [0,1]$, we have either $f^L(x) = s$ or $f^R(x) = s$. Let us fix $x \leq y \leq z$. If $f^L(y) = s$, then $f^L(z) = s$. In addition, $f^R(y) \geq f^R(z)$. Now, since $\bar{\wedge}$ is non-decreasing, we have $(f^L \bar{\wedge} f^R)(y) \geq (f^L \bar{\wedge} f^R)(z)$ and therefore $(f^L \bar{\wedge} f^R)(y) \geq ((f^L \bar{\wedge} f^R)(x)) \wedge ((f^L \bar{\wedge} f^R)(z))$. The case for $f^R(x) = s$ is similar.

As a consequence, $f^L \bar{\wedge} f^R \in \mathbf{C}$, for all $f \in \mathbf{M}$. Now, by [9, Theorem 3], we know that $\blacktriangle$ and $\blacktriangledown$ are closed in **C** and hence $\curlywedge$ and $\curlyvee$ are also closed in **C**.

In [9] the authors showed that the particular operator $\curlywedge$ ($\curlyvee$) denoted by $\sqcap$ ($\sqcup$) is monotonically increasing in **C** respect to parcial order $\sqsubseteq$ ($\preceq$). In the following proposition, we will verify that $\curlywedge$ and $\curlyvee$ do not always satisfy this condition in **C**. Therefore, it is a counterexample that ensures, in general, that $\curlywedge$ and $\curlyvee$ are neither t-norm nor t-conorm on **C** (and consequently on **M**) with respect to $\sqsubseteq$ or $\preceq$.

**Proposition 2.** *Let the operators $\star = \triangle = \wedge$, $\triangledown = \vee$ and $\bar{\wedge} = T_p$ (the product t-norm), in the operations given in Definition 8 and Definition 10. In this case, $\curlywedge$ and $\curlyvee$ are not increasing in every argument on $\boldsymbol{C}$, with respect to any of the orders $\sqsubseteq$ and $\preceq$.*

*Proof.* Let $f, g, h \in \mathbf{C}$ such that $f(x) = \frac{3x}{4}$, for all $x \in [0,1]$,

$$g(x) = \begin{cases} 2x & \text{if } x \in [0, 0.25] \\ 0 & \text{otherwise} \end{cases} \quad \text{and} \quad h(x) = \begin{cases} 2x & \text{if } x \in [0, 0.5] \\ 1 & \text{otherwise.} \end{cases}$$

In this case, according to Theorem 1, $g \sqsubseteq h$. Nevertheless, $(f \curlywedge g) \not\sqsubseteq (f \curlywedge h)$. For instance, it is straightforward to check that $((f^L \barwedge f^R) \blacktriangle (g^L \barwedge g^R))^R(0.125) \wedge ((f^L \barwedge f^R) \blacktriangle (h^L \barwedge h^R))(0.125) > ((f^L \barwedge f^R) \blacktriangle (g^L \barwedge g^R))(0.125)$.

For the operator $\curlyvee$ we have $(p \curlyvee g) \not\sqsubseteq (p \curlyvee h)$ where $p(x) = \frac{3(1-x)}{4}$, for all $x \in [0,1]$. For example, $((p^L \barwedge p^R) \blacktriangledown (g^L \barwedge g^R))^R(0.125) \wedge ((p^L \barwedge p^R) \blacktriangledown (h^L \barwedge h^R))(0.125) > ((p^L \barwedge p^R) \blacktriangledown (g^L \barwedge g^R))(0.125)$.

With respect to the order $\preceq$, we will use the following functions:

$$q(x) = \begin{cases} 2(1-x) & \text{if } x \in [0.75, 1] \\ 0 & \text{otherwise} \end{cases} \quad \text{and} \quad s(x) = \begin{cases} 2(1-x) & \text{if } x \in [0.5, 1] \\ 1 & \text{otherwise.} \end{cases}$$

In this case, according to Theorem 1, $s \preceq q$. However, $(p \curlyvee s) \not\preceq (p \curlyvee q)$ since $((p^L \barwedge p^R) \blacktriangledown (q^L \barwedge q^R))^L(0.875) \wedge ((p^L \barwedge p^R) \blacktriangledown (s^L \barwedge s^R))(0.875) > (p^L \barwedge p^R) \blacktriangledown (q^L \barwedge q^R))(0.875)$.

For the operator $\curlywedge$ we have that $(f \curlywedge s) \not\preceq (f \curlywedge q)$, since, $((f^L \barwedge f^R) \blacktriangle (q^L \barwedge q^R))^L(0.875) \wedge ((f^L \barwedge f^R) \blacktriangle (s^L \barwedge s^R))(0.875) > (f^L \barwedge f^R) \blacktriangle (q^L \barwedge q^R))(0.875)$.

## 4 Analysis of the New Operators with Respect to Some Preorders on M

In the previous section we verified that the operators $\curlywedge$ and $\curlyvee$, in general, were neither t-norms nor t-conorms on $\mathbf{C}$, since monotony failed with respect to the usual partial orders $\sqsubseteq$ and $\preceq$. In order to obtain a suitable framework where these operators are, respectively, t-norm and t-conorm, we introduce a relaxed version of the aforementioned orders. These new relations will be the following preorders denoted by $\trianglelefteq$ and $\Subset$.

**Definition 11.** *Let $f, g \in \mathbf{M}$. The following relations $\trianglelefteq$ and $\Subset$ are defined on $\mathbf{M}$, as follows:*

$$f \trianglelefteq \bar{1}, \forall f \in \mathbf{M};\ \bar{1} \not\trianglelefteq f, \forall f \neq \bar{1}. \ \textit{Otherwise}, f \trianglelefteq g \ \Leftrightarrow \ f \leq g^R,$$

$$\bar{0} \Subset f,\ \forall f \in \mathbf{M};\ f \not\Subset \bar{0},\ \forall f \neq \bar{0}. \ \textit{Otherwise}, f \Subset g \ \Leftrightarrow \ g \leq f^L.$$

*Remark 1.* – Under the conditions given in Definition 11 it is established that $\bar{1}$ is the largest element of $\trianglelefteq$, and $\bar{0}$ is the smallest element of $\Subset$, on $\mathbf{M}$.

- These relations do not satisfy the antisymmetry property, therefore they are not partial orders. For example, let:

$$f(x) = \begin{cases} 1 & \text{if } x \in [0.75, 1], \\ 0 & \text{otherwise,} \end{cases} \qquad g(x) = \begin{cases} 1 & \text{if } x \in [0.8, 1], \\ 0 & \text{otherwise,} \end{cases}$$

$$h(x) = \begin{cases} 1 & \text{if } x \in [0, 0.25], \\ 0 & \text{otherwise,} \end{cases} \quad \text{and} \quad k(x) = \begin{cases} 1 & \text{if } x \in [0, 0.3], \\ 0 & \text{otherwise.} \end{cases}$$

In this case, $f \trianglelefteq g$ and $g \trianglelefteq f$, but $f \neq g$. Moreover, $h \Subset k$ and $k \Subset h$, nevertheless $h \neq k$. Although these relations are not antisymmetric, in the following Proposition 3 we will establish that they satisfy the axioms (reflexivity and transitivity) of a preorder.

**Proposition 3.** *$\trianglelefteq$ and $\Subset$ are preorders on* $\mathbf{M}$.

*Proof.* Let us first analyze the operation $\trianglelefteq$ starting with the reflexivity. Let $f, g, h \in \mathbf{M}$. By Definition 11, we have that $\bar{1} \trianglelefteq \bar{1}$ and in any other case, we know that $f \leq f^R$ (see [16] for more information about the properties of the function $f^R$) and thus that $f \trianglelefteq f$.

Now we will show that it is transitive. Let $f \trianglelefteq g$ and $g \trianglelefteq h$. If $h = \bar{1}$, then, by Definition 11, transitivity is trivial. Let us suppose that $h \neq \bar{1}$ and, consequently, $f, g \neq \bar{1}$. Therefore, $f \leq g^R$ and $g \leq h^R$. From this last relation, $g^R \leq (h^R)^R$ (see Definition 5), i.e., $g^R \leq h^R$. Hence, $f \leq g^R \leq h^R$ and then $f \trianglelefteq h$ which guarantees the transitivity.

The proof to show that the relation $\Subset$ is a preorder on $\mathbf{M}$ is similar.

*Remark 2.* For the functions in $\mathbf{M}$, and in $\mathbf{C}$ in particular, the following statements are true:

- If $f \sqsubseteq g$, then $f \trianglelefteq g$ and if $f \preceq g$ then $f \Subset g$. This is a consequence of Theorem 1 and references [15,16]. This is why we say that the conditions of $\sqsubseteq$ and $\preceq$ are relaxed in the new preorders.
- The function $\mathbf{0} \in \mathbf{M}$ such that $\mathbf{0}(x) = 0$ for all $x \in [0, 1]$ is the smallest and largest element of the preorders $\trianglelefteq$ and $\Subset$, respectively (see Definition 11).
- When we impose the restriction of only using functions on $\mathbf{N}$, $\bar{0}$ and $\bar{1}$ are the smallest and largest element, respectively, of both preorders $\trianglelefteq$ and $\Subset$.

The following proposition establishes that $\curlywedge$ ($\curlyvee$) satisfy the axioms 1, 2 and 3 (1, 2 and 3') of t-norm (t-conorm) on $\mathbf{M}$. In addition, the absorbent elements of these operations are determined.

**Proposition 4.** *The operations $\curlywedge$ and $\curlyvee$ given in Definition 10 are commutative and associative on $\mathbf{M}$. Moreover, $f \curlywedge \bar{1} = f$, $f \curlyvee \bar{0} = f$, $f \curlywedge \mathbf{0} = \mathbf{0}$, and $f \curlyvee \mathbf{0} = \mathbf{0}$, for all $f \in \mathbf{M}$.*

*Proof.* The proof follows directly from Definition 10 and some properties (commutativity, associativity, etc.) of ▲ and ▼ established in [12].

The following Proposition 5 will be useful to prove Proposition 6 where we will establish that, under certain conditions, the operations $\curlywedge$ and $\curlyvee$ satisfy t-norm axiom 4 with respect to $\trianglelefteq$ and $\Subset$, respectively.

**Proposition 5.** *For all $f, g \in \mathbf{M}$, the following holds:*

- $f \blacktriangle g = \bar{1}$ *if and only if* $f = \bar{1}$ *and* $g = \bar{1}$; *and* $f^L \,\bar{\wedge}\, f^R = \bar{1}$ *if and only if* $f = \bar{1}$.
- $f \blacktriangledown g = \bar{0}$ *if and only if* $f = \bar{0}$ *and* $g = \bar{0}$; *and* $f^L \,\bar{\wedge}\, f^R = \bar{0}$ *if and only if* $f = \bar{0}$.

*Proof.* Let us prove that $f \blacktriangle g = \bar{1} \iff f = \bar{1}$ and $g = \bar{1}$:

($\Leftarrow$) Trivial since $f \blacktriangle \bar{1} = \bar{1} \blacktriangle f = f$, $\forall f \in \mathbf{M}$, see [12, Propositions 1, 3].

($\Rightarrow$) If $f \blacktriangle g = \bar{1}$ then $1 = \bar{1}(1) = (f \blacktriangle g)(1) = \sup\{f(y) \star g(z) : y \vartriangle z = 1\} = f(1) \star g(1)$, thus $f(1) = 1$ and $g(1) = 1$ since $\vartriangle$ and $\star$ are t-norms in $[0, 1]$.

We assume that $f \neq \bar{1}$, then there exist, $c < 1$ such that $f(c) > 0$. Therefore, $(f \blacktriangle g)(c) = \sup\{f(y) \star g(z) : y \vartriangle z = c\} \geq f(c) \star g(1) = f(c) > 0$, and so $f \blacktriangle g \neq \bar{1}$. Similarly, it is verified for $g \neq \bar{1}$.

Now, let us prove that $f^L \,\bar{\wedge}\, f^R = \bar{1} \iff f = \bar{1}$. To respect, if $f = \bar{1}$ it is easy to check that $f^L \,\bar{\wedge}\, f^R = \bar{1}$ for every t-norm $\bar{\wedge}$, since $1 \,\bar{\wedge}\, 0 = 0 \,\bar{\wedge}\, 1 = 0$ and $1 \,\bar{\wedge}\, 1 = 1$.

Let us consider now $f \neq \bar{1}$. Note first that $(f^L \bar{\wedge} f^R)(1) = \bar{1}(1) = 1$ if and only if $f^L(1) = 1$ and $f^R(1) = 1$. This last condition implies that $f(1) = f^R(1) = 1$. However, since $f \neq \bar{1}$ and $f(1) = 1$ there must exist $a < 1$ such that $f(a) > 0$, and therefore $f^L(a) > 0$. Furthermore, $1 = f^R(1) = f^R(x)$ for all $x \in [0, 1]$, and then $f^L(a) \,\bar{\wedge}\, f^R(a) = f^L(a) \,\bar{\wedge}\, 1 = f^L(a) > 0$. This means that $f^L \,\bar{\wedge}\, f^R \neq \bar{1}$. In conclusion, $f^L \,\bar{\wedge}\, f^R = \bar{1}$ if and only if $f = \bar{1}$.

The other properties of this Proposition 5 can be proven in a similar way.

The following result establishes a fundamental property for the proposed operators, thereby enabling their utilization as t-norms.

**Proposition 6.** *Let $\curlywedge$ and $\curlyvee$ be calculated with $\bar{\wedge}$ any continuous t-norm in $[0, 1]$. Then, $\curlywedge$ is increasing in each argument on $\mathbf{M}$ with respect to $\trianglelefteq$ and $\curlyvee$ is increasing in each argument with respect to $\Subset$.*

*Proof.* Let us determine if $\curlywedge$ is increasing in each argument with respect to the preorder $\trianglelefteq$. Let $f, g, h \in \mathbf{M}$ with $g \trianglelefteq h$. The following cases may occur:

1. If $f = \bar{1}$, then, $(f \curlywedge g) = g \trianglelefteq h = (f \curlywedge h)$.
2. If $f \neq \bar{1}$ and $g = \bar{1}$. Then, by Definition 11, $h = \bar{1}$. In this case, $(f \curlywedge g) = f \trianglelefteq f = (f \curlywedge h)$.
3. If $f, g \neq \bar{1}$ and $h = \bar{1}$. In this particular case, $f \curlywedge g = (f^L \,\bar{\wedge}\, f^R) \blacktriangle (g^L \,\bar{\wedge}\, g^R)$ and $f \curlywedge h = f$. Here, we must prove that:

$$(f^L \,\bar{\wedge}\, f^R) \blacktriangle (g^L \,\bar{\wedge}\, g^R) \leq f^R. \tag{1}$$

In this regard, we know that $(f^L \bar{\wedge} f^R) \leq (f^L \wedge f^R) \leq f^R$ and $(g^L \bar{\wedge} g^R) \leq \mathbf{1}$ where $\mathbf{1}(x) = 1$ for all $x \in [0,1]$. Therefore, by [12, Proposition 1] and [12, Corollary 1] the next chain of inequalities hold:

$$(f^L \bar{\wedge} f^R)\blacktriangle(g^L \bar{\wedge} g^R) \leq (f^R \blacktriangle \mathbf{1}) = (f^R)^R = f^R$$

i.e., the inequality (1) is satisfied.

4. If $f, g, h \neq \bar{1}$. Then, $f \curlywedge g = (f^L \bar{\wedge} f^R)\blacktriangle(g^L \bar{\wedge} g^R)$ and $f \curlywedge h = (f^L \bar{\wedge} f^R)\blacktriangle(h^L \bar{\wedge} h^R)$. In this particular case, by Proposition 5, it follows that $(f \curlywedge g) \neq \bar{1}$ and $(f \curlywedge h) \neq \bar{1}$. Therefore, it must be proven that $(f \curlywedge g) \leq (f \curlywedge h)^R$. That is

$$(f^L \bar{\wedge} f^R)\blacktriangle(g^L \bar{\wedge} g^R) \leq ((f^L \bar{\wedge} f^R)\blacktriangle(h^L \bar{\wedge} h^R))^R. \tag{2}$$

Regarding this, we have that $((f^L \bar{\wedge} f^R)\blacktriangle(h^L \bar{\wedge} h^R))^R = (f^L \bar{\wedge} f^R)^R \blacktriangle(h^L \bar{\wedge} h^R)^R$, see [12] for more details. Obviously, $(f^L \bar{\wedge} f^R) \leq (f^L \bar{\wedge} f^R)^R$. Therefore, in order for inequality (2) to hold, we only need to prove that:

$$(g^L \bar{\wedge} g^R) \leq (h^L \bar{\wedge} h^R)^R. \tag{3}$$

In this case, since $g \trianglelefteq h$, then $g \leq h^R$, which implies that $g^R \leq (h^R)^R = h^R$. Let $a = \sup g$ and $b = \sup h$. Since $g^R \leq h^R$ then $a \leq b$. Recall that, for any $x \in [0,1]$, we have that $g^L(x) = a$ and $g^R(x) \leq a$, or $g^R(x) = a$ and $g^L(x) \leq a$. Likewise, $h^L(x) = b$ and $h^R(x) \leq b$, or $h^R(x) = b$ and $h^L(x) \leq b$. Furthermore, note that, since $h^L(1) = b$, there exists $c = \inf\{x \in [0,1] \mid h^L(x) = b\}$. Now, we will distinguish between the cases where this infimum is in the set or not. That is:

(a) If $h^L(c) = b$, then for all $x \in [c, 1]$ it is clear that $h^L(x) = b$ and therefore:

$$\begin{aligned}(h^L \bar{\wedge} h^R)^R(x) &\geq (h^L \bar{\wedge} h^R)(x) = h^L(x) \bar{\wedge} h^R(x) = b \bar{\wedge} h^R(x) \\ &\geq a \bar{\wedge} g^R(x) \geq (g^L \bar{\wedge} g^R)(x)\end{aligned} \tag{4}$$

by the monotonicity of the t-norm $\bar{\wedge}$. Let us fix then $x \in [0, c)$. When $h^R(c) = b$ we have:

$$\begin{aligned}(h^L \bar{\wedge} h^R)^R(x) &\geq (h^L \bar{\wedge} h^R)(c) = h^L(c) \bar{\wedge} h^R(c) \\ &= b \bar{\wedge} b \geq a \bar{\wedge} a \geq (g^L \bar{\wedge} g^R)(x)\end{aligned}$$

which would conclude the proof. Otherwise, if $h^R(c) < b$ then $h(c) < b$. In this situation, by [2, Lemma 2.24]:

$$\begin{aligned}b = h^L(c) &= \sup\{h(y) \mid y \leq c\} \\ &= h(c) \vee \sup\{h(y) \mid x < y < c\} \vee \sup\{h(y) \mid y \leq x\} \\ &= h(c) \vee \sup\{h(y) \mid x < y < c\} \vee h^L(x).\end{aligned}$$

By definition of $c$, taking into account that $x < c$ we know that $h^L(x) < b$ an thus $b = \sup\{h(y) \mid x < y < c\}$. Additionally, as $b = h^L(y) \vee h^R(y)$ for all $y \in [0,1]$, it is clear that $h^R(y) = b$ for all $y \in (x,c)$ and thus:

$$\begin{aligned}(h^L \bar{\wedge} h^R)^R(x) &= \sup\{(h^L \bar{\wedge} h^R)(y) \mid y \geq x\} \\ &\geq \sup\{h^L(y) \bar{\wedge} h^R(y) \mid x < y < c\} \\ &= \sup\{h^L(y) \bar{\wedge} b \mid x < y < c\} = \sup\{h^L(y) \mid x < y < c\} \bar{\wedge} b \qquad (5) \\ &\geq \sup\{h(y) \mid x < y < c\} \bar{\wedge} b = b \bar{\wedge} b \geq (g^L \bar{\wedge} g^R)(x)\end{aligned}$$

The identity in line (5) is a consequence of the continuity of $\bar{\wedge}$ by means of [1, Lemma 2.85].

(b) If $h^L(c) < b$, from the definition of $c$ it can be deduced that $h^L(x) = b$ for all $x \in (c,1]$ and the reasoning in (4) also holds. Therefore, let us suppose that $x \in [0,c]$. Hence:

$$\begin{aligned}(h^L \bar{\wedge} h^R)^R(x) &= \sup\{(h^L \bar{\wedge} h^R)(y) \mid y \geq x\} \\ &\geq \sup\{h^L(y) \bar{\wedge} h^R(y) \mid c < y \leq 1\} \\ &= \sup\{b \bar{\wedge} h^R(y) \mid c < y \leq 1\} \\ &= b \bar{\wedge} \sup\{h^R(y) \mid c < y \leq 1\} \\ &\geq b \bar{\wedge} \sup\{h(y) \mid c < y \leq 1\} = b \bar{\wedge} b \geq (g^L \bar{\wedge} g^R)(x)\end{aligned}$$

where the last identity is a consequence of the hypothesis $h^L(c) < b$ as can be checked in the following expression:

$$b = h^L(1) = h^L(c) \vee \sup\{h(y) \mid c < y \leq 1\} = \sup\{h(y) \mid c < y \leq 1\}.$$

Based on the above, it is clear that $\curlywedge$, calculated with a continuous t-norm $\bar{\wedge}$, is increasing in each argument with respect to the preorder $\trianglelefteq$. Similarly, it can be shown that $\curlyvee$, calculated with a continuous t-norm $\bar{\wedge}$, is increasing in each argument with respect to the preorder $\Subset$.

*Remark 3.* Next, we will work with $\bar{\wedge}$ any continuous t-norm in [0,1], on the sets **C** and **M**. In item 1) we will verify that $\curlywedge$ is not increasing in each argument in the preorder $\Subset$, and in item 2) we will verify that $\curlyvee$ is not increasing in each argument in the preorder $\trianglelefteq$.

1) Let $f(x) = 0.1$, $g(x) = 1$ and $h(x) = \bar{1}(x)$, for all $x \in [0,1]$. In this case, $g \Subset h$, but $(f \curlywedge g) \not\Subset (f \curlywedge h)$.
2) Let $f(x) = 0.3$, $g(x) = \bar{0}$ and $h(x) = 1$, for all $x \in [0,1]$. In this case, $g \trianglelefteq h$, however $(f \curlyvee g) \ntrianglelefteq (f \curlyvee h)$.

The next corollary states that the proposed operators can be used as t-norm and t-conorm respectively.

**Corollary 1.** $\curlywedge$ *calculated with any continuous t-norm* $\overline{\wedge}$ *in [0,1], is t-norm on* $\boldsymbol{C}$*,* $\boldsymbol{N}$*,* $\boldsymbol{K}$*,* $\boldsymbol{K}_c^F$*,* $\boldsymbol{L}$ *and* $\boldsymbol{M}$*, respect to the preorder* $\trianglelefteq$*.*

$\curlyvee$ *calculated with any continuous t-norm* $\overline{\wedge}$ *in [0,1], is t-conorm on* $\boldsymbol{C}$*,* $\boldsymbol{N}$*,* $\boldsymbol{K}$*,* $\boldsymbol{K}_c^F$*,* $\boldsymbol{L}$ *and* $\boldsymbol{M}$*, respect to the preorder* $\Subset$*.*

*Remark 4.*
- On $\mathbf{C}$ and all $\mathbf{M}$, $\mathbf{0}$ and $\bar{1}$ are the absorbent and neutral elements, respectively, of $\curlywedge$. In addition, $\mathbf{0}$ and $\bar{0}$ are the absorbent and neutral elements, respectively, of $\curlyvee$.
- On $\mathbf{N}$, $\mathbf{K}$, $\mathbf{K}_c^F$ and $\mathbf{L}$, $\bar{0}$ and $\bar{1}$ are the absorbent and neutral elements, respectively, of $\curlywedge$. In addition, $\bar{1}$ and $\bar{0}$ are the absorbent and neutral elements, respectively, of $\curlyvee$.
- On $\mathbf{C}$ and $\mathbf{M}$, generally, $\curlywedge$ is not t-norm respect to preorder $\Subset$. And, generally, $\curlyvee$ is not t-conorm respect to preorder $\trianglelefteq$.

## 5 Conclusions

In this paper, we have defined the operations $\curlywedge$ and $\curlyvee$, which are extensions of the operations $\perp$ and $\top$, introduced in [9]. While $\curlywedge$ and $\curlyvee$ employ any t-norm in [0,1], $\perp$ and $\top$ are restricted to the *minimum* t-norm in [0,1]. In the present work it was determined that $\curlywedge$ and $\curlyvee$ are closed in $\mathbf{C}$, and satisfy, respectively, the axioms of t-norms and t-conorms (see Definitions 6, 7), except axiom 4 (monotonicity in each argument) on $\mathbf{C}$ and $\mathbf{M}$, with respect to the usual partial orders $\sqsubseteq$ and $\preceq$. Therefore, $\curlywedge$ and $\curlyvee$ are not t-norms nor t-conorms on $\mathbf{C}$ and $\mathbf{M}$, in these partial orders. Consequently, two preorders $\trianglelefteq$ and $\Subset$ were defined and determined on $\mathbf{M}$, and the monotony of the mentioned operations on these preorders was analyzed. In this respect, it was determined that $\curlywedge$ and $\curlyvee$ calculated with $\overline{\wedge}$ continuous t-norm in [0,1], on $\mathbf{C}$, $\mathbf{N}$, $\mathbf{K}$, $\mathbf{K}_c^F$, $\mathbf{L}$ and $\mathbf{M}$, satisfy that, in these conditions, $\curlywedge$ is t-norm with respect to the preorder $\trianglelefteq$ and $\curlyvee$ is t-conorm with respect to the preorder $\Subset$.

In future works it is interesting to analyze if operators that did not satisfy the monotony in the usual partial orders, satisfy them in the preorders established in this work, or in other orders or preorders.

**Acknowledgements.** This paper has been partially supported by the Spanish Ministerio de Ciencia e Innovación/AEI/EU FEDER Funds (grant PID2021-122905NB-C22 and PID2022-139886NB-I00). Pablo Hernández thanks the Vicerrectoría de Investigación y Doctorados de la Universidad San Sebastián, Chile–USS–FIN–24–PASI–11. Francisco Javier Talavera acknowledges the grant from Asociación de Amigos de la Universidad de Navarra.

**Disclosure of Interests.** The authors have no competing interests to declare.

## References

1. Belohlavek, R.: Fuzzy Relational Systems: Foundations and Principles, vol. 20. Springer (2012)

2. Davey, B. A.: Introduction to Lattices and Order. Cambridge University Press, Cambridge (2002)
3. De Baets, B., Mesiar, R.: Triangular norms on product lattices. Fuzzy Sets Syst. **104**, 61–75 (1999)
4. De Cooman, G., Kerre, E.: Order norms on bounded partially ordered sets. J. Fuzzy Math. **2**, 281–310 (1994)
5. Gera, Z., Dombi, J.: Exact calculations of extended logical operations on fuzzy truth values. Fuzzy Sets Syst. **159**(11), 1309–1326 (2008)
6. Gehrke, M., Walker, C., Walker, E.: Some comments on interval-valued fuzzy sets. Int. J. Intell. Syst. **11**, 751–759 (1996)
7. Harding, J., Walker, C., Walker, E.: Convex normal functions revisited. Fuzzy Sets Syst. **161**, 1343–1349 (2010)
8. Harding, J., Walker, C., Walker, E.: Lattices of convex normal functions. Fuzzy Sets Syst. **159**, 1061–1071 (2008)
9. Hernández, P., Talavera, F., Cubillo, S., Torres-Blanc, C., Elorza, J.: Definition of triangular norms and triangular conorms on subfamilies of type-2 fuzzy sets. Axioms **14**(1), 27 (2025)
10. Hernández, P., Cubillo, S., Torres-Blanc, C.: Negations on type-2 fuzzy sets. Fuzzy Sets Syst. **252**, 111–124 (2014)
11. Hernández, P., Cubillo, S., Torres-Blanc, C.: Nuevas operaciones binarias sobre los conjuntos borrosos de tipo 2. In: Actas Multiconferencia CAEPIA 2013, Madrid, Spain, pp. 1250–1259 (2013)
12. Hernández, P., Cubillo, S., Torres-Blanc, C.: On t-norms on type-2 fuzzy sets. IEEE Trans. Fuzzy Syst. **23**(4), 1155–1163 (2015)
13. Mendel, J., Jhon, R.: Type-2 fuzzy sets made Simple. IEEE Trans. Fuzzy Syst. **10**(2), 117–127 (2002)
14. Mizumoto, M., Tanaka, K.: Fuzzy sets of type-2 under algebraic product and algebraic sum. Fuzzy Sets Syst. **5**, 277–290 (1981)
15. Mizumoto, M., Tanaka, K.: Some properties of fuzzy sets of type-2. Inf. Control **31**, 312–340 (1976)
16. Walker, C., Walker, E.: The algebra of fuzzy truth values. Fuzzy Sets Syst. **149**, 309–347 (2005)
17. Walker, C., Walker, E.: T-norms for type-2 fuzzy sets. In: IEEE Proceedings of the International Conference on Fuzzy Systems, 16–21 July 2006, Vancouver, Canadá, pp. 1235–1239 (2006)
18. Wu, X., Chen, G.: Answering an open problem on t-norms for type-2 fuzzy sets. Inform. Sci. **522**, 124–133 (2020)
19. Wu, X., Chen, G., Wang, L.: On union and intersection of type-2 fuzzy sets not expressible by the sup-t-norm extension principle. Fuzzy Sets Syst. **441**, 241–261 (2022)
20. Zadeh, L.: Fuzzy sets. Inf. Control **20**, 301–312 (1965)
21. Zadeh, L.: The concept of a linguistic variable and its application to approximate reasoning-I. Inf. Sci. **8**(3), 199–249 (1975)
22. Zadeh, L.: The concept of a linguistic variable and its application to approximate reasoning-II. Inf. Sci. **8**(4), 301–357 (1975)

# Advancements and Applications of Fuzzy Theory

# Enhanced Anti-Money Laundering Transaction Monitoring via Fuzzy Equivalence in Rule-Based Systems

Igor Rodin[1](✉) and Jelizaveta Jelinska[2]

[1] Elcoin.ai, Lielirbes iela 1, Riga, Latvia
Rodin@elcoin.ai
[2] Institute of Applied Mathematics, Riga Technical University, Riga 1048, Latvia
jelizaveta.jelinska@edu.rtu.lv
http://www.elcoin.ai

**Abstract.** This paper introduces a novel, parsimoniously designed fuzzy logic architecture for Anti-Money Laundering (AML) transaction monitoring (TxM). In contrast to traditional Boolean rule-based systems, our approach employs a minimal yet sufficient fuzzy rule design framework that integrates essential components—flexible membership functions, semantic variable transformation, and statistical test results—to capture the inherent uncertainties in financial transactions. By leveraging a proprietary synthetic dataset that closely mirrors real banking behaviors, our model demonstrates significant improvements in recall, while mitigating vulnerabilities such as threshold manipulation. The parsimony of our design ensures that the architecture remains simple and interpretable, proving that a lean, carefully calibrated fuzzy logic system can effectively address key weaknesses in conventional AML monitoring approaches.

**Keywords:** Fuzzy sets · Anti-Money Laundering · Transaction Monitoring Systems

## 1 Introduction

The rapid adoption of artificial intelligence (AI) and machine learning (ML) in financial systems has revolutionized how organizations detect and mitigate suspicious activities. However, despite advancements in technology, implementing effective solutions remains a challenge due to the complexity of financial data, the rarity of suspicious transactions, and the need for scalable, interpretable models. The objective of this paper is to prove that a lean, carefully calibrated fuzzy logic system can effectively address key weaknesses in conventional Anti-Money Laundering (AML) monitoring approaches.


M. Baczyński et al. (Eds.): EUSFLAT 2025, LNCS 15884, pp. 263–274, 2025.
https://doi.org/10.1007/978-3-031-97228-7_22

## 2 Problem Description

Transaction monitoring (TxM) plays a critical role in identifying financial crimes such as money laundering, terrorist financing, insider trading, and transaction manipulation. These illicit activities pose severe risks to financial institutions, including regulatory penalties, reputational harm, and financial losses. Despite advancements in artificial intelligence (AI) and machine learning (ML), effective AML solutions remain elusive due to inherent complexities such as the rarity of suspicious transactions, scalability requirements, and the need for model interpretability. All approaches typically suffer from low precision and recall. Although such performance statistics are highly confidential and vary by institution, based on over 25 years of practical experience in the field, the author observes that precision is often as low as 10%. This implies that only one in ten alerts ultimately results in a suspicious activity or transaction report (SAR/STR). Furthermore, financial institutions are generally unable to accurately quantify the rate of false negatives, relying instead on back-tests that do not capture complete detection. There are no reliable assessments of how many money laundering transactions within the banking systems are eventually identified [1].

Financial institutions commonly rely on predefined Boolean rule-based systems due to their transparency and ease of regulatory auditing. A typical rule, for example, flags transactions exceeding a monetary threshold within a short timeframe. However, these rigid systems fail to adapt to evolving fraud patterns, rendering them increasingly inadequate.

Additionally, fixed-threshold transaction monitoring systems are inherently vulnerable to exploitation by illicit actors. The Swedbank money laundering case [2] exemplifies how rigid, threshold-based detection mechanisms can be systematically circumvented. Investigations revealed that criminals strategically structured transactions just below the €8,000 threshold to avoid triggering alerts. This tactic enabled them to execute 600 transactions totaling €5 million without raising sufficient suspicion, thereby exposing a critical flaw in conventional threshold-based systems.

Lastly, the use of Boolean rules—with their strict, bivalent logic—is not well suited to handling the complexity of multiple continuous or categorical variables. The process of setting arbitrary thresholds results in significant information loss. For example, country risk is typically categorized using external vendor risk scoring models, such as the Basel AML Index, which generate continuous scores (e.g., 0–9.99) [3]. When a cutoff of 4.00 is used to define a *medium risk* category, a transaction involving Luxembourg (risk score 3.99) may not trigger an alert, whereas one involving Australia (risk score 4.04) will, despite the negligible difference in their actual risk levels. This oversimplification can lead to an inadequate assessment of the true risk associated with transactions.

Despite their limitations, institutions continue to depend on rule-based systems for several reasons, including interpretability, sunk costs, and a flat learning curve for users. Regulators frequently prefer rule-based approaches due to their transparency and straightforward auditing processes. While promising, machine learning alternatives face significant hurdles such as severe class imbalance, data scarcity, and problematic assumptions about clear ground truth labels. Interpretability remains crucial, as outputs directly impact regulatory and legal decisions. Consequently, the current application of AI and ML in transaction monitoring is mainly restricted to assisting human reviewers by speeding up the processing of alerts generated by rule-based systems, a practice known as alert triage. Alert triage places fewer demands on AI interpretability and reliability.

## 3 Originality of the Paper

The originality of our paper lies in our innovative approach—a minimal yet sufficient fuzzy rule design framework. This approach integrates essential components including flexible membership functions, semantic variable transformations, and statistical test results to encapsulate the inherent uncertainties in financial transactions. By leveraging a proprietary synthetic dataset closely mirroring actual banking behaviors, we showcase substantial improvements in recall while significantly reducing vulnerabilities such as threshold manipulation. Our fuzzy logic architecture remains parsimonious, simple, and interpretable, demonstrating that an optimally calibrated fuzzy system can robustly enhance traditional AML monitoring methods. Through our proposed approach we aim to demonstrate how fuzzy methods can effectively integrate multiple knowledge sources, including expert heuristics, statistical testing, and back- testing data, thus addressing crucial gaps in existing AML methodologies and advancing practical capabilities in real-world financial environments.

## 4 Fuzzy Rule-Based Systems in Transaction Monitoring

### 4.1 Fuzzy Rule-Based Systems

Lotfi Zadeh is renowned not only for his foundational work in fuzzy set theory but also for his axiomatic "Vodka Principle"—the tongue-in-cheek notion that, regardless of the problem, vodka will solve it [4]. This quip highlights that even genius mathematicians appreciate both common sense and humor. Beyond this witty remark, Zadeh's contributions to modern mathematics have been profound, laying the groundwork for fuzzy logic.

As discussed, when classifying transactions into the two strict categories of suspicious and non-suspicious, a clear "ground truth" is absent; the boundaries between classes are inherently fuzzy. Given that uncertainty permeates nearly every aspect of AML—from expert opinions to machine learning outputs, whether due to ontological ambiguity or measurement imprecision—the application of fuzzy logic to the AML domain is almost self-evident. This approach assigns degrees of truth rather than forcing rigid binary outcomes, thereby capturing the nuanced complexity of AML data. Consequently, fuzzy algorithms could potentially model complex scenarios more accurately and adaptively, effectively accommodating the inherent variations and uncertainties in financial transactions.

The purpose of our work was to demonstrate that fuzzy techniques can be seamlessly integrated into existing rule-based systems. Rather than replacing these systems entirely, our approach augments them by incorporating fuzzy rule-based systems alongside other strategies such as machine learning and expert analysis. This hybrid methodology leverages the strengths of each technique, resulting in a more robust and nuanced framework for AML transaction monitoring.

### 4.2 Prior Applications of Fuzzy Rule-Based Systems in Transaction Monitoring

Fuzzy rule-based systems have been explored as enhancements to existing methods in financial crime detection, including domains of AML and fraud prevention. Their inherent ability to handle uncertainty and imprecise information renders them useful in multiple scenarios:

1. One widely adopted application is fuzzy name matching for entity recognition. These techniques are primarily employed in sanction screening, where they help identify variations in names that may otherwise elude traditional exact-matching algorithms. Although fuzzy name matching is well documented and has been successfully integrated into financial systems, it is not the central focus of this study. Comprehensive reviews of these methods are available in the literature [5].
2. Another notable application is the use of adaptive fuzzy clustering for anomaly detection. Techniques such as Fuzzy C-Means (FCM) have been shown to improve anomaly detection by uncovering non-obvious groupings in transaction data—groupings that may indicate patterns of money laundering or fraud [6]. By adapting cluster boundaries based on the degree of membership of data points, these methods capture subtle variations that traditional unsupervised learning techniques might miss. Anomaly detection using unsupervised methods are outside the scope of our research.

### 4.3 Gaps in Current Research that This Paper Addresses

Existing research on fuzzy rule-based systems in AML transaction monitoring exhibits several critical shortcomings. Notably, no study has yet demonstrated the application of fuzzy rule-based systems on realistic transaction datasets. Even when datasets are deemed realistic, most ML and AI experiments assume perfectly labeled data and the existence of a clear ground truth—assumptions that rarely hold in real-world financial environments. Furthermore, when diverse sources of information are available—such as expert heuristics on criminal typologies, manual or automated back-testing, and statistical data from SAR/STR reports—there is a tendency to treat the latter as definitive ground truth. This oversimplification fails to account for the inherent complexities and inconsistencies among these data sources.

The challenge of constructing a fuzzy equivalence-based system can be reframed as the task of incorporating multiple knowledge sources into the rule parameters, particularly within the membership functions. An optimal transaction monitoring system must be capable of modeling, fusing, and interpreting knowledge from heterogeneous and typically inconsistent information streams. No research proposed a practical solution for integrating several sources such as: a priori expert knowledge of criminal typologies, which informed the design of rules and the selection of thresholds; and a posteriori statistics including those derived from back-testing.

# 5 Methodology

## 5.1 Description of the Current Boolean Rule System

Traditional rule-based systems in AML transaction monitoring rely on a set of predefined, expert-crafted rules to identify suspicious financial activities. Each rule is designed to flag specific risk scenarios by checking if a transaction meets certain criteria. For instance, one rule targets the rapid movement of funds by monitoring transactions that occur in high-risk regions within a short time frame: if a transaction involves moving funds of €10,000 or more within three days and the counterparty country has a risk rating of at least "medium", an alert is triggered. This rule encapsulates the idea that both the amount of money moved and the country's risk level contribute to identifying potentially suspicious activities. Below is a pseudocode representation of this rule:

```
IF
(CountryRisk = "medium") AND (MovementAmount >= 10000)
AND (MovementTime <= 3 days)
THEN GenerateAlert("Rapid movement of funds detected")
ENDIF
```

## 5.2 Design of the Fuzzy Logic System

Using the above example, fuzzification of the rapid movement of funds rule consists of several key steps. The first step is to convert the crisp term such as "medium" into a fuzzy semantic variable. We define a trapezoidal membership function for the country risk score that assigns a degree of membership to the linguistic term "medium". This function allows countries with risk scores near the threshold to exhibit partial membership, reflecting the gradual transition between risk levels following Basel AML Index. Similarly, fuzzy sets can be defined for the movement amount and the transaction time window to capture uncertainty around the €10,000 and three-day thresholds, respectively.

In the strict rule, the logical AND operator is used to combine the individual conditions. In the fuzzy framework, this operator is replaced by a fuzzy aggregation function—typically a T-norm operator (see Sect. 5.4). While the minimum operator is a common choice, our approach involves the selection or construction of a parameterized aggregation function that is optimized based on empirical data. This optimization adjusts the parameters to best reflect the relative importance of each condition and the degree to which they must all be satisfied. Essentially, the aggregation function serves to combine the fuzzy membership values of the individual conditions into a single overall degree of suspicion.

### 5.3 Defuzzification and Evaluation

To evaluate the efficacy of the fuzzy equivalence-based system in enhancing AML decision-making, we consider two complementary approaches. First, a threshold-based classification method applies an empirically determined cutoff to the similarity scores, enabling the computation of standard performance metrics such as recall, precision, and F1 score. Although this method simplifies evaluation, it may obscure nuanced differences by converting continuous scores into binary outcomes. This first approach was used for our experiments.

Second, a continuous similarity scoring approach ranks transactions based on their similarity scores, thereby providing a prioritized list of cases for investigation. While this ranking aids in resource allocation and risk management, it complicates the direct application of traditional classification metrics. This is approach likely to be preferred for a production system since it facilitates alert triage.

### 5.4 Theoretical Foundations

To quantify the degree of 'suspiciousness' in transactions, we leverage fuzzy relations within the established theoretical framework. Below, we outline the key mathematical foundations underlying our approach.

**Definition 1** *(see e.g. [7]). A fuzzy binary relation $E : X \times X \to [0;1]$ on a set $X$ is called a fuzzy equivalence relation with respect to a t-norm $T$ (or $T$-equivalence), if and only if the following three axioms are fulfilled for all $x, y, z \in X$:*

1. *$E(x, x) = 1$ reflexivity;*
2. *$E(x, y) = E(y, x)$ symmetry;*
3. *$T(E(x, y), E(y, z)) \leq E(x, z)$ $T$-transitivity.*

The following result establishes the principles of construction of fuzzy equivalence relations using pseudo-metrics.

**Theorem 1** [7]. *Let $T$ be a continuous Archimedean t-norm with an additive generator $g$. For any pseudo-metric $d$, the mapping*

$$E_d(x, y) = g^{(-1)}(d(x, y)) \tag{1}$$

*is a $T$-equivalence.*

We will use Hamacher [8] equivalence, which is calculated as:

$$E(x, y) = \frac{\lambda}{e^{d(x,y)} - 1 + \lambda} \tag{2}$$

In our work, we will calculate the equivalence (called also similarity) relations of a value with a given threshold. For example, returning to our rule given in Sect. 4.1 – 2 equivalence scores will be calculated. One for *Movement Amount*, another for *Movement Time*. Note that *Country Risk* is used for filtering, and since there are many rules, other ones cover cases with other levels of country risk (such as high or low).

After we have equivalence scores both for *Movement Amount* and *Movement Time*, we need to aggregate them. That leads to the next theoretical concept.

**Definition 2** *(see e.g. [9]). A function*

$$\boldsymbol{A} : \cup_{n \in N} [0, 1]^n \rightarrow [0, 1]$$

*is called an aggregation operator if it fulfills the following properties:*

*(A1)* $\boldsymbol{A}(x_1, ..., x_n) \leq \boldsymbol{A}(y_1, ..., y_n)$ *whenever* $x_i \leq y_i$ *for all* $i \in 1, ..., n$*;*
*(A2)* $\boldsymbol{A}(x) = x$ *for all* $x \in [0, 1]$*;*
*(A3)* $\boldsymbol{A}(0, ..., 0) = 0$ *and* $\boldsymbol{A}(1, ..., 1) = 1$.

Building on the theoretical foundations outlined in [10], we employ the following formula to compute the similarity score:

**Corollary 1.** *Let* $\boldsymbol{A} : \cup_{n \in N} [0, 1]^n \rightarrow [0, 1]$ *be an aggregation operator defined as:*

$$\boldsymbol{A}(x_1, ..., x_n) = g^{(-1)}\left(\sum_{i=1}^{n} p_i g(x_i)\right), \tag{3}$$

*where*

- $g$ *- additive generator of a t-norm* $T$*;*
- $p_i$ *- weights such that* $1 \leq \sum_{i=1}^{n} p_i$*,*

*then*

$$\begin{aligned} E(x, y) &= E((x_1, ..., x_n), (y_1, ..., y_n)) \\ &= \boldsymbol{A}(E_1(x_1, y_1), ..., E_n(x_n, y_n)) \end{aligned} \tag{4}$$

*is the fuzzy equivalence relation (*$T$*-equivalence) if* $E_i$ *are fuzzy equivalence relations (*$T$*-equivalence) for all* $i = 1, ..., n$*.*

In our work we choose to use Hamacher t-norm equivalence as in 2, and the corresponding aggregated function is:

$$E(d_1, ..., d_n) = \frac{\lambda}{e^{\sum_{i=1}^{n} p_i d_i(x_i, y_i)} - 1 + \lambda} \tag{5}$$

where $\lambda \neq 0$ and optimal $\lambda$ is chosen using techniques as in [11], $p_i$ represents weights satisfying $1 \leq \sum_{i=1}^{n} p_i$, and $d$ denotes the absolute difference between the observed value and the predefined threshold. In our case $n = 2$, but that can be extrapolated to many more dimensions.

# 6 Experimental Setup

## 6.1 Description of the Proprietary Synthetic Dataset

The synthetic dataset was generated using a hybrid approach that combined statistical simulation techniques with extensive manual refinement to mirror authentic banking transaction patterns. Initially, real banking data was analyzed to extract key statistical properties, such as the distribution of transaction amounts, frequencies, and temporal patterns. These properties informed the design of the simulation model, which was tasked with generating 800,000 rows of transactional data across 3,000 unique accounts. The dataset covers 3 month period. Each synthetic transaction replicates critical attributes observed in real data, including the transaction amount, the originating account, debit/credit designation, counterparty account number, and the country associated with the counterparty.

## 6.2 Experimental Design to Compare Boolean and Fuzzy Logic Systems

To evaluate the effectiveness of our proposed method, we iterate through the dataset (which, as a reminder, contains three months of transactional data from 3,000 unique accounts) using a sliding window of four days. This choice is based on the fact that one of the rule dimensions spans a three-day period, but one of the dimensions is about time when threshold of 10000 was reached. *For example, if the threshold of 10000 was reached in 68 h, similarity score is 1. If the threshold was reached in 78 h, similarity score is less than 1.* In the Fig. 1 the similarity score, calculated using 2, is shown for the movement of time dimension.

As a result, we obtain 80 recall and precision scores. We then compare these scores with those obtained using the original rule-based system.

To calculate the recall and precision of our proposed method, we use a similarity score cut-off value of 0.8. If the similarity score is greater than or equal to 0.8, the account is classified as suspicious. The cut-off value was determined empirically to maximize recall.

The graphical results are presented in Fig. 2, while Table 1 provides a summary of the comparative performance of both methods in terms of recall and precision.

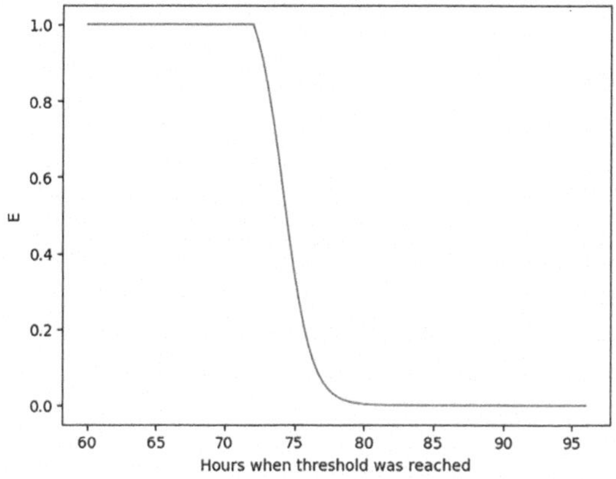


**Fig. 1.** Similarity score depending on the time when threshold was reached.

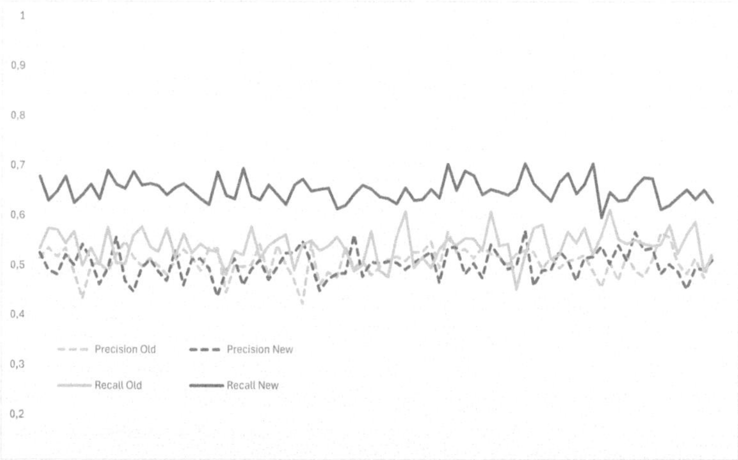


**Fig. 2.** Comparison of precision and recall scores on 80 folds of the dataset.

# 7 Results and Discussion

## 7.1 Comparative Analysis of System Performance

Our results indicate a significant improvement in recall, which increased by 11.61% points—from 54.06% to 65.67%—demonstrating that the fuzzy rule system is more effective at capturing true positives. Although precision experienced a marginal decline of 1.04% points (from 51.42% to 50.38%), this trade-off is acceptable because false negatives—undetected suspicious transactions—can result in severe reputational damage and regulatory penalties, whereas false positives typically lead only to additional investigative effort.

The optimal balance between precision and recall depends on the risk tolerance of the financial institution and the operational costs associated with pro-

**Table 1.** Table of quartiles of the old and the new proposed method.

| Metric | Old Q2 (Q1–Q3) in % | New Q2 (Q1–Q3) in % |
|---|---|---|
| Recall | 54.06 (52.31–55.87) | 65.67 (63.38–66.49) |
| Precision | 51.42 (48.61–53.22) | 50.38 (48.03–51.98) |

cessing false positive alerts [12]. Most banks prioritize enhancing the overall effectiveness of their transaction monitoring systems, placing a higher value on recall given the significant consequences of missed detections. Thus, the substantial improvement in recall observed in our study represents a highly favorable outcome, even when accompanied by a slight reduction in precision.

In summary, the fuzzy rule system offers a beneficial trade-off, improving the detection of suspicious transactions while maintaining an acceptable level of precision. This trade-off aligns well with the operational priorities of financial institutions.

### 7.2 Mitigation of Threshold Exploitation Vulnerabilities

The Swedbank case exemplifies the critical limitations of fixed-threshold transaction monitoring systems and has clearly demonstrated the necessity for such an adaptive rule design. Our approach ensures that even transactions marginally below the defined threshold remain under scrutiny if they exhibit other suspicious characteristics, such as frequency, counterparties, or geographic risk indicators.

By incorporating fuzzy sets, a transaction amount of €9,999 may still trigger a risk score rather than being completely ignored, particularly if it aligns with other risk factors. Our system generates alerts dynamically, considering overlapping risk zones rather than rigid binary classifications. This significantly reduces the vulnerability of AML systems to "structured deposits" designed to avoid regulatory red flags.

### 7.3 Data Enrichment Through Semantic Variable Transformation

We demonstrated that the loss of entropy inherent in rigid classification schemes can negatively impact AML systems by erasing important risk differentiations and limiting the system's ability to identify nuanced suspicious behavior. In contrast, fuzzy logic offers a more sophisticated approach by preserving the richness of the original data. Rather than imposing rigid classifications, fuzzy logic introduces semantic risk variables—such as "low", "medium", "high", and "very high"—that enable continuous gradations in risk assessment. These semantic variables are constructed using manually designed trapezoidal membership functions, effectively capturing subtle variations in risk that are lost in traditional threshold-based approaches.

## 8 Data Availability Statement

The data supporting the findings of this study were obtained under a commercial license from a third-party provider and are subject to confidentiality agreements. Consequently, these data are not publicly available. Researchers interested in accessing the data may contact office@elcoin.ai to inquire about potential access under similar licensing terms.

## 9 Future Research Perspectives

Several avenues remain open for further investigation to enhance and validate the proposed fuzzy logic AML transaction monitoring framework. Firstly, future studies should test our fuzzy equivalence-based approach using larger, real-world banking datasets. Such validation in actual financial environments would strengthen empirical evidence and facilitate broader adoption. Additionally, there is considerable scope for refining the fuzzy aggregation functions through systematic hyperparameter optimization. Developing methodologies to determine optimal T-norm parameters empirically will help further improve model performance and adaptability to specific institutional risk profiles. Another promising research direction involves the design and implementation of advanced methodologies and practical tools specifically aimed at effectively fuzzifying categorical variables. Enhancements in this area could reduce information loss and substantially improve the model's ability to handle complex, real-world financial data.

## 10 Conclusions

Our research advances the field by proposing a novel rule-based design that leverages fuzzy rule-based systems to significantly outperform traditional Boolean-rule systems in AML transaction monitoring. By using parameterized aggregation function that is optimized based on empirical data we offer a robust approach for designing fuzzy-rule systems.

In contrast to earlier works, we validated the performance of fuzzy rule-based systems using realistic datasets, thereby demonstrating their practical utility in complex, real-world environments. Our study further illustrates how the incorporation of linguistic variables into rule antecedents yields a more nuanced risk assessment compared to conventional, binary logic-based approaches.

Finally, our findings highlight the ability of fuzzy rule-based systems to mitigate the risk of rule exploitation by adversaries.

## References


1. FATF. https://www.fatf-gafi.org/en/publications/Digitaltransformation/Opportunities-challenges-new-technologies-for-aml-cft.html. Accessed 20 Feb 2025
2. Baltic News Network. https://shorturl.at/fq2x4. Accessed 20 Feb 2025
3. Basel AML Index. https://index.baselgovernance.org/ranking. Accessed 20 Feb 2025
4. Zadeh, L., Liu, P., Li, H.: Fuzzy Neural Network Theory and Application (2004)
5. Chen, Y., Mathe, J.: Fuzzy computing applications for anti-money laundering and distributed storage system load monitoring. In: World Conference on Soft Computing (2011)
6. Grigorenko, O., Mihailovs, V.: Aggregated fuzzy equivalence relations in clustering process. In: Ciucci, D., et al. (eds.) IPMU 2022. CCIS, vol. 1601, pp. 448–459. Springer, Cham (2022). https://doi.org/10.1007/978-3-031-08971-8_37
7. Zadeh, L.A.: Similarity relations and fuzzy orderings. Inf. Sci. **3**, 177–200 (1971)
8. De Baets, B., Mesiar, R.: Pseudo-metrics and $T$-equivalences. J. Fuzzy Math. **5**, 471–481 (1997)
9. Grabisch, M., Marichal, J.L., Mesiar, R., Pap, E.: Aggregation Functions. Cambridge University Press, Cambridge (2009)
10. Jelinska, J., Grigorenko, O.: Metric-based fuzzy equivalence and inequality relations. In: Lesot, M.J., et al. (eds.) IPMU 2024. LNNS, vol. 1174, pp. 298–309 Springer, Cham (2024). https://doi.org/10.1007/978-3-031-74003-9_24
11. Grigorenko, O., Zemlītis, M.: Fuzzy equivalence relations for solving a multiple objective linear programming problem. In: Lecture Notes in Computer Science, vol. 14069, pp. 112–123 (2023)
12. Rodin, I., Schmuck, R., Hirtreiter, M., Deloitte. https://www.deloitte.com/de/de/services/financial-advisory/perspectives/kuenstliche-intelligenz-geldwaeschebekaempfung.html. Accessed 20 Feb 2025

# An Enhanced Multi Criteria Decision Making Model for Delivery Locker Placement Using TOPSIS and Einstein Operators in a Pythagorean Fuzzy Framework

Gvantsa Tsulaia(✉)

Business and Technology University, I. Chavchavadze Avenue 82, 0162 Tbilisi, Georgia
gvantsa.tsulaia@btu.edu.ge

**Abstract.** Multi Attribute Decision Making (MADM) is vital for evaluating diverse criteria in real-world scenarios. With the rise of e-commerce, efficient delivery systems are essential, particularly in urban areas facing demand for sustainable logistics. Delivery lockers streamline last-mile deliveries, reduce traffic congestion, and minimize environmental impact. This study proposes a robust MADM model to optimize locker placement using the Technique for Order of Preference by Similarity to Ideal Solution (TOPSIS) method with Einstein operators in a Pythagorean fuzzy context. Criteria such as proximity, accessibility, costs, security, and scalability are assessed. Expert judgments are aggregated via Einstein operators to enhance decision stability. The Pythagorean fuzzy TOPSIS approach ranks locations by closeness to the ideal solution. This model offers a scalable, reliable framework for optimizing locker placements, supporting operational efficiency and sustainability in urban areas.

**Keywords:** Pythagorean Fuzzy Sets · Einstein Operators · TOPSIS Approach

## 1 Introduction

The rapid growth of e-commerce has transformed the delivery industry, emphasizing the need for efficient, sustainable systems to address rising demand in urban areas. Delivery lockers have emerged as an effective strategy to reduce congestion, lower environmental impact, and improve operational efficiency. However, realizing these benefits critically depends on the strategic selection of locker locations. The MADM techniques provide a systematic framework for evaluating potential sites across diverse and often conflicting criteria. Nevertheless, conventional approaches frequently encounter challenges in addressing uncertainty and hesitation in expert assessments. To overcome these limitations, this study proposes an enhanced decision-making framework that integrates the TOPSIS within a Pythagorean Fuzzy environment, employing Einstein aggregation operators for improved robustness. The novelty of this study lies in combining the strengths of TOPSIS and Einstein operators to better handle complex urban logistics


M. Baczyński et al. (Eds.): EUSFLAT 2025, LNCS 15884, pp. 275–287, 2025.
https://doi.org/10.1007/978-3-031-97228-7_23

problems under uncertainty. Furthermore, a comparative methodological analysis confirms the advantages of the proposed approach in terms of stability and decision-making consistency.

This paper is structured as follows: Sect. 2 reviews MADM, TOPSIS, and Fuzzy Decision-Making methodologies. Section 3 details the proposed methodology with a focus on Einstein Operators. Section 4 provides a numerical example to illustrate the approach. Section 5 provides a comparative methodological justification, and Sect. 6 concludes with key findings and directions for future research.

## 2 Literature Review and Methodological Background

The problem of MADM entails identifying an optimal alternative that maximizes satisfaction across a set of feasible options evaluated against multiple criteria. MADM problems frequently occur in diverse real-world scenarios. To address the inherent ambiguity of human preferences and the uncertainty associated with the objects being evaluated, Bellman and Zadeh [2] introduced the theory of fuzzy sets as a solution to challenges in Multi Attribute Decision Making. **I**ntuitionistic **F**uzzy **S**ets (**IFS**) were introduced by Atanassov [1] as a generalization of Zadeh's **F**uzzy **S**ets (**FS**) [14]. Each component of IFS, characterized as an **I**ntuitionistic **F**uzzy **N**umber (**IFN**) represented by the tuple $(\mu, v)$, possesses a membership degree $(\mu)$, a non-membership degree $(v)$, and a hesitancy degree $(1 - \mu - v)$. Consequently, IFS is more adept at addressing uncertainty and imprecision compared to classical FS. IFS theory has been extensively examined and implemented across a diverse range of disciplines. However, an IFN denoted as $(\mu, v)$ is subject to a significant constraint: the summation of the degrees of membership and non-membership must be equal to or less than 1. In certain instances, a Decision Maker (DM) may present data for a specific attribute such that the sum of two degrees exceeds 1 (i.e., $\mu + v > 1$). In the works of Yager [11, 12], the author introduced the concept of the **Pythagorean Fuzzy Set (PFS)** as an extension of IFS. This framework features the **Pythagorean Fuzzy Number (PFN)**, denoted as $(\mu, v)$, which imposes a less stringent constraint: the square sum of the degrees of membership and non-membership must be less than or equal to 1 $\left(\mu^2 + v^2 \leq 1\right)$. In general, for practical problems, the PFSs can identify significant decisions that cannot be attained through IFSs. Consequently, the PFSs exhibit enhanced capabilities in processing uncertain information and addressing complex decision-making challenges.

**Definition 2.1 [9, 10].** Let $A$ be a fixed ordinary set. **A q-Rung Orthopair Fuzzy Set** on $A$ is defined as membership grades:

$$A = \{\langle s, \mu_A(s), \nu_A(s)\rangle | s \in S\}, \tag{1}$$

where the functions $\mu_A(s)$ indicates support for membership of $s$ in $A$ and $\nu_A(s)$ indicates support against membership of $s$ in $A$, satisfying the conditions:

$$q \geq 1, 0 \leq \mu_A(s) \leq 1, 0 \leq \nu_A(s) \leq 1, 0 \leq (\mu_A(s))^q + (\nu_A(s))^q \leq 1. \tag{2}$$

The hesitancy associated with a $q$-Rung Orthopair Membership Grade is defined as:

$$Hes_q(s) = \sqrt[q]{1 - ((\mu_A(s))^q + (\nu_A(s))^q)} \tag{3}$$

The strength of commitment viewed at rung $q$ is given by:

$$Str_q(s) = \sqrt[q]{(\mu_A(s))^q + (\nu_A(s))^q} \tag{4}$$

In his 2017 study, Yager demonstrated that Atanassov's Intuitionistic Fuzzy Sets, initially introduced in 1986, can be classified as (q = 1)-rung Orthopair Fuzzy Sets. Furthermore, Yager established that his Pythagorean Fuzzy Sets, developed in 2013, correspond to **(q = 2)-rung Orthopair Fuzzy Sets**. For clarity and convenience, the authors define, for each $s \in S$, $\alpha = \langle s, \mu_\alpha(s), \nu_\alpha(s) \rangle$ as **a (q)-Rung Orthopair Fuzzy Number (q-ROFN)** [9–12]. This is subsequently denoted as $\alpha = (\mu_\alpha, \nu_\alpha)$.

**Definition 2.2 [7, 11].** Suppose $\alpha = (\mu_\alpha, \nu_\alpha)$ is a PFN. A score function $Sc$ of $\alpha$ is defined as:

$$Sc(\alpha) = \mu_\alpha^2 - \nu_\alpha^2. \tag{5}$$

An accuracy function $Ac$ of $\alpha$ is defined as:

$$Ac(\alpha) = \mu_\alpha^2 + \nu_\alpha^2. \tag{6}$$

**Definition 2.3 [7, 11].** Suppose $\alpha = (\mu_\alpha, \nu_\alpha)$ and $\beta = (\mu_\beta, \nu_\beta)$ are any two PFNs, and $Sc(\alpha)$, $Sc(\beta)$ are the score functions, while $Ac(\alpha), Ac(\beta)$ are the accuracy functions of $\alpha$ and $\beta$ respectively. The following rules apply:

$$\begin{aligned} &a)\ \text{if } \mathrm{Sc}(\alpha) > \mathrm{Sc}(\beta),\ \text{then } \beta < \alpha; \\ &b)\ \text{if } \mathrm{Sc}(\alpha) > \mathrm{Sc}(\beta),\ \text{then}: \\ &\text{if } \mathrm{Ac}(\alpha) > \mathrm{Ac}(\beta),\ \text{then } \beta < \alpha. \\ &\text{if } Ac(\alpha) = Ac(\beta),\ \text{then } \beta = \alpha. \end{aligned} \tag{7}$$

**Definition 2.4 [7, 8, 11].** Let $\alpha = (\mu_\alpha, \nu_\alpha)$ represent PFN. For specific cases of $\alpha_1$ and $\alpha_2$, the following fundamental operations are defined:

a) *Complement:*

$$\alpha^c = (\nu_\alpha, \mu_\alpha). \tag{8}$$

b) *Addition:*

$$\alpha_1 \oplus \alpha_2 = \left(\sqrt{\mu_{\alpha_1}^2 + \mu_{\alpha_2}^2 - \mu_{\alpha_1}^2 \cdot \mu_{\alpha_2}^2},\ \nu_{\alpha_1} \cdot \nu_{\alpha_2}\right). \tag{9}$$

c) *Multiplication:*

$$\alpha_1 \otimes \alpha_2 = \left(\mu_{\alpha_1} \cdot \mu_{\alpha_2},\ \sqrt{\nu_{\alpha_1}^2 + \nu_{\alpha_2}^2 - \nu_{\alpha_1}^2 \cdot \nu_{\alpha_2}^2}\right). \tag{10}$$

d) *Minimum:*

$$Min(\alpha_1, \alpha_2) = \left(min\left(\mu_{\alpha_1}, \mu_{\alpha_2}\right),\ max\left(\nu_{\alpha_1}, \nu_{\alpha_2}\right)\right). \tag{11}$$

e) *Maximum:*

$$Max(\alpha_1, \alpha_2) = \left(max\left(\mu_{\alpha_1}, \mu_{\alpha_2}\right),\ min\left(\nu_{\alpha_1}, \nu_{\alpha_2}\right)\right). \tag{12}$$

f) *Scalar Multiplication:*

$$\lambda \cdot \alpha = \left(\sqrt{1-(1-\mu_\alpha^2)^\lambda}, \nu_\alpha^\lambda\right),\ \lambda > 0. \tag{13}$$

g) *Power:*

$$\alpha^\lambda = \left(\mu_\alpha^\lambda, \sqrt{1-(1-\nu_\alpha^2)^\lambda}\right), \lambda > 0. \tag{14}$$

**Definition 2.5 [8].** Suppose $\alpha = (\mu_\alpha, \nu_\alpha)$ and $\beta = \left(\mu_\beta, \nu_\beta\right)$ are any two PFNs. The distance between them is calculated as follows:

$$d(\alpha, \beta) = \frac{1}{2} \cdot \left(\left|\mu_\alpha^2 - \mu_\beta^2\right| + \left|\nu_\alpha^2 - \nu_\beta^2\right|\right) \tag{15}$$

**Definition 2.6 [4,7,11].** Let $\alpha = (\mu_\alpha, \nu_\alpha)$ and $\beta = \left(\mu_\beta, \nu_\beta\right)$ be two PFNs. The Einstein Product and the Einstein Sum, based on the Einstein t-norm and Einstein t-conorm is defined as follows:

$$\alpha \otimes_E \beta = \left(\frac{\mu_\alpha \cdot \mu_\beta}{\sqrt{1+(1-\mu_\alpha^2)\cdot(1-\mu_\beta^2)}}, \frac{\sqrt{\nu_\alpha^2+\nu_\beta^2}}{\sqrt{1+\nu_\alpha^2\cdot\nu_\beta^2}}\right) \tag{16}$$

$$\alpha \otimes_E \beta = \left(\frac{\sqrt{\mu_\alpha^2+\mu_\beta^2}}{\sqrt{1+\mu_\alpha^2\cdot\mu_\beta^2}}, \frac{\nu_\alpha \cdot \nu_\beta}{\sqrt{1+(1-\nu_\alpha^2)\cdot(1-\nu_\beta^2)}}\right) \tag{17}$$

**Definition 2.7 [4, 11].** Let $\alpha_{ij}^k = \left(\mu_{ij}^k, \nu_{ij}^k\right)$ represent the Pythagorean fuzzy evaluation provided by the k-th decision maker for the i-th alternative with respect to the j-th criterion. Let $\omega = (\omega_1, \omega_2, \ldots, \omega_k)^T$ denote the associated weight vector, satisfying $\sum_{s=1}^k \omega_s = 1$ and $\omega_s \in [0,1]$. The aggregation with **PFEWG operator** is defined as follows:

***Aggregated Membership Degree:***

$$\mu_{ij} = \frac{\sqrt{2 \cdot \prod_{s=1}^{k} ((\mu_{ij}^{s})^2)^{\omega_s}}}{\sqrt{\prod_{s=1}^{k} (2 - (\mu_{ij}^{s})^2)^{\omega_s} + \prod_{s=1}^{k} ((\mu_{ij}^{s})^2)^{\omega_s}}}. \tag{18}$$

***Aggregated Non-Membership Degree:***

$$v_{ij} = \frac{\sqrt{\prod_{s=1}^{k} (1 + (v_{ij}^{s})^2)^{\omega_s} - \prod_{s=1}^{k} (1 - (v_{ij}^{s})^2)^{\omega_s}}}{\sqrt{\prod_{s=1}^{k} (1 + (v_{ij}^{s})^2)^{\omega_s} + \prod_{s=1}^{k} (1 - (v_{ij}^{s})^2)^{\omega_s}}}. \tag{19}$$

The integration of Einstein aggregation operators with Pythagorean fuzzy sets through the **Pythagorean Fuzzy Einstein Weighted Geometric (PFEWG)** operator provides a robust framework for managing uncertainty and subjectivity in complex decision-making. This advanced technique enhances reliability and insight, making it highly effective for Multi Criteria Decision Making applications. The TOPSIS introduced by Hwang and Yoon in 1981 [5], is a prominent method for ranking alternatives by minimizing their distance to the positive-ideal solution (PIS) and maximizing their distance from the negative-ideal solution (NIS). When combined with fuzzy set theory, it effectively addresses ambiguity and uncertainty in real-world scenarios [3, 6, 8, 13, 15]. By uniting these methodologies, this study establishes a robust framework to tackle Multi Criteria Decision Making challenges, effectively managing uncertainties and enhancing decision quality.

## 3 Overview of the TOPSIS Methodology for Delivery Locker Selection Using Pythagorean Fuzzy Data

This section outlines the development of a fuzzy Multi Attribute Decision Making approach to solve the delivery locker selection problem. The methodology leverages the fuzzy TOPSIS framework to rank and select optimal locker locations based on multiple criteria. The proposed algorithm for selecting delivery locker locations is structured into the following steps:

**Step 1: Criteria Identification**
A comprehensive framework of evaluation criteria is developed, incorporating industry standards and expert insights to enhance the effectiveness and practicality of the Decision-Making Process. Accordingly, let $C = \{c_1, c_2, \ldots, c_m\}$ represent the set of m attributes, transformed into benefit attributes, used to evaluate and guide the selection of these locations.

**Step 2: Definition of Candidate Locker Locations**
This step identifies a predefined set of candidate locations for delivery locker placement through expert analysis and urban planning. Let the set of potential delivery locker locations be represented as: $\mathcal{L} = \{\ell_1, \ell_2, \ldots, \ell_n\}$, where each $\ell_i$ corresponds to a preselected and feasible candidate location for installing a delivery locker.

**Step 3: Assigning Criteria Ratings to Candidate Locations**

Let DM $= \{\mathrm{dm}_1, \mathrm{dm}_2, \ldots, \mathrm{dm}_k\}$ represent the set of k DMs, who are invited experts contributing to the evaluation process. Based on this notation, let $A_k = \left\{\alpha_{ij}^k \in PFNs, i = 1, \ldots, n; j = 1, \ldots, m\right\}$ denote the performance ratings provided by each expert $dm_k(k = 1,2, .., t)$ for each candidate site $\ell_i(i = 1,2, .., n)$ with respect to the attributes $c_j(j = 1,2, .., m)$.

**Step 4: Construction of Pythagorean Fuzzy Decision Matrices**

In this step, the Pythagorean Fuzzy Decision Making Matrices $D^s = \left[\alpha_{ij}^s\right]_{n\times m} (s = 1,,2, \ldots, t)$ are constructed, where n represents the number of candidate locations, m represents the number of criteria, and t denotes the number of experts providing evaluations. If the criteria consist of both ***benefit-type (BT)*** and ***cost-type (CT)*** attributes, the Pythagorean Fuzzy Decision Matrices $D^s = \left[\alpha_{ij}^s\right]_{n\times m}$ are converted into normalized Pythagorean Fuzzy Decision Matrices $R^s = \left[r_{ij}^s\right]_{n\times m}$,

where:

$$r_{ij}^s = \begin{cases} \alpha_{ij}^s, for\ benefit\ criteria\ c_j \\ \alpha_{ij}^{s\,c}, for\ cost\ criteria\ c_j \end{cases} \tag{20}$$

Here, $\alpha_{ij}^{s\,c}$ is the complement of $\alpha_{ij}^s$, calculated to transform CT criteria into BT criteria. If all criteria are BT, normalization is not required.

**Step 5: Aggregation of Expert Evaluations Using PFEWG Operator**

To aggregate the expert evaluations into a Unified Decision-Making Matrix $R = \left\{\alpha_{ij} | i = 1, .., n; j = 1,2, \ldots, m\right\}$, we use the PFEWG operator. This operator ensures a robust aggregation process by accounting for both the weights of the experts and the Einstein Aggregation rules. The weight vector of the decision makers is denoted as $\omega = (\omega_1, \omega_2, \ldots, \omega_k)^T$, where $\omega_s \in [0,1]$ represents the weight (importance) of the decision maker $dm_s$ for $s = 1,2, \ldots, k$. The sum of the weights satisfies the condition $\sum_{s=1}^k \omega_s = 1$. The aggregated evaluation $\alpha_{ij}$ for alternative $\ell_i$ with respect to attribute $c_j$ is computed using the **PFEWG operator** as follows:

$$\alpha_{ij} = PFEWG\ Aggregation\left(\alpha_{ij}^1, \alpha_{ij}^2, \ldots, \alpha_{ij}^k; \omega_1, \omega_2, \ldots, \omega_k\right)$$

where $\alpha_{ij}^k = \left(\mu_{ij}^k, v_{ij}^k\right)$ is the Pythagorean fuzzy evaluation provided by expert $dm_k$; The membership $\mu_{ij}^k$ and non-membership $v_{ij}^k$ values are aggregated according to Formulas 18, 19.

**Step 6: Calculation of PIS and NIS**

In this step, the TOPSIS method evaluates how closely each locker location aligns with the ideal and least ideal solutions, guiding decision makers toward optimal placement. The PIS and NIS represent the best and worst alternatives based on the evaluation criteria, as defined below:

$$\boldsymbol{PIS}: \quad \ell^+ = \left\{c_j, \alpha_j^+ | \alpha_j^+ \equiv \max_i(\alpha_{ij}), j = 1,2, \ldots, m\right\} \tag{21}$$

where $\alpha_j^+$ is the highest membership degree for attribute $c_j$ across all alternatives.

$$NIS: \quad \ell^- = \left\{c_j, \alpha_j^- | \alpha_j^- \equiv \min_i(\alpha_{ij}), j = 1,2, \ldots, m\right\} \tag{22}$$

where $\alpha_j^-$ is the lowest membership degree for attribute $c_j$ across all alternatives.

**Step 7: Identify Weighted Vector of Criteria**

The weighted vector of the attributes is denoted as $w = (w_1, w_2, \ldots, w_m)^T$, where $w_j \in [0,1]$ represents the relative importance of the j-th attribute $c_j (j = 1,2, \ldots, m)$. The condition $\sum_{j=1}^m w_j = 1$ ensures that the weights are normalized and reflect a consistent distribution of importance across all evaluation criteria.

**Step 8: Calculating Distances to Pythagorean Fuzzy PIS and NIS**

In this step, the weighted distances between each candidate locker location and the Pythagorean fuzzy PIS and NIS are calculated. These distances reflect how closely each candidate aligns with the ideal and least ideal solutions, incorporating the importance of each criterion into the decision-making process. Using the weighted distance measure, the distance between a candidate location $\ell_i$ and the Pythagorean fuzzy PIS and NIS is calculated as the weighted sum of differences between the evaluated PFNs and the extreme solutions. This approach effectively integrates the importance of each criterion into distance calculation, as shown in the following formula:

$$\begin{aligned} D(\ell_i, \ell^+) &= \textstyle\sum_{j=1}^m w_j d_q(\alpha_{ij}, \alpha_j^+) \\ &= \tfrac{1}{2} \cdot \textstyle\sum_{j=1}^m w_j (|(\mu_{\alpha_{ij}})^2 - (\mu_{\alpha_j^+})^2 |\mathrm{D} + |(\nu_{\alpha_{ij}})^2 - (\nu_{\alpha_j^+})^2|) \end{aligned} \tag{23}$$

$$\begin{aligned} D(\ell_i, \ell^-) &= \textstyle\sum_{j=1}^m w_j d_q(\alpha_{ij}, \alpha_j^-) \\ &= \tfrac{1}{2} \cdot \textstyle\sum_{j=1}^m w_j (|(\mu_{\alpha_{ij}})^2 - (\mu_{\alpha_j^-})^2| + |(\nu_{\alpha_{ij}})^2 - (\nu_{\alpha_j^-})^2|) \end{aligned} \tag{24}$$

where:

- $\mathrm{D}(\ell_\mathrm{i}, \ell^+)$ and $\mathrm{D}(\ell_\mathrm{i}, \ell^-)$ denote the distances between the i-th candidate location and the PIS and NIS, respectively.
- $\mathrm{w}_\mathrm{j}$ is the weight of the j-th criterion.
- $\alpha_{ij}$ is the Pythagorean fuzzy evaluation of the i-th candidate location concerning the j-th criterion.
- $\alpha_j^+$ and $\alpha_j^-$ represent the PIS and NIS for the j-th criterion.
- $\mu_{\alpha_{ij}}$ and $\nu_{\alpha_{ij}}$ are the membership and non-membership degrees of $\alpha_{ij}$, respectively.

**Step 9: TOPSIS Aggregation as a Site's Selection Index for Every Alternative**

In the context of the TOPSIS methodology, the performance of each candidate locker location is evaluated based on its proximity to the PIS and its distance from the NIS. Generally, the larger the distance from the NIS $D(\ell_i, \ell^-)$ and the smaller the distance from the PIS $D(\ell_i, \ell^+)$, the better the alternative $\ell_i$ is considered. To quantify this relationship, the **R**elative **C**loseness (**RC**) of each candidate site to the ideal solution is calculated. This measure serves as the site's selection index and is defined as follows:

$$\delta_i \equiv RC(\ell_i) = \frac{D(\ell_i, \ell^-)}{D(\ell_i, \ell^+) + D(\ell_i, \ell^-)}, i = 1, \ldots, n. \quad (25)$$

where:

- $\delta_i$ represents the selection index or the relative closeness of the i-th candidate locker location.
- $D(\ell_i, \ell^+)$ is the distance between the candidate location $\ell_i$ and the PIS.
- $D(\ell_i, \ell^-)$ is the distance between the candidate location $\ell_i$ and the NIS.

**Step 10: Ranking of the Candidate Locker Locations Based on RC Coefficients**
In this final step, the candidate locker locations $\ell_i$, $(i = 1, 2, \ldots, n)$ are ranked according to their ***RC Coefficients*** $\delta_i$, $(i = 1, 2, \ldots, n)$, calculated in the previous steps using the Pythagorean Fuzzy TOPSIS method. A higher $\delta_i$ value indicates a more desirable locker location. The ranking is performed according to the following rule:

For any two alternatives $A_\alpha$ and $A_\beta$:

$$A_\alpha \succcurlyeq A_\beta \text{if and only if } \delta_\alpha \geq \delta_\beta \quad (26)$$

where $\succcurlyeq$ denotes the preference relation on the set of alternatives A. If $\delta_\alpha > \delta_\beta$, then alternative $A_\alpha$ is strictly preferred over $A_\beta$. If $\delta_\alpha = \delta_\beta$, then alternatives $A_\alpha$ and $A_\beta$ are considered equally preferable. If $\delta_\alpha \geq \delta_\beta$, then alternative $A_\beta$ is preferred over $A_\alpha$. This final step ranks all alternatives objectively, enabling logistics providers to optimize their delivery network efficiently. By ranking all candidate locker locations based on their $\delta_i$ values, decision makers can select the most optimal sites for delivery lockers. The locker with the highest $\delta_i$ is the most suitable location, while those with lower values are less favorable.

## 4 Numerical Example for Delivery Locker Location Selection

**Step 1: Criteria Identification**
The selection of evaluation criteria was based on an analysis of real-world urban logistics practices and market needs, ensuring relevance to last-mile delivery optimization. The key criteria for evaluating potential delivery locker locations include: *Proximity to High-Demand Areas* ($c_1$) *– BT, Accessibility by Transport* ($c_2$)*- BT, Installation and Maintenance Costs* ($c_3$) *– CT, Security Measures* ($c_4$)*-BT, Customer Convenience* ($c_5$)*-BT, Scalability* ($c_6$)*-BT, Network Infrastructure* ($c_7$)*-BT.*

**Step 2: Definition of Candidate Locker Locations**
In this numerical example, we assume that the selection of potential delivery locker locations has already been completed. Based on expert evaluations and analysis of urban logistics, five candidate locker locations have been pre-identified for further evaluation. These locations are strategically selected to align with operational efficiency, accessibility, and regulatory compliance. Let the set of these candidate locker locations be represented as: $\mathcal{L} = \{\ell_1, \ell_2, \ell_3, \ell_4, \ell_5\}$, where: $\ell_1$: Locker 1 – Located near a major

residential area; $\ell_2$: Locker 2 – Situated close to a busy shopping center; $\ell_3$: Locker 3 – Positioned near a public transport hub; $\ell_4$: Locker 4 – Located within a corporate business district; $\ell_5$: Locker 5 – Placed near a university campus.

**Step 3: Assigning Criteria Ratings to Candidate Locations**

In this step, three DMs provide their evaluations for five candidate locker locations across seven criteria. These evaluations are expressed using Pythagorean Fuzzy Numbers to effectively capture uncertainty and subjectivity in the decision-making process. The performance ratings are organized into decision matrices for each expert. To ensure clarity, the following notations are used in this example (see Table 1):

- $\text{DM} = \{\text{dm}_1, \text{dm}_2, \text{dm}_3\} \rightarrow$ Set of 3 decision-makers.
- $\mathcal{L} = \{\ell_1, \ell_2, \ell_3, \ell_4, \ell_5\} \rightarrow$ Set of 5 alternatives (Locker 1 to Locker 5).
- $\text{C} = \{\text{c}_1, \text{c}_2, \text{c}_3, \text{c}_4, \text{c}_5, \text{c}_6, \text{c}_7\} \rightarrow$ Set of 7 criteria.
- $A_k = \left\{\alpha_{ij}^k \in PFNs, i = 1, \ldots, 5; j = 1, \ldots, 7\right\} \rightarrow$ Performance rating of decision-maker $\text{dm}_k$ for locker $\ell_i$ concerning criterion $\text{c}_j$.

**Table 1.** Evaluation Matrix $A_1$ by expert 1.

| $l_i/c_j$ | $c_1$ | $c_2$ | $c_3$ | $c_4$ | $c_5$ | $c_6$ | $c_7$ |
|---|---|---|---|---|---|---|---|
| $\ell_1$ | (0.85,0.10) | (0.80, 0.15) | (0.60, 0.30) | (0.75, 0.20) | (0.82, 0.12) | (0.78, 0.18) | (0.83, 0.13) |
| $\ell_2$ | (0.78, 0.18) | (0.75, 0.22) | (0.65, 0.28) | (0.70, 0.25) | (0.80, 0.15) | (0.74, 0.22) | (0.79, 0.17) |
| $\ell_3$ | (0.80, 0.15) | (0.82, 0.12) | (0.70, 0.25) | (0.78, 0.18) | (0.85,0.10) | (0.76, 0.20) | (0.81, 0.14) |
| $\ell_4$ | (0.75, 0.22) | (0.70, 0.25) | (0.55, 0.35) | (0.68, 0.28) | (0.77, 0.18) | (0.72, 0.25) | (0.75, 0.22) |
| $\ell_5$ | (0.88, 0.08) | (0.85, 0.10) | (0.75, 0.20) | (0.82, 0.12) | (0.87, 0.08) | (0.80,0.15) | (0.86, 0.10) |

**Step 4 Construction of Pythagorean Fuzzy Decision Matrices**

In this step, the evaluation matrices provided by the three experts are transformed into Pythagorean Fuzzy Decision Matrices. To ensure a consistent evaluation process, all criteria are normalized to be treated as BT. Specifically, the CT criterion ($c_3$) is converted into a BT criterion using the complement operation. The complement of a Pythagorean Fuzzy Number $\alpha_{ij}^s = (\mu_{ij}, \nu_{ij})$ is calculated as Definition 2.4, Formula 8.

***Note***: *Tables for $A_2$ and $A_3$ evaluation matrices (Step 3) and the normalized matrices (Step 4) are omitted due to space constraints.*

**Step 5: Aggregation of Expert Evaluations Using PFEWG Operator**

In this step, the expert evaluations are aggregated into a unified decision-making matrix $R = \left\{\alpha_{ij} | i = 1, .., 5; j = 1,2, \ldots, 7\right\}$ using the **PFEWG** operator. The aggregation is performed based on Formulas 18, 19, ensuring a balanced and robust combination of expert evaluations by incorporating the relative importance of each expert. The weight vector of the decision-makers is defined as: $\omega = (0.40{,}035{,}0.25)^T$. The weights were assigned based on the experts' years of professional experience in urban logistics and their involvement in decision-making projects. The most experienced expert received the highest weight, reflecting their leading role in the evaluation process. The condition $\sum_{s=1}^{3} \omega_s = 1$ is satisfied, ensuring a valid and consistent aggregation (Table 2).

**Table 2.** Aggregated Evaluation Matrix R.

| $\ell_i/c_j$ | $c_1$ | $c_2$ | $c_3$ | $c_4$ | $c_5$ | $c_6$ | $c_7$ |
|---|---|---|---|---|---|---|---|
| $\ell_1$ | (0.1109, 0.1098) | (0.0922, 0.1660) | (0.0042, 0.6147) | (0.0779, 0.2097) | (0.0994, 0.1361) | (0.0854, 0.1897) | (0.1057, 0.1336) |
| $\ell_2$ | (0.0854, 0.1897) | (0.0758, 0.2211) | (0.0034, 0.6647) | (0.0633, 0.2658) | (0.0899, 0.1660) | (0.0728, 0.2297) | (0.0888, 0.1712) |
| $\ell_3$ | (0.0958, 0.1528) | (0.1019, 0.1212) | (0.0022, 0.7148) | (0.0876, 0.1872) | (0.1109, 0.1098) | (0.0876, 0.1859) | (0.0982, 0.1436) |
| $\ell_4$ | (0.0738, 0.2396) | (0.0633, 0.2633) | (0.0073, 0.5709) | (0.0546, 0.2896) | (0.0821, 0.1897) | (0.0669, 0.2475) | (0.0779, 0.2175) |
| $\ell_5$ | (0.1232, 0.0836) | (0.1135, 0.1013) | (0.0011, 0.7648) | (0.1019, 0.1298) | (0.1190, 0.0899) | (0.0946, 0.1573) | (0.1176, 0.1036) |

**Step 6: Calculation of PIS and NIS**
In this step, PIS and NIS are determined based on the aggregated evaluation matrix obtained in Step 5, using Formulas 21, 22 (Table 3).

**Table 3.** Calculated PIS and NIS.

| | $c_1$ | $c_2$ | $c_3$ | $c_4$ | $c_5$ | $c_6$ | $c_7$ |
|---|---|---|---|---|---|---|---|
| PIS | (0.1232, 0.0836) | (0.1135, 0.1013) | (0.0073, 0.5709) | (0.1019, 0.1298) | (0.1190, 0.0899) | (0.0946, 0.1573) | (0.1176, 0.1036) |
| NIS | (0.0738, 0.2396) | (0.0633, 0.2633) | (0.0011, 0.7648) | (0.0546, 0.2896) | (0.0821, 0.1897) | (0.0669, 0.2475) | (0.0779, 0.2175) |

The PIS represents the most desirable (best) values for each criterion, while the NIS reflects the least desirable (worst) values.

**Step 7: Identify Weighted Vector of Criteria**
The weight vector of the criteria is defined as:

$$w = (0.20, 0.20, 0.15, 0.15, 0.15, 0.10, 0.05)^T.$$

This vector reflects the relative importance of each criterion in the decision-making process: Proximity ($c_1$) and Accessibility ($c_2$) are assigned to have the highest weights ($w_1 = w_2 = 0.20$) due to their critical role in ensuring efficient delivery and customer convenience. Cost ($c_3$), Security ($c_4$), and Convenience ($c_5$) are moderately weighted ($w_3 = w_4 = w_5 = 0.15$), reflecting their significant but balanced impact on decision-making. Scalability ($c_6$) is assigned to a lower weight ($w_5 = 0.10$), as it is more relevant for future planning than immediate operations. Network Infrastructure ($c_7$) has the lowest weight ($w_7 = 0.05$), as it is essential but less critical compared to other criteria in the current context. The condition $\sum_{j=1}^{7} w_j = 1$ is satisfied, ensuring a consistent and balanced weighting scheme.

**Step 8: Calculating Distances to Pythagorean Fuzzy PIS and NIS**
The computed distances between the candidate lockers and the PIS and NIS are presented below (Table 4):

**Table 4.** Calculated Distances.

| | Distance to PIS | Distance to NIS |
|---|---|---|
| $\ell_1$ | 0.0112 | 0.0324 |
| $\ell_2$ | 0.0256 | 0.0180 |
| $\ell_3$ | 0.0197 | 0.0239 |
| $\ell_4$ | 0.0242 | 0.0194 |
| $\ell_5$ | 0.0194 | 0.0242 |

Locker 1 ($\ell_1$) has the shortest distance to the PIS and the longest distance to the NIS, making it the most desirable candidate. Locker 2 ($\ell_2$) has the longest distance to the PIS and the shortest distance to the NIS, making it the least favorable choice.

**Step 9: TOPSIS Aggregation**
Using the distances $D(cl_i, cl^+)$ and $D(cl_i, cl^-)$ calculated in Step 8, the RC to the ideal solution is computed for each candidate locker location using Formula 25. The computed RCs ($\delta_i$, $i = 1, \ldots, 5$) values are as follows:

$$\delta_1 = 0.7431;\ \delta_2 = 0.4128;\ \delta_3 = 0.5482;\ \delta_4 = 0.4450;\ \delta_5 = 0.5550;$$

The locker location with the highest $\delta_i$ value is considered the most suitable for placement. This ranking method ensures that the selection balances proximity to the PIS and distance from the NIS.

**Step 10: Ranking of the Candidate Locker Locations Based on RC Coefficients**
Based on the Relative Closeness Coefficients $\delta_i$, (i = 1,2, ..., 5), calculated in Step 9, The ranking results are as follows:

$$\ell_1 \succcurlyeq \ell_5 \succcurlyeq \ell_3 \succcurlyeq \ell_4 \succcurlyeq \ell_2.$$

Locker 1 ($\ell_1$) has the highest $\delta_i$ value (0.7431) and is the most suitable location for the delivery locker. Locker 2 ($\ell_2$) has the lowest $\delta_i$ value (0.4128), making it the least favorable option. This step provides decision makers with a clear and objective ranking of the candidate locker locations, enabling them to select the most optimal sites for delivery lockers.

## 5 Comparative Analysis and Methodological Justification

In the proposed model, TOPSIS was selected due to its ability to simultaneously minimize the distance from the PIS and maximize the distance from the NIS, providing a balanced and intuitive framework for evaluating alternatives under multiple conflicting criteria. Unlike other MADM methods such as AHP or VIKOR, TOPSIS offers computational simplicity and a natural extension to fuzzy contexts, making it highly suitable for practical, uncertainty-prone logistics problems. Traditional aggregation techniques such as the arithmetic mean, or weighted average often struggle with extreme evaluations and high hesitancy levels characteristic of Pythagorean fuzzy sets. To overcome these limitations, Einstein aggregation operators were adopted. Their mathematical structure effectively mitigates the influence of outliers and better models the interaction between membership, non-membership, and hesitancy degrees, ensuring more robust aggregation results. Thus, the combination of TOPSIS with Einstein aggregation operators provides a more reliable, stable, and theoretically consistent framework for complex multi-criteria decision-making problems involving uncertainty, such as the delivery locker placement problem addressed in this study. A comparative analysis between traditional aggregation operators and the Einstein-based approach was conducted during the model validation phase. Given the page limit restrictions, detailed numerical results are not reported here. However, the findings confirmed that Einstein operators provided enhanced stability and consistency in decision outcomes, particularly under high uncertainty conditions.

## 6 Conclusion and Future Plans

This study presents a comprehensive multi-criteria decision-making framework for selecting delivery locker locations by integrating the fuzzy TOPSIS methodology with the PFEWG operator in a Pythagorean fuzzy environment. The model effectively addresses uncertainty and incorporates expert opinions of varying importance, offering a robust and structured solution for last-mile logistics optimization. While the numerical case is illustrative, the criteria selection and expert inputs are based on realistic urban logistics scenarios, supporting the model's practical relevance. Although real-world implementation is beyond the scope of this study, the proposed framework offers insights that may inform urban logistics strategies and guide future applications in policy-related contexts. Future research may focus on incorporating IoT-based real-time data and exploring machine learning techniques for dynamic criteria weighting to enhance adaptability and scalability.

**Acknowledgments.** The author sincerely thanks the anonymous reviewers for their insightful comments and constructive feedback.

## References


1. Atanassov, K.: Intuitionistic fuzzy sets. Fuzzy Sets Syst. **20**, 87–96 (1986)
2. Bellman, R., Zadeh, L.A.: Decision making in a fuzzy environment. Manage. Sci. **17**(4), 141–164 (1970)
3. Chu, T.C.: Facility location selection using fuzzy TOPSIS under group decisions. Internat. J. Uncertain. Fuzziness Knowl.-Based Syst. **10**(6), 687–701 (2002)
4. Garg, H.: Generalized Pythagorean fuzzy Einstein aggregation operators using entropy measures for multi attribute decision making. J. Intell. Fuzzy Syst. (2017)
5. Hwang, C.L., Yoon, K.: Multiple Attribute Decision Making: Methods and Applications. Springer-Verlag, New York (1981)
6. Jahanshahloo, G.R., Hosseinzadeh Lotfi, F., Izadikhah, M.: Extension of the TOPSIS method for decision-making problems with fuzzy data. Appl. Math. Comput. **181**, 1544–1551 (2006)
7. Rahman, K., Abdullah, S., Ahmad, R., Ullah, M.: Pythagorean fuzzy Einstein weighted geometric aggregation operator and their application to multiple attribute group decision making. J. Intell. Fuzzy Syst. **33**(2), 635–647 (2017)
8. Sirbiladze, G., Sikharulidze, A.: Pythagorean fuzzy TOPSIS approach to facility location selection problem in extreme environments. WSEAS Trans. Circ. Syst. **18**, 167–173 (2019)
9. Yager, R.R.: Aspects of generalized orthopair fuzzy sets. Int. J. Intell. Syst. **33**(11), 2154–2174 (2018)
10. Yager, R.R.: Generalized orthopair fuzzy sets. IEEE Trans. Fuzzy Syst. **25**(5), 1222–1230 (2017)
11. Yager, R.R.: Pythagorean fuzzy subsets. In: Proceedings of the Joint IFSA Congress and NAFIPS Meeting, pp. 357–361 (2013)
12. Yager, R.R.: Pythagorean membership grades in multicriteria decision making. IEEE Trans. Fuzzy Syst. **22**(4), 958–965 (2014)
13. Yong, D.: Plant location selection based on fuzzy TOPSIS. Int. J. Adv. Manuf. Technol. **28**, 839–844 (2006)
14. Zadeh, L.A.: Fuzzy sets. Inf. Control **8**, 338–353 (1965)
15. Zhang, X., Xu, Z.: Extension of TOPSIS to multiple criteria decision making with Pythagorean fuzzy sets. Int. J. Intell. Syst. **29**, 1061–1078 (2014)

# How to Share a Success, How to Share a Crisis, and How All This is Related to Fuzzy

Olga Kosheleva[1] and Vladik Kreinovich[2](✉)

[1] Department of Teacher Education, University of Texas at El Paso, 500 W. University, El Paso, TX 79968, USA
olgak@utep.edu

[2] Department of Computer Science, University of Texas at El Paso, 500 W. University, El Paso, TX 79968, USA
vladik@utep.edu

**Abstract.** In many practical situations, a group of people needs to share a success. What is the fair way to share this success? Nobelist John Nash showed that under reasonable conditions, the group should select the alternative for which the product of utility gains is the largest possible. This solution makes perfect sense from the fuzzy-formalized commonsense viewpoint: it maximizes the degree of confidence that all participants are happy. A natural question is: can we extend this result to a different class of situations, when a group of people needs to share sacrifices caused by a crisis? In this paper, we prove that in this case, no solution satisfies the same set of conditions. We also explain how to actually fairly distribute needed sacrifices in the case of a crisis.

**Keywords:** fair division · fair distribution of sacrifices · Nash's bargaining solution · fuzzy techniques

## 1 Formulation of the Problem

**How to Share a Success: A Problem.** Often, a group of people has an opportunity to benefit all its members. For example, family members get an inheritance in which their late relative did not specify who gets what. In many such cases, there are many possible alternative decisions. In some of these possible alternatives, some of the participants benefit more, in others, other participants benefit more. Which of these alternatives should we choose?

**Known Solution: Nash's Bargaining Solution and its Relation to Fuzzy.** This problem is well studied in decision theory; see, e.g., [2,3,5,6,10, 11,14]. The solution to this problem was provided by John Nash – who later won a Nobel prize for his research; see, e.g., [6,8,9]. He showed that under some reasonable requirements (that we will describe later), the group should select an


M. Baczyński et al. (Eds.): EUSFLAT 2025, LNCS 15884, pp. 288–298, 2025.
https://doi.org/10.1007/978-3-031-97228-7_24

alternative for which the product $U_1 \cdot U_2 \cdot \ldots \cdot U_n$ of their utility gains $U_i$ is the largest possible. This solution is known as *Nash's bargaining solution.*

This solution has a natural interpretation in fuzzy logic; see, e.g., [1,4,7, 12,13,15]. Indeed, it is reasonable to make sure that everyone is as happy as possible, i.e., that the 1st person is happy *and* the 2nd person is happy, etc. Thus, it makes sense to select an alternative for which our degree of confidence in the statement "the 1st person is happy and the 2nd person is happy, etc." is the largest possible. It is natural to use utility gain $U_i$ as the measure of happiness. To combine these degrees, we can use one of the most widely used "and"-operations: algebraic product. Then, our degree of confidence that an alternative makes everyone happy is equal to the product of utilities – which is exactly what Nash's bargaining solution is about.

**But What if There is a Crisis?** Nash's bargaining solution is only applicable in situations of success, when everyone gains. But sometimes, we encounter the opposite situation – of a crisis, when everyone needs to sacrifice. For example, there is an overall budget cut, and some salaries need to be cut: what is the fair way to do it? In general, what is the fair way to share a crisis?

**What We do in this Paper.** In this paper, we analyze what is the fair way to share a crisis, i.e., a situation when we need to decrease utilities.

Since our starting point is utility-based Nash's bargaining solution, we start the paper with Sect. 2 that reminds the reader what is utility and how Nash's bargaining solution is justified. In Sect. 3, we show that a similar approach – based on natural requirements – does not work for the case of a crisis. In Sect. 4, we provide a different set of requirements and show that it enables us to come up with an (almost) unique fair solution. For readers' convenience, all the proofs are placed in special Sect. 5.

## 2 Utility and Nash's Bargaining Solution: A Brief Reminder

**What is Utility.** One of the main objectives of decision theory is to help people make decisions in complex situations. In situations in which there is a very large number of alternatives, it is not possible for a person to process all this data by hand, we need to use computers.

Information about different alternatives comes in different formats, with words, etc. Computers, however, are not very good in processing words, they are much better in processing numbers – this is what they were originally designed for. So, to effectively use computers, we need to describe all the available information in numerical terms. In particular, we need to describe people's preferences in numerical form. For this description, the notion of utility was invented.

This notion allows us to assign, to each alternative $a$, a number $u(a)$ – called its *utility* – so that $a$ is preferable to $b$ if and only if $u(a)$ is larger than $u(b)$. To describe the utilities, we need to select two extreme alternatives, ideally not realistic:

- a very bad alternative $a_-$ which is worse than any actual alternatives, and
- a very good alternative $a_+$ which is better than any actual alternative.

Once these alternatives are selected, we can form, for each value $p$ from the interval $[0, 1]$, a *lottery* $L(p)$ in which we get $a_+$ with probability $p$ and $a_-$ with the remaining probability $1-p$. Of course, the larger the probability $p$ of getting a very good outcome, the better the lottery: if $p > p'$ then, for the user, the lottery $L(p)$ is better than the lottery $L(p')$; we will denote this preference by $L(p) \succ L(p')$.

To find a numerical value $u(a)$ corresponding to an alternative $a$, we need to compare $a$ with lotteries $L(p)$ corresponding to different values $p \in [0, 1]$. For each $p$:

- either $a$ is better ($a \succ L(p)$),
- or the lottery is better ($L(p) \succ a$),
- or the alternative has the same value to the user as the lottery; we will denote this by $a \sim L(p)$.

When $p$ is small, the lottery $L(p)$ is close to the very bad alternative $a_-$ and is, therefore, worse than $a$: $a \succ L(p)$. On the other hand, when $p$ is close to 1, the lottery $L(p)$ is close to the very good alternative $a_+$ and is, therefore, better than $a$: $L(p) \succ a$. One can show that there exists a threshold value $u(a)$ that separates the values $p$ for which $a \succ L(p)$ from the values $p$ for which $L(p) \succ a$: this value is equal to

$$u(a) = \sup\{p : a \succ L(p)\} = \inf\{p : L(p) \succ a\}.$$

This threshold value is called the utility of the alternative $a$.

It can be proven that for any set of alternatives $a_1, \ldots, a_n$, if we consider a lottery in which we get $a_i$ with probability $p_i$, then the utility of this lottery is equal to $p_1 \cdot u(a_1) + \ldots + p_n \cdot u(a_n)$.

*Comments.*

- At first glance, this notion may appear to be not very practical: there are infinitely many possible values $p$, so comparing the alternative $a$ with all these lotteries may take forever. However, this is not an obstacle: we can find the utility value really fast if we use bisection. Namely, we start with the interval $[\underline{u}, \overline{u}] = [0, 1]$ that contains the actual (unknown) value $u(a)$. At each iteration, we decrease this interval – while making sure that the shrank interval still contains $u(a)$. Namely, we compute the midpoint $\widetilde{u}$ of the current interval, and compare the alternative $a$ with the lottery $L(\widetilde{u})$.
  - If $a$ is better than $L(\widetilde{u})$, this means that $u(a)$ is located in the interval $[\widetilde{u}, \overline{u}]$.
  - If $a$ is worse than $L(\widetilde{u})$, this means that $u(a)$ is located in the interval $[\underline{u}, \widetilde{u}]$.

  On each iteration, we make one comparison, and the interval becomes twice narrower. In $k$ iterations, we thus get the interval of width $2^{-k}$. We stop when the width of this interval because smaller than a given accuracy $\varepsilon$. This way, the midpoint of the resulting interval approximates $u(a)$ with accuracy $\varepsilon/2$. So, in 6 iteration, we reach accuracy 1%, and in 9 iterations, we reach accuracy 0.1%.

- Please note that the notion of utility is simply a reflection of the person's preferences, it does not mean that this person only cares about him/herself. In general, a person's preferences depend not only on this person's gains or losses, they are affected by gains and losses of others. Accordingly, the person's utility of each alternative depends not only on this person's gains and losses, it also depends on gains and losses of others.

**Utility is Defined Modulo a Strictly Increasing Linear Transformation.** The above definition of utility depends on the selection of the two extreme alternatives $a_-$ and $a_+$. If we select a different pair $(a'_-, a'_+)$, then, in general, we get different numerical values of the utility. It can be proven that the new utility values $u'(a)$ can be obtained from the original ones $u(a)$ by a strictly increasing linear transformation. In precise terms, there exist constants $c > 0$ and $d$ for which, for every alternative $a$, we have $u'(a) = c \cdot u(a) + d$.

**Nash's Bargaining Solution: Natural Requirements and the Resulting Criterion.** In the success situations, we start with some starting state, which is known as the *status quo* state, in which the participants' utilities form a tuple $s \stackrel{\text{def}}{=} (s_1, \ldots, s_n)$. We have the set $S$ of different possible alternative in which everyone gains, i.e., in which for the resulting utilities $u = (u_1, \ldots, u_n)$ we have $u_i > s_i$ for all $i$. For each two possible alternatives $u$ and $u'$, it is also possible, for each value $p \in [0, 1]$, to have a lottery in which we get $u$ with probability $p$ and $u'$ with the remaining probability $1 - p$. As we have mentioned, the utility of this lottery is equal to $p \cdot u + (1 - p) \cdot u'$. This is an example of a convex combination of the two vectors $u$ and $u'$. Thus, the set $S$ should contain, with every two vectors, its convex combination – i.e., $S$ should be a convex set. We need to come up with a group-based preference relation $\succ_s$ between the tuples.

Let us list natural requirements. First is what is called *Pareto optimality*: if $u_i > u'_i$ for all $i$ (we will denote it by $u > u'$), then we should have $u \succ_s u'$. Second, the preference relation should only depend on the preferences, it should not depend on the choice of $a_-$ and $a_+$ for each person. In other words, for every two tuples $c = (c_1, \ldots, c_n)$ with $c_i > 0$ for all $i$ and $d = (d_1, \ldots, d_n)$, if we denote

$$T_{c,d}(u) \stackrel{\text{def}}{=} (c_1 \cdot u_1 + d_1, \ldots, c_n \cdot u_n + d_n),$$

then $u \succ_s u'$ should imply $T_{c,d}(u) \succ_{T_{c,d}(s)} T_{c,d}(u')$. Third, preferences should not depend on how we number the participants. If we swap $i$ and $j$ – we will denote this transformation by $\pi_{i,j}$ – then preference should not change, i.e., $u \succ_s u'$, then $\pi_{i,j}(u) \succ_{\pi_{i,j}(s)} \pi_{i,j}(u')$.

Finally, the solution should be fair: equal participants should get equal benefit. In precise terms, if both the status quo state $s$ and the set $S$ do not change under the swap, i.e., if $\pi_{i,j}(s) = s$ and $\pi_{i,j}(S) = S$, then for every vector $u \in S$

there should exist a vector $u'$ which is either better or of the same quality as $u$ (we will denote it by $u' \succeq_s u$) for which $\pi_{i,j}(u') = u'$.

Let us describe these conditions in precise terms.

**Definition 1.** *Let $n > 1$ be an integer. A binary relation $\succeq$ on a set $A$ is called a* total pre-order *if it satisfied the following three conditions for all $a$, $b$, and $c$:*

- *if $a \succeq b$ and $b \succeq c$, then $a \succeq c$ (*transitivity*),*
- *$a \succeq a$ (*reflexivity*), and*
- *$a \succeq b$ or $b \succeq a$ (*totality*).*

*Notations.* For each such relation:

- if $a \succeq b$ and $b \not\succeq a$, we will denote it by $a \succ b$, and
- if $a \succeq b$ and $b \succeq a$, we will denote it by $a \sim b$.

**Definition 2.** *Let $n > 1$ be an integer. We say that we have a* preference relation *if for every vector $s \in \mathbb{R}^n$, we have a total pre-order relation $\preceq_s$ on the set of all tuples $x$ for which $x > s$. We say that a preference relation is:*

- Pareto-optimal *if $u < u'$ implies $u \succ u'$;*
- scale-invariant *if for every two tuples $c = (c_1, \ldots, c_n)$ with $c_i > 0$ for all $i$ and $d = (d_1, \ldots, d_n)$, $u \succeq_s u'$ implies $T_{c,d}(u) \succeq_{T_{c,d}(s)} T_{c,d}(u')$, where we denoted $T_{c,d}(u) \stackrel{\text{def}}{=} (c_1 \cdot u_1 + d_1, \ldots, c_n \cdot u_n + d_n)$;*
- anonymous *if for every $i$ and $j$, $u \succeq_s u'$ implies $\pi_{i,j}(u) \succeq_{\pi_{i,j}(s)} \pi_{i,j}(u')$, where $\pi_{i,j}$ swaps elements $u_i$ and $u_j$ in a vector; and*
- fair *if for every vector $s$ and for every convex set $S$ all of whose elements $x$ satisfy the condition $x > s$, once $\pi_{i,j}(s) = s$ and $\pi_{i,j}(S) = S$, then for every vector $u \in S$ there should exist a vector $u'$ which is either better or of the same quality as $u$ (we will denote it by $u' \succeq_s u$) for which $\pi_{i,j}(u') = u'$.*

**Proposition 1.** *For every $n$, for every preference relation $\succeq_s$, the following two conditions are equivalent:*

- *the preference relation is Pareto-optimal, scale-invariant, anonymous, and fair;*
- *the preference relation has Nash's form*

$$u \succeq_s u' \leftrightarrow \prod_{i=1}^{n} U_i \geq \prod_{i=1}^{n} U_i',$$

*where we denoted $U_i \stackrel{\text{def}}{=} u_i - s_i$ and $U_i' \stackrel{\text{def}}{=} u_i' - s_i$.*

*Comment.* In our proof, we will show that we do not actually need the fairness condition: in this case, it follows from the other three conditions. However, we keep this reasonable condition in the definition, since, as we show later, in the crisis case, it does not automatically follow from the other conditions.

## 3 Can a Similar Approach Find a Fair Way to Share a Crisis? Unfortunately, No

**Discussion.** In case of a crisis, when we can no longer maintain the status quo level, fairness means that everyone should contribute, i.e., that we only consider vectors $x$ for which $u_i < s_i$ for all $i$. In this case, it is reasonable to make similar requirements about preferences as in the case of success – Pareto-optimality, scale-invariance, etc. Unfortunately, in this case, it is not possible to satisfy all these four conditions.

**Definition 3.** *Let $n > 1$ be an integer. We say that we have a* crisis-related preference relation *if for every vector $s \in \mathbb{R}^n$, we have a total pre-order relation $\preceq_s$ on the set of all tuples $x_i$ for which $x_i < s_i$ for all $i$.*

**Proposition 2.** *No crisis-related preferences relation is Pareto-optimal, scale-invariant, anonymous, and fair.*

*Comment.* As we can see from the proof, if we do not impose the fairness condition, then the smaller the product of losses $s_i - u_i$, the better. In this case, there is no best outcome, but we can get as close to the best if we let at least one participant to keep almost everything, i.e., to have $u_i \approx s_i$ – while others will suffer. This is clearly not a fair solution.

## 4 So What is a Fair Way to Share a Crisis?

**Discussion.** The negative result from the previous section shows that we cannot come up with a fair solution if all we know is the current state – the status quo state $s$. So, to come up with a fair solution, a natural idea is to also take into account the state $s'$ at some previous moment of time.

So, we need a mapping – or maybe several possible mappings – that will, given two vectors $s$ and $s'$, compute the reduced-gain vector $u$, with $u_i < s_i$. Similarly to the case of sharing a gain, it makes sense to require scale-invariance. Thus, we arrive at the following definition.

**Definition 4.** *By* crisis-related decision function, *we mean a continuous function $F(s, s')$ that transforms pair of tuples into a new tuple $s''$ for which $s'' \le s$. We say that the decision function is:*

- scale-invariant *if for every two tuples $c > 0$ and $d$, $s'' = F(s, s')$ implies $T_{c,d}(s'') = F(T_{c,d}(s), T_{c,d}(s'))$;*
- anonymous *if for every $i$ and $j$, $s'' = F(s, s')$ implies*

$$\pi_{i,j}(s'') = F(\pi_{i,j}(s), \pi_{i,j}(s')).$$

**Proposition 3.** *For each crisis-related decision function $F(s, s')$, the following two conditions are equivalent to each other:*

- *the function $F(s, s')$ is scale-invariant and anonymous, and*
- *there exist values $\alpha_+ \geq 0$ and $\alpha_- \geq 0$ for which, for all $s$ and $s'$, the components of the tuple $s'' = F(s, s')$ have the following form: $s''_i = s_i - \alpha_+ \cdot (s_i - s'_i)$ when $s_i \leq s'_i$ and $s''_i = s_i - \alpha_- \cdot (s'_i - s_i)$ when $s'_i \leq s_i$.*

### Discussion

- When for all $i$, we have $s'_i \leq s_i$, then we only need to use the parameter $\alpha_+$. The smaller $\alpha_+$, the better. Thus, in this case, Proposition 3 uniquely determines the optimal strategy: we need to select the smallest possible value $\alpha_+$.
- Similarly, when for all $i$, we have $s'_i \leq s_i$, then we only need to use the parameter $\alpha_-$. The smaller $\alpha_-$, the better. Thus, in this case, Proposition 3 uniquely determines the optimal strategy: we need to select the smallest possible value $\alpha_-$.
- In the general case, when for some $i$, we have $s'_i < s_i$ while for other indices $j$, we have $s_j < s'_j$, we have a whole family of possible solutions: namely, a 1-D family corresponding to Pareto-optimal solutions, i.e., in this case, pairs $(\alpha_+, \alpha_-)$ of values.

## 5 Proofs

### Proof of Proposition 1

1°. It is easy to see that the Nash's preference relation satisfies the first three conditions. To get the fourth condition, it is sufficient to take the vector $u' = 0.5 \cdot u + 0.5 \cdot \pi_{i,j}(u)$, i.e., a vector in which we replace both values $u_i$ and $u_j$ with their arithmetic average. Indeed, in this case, we keep all the other terms in the product intact and replace the product $U_i \cdot U_j$ with the value $U'_i \cdot U'_j$, where

$$U'_i = U'_j = \frac{U_i + U_j}{2},$$

and one can show that

$$\left(\frac{U_i + U_j}{2}\right)^2 \geq U_i \cdot U_j :$$

indeed, the difference between the left-hand side and the right-hand side is equal to

$$\left(\frac{U_i - U_j}{2}\right)^2 \geq 0.$$

So, to complete the proof of Proposition 1, it is sufficient to prove that every preference relation that satisfies the first three conditions has the Nash's form.

2°. Let us show that because of scale-invariance, we can reduce the family of total pre-orders to a single total pre-order. Indeed, for $c_i = 1$ for all $i$ and $d = -s$, scale-invariance implies that $u \succeq_s u'$ if and only if $U \succeq_0 U'$, where we denoted $U = u - s$ and $U' = u' - s$.

3°. Let us now prove that for every $U$, we have $\pi_{i,j}(U) \sim_0 U$.

Indeed, since the relation $\sim_0$ is total, we have either $\pi_{i,j}(U) \sim_0 U$, or $\pi_{i,j}(U) \succ_0 U$, or $U \succ_0 \pi_{i,j}(U)$.

- In the second case, anonymity would lead to $\pi_{i,j}(\pi_{i,j}(U)) \succ_0 \pi_{i,j}(U)$, i.e., to $U \succ_0 \pi_{i,j}(U)$, which contradicts to $\pi_{i,j}(U) \succ_0 U$.
- In the third case, anonymity would lead to $\pi_{i,j}(U) \succ_0 \pi_{i,j}(\pi_{i,j}(U))$, i.e., to $\pi_{i,j}(U) \succ_0 U$, which contradicts to $U \succ_0 \pi_{i,j}(U)$.

Thus, the only remaining option is $\pi_{i,j}(U) \sim_0 U$.

4°. Let us now prove that for every vector $U$ and for all $i$ and $j$, $U$ is equivalent to a vector $U'$ in which both components $U_i$ and $U_j$ are replaced by their geometric mean $\sqrt{U_i \cdot U_j}$.

Indeed, due to Part 3 of this proof, we have

$$(\ldots, \sqrt{U_i}, \ldots, \sqrt{U_j}, \ldots) \sim_0 (\ldots, \sqrt{U_j}, \ldots, \sqrt{U_i}, \ldots).$$

Due to scale-invariance for $d = 0$, $c_i = \sqrt{U_i}$, $c_j = \sqrt{U_j}$, and $c_k = 1$ for all other $k$, we indeed conclude that

$$(\ldots, U_i, \ldots, U_j, \ldots) \sim_0 (\ldots, \sqrt{U_i \cdot U_j}, \ldots, \sqrt{U_i \cdot U_j}, \ldots).$$

5°. Let us now prove that every vector $U$ is equivalent to the vector consisting of $n$ geometric means $\overline{U} \stackrel{\text{def}}{=} \sqrt[n]{U_1 \cdot \ldots \cdot U_n}$.

Indeed, we will use Part 4 of this proof to prove, by induction over $i = 0, 1, \ldots, n$, that for each $i$, the vector $U$ is equivalent to some vector of the type $(\overline{U}, \ldots, \overline{U}, U'_{i+1}, \ldots)$ in which the first $i$ terms are equal to $\overline{U}$.

The base case is easy: for $i = 0$, as the desired vector, we can take the same vector $U$.

The induction step is as follows. Let us assume that we have such a representation for $i$:

$$U \sim_0 (\overline{U}, \ldots, \overline{U}, U'_{i+1}, U'_{i+2}, \ldots).$$

Then, due to Part 4 of the proof, we have

$$(\overline{U}, \ldots, \overline{U}, U'_{i+1}, U'_{i+2}, U'_{i+3} \ldots) \sim_0 (\overline{U}, \ldots, \overline{U}, \overline{U}, U''_{i+2}, U'_{i+3} \ldots)$$

as long as $U'_{i+1} \cdot U'_{i+2} = \overline{U} \cdot U''_{i+2}$. So this equivalence holds for

$$U''_{i+1} = \frac{U'_{i+1} \cdot U'_{i+2}}{\overline{U}}.$$

The induction is proven. So, for $i = n$, we get the desired result.

6°. So, due to Part 5, every vector $U$ is equivalent to a vector $(\overline{U}, \ldots, \overline{U})$, where $\overline{U}$ is the $n$-th root of the product of the values $U_i$. Thus, every two vectors with the same product are equivalent to each other. Due to Pareto optimality, if the product is larger, the vector is better. So indeed, the preference relation that satisfies the first three condition has the Nash's form.

The proposition is proven.

**Proof of Proposition 2.** Similarly to the proof of Proposition 1, we can prove that under the first three conditions, every tuple $U$ is equivalent to a tuple $(\overline{U}, \ldots, \overline{U})$, where $\overline{U} = \sqrt[n]{U_1 \cdot \ldots \cdot U_n}$, except for this time $U_i \stackrel{\text{def}}{=} s_i - u_i$. Due to Pareto optimality, the smaller $\overline{U}$, the better. So the only preference relation that satisfies the first three conditions is the relation $u \succeq_s u' \leftrightarrow \overline{U} \geq \overline{U}'$.

To complete the proof, we will show that this preference relation does not satisfy the fourth condition. Indeed, let us take $s = 0$ and

$$S = \{(-x, -(3-x), -1, \ldots, -1) : 0 < x < 3\}.$$

Both the status quo state and the set $S$ do not change if we swap participants 1 and 2. For the vector $u = (-2, -1, -1, \ldots, -1)$, we have $\overline{U} = \sqrt[n]{2}$. However, the only outcome which is invariant with respect to the 1–2 swap is $u' = (-1.5, -1.5, -1, \ldots, -1)$. For this outcome, $\overline{U}' = \sqrt[n]{1.5 \cdot 1.5} = \sqrt[n]{2.25} > \overline{U}$. Thus, here $u \succ_s u'$ – and hence, the preference relation violates the fairness condition.

The proposition is proven.

**Proof of Proposition 3**

1°. It is easy to show that for each $\alpha_+ \geq 0$ and $\alpha_- \geq 0$, the corresponding function is scale-invariant and anonymous. So, to complete the proof, we need to show that, vice versa, every scale-invariant anonymous function has the desired form.

2°. Due to scale-invariance for $c_i = 1$ and $d_i = -s_i$, $s'' = F(s, s')$ implies that $s'' - s = F(0, s' - s)$, i.e., that $s'' = F(s, s') = G(s' - s) + s$, where we denoted $G(U) \stackrel{\text{def}}{=} F(0, U)$. Thus, to describe all possible scale-invariant anonymous functions $F(s, s')$, it is sufficient to describe functions $G(U) = F(0, U)$. Since $T_{c,0}(0) = 0$, for this new function, scale-invariance means that for every $c > 0$, if $U' = G(U)$, then $T_c(U') = G(T_c(U))$. In other words, we have $T_c(G(U)) = G(T_c(U))$.

3°. When $U_i = 0$ for some $i$, then for $c_i = 2$ and $c_j = 1$ for all other $j$, we have $T_c(U) = U$. Thus, scale-invariance implies that $T_c(G(U)) = G(U)$. For the $i$-th component of the vector $U' = G(U)$, this means $U_i' = 2U_i'$, thus $U_i' = 0$.

4°. For the values $i$ for which $U_i \neq 0$, we can use $c_i = 1/|U_i|$. Then, the vector $e \stackrel{\text{def}}{=} T_c(U)$ contains only components that are equal to 1, $-1$, and 0. Let $n_-$ be the number of values equal to $-1$, $n_+$ equal to the number of values equal to 1, and $n_0$ be the number of values equal to 0. For every triple $N = (n_+, n_-, n_0)$ different vectors $e$ corresponding to this case can obtained from each other by permutation. Thus, due to anonymity:

- all $n_+$ participants $i$ with $e_i = 1$ get the same value $t_i$ which we will denote by $\alpha_+(N)$, and
- all $n_+$ participants $i$ with $e_i = -1$ get the same value $t_i$ which we will denote by $\alpha_-(N)$, and

By using scale-invariance, we can conclude that the values $U'_i$ have the desired form – with the only exception that now, the values $\alpha_+$ and $\alpha_-$, in general, depend on the vector $N$. To complete the proof, we need to prove that the values $\alpha_+$ and $\alpha_-$ are the same for all triples $N$.

5°. Let us pick the value $i$ for which $e_i = 1$. Let us consider a family of vectors that are obtained by multiplying all the values $U_j$ (except for $U_i$) by some value $\varepsilon$ – while $U_i$ remains intact. For all $\varepsilon > 0$, we have the same vector $N$, so we have the same formulas for $U'_i$ – with the coefficients $\alpha_+$ corresponding to this vector $N$. In the limit $\varepsilon \to 0$, $s''_i$ tends to a vector in which there is only one non-zero component, i.e., for which the corresponding vector $N'$ has the form $(1, 0, n-1)$.

Since the function $F(s, s')$ is continuous, the value $s''_i$ corresponding to the limit vector $N'$ should be equal to the limit of the values corresponding to $N$. For all $\varepsilon > 0$, the value $s''_i$ is the same – corresponding to $\alpha_+(N)$. So, in the limit, this value should remain the same as well. However, for $\varepsilon > 0$, we have $\alpha_+(N)$ corresponding to the original vector $N$, while in the limit, we have the value $\alpha_+(N')$. Thus, for each vector $N$, the value $\alpha_+(N)$ is the same as in the case when only coefficient is different from 0. So $\alpha_+(N)$ does not depend on $N$.

Similarly, the value $\alpha_-(N)$ does not depend on $N$. The proposition is proven.

## 6 Conclusions

How can we share a success? How can we fairly divide the gains between people who contributed to this gain? Decision theory provides an answer to this question: namely, as shown by the Nobelist John Nash, reasonable conditions uniquely determine the fair division. This division is known as Nash's bargaining solution. It has a natural interpretation in fuzzy terms, as a solution for which the desired statement – that all participants are happy – is satisfied to the largest degree.

At first glance, it may seem that a similar approach can be applied to crisis situations, when there is a need for sacrifices – e.g., for salary cuts – and we are looking for the most fair way to share the crisis. Somewhat surprisingly, we show that in the case of a crisis, no solution satisfies all Nash's requirements. We then describe a weaker set of requirements – that (almost) uniquely determine how to share a crisis.

**Acknowledgments.** This work was supported in part by the National Science Foundation grants 1623190 (A Model of Change for Preparing a New Generation for Professional Practice in Computer Science), HRD-1834620 and HRD-2034030 (CAHSI Includes), EAR-2225395 (Center for Collective Impact in Earthquake Science C-CIES), and by the AT&T Fellowship in Information Technology.

It was also supported by a grant from the Hungarian National Research, Development and Innovation Office (NRDI), and by the Institute for Risk and Reliability, Leibniz Universitaet Hannover, Germany.

The authors are thankful to the anonymous referees for valuable suggestions.

## References

1. Belohlavek, R., Dauben, J.W., Klir, G.J.: Fuzzy Logic and Mathematics: A Historical Perspective. Oxford University Press, New York (2017)
2. Fishburn, P.C.: Utility Theory for Decision Making. Wiley, New York (1969)
3. Fishburn, P.C.: Nonlinear Preference and Utility Theory. The John Hopkins Press, Baltimore (1988)
4. Klir, G., Yuan, B.: Fuzzy Sets and Fuzzy Logic. Prentice Hall, Upper Saddle River (1995)
5. Kreinovich, V.: Decision making under interval uncertainty (and beyond). In: Guo, P., Pedrycz, W. (eds.) Human-Centric Decision-Making Models for Social Sciences, pp. 163–193. Springer, Cham (2014)
6. Luce, R.D., Raiffa, R.: Games and Decisions: Introduction and Critical Survey. Dover, New York (1989)
7. Mendel, J.M.: Explainable Uncertain Rule-Based Fuzzy Systems. Springer, Cham (2024)
8. Nash, J.: The bargaining problem. Econometrica **18**(2), 155–162 (1950)
9. Nguyen, H.P., Bokati, L., Kreinovich, V.: New (simplified) derivation of Nash's bargaining solution. J. Adv. Comput. Intell. Intell. Inform. (JACIII) **24**(5), 589–592 (2020)
10. Nguyen, H.T., Kosheleva, O., Kreinovich, V.: Decision making beyond Arrow's 'impossibility theorem', with the analysis of effects of collusion and mutual attraction. Int. J. Intell. Syst. **24**(1), 27–47 (2009)
11. Nguyen, H.T., Kreinovich, V., Wu, B., Xiang, G.: Computing Statistics Under Interval and Fuzzy Uncertainty. Springer, Heidelberg (2012)
12. Nguyen, H.T., Walker, C.L., Walker, E.A.: A First Course in Fuzzy Logic. Chapman and Hall/CRC, Boca Raton (2019)
13. Novák, V., Perfilieva, I., Močkoř, J.: Mathematical Principles of Fuzzy Logic. Kluwer, Boston (1999)
14. Raiffa, H.: Decision Analysis. McGraw-Hill, Columbus (1997)
15. Zadeh, L.A.: Fuzzy sets. Inf. Control **8**, 338–353 (1965)

# Prostate Cancer Diagnosis: A Geometric Approach Based on the Beer Index

M. A. Serra-Moll[1,2](✉), A. Mir-Fuentes[1,2], A. Burguera Burguera[1,2], and O. Valero[1,2]

[1] Department of Mathematics and Computer Science, Universitat de les Illes Balears, Ctra. de Valldemossa km. 7.5, 07122 Palma de Mallorca, Illes Balears, Spain
{m.serra,a.mir}@uib.cat, {antoni.burguera,o.valero}@uib.es

[2] Health Research Institute of the Balearic Islands (IdISBa), Hospital Universitari Son Espases, 07120 Palma de Mallorca, Illes Balears, Spain

**Abstract.** Convexity is a well-known property of sets, but it is still not clear how to measure the degree of convexity of a set. In this paper, we seek to measure the degree of convexity of a set making use of the Beer index, which is based on the visibility of its points. The aforesaid index involves the so-called visibility function, a continuous function that allows to compute the area of the region that sees every point. An application of this method for measuring the convexity degree to prostate cancer diagnosis is presented. Here, pathologists aim to determine whether a patient has a potential risk of cancer. In our case, the Beer index is used to determine the state of individual glands present in biopsy samples by determining the degree of convexity of the lumens. This is done to help pathologists to assess whether these glands are healthy or exhibit a cancerous state. Thus, the main objective in this work is to show that the Beer index captures and reflects a morphological feature which is inherent in prostatic glands and, therefore it allows the distinction between healthy and pathological glands.

**Keywords:** Convexity · Visibility Function · Beer index · Prostate Cancer

## 1 Introduction

Convexity is a significant property to describe geometrical objects. Furthermore, it is a topic of mathematics and computer science that has many applications to functional analysis, differential geometry, computational geometry, data analysis and modeling, among others.

Convex optimization is a topic that has been discussed for about a century, but recent developments have sparked interest in the topic (see, for example, [6]). These developments have been:

Dedicated to the memory of Professor Alexander Šostak.


M. Baczyński et al. (Eds.): EUSFLAT 2025, LNCS 15884, pp. 299–310, 2025.
https://doi.org/10.1007/978-3-031-97228-7_25

- The recognition of interior-point methods to solve convex optimization problems.
- Convex optimization problems are more usual than were previously thought.

In many convex optimization problems, the set where the optimization is applied must be convex. However, it could sometimes be applied to more general sets. Indeed, if we define a convexity index that allows to measure the degree of convexity, we could apply the optimization problem to sets with a convexity index greater than a certain threshold.

Another area of computer science where convex sets are analyzed and studied is computational geometry [1,5,15]. It is a branch of computer science devoted to the study of algorithms which can be stated in terms of geometrical concepts. Many recent results in computational geometry have relied on the attribute of convexity, and they have failed to be adapted to more general geometrical contexts. So, in many cases, the choice is to divide the involved objects into convex pieces where the computational technique works well. The study of this approach to overcome the convexity handicap can be seen in [3,18,19].

Regarding the definition of convexity, essentially, we say that a set $S$ is convex if every segment between two points is inside $S$. In the area of fuzzy logic, where fuzzy sets in the sense of [21] play a central role, is also defined what does it mean for a fuzzy set to be convex. Different properties of convex fuzzy sets are described in [9,10]. Also, other definitions of convex fuzzy set are given in [2] and appropriate notion of convexity for interval-valued fuzzy sets has been introduced in [12], where the notion of admissible order is used as given in [7]. However, this point of view only gives a crisp definition of convexity for fuzzy objects. So, it also seems interesting to give a fuzzy definition of convexity, because it would allow us to compare the convexity of many different crisp sets, even if they were not convex in the usual sense. To explore the possibility of designing fuzzy indexes that try to compute the degree of convexity of a set is the main focus, and a solid idea of how to compare the convexity of two general sets is needed.

In this paper, we introduce a perspective in which convexity is presented as a gradual property, as opposed to its classical interpretation as a strictly binary attribute. This approach enables a fuzzy understanding of convexity. To quantify the degree of convexity of a set, we employ a particular index, the Beer index (BI) given in [4]. This index provides a rigorous and consistent framework for evaluating how closely a given set approximates convexity. Moreover, by using this index, we develop a methodology with clear interpretability useful for prostate cancer diagnosis. Specifically, the Beer index captures and reflects a morphological feature which is inherent in prostatic glands and, therefore it allows the distinction between healthy and pathological glands. Thus, our methodology determines the state of individual glands present in biopsy samples by determining the degree of convexity of the lumens. This is done to help pathologists to assess whether these glands are healthy or exhibit a cancerous state.

The rest of the paper is organized as follows. In Sect. 2, we recall the basic notions about convexity necessary for introducing the concepts of visibility and visibility function. In addition, we relate these notions with the notion of convexity. In Sect. 3, we present the convexity index introduced by G. Beer in [4], hereinafter referred to as Beer index. Also the application to medical diagnosis is presented. In this context, the BI is used to determine the state of individual glands present in biopsy samples, in order to help pathologists to assess whether these glands are healthy or exhibit a cancerous state. Finally, conclusions and future work are discussed in Sect. 4.

## 2 Preliminaries

In this section, we give some auxiliary notions in order to have a complete understanding of the further discussion. Specifically, we introduce the notion of visibility within a set, as this concept serves as the cornerstone for quantifying and analyzing the convexity of sets in our subsequent study. Unless otherwise stated, all points and sets considered here are assumed to be in $\mathbb{R}^2$ and with strictly positive measure (notice that or our purpose Jordan's measure is sufficient, although Lebesgue's measure could also be considered). So the considered subsets $S$ satisfy that $S \subset \mathbb{R}^2$. Moreover, given $x, y \in \mathbb{R}^2$ we will denote by $[x, y]$ the line segment between $x$ and $y$, i.e., $[x, y = \{\lambda x + (1 - \lambda)y : \lambda \in [0, 1]\}]$.

Let us recall the notion of visibility.

**Definition 1** [4]. *Let $x, y \in S$. A point $x$ is said to* see $y$ via $S$ *if and only if the line segment $[x, y]$ is contained in $S$, that is, $[x, y] \subseteq S$. The set all points in $S$ that can be seen by $x$ via $S$ will be denoted by $st(x; S)$, i.e.,*

$$st(x; S) = \{y \in S \mid [x, y] \subseteq S\}.$$

Now the notion of visibility is introduced, let us define the concept of clear visibility.

**Definition 2** [8]. *Let $x, y \in S$. A point $x$ is said to* see clearly $y$ via $S$ *if and only if, there exists a neighborhood $U_y$ of $y$ such that $U_y \subset st(x; S)$. The set all points in $S$ that can be seen clearly by $x$ via $S$ will be denoted by $cl(x; S)$.*

In view of the preceding notion the set of restricted visibility can be introduced.

**Definition 3** [8]. *Given a point $x \in S$, the set of restricted visibility of $x$ in a set $S$ is defined as the set $rv(x; S)$ which is given by $rv(x; S) = st(x; S) - cl(x; S)$.*

Notice that, given $x \in S$, the set $rv(x; S)$ is the set of all points of $S$ that see $x$ through $S$ but do not see it clearly.

Finally, we introduce the concept of visibility function which will result in a useful tool for analyzing convexity. To this end, let us denote by $\mathbb{R}_+$ the set of nonnegative real numbers.

**Definition 4** [4]. *Given an arbitrary set $S$, the visibility function $v_S : S \longrightarrow \mathbb{R}^+$ is defined by $v_S(x) = \mu(st(x; S))$ for all $x \in S$, where $\mu(st(x; S))$ is the area of $st(x; S)$ (the Jordan measure of $st(x; S)$).*

The following result ensure the regularity of the visibility function.

**Theorem 1** [8]. *Let $S$ be a compact subset. If $x \in S$ such that $\mu(st(x;S)) = \mu(cl(x;S))$, then the visibility function $v_S$ is continuous at $x$.*

From now on, we will assume that the sets $S$ under consideration are compact and satisfy that $\mu(st(x;S)) = \mu(cl(x;S))$ for every point $x$. This assumption guarantees that the visibility function $v_S$ is continuous at every $x \in S$.

We now introduce the geometric property that will serve as the central focus of this work: convexity. While convexity is a well-established concept in mathematics, the aim of this work is to determine how this property can be measured as a gradual feature.

**Definition 5.** *A set $S$ is said to be* convex *provided that $[x,y] \subseteq S$ for all $x, y \in S$.*

Note that a set $S$ is convex when the line segment joining $x$ and $y$, $[x,y]$, is entirely contained within $S$.

The concepts of convexity and the visibility function are fundamentally related, as convexity ensures a property of full visibility within a set. In the following, we explore this relationship in detail.

In a convex set $S$, for any two points $x, y \in S$, the segment $[x,y]$ lies within $S$. This is equivalent to $v_S(x) = \mu(S)$ for all $x \in S$. So the visibility function encapsulates the geometric essence of convexity by determining whether all pairs of points in a set $S$ can "see" each other through $S$.

While convexity is traditionally considered a binary property (a set is either convex or not), the visibility function allows for a more gradual evaluation. By analyzing, for every $x \in S$, the portion of the area of $S$ that it can see, one can determine the degree to which the set $S$ retains the property of convexity. This fact will be useful to introduce Beer's index as a fuzzy convexity index in the next section.

## 3 The Beer Index and its Application to Medical Diagnosis

In this section, we introduce a perspective in which convexity is presented as a gradual property, as opposed to its classical interpretation as a strictly binary attribute. This approach enables a fuzzy understanding of convexity, allowing us to measure and compare how "nearly convex" different sets are. To quantify the degree of convexity of a set, we employ a particular index, the Beer index as introduced in [4]. This index provides a rigorous and consistent framework for evaluating how closely a given set approximates convexity. Thus, by applying the aforementioned index, we can obtain a numerical representation, belonging to $[0,1]$, of the convexity of a given set. This approach facilitates a deeper understanding of convexity as a gradual property and it allows different applications to various theoretical and practical contexts, especially in medical imaging. Here, it is shown how the BI appears to have an interesting application to the medical diagnosis in the case of prostate cancer.

Next let us remind the definition of the Beer index.

**Definition 6.** *Let $S \subset \mathbb{R}^2$ with strictly positive measure satisfying conditions in Theorem 1. The Beer index of $S$, $I_B(S)$, is defined as follows*

$$I_B(S) = \frac{1}{\mu(S)^2} \int_S v_S(x)\, dx.$$

Observe that Theorem 1 warranties that the Beer index is well-defined because the continuity of the visibility function gives that it is a Riemann integrable function.

The Beer index is one of the first convexity indices in the literature. Notice that it is based on the previously introduced visibility function and in addition, it presents a very intuitive approach to determine how convex a set is. Moreover, $I_B(S) \in [0, 1]$ and $I_B(S) = 1 \Leftrightarrow S$ is convex.

In the light of the preceding notion, we proceed to illustrate its use by developing the promised application.

It goes without saying that cancer is a major health matter around the world. It is characterized by an uncontrolled cell division caused by abnormal cells. Still, a huge number of people continue to be diagnosed with cancer every day and therefore, it remains between the top 10 causes for morbidity and mortality on a global scale. Hence, the progress of determining successful premature diagnostics is crucial [11].

Particularly, prostate cancer is among the most common kind of cancers in men. It consist in the development of cancer cells in the prostate gland. Here, pathologists work on determining whether a patient has a potential risk of prostate cancer. Early detection is essential as it notably improves the probability of finding a treatment and the survival of the patient. Despite improvements in bio-medical technology, the appropriate diagnosis of prostate cancer remains challenging due to the diversity of the disease and the subjectivity involved in the pathological evaluation [20]. Currently, the diagnosis of prostate cancer implies a visual review of tissue samples, which are examined by a pathologist. This manual evaluation is time-consuming and it is also subject to a high degree of subjectivity among different experts.

As said before, prostatic glands are examined so as to identify possible cancer signs. These glands, exemplified in Fig. 1, are composed of the nuclei (darker blue elements), the cytoplasm (lighter purple regions), the stroma (pink areas), and the lumens (white areas surrounded by cytoplasm and nuclei). Pathologists use the structure of the lumen as a reference to determine the state of the gland. According to medical literature (see [14]), the area of the lumen is a good indicator for determining whether prostate tissue is healthy or cancerous. Usually, larger with complex branching lumens indicate benign tissues, in contrast, small size, simplified architecture and round or oval lumens are more associated with cancerous tissue, according to the Gleason scale classification. Figure 2a shows an example of a healthy tissue while Fig. 2b exemplifies a diseased one. In both figures, a more detailed view is also provided so as to display the appearance of a healthy and a diseased lumen respectively. Observe that the diseased lumen is substantially more convex than the healthy one.

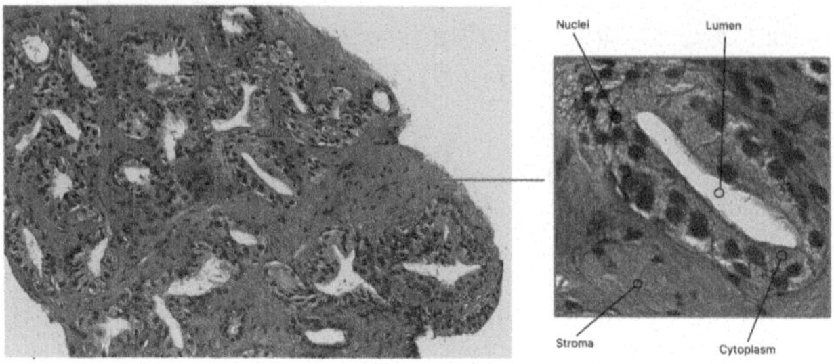


**Fig. 1.** A prostatic gland and its different parts. Source: [13].

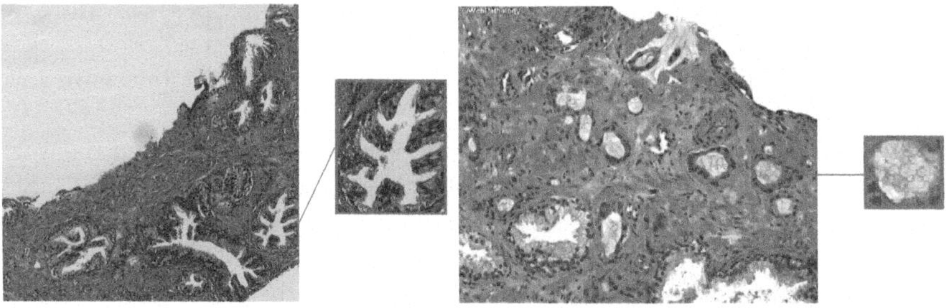

(a) (b)

**Fig. 2.** (a) Sample of benign tissue. Source: [13]. (b) Sample of pathological tissue. Source: [16].

Next, we present an example of an application derived from the Beer index for premature prostate cancer diagnosis. Our contribution lies in using the BI to design an explicable algorithm to determine the state of individual glands present in biopsy samples, in order to help pathologists to assess whether these glands are healthy or exhibit a cancerous state. For this reason, in first place we will detect and segment the glandular regions, specifically the lumens, and then compute the associated BI of the identified ones (notice that the details about the mentioned segmentation falls outside the scope of this paper). Thus, the main objective here is to show that the BI captures and reflects a morphological feature which is inherent in prostatic glands and, therefore it allows the distinction between healthy and pathological glands.

In this section, all the results and images presented are extracted from the public datasets [13] and [16]. To sum up, we show that the Beer index can be used as another reference for pathologists to assess whether these glands are healthy or present a cancerous state. It is important to clarify that we present this new methodology only as an assistance system for pathologists, who will take the final decision on the gland state. The application has been carried out following the process detailed below:

1. **Extraction of regions of interest from the samples.**
First of all, slides[1] with biopsied prostate tissue samples are analyzed in order to identify regions of interest as the example seen in Fig. 3. Concretely, this is an example of a benign tissue. This is performed by means of an image processing pipeline that we have designed, implemented and tested. The description of this pipeline falls outside of the scope of this paper.

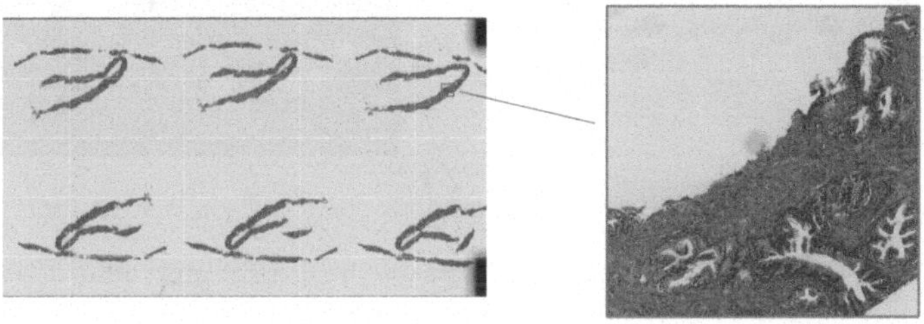

**Fig. 3.** Slides with biopsied prostate tissue samples from which histological images (Fig. 2a) are obtained with a zoom of one particular region.

2. **Identification of the lumens.**
Next step is the identification and segmentation of the lumens as independent objects. Observe that the segmentation algorithm returns a closed polygon, which ensures us that the area that is clearly visible for an arbitrary point is the same as the area of the points that it generally sees. Then, if $S$ is the set of points that we classify as a lumen, we have that $\mu(st(x;S)) = \mu(cl(x;S))$ for any $x \in S$, fulfilling the hypothesis of Theorem 1. The result of applying this segmentation process to the images in Fig. 2a and 2b are shown in Figs. 4 and 5 respectively. This is also performed following an image processing pipeline that falls outside of the scope of this paper. In this study, a total of 211 lumens

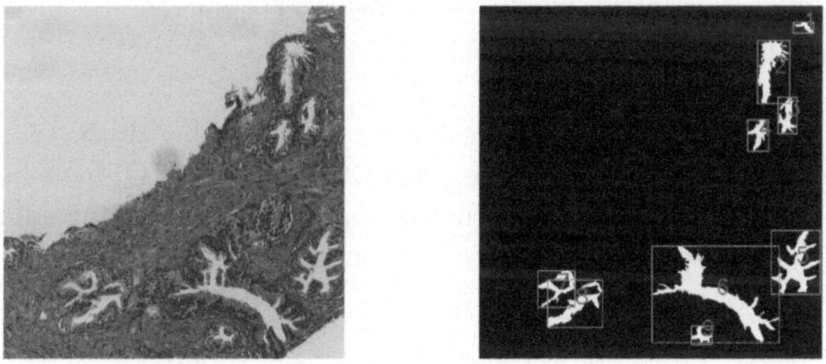

(a) (b)

**Fig. 4.** (a) Histological image 2a, (b) Lumens of the histological image.

[1] Slides are obtained from the dataset [13] while the other data source [16] directly provides histological images.

from 24 histological images have been segmented and analyzed, of which 106 correspond to benign lumens and 105 to pathological ones.

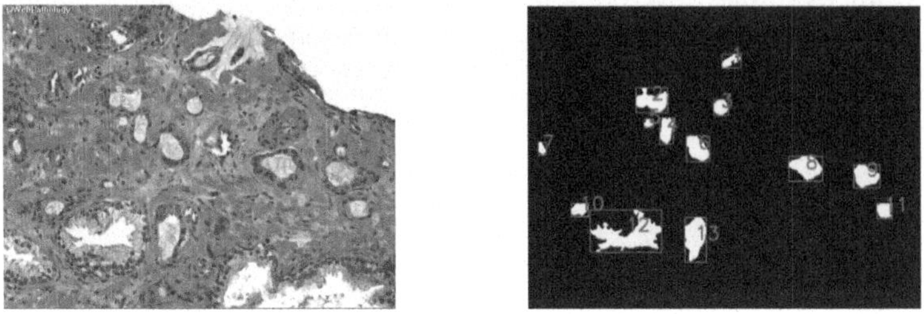

(a) (b)

**Fig. 5.** (a) Histological image 2b, (b) Lumens of the histological image.

3. **Calculation of the Beer index for each lumen.**
   Once we have identified all potential lumens, we calculate[2] the Beer index for each one. Table 1 presents the results of the Beer index applied to all lumens from the benign histological image in Fig. 2a. Each lumen has been classified as benign (NC) or cancerous (C) according to the provided ground truth in [13].
   The same procedure was performed to the pathological histological image in Fig. 2b. Table 2 displays the BI results for each lumen along with its corresponding label, determined by the descriptions in [16].
   Finally, Fig. 6 illustrates the complete analyzed dataset, which includes also the previous displayed results, showing the number of C and NC cases for each specific BI range. Here, it is easy to notice that lumens labelled as C have a substantially higher value of the Beer index than those which are classified as NC. However, some NC samples have a BI close to 1, but the number of C samples with a BI near 1 is significantly larger. Thus, while BI alone may not be sufficient to fully distinguish between C and NC, it clearly provides highly valuable information.
4. **Modeling.**
   The next step consists in a BI threshold study to deal with the binary classification problem. Here, some different thresholds ($THOLD$) have been applied to the BI in order to develop a model capable of classifying lumens ($\hat{y}$) as healthy (0) or potentially cancerous (1) as shown in the following:

$$\hat{y} = \begin{cases} 1 & \text{if } BI \geq THOLD \\ 0 & \text{if } BI < THOLD \end{cases}.$$

   Threshold (THOLD) values ranging from 0.1 to 0.9 in 0.1 increments have been experimentally assessed. Each lumen was classified as C or NC based on

[2] The mentioned calculation or code script can be consulted or downloaded from the following GitHub repository: https://github.com/mserrauibcat/Beer-Index.git.

**Table 1.** Beer index and Label for each Lumen (Image: 2a)

| Lumen | Beer index | Label |
|---|---|---|
| 1 | 0.74 | NC |
| 2 | 0.59 | NC |
| 3 | 0.62 | NC |
| 4 | 0.78 | NC |
| 5 | 0.39 | NC |
| 6 | 0.41 | NC |
| 7 | 0.29 | NC |
| 8 | 0.41 | NC |
| 9 | 0.69 | NC |

**Table 2.** Beer index and Label for each Lumen (Image: 2b)

| Lumen | Beer index | Label |
|---|---|---|
| 1 | 0.74 | C |
| 2 | 0.88 | C |
| 3 | 1 | C |
| 4 | 0.99 | C |
| 5 | 1 | C |
| 6 | 0.99 | C |
| 7 | 1 | C |
| 8 | 0.99 | C |
| 9 | 1 | C |
| 10 | 0.99 | C |
| 11 | 0.99 | C |
| 12 | 0.62 | NC |
| 13 | 0.98 | C |

whether its BI was below or above the threshold. Each threshold was evaluated using a confusion matrix, along with the main classification metrics: Precision, Sensibility (Recall), F1-Score, Accuracy and Miss Rate, in Table 3. Notice that a confusion matrix provides an insightful method for evaluating the classification performance, which is crucial in data science. Moreover, the aforementioned metrics are highly helpful in the decision-making process for real-world data challenges [17].

First, we have to clarify that as we are working with a medical binary classification model, it is essential to minimize FN predictions, which will, in turn, result in high recall values. The main reason is that the model is designed to assist pathologists by identifying positive or potentially cancerous lumens. Then, the experts will review those potentially cancerous results to verify if they are truly diseased. Nevertheless, if the model classifies a lumen as benign, the idea is that it will not be further reviewed by the pathologist.

Notice that as the threshold is higher, lower is the sensibility but higher the rest of the metrics. Nevertheless, sensibility remains the maximum till $THOLD = 0.6$.

Thus, the model with both, the highest threshold and the highest recall is $THOLD = 0.5$, indicating that it correctly identifies all positive samples from the actual positive cases in the dataset. This corresponds the lowest number of FN predictions or Miss Rate, which is zero. However, its precision is only of 57.92% predicted positive results being correct. The accuracy is 0.6351, implying that 63.51% of all observations are correctly classified.

With $THOLD = 0.6$, recall decreases first to 97.17% due to an increase in

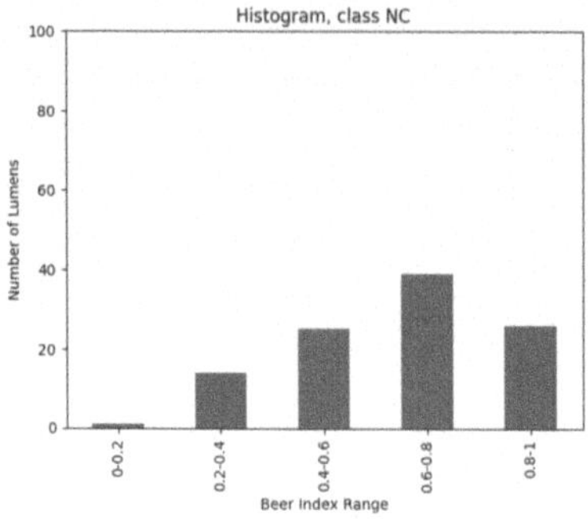


(a)

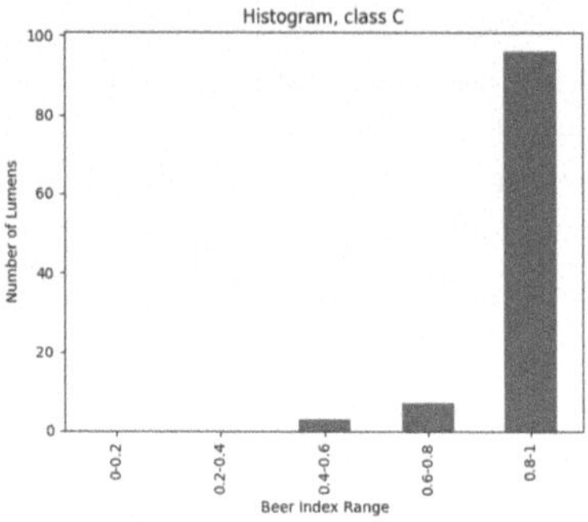


(b)

**Fig. 6.** Complete dataset: (a) Histogram, class NC. (b) Histogram, class C.

**Table 3.** Summary of Confusion Matrix and Classification Metrics.

| Threshold | $TP$[a] | $TN$[b] | $FP$[c] | $FN$[d] | Precision | Recall | F1-Score | Accuracy | Miss Rate |
|---|---|---|---|---|---|---|---|---|---|
| 0.1 | 106 | 0 | 105 | 0 | 0.5024 | 1 | 0.6688 | 0.5024 | 0 |
| 0.2 | 106 | 1 | 104 | 0 | 0.5048 | 1 | 0.6709 | 0.5071 | 0 |
| 0.3 | 106 | 8 | 97 | 0 | 0.5222 | 1 | 0.6861 | 0.5403 | 0 |
| 0.4 | 106 | 15 | 90 | 0 | 0.5408 | 1 | 0.702 | 0.5735 | 0 |
| 0.5 | 106 | 28 | 77 | 0 | 0.5792 | 1 | 0.7336 | 0.6351 | 0 |
| 0.6 | 103 | 40 | 65 | 3 | 0.6131 | 0.9717 | 0.7518 | 0.6777 | 0.0283 |
| 0.7 | 101 | 62 | 43 | 5 | 0.7014 | 0.9528 | 0.808 | 0.7725 | 0.0471 |
| 0.8 | 96 | 79 | 26 | 10 | 0.7869 | 0.9057 | 0.8421 | 0.8294 | 0.0943 |
| 0.9 | 85 | 95 | 21 | 10 | 0.8947 | 0.8019 | 0.8458 | 0.8531 | 0.1981 |

[a] True Positive. [b] True Negative. [c] False Positive. [d] False Negative.

the number of FN (3 cases). However, precision and accuracy are improved to 61.31% and 67.77% respectively.
At the highest threshold (BI = 0.9), recall decreases to 80.19% as the number of FN is increased to 10. Despite this, precision and accuracy are improved substantially, reaching 89.47% and 80.19% respectively. For these reasons, it seems that de BI has an accurate capacity to classify lumens as healthy or diseased reaching up to an accuracy of 85.31% in $THOLD = 0.9$.
Finally, according to minimize FN predictions is essential, it seems advantageous to apply the threshold $BI = 0.5$, since it results in zero FN. However, metrics such precision and accuracy are significantly penalized.

## 4 Conclusions

As a theoretical review, we have seen that convexity is a well-known property of sets, but it is still not clear how to measure the degree of convexity of a set. In addition, we have seen how the visibility function and convexity are related and finally the Beer index has been introduced.

Next, an application to medical diagnosis has been presented. Here, it is shown how the Beer index appears to have an interesting application in the medical field, specifically in the case of prostate cancer. In this context, the Beer index has been used to determine the state of individual glands present in biopsy samples by determining the degree of convexity of the lumens. The main objective was to establish the start point for the development of a decision support toolkit that helps pathologists to assess whether these glands are healthy or exhibit a cancerous state.

After a detailed analysis, we have shown that the Beer index captures and reflects a morphological feature which is inherent in prostatic glands and, therefore it allows the distinction between healthy and pathological glands. Concretely, we have performed a threshold analysis along with a confusion matrix and some classification metrics. It is important to consider that as are working with a medical binary classification model it is essential to minimize FN predictions.

In conclusion, we have introduced an analytical technique which could prove to be really helpful for pathologists, as it allows for an initial screening that could significantly reduce their workload. One the one hand, it reduces subjectivity, one of the main challenges that experts face when labelling lumens, hence, being reasonable and appropriate for the assessment of the lumens classification. On the other hand, some other advantages must be mentioned. It is an explainable methodology with a unique variable, it does not require training data, and therefore it is not considered a black box unlike other AI models.

As a further work, a study on the definition of new indexes will be made in order to improve the results and their associated metrics. Moreover, an AI model will be developed incorporating in addition the BI, a few new variables of interest to pathologists in order to improve the classification. Furthermore, it seems interesting to develop a software tool, which could be incorporated in the expert's control panel with the aim of analyzing various scenarios, giving the expert more support for decision-making.

**Acknowledgments.** This research is part of project PID2022-139248NB-I00 funded by MICIU/AEI/10.13039/501100011033 and ERDF/EU. The authors thank the support from *Programa de Foment de la Recerca i la Innovació de la Universitat de les Illes Balears 2024–2026* and ITS2023-086-Programa de Foment a la recerca.

**Disclosure of Interests.** The authors have no competing interests to declare that are relevant to the content of this article.

## References

1. Ahn, H., Cheong, O., Park, C., Shin, C., Vigneron, A.: Maximizing the overlap of two planar convex sets under rigid motions. Comput. Geom. **37**(1), 3–15 (2007)
2. Ammar, E.E.: Some properties of convex fuzzy sets and convex fuzzy cones. Fuzzy Sets Syst. **106**(3), 381–386 (1999)
3. Bajaj, C.L., Dey, T.K.: Convex decomposition of polyhedra and robustness. SIAM J. Comput. **21**(2), 339–364 (1992)
4. Beer, G.: The index of convexity and the visibility function. Pac. J. Math. **44**(1), 59–67 (1973)
5. de Berg, M., van Kreveld, M., Overmars, M.: Computational Geometry. Springer (1997)
6. Boyd, S., Vandenberghe, L.: Convex Optimization. Cambridge University Press (2009)
7. Bustince, H., Fernandez, J., Kolesárová, A., Mesiar, R.: Generation of linear orders for intervals by means of aggregation functions. Fuzzy Sets Syst. **220**, 69–77 (2013)
8. Cunto, A.F., Losada, M.P., Toranzos, F.A.: The visibility function revisited. J. Geom. **65**(1), 101–110 (1999)
9. Drewniak, J.: Convex and strongly convex fuzzy sets. J. Math. Anal. Appl. **126**(1), 292–300 (1987)
10. Dubois, D.J.: Fuzzy Sets and Systems: Theory and Applications, vol. 144. Academic Press (1980)
11. Ferlay, J., et al.: Cancer statistics for the year 2020: an overview. Int. J. Cancer **149**(4), 778–789 (2021)
12. Huidobro, P., Alonso, P., Janiš, V., Montes, S.: Convexity and level sets for interval-valued fuzzy sets. In: Fuzzy Optimization and Decision Making, pp. 1–28 (2022)
13. Koziarski, M., et al.: DiagSet: a dataset for prostate cancer histopathological image classification. Sci. Rep. **14**(1), 6780 (2024)
14. Nguyen, K., Sabata, B., Jain, A.K.: Prostate cancer grading: gland segmentation and structural features. Pattern Recogn. Lett. **33**(7), 951–961 (2012)
15. O'Rourke, J.: Computational Geometry in C. Cambridge University Press (1998)
16. Ramnani, D.: Webpathology - a collection of surgical pathology images. (2025). https://www.webpathology.com/ Accessed Feb 2025
17. Sathyanarayanan, S., Tantri, B.R.: Confusion matrix-based performance evaluation metrics. Afr. J. Biomed. Res. **27**(4), 4023–4031 (2024)
18. Siciliano, B., Sciavicco, L., Villani, L., Oriolo, G.: Robotics. Moelling, Planinng and Control. Springer (2009)
19. Tor, S.B., Middleditch, A.E.: Convex decomposition of simple polygons. ACM Trans. Graph. (TOG) **3**(4), 244–265 (1984)
20. Tzelepi, V.: Prostate cancer: pathophysiology, pathology and therapy. Cancers **15**(1), 281 (2022)
21. Zadeh, L.: Fuzzy sets. Inf. Control **8**(3), 338–353 (1965)

# Author Index


**A**

Aguzzoli, Stefano I-322
Asmus, Tiago C. I-270
Asmuss, Svetlana I-127

**B**

Bajārs, Jānis II-15
Baz, Juan I-245, I-258
Bianchi, Matteo I-322
Bibiloni-Femenias, M. D. M. I-54, I-91
Botur, Michal I-309
Bouchon-Meunier, Bernadette I-193
Bula, Inese II-134
Burguera Burguera, A. II-299
Bustince, Humberto I-270, I-282

**C**

Cabrerizo, Francisco Javier I-66
Camargo, Heloisa A. I-270
Cardin, Marta II-66
Castronovo, Lydia II-76
Cazzorla, Davide II-173
Christen, Ramón I-39
Cubillo, Susana II-237, II-249

**D**

De Baets, Bernard II-41
de Oliveira, Lucas Dantas I-141
Destercke, Sébastien II-158
Díaz, Irene I-245, I-294
Dimuro, Graçaliz P. I-270

**E**

Elorza, Jorge II-237, II-249
Ertuğrul, Ümıt II-122
Esteva, Francesc I-335

**F**

Fiala, Karel I-153
Filippone, Giuseppe II-76, II-98
Flaminio, Tommaso I-347
Freitas, Guilherme II-3

**G**

Galici, Mario II-76, II-98
Gispert, Joan I-335
Godo, Lluís I-335
Gómez, Daniel I-282
Gomide, Fernando II-3
González, Xabier I-282
González-Quesada, Juan Carlos I-66
Grigorenko, Olga I-207
Gromov, Dmitry II-15
Grzegorzewski, Przemysław II-198
Grzegorzewski, Przemyslaw II-211
Gupta, Megha I-15
Gutiérrez, Inmaculada I-282

**H**

Hernández-Varela, Pablo II-237, II-249
Huidobro, Pedro II-237, II-249
Hundertmark, Sophie I-39

**I**

Isaks, Reinis I-207
Iturrate-Bobes, Marina II-53

**J**

Jaume-Martin, G. I-54, I-91
Jayaram, Balasubramaniam I-15
Jelinska, Jelizaveta II-263

**K**

Kacprzyk, Janusz II-29
Kalvāns, Dāvis II-15
Karacaır, Kübra II-122
Karaçal, Funda II-122
Kokainis, Martins I-127
Kollár, Igor I-26




M. Baczyński et al. (Eds.): EUSFLAT 2025, LNCS 15884, pp. 311–312, 2025.
https://doi.org/10.1007/978-3-031-97228-7

Kosheleva, Olga I-117, II-91, II-288
Kreinovich, Vladik I-117, II-91, II-288

L
La Rosa, Gianmarco II-76, II-98
López-Rodríguez, Domingo II-146
Lucca, Giancarlo I-270

M
Maciel, Leandro II-3
Marco-Detchart, Cedric I-270
Marsala, Christophe I-193
Martorell-Cunill, O. I-78
Mata, Francisco I-66
Mencar, Corrado II-173
Miķelsone, Elīna II-134
Miñana, Juan-José I-219
Mir-Fuentes, A. I-104, II-299
Močkoř, Jiří I-3
Montero, Javier I-282
Montes, Ignacio II-41, II-53
Montes, Susana I-245
Mulet-Forteza, C. I-78
Murinová, Petra I-153, I-166

N
Nanavati, Kavit I-15
Nazato, Vinicius II-3
Novák, Vilém I-166

O
Ojeda-Hernández, Manuel II-146
Onbaşıoğlu Altuhovs, Şuara I-229
Ontkovičová, Zuzana I-181

P
Paseka, Jan I-309
Pazar Varol, Banu I-229
Peiseniece, Līga II-134
Pellerey, Franco I-258
Pérez, Ignacio Javier I-66
Pérez-Fernández, Raúl II-41, II-53
Perfilieva, Irina I-117
Petturiti, Davide II-185
Pintanel, Alice I-270
Portmann, Edy I-39

R
Reiser, Renata H. S. I-270
Rico, Agnès II-158
Rico, Noelia I-294
Rifqi, Maria II-185
Rijkure, Astrīda II-134
Rodin, Igor II-263
Rodríguez, J. Tinguaro I-282
Romaniuk, Maciej II-198, II-223

S
Santos, Helida S. I-270
Serra-Moll, M. A. I-78, II-299
Siwek, Joanna II-110
Smolka, Richard I-309
Spilbergs, Aivars II-134
Špirková, Jana I-26
Stachowiak, Anna II-110
Subirana, Lluis I-347
Sussner, Peter I-141

T
Tabacchi, Marco Elio II-76, II-98
Talavera, Francisco Javier II-237, II-249
Talia, Simona I-219
Torra, Vicenç I-181
Torres-Blanc, Carmen II-237, II-249
Trillo, José Ramón I-66
Tsulaia, Gvantsa II-275

U
Ulloa, Juan II-91
Uvarova, Inga II-134

V
Valero, O. I-54, I-78, I-91, I-104, II-299
Velasco, Aaron II-91
Villar, Mario I-294

Y
Yamin, Adenauer C. I-270

Z
Zadrożny, Sławomir II-29
Zámečniková, Hana I-117
Żywica, Patryk II-110

The manufacturer's authorised representative in the EU is Springer Nature Customer Service Centre GmbH, Europaplatz 3, 69115 Heidelberg, Germany. If you have any concerns regarding our products, please contact ProductSafety@springernature.com

Printed and bound by CPI Group (UK) Ltd, Croydon, CR0 4YY
29/04/2026
02099461-0010